CIRCULATION AND CONTROL

Circulation and Control

Artistic Culture and Intellectual Property in the Nineteenth Century

Edited by Marie-Stéphanie Delamaire and Will Slauter

OpenBook Publishers

https://www.openbookpublishers.com

Digital material and resources associated with this volume are available at https://doi.org/10.11647/OBP.0247#resources

ISBN Paperback: 9781800641464
ISBN Hardback: 9781800641471
ISBN Digital (PDF): 9781800641488
ISBN Digital ebook (epub): 9781800641495
ISBN Digital ebook (mobi): 9781800641501
ISBN XML: 9781800641518
DOI: 10.11647/OBP.0247

Cover image: 16 tintype portraits of an unidentified sitter on a single plate, Division of Work and Industry, National Museum of American History, Smithsonian Institution.
Cover design by Anna Gatti.

Contents

Contributor Biographies

Isabella Alexander is a Professor in the Faculty of Law at the University of Technology Sydney (Australia). She is a specialist of the history of copyright and is the author of *Copyright and the Public Interest in the Nineteenth Century* (Hart Publishing, 2010). She is currently working on a project on the history of copyright and cartography (www.copyrightcartography.org) and is lead CI on the Australian Research Council Discovery Grant *Hacking Copyright Law in the 21st Century: Art, Law, History and Technology.*

Oren Bracha is the William C. Conner Chair in Law at the University of Texas School of Law. He is the author of *Owning Ideas: The Intellectual Origins of American Intellectual Property 1790–1909* (Cambridge University Press, 2016) as well as numerous articles on the history of intellectual property.

Elena Cooper is Leverhulme Early Career Fellow at CREATe, School of Law, University of Glasgow, having joined CREATe in 2014. Prior to this, she was Orton Fellow in Intellectual Property Law at Trinity Hall Cambridge. Her first monograph — *Art and Modern Copyright: The Contested Image* (Cambridge University Press, 2018) — is the first in-depth account of artistic copyright law in the nineteenth and early twentieth centuries and was shortlisted for the Birks Book Prize for Outstanding Legal Scholarship by the Society of Legal Scholars in 2020. This significantly extends her PhD thesis, completed under the supervision of Prof. Lionel Bently, University of Cambridge, which was awarded a Yorke Prize by the Faculty of Law, Cambridge, in 2011. Elena is a member of the British Art Network (organized by the Tate to connect experts in British art) and was elected a Fellow of the Royal Society of Arts in 2020.

Marie-Stéphanie Delamaire is the Associate Curator of Fine Arts at the Winterthur Museum, Garden & Library, and an affiliated assistant professor at the University of Delaware/Winterthur Program in American Material Culture. Her research interests include artistic encounters in the post-colonization period, printmaking, and the transnational art market. The author of several articles and book chapters on the circulation and appropriation of printed images, she is also the project director of *The Denig Illuminated Manuscript of 1784: A Digital Project Exploring Artmaking in the Early American Borderlands.*

Jill Haley is Curator Human History at Canterbury Museum in Christchurch, New Zealand. Her work explores the material and social aspects of photography in nineteenth-century New Zealand. She is currently investigating the contributions that women made to the development of commercial photography in the colony.

Marta Iljadica is Senior Lecturer in Intellectual Property at the University of Glasgow. She completed her PhD in law at King's College London under the supervision of Prof. Tanya Aplin and Prof. Penny Green and was previously Lecturer in Law at the University of Aberdeen and the University of Southampton. Marta researches within (the intersection of) intellectual property and land law including on copyright law and geography, and creativity and non-legal norms. Her current research projects engage with copyright and freedom of panorama, and the digitization and circulation of cultural heritage in European cities. Her monograph on UK copyright law and graffiti norms, *Copyright Beyond Law: Regulating Creativity in the Graffiti Subculture* (Hart Publishing, 2016) was shortlisted for the Birks Book Prize for Outstanding Legal Scholarship by the Society of Legal Scholars in 2018.

Karen Lemmey is the Lucy S. Rhame Curator of Sculpture at the Smithsonian American Art Museum. She holds a PhD in art history and a Certificate in American Culture from the Graduate Center of the City University of New York. She previously worked as a research associate at the Metropolitan Museum of Art and as monuments coordinator for the City of New York's Parks & Recreation Department. Her research interests include public art and monuments, the history of materials and methods, American artist colonies in nineteenth-century Italy, the construction of race in American sculpture, the history of sculpture conservation, and direct carving.

Cristina S. Martinez holds a PhD from Birkbeck College, University of London, and teaches in the Department of Visual Arts at the University of Ottawa. Her research focuses on graphic satire, the history of copyright law and encounters between art and law. She is currently completing the book *Art, Law and Order: The Legal Life of Artists in Eighteenth-Century Britain* which is to be published by Manchester University Press, and is co-editor for the forthcoming collection *Female Printmakers, Printsellers and Publishers in the Eighteenth Century: The Imprint of Women in Graphic Media, 1735–1830*, under contract with Cambridge University Press.

Katherine Mintie is the Senior Researcher in Art History at the Lens Media Lab at the Institute for the Preservation of Cultural Heritage at Yale University. She received her PhD in the History of Art from the University of California, Berkeley. Before joining the Lens Media Lab, she was the John R. and Barbara Robinson Family Curatorial Fellow in Photography at the Harvard Art Museums.

Shannon Perich is Curator of the Photographic History Collection at the Smithsonian's National Museum of American History. Her publications include *When the Circus Came to Town: An American Tradition in Photographs* (Smithsonian Institution Scholarly Press, 2020), *The Changing Face of Photography: Daguerreotype to Digital* (Smithsonian, 2011) and *Portrait of a Family: Richard Avedon's Photographs of the Kennedys* (Harper Collins, 2007). Perich has curated and co-curated a number of exhibitions including the Smithsonian Institution's Traveling Exhibition Service's *Billie Holiday at Sugar Hill: Photographs by Jerry Dantzic* that is currently traveling. She has curated several exhibitions of Richard Avedon's photographs of the John F. Kennedy family for SITES and NMAH. Her exhibition *Laughing Matters* explored women and comedy. She co-curated *Country: Portrait of a Sound* at the Annenberg Center for Photography in Los Angeles with curators from the Country Music Hall of Fame and Museum. Perich has taught history of photography at Maryland Institute College of Art. Her blogs can be found on the NMAH and NPR websites. Perich is the project director and co-content manager for *Stories of 2020*, a story-gathering and archiving website for NMAH. Her photography research and collecting interests are broad, building upon the history of the medium and intersections with national narratives to explore how we can better see and understand history.

Erika Piola is Curator of Graphic Arts and Director of the Visual Culture Program at the Library Company of Philadelphia. In addition to her work in collections stewardship and public exhibitions, Piola has authored or edited a number of publications on nineteenth-century American art and visual culture, including *Philadelphia on Stone: Commercial Lithography in Philadelphia, 1828–1878* (Penn State University Press, 2012).

Rose Roberto's interdisciplinary research covers nineteenth- and early twentieth-century visual culture, the intellectual, economic and social history of the transnational book trade, and the hidden histories related to class, gender, race, and personal identity imbedded in material culture. Rose manages two library special collections at Bishop Grosseteste University, where she also lectures part-time on history and heritage education courses. She has previously lectured in the Department of Information Studies at UCLA.

Will Slauter is a professor at Sorbonne Université. His research interests include the history of publishing, the history of news and journalism, and the history of copyright law in the United Kingdom and the United States. He is the author of *Who Owns the News? A History of Copyright* (Stanford, 2019) and editor of a special issue of *Victorian Periodicals Review* on 'Copyright Law and Publishing Practice in the Nineteenth-Century Press' (2018).

Thomas Smits is a historian of nineteenth- and twentieth-century visual (news) culture. He applies Artificial Intelligence (AI) techniques to analyse large collections of historical images and is the author of the prize-winning *The European Illustrated Press and the Emergence of a Transnational Visual Culture of the News, 1842–1870* (Routledge, 2019).

Simon Stern is Professor of Law and Director of the Centre for Innovation Law & Policy at University of Toronto. He works at the borders of law and literature, and has published extensively on the history of copyright and the public domain in Great Britain. He is co-editor of the *Oxford Handbook of Law and Humanities* (Oxford University Press, 2020), and is completing a book titled *Reasonable Doubters*, on changing ideas about deception, proof, and verification in Anglo-American culture from the eighteenth century to the present.

Acknowledgements

This book is the result of several years of exchanges among the editors, the contributors, and a wider group of scholars that shared their work and expertise at two international symposia. The first event was hosted by the Winterthur Museum, Garden, & Library in 2018 and consisted of public presentations of original research, not only by the contributors to this volume, but also by other speakers, session chairs, and commentators whom we would like to thank publicly here: Georgia Barnhill, Barbara Cohen-Stratyner, Mazie M. Harris, Jason Hill, Peter Jaszi, Michael Knies, Lía Munilla Lacasa, Jessica Lake, Christopher J. Lukasik, Anne McCauley, Jessica Silbey, Nora Slonimsky, Amy Sopcak-Joseph, Eva E. Subotnik, Sandra M. Szir, Anne Verplanck, and Amy Werbel. The second meeting, hosted by Columbia University Global Centers Paris (Reid Hall) in 2019, took the form of a workshop featuring intensive discussion and peer review of the draft chapters for this book.

These symposia — and the present book — would not have been possible without the generous financial support of the Terra Foundation for American Art and the Samuel H. Kress Foundation. On behalf of all participants, we would like to express our gratitude to both organizations for their funding. Crucial support also came from the Institut universitaire de France (IUF), which enabled us to defray expenses associated with the two symposia and the preparation of this book.

We would like to thank our colleagues for their help in planning the two events. At Winterthur, these include Giovanna Urist, who provided expert assistance with several grant applications; the late Linda Eaton, Senior Curator Emerita of textiles, who supported our project; and Janice Kraft and Jean McCuskey, who were crucial to the success of the first symposium. We are also grateful to the late François Brunet, who as head of the Laboratoire de recherches sur les cultures anglophones (Université de Paris/ CNRS, UMR 8225), supported this project from the beginning, and to LARCA's Jean-Marie Boeglin, who provided indispensable administrative support. The Paris workshop was facilitated by the staff of Columbia Global Centers Paris, especially Loren Wolfe and Krista D. Faurie. Courtney Traub of WordTailors provided expert copyediting on a tight deadline. We are grateful for the anonymous peer reviewer who offered detailed comments on the individual chapters. Finally, we owe thanks to Alessandra Tosi for her encouragement and advice throughout the publication process, and to the superb editorial staff of Open Book Publishers, including Lucy Barnes, Anna Gatti, and Melissa Purkiss. As this book was going to press, we learned the sad news of the passing of William St Clair, Chairman of Open Book Publishers, whose scholarly contributions to the history of intellectual property and access to knowledge and culture were formidable.

Marie-Stéphanie Delamaire
Will Slauter

1. Law, Culture, and Industry

Toward a History of Intellectual Property for Visual Works in the Long Nineteenth Century

Marie-Stéphanie Delamaire and Will Slauter

The nineteenth century witnessed a series of revolutions in the production, circulation, and reproduction of images. Thanks to changes in printing and imaging technology and shifts in the practices of artists, publishers, and photographers, images became more readily available, in a wider range of media than ever before. Working in the new field of lithography, artists produced portraits, landscapes, caricatures, and depictions of events done 'on the spot', which were distributed quickly and cheaply. The development of photography led to the circulation of radically new forms of images such as daguerreotypes, ambrotypes, tintypes, *cartes-de-visite,* and stereographs. The quest to reproduce paintings and photographs spurred numerous experiments with printing techniques and photomechanical processes; meanwhile, a 'mechanical turn' in sculpture led producers and artists to invent materials and practical machines for the mass production of their work.[1] Engravings became a common feature in books, magazines, and newspapers, profoundly affecting the experience of reading.

1 The impact of industrialization on nineteenth-century sculpture remains an under-explored area in the history of art and visual culture. In England, new materials such as fired artificial stone — also known as 'Coade Stone' — were widely used in architecture and sculpture in the Georgian era. See Caroline Stanford, 'Revisiting the Origins of Coade Stone', *The Georgian Group Journal,* XXIV (2016), 95–114. For U.S.

 https://doi.org/10.11647/OBP.0247.01

The circulation of images across various formats and media, and the ways in which such circulation can transform the viewing experience, have generated considerable interest among specialists of art history and visual culture.[2] But the role that intellectual property laws played in shaping the production and dissemination of visual works has received far less attention. The increasing ease with which images circulated often went hand-in-hand with a desire — on the part of artists, publishers, collectors, and others — to exert some form of control over that circulation. The title of this book, *Circulation and Control*, evokes this tension, which has often been at the heart of debates about the ownership, reproduction, and appropriation of creative works envisioned as a form of intellectual property. Although other areas of law have undeniably had an impact on the circulation of images (censorship and obscenity law immediately come to mind), the essays in this book are concerned with intellectual property (IP), a broad area of law whose most well-known branches are copyright, patent, and trademark.[3] In the

---

artists' interest in mechanical means of reproduction, see Albert TenEyck Gardner, *Yankee Stonecutters: The First American School of Sculpture 1800–1850* (New York: Columbia University Press for the Metropolitan Museum of Art, 1945), especially Chapter 6: 'The Ingenuous Yankee Mechanic, or the Statuary Business', pp. 52–56.

2 A rich scholarship has explored the impact of nineteenth-century technology on theories and practices of vision. Jonathan Crary's influential monographs, *Techniques of the Observer: On Vision and Modernity in the Nineteenth Century* (Cambridge, MA: MIT Press, 1992) and *Suspensions of Perception: Attention, Spectacle, and Modern Culture* (Cambridge, MA: MIT Press, 1999) have been fundamental for our understanding of the historical conditions of viewing in the modern era, combining a subjective model of visual experience with the disciplinary and standardizing forces of industrialization. For an overview of the historiography of nineteenth-century visual culture, see *The Nineteenth-Century Visual Culture Reader*, ed. by Vanessa Schwartz and Jeannene Przyblyski (New York and London: Routledge, 2004). For a historiography in the American context, see François Brunet, 'Introduction: No Representation without Circulation', in *Circulation*, ed. by François Brunet (Chicago: Terra Foundation for American Art/University of Chicago Press, 2017), pp. 10–39, as well as the other essays in that volume. See also Patricia Mainardi, *Another World: Nineteenth-Century Illustrated Print Culture* (New Haven: Yale University Press, 2017).

3 On obscenity and censorship in particular, see *Law and the Image: The Authority of Art and the Aesthetics of Law*, ed. by Costas Douzinas and Lynda Nead (Chicago: University of Chicago Press, 1999); and Amy Werbel, *Lust on Trial: Censorship and the Rise of American Obscenity in the Age of Anthony Comstock* (New York: Columbia University Press, 2018), https://doi.org/10.7312/werb17522. Other areas of IP include trade secrets, industrial design rights, geographic indications, and traditional cultural expressions. Major histories of IP that treat the period covered by the present volume include: Brad Sherman and Lionel Bently, *The Making of Modern Intellectual Property Law: The British Experience, 1760–1911* (Cambridge:

visual arts, IP laws have often been looked to as a means of exerting some kind of control, such as by reserving the exclusive right to display or reproduce a work of art, or by licensing the right to use a particular technical process for making or duplicating visual works. Yet the history of such efforts has so far received relatively little scholarly attention, especially compared to the history of copyright for books and other printed texts.[4]

With contributions by scholars in law, art history, the history of publishing, and specialists of painting, photography, sculpture, and graphic arts, this book considers the multifaceted relationships between IP laws, artistic practices, and business strategies that shaped the production and circulation of images in the United States, the United Kingdom, and one of its colonies (New Zealand) during the 'long' nineteenth century. Many of the essays in this volume explore contested rights to make and sell copies or reproductions of visual works, to reproduce their design in a new format or medium, or to make what are now called 'derivative works' (that is works directly inspired by a copyrighted work, such an illustration from a famous novel). In this respect, the area of IP law that is given the most attention in this volume is copyright. However, patent law is also considered by two of the essays, which explore how individuals and groups attempted to use patents to protect photographic processes and the designs of sculptures. Although art's relationship to trademark law is not addressed here, recent work has explored how designers and firms looked to trademark law as a mechanism for controlling the reproduction of images, not least for advertising posters produced through the new medium of lithography.[5]

Cambridge University Press, 1999); Adrian Johns, *Piracy: The Intellectual Property Wars from Gutenberg to Gates* (Chicago: University of Chicago Press, 2009), https://doi.org/10.7208/chicago/9780226401201.001.0001; Isabella Alexander, *Copyright Law and the Public Interest in the Nineteenth Century* (Oxford: Hart Publishing, 2010), https://doi.org/10.5040/9781472565013; Oren Bracha, *Owning Ideas: The Intellectual Origins of American Intellectual Property, 1790–1909* (Cambridge: Cambridge University Press, 2016), https://doi.org/10.1017/9780511843235; Stina Teilmann-Lock, *The Object of Copyright: A Conceptual History of Originals and Copies in Literature, Art and Design* (London: Routledge, 2016), https://doi.org/10.4324/9781315814476.

4 There are some recent exceptions. See the section entitled 'Existing Studies and New Lines of Inquiry' later in this chapter.

5 See, for example, Amanda Scardamaglia, 'A Legal History of Lithography', *Griffith Law Review*, 26 (2017), 1–27, https://doi.org/10.1080/10383441.2017.1310011. On the intersection of copyright law and design law, see the essays in *The Copyright/Design*

Indeed, it should be mentioned at the outset that our volume makes no claim to exhaustively cover the full gamut of IP law during this formative period, nor does it adequately treat the immense range of creative productions that might be considered under the umbrella of art and visual culture. As research progresses, it may be possible to write a succinct history of IP legislation and case law as it affected various branches of the visual arts. The collaborative project that led to this volume has, however, a different aim: to bring together an interdisciplinary group of scholars from law and the humanities — as well as specialists of nineteenth-century art and visual culture based in museums and libraries — to produce a series of case studies that examine interactions between artistic practices, business strategies, and questions of IP as they emerged throughout the nineteenth century.[6] A mix of disciplinary backgrounds and expertise enables us to better understand the interactions between law, culture, and industry, and to better appreciate the specific factors that made different conceptions of IP in visual works seem relevant (or not) to various artists, distributors, and collectors of artworks. In short, we endeavor to consider how artistic practices and legal norms shaped each other. In that respect, this book builds on an interdisciplinary approach to the history of IP that does not limit itself to changes in legislation and judicial interpretation, but also considers the development of cultural norms and business practices that individuals and groups used in an effort to exert some degree of control over the conditions of copying and reuse of creative works.[7]

Interface: Past, Present and Future, ed. by Estelle Derclaye (Cambridge: Cambridge University Press, 2018), https://doi.org/10.1017/9781108182676.

6 The topics and methodological approaches that are explored in the individual chapters, as well as gaps in coverage that readers may identify, result in part from the way the project proceeded. The editors of the present volume issued a call for papers in 2016 for a conference on the general theme of 'Images, Copyright, and the Public Domain in the Long Nineteenth Century', which was held at the Winterthur Museum, Garden & Library in the spring of 2018. In part because of restrictions related to funding and in part owing to our own institutional affiliations, we limited the geographic scope to the United States, the United Kingdom, and its colonies during the nineteenth century. We received many more proposals than we possibly could have accommodated, but did our best to include a mix of professional and disciplinary backgrounds among the contributors, and to cover a range of artistic fields. Some of the gaps that we identified at the first conference were filled by soliciting new contributions in advance of a second meeting, held in Paris in 2019, but certain areas remain under-represented.

7 Important touchstones in the development of this approach include *The Construction of Authorship: Textual Appropriation in Law and Literature*, ed. by Martha Woodmansee

This introductory chapter will begin by offering an overview of some of the period's major developments in artistic media and visual culture. It will then survey existing scholarship on the history of intellectual property by considering the small but growing literature on copyright for visual works in relation to the much larger historiography on copyright for printed texts. Finally, it will discuss the structure and main themes of the volume. Like the other contributors to this book, we have written with a broad audience in mind. While some readers may be more familiar with the legal scholarship than with the history of art and visual culture, others may be well-versed in the history of technology or the art market but not as familiar with legal concepts and sources. With such differences in mind, we have included a broad range of references in the notes.[8]

New Visual Media and Artistic Practices

One of the defining features of the nineteenth century is how science, technology, and industry produced new visual media, transforming artistic processes of creation and conditions of viewing. Building on recent developments in chemistry, new media such as lithography and photography produced images that created new visual experiences of the world with representations ranging from the fine arts to the documentation of people, events, landscapes, and natural or scientific phenomena. Lithography (derived from the Greek for 'writing on a stone') was developed in Germany by a playwright, Alois Senefelder, at the end of the eighteenth century. A planographic printing process based on the principle that water and oil do not mix, lithography entailed the direct drawing of a design with a greasy medium on a limestone slab. Using the properties of gum arabic and acid to affix the image on the

and Peter Jaszi (Durham, NC: Duke University Press, 1994); *Privilege and Property: Essays on the History of Copyright*, ed. by Ronan Deazley, Martin Kretschmer and Lionel Bently (Cambridge: Open Book Publishers, 2010), https://www.openbookpublishers.com/product/26/; and Johns, *Piracy*.

8 Readers who are less familiar with the abbreviations used in citing legislation and court decisions may find it useful to consult the Cardiff Index to Legal Abbreviations, http://www.legalabbrevs.cardiff.ac.uk. Another excellent web resource for copyright history, which is cited by many of the chapters that follow, is *Primary Sources on Copyright (1450–1900)*, ed. by Lionel Bently and Martin Kretschmer, http://www.copyrighthistory.org/cam/index.php.

stone, the lithographer then inked the stone and passed it through a flat-bed press, transferring the design to the paper.[9]

The design process in lithography, once mastered, was faster than intaglio engraving or etching, and produced an infinitely greater number of copies. These qualities made lithography an ideal medium for the dissemination of reproductions of artworks to an expanding consumer public, the topic explored in Erika Piola's contribution to this volume. Additionally, the hand-drawn quality of a lithographic image was one of the technique's defining characteristics. Allowing the direct transfer of a design from stone to sheet of paper, lithography created what was first conceived as a multiplicity of autographic originals. Artists produced a wide range of images, including portraits, landscapes, social and political caricatures, scenes of everyday life, and depictions of events, such as fires and steamboat accidents. Lithographs could be produced with a virtually infinite print run as long as the stone itself was properly maintained. It is this latter feature that positioned the medium at the forefront of the transformations taking place in the printing industry, and which contributed to the rise of mass visual culture. Making the quick and cheap publication of images possible, lithography could respond to the latest event or talk of the town and lead to a variety of unauthorized reproductions — a practice that seems to have been rampant in the United States.[10]

9 Simple in principle, lithography was a demanding technique and a chemical form of printing that entailed the production of new materials and tools in order to obtain a satisfactory image. See Michael Twyman, 'The Process of Lithography and the Technique of Drawing on Stone', in Twyman, *Lithography 1800–1850: The Techniques of Drawing on Stone in England and France and their Application in Works of Topography* (London, New York, and Toronto: Oxford University Press, 1970), pp. 61–163. The problems of achieving a consistent, good quality lithographic paper that would remain mechanically and chemically stable in printing was a major difficulty, especially when the nascent art form of lithography met the developing technology of the paper machine in the early decades of the nineteenth century. See Marie-Stéphanie Delamaire and Joan Irving, 'Fine or Commercial Lithography? A Reappraisal of Fanny Palmer's Prints Published by Currier & Ives', in *Laid Down on Paper: Printmaking in America 1800 to 1865*, ed. by Caroline Sloat (Gloucester, MA: Cape Ann Museum, 2020), pp. 41–44.

10 See Erika Piola, 'Drawn on the Spot: Philadelphia Sensational News-Event Lithographs', in *Philadelphia on Stone: Commercial Lithography in Philadelphia, 1828–1878*, ed. by Erika Piola (University Park: Pennsylvania State University Press, 2012), pp. 177–200; and Elizabeth Hodermarsky, 'The Kellogg Brothers' Images of the Mexican War and the Birth of Modern-Day News', in *Picturing Victorian America: Prints by the Kellogg Brothers of Hartford, Connecticut, 1830–1880*, ed. by Nancy Finlay (Hartford: Connecticut Historical Society, 2009), pp. 73–83.

Chromolithography, an extension of the medium to color printing, was developed towards the end of the 1830s. It involved multiple stone drawings, each printed with one colored ink. In contrast to lithography, which found rich creative terrain both in the fine and commercial arts, chromolithography became the dominant medium of commercial printing, and served particularly well firms specializing in the production of advertisements, product labels, etc. Some firms, like L. Prang and Company in Boston, improved on the methods of chromolithography to produce high quality reproductions of paintings which imitated not only the colors of the original work but also its texture and the surface of the painter's brush strokes. These reproductive prints became known as 'chromos'. They were so perfect in their imitation of the original paintings that they not only sparked debates about the merits of art reproduction in artistic circles but also led to the singularization of 'chromo' as a specific category for copyright protection in the US Copyright Act of 1870.[11]

Photography, a means of producing an image based on the chemistry of silver, was developed through the application of recent discoveries in chemistry, combined with the use of materials that had long been part of artistic practice, such as the portable camera obscura, a light-tight box equipped with a lens that projects an image of the outside world onto its interior wall. The first commercially successful photographic process, the daguerreotype, produced a stable unique positive image on a silver-coated copper plate brought out by exposure to light in a camera obscura. In 1839, the daguerreotype was given free circulation by the French Government's purchase of Louis-Jacques Mandé Daguerre's process, leading to its popularity beyond national borders. Around the same time, William Henry Fox Talbot in England used sensitized paper for his photographic experiments. His technique, patented in 1841, created a negative that could be used to make multiple identical

11 Jay T. Last, *The Color Explosion: Nineteenth Century American Lithography* (Santa Ana, CA: Hillcrest Press, 2005); Peter Marzio, *The Democratic Art: Pictures for a Nineteenth-Century America: Chromolithography 1840–1900* (Fort Worth, TX: Amon Carter Museum, 1979); Michael Twyman, *A History of Chromolithography: Printed Colour for All* (New Castle, DE and London: Oak Knoll Press/British Library, 2013). On the relationship between chromolithography and copyright see Robert Brauneis, 'Understanding Copyright's First Encounter with the Fine Arts: A Look at the Legislative History of the Copyright Act of 1870', *Case Western Reserve Law Review*, 71 (2020), 585-625.

positive prints. Talbot's negative process made it possible to envision a photograph as a multiple rather than a single original. At the crossroads of art and science, photography transformed the status of an image as representation: its seemingly indexical relationship to the world brought about a new framework for the discourse on objectivity and truth in visual representation.[12] But as Shannon Perich's chapter in this book suggests, the history of photographic practices and materials was also shaped by patent claims and licensing deals. Unlike Talbot's calotype, Daguerre's process was widely publicized and its use unimpeded by patent claims. In the United States, various efforts by inventors and photographers to claim exclusive rights over new inventions or improvements on existing processes were part and parcel of the cultural and material history of photography in the nineteenth century.

In parallel with the development of lithography and photography, wood engraving generated an immense number of images produced through a combination of artistic talent, technological innovation, and mechanical operations. Thomas Bewick developed the wood-engraving technique in Britain at the end of the eighteenth century. In contrast to woodcuts, which used the plank of the wood and traditional wood-carving tools, Bewick used an engraver's burin to carve the end grain of the wood, resulting in small but highly-detailed images. Wood-engraved blocks could be printed together with texts and became part and parcel of the industrialization of the publishing industry in the nineteenth century, driving the expansion of the illustrated press. With the development of stereotyping and electrotyping processes that duplicated a relief-printing matrix, the matrices of individual wood engravings could be reproduced on metal and sold to other publishers, creating a secondary market for images. Focusing on illustrated newspapers, Thomas Smits's contribution to this volume explores the business opportunities and legal challenges involved in the transnational trade in wood engravings depicting current events.

While photography initially appeared ill-suited to the large-scale production of images, two crucial technical developments turned it into a medium that was well-adapted to the visual industry: the invention

---

12 There are numerous references for this idea, but see especially François Brunet, *The Birth of the Idea of Photography*, trans. by Shane B. Ellis (Cambridge, MA: MIT Press, 2019) [originally published in French as *La naissance de l'idée de photographie* (Paris: Presses universitaires de France, 2000)].

of a transparent support for the photographic image, which enabled its transfer onto a sensitized printing matrix (woodblock, lithographic stone, or metal plate), and the development of a mass-produced sensitized paper. Photomechanical processes, or the production of a printing matrix with the help of a photographic image, were a major interest of the printing industry early on, finding applications in all areas of visual culture, from the illustrated press to fine art publishing. Photogravure, which involved the transfer of a photograph onto an intaglio plate, combined the fine tonal gradations of a photograph and the rich material qualities and stability of an intaglio print. Intaglio engravings were costly to produce and thus often used for the high-quality reproduction of a work of art. By contrast, wood engravings were relatively cheap to produce. The illustrated press started transferring photographs to wood blocks for engraving in the late 1850s, a process initially known as photoxylography. The transferred image was manually cut using the original sketch or photograph as a guide. Later, the relief line block process used a sensitized gelatin that hardened with light and required less manual intervention. Both processes preceded the half-tone by several decades and gave the image departments of illustrated magazines and newspapers many opportunities to appropriate and adapt existing photographs or wood engravings for their purposes. The artists who transferred the image to the block were free to alter its size and orientation, or to work from fragments of several images, which could be rearranged or combined into an entirely new composition.[13]

In the photographic studio, the development of prints on albumen paper, an improvement on Talbot's salted paper negative, played a critical role in the rise of commercial photography, leading to the development of two characteristic products of the nineteenth century: the *carte-de-visite* and the stereoscopic view. Introduced in 1851 by

---

13 Gerry Beegan, 'The Mechanization of the Image: Facsimile, Photography, and Fragmentation in Nineteenth-Century Engraving', *Journal of Design History*, 8 (1995), 257–275, https://doi.org/10.1093/jdh/8.4.257; Estelle Jussim, *Visual Communication and the Graphic Arts: Photographic Technologies in the Nineteenth Century* (New York: R. R. Bowker & Co., 1974); Tom Gretton, 'Reincarnation and Reimagination: Some Afterlives of Géricault's "Raft of the Medusa" from c. 1850 to c. 1905', and Marie-Stéphanie Delamaire, 'De l'utilisation de la peinture d'histoire dans le cartoon politique américain (1865–1876)', in *L'image recyclée*, ed. by Georges Roque and Luciano Cheles, special issue of *Figures de l'art: Révue d'études esthétiques*, 23 (2013), 77–94; 95–109.

Louis-Désiré Blanquart-Evrard, albumen paper allowed for a much better reproduction of details, which was particularly well adapted to the collodion glass negative. Most importantly, albumen paper could be manufactured on an industrial scale. Albumen prints soon became the most widely-used means of producing a photographic print. *Cartes-de-visite* were typically full-length portraits printed on albumen paper and pasted onto a paper board the size of a visiting card. They became immensely popular. Portraits of celebrities in particular sold by the thousands to people of widely different backgrounds and means. They were often collected and stored together with family portraits in albums. Stereoscopic views, or stereographs, were pairs of photographs of the same subject taken with a two-lens camera. When viewed with a device that also included two lenses, eye-distance apart, a single image of startling depth appeared, creating a new virtual experience of the world. Stereographs, which are discussed in Will Slauter's chapter, encouraged the viewer's mental projection into the realm of representation, be it a *tableau vivant*, an exotic locale, a military encampment, or an international exhibition.[14]

Nineteenth-century technological developments not only led to the genesis of radically new (and often cheap) types of images. They also affected the production and consumption of older artistic media such as painting and sculpture, and accompanied new sorts of visual experiences that became more common and accessible: art exhibitions, fairs, performances, panoramas, lantern-slide shows, sightseeing and window shopping all became essential features of nineteenth-century cultural life. Public exhibitions of paintings, often shown together with drawings, lithographs, photographs, watercolors, and sculpture, took place at mechanics' institutes, athenaeums, art-union galleries, local and international fairs, theaters, photographic studios, frame-makers and print-sellers' shops, and other venues. Viewing a painting often went hand-in-hand with being offered a subscription to its intaglio engraving, reading about it and looking at its wood-engraving reproduction in an illustrated newspaper, or finding it in another medium at the print shop. Similarly, the experience of seeing a famous marble sculpture such as

14 There is a considerable body of literature on *cartes-de-visite* and stereographs. See Anne McCauley, *Industrial Madness: Commercial Photography in Paris 1848–1871* (New Haven: Yale University Press, 1994); and the references in Chapter 5 of the current volume.

Hiram Powers's *The Greek Slave* — further discussed in Karen Lemmey's chapter — was often mediated by graphic reproductions, industrially produced replicas in plaster, or newly-developed ceramic processes like Parian ware.

This proliferation of art objects and reproductions was noted by writers, publishers, and artists — the latter often finding out about an unauthorized replica by seeing it for sale in a shop. Some commentators decried the danger of blurring the distinctions between an artist's creative genius present in the original work and a soulless, mechanically-produced copy. Others applauded what they called the democratization of art enabled by reproductions, and the shift from an art world supported by elite patronage to one rooted in the marketplace. At the same time, as imaging and printing technologies expanded, so did the markets and networks for the distribution of their products. Although artists and publishers sometimes expressed concern about a lack of control over the uses and reuses of their works, they also benefited from the exponential growth in markets for visual works. This growth was supported by informal networks connecting dealers and publishers across national borders and oceans, and by European and American imperial expansion. Consequently, the visual arts and experiences that emerged out of nineteenth-century urban culture impacted and reached a more socially, ethnically, and racially diverse range of people than ever before. Yet as the markets for visual works grew across regional, national, and imperial boundaries, the ability of artists, owners of artworks, and subjects (such as sitters in paintings or photographs) to control the circulation of a given work and the commercial exploitation of it became more uncertain.

Existing Studies and New Lines of Inquiry

The history of intellectual property is a growing interdisciplinary field that attracts scholars from law, the humanities, and the social sciences.[15] The history of copyright in particular has benefited from cross-disciplinary

15 The International Society for the History and Theory of Intellectual Property (ISHTIP) was founded in 2008, with the literary scholar Martha Woodmansee and the legal scholar Lionel Bently as the first executive directors. ISHTIP holds annual workshops that bring together scholars from a range of disciplines interested in the historical and theoretical aspects of IP. The programs of these workshops, available

exchanges among legal scholars, literary historians, and specialists of the history of printing and publishing. Such cross-fertilization has had a lasting impact on how the history of copyright for books and other printed texts is understood, and provides an important source of inspiration for the current volume. Lyman Ray Patterson's classic book *Copyright in Historical Perspective* (1968) drew upon research by bibliographers and historians of printing to chart the transition from the system of licensing and royal privileges in early modern England to the first copyright statutes on both sides of the Atlantic in the eighteenth century.[16] The literary scholars Martha Woodmansee and Mark Rose offered pioneering studies of the construction of authorship that connected debates about literary property to the commercial practices of the book trade in the eighteenth century.[17] More direct collaboration between literary scholars, book historians, and law professors working in this area was promoted by the gatherings organized by Woodmansee and Peter Jaszi that led to their co-edited volume, *The Construction of Authorship: Textual Appropriation in Law and Literature* (1994). Major works by John Feather, Adrian Johns, William St Clair, and others offered historical studies of copyright and piracy that foregrounded the cultural norms, business strategies, and rivalries that determined which books were produced where, and how unauthorized (but not necessarily illegal) reprints affected access to culture and knowledge.[18] Studying disputes over exclusive rights (such as copyright) has also revealed power struggles among communities over questions of appropriation, as well as important forms of cultural and political resistance, as Phillip Round's work on Native American printing and book cultures has shown.[19]

---

at https://www.ishtip.org, provide an indication of the range of work being undertaken in this field.

16 Lyman Ray Patterson, *Copyright in Historical Perspective* (Nashville: Vanderbilt University Press, 1968).

17 Martha Woodmansee, 'The Genius and the Copyright: Economic and Legal Conditions of the Emergence of the "Author"', *Eighteenth-Century Studies*, 17 (1984), 425–448, https://doi.org/10.2307/2738129; Mark Rose, *Authors and Owners: The Invention of Copyright* (Cambridge, MA: Harvard University Press, 1993).

18 John Feather, *Publishing, Piracy and Politics: An Historical Study of Copyright in Britain* (London: Mansell, 1994); William St Clair, *The Reading Nation in the Romantic Period* (Cambridge: Cambridge University Press, 2004); Johns, *Piracy*. See also Peter Baldwin, *The Copyright Wars: Three Centuries of Trans-Atlantic Battle* (Princeton: Princeton University Press, 2014).

19 Phillip Round, *Removable Type: Histories of the Book in Indian Country, 1663–1880* (Chapel Hill: University of North Carolina Press, 2010).

The slow and contentious process of establishing international copyright agreements during the nineteenth century, and the recurring problem of cross-border 'piracy'(the term was often used even in situations where the reprinting was not illegal) became an important topic of study for literary historians such as Melissa Homestead and Meredith L. McGill, as well as for legal scholars such as Catherine Seville and Robert Spoo.[20] More generally, several generations of scholarship at the crossroads of book history and copyright history have revealed the value of studying the law in relation to the organizational structure of the book trade and shifts in the practices of writers, publishers, and readers. Such work has highlighted how, in many circumstances, copyright statutes and their judicial construction mattered less than the cultural norms and trade customs that individuals and groups established (or sought to establish) in an effort to regulate the production and circulation of texts.[21] It is therefore necessary to study how law, culture, and business shaped one another, and to think of the history of IP as a history of norms and practices, rather than solely a history of legislative and judicial developments.

This book focuses on the visual arts in the nineteenth century, a topic which has not hitherto benefited from as much interdisciplinary inquiry into the relationships between IP, cultural norms, and business practices as has the realm of printed texts. But like writers, artists were concerned

20 James J. Barnes, *Authors, Publishers and Politicians: The Quest for an Anglo-American Copyright Agreement 1815–1854* (Columbus: Ohio State University Press, 1974); Meredith L. McGill, *American Literature and the Culture of Reprinting, 1834–1853* (Philadelphia: University of Pennsylvania Press, 2003); Melissa Homestead, *American Women Authors and Literary Property, 1822–1869* (Cambridge: Cambridge University Press, 2005); Melissa Homestead, 'American Novelist Catharine Sedgwick Negotiates British Copyright, 1822–1857', *Yearbook of English Studies*, 45 (2015), 196–215; Catherine Seville, *The Internationalisation of Copyright Law: Books, Buccaneers and the Black Flag in the Nineteenth Century* (Cambridge: Cambridge University Press, 2009); and Robert Spoo, *Without Copyrights: Piracy, Publishing, and the Public Domain* (Oxford: Oxford University Press, 2013).

21 For an overview of the vast literature that lies at the crossroads of copyright law and book history, see Meredith L. McGill, 'Copyright and Intellectual Property: The State of the Discipline', *Book History*, 16 (2013), 387–427, https://doi.org/10.1353/bh.2013.0010. The history of copyright for non-book forms of print, such as contributions to newspapers and periodicals, have also begun to receive more attention. See *Copyright Law and Publishing Practice in the Nineteenth-Century Press*, ed. by Will Slauter, special issue of *Victorian Periodicals Review*, 51 (2018), 583–737; and Slauter, *Who Owns the News? A History of Copyright* (Stanford, CA: Stanford University Press, 2019).

with the relationship between their creative work and what preceded it; they were also interested in their work's future prospects and their own posterity as creators. Painters, sculptors, graphic artists, and architects took steps to ensure that their work continued to live in various forms and media. In order to shape the circumstances in which their creations were made public, they collaborated with or disputed with their peers, art institutions, patrons who sat for portraits, collectors who owned their work, and printmakers and publishers who reproduced it. They worried about such questions as who had the right to display or copy their work, in what circumstances, and in what format, medium, or manner. They lobbied for new legislation or initiated lawsuits to defend what they believed to be their rights over the products of their creative labor. In these endeavors, creators did not always present a unified front. Additionally, their concerns often collided with those of other stakeholders — be it a competitor, the purchaser or commissioner of an artwork, or the sitter in a portrait — over questions of ownership in an object and its 'design', or the right to control reproductions of a person's likeness.

The relative paucity of scholarship that examines legal questions raised by the copying and reproduction of artworks in relation to commercial and artistic practices is all the more surprising given the fundamental role that imitation, emulation, copying, originality, and influence have long played in artistic discourse and practice, as well as in the foundational texts of art history. Artists and writers have employed various concepts to characterize the subtle and complex relationships that connect a work of art to its antecedents. Mimesis, imitation, emulation, and copying are terms usually associated with the early modern period in Europe and the writings of Roger de Piles, Denis Diderot, and Johann Joachim Winckelmann. Originality, reproduction, influence, *plagiat*, appropriation, translation, citation, repetition, replication, and *détournement* are all terms associated with prolific modern and post-modern artistic discourse and practices located in the interconnected and global art world that resulted from European and North American colonial expansion in the eighteenth and nineteenth centuries.[22] Originality, a notion that indexes the artist's subjectivity

22 For a recent discussion of these concepts over various geographical areas and periods, see Georg Baselitz et al., 'Notes from the Field: Appropriation: Back Then,

and authorship in the work of art, gained traction in European and North American artistic practices over the course of the nineteenth century, the period examined in this book. This concept tended to focus attention on an individual artist's agency at the expense of the structure of the art world with its studios, institutions, and exhibition practices, its patronage system, and its expanding consumer market with links to the printing and publishing trades. Necessarily embedded in a dialectical relationship with its opposite — be it reproduction, copy, or replica — originality not only constituted itself in artist's studios and literary and aesthetic discourse, but also in the way creators, patrons, and business partners negotiated and articulated their rights over visual representations. These aesthetic and commercial developments shaped discussions of copyright reform, leading to the notion of originality being incorporated into the language of copyright statutes. In the United Kingdom, for example, the Fine Arts Copyright Act of 1862 explicitly protected 'original' drawings, paintings, and photographs, affirming a statutory threshold of 'originality' that would necessarily lead to debates about what constituted an 'original' photograph, for example.[23]

Although the role that artists, their patrons, and business partners played in shaping legal norms — and how such norms interacted with artistic creation during this period — have remained on the margins of art historical inquiries, this book builds upon a small but growing literature on the topic. In the contemporary art world, the seemingly boundless circulation of images that has accompanied the rise of new media in recent decades has led to new practices and critical inquiries centered on creative reuses and transformations. Interest in how

In Between, and Today', *The Art Bulletin*, 94 (2012), 166–186. This series of short essays written by specialists of various fields foregrounds the fundamentally appropriative and transformative nature of artistic creation, and therefore the critical importance of specific approaches and conditions in which artists have utilized and positioned their own creative practice vis-à vis what preceded them. Only one of the contributions in this series evokes the regulatory power of intellectual property law, and the way it signals connections between the aesthetics and politics of culture in today's global art world.

23 Ronan Deazley, 'Commentary on Fine Arts Copyright Act 1862', in *Primary Sources on Copyright*, ed. by Bently and Kretschmer, http://www.copyrighthistory.org/cam/tools/request/showRecord?id=commentary_uk_1862. As Deazley notes, the 1814 Sculpture Copyright Act had contained the phrase 'new and original'. On these questions, see also the more recent work by Elena Cooper cited later in this chapter.

copyright law affects artists' practices and legacies was one of the motivations for a 2002 volume edited by Daniel McClean, a specialist of art and cultural property law, and Karsten Schubert, a contemporary art dealer and publisher. Titled *Dear Images: Art, Copyright, and Culture,* the volume also included two chapters on the nineteenth-century UK, as well as a historiographic essay by Kathy Bowrey that began with the following observation: 'The history of copyright has overwhelmingly been concerned with literature and not art'.[24] Since that time, a number of important articles and book chapters have appeared, by both legal scholars and historians of art and photography, treating various aspects of the history of copyright for engravings, maps, and photographs.[25] Some of these studies were related to an AHRC-funded web resource launched in 2008 entitled *Primary Sources on Copyright (1450–1900)*.[26] This indispensable open-access site features primary sources (including statutes, proposed bills, reported court opinions, and polemical literature such as pamphlets) from several countries, as well as scholarly commentaries that situate the documents in their historical contexts. Members of the editorial team of *Primary Sources on Copyright*, along with other scholars in law and the humanities, also produced *Privilege*

24 *Dear Images: Art, Copyright and Culture*, ed. by Daniel McClean and Karsten Schubert (London: Ridinghouse/ ICA, 2002); Kathy Bowrey, 'Who's Painting Copyright's History?', in *Dear Images*, ed. by McLean and Schubert, pp. 257–274 (p. 257). In the same volume, see the essays by Lionel Bently, 'Art and the Making of Modern Copyright Law' (pp. 331–351); and Simon Stokes, 'Graves' Case and Copyright in Photographs'(pp. 108–121). See also *Artist, Authorship, and Legacy: A Reader*, ed. by Daniel McClean (London: Ridinghouse, 2018); Simon Stokes, *Art and Copyright* (Oxford: Hart Publishing, 2003); and *Art and Law: The Copyright Debate*, ed. by Morten Rosenmeier and Stina Teilmann (Copenhagen: DJØF Publishing, 2005).

25 David Hunter, 'Copyright Protection for Engravings and Maps in Eighteenth-Century Britain', *The Library* 6th ser. 9 (1987), 128–147, https://doi.org/10.1093/library/s6-IX.2.128; Ronan Deazley, 'Commentary on the Engravers' Act (1735)', in *Primary Sources on Copyright* ed. by Bently and Kretschmer, http://www.copyrighthistory.org/cam/tools/request/showRecord?id=commentary_uk_1735. Photography is by far the subject that has received the most attention. See Ronan Deazley, 'Struggling with Authority: The Photograph in British Legal History', *History of Photography*, 27 (2003), 236–246, https://doi.org/10.1080/03087298.2003.10441249; Anne McCauley, '"Merely Mechanical": On the Origins of Photographic Copyright in France and Great Britain', *Art History*, 31 (2008): 57–78, https://doi.org/10.1111/j.1467-8365.2008.00583.x; Kathy Bowrey, '"The World Daguerreotyped: What a Spectacle!" Copyright Law, Photography and the Economic Mission of Empire', in *Copyright and the Challenge of the New*, ed. by Brad Sherman and Leanne Wiseman (Alphen aan den Rijn, The Netherlands: Wolters Kluwer, 2012), pp. 11–42.

26 *Primary Sources on Copyright*, ed. by Bently and Kretschmer, http://www.copyrighthistory.org.

and Property: Essays in the History of Copyright (2010), a wide-ranging set of essays covering several countries and time periods.[27] Though most of the essays focus on printed texts, three of them do explore copyright in relation to the visual arts. Moreover, the general approach of that volume — which studies copyright law in relation to social norms, cultural developments, and business practices — was an important inspiration for this book.[28]

Another milestone was reached in 2018, when two major book-length studies of the history of copyright for art appeared: one, by the art historian Katie Scott, focuses on early modern France, and reveals the interplay between art theory, royal institutions, the economy of the print trade, and notions of IP in the visual arts.[29] The other, by the legal scholar

27 *Privilege and Property*, ed. by Deazley, Kretschmer, and Bently, https://www.openbookpublishers.com/product/26. The essays by Ronan Deazley, Frédéric Rideau, and Katie Scott discuss selected aspects of the history of artistic copyright. Since then, other important collections on the history of copyright have appeared, including *Copyright and Piracy: An Interdisciplinary Critique*, ed. by Lionel Bently, Jennifer Davis, and Jane C. Ginsburg (Cambridge: Cambridge University Press, 2010), https://doi.org/10.1017/cbo9780511761577, which includes essays by Daniel McClean and Jonathan Griffiths on copyright's relationship to the contemporary art market; and *Research Handbook on the History of Copyright Law*, ed. by Isabella Alexander and H. Tomás Gómez-Arostegui (Cheltenham: Edward Elgar, 2016), https://doi.org/10.4337/9781783472406, which includes an important essay by Elena Cooper, 'How Art was Different: Researching the History of Artistic Copyright' (pp. 158–173).

28 As the editors of the volume state in the introduction: '"Copyright law" needs to be understood as having been only one mechanism for the articulation of proprietary relationships: other legal norms (personal property, contract, bailment), and, more interestingly, other social norms, allowed for systems of ascription and control, flows of money, as well as the transfer and sharing of ideas and expression. Copyright history is not just another branch of positive law'. Martin Kretschmer, with Lionel Bently and Ronan Deazley, 'The History of Copyright History: Notes from an Emerging Discipline', in *Privilege and Property*, ed. by Deazley, Kretschmer and Bently, pp. 1–20 (p. 6).

29 Katie Scott, *Becoming Property: Art, Theory and Law in Early Modern France* (New Haven: Yale University Press, 2018). Specialists of the sixteenth and seventeenth centuries have revealed that efforts to control the circulation of visual works have a long history. David Landau and Peter Parshall, *The Renaissance Print, 1470–1550* (New Haven: Yale University Press, 1994) is essential reading on the topic. See in particular the study of the origins of the reproductive print in the fourth section of the book, entitled 'From Collaboration to Reproduction in Italy'. See also Caroline Karpinski, 'Preamble to a New Print Typology', in *Coming About: A Festschrift for John Shearman*, ed. by Lars Jones and Louisa Matthew (Cambridge, MA: Harvard University Art Museums, 2001), pp. 375–379; Lisa Pon, *Raphael, Dürer, and Marcantonio Raimondi: Copying and the Italian Renaissance Print* (New Haven: Yale University Press, 2004); and *Paper Museums: The Reproductive Print in Europe 1500–1800*, ed. by Rebecca Zorach and Elizabeth Rodini (Chicago: The David and Alfred

Elena Cooper (who is also a contributor to the present volume), covers the United Kingdom from the mid-nineteenth century through the early twentieth century.[30] Scott's study shows that the complex system of royal and corporate privileges that developed in France between the sixteenth and eighteenth centuries was grounded in conceptions of artists' rights and obligations as formulated in art theory, at the academy, and in artists' studios. Evolving notions of imitation, emulation, and invention are crucial to this history. Importantly, Scott shows that the notion of intellectual property that emerged in the entanglement of privilege, artistic discourse, and commercial practice in France became so closely tied to the identity of the artist that this property could not be easily alienated with the sale of the artwork. Scott's book reveals the eighteenth-century roots of a fundamental question that works of art raised as artists envisioned the status of their work as property: whether the intellectual property in the work of art was independent of the possession of the material work itself. This question also preoccupied artists in Britain and North America during the period; Marie-Stéphanie Delamaire's chapter in the present volume highlights how it motivated Gilbert Stuart's attempts to control the reproduction of his iconic portrait of George Washington in the United States.

Like Scott, Cooper also situates the development of legislation and case law in relation to cultural, aesthetic, and commercial trends. Her account of the lobbying that ultimately led to the 1862 Fine Arts Copyright Act in the United Kingdom — and the debates about copyright reform that continued for several decades after 1862 — highlights the different and sometimes conflicting interests of individuals and groups representing various fields of artistic endeavor. Sculptors, painters, engravers, print sellers, and photographers often had different ideas about what copyright should protect, and these ideas reflected economic interests and institutional connections, as well as the aesthetic and political ideals that these groups sought to promote.

Smart Museum of Art, the University of Chicago, 2005). It is important to note, however, that the notion of a 'reproductive print' itself is a modern concept, coined by Franz Wickhoff in 1899, and denotes a late nineteenth-century development. Franz Wickhoff, 'Beiträge zur Geschichte der Reproducirenden Künste: Macantons Eintritt in den Kreis Römischer Künstler', *Jahrbuch der kunsthistorischen Sammlungen des allerhöchsten Kaiserhauses*, 20 (1899), 181–194.

30 Elena Cooper, *Art and Modern Copyright: The Contested Image* (Cambridge: Cambridge University Press, 2018), https://doi.org/10.1017/9781316840993.

Cooper shows that in order to understand the convoluted path that copyright for visual works took in the nineteenth and early twentieth centuries, it is crucial to examine the complex and evolving relationships among the different groups that made up the art world, including the role of art patrons and collectors (whose interests were not always aligned with those of artists), public galleries (which sought to broaden public access to art), and publishers, whose arrangements with artists and disputes with rivals fundamentally shaped the debates, litigation, and legislative lobbying that took place during the period.[31] Cooper and Marta Iljadica, in their jointly-authored contribution to this volume, extend this line of analysis by reconstructing the different interests of architects, painters, photographers, and the public, revealing how and why architects failed to achieve the sort of copyright protection they sought. Cooper's monograph, building on articles and chapters by legal scholars such as Lionel Bently and Ronan Deazley and art historians such as Anne McCauley, has helped to elucidate the development of copyright law for artistic works in nineteenth-century Britain. The present volume includes several new essays on Britain and one of its colonies, New Zealand. These chapters explore aspects that have received less attention, such as protection for architecture and illustrations of the news, as well as the experiences of women and indigenous people as creators or subjects of protected works.

In the case of the United States, the other main country under consideration here, the existing literature on art and intellectual property is far more limited. Major studies, such as Oren Bracha's book on the history of IP in the United States, have acknowledged some of the challenges faced by those who sought protection for artistic works under a copyright regime built around notions of literary authorship and the commercial practices of the book trade.[32] Recently, Robert Brauneis has taken a closer look at the legislative history of the 1870 Copyright Act, which extended protection to drawings, paintings, and sculpture (photography was protected under a separate statute passed in 1865).[33] As Brauneis shows, it was not inevitable that works of fine art would simply be assimilated into the existing framework of copyright

31 Cooper, *Art and Modern Copyright*; and Cooper, 'How Art was Different'.
32 Bracha, *Owning Ideas*, pp. 88–93, 120–123.
33 Brauneis, 'Understanding Copyright's First Encounter with the Fine Arts'.

law; among the proposals for artistic copyright in the years leading up to the 1870 act, some would have recognized the specific concerns of artists by introducing different rules and procedures than those already existing for printed texts.

Much of the existing scholarship on the history of copyright for artistic works has been produced by legal scholars, who have considered the relationship between literary and artistic copyright and the extent to which the visual arts challenged existing legal frameworks and thereby influenced the overall history of copyright. As Cooper put it, 'Contests over nineteenth-century images, in presenting the law with new questions and different changing technological, commercial, and aesthetic contexts, resulted in powerful, varied and rich debates about the concept or "image" of copyright'.[34] The notion that visual works were different from texts, and that distinct genres of art should be subject to specific copyright rules, was expressed on numerous occasions during the nineteenth century.[35] The world of art raised new questions and pushed policy debates in unforeseen directions. In particular, the relationships among artists working in different media, with different aesthetic ideals and institutional affiliations, and the different business models that they developed, led to different sorts of legal and commercial arrangements to those that existed for literary works. The development of IP norms for visual works was therefore related to, but also sometimes in tension with, the history of copyright for printed texts.

In the world of books, the exclusive right to print and sell a particular work had long been seen by publishers as a means of protecting their investments in producing and distributing the book. The business was based on selling multiple printed copies of the author's work. The economics of image circulation were often quite different, and business strategies evolved in important ways during the period under consideration in this volume. First, the rise of mass visual culture led to a profound transformation of print culture as the acquisition and publication of images became an increasingly important part of book and periodical publishing. Rose Roberto's chapter on illustrated reference books, Thomas Smits's chapter on illustrated newspapers,

---

34 Cooper, *Art and Modern Copyright*, p. 249.

35 See Cooper, 'How Art Was Different'; and Brauneis, 'Understanding Copyright's First Encounter with the Fine Arts'.

and Oren Bracha's chapter on the textual and visual iterations of the bestselling novel *Ben-Hur* explore, each in their own way, the shifting relationships among printed texts, visual culture, and copyright law. Second, the relationship between a work of art's value and its publication was also changing during the nineteenth century as a result of far-reaching transformations that affected the national and international art market and the expansion of art's consumer base to various groups whose interests did not necessarily coincide.[36] One of the major changes that affected the art market was the growing importance of a group of buyers and collectors who came from a new social class: an increasingly rich and powerful middle class that supplanted traditional patronage (royalty, aristocracy, and state commissions) and brought with them a new speculative outlook on art buying and collecting.[37]

Cooper's study of the British context that led to the 1862 Fine Arts Copyright Act elucidates how some of these concerns affected the relationships among the different groups that constituted the British

36 The commodification of the fine arts has long been seen as a fundamental shift happening in Europe and the United States during the middle decades of the nineteenth century, a shift theorized by influential writers in the last century. Walter Benjamin, in his *Arcade Project*, not only brought to the fore the new conditions of art production but also elaborated on the new accessibility of the visual arts to the masses, and what he saw as the consequent loss of 'aura' in the original work of art. Recent studies by art historians interested in mass visual culture and business practices have refined our understanding of this paradigmatic shift and its impact on artistic value. See Michael Leja, 'Fortified Images for the Masses', *Art Journal*, 70 (2011), 60–83, https://doi.org/10.1080/00043249.2011.10791072; and Michael Leja, 'Mass Art', in *Encyclopedia of Aesthetics*, ed. by Michael Kelly, 2nd ed. (Oxford: Oxford University Press, 2014), https://doi.org/10.1093/acref/9780199747108.001.0001.

37 The scholarship on the nineteenth-century art market has recently seen a flurry of studies based on the application of digital tools and quantitative data. The online journal *Nineteenth-Century Art Worldwide* has published several of these studies. See in particular Pamela Fletcher and Anne Helmreich, with David Israel and Seth Erickson, 'Local/Global: Mapping Nineteenth-Century London's Art Market', *Nineteenth-Century Art Worldwide*, 11 (2012), http://www.19thc-artworldwide.org/autumn12/fletcher-helmreich-mapping-the-london-art-market; Diana Seave Greenwald, 'Colleague Collectors: Project Narrative', in Diana Seave Greenwald, with Allan McLeod, 'Colleague Collectors: A Statistical Analysis of Artists' Collecting Networks in Nineteenth-Century New York', *Nineteenth-Century Art Worldwide*, 17 (2018), https://doi.org/10.29411/ncaw.2018.17.1.14; and Agnès Penot, 'The Perils and Perks of Trading Art Overseas: Goupil's New York Branch', *Nineteenth-Century Art Worldwide*, 16 (2017), https://doi.org/10.29411/ncaw.2017.16.1.4; Jan Dirk Baetens, 'Artist-Dealer Agreements and the Nineteenth-Century Art Market: The Case of Gustave Coûteaux', *Nineteenth-Century Art Worldwide*, 19 (2020), https://doi.org/10.29411/ncaw.2020.19.1.2.

art world, and informed debates over intellectual property in the UK at that time.[38] Tensions between elite viewers and the masses were equally important to court cases brought against alleged copyright infringers during the period. The chapters by Simon Stern and Will Slauter in this volume hint at some of the tensions between social classes and aesthetic hierarchies in reproductive media, and at how these tensions played out in copyright disputes in the UK. Indeed, the technical transformations that affected the work of art in reproduction not only made a work of art more accessible to the masses; they also affected the work's status and the value associated with an original.[39]

Authorship in original artworks and reproductions was a layered concept. A painting often existed in more than one copy — each version differing from the other in size and small iconographic details. Additionally, paintings and sculptures (and their reproductions) often entailed the intervention of more than one hand, as can be seen in Karen

38 Cooper, *Art and Modern Copyright*.

39 The role of the multiple image and the shifting meaning of originality in nineteenth-century art has been a rich area of art-historical research for several decades, particularly but not exclusively in relation to French art. Several scholars have highlighted how the pervasive phenomenon of repetition associated with the early modern art world remained undiminished in the nineteenth century, and flourished both among painters associated with academic institutions and those of the avant-garde. How such practices continued to thrive in spite of, or rather in relation to, the development of new modes of art reproduction and the invention of photography has been explored by Stephen Bann. See Stephen Bann, *Parallel Lines. Printmakers, Painters, and Photographers in Nineteenth-Century France* (New Haven: Yale University Press, 2001); and Bann, *Distinguished Images: Prints in the Visual Economy of Nineteenth-Century France* (New Haven: Yale University Press, 2013). See also Rosalind E. Krauss, *The Originality of the Avant-Garde and Other Modernist Myths* (Cambridge, MA: MIT Press, 1985); Richard Shiff, 'The Original, the Imitation, the Copy, and the Spontaneous Classic: Theory and Painting in Nineteenth-Century France', *Yale French Studies*, 66 (1984), 27–54, https://doi.org/10.2307/2929861; and *The Repeating Image: Multiples in French Painting from David to Matisse*, ed. by Eik Kahng (Baltimore: The Walters Art Museum, distributed by Yale University Press, 2007). Some scholars have taken a transnational approach to the topic in light of the art market's significant geographic expansion. Several of the mid-nineteenth-century's most successful artistic careers depended on their connections to transnational dealers and publishers who simultaneously operated in Britain, France, Germany, the Netherlands, and the United States. See Robert Verhoogt, *Art in Reproduction: Nineteenth-Century Prints after Lawrence Alma-Tadema, Jozef Israëls, and Ary Scheffer* (Amsterdam: Amsterdam University Press, 2007); and Marie-Stéphanie Delamaire, 'Woodville and the International Art World', in *New Eyes on America: The Genius of Richard Caton Woodville*, ed. by Joy Peterson Heyrman (Walters Art Museum, distributed by Yale University Press, 2013), pp. 51–64.

Lemmey's contribution to this book. Even though we tend to look at an engraving after a painting as a derivative image that is not fundamentally different from a photographic reproduction, its status and place in the visual economy of the nineteenth century was entirely distinct. Prints that we call 'reproductive' today were then considered translations of the original painting, and the creative role of the interpreter was acknowledged in the collaborative authorship at play in its production. In addition, the fundamental notions of emulation, invention, and imitation that had dominated artistic theory and practices since the seventeenth century lost traction over the course of the nineteenth century. This was a very slow process, in which the industrialized manufacture of art reproductions only gradually shifted attention to the dichotomy between originality and creation, on the one hand, and copy and reproduction on the other. During most of the period covered by this book, numerous artistic practices of repetition and collaboration co-existed, and involved a range of practitioners whose livelihood depended on the production and sales of images based on other works of art. Their actions raised new questions about the boundaries between acceptable appropriation and illegitimate copying. Slauter's chapter in this volume highlights such a case of questionable appropriation, and in the process shows how the producer of a *tableau vivant* stereoscopic view after a painting envisioned his own artistic creation during an important transition period in the history of photography and its relation to the other visual arts.

Another important change was the transnational expansion of major art dealers and publishers, who did not always adopt the trade practices and legal frameworks of the countries in which they operated, and thus introduced new norms and contractual arrangements based on their own understandings of what constituted 'property' in a visual work. The international and colonial dimensions of copyright for artistic works remains to be studied in more detail, though some of the chapters in this book do contribute to this area of inquiry. Thomas Smits's chapter explores the international trade in illustrations of the news, and the difficulties faced by those who sought to use existing copyright laws to claim exclusive rights over images first published in a foreign periodical; Jill Haley discusses photographic copyright law and commercial practices in colonial New Zealand; Rose Roberto studies a transatlantic partnership between major publishers of illustrated reference works. Marie-Stéphanie Delamaire examines both the transatlantic context in which Gilbert Stuart worked and the international origins of the unauthorized reproductions of his portraits; these were created in China and shipped to the United States, where they would have competed directly with Stuart's own originals. It is nevertheless clear that the international dimensions of IP norms and practices deserve further study. Works circulated across national borders. Bilateral and multilateral copyright agreements (most famously the Berne Convention from 1886 onward) represented attempts to create effective international protection, but there has been very little study of how the various treaties (and the national laws passed in accordance with those treaties) actually affected the production and circulation of visual works. The shared customs and business arrangements that creators and distributors of art works attempted to use to control the cross-border copying and reuse of visual works also merits further study.

As several of the chapters in this book reveal, the different uses to which photography was put over time threatened to upset existing relationships and business models. The history of copyright for photography in the United States has received a fair amount of attention, but most of the existing scholarship crystallizes around an 1884 Supreme Court decision involving an unauthorized reproduction (via lithography) of a photograph of Oscar Wilde by Napoleon Sarony.[40] The earlier period, just before and after the passing of the 1865 Copyright Act Amendment (which extended copyright to photographs in the United States), has recently begun to attract some attention.[41] Even within

40 The Oscar Wilde case is *Burrow-Giles Lithographic Co.* v. *Sarony*, 111 U.S. 53 (1884). Studies include Jane M. Gaines, *Contested Culture: The Image, the Voice, and the Law* (Chapel Hill: University of North Carolina Press, 1991), Chapter 2; Christine Haight Farley, 'The Lingering Effects of Copyright's Response to the Invention of Photography', *University of Pittsburgh Law Review*, 65 (2004), 385–456, https://doi.org/10.5195/lawreview.2004.10; Justin Hughes, 'The Photographer's Copyright: Photograph as Art, Photograph as Database', *Harvard Journal of Law and Technology* 25 (2012), 339–428; Mark Rose, *Authors in Court: Scenes from the Theater of Copyright* (Cambridge, MA: Harvard University Press, 2016), Chapter 4; and David Newhoff, *Who Invented Oscar Wilde? The Photograph at the Center of Modern American Copyright* (Lincoln, NE: University of Nebraska Press, 2020).

41 Zvi Rosen has recently located a draft copyright bill dated 1864, which differs in interesting ways from the law that was ultimately passed in 1865. Zvi Rosen, 'The Forgotten Origins of Copyright for Photographs', *Mostly IP History* (blog), 10

the realm of photography, there is significant space for future work on how notions of IP were shaped by the practices of photographers, and several of the contributors to this volume offer new insights in this area. Shannon Perich, for example, explores a series of attempts to use patent laws to license photographic processes in nineteenth-century America, uncovering the strategies of the individuals involved and the extent to which their actions succeeded or failed. The collective efforts of photographers to have their rights recognized, and to receive payment and credit for their work, is examined in Katherine Mintie's chapter on American photographers' struggles against newspaper publishers at the end of the nineteenth century.

The question of IP in other fields of visual culture, such as painting, sculpture, architecture, and the graphic arts, has received far less attention than photography, and this book seeks to help correct that imbalance. The essay by Delamaire, for example, studies how the painter Gilbert Stuart responded to unauthorized reproductions of one of his famous portraits of George Washington to explore emerging concepts of artistic property in the late-eighteenth and early- nineteenth centuries. In the realm of sculpture, Karen Lemmey details how several American artists sought to use design patents to protect and monetize their work, though not always successfully. Elena Cooper and Marta Iljadica focus on copyright for architecture, situating efforts by British architects to secure protection for their buildings in relation to the claims of painters and other artists to freely portray the urban landscape. And with respect to prints and lithographs in nineteenth-century America, Erika Piola highlights the crucial role of lithographic publishers and other intermediaries such as frame makers and art associations.

October 2017, http://zvirosen.com/2017/10/10/the-forgotten-origins-of-copyright-for-photographs/. Jason Lee Guthrie has explored how Mathew Brady attempted to use copyright to protect his photographs of the Civil War. Jason Lee Guthrie, 'Ill-Protected Portraits: Mathew Brady and Photographic Copyright', *Journalism History*, 45 (2019), 135–156, https://doi.org/10.1080/00947679.2019.1603053. Beginning in an even earlier period, Mazie Harris has explored the interplay between photography, business history, and IP law (both patent and copyright). Mazie M. Harris, 'Inventors and Manipulators: Photography as Intellectual Property in Nineteenth-Century New York' (unpublished Doctoral dissertation, Brown University, 2014).

Structure and Common Themes

In order to draw attention to certain shared themes and preoccupations, the book is divided into three parts. The first part, titled 'Who Owns What?', spans the period from 1735 (when the first statute extending copyright protection to engravings was passed in Britain) through the early twentieth century. The five chapters in this part proceed in roughly chronological order, but alternate between developments in the British Isles and in the United States to explore some of the ways that visual works challenged established frameworks of copyright law. Isabella Alexander and Cristina S. Martinez examine a court case brought under the first British statute designed to protect visual works, the Engravings Act of 1735. The litigation introduced important questions that continued to be debated during the nineteenth century: what kinds of works were eligible for protection? Who could qualify as the owner of the copyright? How would courts interpret terms such as 'invention' and 'design' in determining a work's eligibility for copyright and the scope of protection? The case discussed by Alexander and Martinez was brought by a woman, Elizabeth Blackwell, in an effort to protect botanical illustrations after nature, and thus provides an opportunity to study the complex relationships between gender, creativity, scientific knowledge, and copyright law.

The case studies featured in Part 1 center on individual creators and entrepreneurs working in specific media and genres, who acted as plaintiffs or defendants in litigation aimed at upholding exclusive rights over a particular work. The arguments of the parties, the published judicial opinions, and the outcomes of the cases are analyzed not only for their contribution to copyright doctrine, but also for what these disputes reveal about contemporary artistic and commercial practices. Focusing on such disputes uncovers what individual artists and entrepreneurs thought should be protected by copyright law and why. Litigation was the exception rather than the rule, since most parties sought to avoid the expense and trouble of going to court. It should not be assumed that the positions taken by the parties represent universally-held values within a given field; indeed, sometimes individuals went to court in an effort to impose new rules or to obtain legal clarification of principles that were disputed at the time. But by forcing the parties to articulate their claims, such disputes often brought to the surface routine business practices and cultural norms that might not otherwise be made explicit if the parties had not felt strongly enough to proceed with litigation and continue all the way to a judgment. Many disputes were settled out of court, and therefore left fewer traces in the historical record.

Disputes over partial and trans-media copying are given particular attention in Part 1, since they raised the fraught question of what constituted a copy. To take an example from Simon Stern's chapter, did a panorama based on the design of a famous painting or engraving count as an infringing copy, given that the public paid to view the panorama but did not actually purchase any tangible 'copy' of it? In the case analyzed by Oren Bracha, could the copyright owner of a bestselling novel stop others from producing a magic lantern show that illustrated scenes from the novel? The case studies in the first section span almost two centuries, and much of their value lies in how they contextualize the disputes. But taken together, they also confirm a general trend of expansion in terms of the rights of copyright owners — from literal, verbatim copying of texts to the right to control 'derivative' works — such as the magic-lantern slide show of *Ben-Hur* at the heart of the dispute in Bracha's chapter. However, this history is neither smooth nor linear, since each new combination of technology, artistic practice, and business strategy provided an occasion to test the limits of the law, lobby for new forms of protection, or ignore the law in favor of other shared norms or commercial arrangements.

Whereas Part 1 focuses on specific disputes, many of which resulted in court rulings, Part 2, titled 'Agents of Circulation', draws attention to different individuals and groups involved in the production, distribution, and reuse of images. In some cases, commercial arrangements and rivalries sparked discussions of IP or attempts to obtain legal protection of some kind. Some of these entrepreneurs, such as the publishers of illustrated newspapers examined by Thomas Smits, went to court in an effort to enforce exclusive rights against rivals in their field, only to find that existing laws were poorly suited to their needs. Others, such as the major publishers of reference books that feature in Rose Roberto's chapter, created international business partnerships in an attempt to forestall piracy and exploit the market on both sides of the Atlantic. The makers and distributors of lithographic prints discussed in Erika

Piola's chapter did not make systematic use of copyright (some of the works were registered for copyright while others were not); the art unions seem to have been more likely to have recourse to copyright, but this isn't the heart of the story, since what mattered was unions' role in making reproductions of artworks available to a broad audience through a membership subscription system.

The chapters in Part 3, 'Navigating Intellectual Property', further explore the interplay of law, artistic practice, and business strategy by highlighting how individuals and groups dealt with questions of exclusivity, authorial credit, and control over their works. Some lobbied for new legislation, either independently or as part of professional associations, as can be seen in the chapter on architects and painters by Elena Cooper and Marta Iljadica, and in Katherine Mintie's chapter on photographers and newspaper publishers. Other artists tried to take advantage of existing laws, as the essays by Karen Lemmey and Shannon Perich on two different types of patents (design patents as applied to sculpture and utility patents as applied to photographic processes) reveal. Others went to court to test a new law, as in Jill Haley's study of an early photographic copyright suit in New Zealand; here the litigation exposed interesting questions about the rights of photographic subjects and the emergence of a celebrity culture surrounding the indigenous Māori people.

Further research is needed on the interactions between artistic practices, IP laws, and the commercialization of artworks, not only in the countries covered here, but in other parts of the world and the connections among them. Our approach was not to commission a series of essays on designated topics by known specialists to be as comprehensive as possible. Rather, we organized two international conferences in 2018 and 2019 in an effort to identify emerging research in this area and to encourage individual scholars to develop essays based on their own expertise. Given this process, the shape of the volume reflects a number of common concerns that emerged from our discussions, while simultaneously offering a range of individual perspectives and examples that we hope will inspire further research in this exciting field.

Bibliography

Alexander, Isabella, *Copyright Law and the Public Interest in the Nineteenth Century* (Oxford: Hart Publishing, 2010), https://doi.org/10.5040/9781472565013.

Alexander, Isabella, and H. Tomás Gómez-Arostegui, eds., *Research Handbook on the History of Copyright Law* (Cheltenham: Edward Elgar, 2016), https://doi.org/10.4337/9781783472406.

Baetens, Jan Dirk. 'Artist-Dealer Agreements and the Nineteenth-Century Art Market: The Case of Gustave Coûteaux', *Nineteenth-Century Art Worldwide*, 19 (2020), https://doi.org/10.29411/ncaw.2020.19.1.2.

Baldwin, Peter, *The Copyright Wars: Three Centuries of Trans-Atlantic Battle* (Princeton: Princeton University Press, 2014).

Bann, Stephen, *Parallel Lines. Printmakers, Painters, and Photographers in Nineteenth-Century France* (New Haven: Yale University Press, 2001).

——, *Distinguished Images: Prints in the Visual Economy of Nineteenth-Century France* (New Haven: Yale University Press, 2013).

Barnes, James J., *Authors, Publishers and Politicians: The Quest for an Anglo-American Copyright Agreement 1815–1854* (Columbus: Ohio State University Press, 1974).

Beegan, Gary, 'The Mechanization of the Image: Facsimile, Photography, and Fragmentation in Nineteenth-Century Engraving', *Journal of Design History*, 8 (1995), 257–275, https://doi.org/10.1093/jdh/8.4.257.

Bently, Lionel, 'Art and the Making of Modern Copyright Law' in *Dear Images: Art, Copyright and Culture*, ed. by Daniel McClean and Karsten Schubert (London: Ridinghouse/ ICA, 2002), pp. 331–351.

Bently, Lionel, Jennifer Davis, and Jane C. Ginsburg, eds., *Copyright and Piracy: An Interdisciplinary Critique* (Cambridge: Cambridge University Press, 2010), https://doi.org/10.1017/cbo9780511761577.

Bently, Lionel, and Martin Kretschmer, eds., *Primary Sources on Copyright (1450–1900)*, http://www.copyrighthistory.org/.

Bowrey, Kathy, 'Who's Painting Copyright's History?' in *Dear Images: Art, Copyright and Culture*, ed. by Daniel McClean and Karsten Schubert (London: Ridinghouse/ ICA, 2002), pp. 257–274.

——, '"The World Daguerreotyped: What a Spectacle!" Copyright Law, Photography and the Economic Mission of Empire' in *Copyright and the Challenge of the New*, ed. by Brad Sherman and Leanne Wiseman (Alphen aan den Rijn, The Netherlands: Wolters Kluwer, 2012), pp. 11–42.

Bracha, Oren, *Owning Ideas: The Intellectual Origins of American Intellectual Property, 1790–1909* (Cambridge: Cambridge University Press, 2016), https://doi.org/10.1017/9780511843235.

Brauneis, Robert, 'Understanding Copyright's First Encounter with the Fine Arts: A Look at the Legislative History of the Copyright Act of 1870', *Case Western Reserve Law Review*, 71 (2020), 585-625.

Brunet, François, *The Birth of the Idea of Photography*, translated by Shane B. Ellis (Cambridge, MA: MIT Press, 2019) [originally published in French as *La naissance de l'idée de photographie* (Paris: Presses universitaires de France, 2000)].

——, 'Introduction: No Representation without Circulation' in *Circulation*, ed. by François Brunet (Chicago: Terra Foundation for American Art/University of Chicago Press, 2017), pp. 10–39.

Cooper, Elena, *Art and Modern Copyright: The Contested Image* (Cambridge: Cambridge University Press, 2018), https://doi.org/10.1017/9781316840993.

——, 'How Art was Different: Researching the History of Artistic Copyright' in *Research Handbook on the History of Copyright Law*, ed. by Isabella Alexander and H. Tomás Gómez-Arostegui (Cheltenham: Edward Elgar, 2016), pp. 158–173, https://doi.org/10.4337/9781783472406.00015.

Crary, Jonathan, *Techniques of the Observer: On Vision and Modernity in the Nineteenth Century* (Cambridge, MA: MIT Press, 1992).

——, *Suspensions of Perception: Attention, Spectacle, and Modern Culture* (Cambridge, MA: MIT Press, 1999).

Deazley, Ronan, 'Commentary on the Engravers' Act (1735)' in *Primary Sources on Copyright (1450–1900)*, ed. by Lionel Bently and Martin Kretschmer, http://www.copyrighthistory.org/cam/tools/request/showRecord?id=commentary_uk_1735.

——, 'Commentary on Fine Arts Copyright Act 1862' in *Primary Sources on Copyright (1450–1900)*, ed. by Lionel Bently and Martin Kretschmer, http://www.copyrighthistory.org/cam/tools/request/showRecord?id=commentary_uk_1862.

——, 'Struggling with Authority: The Photograph in British Legal History', *History of Photography*, 27 (2003), 236–246, https://doi.org/10.1080/03087298.2003.10441249.

Deazley, Ronan, Martin Kretschmer, and Lionel Bently, eds., *Privilege and Property: Essays on the History of Copyright* (Cambridge, UK: Open Book Publishers, 2010), https://www.openbookpublishers.com/product/26/.

Delamaire, Marie-Stéphanie, 'De l'utilisation de la peinture d'histoire dans le cartoon politique américain (1865–1876)' in *L'image recyclée*, ed. by Georges Roque and Luciano Cheles, special issue of *Figures de l'art: Révue d'études esthétiques*, 23 (2013), 95–109.

——, 'Woodville and the International Art World' in *New Eyes on America: The Genius of Richard Caton Woodville*, ed. by Joy Peterson Heyrman (Walters Art Museum, distributed by Yale University Press, 2013), pp. 51–64.

Delamaire, Marie-Stéphanie, and Joan Irving, 'Fine or Commercial Lithography? A Reappraisal of Fanny Palmer's Prints Published by Currier & Ives' in *Laid Down on Paper: Printmaking in America 1800 to 1865*, ed. by Caroline Sloat (Gloucester, MA: Cape Ann Museum, 2020), pp. 41–44.

Derclaye, Estelle, ed., *The Copyright/Design Interface: Past, Present and Future* (Cambridge: Cambridge University Press, 2018), https://doi.org/10.1017/9781108182676.

Douzinas, Costas, and Lynda Nead, eds., *Law and the Image: The Authority of Art and the Aesthetics of Law* (Chicago: University of Chicago Press, 1999).

Farley, Christine Haight, 'The Lingering Effects of Copyright's Response to the Invention of Photography', *University of Pittsburgh Law Review*, 65 (2004), 385–456, https://doi.org/10.5195/lawreview.2004.10.

Feather, John, *Publishing, Piracy and Politics: An Historical Study of Copyright in Britain* (London: Mansell, 1994).

Fletcher, Pamela, and Anne Helmreich, with David Israel and Seth Erickson, 'Local/Global: Mapping Nineteenth-Century London's Art Market', *Nineteenth-Century Art Worldwide*, 11 (2012), http://www.19thc-artworldwide.org/autumn12/fletcher-helmreich-mapping-the-london-art-market.

Gaines, Jane M., *Contested Culture: The Image, the Voice, and the Law* (Chapel Hill: University of North Carolina Press, 1991).

Gardner, Albert TenEyck, *Yankee Stonecutters: the First American School of Sculpture 1800–1850* (New York: Columbia University Press for the Metropolitan Museum of Art, 1945).

Greenwald, Diana Seave, with Allan McLeod, 'Colleague Collectors: A Statistical Analysis of Artists' Collecting Networks in Nineteenth-Century New York', *Nineteenth-Century Art Worldwide*, 17 (2018), https://doi.org/10.29411/ncaw.2018.17.1.14.

Gretton, Tom, 'Reincarnation and Reimagination: Some Afterlives of Géricault's "Raft of the Medusa" from c. 1850 to c. 1905' in *L'image recyclée*, ed. by Georges Roque and Luciano Cheles, special issue of *Figures de l'art: Révue d'études esthétiques*, 23 (2013), 77–94.

Guthrie, Jason Lee, 'Ill-Protected Portraits: Mathew Brady and Photographic Copyright', *Journalism History*, 45 (2019), 135–156, https://doi.org/10.1080/00947679.2019.1603053.

Harris, Mazie M. 'Inventors and Manipulators: Photography as Intellectual Property in Nineteenth-Century New York' (unpublished doctoral dissertation, Brown University, 2014).

Hodermarsky, Elizabeth, 'The Kellogg Brothers' Images of the Mexican War and the Birth of Modern-Day News' in *Picturing Victorian America: Prints by the Kellogg Brothers of Hartford, Connecticut, 1830–1880*, ed. by Nancy Finlay (Hartford: Connecticut Historical Society, 2009), pp. 73–83.

Homestead, Melissa, 'American Novelist Catharine Sedgwick Negotiates British Copyright, 1822–1857', *Yearbook of English Studies*, 45 (2015), 196–215.

——, *American Women Authors and Literary Property, 1822–1869* (Cambridge: Cambridge University Press, 2005).

Hughes, Justin, 'The Photographer's Copyright: Photograph as Art, Photograph as Database', *Harvard Journal of Law and Technology*, 25 (2012), 339–428.

Hunter, David, 'Copyright Protection for Engravings and Maps in Eighteenth-Century Britain', *The Library* 6th ser. 9 (1987), 128–147, https://doi.org/10.1093/library/s6-IX.2.128.

Johns, Adrian, *Piracy: The Intellectual Property Wars from Gutenberg to Gates* (Chicago: University of Chicago Press, 2009), https://doi.org/10.7208/chicago/9780226401201.001.0001.

Jussim, Estelle, *Visual Communication and the Graphic Arts: Photographic Technologies in the Nineteenth Century* (New York: R. R. Bowker & Co., 1974).

Kahng, Eik, ed., *The Repeating Image: Multiples in French Painting from David to Matisse* (Baltimore: The Walters Art Museum, distributed by Yale University Press, 2007).

Karpinski, Caroline, 'Preamble to a New Print Typology' in *Coming About: A Festschrift for John Shearman*, ed. by Lars Jones and Louisa Matthew (Cambridge, MA: Harvard University Art Museums, 2001), pp. 375–379.

Krauss, Rosalind E. *The Originality of the Avant-Garde and Other Modernist Myths* (Cambridge, MA: MIT Press, 1985).

Landau, David, and Peter Parshall, *The Renaissance Print, 1470–1550* (New Haven: Yale University Press, 1994).

Last, Jay T. *The Color Explosion: Nineteenth Century American Lithography* (Santa Ana, CA: Hillcrest Press, 2005).

Leja, Michael, 'Fortified Images for the Masses', *Art Journal*, 70 (2011), 60–83, https://doi.org/10.1080/00043249.2011.10791072.

——, 'Mass Art' in *Encyclopedia of Aesthetics*, ed. by Michael Kelly, 2nd ed. (Oxford: Oxford University Press, 2014), https://doi.org/10.1093/acref/9780199747108.001.0001.

Mainardi, Patricia, *Another World: Nineteenth-Century Illustrated Print Culture* (New Haven: Yale University Press, 2017).

Marzio, Peter, *The Democratic Art: Pictures for a Nineteenth-Century America: Chromolithography 1840–1900* (Fort Worth, TX: Amon Carter Museum, 1979).

McCauley, Anne, *Industrial Madness: Commercial Photography in Paris 1848–1871* (New Haven, CT: Yale University Press, 1994).

——, '"Merely Mechanical": On the Origins of Photographic Copyright in France and Great Britain', *Art History*, 31 (2008). 57–78, https://doi.org/10.1111/j.1467-8365.2008.00583.x.

McClean, Daniel, ed., *Artist, Authorship, and Legacy: A Reader* (London: Ridinghouse, 2018).

McClean, Daniel, and Karsten Schubert, eds., *Dear Images: Art, Copyright and Culture* (London: Ridinghouse/ ICA, 2002).

McGill, Meredith L., 'Copyright and Intellectual Property: The State of the Discipline', *Book History*, 16 (2013), 387–427, https://doi.org/10.1353/bh.2013.0010.

——, *American Literature and the Culture of Reprinting, 1834–1853* (Philadelphia: University of Pennsylvania Press, 2003).

Newhoff, David, *Who Invented Oscar Wilde? The Photograph at the Center of Modern American Copyright* (Lincoln, NE: University of Nebraska Press, 2020).

Patterson, Lyman Ray. *Copyright in Historical Perspective* (Nashville: Vanderbilt University Press, 1968).

Penot, Agnès, 'The Perils and Perks of Trading Art Overseas: Goupil's New York Branch', *Nineteenth-Century Art Worldwide*, 16 (2017), https://doi.org/10.29411/ncaw.2017.16.1.4.

Piola, Erika, 'Drawn on the Spot: Philadelphia Sensational News-Event Lithographs' in *Philadelphia on Stone: Commercial Lithography in Philadelphia, 1828–1878*, ed. by Erika Piola (University Park: Pennsylvania State University Press, 2012), pp. 177–200.

Pon, Lisa, *Raphael, Dürer, and Marcantonio Raimondi: Copying and the Italian Renaissance Print* (New Haven: Yale University Press, 2004).

Rose, Mark, *Authors and Owners: The Invention of Copyright* (Cambridge, MA: Harvard University Press, 1993).

——, *Authors in Court: Scenes from the Theater of Copyright* (Cambridge, MA: Harvard University Press, 2016).

Rosen, Zvi, 'The Forgotten Origins of Copyright for Photographs', *Mostly IP History* (blog), 10 October 2017, http://zvirosen.com/2017/10/10/the-forgotten-origins-of-copyright-for-photographs/.

Rosenmeier, Morten, and Stina Teilmann, eds., *Art and Law: The Copyright Debate* (Copenhagen: DJØF Publishing, 2005).

Round, Phillip, *Removable Type: Histories of the Book in Indian Country, 1663–1880* (Chapel Hill: University of North Carolina Press, 2010).

Scardamaglia, Amanda, 'A Legal History of Lithography', *Griffith Law Review*, 26 (2017), 1–27, https://doi.org/10.1080/10383441.2017.1310011.

Shiff, Richard, 'The Original, the Imitation, the Copy, and the Spontaneous Classic: Theory and Painting in Nineteenth-Century France', *Yale French Studies,* 66 (1984), 27–54, https://doi.org/10.2307/2929861.

Schwartz, Vanessa, and Jeannene Przyblyski, eds., *The Nineteenth-Century Visual Culture Reader* (New York and London: Routledge, 2004).

Scott, Katie, *Becoming Property: Art, Theory and Law in Early Modern France* (New Haven: Yale University Press, 2018).

Seville, Catherine, *The Internationalisation of Copyright Law: Books, Buccaneers and the Black Flag in the Nineteenth Century* (Cambridge: Cambridge University Press, 2009).

Sherman, Brad, and Lionel Bently, *The Making of Modern Intellectual Property Law: The British Experience, 1760–1911* (Cambridge: Cambridge University Press, 1999).

Slauter, Will, ed., *Copyright Law and Publishing Practice in the Nineteenth-Century Press,* special issue of *Victorian Periodicals Review,* 51 (2018), 583–737.

——, *Who Owns the News? A History of Copyright* (Stanford, CA: Stanford University Press, 2019).

Spoo, Robert, *Without Copyrights: Piracy, Publishing, and the Public Domain* (Oxford: Oxford University Press, 2013).

St Clair, William, *The Reading Nation in the Romantic Period* (Cambridge: Cambridge University Press, 2004).

Stokes, Simon, *Art and Copyright* (Oxford: Hart Publishing, 2003).

——, 'Graves' Case and Copyright in Photographs', in *Dear Images: Art, Copyright and Culture,* ed. by Daniel McClean and Karsten Schubert (London: Ridinghouse/ ICA, 2002), pp. 108–121.

Teilmann-Lock, Stina, *The Object of Copyright: A Conceptual History of Originals and Copies in Literature, Art and Design* (London: Routledge, 2016), https://doi.org/10.4324/9781315814476.

Twyman, Michael, *A History of Chromolithography: Printed Colour for All* (New Castle, DE and London: Oak Knoll Press/British Library, 2013).

——, *Lithography 1800–1850: The Techniques of Drawing on Stone in England and France and their Application in Works of Topography* (London, New York, and Toronto: Oxford University Press, 1970).

Verhoogt, Robert. *Art in Reproduction: Nineteenth-Century Prints after Lawrence Alma-Tadema, Jozef Israëls, and Ary Scheffer* (Amsterdam: Amsterdam University Press, 2007).

Werbel, Amy, *Lust on Trial: Censorship and the Rise of American Obscenity in the Age of Anthony Comstock* (New York: Columbia University Press, 2018), https://doi.org/10.7312/werb17522.

Wickhoff, Franz, 'Beiträge zur Geschichte der Reproducirenden Künste: Macantons Eintritt in den Kreis Römischer Künstler', *Jahrbuch der kunsthistorischen Sammlungen des allerhöchsten Kaiserhauses*, 20 (1899), 181–194.

Woodmansee, Martha, 'The Genius and the Copyright: Economic and Legal Conditions of the Emergence of the "Author"', *Eighteenth-Century Studies*, 17 (1984), 425–448, https://doi.org/10.2307/2738129.

Woodmansee, Martha, and Peter Jaszi, eds., *The Construction of Authorship: Textual Appropriation in Law and Literature* (Durham, NC: Duke University Press, 1994).

Zorach, Rebecca, and Elizabeth Rodini, eds., *Paper Museums: The Reproductive Print in Europe 1500–1800* (Chicago: The David and Alfred Smart Museum of Art, the University of Chicago, 2005).

PART I

WHO OWNS WHAT? IMAGES AND COPYRIGHT LAW

2. The First Copyright Case under the 1735 Engravings Act

The Germination of Visual Copyright?

Isabella Alexander and Cristina S. Martinez[1]

Introduction

In 1735, the British Parliament passed the world's first copyright statute in relation to visual works of art: the Engravings Act, commonly known as Hogarth's Act due to the role played by the famous artist in its enactment. William Hogarth was also involved in the first court case to invoke the Act's protection, *Blackwell* v. *Harper* (1740); however, he played a supporting role in that litigation, as a mere witness. The central character, one of the plaintiffs and the artist whose works were copied, was Elizabeth Blackwell. This legal suit, brought by Elizabeth and her husband, Alexander, in the Court of Chancery against a number of prominent London printsellers was not only the first case to invoke the protection of the Engravings Act 1735 but also the first copyright case with a woman plaintiff involving works created by a female artist. It was also the first case to grapple with the question of whether there was a threshold of creativity that would qualify a work for protection

1 The authors wish to thank Stéphanie Delamaire and Will Slauter for their invitation to participate in this volume. They also wish to thank Tomás Gómez-Arostegui for his feedback as well as invaluable assistance in locating and accessing primary source material, participants at the IP in the Trees Seminar at Lewis & Clark Law School (2019), and Oren Bracha for reading an early draft of this paper and for his helpful suggestions.

 https://doi.org/10.11647/OBP.0247.02

by copyright law, through a consideration of the meaning of the word 'invention'.

Elizabeth was a highly unusual litigant. Her creative labor gave rise to the property rights in question but, as a married woman, she was in principle unable to own property or bring legal proceedings under the doctrine of coverture. Moreover, as a married woman with scientific aspirations rather than a professional (male) engraver embedded in the artistic community, she was hardly the kind of author to whom the Act's drafters had foreseen offering protection. Furthermore, the artistic works being litigated were not the imaginative engravings envisioned by the statute's proponents but botanical illustrations — works 'copied from nature'. Elizabeth's works therefore tested the applicability of the very first law for the protection of images, establishing a key precedent for its future application and determining the legal fate of botanical illustrations.

This chapter explores the case of *Blackwell* v. *Harper* in detail, drawing on the legal archival record to investigate how the law was interpreted and applied, and uncovering the historical legal and social background against which the case was brought. It focuses in particular on the two unusual aspects of the case noted above. The first of these is its distinct subject matter, which threw into question the kinds of engravings that the Act was intended to protect. For reasons which are explained below, the court was required to interpret the meaning of the word 'invention', opening up the potential for conflict between the way the concept was understood in the world of art and the way it would be understood in the world of law. The second remarkable aspect is the plaintiff herself, Elizabeth Blackwell, one of only a handful of women to become involved in copyright litigation in the period. A detailed examination of Elizabeth's role therefore allows us to reflect on the gendered nature of copyright law, and to trace it back to the very earliest statutes and decided cases. It also requires consideration of how a woman exercised artistic, intellectual, and commercial agency in the male-dominated society and competitive marketplace of eighteenth-century Britain.

We start by briefly setting out the background to the 1735 Act, including its relationship to the Statute of Anne, and its key provisions. We then consider how 'invention' was understood by artists and their patrons in the mid-eighteenth century. Next, we narrate how Elizabeth came to produce *A Curious Herbal*, the volume containing her botanical illustrations, and explore the social and legal contexts in which she was operating, before turning to the litigation itself. Finally, we reflect upon what a case that lies at the intersection of gender, authorship, and art can tell us about the development of copyright law in the visual domain.

The Statutory Background: The Statute of Anne (1710) and the Engravings Act (1735)

The Statute of Anne, which entered into force in April 1710, created a statutory copyright for books, lasting fourteen years from first publication, with a possible second term of fourteen years if the author was still alive at the expiration of the first.[2] The right was held by the author of the work in question and, if infringed, the infringer would be liable for forfeitures and penalties. These remedies were dependent upon the book being registered before publication in the register book of the Company of Stationers.[3] Importantly, it was not necessary to be a member of the Stationers' Company to register a book, which represented a sharp distinction from prior practice.[4]

Prints published as or within books would probably have been protected by the provisions of the Statute of Anne. Individual prints were sometimes registered at Stationers' Hall as well.[5] Yet clearly, there remained a gap in protection for prints. In 1735, William Hogarth

2 Act for the Encouragement of Learning, by Vesting the Copies of Printed Books in the Authors or Purchasers of Such Copies, during the Times therein mentioned, 8 Anne c. 19 (1710) (hereafter Statute of Anne).

3 Statute of Anne, s.2.

4 See H. Tomás Gómez-Arostegui, 'The Untold Story of the First Copyright Suit Under the Statute of Anne', *Berkeley Technology Law Journal*, 25 (2010), 1247–1350 (pp. 1254–1257).

5 Malcolm Jones, in a study of the Stationers' Registers from 1562–1656, states that 'the number of prints as opposed to books recorded in the *Registers* is trivial — less than one per cent of all entries — and yet, for all that, there are well over 300 such "prints"'. Malcolm Jones, 'Engraved Works Recorded in the "Stationers' Registers", 1562–1656: A Listing and Commentary', *The Volume of the Walpole Society*, 64 (2002), 1–68 (p. 1). A similar study for the eighteenth century has yet to be made, but a few examples indicate that the practice of recording prints was still employed. This is the case of Reverend John Watson who, in 1761, registered two copperplates — *The South East View of the Town of Halifax* and *A South East Prospect of Halifax Church* — and later published a book, also registered at Stationers' Hall, which incorporated them.

and six fellow engravers presented a petition to Parliament asking for protection against 'divers Printsellers and Printers' who had lately too frequently taken the liberty of copying, printing and publishing 'great Quantities of base, imperfect, and mean, Copies and Imitations.'[6] The other six artists (George Lambert, Isaac Ware, John Pine, George Vertue, Joseph Goupy, and Gerard Vandergucht) were also prominent engravers of the time. A bill was introduced and passed through both Houses of Parliament, receiving Royal Assent on 15 May 1735. The new Act gave exclusive printing rights to any person who 'shall invent and design, engrave, etch or work in *Mezzotinto* or *Chiaro Oscuro* [...] any historical or other print' for a term of fourteen years from first publication. It also protected anyone who 'from his own Works and Invention shall cause to be designed and engraved, etched or worked in *Mezzotinto* or *Chiaro Oscuro*, any historical or other Print or Prints'.[7] Anyone who copied and engraved, etched or printed any such print without the consent of the owner, or who knowingly sold or imported such a print would be liable to forfeit the plates, the printed sheets, and the sum of five shillings for every print found in their custody. The plates and prints would be destroyed, while the money would be shared between the King and the person bringing the action.[8] The penalties would not, however, be incurred by a person who had purchased the plates from the original proprietor and sought to print from them.[9] This provision seems designed to clarify that copyright did not pass automatically with the physical copper plates, while allowing those who may have purchased plates intending to print from them to do so without fear of legal action. In other words, that person would receive a copyright license rather than an assignment.[10]

---

6 *Journal of the House of Commons*, 22, p. 364. See also Ronan Deazley, 'Commentary on the Engravers' Act (1735)', in *Primary Sources on Copyright (1450–1900)*, ed. by Lionel Bently and Martin Kretschmer, http://www.copyrighthistory.org/cam/tools/request/showRecord?id=commentary_uk_1735.

7 An Act for the encouragement of the Arts of Designing, Engraving and Etching Historical and other Prints, by vesting the Properties thereof in the Inventors and Engravers, during the Time therein mentioned 1735 (8 Geo II c.13) (hereafter Engravings Act 1735).

8 Ibid., s.1.

9 Ibid., s.2.

10 Ronan Deazley, *On the Origin of the Right to Copy: Charting the Movement of Copyright Law in Eighteenth-Century Britain (1695–1775)* (Oxford: Hart Publishing, 2004), p. 93, https://doi.org/10.5040/9781472563064.

The phrasing of the Act was unclear in several respects. Two of these would require interpretation by the court in *Blackwell* v. *Harper*. One question related to the information that needed to be included on each print in order to claim the penalties under the Act. The 1735 Act did not replicate the requirement in the Statute of Anne that works be registered at Stationers' Hall. That requirement represented a point of continuity for the book trade that dated back to the licensing era, but there was no parallel practice for the print trade. Instead, the more common practice was to insert the name of the engraver on each print, and it was this practice that was adapted for inclusion in the Engravings Act. The Act thus set out that the date of protection would 'commence from the Day of first publishing thereof, which shall be Truly engraved, with the name of the Proprietor on each Plate, and printed on every such Print or Prints'.[11]

A second issue was the role to be played by the words 'invention' and 'design' in limiting the type of engravings to which the Act applied. Timothy Clayton, in his description of Hogarth's role in the passing of the Act, emphasizes the word 'design', stating that '[t]he Act protected only designers who published their own prints'.[12] Yet, paying close attention to the phrasing and punctuation of the Act, it would appear to require the proprietor of a print to have invented *and either* designed, *or* engraved, *or* etched *or* worked the print in *Mezzotinto* or *Chiaro Oscuro*. The Act thus seems to offer protection mainly to 'inventors' — but what did this mean and, for our purposes, could it cover botanical illustrations, copied from nature? Was an 'inventor' the same as a 'designer', as Clayton assumes? The question is difficult because it requires a consideration of whether 'invention' and 'design' meant the same thing to the engravers whose works were the subject of the Act as it did to the court enforcing it. Before we turn to the court's approach to this question, it is therefore important to consider how artists, engravers and printsellers would have interpreted the terms 'invention' and 'design' in the mid-eighteenth century.

11 Engravings Act 1735, s.1.

12 Timothy Clayton, *The English Print 1699–1802* (New Haven and London: Paul Mellon Centre for Studies in British Art & Yale University Press, 1997), p. 87.

The Meaning of Invention and Design

The first point to observe in the 1735 Act is the sheer number of times that the words 'invention' and 'design' appear as well as their different combinations, including 'arts of designing', 'invented and engraved', 'invent and design', 'from his own works and invention', and 'shall cause to be designed and engraved'. The use of these terms and their Latin abbreviations on prints varied (for example, *invenit* or *invent* for the person who conceived the image, *sculpt* or *sculpsit* for the engraver, and *delint*, *delt* or *delineavit* for the person who created the drawing). It is of interest to note that Hogarth employed some of these Latin forms in early works — *The Lottery* (1724) has 'Willm. Hogarth Invt. et Sculpt.' inscribed within the image itself; *Perseus Rescuing Andromeda* is lettered at the lower right 'WH fecit' (WH has made); and his series *A Harlot's Progress* (1732) sees the inscription 'invt. pinxt. et sculpt.';[13] but after the passing of the Act, Hogarth's phrases and formulae are more consistently provided in English, as if moving away from the continental tradition. This can be seen in the series of *A Rake's Progress* (1735), 'Invented Painted Engrav'd & Publish'd by Wm. Hogarth' as well as in Plates I and II of the *Analysis of Beauty* (1753), 'Designed, Engraved, and Publish'd by Wm. Hogarth'; and in the subscription ticket *Crowns, Mitres, Maces, Etc.* (1754), 'Design'd, Etch'd & Publish'd by Wm. Hogarth', amongst others.[14] Did Hogarth use the words 'Invented' and 'Designed' interchangeably or with discretion? These examples and the wording of the Act itself reveal the complex underpinnings behind each of these terms from both a legal standpoint and the perspective of art theory. As the art historian Katie Scott has observed, the word 'invention' refers to some 'slippery concepts'.[15]

13 Digital images are available from the Lewis Walpole Library, Yale University: *The Lottery* (1724), lwlpr26065a, https://findit.library.yale.edu/catalog/digcoll:4048164; *Perseus Rescuing Andromeda*, lwlpr26106b, https://findit.library.yale.edu/catalog/digcoll:4048363; *A Harlot's Progress*, Plate 2, lwlpr22339, https://findit.library.yale.edu/catalog/digcoll:2807169.

14 Digital images are available from the Lewis Walpole Library, Yale University: *A Rake's Progress* (1735), Plate 1, lwlpr22206, https://findit.library.yale.edu/catalog/digcoll:2808268; *Analysis of Beauty* (1753), Plate 1, lwlpr22275, https://findit.library.yale.edu/catalog/digcoll:2808334, and Plate 2, lwlpr22276, https://findit.library.yale.edu/catalog/digcoll:2808335; *Crowns, Mitres, Maces, Etc.* (1754), lwlpr15021, https://findit.library.yale.edu/catalog/digcoll:2782448.

15 Katie Scott, *Becoming Property: Art, Theory, and Law in Early Modern France* (New Haven and London: Yale University Press, 2018), p. 247.

In law, invention could refer to the kind of new mechanical or chemical process that might be the subject of a patent, but in relation to copyright for literary works protection was linked to an act of authorship that was *not* mechanical. In 1720, counsel for the plaintiff in *Burnett* v. *Chetwood* argued that a translation was not an infringement under the Statute of Anne because 'the translator may be said to be an author, in as much as some skill in language is requisite thereto, and not barely a mechanic art, as in the case of reprinting in the same language'.[16] The concept of inventiveness was also specifically used by courts making decisions in relation to literary copying.[17] For example, in the 1740 decision of *Gyles* v. *Wilcox*, Lord Hardwicke observed that 'abridgments may with great propriety be called a new book, because not only the paper and print, but the invention, learning and judgment of the author is shewn in them'.[18]

The debate surrounding the division between mind and hand (or intellectual rather than manual labor) first emerged in the Renaissance, and the use of the word 'design' in the Engravings Act 1735 might very well stem from the Renaissance concept of *disegno*. The Italian painter and biographer Giorgio Vasari writes in *The Lives* that *disegno* 'is none other than a visible expression and declaration of the inner concept and of that which one has imagined and fabricated in the mind'.[19] For Vasari, however, the expression of a thought (invention) also necessitated manual ability (execution), and these two principles of *disegno* are what the Act seemed to have wanted, and demanded, for engravings.

Not all prints and drawings could be properly called inventive. Jonathan Richardson, in his discourses on art published in 1719, made the distinction between prints 'Such as are done by the Masters themselves whose Invention the Work is; and such as are done by Men not pretending to invent, but only to Coppy (in Their way) Other men's Works'.[20] Similarly, the architect John Gwynn's 1749 *Treatise on Drawing*

16 *Burnet* v. *Chetwood* (1720) 2 Mer 441, 441.

17 This observation was made by Catherine Gallagher, *Nobody's Story: The Vanishing Acts of Women Writers in the Marketplace 1670–1820* (Berkeley: University of California Press, 1995), p. 157.

18 *Gyles* v. *Wilcox* (1740) 2 Atk 141, 143.

19 Giorgio Vasari, *Lives of the Most Eminent Painters, Sculptors and Architects*, ed. by Gaston Du C. De Vere (New York: AMS Press, 1976), 10 vols., vol. 1, p. 111.

20 Jonathan Richardson, '*An Essay on the whole Art of Criticism* as it relates to Painting', in *Two Discourses* (London: W. Churchill, 1719), p. 194.

distinguished between the mechanical and the inventive using the notion of design:

> *Drawing* is mechanical, and may therefore be taught, in some Measure, to any Person of moderate Talents, who applieth sufficiently to the Practice of it: But *Design* is the Child of Genius, and cannot be wholly infused: The Principle of it must exist in the Soul, and can be called forth only by Education, and improv'd by Practice.[21]

However, because the Act's phrasing sets up 'invent' as a cumulative condition alongside the alternatives of 'design', 'engrave', 'etch' or 'work in *Mezzotinto* or *Chiaro Oscuro*', it appears that the word 'design' was employed to convey the mechanical act, while 'invent' was used to express the creative act.[22] The precise nature of Parliament's intention cannot be known, but the result was that debates previously confined to the artistic sphere spilled into the legal sphere. Before turning to consider the complex interactions between the theory and practice of art in *Blackwell* v. *Harper*, it is necessary to provide some background to the parties and the works involved.

Who Was Elizabeth Blackwell?

Elizabeth Blackwell is remembered in history as the author and artist of *A Curious Herbal*.[23] Yet, as is the case with the many British women involved in the print and publishing trade of the eighteenth century, we know very little about Elizabeth herself. A short entry on her exists in the *Oxford Dictionary of National Biography* and biographical detail can also be found in John Nichols's *Literary Anecdotes* and Blanche Henrey's magnum opus *British Botanical and Horticultural Literature before 1800*.[24] It

21 John Gwynn, *An Essay on Design: Including Proposals for Erecting a Public Academy to Be Supported by Voluntary Subscription ... For Educating the British Young in Drawing and the Several Arts depending thereon* (Dublin: George Faulkner, 1749), Preface, p. i.

22 Engravings Act 1735, s.1.

23 *A Curious Herbal, Containing Five Hundred Cuts, of the most useful Plants, which are now used in the Practice of Physick. Engraved on folio Copper Plates, after Drawings, taken from the Life. By Elizabeth Blackwell. To which is added a short Description of yͤ Plants; and their common Uses in Physick* (London, Printed for John Nourse at the Lamb without Temple Bar), 2 vols., [1737–]1739. Lindley Library, London, 615.3 BLA VOL I and 615.3 BLA VOL II.

24 See Doreen A. Evenden, 'Blackwell [née Blachrie], Elizabeth (bap. 1707, d. 1758)', Oxford Dictionary of National Biography, 27 May 2010, https://doi.org/10.1093/

should be noted, however, that the stories told about Elizabeth appear to be based on two main sources, which are themselves contradictory in places.[25] Moreover, recently discovered records from the legal case cast further doubt on some of the information therein.

The first point of confusion relates to Alexander and Elizabeth's parentage. Piecing together the evidence, it seems most likely that Alexander's parents were Thomas Blackwell, a professor of theology and the principal of Marischal College in Aberdeen, and his wife Christian, who was the sister of John Johnstoun, a physician and professor of medicine at the University of Glasgow. Alexander's brother was the classical scholar, also called Thomas Blackwell.[26] One of the dedications in Elizabeth's *Curious Herbal* is made to John Johnstoun, identifying herself as his 'much obliged Niece & humble Servant'.[27] In respect of Elizabeth, new research reveals that previous statements about her parents are incorrect. One of the depositions in the court case is from Alice Simpson, who states under oath that she is Elizabeth's mother.[28] Who Elizabeth's father might have been remains unknown. It seems almost impossible to imagine that Elizabeth had no training in either drawing or the craft of

ref:odnb/2540; John Nichols, *Literary Anecdotes of the Eighteenth Century* (London: Nichols, 1812), vol. 2, p. 93; and Blanche Henrey, *British Botanical and Horticultural Literature before 1800, Comprising a History and Bibliography of Botanical and Horticultural Books Printed in England, Scotland, and Ireland from the Earliest Times until 1800* (London: Oxford University Press, 1975). Stories about Elizabeth's background can also be found online, see 'Elizabeth Blackwell: Prison, Plotting and the Curious Herbal', https://www.rcpe.ac.uk/heritage/elizabeth-blackwell-prison-plotting-and-curious-herbal; and Katherine Tyrell, 'An introduction to Elizabeth Blackwell and "A Curious Herbal"', https://www.botanicalartandartists.com/about-elizabeth-blackwell.html.

25 'Abstract of a Letter concerning Dr Blackwell' from the *Bath Journal*, 14 September 1747, *Gentleman's Magazine*, 17 (1747), pp. 424–26; *A Genuine Copy of a Letter from a Merchant in Stockholm to his Correspondent in London Containing an Impartial Account of Doctor Alexander Blackwell, His Plot, Trial, Character, and Behaviour, both under Examination, and at the Place of Execution. Together with a Copy of a Paper deliver'd to a Friend upon the Scaffold* (London, [1747?]).

26 Evenden, *Blackwell, Elizabeth*; 'Abstract of a Letter', p. 424. This information is to be preferred as it is corroborated in writings on Thomas Blackwell which refer to his son. For example, see William T. Steven, *'The Life and Work of David Fordyce, 1711–1751'* (unpublished doctoral thesis, University of Glasgow, May 1978), p. 86, http://theses.gla.ac.uk/2766/1/1978stevenphd.pdf.

27 Blackwell, *A Curious Herbal*, vol. [2], 1739 (Lindley Library, 615.3 BLA VOL II). The acknowledgment is dated 'Chelsea January ye 17th 1739', [between Plates 452–453].

28 Deposition of Alice Simpson, 14 May 1740, The National Archives (NA), Kew, C24/1547/2.

engraving prior to producing her skillfully executed prints, and it is not known to what extent her family was involved in the print trade.

The second point of confusion is Elizabeth and Alexander's marriage. Although several sources claim they eloped and lived in Aberdeen, records reveal that an Elizabeth Simpson of St Paul's Covent Garden married Alexander Blackwell of St Mary le Strand on 1 October 1733 in Lincoln's Inn Chapel, Holborn, London.[29] One fact about Alexander and Elizabeth that is mentioned in the above accounts, and which has been verified by the archival record, is that a commission of bankruptcy was issued against Alexander in September 1734.[30] Intriguingly, the creditor who initiated the bankruptcy is one Thomas Blackwell. Could this have been Alexander's own brother? At least one source alleges Alexander assisted in the publication of Thomas Blackwell's *Life of Homer* prior to his bankruptcy.[31] According to a sympathetic report in the *Bath Journal*, after the bankruptcy, one of Alexander's creditors arrested him and he was sent to prison, where he spent nearly 'two years, in a very helpless condition'.[32] The report further claims that it was the bankruptcy and imprisonment that spurred Elizabeth into action. She took a house close to the Chelsea Physic Garden and began to collect, draw and engrave botanical illustrations with the object of selling them to provide for herself and secure her husband's release.[33] This narrative was endorsed

29 *Records of the Honourable Society of Lincoln's Inn*, vol. 2 (Lincoln's Inn, 1896), p. 595. The marriage allegation (FM I/68) and bond (FM II/70) are held at Lambeth Palace Library, London. Different claims have been made as to children of the marriage. The only child whose birth has been verified by the archival record to date is Alexander Blackwell, baptised 7 September 1742 at St Paul's Church, Covent Garden: *The Registers of St Paul's Church, Covent Garden* (London, 1906), p. 267.

30 The notice of commission of bankruptcy can be found in the National Archives at B8/4. See also *London Gazette*, 10 September 1734 and 26 November 1734. According to the anonymous letter in the *Gentleman's Magazine*, an action was brought against him because he had not served a proper apprenticeship in the trade. We have not been able to locate any records of this action. 'Abstract of a Letter', p. 425.

31 Steven, *The Life and Work of David Fordyce*, p. 86. The book itself has no printer or publisher names on its title page, so these details cannot be verified: Thomas Blackwell, *An Enquiry into the Life and Writings of Homer* (London, 1735).

32 'Abstract of a Letter', p. 425. The commission of bankruptcy should have protected him against imprisonment, if the creditors assented to the certificate, but we have not been able to locate any material that indicates whether or not all the creditors did so assent, nor have we found any record of Alexander's imprisonment.

33 Ibid. Henrey has verified that the house at 4 Swan Walk was leased to Alexander Blackwell between 1736 and 1739: Henrey, *British Botanical and Horticultural Literature*, vol. 2, p. 228 fn. 2.

by the botanical author Richard Pulteney, who wrote in 1790 that 'It is a singular fact, that physic is indebted for the most complete set of figures of the medicinal plants, to the genius and industry of a lady, exerted on an occasion that redounded highly to her praise'.[34]

Making and Selling *A Curious Herbal*

Herbals formed a genre of published literary works which had steadily grown in popularity since the first introduction of the printing press. These books generally contained the names and descriptions of plants and herbs, together with their properties and virtues both for nourishment and medicine. In the period between 1500 and 1600, around nineteen botanical and horticultural books were published in England. Between 1600 and 1700 this number increased fivefold, to around one hundred, and in the following century around 600 individual new titles were published.[35] Such books were a necessary tool of trade for herbalists, botanists, physicians, and apothecaries, but were also indispensable to housewives, who treated minor medical complaints of household members, as well as more serious ones when the costs of a physician lay beyond their means.

Despite this growing market, Elizabeth appears to have identified a gap for a work such as hers. She explains in the introduction that her object was to 'make this Work more useful to such as are not furnished with other Herbals'.[36] To do this she gave a short description of each plant, including its names in different languages as well as the time of flowering, the place of growth, and common uses in 'physick', or what we would today call medicinal botany.[37] Some sources assert that Alexander provided the Latin names, but Elizabeth herself claimed to have used Joseph Miller's *Botanicum Officinale* as her reference.[38]

34 Richard Pulteney, *Historical and Biographical Sketches of the Progress of Botany in England, From its Origin to the Introduction of the Linnaean System*, vol. 2 (1790), p. 251, cited by Henrey, *British Botanical and Horticultural Literature*, vol. 2, p. 228.

35 Henrey, *British Botanical Literature*, vol. 1, pp. 3, 77; vol. 2, p. 3.

36 Blackwell, *A Curious Herbal*, vol. 1 (London: John Nourse, 1739), Introduction.

37 See *London Evening Post*, 17 February 1736; *Country Journal; or, The Craftsman*, 27 March 1736.

38 'An abstract of a Letter', p. 425; Blackwell, *A Curious Herbal*, vol. 1 (London: John Nourse, 1739), Introduction.

Elizabeth's botanical prints were created by intaglio engraving. The process and technology involved in making such engravings changed very little between the sixteenth and early nineteenth centuries. The process almost always began with a drawing or painting. Copper plates were then prepared with a white wax ground, and the design was then transferred to the ground by pricking or scratching through the wax. The wax was subsequently removed and the design was completed using a burin to engrave the lines. Lettering was added to the plates after the design was finished. Since the letters, like the design, had to be done as a mirror-image, this was a specialist task usually done by letter engravers. The copper plates would then be printed off using a rolling press, and later colored, if desired. It would be normal for each of these activities to be carried out by a different specialist.[39] Elizabeth was, if not unique, certainly unusual in carrying out the drawing, engraving of both design and lettering, and coloring herself.

Once printed and colored, Elizabeth's prints were issued in weekly parts. Publishing in installments was a new strategy developed by booksellers during the eighteenth century; this allowed them to reach customers who would not have been able to afford large, expensive books, by selling reasonably priced segments. The practice accelerated rapidly after 1732 and was commonly used for the more expensive horticultural and botanical books.[40] Each installment would consist of a small batch of printed sheets and was known as a part, fascicle, or number delivered at weekly, fortnightly, or monthly intervals. The sheets would be folded, collated, and stitched in blue paper. When the set was complete, the blue wrapper would be removed and the full set would be taken to a binder for leather binding.[41]

The creation of such a volume as A *Curious Herbal* was an enormous undertaking, both in terms of time, labor, and expense. The strategy of selling in weekly installments would have been attractive to Alexander and Elizabeth, given their recent financial difficulties, as it required less

39 See Antony Griffiths, *The Print Before Photography: An Introduction to European Printmaking 1550–1820* (London: British Museum, 2016), pp. 28–48, https://doi.org/10.1093/library/18.1.106.

40 R.M. Wiles, *Serial Publication in England before 1750* (Cambridge: Cambridge University Press, 1957), pp. 2–5; Henrey, *British Botanical Literature*, vol. 2, p. 660.

41 Wiles, *Serial Publication in England*, p. 195; Henrey, *British Botanical Literature*, vol. 2, p. 661.

initial capital and allowed them to recuperate costs as they went along. The weekly *Numbers* contained four prints (available uncolored at 1s. and colored at 2s.), and these were distributed to customers until the set was complete.[42] Each print which she titled at the bottom and numbered at the top right (a practice she adopted throughout the series) also included, in the lower left-hand corner, the following inscription: 'Eliz. Blackwell delin sculp et Pinxt'. This was the common abbreviation for 'Elizabeth Blackwell delineavit sculpsit et Pinxit' or, in English, 'drawn, engraved and painted by Elizabeth Blackwell'.

In 1736 the *London Evening Post* announced that 'Elizabeth Blackwell, according to the late *Act of Parliament*, has consented that the said Samuel Harding (only) shall sell these her *Prints*'.[43] The Act to which the advertisement was referring was clearly the Engravings Act 1735. At this stage, the prints had not been collected into a book, so this was the only statute which could have protected them from piracy.[44] However, a book was the desired end product and thus, on 28 September 1737, Alexander entered into a contract with the bookseller John Nourse. Nourse was an established London publisher and retail bookseller and, having arranged for their own printing and publishing of the book through Harding, the Blackwells may well have needed his connections to assist with sales.[45]

The 1737 contract sold Nourse a one-third share of 'Elizabeth Blackwell's Herbal, which is to contain five hundred specimens of Officinal Plants engraved on five hundred Copper-Plates, and also the Third Share of the Explanation Plates, which are to be the Hundred and Twenty Five'.[46] Importantly, the Blackwells were not selling him the copyright but rather a one-third share in the plates and in any profits. The price was 150 pounds, and as a security measure a third of the copper plates were delivered into Nourse's possession. This contract reveals

42 *London Evening Post*, 17 February 1736; *London Evening Post*, 19–22 June 1736.

43 *London Evening Post*, 17 February 1736.

44 As noted above, the Statute of Anne only applied to books, not individual prints produced by engraving.

45 It is possible that the Blackwells knew Nourse more personally through their mutual connection to the Society for the Encouragement of Learning. Nourse was one of the Society's booksellers between 1735 and 1749 and Alexander unsuccessfully stood for the post of secretary of the Society in 1739. John Feather, 'John Nourse and his Authors', *Studies in Bibliography*, 34 (1981), 205–226, p. 206.

46 British Library (BL), MS Add 38729, [31].

that, at this time, 320 of the plant plates had already been engraved, as well as forty-five of the explanation plates. In addition, Nourse was granted the right to a one- third share in any future work by Elizabeth 'relating to Plants Fruits or Flowers'.[47]

There are several points of interest to note in relation to this contract. First, as John Feather has remarked, the transaction was more comparable to granting a security against a loan than it was to the usual trading in shares of copies in the book trade.[48] Second, the contract referred to the book in terms that recognized Elizabeth's authorship, but the contracting parties were Nourse and Alexander. Interestingly, five months later, on 22 February 1738, Elizabeth added a statement to the *verso* side of the contract declaring that the deed of assignment was made with her consent and approbation.[49] This highlights the legal challenges posed by the author's gender. Under the doctrine of *feme covert*, Elizabeth and Alexander were regarded as one person.[50] While the basic rule was that married women could own no property of their own, the law in relation to the property rights, both real and personal, of married and unmarried women was in fact both complex and unclear. It could only have been more so in relation to such a new right as that of copyright in engravings.[51]

In everyday life, the strict rules of coverture were frequently not observed, and many wives carried on businesses and entered into commercial transactions. Indeed, as Tim Stretton and Krista Kesselring point out, 'If followed to the letter, the legal restrictions of coverture would have made ordinary life all but impossible'.[52] Ensuring that the

47 Ibid.

48 Feather, 'John Nourse and his Authors', p. 226.

49 BL MS Add 38729, [31].

50 *A Treatise of Feme Covert or, the Lady's Law* (London, 1735), p. v.

51 The *Treatise of Feme Covert* stated, somewhat obliquely: 'Chattels Real, being of mixt Nature, partly in Possession, and partly in Action, which accrue, during the Coverture, the Husband is intitled to by the Marriage, if he survive his Wife, albeit he reduceth them not in to Possession in her Life-time.' (at 53). Yet, over 150 years later, lawyers were still debating whether copyright was a chose in action or a chose in possession, a categorisation which impacted how they would be treated if owned or assigned to a woman, married or otherwise. See T. Cyprian Williams, 'Property, Things in Action and Copyright' (1895) 11 *LQR*, p. 223; Spencer Broadhurst, 'Is copyright a chose in action?' (1895) 11 *LQR*, p. 64; Charles Sweet, 'Choses in action' (1895) 11 *LQR*, p. 238.

52 Tim Stretton and Krista J Kesselring, 'Introduction: Coverture and Continuity' in *Married Women and the Law: Coverture in England and the Common Law World*, ed.

assignment had the consent of both husband and wife — particularly in light of the litigation they were no doubt at that time preparing to launch — was a sensible strategy. A third point of interest to note regarding the initial contract with Nourse is that the money was to be paid in two cheques of seventy-five pounds, both payable to Elizabeth's mother, Alice Simpson. Was this an attempt to shield the money from Alexander's creditors? Or were there other, personal, reasons for this? Again, the historical record is frustratingly silent.

In February 1739, the Blackwells clearly needed more money, perhaps to pay for the Chancery proceedings now underway, or perhaps to continue to cover their publication costs; they thus entered into another agreement with Nourse. For £319 6*s.* 1*d.*, Alexander granted Nourse 'the copy right and sole privilege of printing reprinting publishing and selling of all that book compiled written or engraved by Elizabeth the wife of the said Alexander Blackwell entitled "A Curious Herbal...,"' as well as all the copper plates and unsold books in the Blackwells' possession. However, the indenture went on to specify that the copyright be further divided into thirds, one third of which would be held by Nourse, and two-thirds of which were to be held by Nourse upon trust for Alexander and re-conveyed to him once he had paid Nourse the sum of £169 4*s.* 1*d.*, as well as any expenses Nourse had incurred in publishing the book.[53]

On 2 October 1740, both Alexander and Elizabeth signed an assignment to Nourse of a one-sixth share of the copyright, copper plates and copies of the *Curious Herbal* in exchange for 75 pounds, stating that this meant Nourse now owned half of the book outright, when combined with the one-third share he had bought in September 1737, and continued to hold the other half on trust for Alexander.[54] In April 1747, Elizabeth sold Nourse the remaining half of her copyright. She entered into this transaction on her own as Alexander was now living in

---

by Tim Stretton and Krista J Kesselring (Montreal & Kingston: McGill-Queen's University Press, 2013), pp. 3–23 (p. 8).

53 BL MS Add 38729, [37]. On 29 March 1739, there is an entry in Blackwell's account with Nourse referring to Alexander having received £11 4*s.* 2*d.* from Harding, indicating a possible date when their relationship ended: see Henrey, vol. 2, 234, fn 43b. At this point the title-leaves of both volumes were cancelled, and cancellantes dated 1739 were printed with Nourse's name replacing Harding's. There are some mixed sets, including the one held in the British Library: J. Feather, 'John Nourse and his Authors', p. 206.

54 BL MS Add 38729, [38].

Sweden and had given her a power of attorney.[55] At this time, Elizabeth still owed Nourse £108 13*s*., and the remainder of the copyright, the unsold copies of the books and the copper plates were sold for £20 in addition to the cancellation of that debt.

The contracts with Nourse provide a rich source of information on the publication history of the *Curious Herbal*, yet some mysteries remain in addition to those already mentioned. The way that the book was issued and compiled means that all extant copies are slightly different. It is unclear when the second volume was published, although it seems likely to have been in 1739, as it contains a dedication to John Johnstoun dated 17 January 1739.[56] The dedications and the commendation are particularly striking aspects of the book, both in nature and number, and owing to the additional background information they provide.[57] Most extant copies of the first volume of the *Herbal* contain a commendation from the Royal College of Physicians, dated 1 July 1737, with the names of the College President, Thomas Pellett, and those of the four censors, Henry Plumptre, Richard Tyson, Peirce Dod and William Wasey. It is accompanied by an illustration that one supposes Elizabeth intended to represent the arms of the College, but which contains two modifications: the arm emerges from the left side of the shield and, as underlined by Henrey, the pomegranate is depicted more like a thistle.[58]

Inserted in different versions of the work are a number of additional dedications. These include a dedication to Richard Mead, physician to George II, who Elizabeth states was first to advise her to publish the work; to Sir Hans Sloane, who gave the author permission to draw such foreign plants from his specimens 'as were not to be found in England', and to the physician Alexander Stuart, who showed 'some of the first drawings at a publick herbarizing of the worshipful Company

55 BL MS Add 38729, [39].

56 Henrey, *British Botanical Literature*, vol. 2, p. 233.

57 Not all editions include the informative and personal dedications. The two volumes held at the Lindley Library (London) seem to be the most complete, 615.3 BLA VOL I and 615.3 BLA VOL II. The British Museum holds editions from 1737, 1739 and 1782, as follows: 1737 (shelfmark 452.f.1,2) — this copy was formerly owned by Sir Joseph Banks; 1739 (shelfmark 34.i.12,13) — formerly owned by King George II, and 1782 (shelfmark 445.h.6,7) — possibly no former owner, the original British Museum Library copy.

58 Henrey, *British Botanical Literature*, vol. 2, p. 231.

of apothecaries' and who recommended the author to the friendship of Isaac Rand of Chelsea. Isaac Rand, apothecary and director of the Chelsea Physic Garden, was another dedicatee, Elizabeth says that without his assistance and instruction this undertaking 'wou'd have been very imperfect' as she claims (perhaps modestly) that she has 'no skill in botany'.[59] Other dedicatees include the physician and botanist James Douglas, Henry Plumptre, later President of the Royal College of Physicians, Dr. John Johnstoune, as mentioned above, and the apothecary Robert Nicholls, who gave a deposition in the court proceedings (see below).[60] While it was common for botanical and horticultural works to be dedicated to well-known physicians, apothecaries and botanists (Richard Mead being a popular dedicatee), the sheer number included by Elizabeth stands out. Was she emphasizing her scientific credentials and connections to balance out gender bias?

The use of dedications also assisted with sales, and many of those to whom the book was dedicated were also purchasers.[61] Nourse invested in advertising the work, and the accounts reveal he spent £5 8*s*. for advertisements in the country papers, and £5 6*s*. 6*d*. for advertising in the London papers.[62] The advertisements state that the 'setts are colour'd by Mrs. Eliz. Blackwell' and engraved 'from Drawings taken after the Life.'[63] They also include references to the endorsements by the Royal College of Physicians.[64] The work's appeal derived from its scientific and systematic approach as well as its entertaining nature. The prints were advertised as 'curious and useful' and aimed at an educated public of scientists and taxonomists, botanical enthusiasts

59 Blackwell, *A Curious Herbal*, vol. [2], 1739 (Lindley Library, 615.3 BLA VOL II., between Plates 400–401).
60 Henrey, *British Botanical Literature*, vol. 2, p. 235; and vol. 3, pp. 9–10.
61 BL MS Add 38729, Account of Outstanding Debts on Acct of the Herbal [32].
62 Wiles, *Serial Publication in England*, pp. 183–4.
63 *London Evening Post*, 23–26 May 1747; *Country Journal; or, The Craftsman*, 27 March 1736.
64 The important endorsement from the Royal College of Physicians is mentioned in newspaper advertisements. See for example *London Evening Post*, 17–19 June 1736; and *Country Journal: Or The Craftsman*, 27 March 1736. The *Old Whig: Or The Consistent Protestant* (7 July 1737) states that 'Mrs. Blackwell was introduced to the President and Censors of the College of Physicians by Mr. Rand, when she had the Honour to present them with the first Volume of her Plants, colour'd, which they were pleased to accept; and as a Mark of their Approbation, they honoured her with [a] [...] publick Recommendation' endorsed by Thomas Pellet, Henricus Plumtre, Richardus Tyfon, Peircius Dod, and Gulielmus Wafey.

and print collectors.[65] We know that purchasers of the volume also included the Duke of Richmond, the Countess of Aylesford, and the Bishop of St Asaph.[66]

The Proceedings in Chancery

Elizabeth's connections in the world of science and botany were not sufficient to protect her from the cut-throat world of the print trade, nor from the unauthorized copying which was endemic to it. Nor was she the first author of a botanical work to complain of piracy. On 18 March 1732 a notice appeared in *Fog's Weekly Journal* warning readers against a pirated edition of Robert Furber's *Twelve months of flowers*.[67] Elizabeth was, however, the first to take legal action.[68] On 9 March 1738, Elizabeth and Alexander commenced proceedings in the Court of Chancery by bringing a Bill of Complaint against a number of London printsellers whom they accused of copying Elizabeth's prints.[69] As previously noted, there was only one authorized seller of Elizabeth's prints. An advertisement in the *Country Journal; or, the Crafstman*, dated 6 May 1738, states that the 'first Volume and what is finish'd of the second, is sold by Samuel Harding, Bookseller, in St. Martin's-Lane; and no where else'; it emphatically warns

> of a spurious and base Copy of this Original Work; one Number of which has been lately publish'd and sold by the underwritten Printsellers and Engravers, viz. George Bickham, jun., Philip Overton, John King, Thomas Bakewell, John Tinny, Samuel Simpson, Stephen Lye, Thomas Harper.[70]

---

65 See for example, *London Evening Post*, 23–26 May 1747; *General Evening Post*, 7–9 April 1748; and *London Evening Post*, 16–18 May 1749.

66 BL MS Add 38729, Account of Outstanding Debts on Acct of the Herbal [32].

67 Henrey, *British Botanical Literature*, vol. 2, p. 661.

68 It is interesting to note that two years after Elizabeth's suit was commenced, her own mentor Philip Miller discovered that his extremely popular book *Gardener's Calendar* had been pirated; his publisher Rivington sought an injunction in Chancery: *Rivington* v. *Cooper* (1740), National Archives (NA), C11/1566/42.

69 NA, C11/1543/7 no. 1.

70 *Country Journal; or, the Crafstman*, 6 May 1738. The copy of Volume II of the *Curious Herbal* held in the British Library, which indicates it was published by Harding, also states on the title page a publication date of 1737. Based on this advertisement, as well as evidence from the contracts with Nourse discussed above, this date would appear to be false.

These were the defendants against whom the case was being brought. The inclusion of both Blackwells as plaintiffs is of interest. *A Treatise of Feme Covert* (1735) explained: 'Where Baron and Feme [sic] sue for personal things, they shall not join unless such things are in Action, and then it is in the Election of the Husband to join his wife or not. But where they have a joint interest they must join'.[71] The question of who owned the property in question was one that the Court had to consider, and will be examined in more detail below.

It is also important to note that although the advertisement quoted earlier refers to a complete 'Volume' and 'a spurious and base copy', the suit in question was brought not in respect of the *Curious Herbal* as a book, but in respect of four of the engraved prints. The Bill of Complaint stated that Elizabeth had with 'Labour and Expence [...] invented Designed Etched and Engraved [...] Three hundred and sixty prints being the representations of Sundry Official plant or plants'; but, of these, the prints at the subject of the suit were the Dandelion (which she labelled 'Plate 1'), the Garden Cucumber 'Plate 4', the Red Poppy 'Plate 2' and the Pansy, or Heart's Ease 'Plate 44' (see Figs 1–4).[72] Resting the case on the copying of the prints rather than the book meant that it clearly engaged the brand-new Engravings Act.[73]

Certainly, the Blackwells seemed aware that they were the first to make use of the new statute, because their Bill commenced by providing some background to it. They explained to the court that the 1735 Act had been passed as a response to the unauthorized copying of historical and other prints, 'to the very great prejudice and Detriment of the Inventors Designers and proprietors thereof' and its object was to provide a remedy and prevent such practices in the future.[74] They went on to complain that although Elizabeth had made the engravings after the Act was passed

71 *A Treatise of Feme Covert*, p. 88. The uncertainty over whether copyright was a chose in action or a chose in possession is referred to above in note 50.

72 NA, C11/1543/7 no. 1. The reason for this particular selection amongst Blackwell's prints is unknown, but this is the order in which they are listed in the Bill of Complaint (where the dandelion print is given a different number).

73 It does not appear that either the Blackwells, Harding or Nourse ever registered the book at Stationers' Hall. This would have precluded them from obtaining the penalties under the Statute of Anne (s.2) but not from bringing an action for ordinary damages, or indeed common law copyright. For some discussion of this, see Arostegui, 'Untold Story', pp. 1306–1307.

74 NA, C11/1543/7 no. 1.

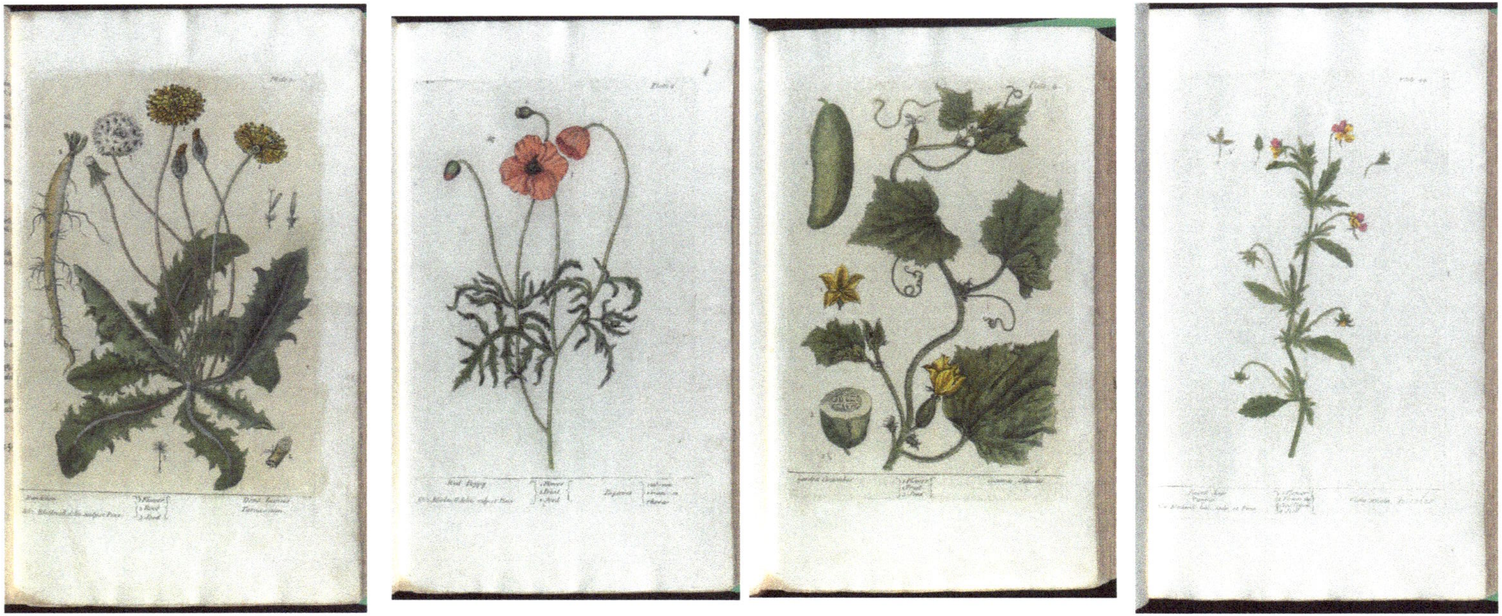

Figs. 1–4 Elizabeth Blackwell, *A Curious Herbal*, vol. 1, John Nourse (1739), Medical Historical Library, Harvey Cushing/John Hay Whitney Medical Library, Yale University. Dandelion ‘Plate 1’; Red Poppy ‘Plate 2’; Garden Cucumber ‘Plate 4’ and Pansy, or Heart’s Ease ‘Plate 44’.

and had published them on 1 July 1737, several printers and printsellers had nevertheless engraved and sold copies of Elizabeth's four works without her permission.

The chief argument of seven of the defendants was that they had been supplied by George Bickham the younger, and that as soon as they had discovered that the Blackwells had asserted their title in the prints they returned all the prints to Bickham.[75] Bickham was a talented political satirist who, according to his biographer Timothy Clayton 'often sailed close to the wind in matters of piracy, obscenity and political acceptability'.[76] The court had to issue a number of additional orders in an attempt to get Bickham to appear and answer the complaint, and he eventually submitted his Answer on 18 December 1738.[77]

In May 1740 a number of depositions were taken. The deponents included the apothecary Robert Nicholls, who testified to Elizabeth's creation of the engravings from specimens of plants he had supplied, and Elizabeth's own mother, Alice Simpson, who testified she had witnessed Elizabeth making the engravings.[78] The most famous of the deponents was William Hogarth himself. Hogarth was appearing as an 'expert witness' on the fact of copying, deposing on 16 May 1740 that the prints sold by Bickham were copies of those made by Elizabeth. It is unfortunate that the short deposition, which includes the letters and numbers identifying each of the four prints and respective copies, is addressed only to the factual question of copying. It does not provide a rationale upon which Hogarth based his evaluation, and rather uninformatively states that 'the time when or by whom' Elizabeth's works were 'reprinted or Copyed this deponent cannot set forth'.[79]

The case was eventually heard by Lord Chancellor Hardwicke on 8 December 1740. By this stage, the defense had been reduced to two key issues: first, whether prints copied from nature fell within the ambit of the statute; and second, whether Elizabeth Blackwell had complied with the terms of the statute so as to bring her engravings within its protection. We now turn to consider each of these issues in more detail.

75 NA, C11/1543/7 no. 2; C11/1543/11.

76 Timothy Clayton, 'Bickham, George (c. 1704–1771)', *Oxford Dictionary of National Biography*, 23 September 2004, https://doi.org/10.1093/ref:odnb/2352.

77 NA, C11/1546/6 no. 2.

78 NA, C24/1547/2.

79 NA, C24/1547/2. Reprinted in Pat Rogers, 'A New Hogarth Document', *Burlington Magazine*, 126 (November 1984), pp. 690–691.

(a) The Meaning of Invention

From the outset, Alexander and Elizabeth anticipated that a chief objection to their claim would focus on whether the prints were 'invented and designed' by Elizabeth. The initial Bill of Complaint emphasized Elizabeth's 'great Labour and Expense' in inventing, designing, etching and engraving the prints and went on to state that the defendants 'pretend that if your Oratrix did design the said prints yet that they being taken from nature are not to be considered as historical or other prints invented by your Oratrix within the meaning of the aforesaid Statute'.[80] They sought to forestall this claim with their evidence by deposition. The apothecary Robert Nicholls deposed that he had provided some of the botanical specimens to Elizabeth as her models, and also stated she had employed others to color some of the completed engravings, copying from 'original prints of her own painting', because she did not have time to paint them all.[81] The assertion is of interest in view of inconsistencies in the treatment of line and color within and between volumes. Such is the case, for example, in Peas 'Plate 83', where the patchy coloring of the legume pods in the first volume of the *Curious Herbal* from the Medical Historical Library at Yale University (see Figure 8) contrasts with the more detailed lines and richer tonal variations of the images in both the Lindley Library and the British Library's volumes.[82] Whether Elizabeth hired or received help from others remains unknown, yet, importantly, Elizabeth's mother deposed that Elizabeth was the 'Inventor and Author', noting that she was best able to assert this as her daughter carried out the engravings in her presence.[83]

George Bickham had several lines of defense. He argued that 'the Engraving or Etching of the Representation of any plant flower or vegetable' is not such an 'Invention or Design' intended by Parliament to fall within the Act, because it is 'only the effect of Labour and not of Genius or Invention'.[84] He also alleged that he had made the engravings

80 NA, C11/1543/7 no. 1

81 NA, C24/1547/2. When Nicholls says 'paint' he is referring to the coloring of the black and white engravings.

82 Blackwell, *A Curious Herbal*, vol. 1, Medical Historical Library, Harvey Cushing/John Hay Whitney Medical Library, Yale University; Lindley Library (615.3 BLA VOL I) and British Library (shelfmark 452.f.1).

83 NA, C24/1547/2.

84 NA, C11/1546/6 no. 2.

without copying Elizabeth's. Here he seems unable to avoid a small dig at Alexander's failure to have been properly apprenticed in the trade, noting that 'having served a regular apprenticeship to an Engraver and having set up and followed that Business,'[85] he (Bickham) had decided it would be profitable to engrave some prints of herbs, flowers and vegetables, and that he did so not by copying from the Complainant but by etching from drawings or the plants themselves. Thus, any likeness between his prints and those of Blackwell 'cannot be avoided they being Representations of the same plants and vegetables'.[86] He went on to argue that *his* prints were 'original Designs [...] taken from Nature and the Similitude of those prints owing to this Defendants own Genius and Invention and done in a manner as he apprehends much better than the Complainants plates'.[87]

It is of particular import to note the inherent contradiction of Bickham's first and third claims. Both assert the centrality of 'genius' and 'invention' to the protection offered by the Act, but the former denies such characteristics to botanical prints, while the latter emphasizes them. This demonstrates the very real uncertainty as to the scope and operation of this new statute, and the interpretation that the court would take of the words 'design' and 'invent'.

There are several sources of the argument and decision before Lord Hardwicke. There are two printed reports: one in Barnardiston's Chancery Reports, and another in Atkyns' Reports.[88] There are also two manuscript reports held by the British Library which appear to be identical as well as Lord Hardwicke's own notes on the case and notes from the collection of shorthand documents by Sir Dudley Ryder.[89] Both Atkyns and the manuscript reports in the British Library include information about the arguments; both state that the Attorney-General's first objection on behalf of the defendant was that Elizabeth could not be considered as falling within the intent of the Act because she was not

85 Ibid.

86 Ibid.

87 Ibid.

88 *Blackwell* v. *Harper* (1740) Barn. C. 209; *Blackwell* v. *Harper* (1740) 2 Atk. 93.

89 BL Add MS 36,015; BL Hargrave MS 412; BL Add MS 36,050; *Blackwell* v. *Harper* (1740), printed in *Sir Dudley Ryder, Ryder Shorthand Documents* (1973), p. 7 (Transcription of legal notes held at Georgetown University Law Library, original manuscripts held in Lincoln's Inn Library. The authors are grateful to Tomás Gómez-Arostegui for sharing his copy with them).

an 'inventor'. According to Atkyns, 'engraving is not properly inventing, and therefore is not within the act, unless it had been something within the mind, and not already in nature, as all these plants certainly are'.[90] Likewise, the MS report recorded the argument as 'she is not within the Intent of the Stat. for these are only Copys from Nature & no Inventions & the Stat: designd this benefit only to persons who form'd designs out of their own Fancy — as Historical — Allegorical Prints &c'.[91]

Lord Hardwicke declined to take such a narrow interpretation of the word 'invention'. The precise words he used vary between the different reports, but all agree he stated something along the following lines: 'I do not think the act confines it merely to invention; as for instance, an allegorical or fabulous representation'.[92] Moreover, the reports agree he went on to explain that the Act could cover a print of something already in nature, and mentioned that prints of a garden, a building and the city of London could all be covered by the Act. The only way that Bickham and the printsellers would be able to escape liability under the Act would be to show that Elizabeth had copied the prints from ones already in existence.[93]

Lord Hardwicke's judgment assisted in interpreting the scope of the Act in one respect — namely that 'design and invent' did not require a depiction of an imagined image. In other words, it extended beyond the fabulous and allegorical prints of William Hogarth to cover many other types of prints that made up the popular print market. Yet it left two gaps: first, the question of whether prints copied from drawings or paintings could be considered the product of 'design and invention'. Indeed, Lord Hardwicke opened this up as an issue in his discussion of the particular provision in the 1735 Act in relation to John Pine's tapestries contained in Section 5 of the Act:

> And whereas John Pine of London, engraver, doth propose to engrave and publish a set of prints copied from several pieces of tapestry in the house of lords, and his Majesty's wardrobe, and other drawings relating to the Spanish invasion, in the year of our Lord one thousand five hundred and eighty eight; be it further enacted by the authority aforesaid, That the said John Pine shall be intitled to the benefit of this act, to all intents and purposes whatsoever, in the same manner as if the said John Pine had been the inventor and designer of the said prints.[94]

90 *Blackwell*, 2 Atk. 93, 93.
91 BL Hargrave MS 412, fol. 131r.
92 *Blackwell*, 2 Atk 93, 94.
93 *Blackwell*, 2 Atk 93, 94–5; Barn C 209, 212; BL Add MS 36,015.
94 Engravings Act 1735, s5.

Lord Hardwicke explained that the existence of this clause was not an argument in favor of the defendants, as it dealt with a different situation. According to Atkyns, he stated: 'If it had not been for the clause thrown in for Mr *Pine's* benefit, any body might have copied the prints of the hangings in the House of Lords, for what is tapestry but copies taken from drawings'.[95] This was explained a little more fully in the Barnardiston report, which stated 'that Print cannot be an Invention, it being only a mere Copy from the Tapestry. All Tapestry is made from Drawings; the Drawing is the Invention, the Tapestry is a Copy from the Drawings, and consequently Mr Pine's Prints are only Copies from Copies'.[96] He went on to say that 'The present Prints are of quite another Nature, and clearly Inventions within the Meaning of the Act'.[97] The explanation, however, requires one to overlook the reality of making any engraving. It would be very rare for the design to be applied directly to the copper plates without the prior creation of preliminary design drawings. The Lord Chancellor's reasoning therefore creates a distinction between drawings made solely for the purpose of being copied onto plates, and drawings (or paintings) with an independent aesthetic value, but this distinction goes entirely unobserved.

Second, Lord Hardwicke markedly failed to provide a legal definition or standard of 'invention'. It is in fact noteworthy that every participant in the case also characterized Elizabeth's prints as factual, precise and objective depictions of plants in actual existence. Yet, this is exactly what they were not and could never be. As Kärin Nickelsen explains, botanical illustration in the eighteenth century was not intended to produce what we could today call 'photographically exact' copies of nature. Rather, draughtsmen 'consciously applied specific strategies (such as simplifying, schematizing and exaggerating details as well as unrealistically combining several stages of development in the life-cycle of a plant) that sometimes rendered their illustrations quite unlike real-life specimens of the depicted species'.[98] Thus, much of the skill and labor expended by Elizabeth was devoted to ensuring that she depicted all of the elements needed to demonstrate the plant's qualities and

95 *Blackwell*, 2 Atk 93, 95.

96 *Blackwell*, Barn C 210, 211.

97 Ibid.

98 Kärin Nickelsen, *Draughtsmen, Botanists and Nature: The Construction of Eighteenth-Century Botanical Illustrations* (Springer Netherlands, 2006), p. 11, https://doi.org/10.1007/978-1-4020-4820-3.

features for its scientifically-minded audience, while at the same time creating the illusion of facticity which gave her work its very authority.

As noted above, Elizabeth was unusual in combining in one person the skills that were more commonly distributed amongst a group of skilled craftsmen: namely, the draughting of the initial design, the engraving (itself a task sometimes divided between those with specific expertise) and the coloring of the completed images. Carl Linnaeus himself wrote in his *Philosophia Botanica* (1751) 'A draughtsman, an engraver and a botanist are equally necessary to produce a praiseworthy image; if one of these is at fault, the image turns out to be flawed'.[99] Yet, Elizabeth appears to have mastered all of these skills, even if she did have the assistance she refers to in her various dedications.

Detail and accuracy of illustrations were a primary concern in botanical works, enabling comparative analyses, identifications, and classifications. In the words of the seventeenth-century English botanist John Ray, many 'looked upon a history of plants without figures as a book of geography without maps'.[100] As with the latter, the choice of what is included or excluded is key and, in fact, as Nickelsen explains 'using the results of successful predecessors was the best way to avoid mistakes and allowed the players to start their work at a comparatively high level'.[101] Elizabeth was not exempt from this practice, but what made hers unusual was that she was careful to acknowledge others when she did copy from them. She in fact copied some of her drawings from Henricum van Rheede, van Draakestein's *Hortus indicus malabaricus*, published in Amsterdam in twelve volumes between 1678–1703; yet acknowledgement is contained in the descriptive text accompanying each plant.[102] In her description of the Indian Berry Tree 'Plate 389' she concedes: 'This Specimen I had from the Malabar Garden. Vol. 7. Tab. 1 & the separate Fruit from Mr. Joseph Millar'.[103] Elizabeth also admits to have copied elements from Mr. Nicholls 'Plate 395' but in the case of the

99 Ibid., p. 68.

100 John Ray, *Correspondence*, 1848, p. 155.

101 Nickelsen, *Draughtsmen, Botanists and Nature*, p. 256.

102 Henrey, *British Botanical Literature*, vol. 2, p. 235, fn. 1. Compare *A Curious Herbal*, vol. 2 plates 389, 391, 395 and 400 with *Hortus indicus malabaricus*, vol. 7 pl 1; vol. 1 pls 57, 37 and 38 respectively. Henricum van Rheede, van Draakestein, *Hortus indicus malabaricus*, 12 vols, Amsterdam, 1678–1703 (Lindley Library, 581.9 (5H) Rhe).

103 Blackwell, *A Curious Herbal*, Vol: [2], 1739. Lindley Library, 615.3 BLA VOL II.

Embrick Myrobalan 'Plate 400', also copied from the Malabar Garden, she specifies: 'the Fruit that is open and divided I did from the Life'.[104] Elizabeth drew from 'life', employing the carefully curated specimens from the Chelsea Physic Garden, and it should be noted that her bright and lively colors distinguish her representations from van Draakestein's uncolored works.

Botanical illustrations were the product of direct observation, yet this did not supplant artistic and technical merit. Elizabeth's creative impulse is evinced in the curious juxtaposition of elements (Water Lilly Roots 'Plate 499', see Figure 5) and her rich and vibrant compositions (Asch Colour'd Lichen 'Plate 336'). Also, it is revealed in her playful yet balanced representations, as seen in a Hart's Tongue 'Plate 138' and Wake Robin 'Plate 228' (as seen in Figures 6–7) which bring to mind the sensual nature of Georgia O'Keeffe's modern works, three centuries later.

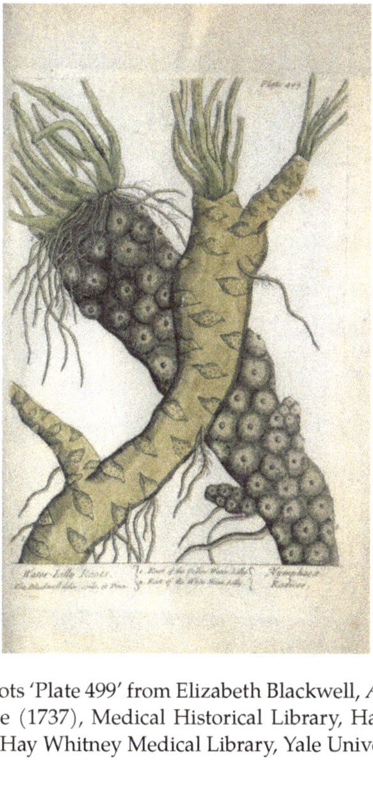

Fig. 5 Water Lilly Roots 'Plate 499' from Elizabeth Blackwell, *A Curious Herbal*, vol. 2, John Nourse (1737), Medical Historical Library, Harvey Cushing/John Hay Whitney Medical Library, Yale University.

104 Ibid.

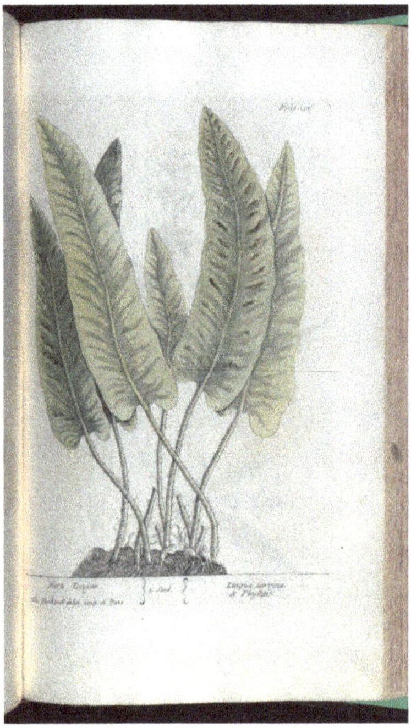
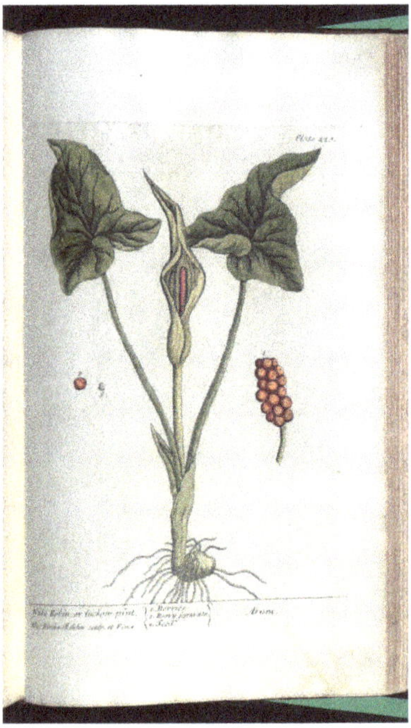

Figs. 6–7 Hart's Tongue 'Plate 138' and Wake Robin 'Plate 228' from Elizabeth Blackwell, *A Curious Herbal*, vol. 1, John Nourse (1739), Medical Historical Library, Harvey Cushing/John Hay Whitney Medical Library, Yale University.

A combination of aesthetic, scientific, and technical mastery of the art of engraving were all necessary in rendering an image of high quality. Elizabeth's reputation resided precisely in the inclusive treatment of all three aspects. Indeed, her work was so respected that it was itself copied. A German edition, *Herbarium Blackwellianum Emendatum*, was published in Nuremberg in five volumes in the 1750s, with a supplementary volume in 1773 of a large number of extra prints. The volumes were edited by Christoph Jacob Trew and the images redrawn and engraved by Nicholaus Friedrich Eisenberger. The title page states that it is an amended and improved version of Elizabeth's work, and although it clearly gives attribution to her authorship, Elizabeth did not receive any monetary compensation.[105] Of course, in the absence of international copyright law there was no legal entitlement for her to seek.

105 *Herbarium Blackwellianum Emendatum*, ed. by Christoph Iacobi Trew, 6 vols. (Nuremberg, [1752] 1757–1773), Lindley Library, 615.3 BLA VOL I–VI.

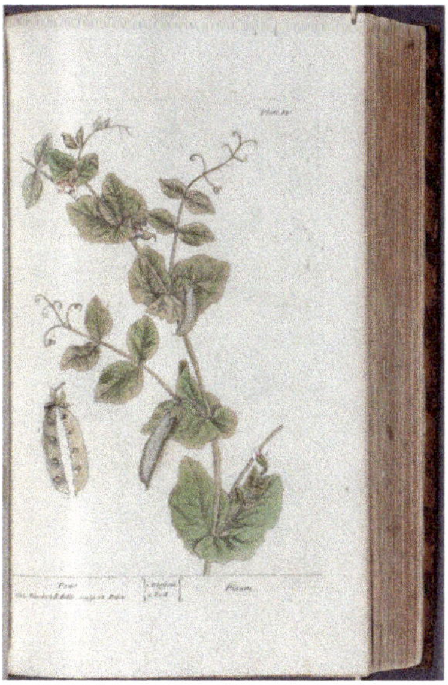

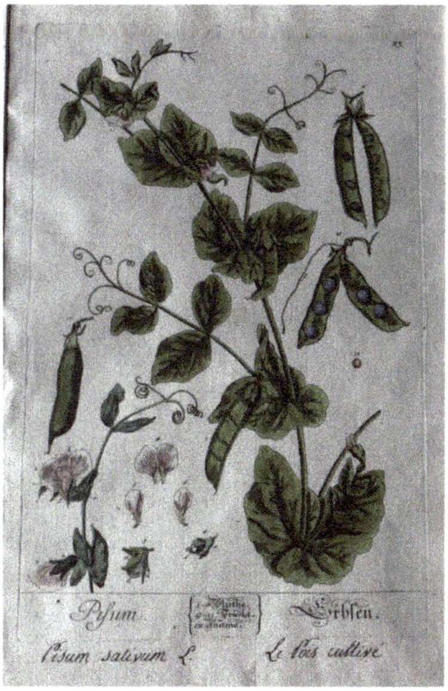

Figs. 8–9 Peas 'Plate 83', from Elizabeth Blackwell, *A Curious Herbal*, vol. 1, John Nourse (1739), Medical Historical Library, Harvey Cushing/John Hay Whitney Medical Library, Yale University; and Peas 'Plate 83' with French titles, individual sheet from an unknown edition, private collection of one of the authors.

Eisenberger closely reproduced Blackwell's prints adding the title and other descriptive terms in German at the bottom of the works, as well as providing other details. For example, his version of the Peas, also numbered 'Plate 83', includes various blossoms of the flowering cycle.[106] Eisenberger's prints seem to have continued to circulate, gaining new information and details in an effort to provide greater knowledge. Figure 9 shows a separate print of the Peas with a French title and the more specific Latin name *Pisum Sativum L.* now inscribed, but whether these additions were made by its owner, a collector, or a seller pursuing the French market remains unknown. A comparison between Blackwell's Peas 'Plate 83' (Figure 8) and the version with the French caption (Figure 9) shows how closely her image was copied. Following the convention of botanical illustrations, each specimen is rendered against a blank background. The image is almost identical except for the appearance

106 See the *Herbarium Blackwellianum Emendatum* in the Lindley Library (615.3 BLA VOL I–VI) and the Toronto Public Library (Baillie Special Collections 581.6 V. 1–6).

of an unopened legume and a detailed flower stem (both on the left) as well as the addition of another split pea and the repositioning of the open pod to the right. The size and appearance of the leaves, stems, and curly tendrils of her artistic composition have all been retained. The similarity with Elizabeth's works is also unmistakable in other images, such as the Citrul or Water melon 'Plate 157', where the arrangement is virtually the same, and where only a few details and dissected parts have been added.

(b) Property and Formalities

Alongside claims about lack of invention, the second main line of defense was that Elizabeth had failed to comply with the requirements of the Engravings Act because she had not included the correct information on each print. The Act stated, somewhat opaquely, that:

> Every person who shall invent and design, engrave, etch, or work in *Mezzotinto* or *Chiaro Oscuro*, or from his own works and invention, shall have the sole Right and Liberty of printing and reprinting the same for the Term of Fourteen years to commence from the Day of first publishing thereof, which shall be Truly engraved, with the name of the Proprietor on each Plate, and printed on every such Print or Prints.[107]

The Attorney-General argued that this provision meant that the name of the proprietor of the copyright must be included on every print, for 'Mrs Blackwell might both delineate and engrave them, and yet not be the proprietor of them'.[108] Further, the day of the first printing ought also to be included 'that all mankind might know when it commences, and when it expires'.[109] As noted above, on each of the prints in question, Elizabeth had included the phrase 'Eliz. Blackwell delin sculp et Pinx', but she had not specifically named herself as proprietor, nor included the day of publication. The question of whether Elizabeth could own property under the doctrine of *feme covert* has been discussed above. The evidence provided by the contracts with Nourse indicates that her husband, Alexander, was the appropriate contracting party, although the inclusion of Elizabeth's endorsement suggests that there may have

107 Engravings Act 1735, s.1.
108 *Blackwell*, 2 Atk 93, 93.
109 Ibid.

been some uncertainty about this. There was, however, no uncertainty in the court. According to Atkyns, Lord Hardwicke stated:

> The second objection is, as to the directions of the act, that Mrs Blackwell has not complied with the terms of it so as to vest the sole property in herself. *Elizabeth Blackwell sculpsit et delineavit* is sufficient, and are the very words of the act of parliament to shew the person to be proprietor.[110]

There is no suggestion here that gender was a consideration for the Lord Chancellor. Indeed, by the time the case was reported, the existence of Alexander seems to have been deemed irrelevant. He is not mentioned at all in the Atkyns report and the Barnardiston report refers to him simply as a long dash ('Wife of — Blackwell').[111]

The Lord Chancellor held that the day of first publishing *did* need to be included. He drew an analogy here with the Statute of Anne and the case of *Baller* v. *Watson*, in which the question had arisen as to whether the book needed to be registered at Stationers' Hall. He concluded that the day of publishing needed only to be included if the owner wished to take advantage of the penalties in the Act.[112] Since Elizabeth had not included this information on the prints, she could be awarded a perpetual injunction, but not the penalties in the Act (5 shillings per print) nor the costs of suit. Moreover, the Lord Chancellor also considered that this was not a case in which it was appropriate to award an account of profits, because the profits involved were so small and it would be unjust to the defendants who had no notice of the date on which the prints were first published.

The litigation was therefore only a partial victory for Elizabeth and does not seem to have solved her financial woes. Before the decree was even handed down, she and Alexander had sold Nourse a further one-sixth share, as noted above. Alexander took up a position as superintendent of works for the Duke of Chandos, but did not entirely

---

110 *Blackwell*, 2 Atk 93, 95.

111 *Blackwell*, Barn C. 209, 209.

112 *Baller* v. *Watson* (1737) 2 Swans 431. Lord Hardwicke's reasoning on this point is not clear to modern eyes. According to Atkyns' Report, he states that the words of the statute are 'only directory and not descriptive of the day, and that they are only necessary to make the penalty incur.' *Blackwell*, 2 Atk 93, 95. The words 'directory' and 'not descriptive' are also referred to in the Barnardiston report, while the MS report refers to the words being 'directory'. He appears to be stating that the requirement is not necessary to enliven the property right itself but only to give access to the statutory remedies. Barn C. 209, 213.

abandon the world of books, publishing *A New Method of Improving Cold, Wet and Clayey Grounds: Particularly Clayey-Grounds ... as practiced in North Britain* in 1741. The work is dedicated to Cockin Sole, Esq. and contains only a few technical illustrations. A year later, in 1742, Alexander traveled to Sweden, where he became involved in political intrigues and was executed for treason on 9 August 1747.[113] Elizabeth apparently remained in London but vanishes from the records to live on only in her *Curious Herbal*. The famous biologists Carl Linnaeus and Albrecht von Haller both mentioned her work.[114] A century later, in 1806, Richard Weston, a well-known writer on agriculture and gardening wrote: 'This work still continues in such esteem as to keep up its original price of six or seven guineas, and 10 on large paper, in the modern sale catalogues'.[115]

Conclusion

The case of *Blackwell* v. *Harper* is both significant and fascinating in the history of visual copyright, lying as it does at the intersection of questions about gender, authorship, and contemporary understandings — both cultural and legal — of what makes a work protectable by copyright law. Today, we might examine this latter question in terms of whether the work can be said to be 'original' and whether that, in turn, means of aesthetic value, demonstrating creativity, an investment of labor and money, or some combination thereof. In 1740, however, the question was couched in terms of what it meant to 'design and invent' under the terms of the Engravings Act of 1735. While the arguments of the parties, and the circumstances in which the prints were created, may have offered Lord Hardwicke the opportunity to provide guidance on what factors might be relevant to establishing the meaning of these words as

113 A.N.L. Grosjean, 'Blackwell, Alexander (bap. 1709, d. 1747)', *Oxford Dictionary of National Biography*, 23 September 2004, https://doi.org/10.1093/ref:odnb/2539.

114 In a letter, dated 11 January 1739, Albrecht von Haller wrote to Carl Linnaeus: 'In England Elizabeth Blackwell has published a herbarium consisting of 500 copper plates, with new illustrations for common plants.' The letter is available online at the Alvin — Platform for digital collections and digitized cultural heritage: www.alvin-portal.org/alvin/view.jsf?pid=alvin-record%3A223184&dswid=5940. In another letter that appears to be between Linnaeus and Jacob Jonas Björnståhl, Den Haag, 28 February 1774, Elizabeth's name and her *Herbal* are listed in a group of 'artists' who 'in recent years [...] have 'produced pictures of plants in color'. See www.alvin-portal.org/alvin/view.jsf?pid=alvin-record%3A233558&dswid=-1718.

115 Henrey, *British Botanical Literature*, vol. 2, p. 235.

a matter of law, he did not do so. Instead, he simply stated what was *not* required: that is, fabulous or allegorical representation. Further, by treating images of plants, alongside those of other objects such as buildings and gardens, as simply 'copied from nature' or the real world, and failing to recognize the artistic skill and aesthetic choices inherent to making such images, he was able to sidestep the question of whether 'invention' required a particular level of creativity, or its relationship to the connotations the word held within the artistic community.

By simply stating that Elizabeth was the proprietor of the copyright in the prints, Lord Hardwicke also sidestepped the question of gender. However, even though gender was not addressed in the court does not mean it was irrelevant. Elizabeth had worked hard to establish her claim to both authorship and authority. Moreover, she had done so in terms that seem to have been carefully calibrated not to upset the paradigm of male authorship. Her numerous dedications to her scientific mentors and champions sought to establish the scientific repute of her work, but she also played down her own contributions with an expected level of feminine modesty. As noted, she insisted that without Rand's assistance her work 'wou'd have been very imperfect' due to her lack of 'skill in botany', and recognized Miller for descriptions and information 'extracted [...] with his consent' and furnishing her with rare specimens.[116]

Even the narrative around Elizabeth's impetus for creation is gendered, with close-contemporary and later accounts all emphasizing her noble motivation to support her family, rescue her husband and pay off his debts. Recently, attention has been paid to the masculine nature of the Romantic author;[117] Mark Rose, for example, has drawn attention to the difficulties caused by 'the [romantic] notion of the author as a creative man who by virtue of imposing the imprint of his unique

116 Blackwell, *A Curious Herbal*, vol. 1 (London: John Nourse, 1739), Introduction.

117 See, for example, Carys Craig, 'Reconstructing the Author-Self: Some Feminist Lessons for Copyright Law', *American University Journal of Gender, Social Policy & the Law*, 15 (2007), 207–268; Carys Craig, 'Feminist Aesthetics and Copyright Law: Genius, Value, and Gendered Visions of the Creative Self' in *Diversity and Intellectual Property: Identities, Interests, and Intersections*, ed. by Irene Calboli and Srividhya Ragavan (Cambridge University Press, 2015) pp. 273–93, https://doi.org/10.1017/cbo9781107588479.015. In the context of art, see Christine Battersby, *Gender and Genius: Towards a Feminist Aesthetics* (London: The Women's Press, 1989) and Rozsika Parker/Griselda Pollock, *Old Mistresses: Women, Art and Ideology* (London and Henley: Routledge, 1981).

personality on his original work makes them his own'.[118] Shelley Wright has also commented upon the impact of possessive individualism in copyright law, explaining:

> The existing definition of copyright [...] presupposes that individuals live in isolation from one another, that the individual is an autonomous unit who creates artistic works and sells them, or permits their sale by others, while ignoring the individual's relationship with others within her community, family, ethnic group, religion — the very social relations out of which and for the benefit of whom the individual's limited monopoly rights are supposed to exist.[119]

Printing in the eighteenth century was still a trade that was carried out mostly in the home; this facilitated participation by women, an aspect that has only begun to be explored.[120] Elizabeth's authorship and its assertion were intrinsically situated in the domestic sphere and in her community: they involved her mother (who witnessed her labors), her husband (whose troubles impelled her), and her relationships with apothecaries, gardeners, physicians, and even the leading painter and engraver of the day, William Hogarth. While the collaborative nature of her work is emphasized in the publication itself through the various dedications, and emerges through the legal documents, the decision of the Lord Chancellor saw only one authorial proprietor — Elizabeth.

Furthermore, legal and other sources tell us almost nothing about the reality of Elizabeth's internal life or motivations. Was she a victim of her husband's improvidence? Was he exploiting her labor for his own gain? Or was she a willing and supportive economic agent in her own right? Did she consider herself an artist expressing her creative and authorial ambitions, or a natural philosopher engaged in furthering knowledge for the public benefit? Certainly, she was far from passive in the story of her life. A treatise published in 1735 entitled *The hardships of the English laws*

---

118 Mark Rose, 'Mothers and Authors: *Johnson v. Calvert* and the New Children of Our Imaginations', *Critical Inquiry*, 22 (1996), 613–633 (p. 614).

119 Shelley Wright, 'A Feminist Exploration of the Legal Protection of Art', *Canadian Journal of Women and Law*, 7 (1994), 59–96 (p. 73).

120 Adrian Johns, *The Nature of the Book: Print and Knowledge in the Making* (Chicago: University of Chicago Press, 1998), pp. 74–79, https://doi.org/10.3138/cjh.35.2.403. The contributions of women to the print trade is the subject of *Female Printmakers, Printsellers and Publishers in the Eighteenth Century: The Imprint of Women 1735–1830*, ed. by Cristina S. Martinez and Cynthia Roman (Cambridge: Cambridge University Press, forthcoming).

in relation to wives attacked coverture and asserted that married women were 'Dead in Law'.[121] But Elizabeth was not dead. She created property rights through her skill and labor, she entered into contracts in relation to these rights, and she brought a legal action enforcing them in which the court clearly recognized her as a proprietor. The case that Elizabeth brought before the courts is significant in terms of copyright's history and the development of copyright doctrine, particularly in relation to how courts approach cases involving artistic works. In addition, attending to gender enriches the story by stimulating insights in relation to the history of women as legal and economic actors more generally.[122]

Examining Elizabeth's story and her involvement in the birth of artistic copyright law also raises questions about the kinds of authors copyright protects and rewards. It reminds us that much of the rhetoric in copyright law and policy is directed at those who create for individual fulfilment and public benefit, rather than those who might create to benefit their family or community, and might prompt us to question whether one set of motivations is inherently more worthy of encouragement or reward. It is hoped that an examination of the case of *Blackwell* v. *Harper* which initiates this volume not only offers the first glimpses into the complexities surrounding the role played by creativity in copyright law — whether addressed in terms of invention or originality — but also serves to give proper recognition to the key role that a woman played in copyright history. In fact, Elizabeth Blackwell's inventive and laborious work planted the seeds for the germination of visual copyright law.

121 *The hardships of the English laws in relation to wives* (London, 1735), p. 51.

122 See, for example, Joanne Bailey, 'Favoured or oppressed? Married women, property and "coverture" in England, 1660–1800', *Continuity and Change* 17 (2002), 351–372; A.L. Erickson, *Women and property in early modern England* (London, 1993); *Women waging law in Elizabethan England*, ed. by Tim Stretton and Krista J. Kesselring (Cambridge: Cambridge University Press, 1998).

Bibliography

Primary Sources

A Treatise of Feme Covert or, the Lady's Law (London, 1735).

Alexander and Elizabeth Blackwell: Assignments etc., of the Herbal: 1737–1747: Upcott Collection, BL MS Add 38729 ff. 31–48.

An Act for the Encouragement of Learning, by Vesting the Copies of Printed Books in the Authors or Purchasers of Such Copies, during the Times therein mentioned, 8 Anne c. 19 (1710) (Statute of Anne).

An Act for the Encouragement of the Arts of Designing, Engraving and Etching Historical and other Prints, by vesting the Properties thereof in the Inventors and Engravers, during the Time therein mentioned 1735 (8 Geo II c. 13) (Engravings Act 1735).

A Curious Herbal, Containing Five Hundred Cuts, of the most useful Plants, which are now used in the Practice of Physick. Engraved on folio Copper Plates, after Drawings, taken from the Life. By Elizabeth Blackwell. To which is added a short Description of ye Plants; and their common Uses in Physick (London: Printed for John Nourse at the Lamb without Temple Bar), 2 vols., [1737-]1739.

Blackwell v. Harper (1740) Barn. C. 209.

Blackwell v. Harper (1740) 2 Atk. 93.

Blackwell v. Harper Bill of Complaint and Answer C11/1543/7 (9 March 1738); Answer C11/1543/11 (3 May 1738); Further Answer C11/1546/6 (16 December 1738); Answer C11/1546/6 (18 December 1738); Various orders in Court Registers at C33 (UK National Archives).

Herbarium Blackwellianum Emendatum, ed. by Christoph Iacobi Trew, 6 vols., [1752] 1757–1773, Nuremberg, Lindley Library, 615.3 BLA VOL I–VI.

Henricum van Rheede, van Draakestein, Hortus indicus malabaricus, 12 vols, Amsterdam, 1678–1703. Lindley Library, 581.9 (5H) RHE TOM I–XII.

Secondary Works

Bailey, Joanne, 'Favoured or Oppressed? Married Women, Property and "coverture" in England, 1660–1800', *Continuity and Change*, 17 (2002), 351–372.

Clayton, Timothy, 'Bickham, George (c. 1704–1771)', *Oxford Dictionary of National Biography*, 23 September 2004, https://doi.org/10.1093/ref:odnb/2352.

——, *The English Print 1699–1802* (New Haven and London: Paul Mellon Centre for Studies in British Art & Yale University Press, 1997).

Craig, Carys, 'Reconstructing the Author-Self: Some Feminist Lessons for Copyright Law', *American University Journal of Gender, Social Policy & the Law*, 15(2) (2007), 207–268.

——, 'Feminist Aesthetics and Copyright Law: Genius, Value, and Gendered Visions of the Creative Self' in *Diversity and Intellectual Property: Identities, Interests, and Intersections*, ed. by Irene Calboli and Srividhya Ragavan (Cambridge: Cambridge University Press, 2015), pp. 273–293, https://doi.org/10.1017/cbo9781107588479.015.

Deazley, Ronan, 'Commentary on the Engravers' Act (1735)', in *Primary Sources on Copyright (1450–1900)*, ed. by Lionel Bently and Martin Kretschmer, www.copyrighthistory.org.

——, *On the Origin of the Right to Copy: Charting the Movement of Copyright Law in Eighteenth-Century Britain (1695 0 1775)* (Oxford: Hart Publishing, 2004), https://doi.org/10.5040/9781472563064.

Erickson, A. L., *Women and Property in Early Modern England* (London: Routledge, 1993).

Evenden, Doreen A., 'Blackwell [née Blachrie], Elizabeth (bap. 1707, d. 1758)', *Oxford Dictionary of National Biography*, 23 September 2004, https://doi.org/10.1093/ref:odnb/2540.

Feather, John, 'John Nourse and his Authors', *Studies in Bibliography*, 34 (1981), 205–226.

Gómez-Arostegui, H. Tomás, 'The Untold Story of the First Copyright Suit Under the Statute of Anne', *Berkeley Technology Law Journal*, 25 (2010), 1247–1350.

Grosjean, A. N. L., 'Blackwell, Alexander (bap. 1709, d. 1747)', *Oxford Dictionary of National Biography*, 23 September 2004, https://doi.org/10.1093/ref:odnb/2539.

Henrey, Blanche, *British Botanical and Horticultural Literature before 1800, Comprising a History and Bibliography of Botanical and Horticultural Books Printed in England, Scotland, and Ireland from the Earliest Times until 1800* (London: Oxford University Press, 1975).

Johns, Adrian, *The Nature of the Book: Print and Knowledge in the Making* (Chicago: University of Chicago Press, 1998), https://doi.org/10.3138/cjh.35.2.403.

Nickelsen, Kärin, *Draughtsmen, Botanists and Nature: The Construction of Eighteenth-Century Botanical Illustrations* (Springer Netherlands, 2006), https://doi.org/10.1007/978-1-4020-4820-3.

Rogers, Pat, 'A New Hogarth Document', *Burlington Magazine*, 126 (November 1984), 690–691.

Rose, Mark, 'Mothers and Authors: *Johnson v. Calvert* and the New Children of Our Imaginations', *Critical Inquiry*, 22 (1996), 613–633.

Scott, Katie, *Becoming Property: Art, Theory, and Law in Early Modern France* (New Haven and London: Yale University Press, 2018).

Stretton, Tim, and Kesselring, Krista J., eds., *Women Waging Law in Elizabethan England* (Cambridge: Cambridge University Press, 1998).

Wright, Shelley, 'A Feminist Exploration of the Legal Protection of Art', *Canadian Journal of Women and Law*, 7 (1994), 59–96.

3. Who Owns Washington?
Gilbert Stuart and the Battle for Artistic Property in the Early American Republic

Marie-Stéphanie Delamaire

'Meaningless, inconsistent, and inadequate': this is how Eaton Drone evaluated the legal provisions that emerged from US-American and British intellectual property law and jurisprudence in 1879.[1] Published a few years after the 1870 statute that granted copyright protection to paintings for the first time in the United States, Drone's innovative treatise on intellectual property regarded past British and US-American judicial decisions as ambiguous at best, and more often incompatible with the general principles of property in intellectual production that he formulated in this volume. Founded on the notion that property was a natural right fundamentally connected to labor — 'what a man creates by his own labor, out of his own materials, is his to enjoy to the exclusion of all others' — Drone defined intellectual property as the product of intellectual labor, no matter the medium; he argued that it was found in various travails of the mind, from literary production to drama, music, sculpture and painting.[2] Grounded in Enlightenment philosophy, Drone's definition of intellectual property has been understood as a

1 Eaton S. Drone, *A Treatise on the Law of Property in Intellectual Productions in Great Britain and the United States* (Boston: Little, Brown, and Company, 1879), p. v. Research for this chapter was supported by a National Endowment for the Humanities Post-doctoral Fellowship at the Library Company of Philadelphia. The author would like to thank Georgia Barnhill, Oren Bracha, Robert Brauneis, Elena Cooper, Jim Green, Peter Jaszi, Will Slauter, and Simon Stern for their comments. I am also grateful to the late Linda Eaton for her support to this project.

2 Ibid., p. 4.

 https://doi.org/10.11647/OBP.0247.03

result of the broadening of the notion of authorship beyond the written word, which has been seen as the driving force behind the belated integration of the fine arts in American copyright law in the act of 1870.[3]

The equivalence between painting and literary creation was not new; it was a concept fundamental to European and American cultures, rooted in Horace's famous phrase 'Ut pictura poesis', literally meaning 'as is painting, so is poetry'. Since the Renaissance, numerous treatises on art and literature have repeatedly remarked on the close relationship between 'the sister arts', as they were called.[4] Artists, writers, and patrons alike invoked Horace's phrase to raise the status of painting as a liberal art, and that of their creator above the status of a craftsman. This argument had become particularly influential in eighteenth-century British art. Furthermore, it found a fertile ground in the early nineteenth-century United States, where the trope of the self-taught artistic genius asserted national authority, not only over Britain, but also over European culture at large.[5]

In spite of a broad consensus on the kinship between literature and painting in artistic and literary circles, the equivalence between painting and literary creation posed certain difficulties when presented as an argument to legislators, or when used as legal evidence in court, even after the United States Congress extended copyright protection to paintings.[6] When, in 1801 and 1802, Congress considered the inclusion

3 Lionel Bently, 'Art and the Making of Modern Copyright Law', in *Dear Images: Art, Copyright and Culture*, ed. by Daniel McClean and Karsten Schubert (London and Manchester: Ridinghouse and the Institute of Contemporary Arts, 2002), pp. 331–351 (pp. 332–334); Fiona MacMillan, 'Is Copyright Blind to the Visual?' in *Visual Communication*, 7 (2008), 97–118 (pp. 97–98); Oren Bracha, *Owning Ideas: The Intellectual Origins of American Intellectual Property, 1790–1909* (New York: Cambridge University Press, 2016), p. 376; Elena Cooper, *Art and Modern Copyright: The Contested Image* (Cambridge: Cambridge University Press, 2018), pp. 15–16. Drone's treatise is discussed further in Bracha's contribution to this volume, in relation to broader transformations affecting US-American literature and visual culture in the late-nineteenth century.

4 For an extensive discussion of the significance of this metaphor in *Ancien Régime* France, see Katie Scott, *Becoming Property: Art, Theory and Law in Early Modern France* (New Haven and London: Yale University Press, 2018), pp. 37–90.

5 Susan Rather, *The American School* (New Haven: Yale University Press, 2016).

6 For more on the legislative history of the 1870 Act, which extended copyright to drawings, paintings and sculpture, see Robert Brauneis, 'Understanding Copyright's First Encounter with the Fine Arts: A Look at the Legislative History of the Copyright Act of 1870', *Case Western Reserve Law Review*, 71 (2020), 585-625. In the United States, the first case that debated the affinity between the written word

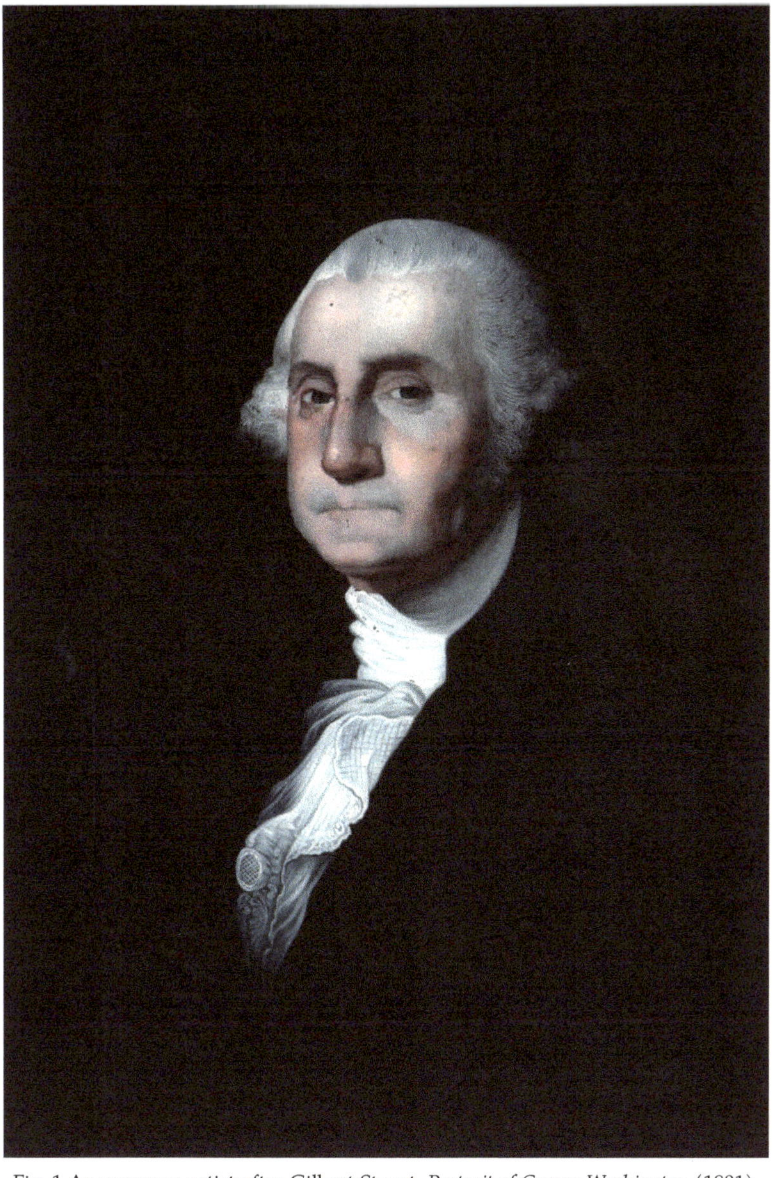

Fig. 1 Anonymous artist after Gilbert Stuart, *Portrait of George Washington* (1801), reverse painting on glass, 1960.0569 A, Winterthur Museum, Garden & Library, Bequest of Henry Francis du Pont, Courtesy of Winterthur Museum.

of visual works in the revisions of the copyright statute of 1790, painters did not lobby en masse to request the addition of paintings to the list of images that could benefit from protection under the new statute.[7] The US Copyright Act of 1802, specifically aimed at encouraging the visual arts, did not include them, limiting itself instead to the 'arts of designing, engraving and etching historical and other prints'.[8] In spite of this limitation, the famous painter Gilbert Stuart went to court against a sea captain who had commissioned unauthorized copies of one of his portraits of George Washington only a couple of weeks after the publication of the new statute, and won his case in court — seemingly substantiating Drone's statement that, by and large, US-American law was marked by a series of erroneous or conflicting decisions.

Court cases relating to intellectual property and the visual arts were the exception rather than the norm in the nineteenth-century United States. The Stuart v. Sword case is the first among a handful for the entire period covered in this book. It registers a moment of uncertainty: one when an artist asked the court for clarification about an object that was not addressed in the statute, and a moment when other artists and print publishers asserted intangible property rights on visual works, whether these could be backed by statute and jurisprudence, or not. Starting with Stuart v. Sword, this chapter examines how various constituencies in the early decades of the American Republic envisioned the nature of artistic property in a painting, even as it remained outside the realm of statutory protection. I investigate how painters and their patrons, publishers, and dealers came to conceptualize a notion of intellectual property in a painting, and how they, together with their lawyers and judges, articulated this notion either in court or in artistic and trade practices. What kind of property did various constituents

---

and the visual language of painting in legal terms took place two years later: *Parton v. Prang* (1872).

7 In February of 1802, the *Carlisle Gazette* (PA) reported that George Helmbold Jr., a Philadelphia printer, publisher and print seller, presented a memorial asking for the extension of copyright protection to several types of images, including paintings. In contrast, the artist writing to 'Mr. Editor' in *The Philadelphia Repository and Weekly Register* a few months earlier only requested the legislative protection of the fine arts by way of engraved images, not paintings. (To 'Mr. Editor' by 'A Young Artist', *The Philadelphia Repository and Weekly Register*, 3 October 1801).

8 1802 Amendment (1802), Primary Sources on Copyright (1450–1900), ed. by Lionel Bently and Martin Kretschmer, http://www.copyrighthistory.org/cam/tools/request/showRecord.php?id=record_us_1802.

think they had when they created or owned a picture? What happened to this property when the artwork was sold or given? Under what conditions could it be copied or reproduced in various media? The notion that painters owned artistic property in the product of their creative genius, separate from its physical utterance in the painting, was, I argue, fundamental to Stuart's decision to seek legal advice and go to court. The concept emerged from the synergy between artistic discourse and practices in the print trade that developed in the art world of London, where Stuart first became a successful and highly regarded artist.

Nevertheless, it did not open a clear legal path for painters' claims to control that property, as it was transformed by reproduction and circulated away from their studio. Neither did it facilitate the enactment of statutory protection for paintings in the United States. The present essay examines these apparent contradictions to understand how, in the absence of statutory protection, American artists reconciled an intellectual conception of artistic property — formulated through academic art theory and practices that flourished in Europe in the eighteenth century — with the new visual media landscape and transnational art market that emerged in the United States during the early decades of the nineteenth century.

Stuart v. Sword: Controlling Copying in Early Nineteenth-Century Philadelphia

Gilbert Stuart, born in 1755 in Newport, Rhode Island and the son of a snuff maker, showed an early talent for drawing. After working for a few years as a portrait painter in Rhode Island and other American colonies, the aspiring artist moved to London in 1775, where he entered the studio of American-born painter Benjamin West. West was a rising star in the London art world, a founding member of the Royal Academy, and historical painter to the court. Stuart was soon immersed in some of West's artistic projects that connected him to John Boydell (1719–1804), the foremost London art publisher. Boydell and West's recent collaboration in the publication of an engraving after the painter's *The Death of General Wolfe* (1776) has been credited with inaugurating a new era of patronage and popularity for English historical pictures[9] (see Figure 5). After Stuart exhibited his first full-length portrait, representing William Grant and titled *Portrait of a Gentleman Skating* at the Royal Academy in 1782 — a painting that brought him widespread recognition — Boydell commissioned Stuart with fifteen portraits of prominent living artists, including that of William Woollett, the engraver of *The Death of General Wolfe* (see Figure 2).[10]

Three portraits from the series were also integrated into Boydell's exhibition of John Singleton Copley's enormously popular picture, *The Death of Major Peirson* (also a Boydell commission), when the painting was on public view at No. 28, Haymarket, and later in the publisher's skylighted gallery: 'Three ovals on the top of the frame, in the center of which is Mr. Copley's portrait, painted by that able artist Mr. Stuart. The portrait of Mr. Heath, who is to engrave the subject on one side, and that of Mr. Joshua Boydell, who is to make the drawing [to be used as model for the engraving] on the other.'[11]

In London, Stuart maintained an extravagant lifestyle, which put him into an increasingly serious amount of debt. Threatened by the dismal state of his financial affairs, the artist fled first for Ireland and later for America, where he arrived in 1794 with the explicit goal of regaining financial stability by painting George Washington. 'There [in America] I expect to make a fortune by Washington alone. I calculate upon making a plurality of his portraits [...]; and if I should be fortunate, I will repay my English and Irish creditors.'[12] Known for his provocative personality, Stuart openly professed to dislike anything else than portraiture: an attitude that won him broad support and patronage in the United States. With numerous commissions for the anticipated portrait, and a letter of introduction from lawyer, statesman, and writer John Jay, Stuart arrived in Philadelphia in November of 1795 to paint the first president. This first sitting resulted in the Vaughan portrait type (after Samuel

9 Sven H. A. Bruntjen, *John Boydell, 1719–1804: A Study of Art Patronage and Publishing* (New York and London: Garland Publishing Inc., 1985), p. 35, and pp. 61–62.

10 Carrie Rebora Barratt and Ellen G. Miles, eds., *Gilbert Stuart* (New York: The Metropolitan Museum of Art, and New Haven and London: Yale University Press, 2004), pp. 51–52.

11 Quoted by Bruntjen, *John Boydell*, p. 210.

12 Quoted by John Hill Morgan, 'A Sketch of the life of Gilbert Stuart 1755–1828', in *Gilbert Stuart: An Illustrated Descriptive List of His Works Compiled by Lawrence Park* (New York: William Edwin Rudge, 1926), pp. 9–70 (p. 44).

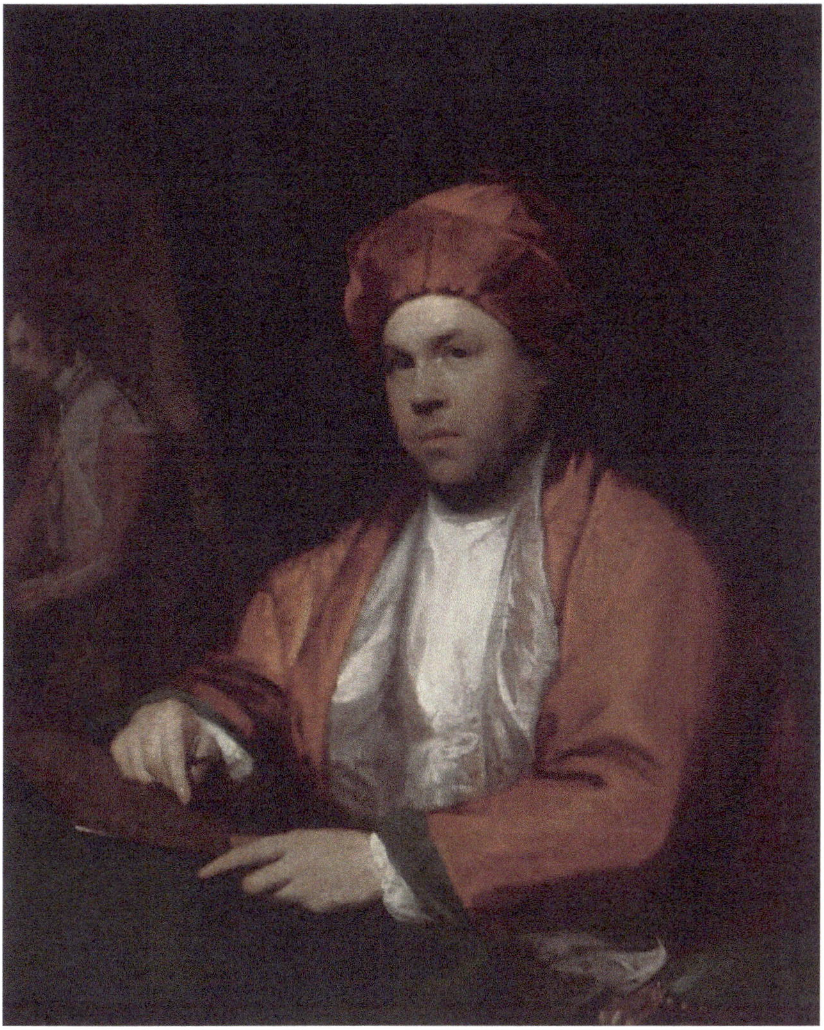

Fig. 2 Gilbert Stuart, *Portrait of William Woollett* (1783), oil on canvas, Tate Britain. Image by The Athenaeum, Wikimedia: https://commons.wikimedia.org/wiki/File:William_Woollett_by_Gilbert_Stuart_1783.jpeg.

Vaughan, one of the artist's patrons who had commissioned a copy in anticipation of its completion): a waist-length portrait showing the right side of Washington's face (see Figure 3).

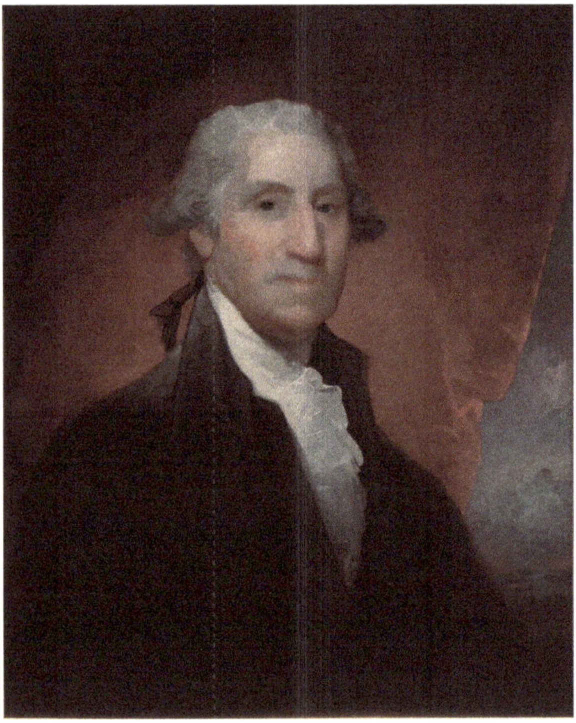

Fig. 3 Gilbert Stuart, *Portrait of George Washington* (1795–1796), oil on canvas, 1957.0857, Winterthur Museum, Garden & Library, Gift of Henry Francis du Pont, Courtesy of Winterthur Museum.

Washington sat for the artist a second time the following year. The portrait that resulted from this April 12, 1796 sitting, also waist-length, was left unfinished, but served as a model for about one hundred subsequent likenesses of Washington painted by Stuart over the next two decades. The second composition is called the Athenaeum type because the original unfinished portrait made during Washington's sitting was purchased by the Boston Athenaeum soon after the painter's death in 1828. All of the Athenaeum-type portraits of the first president were painted on a standard English canvas size of about 25 by 30 inches, known as 'three-quarter length'. Finally, Stuart painted a third type, the portrait of Washington in full length, called the Lansdowne portrait.

It was commissioned for Lord Lansdowne by William Bingham, a Philadelphia merchant, in 1796. This portrait was also based on the April 1796 sitting and shows the left side of the president's face[13] (see Figure 4).

Painting Washington's portrait proved to be the very successful business Stuart had hoped for: In 1795, he wrote a list of thirty-nine patrons for his Washington portraits, and we know that he was selling the smaller portraits of the Athenaeum type for about $150 a piece, a significant sum for the period.[14] For the commission of the large full-length type, he received $1,000 from William Bingham, who intended it as a gift to the Marquis of Lansdowne, Britain's Prime Minister during the final months of the American Revolutionary War, who had secured peace with the United States. It is no wonder that the landing of the *Connecticut* in Philadelphia on April 3, 1802, with 'above one hundred' full-size Athenaeum-type portraits painted on glass in China, felt like a major threat to the painter's flourishing business. The captain of the *Connecticut*, John Sword, had purchased a portrait of Washington directly from Stuart a year earlier. Active in the Atlantic and the China Sea since the 1780s, Sword had taken the painting to Guangzhou where he commissioned the 100 copies. Returning from East Asia, he imported the Chinese copies among the three trunks of personal property listed in the manifest of the *Connecticut* on his arrival.[15]

---

13 Barratt and Miles, *Gilbert Stuart*, p. 130. All the then-known portraits of Washington by Gilbert Stuart are listed in *Gilbert Stuart: An Illustrated Descriptive List of His Works*. Today, we know of four copies of the Lansdowne portrait: two in Washington DC (one at the National Portrait Gallery, one at the White House), one in New York at the Brooklyn Museum, and another at the Pennsylvania Academy of the Fine Arts in Philadelphia.

14 Barratt and Miles, *Gilbert Stuart*, p. 164. By the end of his life, Stuart would paint almost a hundred and twenty-five portraits of the Athenaeum type alone according to Lawrence Park, *Gilbert Stuart: An Illustrated Descriptive List of His Works*, although it is likely that this number is inflated. Later scholars think that the painter's daughter, Jane Stuart, painted some of them.

15 The US-China trade was characterized by smaller ships that heavily relied on consignment, smuggling, and special orders. The *Connecticut* was a ship owned by James Barclay and George Simson of Philadelphia. With an estimated tonnage of 360, the *Connecticut* is on the list of confirmed American ships that traded legally with China, arriving at Whampoa on August 10, 1801. It was recorded back in Philadelphia in early April of 1802. None of the portraits, however, are itemized on the ship's manifest. See Rhys Richards, 'United States Trade with China, 1784–1814', *The American Neptune*, 54: Special Supplement (1994); Libby Lai-Pik Chan with Nina

These copies of Stuart's Washington were made using the popular Chinese technique of reverse paintings on glass. Such paintings were prize Chinese export artifacts that had been circulating throughout the British Empire since the seventeenth and eighteenth centuries. Even though such imports represented a small percentage of the US-China trade, they were popular between the 1780s and the first decade of the nineteenth century, just as a new trend in this type of painting emerged: the copying of European and American prints. Large reverse paintings on glass were luxury goods. Likely one of the portraits that survived the Stuart v. Sword lawsuit, the beautifully crafted Chinese replica of Stuart's painting currently in the Winterthur Museum collection, is a full-size copy of the original work painted on a 25 by 30 sheet of glass (see Figure 1). Considering its fragile medium, it is in remarkable condition. Such large-size paintings would have cost Captain Sword at least $15 to $20 a piece, and represented a significant investment on Sword's part (if he acted alone in this enterprise).[16] Since the portraits on glass were never advertised, we do not know how much Sword intended to sell them in Philadelphia. His investment, however, was certainly calculated to bring a handsome return. Although it is unlikely that they would have reached the price of one of Stuart's own Athenaeum copies, they would nevertheless have not come close to the price of an engraving. At that time, the painter was also investing into the engraved reproduction of his painted portraits of Washington. He advertised plans to produce his own engraving of the full-length portrait, which he intended to sell for $20: quite an expensive price for a reproductive print in the United States.[17] The medium of Chinese reverse painting on glass associated

---

Lai-Na Wan, eds., *The Dragon and the Eagle: American Traders in China, A Century of Trade from 1784 to 1900* (Hong Kong: Maritime Museum, 2018).

16 Carl Crossman discusses the cost of Chinese reverse paintings to American traders, but not the American market: Carl Crossman, *The Decorative Arts of the China Trade* (Woodbridge, Suffolk: Antique Collectors' Club, 1991), pp. 206–216. Advertisements for Chinese paintings on glass appear in numerous newspapers at the time, unfortunately without individual prices. See the *Columbian Centinel* (Mass.), 14 May 1800; the *New England Palladium* (Mass.), 7 June 1803; the *Morning Chronicle* (New York), 15 April 1803. According to Crossman, another series of 10 copies of Gilbert Stuart's Athenaeum portraits made in China were commissioned by Rhode Island merchant Edward Carrington, who was billed by the Chinese artist Foeiqua in 1805 (Crossman, p. 215).

17 'Washington', *The Philadelphia Gazette*, 13 June 1800. Many thanks to Erika Piola for sharing this advertisement. In contrast, the bust-length engraved portrait of Thomas

Sword's unauthorized copies with sumptuous exotic goods. Their materiality would have prevented any collector from mistaking them for Stuart's original paintings. Yet, their size and association with luxury goods would have made them a much closer equivalent to Stuart's paintings than the large (unauthorized) print of the Lansdowne portrait engraved by James Heath, also offered for sale in Philadelphia at the time. The Chinese copies of Stuart's painting on glass were bound to become direct competitors of Stuart's own paintings, on the expansive market of painted likenesses of the American Republic's founding father.

On May 14, 1802, Stuart filed a lawsuit against Captain Sword in the District Court of Pennsylvania. The artist was still a British citizen in 1802, and he filed the lawsuit in the Federal District Court rather than in the State Court.[18] The bill explained that the portrait had been sold to the buyer with specific restrictions regarding the buyer's right to have the painting copied. Stuart explained the conditions of the sale, and its restrictions on copying without giving details as to the medium in which the painting might or might not be copied:

> Your orator thereupon refused to sell the same [the portrait of George Washington] unless the said John E. Sword would promise your orator that no copies should be taken thereof, whereupon the said John E. Sword did promise and assure your orator that no copies thereof should be taken and the better to prevail on your orator to sell him the same, the said John E. Sword alleged and pretended to your orator that he wanted the same for a gentleman in Virginia, whereupon your orator giving faith to his said promise and assurance did sell and deliver to him the said portrait of General Washington.[19]

Jefferson by Cornelius Tiebout was advertised for $2 by Mathew Carey. In 1803, Stuart and the engraver David Edwin copyrighted an engraving after Washington's portrait. (Library of Congress, Copyright Records, Eastern District of Pennsylvania, microfilm reel 61, vol. 262, 1790–1804).

18 Records of the District Court of the United States for the Eastern District of Pennsylvania (National Archives and Records Administration, RG21.40.2 (1790–1804)). The full details around Gilbert Stuart's petition and the judge's reasoning are not recorded in the archive. Stuart's petition and the injunction against Sword were published in Gilbert Stuart, D. Chadwick, E. P. Richardson, Claude Flory and Edward R. Black, 'Notes and Documents', *The Pennsylvania Magazine of History and Biography*, 14:1 (January 1970), 95–103. Stuart's status as a British citizen entitled him to present his case to a Federal Court because the defendant, Captain Sword, was an American citizen. (Many thanks to Robert Brauneis for clarifying this point.)

19 Stuart v. Swords [sic] Bill, filed 14 May 1802. Records of the Circuit Court of Pennsylvania, NARA (microfilm), consulted in February 2018. See also D. Chadwick, E. P. Richardson, Claude R. Flory, and Edward R. Black, 'Notes and

Stuart filed his suit barely a couple of weeks after President Jefferson signed the supplementary act that expanded the reach of copyright statutory protection to printed images, but not to paintings. Nevertheless, Stuart went to court and requested that Sword not only 'be enjoined and restrained from vending or [...] disposing of any of the said copies' but also that he 'may be ordered to deliver us all that remain unsold or otherwise dispose of them'. The Court's injunction, issued the same day against the defendants, went beyond the remedies available at common law, demanding not only that Sword cease selling the unauthorized copies, but that he also have them ready for the Court's further instructions — suggesting forthcoming seizure or destruction. While the lawsuit is a relatively obscure case of jurisprudence, it is well-known among historians of US-American art, for whom it largely represents an example of early art fraud. The case is also seen as evidence of Stuart's preoccupation with profiting from the market in reproductions of his paintings.[20]

It was not the first time Stuart asserted a right to control the production and circulation of images copied after his paintings. Before his dispute with Sword, Stuart had publicly claimed an intangible property in his full-length portrait of George Washington commissioned by William Bingham for Lord Lansdowne. This property gave the painter — Stuart insisted — the authority to control the publication of the painting long after its delivery to Bingham in Philadelphia, and to its final recipient, Lord Lansdowne in Britain. Unfortunately for the artist, however, Stuart discovered that a stipple engraving after his portrait, made by the well-known British engraver James Heath, was offered for sale in Philadelphia (see Figure 4).

In order to defend what he articulated as an intangible property in his own artistic creation, Stuart stated in a letter to the press that Heath's engraving had not been authorized. In a breach of trust, Bingham had not obeyed the painter's specific instructions, that — when delivering the painting — Bingham was to reserve for the painter the right to

---

Documents', *The Pennsylvania Magazine of History and Biography*, 94:1 (Jan. 1970), 95–103.

20 Maggie Cao, 'Washington in China: A Media History of Reverse Painting on Glass', *Commonplace: The Journal of Early American Life*, 15:4 (Summer 2015), n.p., http://commonplace.online/article/washington-in-china-a-media-history-of-reverse-painting-on-glass/.

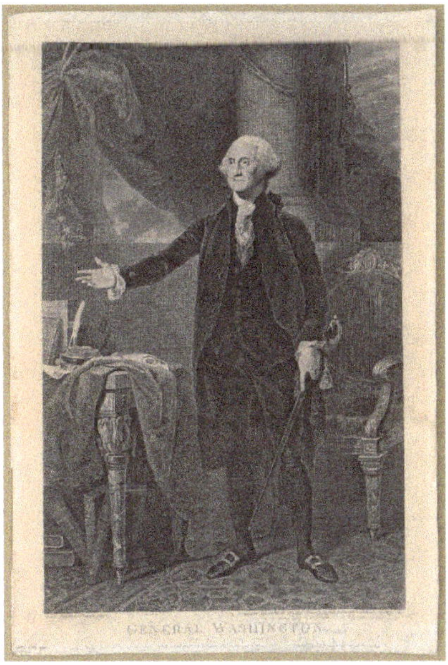

Fig. 4 James Heath after Gilbert Stuart, *Portrait of George Washington* (1800), engraving, Library of Congress, Photographs and Prints Division, https://www.loc.gov/pictures/item/2004667280/.

publish the portrait in print. Dismayed to see an English print after his work for sale in Philadelphia, the artist mounted a public campaign against this unauthorized print:

> Mr. Stuart has the mortification to observe, that without any regard to his property, or feelings, as an Artist, an engraving had recently been published in England; and is now offered for sale in America, copied from one of his Portraits of Gen. Washington. Though Mr. Stuart cannot but complain of this invasion of his Copy-right (a right always held sacred to the Artist, and expressly reserved on this occasion, as a provision for a numerous family) he derives some consolation from remarking, that the manner of executing Mr. *Heath's* engraving, cannot satisfy or supercede [sic.] the public claim, for a correct representation of the American patriot.[21]

In claiming his right to reserve publication for the painter, Stuart was following well-established practices in Britain. The painter's preoccupations with controlling copying, and with reaping the benefits

21 *Philadelphia Gazette*, 13 June 1800, p. 2.

of adapting one's painting in print tied him to the London art world where he trained, and where his peers Benjamin West and John Singleton Copley developed strategies and formed alliances with engravers and the leading publisher John Boydell to control the publication and circulation of their paintings in print. His use of the term 'property' and 'copy-right' in association with a painting, however, was atypical.

Painting as Intellectual Property in Eighteenth-Century London: Art Theory and its Intersection with Artistic and Trade Practices

Through exhibitions, artist-dealer contracts, and in their relationships with patrons, leading British painters asserted an entitlement to oversee the afterlife of their compositions in print, in spite of the lack of statutory law on painting in England. Such a claim was not only based on art theory, which defended the intellectual nature of the painter's art. It also depended on the British print trade's capacity to produce fine reproductive prints that painters would accept as proper expression of their creations. By and large, British printmakers reached this degree of excellence in the second half of the eighteenth century, as result of John Boydell's patronage and business practice in the London print trade.

John Boydell, an engraver by training, would become one of the leading figures of the British art world by the end of the eighteenth century. He not only worked as a publisher and print seller, but also promoted contemporary British painting in various ways. As a publisher, he commissioned, exhibited, and published paintings by living artists. He donated works of art to public institutions, developed a large network of patrons within elite circles, and published several aristocratic collections in print. He also held several public offices, which he used to promote contemporary painting commissions, and fund public building renovations with ambitious painting programs.[22]

Following a regular apprenticeship in engraving, Boydell started as an engraver and print seller in the late 1740s London. In 1751, he purchased a membership in the Stationer's Company and moved to

22 Bruntjen, *John Boydell* is the most complete account of Boydell's various activities in the British art world.

large quarters on the West corner of Queen Street and Cheapside. There, he opened a full-scale shop and decided to distinguish himself from his peers by almost exclusively focusing on selling fine reproductive prints. These high-end commodities had to be imported from France. According to later recollections, the hard cash Boydell had to pay for the prints — no print publisher on the other side of the Channel at that time would accept British prints in exchange — led him to invest in the most promising young English engravers to raise the quality of British reproductive art. He considerably increased premiums paid to engravers — paying amounts for a single plate that had never before been seen in England — to secure the best artists' work for his projects, and to encourage engravers to dedicate their time to the adaptation of celebrated paintings into print.[23] This successful strategy set new standards both in the print trade and the art world at the same time. Boydell was soon able to offer quality engravings on par with foreign imports, which put him in a position to contract with major painters and engravers for the reproduction of famous works by contemporary artists such as Benjamin West (for instance, *The Death of General Wolfe* — see Figure 5). In time, these engravings found a market both in England and on the European continent.[24] More importantly, the growing role of reproductive engravings in contemporary British culture — a role that Boydell strategically brought about and emphasized in high-profile publications, exhibitions, and public works — converged with influential art theory to clear a path for British painters' demand for authorial control in reproduction.

The concept of painting as a liberal art certainly was critical to the emergence of artists' claims of authorship in the eighteenth century.[25]

23 See Boydell's speech made to the Court of Common Council on October 31, 1793, published in Bruntjen, *John Boydell*, pp. 273–376.

24 Tim Clayton, *The English Print* (New Haven: Yale University Press, 1997) discusses the emergence of English reproductive prints in the international print trade during this period. Boydell's prints also circulated in the American colonies.

25 The move towards an abstraction of authorship in the visual arts was previously ascribed to the rise of Romanticism (See Lionel Bently, 'Art and the Making of Modern Copyright Law', in *Dear Images: Art, Copyright and Culture*, ed. by Daniel McClean and Karsten Schubert (London and Manchester: Ridinghouse and the Institute of Contemporary Arts, 2002), pp. 331–351 (p. 331)). In her recent book, Katie Scott convincingly argues for the roots of abstracted authorship in early modern France. See Scott, *Becoming Property*, specifically the first chapter '"Ut Pictura Poesis"', Matters of Privilege and Property, pp. 37–91. The impact of French

However, it is in the relationship drawn between a painting and its publication in print that the seeds of an abstract notion of intellectual property in a painting were sowed. Several authors, in particular Charles Alphonse du Fresnoy (*De Arte Grafica,* translated into English by John Dryden in 1695), Roger de Piles, and Jonathan Richardson were responsible for popularizing the liberal-art status of painting in the British Empire.[26] Their influence expressed itself in the language of the 1735 petition that called for new copyright legislation protecting images. The pamphlet called attention to the 'genius' of the artist and complained about the difficulty of exerting one's 'invention' in the conditions of artistic creation created by the print trade: 'seeing how vain it is to attempt any thing [sic] New and Improving, [...] [the artist] bids farewel [sic] to Accuracy, Expression, Invention, and every thing [sic] that sets one Artist above another, and for bare Subsistence enters himself into the Lists of Drudgery under these Monopolies [of the printsellers].'[27]

Invention and genius are typical critical terms associated with the language of the liberal arts. They were also keywords used in the teachings of the Royal Academy (RA) founded in 1768. Its first president, Sir Joshua Reynolds, was an admirer of Richardson's work, and one

---

artistic practice and theory in eighteenth-century England was not negligible. The writings of theoreticians of art such as Roger de Piles and Charles Alphonse du Fresnoy were influential in eighteenth-century England. In addition, English artists were very much aware of the complex French privilege system and its impact on artistic property rights; see, for instance, references to French art in *The Case of Designers, Engravers, Etchers, &c.* (London, 1735), p. 7, digitized in *Primary Sources on Copyright*, ed. by Bently and Kretschmer, http://www.copyrighthistory.org/cam/tools/request/showRecord.php?id=record_uk_1735a.

26 Johnathan Richardson published *The Theory of Painting* in 1715, the *Essay on the Art of Criticism* in 1719, and *The Science of a Connoisseur* in 1722. Du Fresnoy and Richardson's writings went through multiple editions over the century. Their influence extended far and large into the British Empire: Benjamin West recalled his first encounters with Richardson and du Fresnoy in 1750s Philadelphia, in the workshop of a colonial painter and music teacher, William Williams. West credited the encounter with initiating him to the higher purpose of painting. See Susan Rather, 'Benjamin West's Professional Endgame and the Historical Conundrum of William Williams', *The William and Mary Quarterly*, 59 (2002), 821–864.

27 *The Case of Designers, Engravers, Etchers, &c.*, p. 3. Mark Rose sees the rise of authorship as resulting from a separation between intellectual endeavor and the craft of engraving ('Technology and Copyright in 1735: The Engraver's Act', *The Information Society*, 21 (2005), 63–66. Alexander and Martinez's essay in this volume further discuss the language of the liberal arts in the 1735 act.

of the major proponents of the concept of painting as a liberal art, alongside that of the artist as intellectual genius. Richardson argued that painting's 'business [was] above all to communicate ideas'. Bainbrigg Buckeridge, another influential author who translated Roger de Piles in 1706 and whose writings were published in several editions through 1754, re-introduced Horace's *ut pictura poesis* to argue for the superior mental qualities of the art:

> Painting is sister to Poetry, the muse's darling; and though the latter is more talkative, and consequently more able to push her fortune; yet Painting, by the language of the eyes and the beauty of a more sensible imitation of nature, makes as strong an impression on the soul, and deserves, as well as poetry, immortal honours.[28]

Reynolds expressed his belief in the intellectual nature of artistic creation in the academy's curriculum and in his *Discourses,* which formulated what became the dominant theory of art in England: 'This is the ambition I could wish to excite in your minds,' Reynolds instructed his students, 'and the object I have had in my view, throughout this discourse, is that one great idea which gives to painting its true dignity, that entitles it to the name of a Liberal Art, and ranks it as a sister of poetry'.[29] If painting was a liberal art, it meant that the artist's genius was the true source of a higher realm of artistic creation:

> Neatness and high finishing: a light, bold pencil; gay and vivid colours, warm and sombrous; force and tenderness; all these are [...] beauties of an inferior kind, even when so employed; they are the mechanical parts of painting, and require no more genius or capacity, than is necessary to, and frequently seen in ordinary workmen.[30]

28 Charles Alphonse du Fresnoy and John Dryden (trans.), *De arte graphica. The art of painting, by C. A. Du Fresnoy. With remarks. Translated into English, together with an original preface containing a parallel betwixt painting and poetry. By Mr. Dryden* (London: W. Rogers, 1695); Jonathan Richardson, 'The Science of the Connoisseur', in *The works of Mr. Jonathan Richardson ... all corrected and prepared for the press by his son Mr. J. Richardson* (London: Printed for T. Davis, in Russel-Street, 1773), p. xv. Bainbrigg Buckeridge, *The art of painting, with the lives and characters of above 300 of the most eminent painters* (London: Printed for T. Payne, 1754), p. 50.

29 'A Discourse Delivered to the Students of the Royal Academy, on the Distribution of the Prizes, December 14, 1770, by the President', *Sir Joshua Reynolds, Discourses on Art,* 1901 edition, https://www.gutenberg.org/files/2176/2176-h/2176-h.htm.

30 Richardson, 'Essay on the Art of Criticism', in *The works of Mr. Jonathan Richardson ... all corrected and prepared for the press by his son Mr. J. Richardson* (London: Printed for T. Davis, in Russel-Street, 1773), p. 234. Katie Scott calls attention to the use of the

The greater priority given to artists' genius had profound implications for their status as intellectual authors: genius was not nurtured in a workshop; rather than a learned skill, it was a fundamentally innate and abstract quality, and one specific to individuals. Consequently, as Richardson explained, it would not reveal itself in the material handling of the paint, but would be detected in one particular quality: the artist's capacity for invention.

Giving priority to intangible elements at the expense of material ones, the theory of painting as a liberal art contributed to the detachment of the artist's authorship from the material utterance of the painted work. As will be discussed below, the same writers who advocated for the liberal-art status of painting also encouraged connoisseurs and amateurs of the visual arts to find and contemplate similar abstract features both in the art of painting and in that of engraving. Instead of considering the work of the engraver in its own terms, viewers were to revel in the way prints conveyed the painter's genius and invention. Art theory thus contributed to the mental transfer of the painter's authorship from the painted surface onto the reproductive print. Such notions found a direct translation into the language of the 1735 Copyright Act, which not only offered protection to visual works produced by artists who made their own compositions — what we today consider 'original prints' — but also offered copyright protection to 'every person who [...] from his own works and invention, shall cause to be designed and engraved, etched, or worked in Mezzotinto or Chiaro Oscuro, any historical or other print or prints'.[31] In other words, the 1735 act, although primarily designed to protect the work of artists like William Hogarth, also opened the door for painters to claim proprietorship on their own painted compositions.[32] There is enough evidence in the archive to show that at least some painters did just that.[33] But it was only in the second half of the eighteenth

term 'genius' in the language of the Edict of Saint-Jean-de-Luz (1660), which gave engraving the status of a liberal art in France: an important step leading to French engravers' claim of exclusive rights in the product of their work (Scott, Becoming Property, p. 60).

31 Engravers' Copyright Act 1735 (8 Geo II, c. 13), § 1, available in *Primary Sources on Copyright*, ed. by Bently and Kretschmer, http://www.copyrighthistory.org/cam/tools/request/showRecord.php?id=record_uk_1735.

32 For a discussion of the 1735 act, see Alexander and Martinez's essay in this volume.

33 See the 1764 mezzotint portrait of John Wilkes Esq., after the painting by Robert Edge Pine and engraved by James Watson, which was the subject of a court case

century that reproductive prints — that is, prints after another work of art (usually a drawing or a painting) — became a dominant force in the British print trade.[34] This turn of events, largely due to John Boydell's strategic business decisions and his patronage of contemporary British painters, had an impact on legislation: it drove the expansion of copyright protection to reproductive prints specifically — including prints after old masters, and those made outside of Britain — and opened that protection to publishers as well as artists.[35] Additionally, it affected the way British painters were able to claim intellectual ownership over their paintings, and the privileges that such claims conferred on them: a right to authorize an engraving (or not), irrespective of whether the original painting had been sold and left the painter's studio.

Because of Boydell's intervention in the reproductive print trade — and the financial success of his enterprise — the leading engravers working after 1750 turned their attention to the adaptation of existing compositions, often paintings, by old masters and living artists, rather than creating their own compositions. Reproductive prints had a long tradition in the history of art since the Renaissance: they had played a critical role in the circulation of artistic designs beyond painters, sculptors, and engravers' restricted circles of patronage.[36] Intaglio engravings, or engravings on metal, had come to be considered the highest form in which a painting could be reproduced. As a result, the preeminent engravers' task was the reproduction of an artist's design

decided at the Court of Common Plea in May of 1765. Unfortunately, at the time of writing, I have not been able to access the court's records.

34 See Chapter 1 for a discussion of the concept of reproductive print in its historical context.

35 Engravers' Copyright Act 1766 (7 Geo III, c.38), § 1 & 2, available in *Primary Sources on Copyright*, ed. by Bently and Kretschmer, http://www.copyrighthistory.org/cam/tools/request/showRecord.php?id=record_uk_1766. The act also made illegal the import of a foreign reproductive print after the same work, thus highlighting the changing conditions of the British print trade.

36 This function of the print is key to art historical inquiries concerned with the development of the concept of prints as works of art, and with prints' roles in European artistic practices in early modern and modern Europe. See David Landau and Peter Parshall, *The Renaissance Print* (New Haven: Yale University Press, 1996), pp. 1–3, 6, 43–46, 50–65; Lisa Pon, *Raphael, Dürer, and Marcantonio Raimondi: Copying and the Renaissance Italian Print* (New Haven: Yale University Press, 2004); and Sarah Cree, 'Translating Stone into Paper: Sixteenth-and Seventeenth- Century Prints after the Antique', in *Paper Museums: The Reproductive Print in Europe, 1500–1800*, ed. by Rebecca Zorach and Elizabeth Rodini (Chicago: University of Chicago Press, 2005).

on the copper plate.[37] At the same time, the quality of an engraving was measured in terms of the competence and creativity of the engraver's imitation: 'Engraving, which only imitates Nature, must follow her in every way', explained Abraham Bosse, in what was the most influential treatise in Europe until the end of the eighteenth century.[38] In other words, the critical vocabulary and intellectual framework through which engravings were evaluated did not fundamentally differ from those of the other visual arts (painting and sculpture) which it reproduced and conveyed in a new medium. In England, however, as the print trade turned to the adaptation of old masters and contemporary paintings into prints, the fame of engravers increasingly rested on the status of the living painters whose work they successfully adapted to the copper plate. As commissions to represent contemporary paintings in print became publicized through large single picture exhibitions in London, the significance of the collaboration between painter and engraver took on an increased importance.

The success of the alliance between painter and engraver was evaluated by comparison with a powerful antecedent in the Renaissance: the relationship between Raphael and his contemporary, the printmaker Marcantonio Raimondi. Although 'Marc Antonio's engravings come far

37 Vasari contributed to the establishment of this conception of printmaking with his addition of a chapter specifically dedicated to Marcantonio Raimondi in the second edition of the *Vite* (1568): 'For Vasari the central role of the print was not to invent but to reproduce the *invenzione* and the *disegno* of another work of art' (Landau and Parshall, *The Renaissance Print*, p. 103).

38 After the Renaissance, the most influential treatise on engraving was Abraham Bosse's *Traicté des Manières de Graver en Taille Douce sur l'Airin, Par le Moyen des Eaux Fortes, et des Vernix Durs & Mols* (Paris, 1645), which analyzed the medium in terms of mimesis: 'La Gravure qui n'est qu'une imitation de la Nature doit la suivre dans tous ses effets' (Bosse, *Traicté des Manières de Graver* (Paris, 1745 ed.), p. 79). Bosse's treatise was republished in new and expanded editions in 1701, 1745, and 1758. It was widely influential in Europe, translated and published in England in William Faithorne's *The Art of Graveing and Etching, wherein is expressed the true Way of Graveing in Copper; also the Manner of that famous Callot, and M. Bosse, in their several ways of Etching* (London: A. Roper, 1702); and into German in 1765 (*Die Kunst in Kupfer zu stechen: sowohl vermittelst des Aetzwassers als mit dem Grabstichel; insgleichen die sogenannte schwarze Kunst, und wie die Kupferdrucker-Preße nach ietziger Art zu bauen und die Kupfer abzudrucken sind.* Dresden: Gröll, 1765). Despite the technical additions and aesthetic changes that are reflected in Bosse's successive editions and translations — in particular the mid-eighteenth-century predilection for painterly rather than graphic effects — the framing concept of reproductive engraving remained the notion of imitation. See Michel Roncerel, 'Traités de gravure', *Nouvelles de l'estampe,* 194 (May-June 2004), 19–27.

short of what Raphael himself did,' admitted Richardson, 'all others that have made prints after Raphael come vastly short of him, because he [Marcantonio] has better imitated what is most excellent in that beloved, wonderful man [Raphael] than any other has done.'[39] The market and aesthetic values of a print depended on the close relationship between painter, engraver, and draftsman involved in its production. Archival evidence, in particular contracts between artists and publishers, support the view that Boydell's publications of paintings by the most important contemporary artists were highly collaborative enterprises, through which the painter not only gained financial return but also fully partnered in the project.[40]

Gilbert Stuart's early career was profoundly affected by such artistic partnerships (which included the print publisher as well). His portrait of the engraver William Woollett (see Figure 2) belonged to a large commission of portraits of living artists by Boydell who intended to use them as promotional material. Woollett was an early collaborator of Boydell's, and one of the most sought-after engravers in London. His plate after Benjamin West's *The Death of General Wolfe* (1776) had become the most celebrated engraving of the time.

Stuart called attention to the significance of the collaborative partnership between painter and printmaker in his portrait of Woollett: the picture shows the engraver working on his plate directly with West's painting in the background to emphasize the intimate relationship between the painter's work and the engraver — even though Woollett more likely worked from a drawing after the painting as was customary practice (an intermediary drawing would not only bring the composition to the size of the plate but would also adapt it to a grayscale).

Boydell's public exhibitions of Stuart's portraits also highlighted the close relationship between painter and graphic interpreters. He displayed John Singleton Copley's *Death of Major Peirson* topped with Stuart's portrait of Copley, the painter, at the center, flanked by those of

39 Jonathan Richardson, 'Essay on the Art of Criticism', in *The works of Mr. Jonathan Richardson ... all corrected and prepared for the press by his son Mr. J. Richardson* (London: Printed for T. Davis, in Russel-Street, 1773), pp. 234–235.

40 For examples of contracts for the production of reproductive prints, see Anthony Griffiths, 'Two Contracts for British Prints', *Print Quarterly* 9:2 (June 1992), 184–187. See also Bruntjen, *John Boydell*, pp. 205–211; Clayton, *The English Print*, pp. 195–196, 224–228.

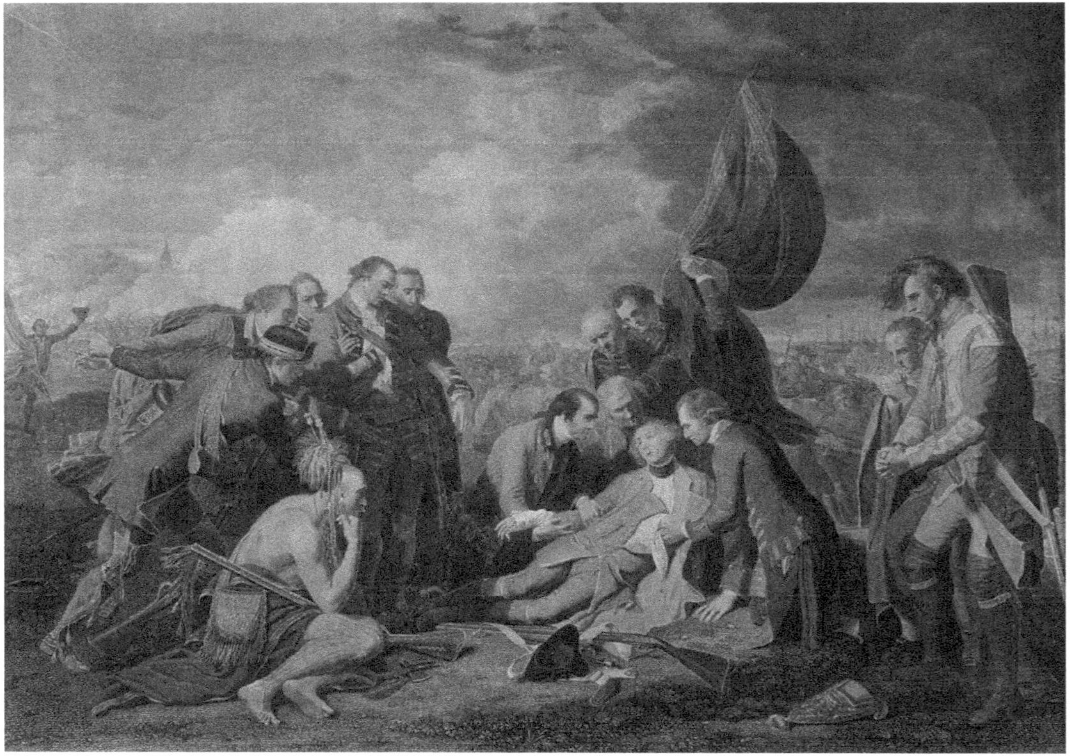

Fig. 5 William Woollett after Benjamin West, *The Death of General Wolfe* (1776), engraving, 1966.0260 A, B, Winterthur Museum, Garden & Library, Museum purchase, Courtesy of Winterthur Museum, Photo funded by NEA.

James Heath (the engraver), and Joshua Boydell (the draftsman who made an intermediary drawing after the painting). The exhibit served to promote both Copley and the engraving — subscription papers were available at the gallery. It not only attested to the collaborative nature of the work that presided over the creation of the engraving, but also implied the painter's endorsement of the printed image. Highlighting the alliance between the genius of the painter and the talent of its interpreters, Boydell's public displays of paintings like Copley's *Death of Major Peirson* anticipated the reference status of the engraving, similar to what Marcantonio's engravings were to Raphael's paintings. This was of critical importance since, as Richardson declared, it was not the painting but the graphic work that would ultimately convey the painter's 'last, [...] utmost thoughts on [a] subject, whatever it be'.[41] Richardson and other theoreticians of art created habits of viewing and appreciating an engraving that was tied to the way the graphic image conveyed the work of the painter-author of the composition. In other words, art theory converged with Boydell and artists' partnerships in publishing and exhibition to facilitate the painters' insistence that they should control when, how, and by whom their work of art would be adapted into print. Benjamin West collaborated with Boydell and with engravers William Woollett and John Hall for the publication of several of his history paintings in print, including *The Death of General Wolfe*, and *Penn's Treaty with the Indians*.[42] John Singleton Copley painted some of his greatest historical paintings for publication. Although he remarked later that 'the difficulties of a Painter began when his picture was finished, if an engraving from it should be his object', the artist was deeply invested in the appearance of his paintings in print, and in their quality.[43] The catalogue of the Sotheby's Copley print sale, held five years after the painter's death in 1815, listed a large number of copper plates after his own works. The quality of a print after a painting was so important to Copley that he was ready to go to court to defend the need for the

41 Richardson, 'Essay on the Art of Criticism', in *The works of Mr. Jonathan Richardson ... all corrected and prepared for the press by his son Mr. J. Richardson* (London: Printed for T. Davis, in Russel-Street, 1773), p. 234.

42 See James Clifton, 'Reverberated Enjoyment: Prints, Printmakers, and Publishers in Late-Eighteenth-Century London', in *American Adversaries. West and Copley in a Transatlantic World* (Houston: The Museum of Fine Arts, 2013), pp. 51–61 (p. 51).

43 Quoted in Clifton, 'Reverberated Enjoyment', p. 57.

highest quality in a reproductive engraving. Dissatisfied with the plate after his *Death of Earl Chatham*, the painter refused to pay the engraver's premium. The disagreement between the two artists led to a famous court case that opposed Copley to his engraver Jean Marie Delattre in 1801.[44] In other words, art theory converged with Boydell's trade practices and with painters and engravers' partnerships to facilitate the painters' aspirations to control when, how, and by whom their work of art would be adapted into print.

At the same time, artistic and trade practices expressed something more than what Ronan Deazley has called a painter's 'engraving rights.'[45] They showed that a painter was the author of an intellectual work, manifest both in the painting and in the print. Boydell's exhibition and publication practices promised subscribers an image that not only communicated the painter's approved authorial presence in the engraving, but also prepared the viewer to experience artistic authorship in the most abstract terms. As Richardson explained, the painter's creation could only be conveyed through the work's most intellectual elements: 'invention, composition, manner of designing, grace and greatness'.[46] The physical ink marks transferred from the copper plate to paper during the printing process were of secondary importance. They attested to another artist's hand, an interpreter whose talent lay in an ability to accurately translate another creator's thoughts in the visual language of lines and dots of printed ink on paper.[47]

44 Jules D. Prown, *John Singleton Copley*, vol. 2: *Copley in England* (Cambridge, MA: Harvard University Press, 1966), includes a transcript of the sale catalogue (pp. 389–394). Copley commissioned Francesco Bartolozzi for the engraving of the *Death of Earl Chatham* and a second smaller plate from Delattre. The engraver sued the painter and won his case in a celebrated court case in which 14 painters gave evidence in support of Copley, while 14 engravers supported Delattre.

45 Ronan Deazley, 'Commentary on the *Models and Busts Act* 1798', in *Primary Sources on Copyright*, ed. by Bently and Kretschmer, http://www.copyrighthistory.org/cam/tools/request/showRecord?id=commentary_uk_1798.

46 Jonathan Richardson, 'The Theory of Painting', in *The works of Mr. Jonathan Richardson ... all corrected and prepared for the press by his son Mr. J. Richardson* (London: Printed for T. Davis, in Russel-Street, 1773), p. 20

47 Writers and artists who focused on the relationship between the painter and the engraver during the second half of the eighteenth century moved towards the literary metaphor of translation to explain the nature of the relationship between painter and engraver. Even though the dominant framing concept of reproductive engraving remained the notion of imitation in England until the turn of the nineteenth century, several writers in France presented this new approach to the art of reproductive engraving, comparing it to literary translation. See Claude-Henri Watelet's article 'Engraving' in Diderot and d'Alembert's *Encyclopedie*: 'The

When subscribers received their engraving or when spectators looked at the engraving through a shop window, what they saw was not the engraver's talent, but the painter's genius. Benjamin West recalled an anecdote from a conversation with the naval hero Horatio Nelson that stresses the importance of this point: 'I never pass a print-shop with your "Death of Wolfe" in the window', West reported Nelson saying, 'without being stopped by it'. Nelson's (and West's) use of the possessive adjective for *The Death of General Wolfe* clearly identifies the painter as the intellectual author (and would-be legitimate proprietor) of the engraved image.[48]

The cultural predominance of the artist-author that this conversation articulates had extensive applications — especially in the relationships between artists and their patrons. While British painters learned to rely on their relationship with publishers, as well as the 1735 and 1766 statutes to exert some control over the afterlife of their painting in print, the absence of legislation on paintings themselves presented potential difficulty when they left the studio before plans for engravings had been made.[49] A dispute that arose between Copley and the owners of one of his portraits, however, sheds light on the extensive power that art theory and trade practices had come to exert over British art patronage at the turn of the nineteenth century. The quarrel never became public. It arose after the death of Anglo-Irish nobleman William Ponsonby, 2nd Earl of Bessborough.

---

engraver is for the painters whose pictures he imitates, what the translator is for the authors whose works he interprets ... One reads a translation, and one considers an engraving only to get acquainted to the original authors'. By the early nineteenth century, the metaphor had become so common that it could be subject to critical comment by various authors. In England, John Landseer, the foremost engraver associated with the Royal Academy, built his defense of the art of reproductive engraving on the comparison between engraving and translation. For further discussion of eighteenth-century French writing on engraving as translation, see Christian Michel, 'Les débats sur la notion de graveur/traducteur en France au XVIIIème siècle', in Marie-Félicie Perez-Pivot and François Fossier, *Delineavit et Sculpsit: dix-neuf contributions sur les rapports dessin-gravure du XVIe au XXe siècle.* Lyon: Presses Universitaires de Lyon, 2003, pp. 151–161.

48 The conversation between West and Nelson is quoted in Clifton, 'Reverberated Enjoyment', p. 51.

49 Although the question of common-law copyright in a manuscript was an important one, debated in literary copyright at the time, there is no evidence — at the time of this writing — that it was legally discussed in cases that involved a painting. See Tomás Gómez-Arostegui, 'Copyright at Common Law in 1774', *Connecticut Law Review*, 47 (2014), 1–57.

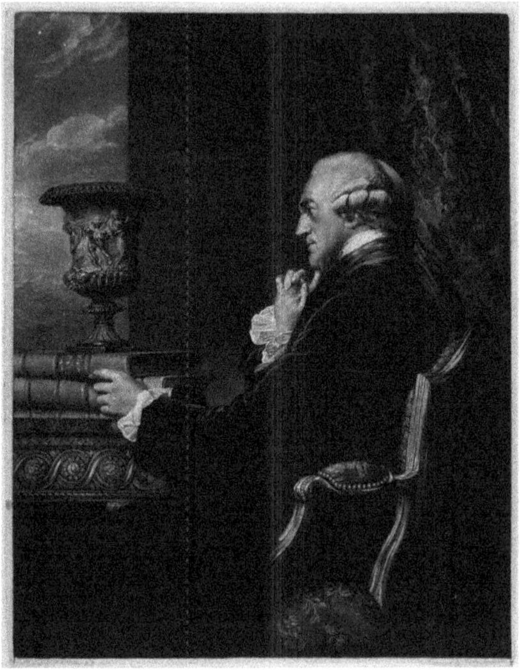

Fig. 6 Robert Dunkarton, after John Singleton Copley, *Portrait of William Ponsonby, Earl of Bessborough* (1794), mezzotint, Harvard Art Museums/Fogg Museum, Transfer from Harvard University, Gift of Gardiner Greene. © President and Fellows of Harvard College.

His heirs desired to pay tribute to Ponsonby's lifelong devotion to art patronage by commissioning a print after a portrait of the earl, painted by Copley in 1790. The deceased's family and friends contacted the best art publisher of the time, John Boydell, to contract for the publication of the mezzotint. The arrangement was to use Admiral Caldwell's copy of Copley's portrait and have it adapted into print by one of Boydell's engravers. Possibly hearing of the project from Boydell himself, Copley wrote to Caldwell to stop what he felt was an unauthorized reproduction of his work, expressing outrage at the owner's lack of awareness of customary practices: 'It is extremely uncommon for an engraving to be made from a picture without first consulting with the Artist who has painted it'.[50] Copley continued, 'I did not make any express agreement

50 Copley to Caldwell, Sheffield Archives WWM F32/1, letter published in Rachel Finnegan, '"An Extreme Cunning Fellow": Copley's Memorial Engraving to the 2nd Earl of Bessborough', *Print Quarterly*, 24:1 (March 2007), 3–11 (pp. 6–7).

to secure myself from that inconvenience because I did not suppose it necessary. [...] I certainly however expected that both the Copy which I painted for Lord Clanbrassel and that which I painted for Admiral Caldwell would be considered as delivered from my possession with the implied condition of their not being published.'[51]

Copley, as we know, was deeply preoccupied with the publication of his paintings, whether portraits or grand manner historical works; according to the same letter, he had already contracted Robert Dunkarton for the work. As Copley's phrasing indicates, his expectations did not rely on legal texts but rather on usage and conventions. The painter would likely not have had any recourse in the law. Yet, in spite of Caldwell's indignant response, the painter's point of view prevailed, thanks at least in part to the printseller's intervention. Boydell recommended that Caldwell and the family's publication project be abandoned, and Copley published a mezzotint of his portrait, made after the copy Copley had painted for the Earl of Clanbrassel. As with several other of his paintings, Copley was the owner of the copyright for the print, *Portrait of William Ponsonby, Earl of Bessborough* (see Figure 6).[52]

Building on the critical art theory that defined painting as a liberal art, and that envisioned engraving's primary purpose in its ability to convey a painter's invention, artistic and publishing practices in eighteenth-century London created a climate in which the predominant relationship that defined the art of engraving was its ability to communicate the essence of an original work of art. Critical discourse and visual experiences of paintings and reproductive engravings redirected viewers' attention away from the contemplation of the object itself to consider the artist's power of invention independent of the medium in which it was expressed. Painters and beholders learned to privilege an intellectual response to a picture and the evocative power of formal elements, including composition and harmony of line and forms. Artists worked with an eye to the appearance of their paintings

51 Ibid.

52 At the sale of Copley's estate in 1820 were numerous copper plates impressions after his paintings, many of which were made by the most famous engravers of the period — such as Bartolozzi, Dunkarton, and Earlom — who also worked with Boydell. See Prown, *John Singleton Copley*; and Emily Ballew Neff and Kaylin H. Weber, eds., *American Adversaries: West and Copley in a Transatlantic World* (Houston: The Museum of Fine Arts, 2013).

in print to ensure their posterity. It was not only critical that a painting be published in engraved form: it was equally important that the painter vetted the engraver commissioned for the job, since painters and beholders were expected to see the painter's extended authorship in the print. In addition to the dominant theory of art and many an artist's experience studying the old masters in print — the most common vehicle that ultimately conveyed their invention in visual form — trade practices and the copyright statute of 1766, all reinforced the painter's authorial presence in reproductive engravings. Many painters thus claimed it in the reproduction. Intellectual ownership of one's painting in the form of an engraving entitled painters to assert a right to limit copying, and the right to authorize a painting's publication as an engraving. In the expanding art world and reproductive print trade of eighteenth-century England, British painters found fertile ground for claims of intellectual ownership over their compositions, and of the right to oversee the conditions of their publication — all elements that Gilbert Stuart would later claim for himself in the less- favorable environment of the new American Republic.

Stuart and the Visual Economy of the Young Republic

The relationship between a painting and its reproduction in an intaglio print, and the painter's customary power to authorize a reproduction, was thus fundamental to the artistic culture in which Gilbert Stuart became an artist. When Stuart demanded that William Bingham not cede his publication right together with the portrait of Washington commissioned for the Marquis of Lansdowne, he was following the established practices that Copley described in his letter to the 2nd Earl of Bessborough's friend. The artist's request to his patron was therefore far from extraordinary. What *was* new in the case of Stuart was that he expressed his claim in property and copyright terms. He was not, moreover, the only one to do so.

In 1800, Rembrandt Peale (1778–1860), the son of Charles Willson Peale and a young, ambitious artist who twenty years later would petition Congress for statutory protection of paintings, monetized the copying of his portrait of Thomas Jefferson as a right to its publication. Although he could not claim prices as high as Stuart for portraying

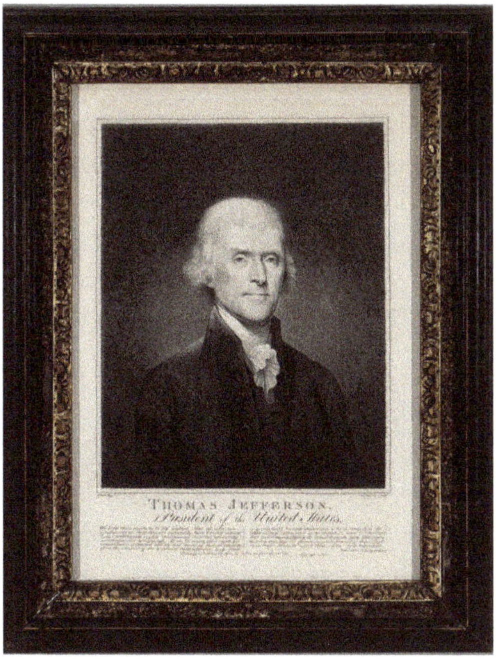

Fig. 7 Cornelius Tiebout after Rembrandt Peale, *Portrait of Thomas Jefferson* (1800), stipple engraving, 1963.0060, Winterthur Museum Garden & Library, Museum purchase, Courtesy of Winterthur Museum, Photo funded by NEA.

his sitters, he followed similar practices. When Thomas Jefferson rose to the presidency in 1800, Rembrandt Peale collaborated with the enterprising Philadelphia publisher Mathew Carey to create the best printed image of the president elect (see Figure 7).[53] Working in concert with the painter on this enterprise, Carey bought from the artist the right to publish the painted portrait of Jefferson as a print for $50. Following in Boydell's steps, the publisher also paid a premium of $150 to the best available Philadelphia engraver, Cornelius Tiebout, to engrave the plate.[54] The sum Peale received for letting Tiebout draw a

53 At the sale of Copley's estate in 1820 were numerous copper plates impressions after his paintings, many by the most famous engravers of the period such as Bartolozzi, Dunkarton, Earlom, who also worked with Boydell. See Prown, *John Singleton Copley;* and Neff and Weber, eds., *American Adversaries*.

54 To Cornelius Tiebout, from Matthew Carey, 19 August 1800: Account Books, no. 5995, Carey Papers, American Antiquarian Society. That sum was three times the amount Carey paid the engraver for engraving biblical illustrations during the same period.

copy of his work for the engraving was significantly higher than what Peale asked for an ordinary copy he would paint himself ($30). This indicates that the money received from Carey was a payment for the right to copy and publish the original work of art in printed form, in addition to the repeated composition.[55] Carey made this explicit when marketing the print: in order to attract attention to the forthcoming plate, he circulated a limited number of unfinished proofs of Tiebout's engraving, together with subscription papers. Carey inscribed the plate with the mention 'Copy Right Secured' in the lower right margin, and gave strict instructions to his agents to not let anyone borrow the print so as to prevent any unauthorized copying.[56] At that time, there was no legislation on copyright for images in the United States. Peale and Carey not only followed what they considered proper trade practices — the purchase of the artist's authorization to copy before publishing. Carey also claimed a monopoly on Peale's depiction of Jefferson, a privilege that he did not legally control in the unregulated context of the early Republic. The risk of piracy was not negligible, making it necessary for the publisher to spell out a claim which asserted an exclusive right in the publication of Peale's image of the newly elected president. This also revealed what the artists and publishers regarded to be the conceptual essence of the long-established trade and artistic practices that had developed in England over the past fifty years.[57] A painter's authorization to have his work copied had monetary value. For Stuart, Peale and Carey, this was a copyright in the painter's image.

---

55 In March 1801 Peale had written to Jefferson about the president's commission of a painted copy of his original portrait: 'I shall feel happy in being able to furnish you with an accurate Copy of your Portrait, at my usual price of 30 Dollars — which shall be immediately begun and finished as soon as possible'. Rembrandt Peale to Thomas Jefferson, Philadelphia, 1 March 1801, Founders Online, National Archives, http://founders.archives.gov/documents/Jefferson/01-33-02-0096, The Papers of Thomas Jefferson, vol. 33, 17 February-30 April 1801, ed. by Barbara B. Oberg (Princeton: Princeton University Press, 2006), p. 114. The practice of repeating a composition is discussed in Chapter 1 of the present volume.

56 'You will not allow any person whatsoever to have it five minutes out of your possession', Carey (quoted without reference) in Noble E. Cunningham, *The Image of Thomas Jefferson in the Public Eye: Portraits for the People, 1800–1809* (Charlottesville: University Press of Virginia, 1981), p. 48.

57 For the many printed portraits of Thomas Jefferson inspired and copied with various degrees of success from Rembrandt Peale's 1800 portrait, see Cunningham, *The Image of Thomas Jefferson*, pp. 23–53.

Gilbert Stuart, Rembrandt Peale, and Mathew Carey were not only trying to set public standards and rules for the trade in the highly competitive and unregulated engraving market in the United States in the first decade of the nineteenth century.[58] They also claimed ownership of an intangible property rooted in a painting, and one not circumscribed by the materials used, nor by the physical traces of an artist's work on its surface. This property was originally tied to the painter's publication of the work in print. At the same time, Stuart's difficulty with Captain Sword makes clear that — in the eye of the artist at least — it applied to any medium, whether they mechanically reproduced an image or not.

Examined in both its local American and its transatlantic contexts, Stuart's bill against Captain Sword indicates that the portraitist fully discerned the conceptual implications of the artistic theory and trade practices that had nurtured his career in London. In the United States, Stuart had to assert what they meant, owing to the absence of well-established rules of trade, art institutions, and the uncertain legal framework that might otherwise defend them in America. For his litigation against Sword, Stuart received legal advice from well-established members of the Philadelphia Bar, who were all among his patrons. Alexander James Dallas (1759–1817), whose portrait Stuart painted in 1800, was the United States Attorney for the District of Pennsylvania where Gilbert Stuart filed his bill. William Lewis (1751–1819), whose portrait by Stuart is known through John Neagle's copy, was a Quaker, and a lawyer involved in the drafting of the act for the gradual abolition of slavery that passed in Pennsylvania in 1780. William Tilghman (1756–1827) was a lawyer and plantation owner from Maryland, who had moved to Philadelphia in 1793, and briefly served as a federal judge of the US Circuit Court in 1801. Last but not least, William Rawle (1759–1836), also a Quaker and another of Stuart's patrons, was a lawyer involved in numerous learned societies and cultural circles. He would contribute to the foundation of the Pennsylvania Academy for the Fine Arts in 1805. Dallas, Lewis, Rawle, and Tilghman were all known for their sympathy for the rights of British citizens. They commissioned and purchased works of art from Stuart. At least one of them, William

58 'Proposals of Matthew Carey, for Publishing by Subscription, an elegant likeness (half length) or Thomas Jefferson, President Elect of the U. States', published in the *Virginia Argus*, March 6, 10, 20, 24, 1801, and dated Philadelphia, January 25.

Rawle, had more than a casual interest in the role of the visual arts in the United States.

In light of the scant archival record, it is unclear under what terms Stuart won his case at court. Nothing in his bill indicates that his lawyers or the presiding judge recognized the legal weight of an artist's claim of intellectual property over a painting in the context of US-American law. Dallas, Lewis, Rawle, and Tilghman more likely saw possibilities in the breach of contract between Stuart and Sword. The remedies Stuart asked for do not, however, shed much light on this question. The bill Stuart presented to the court expressed a concern that his claim would not find sufficient remedies at common law: 'Your orator hath no plain, adequate, and complete relief in the premises at Common Law'. Common law remedies gave the complainant the possibility to recover costs equivalent to damages that could be proven — there are no records of how many of the portrait Sword *did* sell — but they did not permit the confiscation of fraudulent copies. By the time Sword landed in Philadelphia with the copies of the Athenaeum type, we know that Stuart had secured about forty commissions for Washington's portraits. The painter was therefore stretching the well-established practice of repeating one's work of art for several patrons further than anyone has done before him. Scholars have estimated the total output of Stuart's Washington portraits slightly above one hundred, a quantity exactly corresponding to the number of Sword's Chinese copies. Over the course of just a few months, Sword was throwing on the market an equivalent of the painter's life work. The sheer quantity of paintings imported by Sword was a major threat to the artist's livelihood, and their forfeiture was clearly the painter's goal. Stuart therefore requested remedies that the court of Chancery in England could issue — an injunction ordering the delivery and destruction of the fraudulent goods. Stuart's case was solved in favor of the painter, showing that the court likely accepted the validity of the painting's contractual sale, together with its limitations on copying.

The case of Stuart v. Sword, together with Stuart's public campaign against James Heath's unauthorized engraving and Rembrandt Peale's contract with Mathew Carey for the reproduction of his portrait of Jefferson, shows the importance that artists and publishers gave to an abstract concept of artistic property as well as proper trade practices — practices clearly inherited from British antecedents, but that had also not been broadly accepted in the US-American context. Chinese reverse painting on glass, the medium of Sword's unauthorized copies of Stuart's Washington portrait, was not a new type of artwork in the early 1800s Philadelphia. Such paintings — often copies after printed images — had been circulating in Europe and America since the seventeenth century. Nevertheless, the industrial scale of Captain Sword's order of one hundred copies — which likened the final product to luxurious but utilitarian objects like Chinese export porcelain plates — combined with its unique life-size format, made the reverse paintings after Stuart's Athenaeum portrait an utterly new kind of object on the American market. Captain Sword's portraits of Washington, 'made in China' and offered for sale in Philadelphia, were also a direct consequence of the expanded trade routes open to US-American shipping after the country's independence. These exotic objects did not bring an entirely new set of questions to the fore; the right that a painter had to restrict copying of a painting after a painting's sale had its roots in the London art world and could obviously be enforced under certain conditions. However, the new medium in which the copies were executed brought a new and broader set of answers to these questions.

Unlike Heath's engravings, the paintings on glass could not be considered a publication of the original work. Just like Carey's purchase of a right to publish Rembrandt Peale's portrait of Thomas Jefferson, Stuart's approach to stop the sale of about one hundred unauthorized copies of a likeness of Washington, and his press campaign addressing the unauthorized publication of his Lansdowne portrait demonstrate that artists and publishers shared in the opinion that the creator of a work of art had the right to control copying of his original work. They believed that this right should be respected no matter the medium in which a work of art might be reproduced: whether a painted full-size copy made on another continent, or an engraving commissioned in London by the new owner of the work. As Sword and Bingham's undertakings show, not all collectors or purchasers of art agreed with this opinion. Equally important, Stuart's legal and public attempts to control the reproduction of his portraits after sale also reveals the difficulty that artists, print sellers and publishers faced in exerting their prerogative in a new nation, trading far and wide without long-established public advocates or art institutions like the Royal Academy. American independence had opened new channels of direct trade with Asia, and this new pattern of trade had suggested to Captain Sword untried avenues of profit through the multiplication of a portrait of George Washington in a luxurious, exotic format. This represented both a high point in the demand for images of the country's founding father — Washington had died less than two years earlier — and a time of uncertainty with regards to how Congress intended to provide legislation that would protect American artists and their creations.

Stuart, Carey, and Peale's practices expanded on what Ronan Deazley has called a painter's 'engraving rights', expressed through art publishers' contracts with painters like Benjamin West and John Singleton Copley.[59] Stuart's advertisement against the Heath's unauthorized British engraving, Carey's requested inscription below Tiebout's proof engraving, and the Stuart v. Sword litigation demonstrate that American artists and publishers did not defend an 'engraving right' per se, but a broader intangible ownership in a work of art, which meant a right in controlling copying and publication in all media available, prior to and following the sale of the artwork, within and outside the boundaries of the nation state. In the unregulated marketplace of the young American Republic, Stuart, Peale, and Carey claimed that this was properly a 'copy-right' and one that was directly connected to the original work, not just a printed image. This broad claim of authority over copying — in contracts, in the press, and in Stuart v. Sword — was founded on the dematerialization of the painter's authorship over the image, which had been advanced in theoretical discourses on art, and in the relationships between intaglio engravings and paintings: ones that took pride of place decades earlier in exhibitions and high-profile commissions in Britain. Separate from the ownership of the material work, this intellectual property, the creative genius's expression in the painting or in the print, could not be transferred without either a purchase from the painter, or at the very least an official endorsement.

Ultimately, however, the intangible nature of the work of art would not entirely hold in the US-American legal context. One could not simply discard the material and visual dimensions of a picture. This issue became the center of a court case in 1821: Binns v. Woodruff, which concluded that the artistic property in a picture was both intangible

59 Deazley, 'Commentary on the Models and Busts Act 1798'.

and material.[60] John Binns, an Irish-born Philadelphia publisher, had commissioned several artists to draw and engrave the elements of a composition that presented a copy of the Declaration of Independence with facsimiles-signatures framed into an oval made of decorative medallions representing the arms of the thirteen States of the United States, and the portraits of three founding fathers: John Hancock, George Washington, and Thomas Jefferson, capped by the great seal of the United States. He had deposited an incomplete state of the print for copyright in November of 1818, accompanied by a prospectus. In February 1819, a similar design was engraved by William Woodruff, and Binns sued for infringement on his copyright.[61] Binns lost his case at court on the account that he had not drawn the design himself, but only given verbal directions to others; in the end, five artists (Bridport, Valance, Bird, Murray, and Sully) had given the printed image its composition and visual form, not Binns himself. Although the engraving act of 1802 followed the British Engraving act relatively closely, as Robert Brauneis has shown, the language of the American law limited those who could claim copyright protection: the proprietor of an image could be either 'every person [...] who shall invent and design, engrave, etch, or work', or everyone who 'from his own works and inventions, shall cause to be designed and engraved, etched or worked, any historical or other print or prints'.[62] The language of the law indicated the importance of being either the maker or the inventor of a picture in order to claim copyright protection. However, Judge Bushrod Washington interpreted the statute further, explaining that the language of the law indicated without doubt that the person 'intended and described as the proprietor of a copyright' must either be the engraver of the print ('in other words, the entire work, or subject of the copyright is executed by the same person') or the author of the original design in another medium: 'the invention is designed or embodied by the person in whom the right is vested, and the form and completion of the work are executed by another'.[63] The court was clear that the commissioner of a painting could not claim the

60 Binns v. Woodruff, 3 Fed. Cas. 421 (1821).

61 A reprint of that plate was sold recently at Doyle: https://doyle.com/auctions/16bp02-rare-books-autographs-photographs/catalogue/126-declaration-independence-broadside.

62 1802 Amendment, s. 2; Brauneis, 'Understanding Copyright's First Encounter'.

63 Binns, 3 Fed. Cas. at 422.

copyright for a picture since he had not given it visible form on a material support. Calling on the British antecedent of Blackwell v. Harper, Judge Washington remarked that the plaintiff 'not only conceived the idea of making a representation of the medicinal plants, but she also engraved them herself, and the combination of the two afforded the evidence of genius and art which the law intended to encourage'.[64] In the absence of a contract of sale of the image's copyright, the commissioner of the print could not claim property in the print. The use of the terms 'genius' and 'art' in Judge Washington's decision are direct references to a combination of intellectual labor and technical knowledge. Intellectual property in the visual arts was not considered entirely immaterial. Conceiving the idea of a design was no ground for copyright unless one transformed this idea into a visible design. A picture could not entirely be separated from its material form.

Eighteenth-century artistic practices and art theory built the foundation for a broad concept of intellectual property in painting, and its expression in early American trade practices. In spite of the lack of legislation on painting in the United States at that time, the notion that an intangible property in a painting existed outside of statutory law did find traction in the cultural landscape of early nineteenth-century Philadelphia. Even though Stuart v. Sword was not reported in the legal literature at the time, there is little doubt that the conception of painting as intellectual property that painters and publishers like Stuart and Carey envisioned had a profound impact on the next generation of artists to which Rembrandt Peale belonged. Stuart never returned to Britain, but in the United States, he became a founding figure for young painters who sought him out for advice and instruction. One of them, John Neagle, who would become a director of the Pennsylvania Academy of the Fine Arts, recalled discussing these events with the master. Neagle later reported to William Dunlap the Philadelphia merchant's inappropriate conduct vis-à-vis Stuart's Lansdowne portrait, and how Stuart had been deprived of his property in the painting. Dunlap made it an important story in his chapter on Stuart in his 1834 *History of the Rise and Progress of the Arts of Design in the United States*. In 1848, at a time when there was still no legislation on the copyright of paintings, William Sidney Mount, the celebrated genre painter, privately commented on being

64 *Id.* at 424.

compensated for the copyright of *The Power of Music* when the newly established French art dealer and publisher Goupil & Co. contracted him for the painting's publication.

The notion of artistic property in a painting did not find expression in the 1802 statute, which limited copyright protection to printed images. However, Stuart's disputes over his portraits of Washington also anticipated key questions that would be debated in England in the middle decades of the nineteenth century, namely whether one could hold an intellectual property right for an unpublished painting, and if so, under what condition(s) that property might be secured, forfeited, or transferred together with the material work.[65] In the United States, while the 1802 act restrained protection to printed images, the text still offered protection to the author or 'inventor' of a picture, even if she/he did not actually work on the print itself. American jurisprudence reinforced this view with Binns v. Woodruff: painters who necessarily produced material works expressing their intellectual inventions could become proprietors of their own pictures. Expectedly, Stuart took advantage of the law and copyrighted (together with the engraver David Edwin) several of his pictures, including a portrait of Thomas M'Kean, governor of Pennsylvania, and a portrait of Washington in 1803. Stuart's copyright deposits also represent the first scant archival evidence of a painter's interest in using the legal system to protect an intellectual property originating in a painting in the United States. What is surprising, in fact, is how few well-known painters followed in Stuart's steps. The importance of printed images in US-American visual culture only grew in the next decade, and some of the nation's most innovative artists, such as the recent German immigrant John Lewis Krimmel, Thomas Sully, and Asher B. Durand, cultivated close relationships with the publishing industry, not only using reproductive prints as sources for inspiration but also entering into collaborations with local printmakers, publishers, and magazine editors with whom they explored the possibilities offered by the expanding print culture of the Republic. More research on the early American publishing industry and its relationship with artists might yield further insight into the reasons why US-American painters (with the exception of Rembrandt Peale) did

65 These questions are discussed in Cooper, *Art and Modern Copyright*, and in Will Slauter's chapter in this volume.

not pursue legal means of protecting what many privately considered a copyright in their paintings.[66]

Bibliography

8 Geo II, c. 13: An Act for the encouragement of the arts of designing, engraving, and etching historical and other prints, by vesting the properties thereof in the inventors and engravers, during the time therein mentioned (1735) digitized in *Primary Sources on Copyright* (1450–1900), ed. by Lionel Bently & Martin Kretschmer, www.copyrighthistory.org: http://www.copyrighthistory.org/cam/tools/request/showRecord.php?id=record_uk_1735.

7 Geo. III, c.38: An act to amend and render more effectual an act made in the eighth year of the reign of King George the Second, for encouragement of the arts of designing, engraving, and etching, historical and other prints; and for vesting in, and securing to, Jane Hogarth widow, the property in certain prints, 1766 — digitized in *Primary Sources on Copyright* (1450–1900), ed. by L. Bently & M. Kretschmer, www.copyrighthistory.org: http://www.copyrighthistory.org/cam/tools/request/showRecord.php?id=record_uk_1766.

Barratt, Carrie Rebora and Ellen G. Miles, eds., *Gilbert Stuart* (New York: The Metropolitan Museum of Art, and New Haven and London: Yale University Press, 2004).

Bently, Lionel, 'Art and the Making of Modern Copyright Law', in *Dear Images: Art, Copyright and Culture,* ed. by Daniel McClean and Karsten Schubert (London and Manchester: Ridinghouse and the Institute of Contemporary Arts, 2002), pp. 330–351.

Bosse, Abraham, *Traicté des Manières de Graver en Taille Douce sur l'Airin, Par le Moyen des Eaux Fortes, et des Vernix Durs & Mols* (Paris: 1645).

Bracha, Oren, *Owning Ideas. The Intellectual Origins of American Intellectual Property, 1790–1909* (New York: Cambridge University Press, 2016) https://doi.org/10.1017/9780511843235.

Brauneis, Robert, 'Understanding Copyright's First Encounter with the Fine Arts: A Look at the Legislative History of the Copyright Act of 1870', *Case Western Reserve Law Review*, 71 (2020), 585-625.

Bruntjen, Sven H. A., *John Boydell, 1719–1804: A Study of Art Patronage and Publishing* (New York and London: Garland Publishing Inc., 1985).

Buckeridge, Bainbrigg, *The art of painting, with the lives and characters of above 300 of the most eminent painters* (London Printed for T. Payne, 1754).

66 The role of some of the printing industry's intermediaries is the subject of Erika Piola's essay in this volume. Many thanks to Robert Brauneis, whose remarks and suggestions proved tremendously valuable for this chapter, and to the participants of the two conferences who commented on it.

Cao, Maggie, 'Washington in China: A Media History of Reverse Painting on Glass', *Common-Place*, 15:4 (Summer 2015)/Object Lessons, http://commonplace.online/article/washington-in-china-a-media-history-of-reverse-painting-on-glass/.

Carey Papers, Account Books, no. 5995, American Antiquarian Society.

Chadwick, D., E. P. Richardson, Claude Flory and Edward R. Black, eds., '"Notes and Documents," Gilbert Stuart, D.', *The Pennsylvania Magazine of History and Biography*, 14:1 (January 1970), 95–103.

Chan, Libby Lai-Pik and Nina Lai-Na Wan, eds., *The Dragon and the Eagle: American Traders in China, A Century of Trade from 1784 to 1900*, Hong Kong Maritime Museum (2018).

Clayton, Tim, *The English Print* (New Haven: Yale University Press, 1997).

Copyright Records, Pennsylvania, Eastern Circuit Court, Library of Congress, microfilm reel 61, vol. 262, 1790–1804.

Cooper, Elena, *Art and Modern Copyright. The Contested Image* (Cambridge, UK and New York: Cambridge University Press, 2018), https://doi.org/10.1017/9781316840993.

Crossman, Carl, *The Decorative Arts of the China Trade* (Woodbridge, Suffolk: Antique Collectors' Club, 1991).

Cunningham, Noble E., *The Image of Thomas Jefferson in the Public Eye: Portraits for the People, 1800–1809* (Charlottesville: University Press of Virginia, 1981).

Deazley, Ronan, 'Commentary on the *Models and Busts Act* 1798', in *Primary Sources on Copyright*, ed. by Bently and Kretschmer, http://www.copyrighthistory.org/cam/tools/request/showRecord?id=commentary_uk_1798.

Drone, Eaton S., *A Treatise on the Law of Property in Intellectual Productions in Great Britain and the United States* (Boston: Little, Brown, and Company, 1879).

Du Fresnoy, Charles Alphonse, and John Dryden, trans., *De arte graphica. The art of painting, by C. A. Du Fresnoy. With remarks. Translated into English, together with an original preface containing a parallel betwixt painting and poetry. By Mr. Dryden* (London: W. Rogers, 1695).

Finnegan, Rachel, '"An Extreme Cunning Fellow": Copley's Memorial Engraving to the 2nd Earl of Bessborough', *Print Quarterly*, 24:1 (March 2007), 3–11.

Faithorne, William, *The Art of Graveing and Etching, wherein is expressed the true Way of Graveing in Copper; also the Manner of that famous Callot, and M. Bosse, in their several ways of Etching* (London: A. Roper, 1702).

Gómez-Arostegui, Tomás, 'Copyright at Common Law in 1774,' *Connecticut Law Review*, 47:1 (2014), 1–57.

Griffiths, Anthony, 'Two Contracts for British Prints', *Print Quarterly*, 9:2 (June 1992), 184–187.

Landau, David and Peter Parshall, *The Renaissance Print* (New Haven: Yale University Press, 1996).

MacMillan, Fiona, 'Is copyright blind to the visual?' *Visual Communication,* 7:1 (2008), 97–118 (pp. 97–98), https://doi.org/10.1177/1470357207084868.

Michel, Christian, 'Les débats sur la notion de graveur/traducteur en France au XVIIIème siècle,' in Marie-Félicie Perez-Pivot and François Fossier eds., *Delineavit et Sculpsit: dix-neuf contributions sur les rapports dessin-gravure du XVIe au XXe siècle* (Lyon: Presses Universitaires de Lyon, 2003).

Neff, Emily Ballew, and Kaylin H. Weber eds., *American Adversaries: West and Copley and a Transatlantic World* (Houston: Museum of Fine Arts, 2013).

Park, Lawrence, *Gilbert Stuart: An Illustrated Descriptive List of His Works Compiled by Lawrence Park* (New York: William Edwin Rudge, 1926).

Oberg, Barbara B. ed., *The Papers of Thomas Jefferson,* vol. 33, *17 February-30 April 1801* (Princeton: Princeton University Press, 2006).

Pon, Lisa, *Raphael, Dürer, and Marcantonio Raimondi: Copying and the Renaissance Italian Print* (New Haven: Yale University Press, 2004).

Prown, Jules D., *John Singleton Copley,* vol. 2: *Copley in England* (Cambridge, MA: Harvard University Press, 1966).

Rather, Susan, *The American School* (New Haven: Yale University Press, 2016).

——, 'Benjamin West's Professional Endgame and the Historical Conundrum of William Williams', *William and Mary Quarterly,* 59:4 (Oct. 2002), 821–864, https://doi.org/10.2307/3491572.

Reynolds, Sir Joshua, *Seven Discourses on Art* (New York: Cassell and Company, 1901), transcribed and open access on Gutenberg.org: https://www.gutenberg.org/files/2176/2176-h/2176-h.htm.

Richards, Rhys, 'United States Trade with China, 1784–1814', *The American Neptune,* 54: Special Supplement (1994).

Richardson, Jonathan, *The works of Mr. Jonathan Richardson ... all corrected and prepared for the press by his son Mr. J. Richardson* (London: Printed for T. Davis, in Russel-Street, 1773).

Roncerel, Michel, 'Traités de gravure,' *Nouvelles de l'estampe,* no. 194 (May-June 2004): 19–27.

Rose, Mark, 'Technology and Copyright in 1735: The Engraver's Act,' *The Information Society,* 21:1 (2005), 63–66, https://doi.org/10.1080/01972240590895928.

Scott, Katie, *Becoming Property: Art, Theory and Law in Early Modern France* (New Haven and London: Yale University Press, 2018).

Stuart v. Swords [sic] Bill, filed 14, May 1802. Records of the District Court of the United States for the Eastern District of Pennsylvania (National Archives and Records Administration, RG21.40.2 (1790–1804).

The Case of Designers, Engravers, Etchers, &c., London (1735), digitized in *Primary Sources on Copyright* (1450–1900), ed. by L. Bently & M. Kretschmer, www.copyrighthistory.org: http://www.copyrighthistory.org/cam/tools/request/showRecord.php?id=record_uk_1735a.

US Congress, An Act supplementary to an act, intituled 'An act for the encouragement of learning, by securing the copies of maps, charts, and books to the authors and proprietors of such copies during the times therein mentioned' and extending the benefits thereof to the arts of designing, engraving, and etching historical and other prints (1802), digitized in *Primary Sources on Copyright (1450–1900)*, ed. by L. Bently & M. Kretschmer, www.copyrighthistory.org: http://www.copyrighthistory.org/cam/tools/request/showRecord.php?id=record_us_1802.

Watelet, Claude-Henri. 'Print (engraving)', in *The Encyclopedia of Diderot & d'Alembert Collaborative Translation Project* (Ann Arbor: Michigan Publishing, University of Michigan Library, 2018), http://hdl.handle.net/2027/spo.did2222.0003.391. Originally published as 'Estampe (Gravure),' *Encyclopédie ou Dictionnaire raisonné des sciences, des arts et des métiers,* 5: 999–1000 (Paris, 1755).

Zorach, Rebecca, and Elizabeth Rodini, eds., *Paper Museums: The Reproductive Print in Europe, 1500–1800* (Chicago: University of Chicago Press, 2005).

4. The Scope of Artistic Copyright in Nineteenth-Century England[1]

Simon Stern

Modern copyright law abounds in distinctions that were delineated differently, if at all, before the twentieth century — such as distinctions that separate idea from expression, 'fair dealing' from excessive use, and 'verbatim' copies from 'nonliteral' copies that use characters or other distinctive aspects of the work. In 1800, the scope of copyright barely extended beyond direct and complete reproduction of a protected work. Language in various eighteenth-century British statutes and legal cases suggested otherwise, but scholars have yet to find a single instance, before 1800, of a plaintiff who won an infringement case when the defendant had copied less than the entire work.[2] During the first half of the nineteenth century, some plaintiffs prevailed in lawsuits over abridgments, and those decisions, in the area of literary copyright, signaled a conceptual shift that allowed for increasingly broad coverage extending to nonliteral uses. Scholars such as Isabella Alexander, Derek Miller, and Oren Bracha, among others, have discussed the expanding scope of literary copyright in nineteenth-century British and American law.[3] The scope of artistic copyright, in relation to these developments,

1 Thank you to all the participants in the two workshops that led to the publication of this volume, and particularly to Stéphanie Delamaire and Will Slauter.

2 Simon Stern, 'Copyright, Originality, and the Public Domain in Eighteenth-Century England', in *Originality and Intellectual Property in the French and English Enlightenment*, ed. by Reginald McGinnis (New York: Routledge, 2008), pp. 69–101 (p. 78).

3 Isabella Alexander, *Copyright Law and the Public Interest in the Nineteenth Century* (Oxford: Hart, 2010); Derek Miller, *Copyright and the Value of Performance, 1770–1911* (Cambridge: Cambridge University Press, 2018), https://doi.org/10.

 https://doi.org/10.11647/OBP.0247.04

has received less attention. In what follows, I consider the slower process of its expansion in nineteenth-century England. I focus on two forms of copying: uses that include a significant part of an image without reproducing the whole work, and uses that copy the work in a different medium.

Throughout the nineteenth century, when new questions arose as to how copyright applied to certain varieties of artistic productions, or to certain components of them, the arguments tended to repeat those that had already been rehearsed in discussions of literary copyright during the eighteenth century. In elaborating copyright doctrine for visual works, the courts proceeded more slowly and haltingly than they did for literary copyright, in part because the judges were much more at home on textual terrain. As Jessica Silbey has observed, 'lawyers and judges are word people and not picture people'.[4] Most of the lawsuits involved plaintiffs who, as publishers or art dealers, had invested a significant amount in purchasing the copyright of a work of art, or in licensing the copyright and commissioning a new work, usually an engraving. If the defendant was in the same business (e.g., a seller of prints), the preferable solution would be an injunction that removed the infringing version from the market. Plaintiffs often complained that it was too slow and expensive to achieve this result; in 1862, new summary judgment provisions in the Fine Art Copyright Act made the process easier.[5] On the other hand, if the infringement occurred in a newspaper or magazine, injunctive relief achieved nothing: the print run would already be exhausted by the time the plaintiff arrived in court.[6] Moreover, the

1017/9781108349284; Oren Bracha, *Owning Ideas: The Intellectual Origins of American Intellectual Property, 1790–1909* (Cambridge: Cambridge University Press, 2016), https://doi.org/10.1017/9780511843235.

4 Jessica Silbey, 'Images in/of Law', *New York Law School Law Review*, 57 (2012), 171–83 (p. 177).

5 Fine Art Copyright Act 1862, 25 & 26 Vict. c. 68, s. 8, available in *Primary Sources on Copyright (1450–1900)*, ed. by Lionel Bently and Martin Kretschmer, http://www.copyrighthistory.org/cam/tools/request/showRecord.php?id=record_uk_1735; see also Elena Cooper, *Art and Modern Copyright: The Contest Image* (Cambridge: Cambridge University Press, 2018), pp. 182–189, https://doi.org/10.1017/9781316840993.

6 Will Slauter draws a similar contrast between book publishers and publishers of periodicals, with similar consequences for copyright litigation, in 'Toward a History of Copyright for Periodical Writings: Examples from Nineteenth-Century America', in *From Text(s) to Book(s): Studies in Production and Editorial Processes*, ed. by Nathalie Collé-Bak et al. (Nancy: Éditions universitaires de Lorraine, 2014), pp. 65–84.

cheaply produced illustrations in periodicals (using woodcuts or, later, photographs) would have little effect on the sales of fine art prints. Even if the money damages were trifling, however, the plaintiff could demand that the defendant pay the litigation costs (under the English rule imposing these costs on the losing party). Plaintiffs who specialized in a subject that frequently became newsworthy (e.g., theatrical performers or racing scenes) might anticipate the unauthorized use of their images on a recurring basis, and might hope that the cost of underwriting the litigation, more than the damages award, would make the defendant hesitate before offending again.

Throughout the eighteenth century, the scope of literary copyright was limited to verbatim reproductions of an entire text, leaving room for others to publish abridgments, digests, sequels, and imitations. Objections to these works turned on two sorts of arguments. One argument involved reputational concerns: an unauthorized adaptation could harm the author of the source text, because readers might think the author had approved it. Second, writers and publishers objected that partial and imitative works could undermine the sales of the original work, insofar as readers were satisfied with a market substitute.[7] Various eighteenth-century writers complained about sequels, parodies, and works presenting themselves as 'in the style of' a famous author, but litigation stemming from such uses was virtually nonexistent. Samuel Richardson was especially vociferous in his criticisms; he was outraged by the sequels to his novel *Pamela* (1740), and called one of them a 'notorious Invasion of his plan'; but even so, he did not sue those responsible for this 'spurious Continuation'.[8]

The copyright litigation that occurred during this period involved unauthorized reprinting, and almost invariably featured booksellers as plaintiffs, prompted by economic concerns. When the statutory

---

7 For further discussion, see Simon Stern, 'From Author's Right to Property Right', *University of Toronto Law Journal*, 62 (2012), 29–91. A recent study by Douglas Duhaime, drawing from large databases of printed texts, offers valuable new insights into the nature and frequency of reusing material from other sources during the eighteenth century. See Douglas Duhaime, 'Copyright and the Early English Book Market: An Algorithmic Study' (unpublished doctoral thesis, University of Notre Dame, 2019), https://www.earlybookmarket.com/.

8 Advertisement in the *Gazetteer* (London), 7 May 1741, quoted in Thomas Keymer and Peter Sabor, Pamela *in the Marketplace* (Cambridge: Cambridge University Press, 2005), p. 59.

regulation that served, in effect, to prohibit unauthorized reprinting lapsed in 1695, the leading London booksellers who belonged to the Stationers' Guild petitioned repeatedly for legislation that would restore the protection they had lost. In the course of their lobbying efforts, the booksellers insisted that a damages regime would do them no good — a fine for infringement would be ineffective, because publishers of unauthorized copies would profit from their misdeeds, conceal or destroy their remaining copies when sued, and use the proceeds to defend themselves in court, rendering the fine ineffective. The booksellers wanted legislation that would help them prevent the circulation of unauthorized copies as soon as they were detected. The Statute of Anne (1710) failed to offer that solution directly, opting for a fine instead; however, the booksellers used that provision as a means of obtaining an injunction in the court of Chancery, converting the fine into a device for restricting the distribution of unauthorized editions — or, in modern parlance, for turning a property rule into a liability rule.[9]

In the eighteenth century, the reputational argument was far more popular among writers than booksellers. This argument could help to explain why verbatim reprints were impermissible (they were invariably criticized as poorly edited and shoddily produced), but it was less successful when applied to partial copies and imitations. Many writers, in fact, doubted that the reputational argument could extend that far.[10] The courts shared those doubts. When the publisher of Samuel Johnson's novel *Rasselas* sued the owner of the *Grand Magazine of Magazines* for excerpting the book, excising two-thirds of the text by eliminating 'the moral and useful reflections', the magazine version was held to be non-infringing.[11] The publishers were primarily concerned with market substitution, and when the courts finally began to treat partial copies of

9 See Simon Stern, 'Copyright as a Property Right? Authorial Perspectives in Eighteenth-Century England', *UC Irvine Law Review*, 8 (2018), 461–488 (pp. 467–469), https://scholarship.law.uci.edu/ucilr/vol9/iss2/10/; see also Elena Cooper and Sheona Burrow, 'Photographic Copyright and the Intellectual Property Enterprise Court in Historical Perspective', *Legal Studies*, 39 (2019), 143–65, https://doi.org/10.1017/lst.2018.10.

10 See Stern, 'Copyright as a Property Right?', pp. 463, 481–484.

11 Dodsley v. Kinnersley (1761) Amb. 403, at 405.

literary works as infringing, in the course of the nineteenth century, this extension of the law seems to have depended to a significant extent on economic logic.[12]

In the context of visual copyright, artists and dealers confronted largely the same issues. On the one hand, the protection for engravings, under the 1735 statute known as Hogarth's Act, expressly applied to partial copies: it prohibited others from making copies 'in the whole or in part, by varying, adding to, or diminishing from, the main design', and from reprinting any 'print or prints, or any parts thereof', without authorization.[13] The same language appeared in a 1777 statute that strengthened the provisions for damages.[14] The significant legislative changes introduced in 1862, again, prohibited 'copy[ing] [or] colourably imitat[ing]' various kinds of artistic works, and covered not only the work but also 'the design thereof'.[15] Nevertheless, we see no evidence of litigation over partial or imitative uses of visual works during the eighteenth century, and only a few such cases during the nineteenth century; the main concern was with complete reproductions of the same image.

The reasons are not far to seek: as with books, people dealing in unauthorized copies of pictures sought mainly to capitalize on the success of well-known works by offering cheaper copies. In addition, texts and images that revise the source material — even when they use a significant amount — are harder to discover, unless they expressly target the market for the original (for instance, by naming themselves after it, as with the *Pamela* sequels).[16] In literary copyright, abridgments

12 See, e.g., Ronan Deazley, 'The Statute of Anne and the Great Abridgement Swindle', *Houston Law Review*, 47 (2010), 793–818; Catherine Seville, *Literary Copyright Reform in Early Victorian England: The Framing of the 1842 Copyright Act* (Cambridge; Cambridge University Press, 1999), pp. 240–246.

13 Engravers' Copyright Act 1735 (8 Geo. II, c. 13), s. 1, available in *Primary Sources on Copyright*, ed. by Bently and Kretschmer, http://www.copyrighthistory.org/cam/tools/request/showRecord.php?id=record_uk_1735. See also Isabella Alexander and Cristina S. Martinez, 'The First Copyright Case under the 1735 Engravings Act: The Germination of Visual Copyright?' (Chapter 2 of the current volume).

14 Engravers' Copyright Act 1777 (17 Geo. 3, c. 57), available in available in *Primary Sources on* Copyright, ed. by Bently and Kretschmer, http://www.copyrighthistory.org/cam/tools/request/showRecord.php?id=record_uk_1777a.

15 Fine Art Copyright Act, s. 6

16 However, digital search and comparison techniques may now make such discoveries easier; see Duhaime, 'Copyright and the Early English Book Market'.

accounted for the first significant area of doctrinal extension in the nineteenth century, precisely because they might substitute for the original work — but this development had little significance for artistic copyright, since abridgments do not play that role in the art market.[17]

One of the first cases that ostensibly tested the prohibition on partial uses was *West* v. *Francis*, in 1822.[18] The defendant was charged with selling 'seven prints' (probably from woodcuts) characterized as 'copies', or alternatively 'copies in part', of the plaintiff's engraved prints 'representing the characters of performers on the stage in popular dramas'.[19] The plaintiff, William West, was an artist and publisher who specialized in theatrical prints.[20] Because the cursory description quoted above is the only reference in the case report to the particular images in contention, we cannot identify them with any certainty; however, Figure 1, portraying the actress and singer Lucia Elizabeth Vestris in 1820, offers a good example of West's work in this vein. Commentators praised the 'execution and accuracy' of his illustrations, and noted that he 'published scenes and characters of every play and pantomime of the time which attained any degree of popularity'.[21] He was highly entrepreneurial, and has been credited with 'publish[ing] the first cheap theatrical prints as souvenirs of the spectacular melodramas and pantomimes being performed on the London stage at the period', which he sold for '"a penny plain" and "twopence coloured"'.[22] His success brought 'imitators and plagiarists', who undercut his prices by using plates 'carelessly drawn on wood' (whereas West's were 'well executed on copper') and selling the results for a halfpenny 'or even less'. The prints may have been inferior, but 'at least to boys', West's most enthusiastic customers, 'they appeared the same'.[23]

17 Deazley, 'The Statute of Anne'; see also Matthew Sag, 'The Prehistory of Fair Use', *Brooklyn Law Review*, 76 (2011), 1371–1412.

18 *West* v. *Francis* (1822) was reported in 5 B. & Ald. 737, 106 Eng. Rep. 1361, and in 1 Dowl. & Ryl. 400. The latter version is more detailed, and was cited in some contemporaneous treatises, but has been largely overlooked by modern scholars, probably because it was not incorporated into the *English Reports*.

19 *West*, 1 Dowl. & Ryl. at 400.

20 See 'William West', The British Museum, https://research.britishmuseum.org/research/search_the_collection_database/term_details.aspx?bioId=12167.

21 Ralph Thomas, 'West's Toy-Theatre Prints', *Notes and Queries*, 4th series, 12 (1873), 463.

22 'Toy Theatre Gallery: History', https://www.toytheatregallery.com/history/.

23 Thomas, 'West's Toy-Theatre Prints', 463. Thomas writes that West's copiers were 'too numerous to mention', but singles out Martin Skelt as a particular offender.

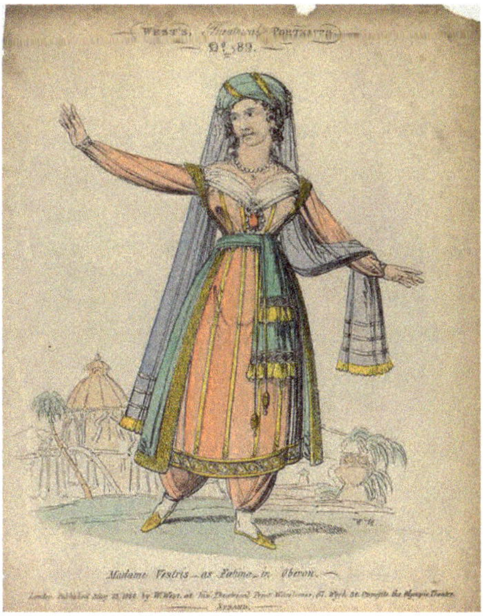

Fig. 1 William West, Madame Vestris as Fatima in *Oberon*, 1820.

As both an artist and proprietor, West would have been particularly sensitive to the threat these imitations posed (in that respect, he recalls Samuel Richardson, who was both a novelist and printer). He sued Francis for violating the Engravings Act of 1777, charging the defendant not with producing the copies but only with selling them (they were created by an unidentified third party).[24] The defense turned on a half-hearted argument that although the statute prohibited artists from copying engravings 'in the whole or in part, by varying, adding to, or diminishing from the main design', the prohibition against selling unauthorized copies, in the latter part of the same sentence, referred only to 'any copy or copies', not to variations. Hence, the defendant hopefully proposed, 'the seller is only liable where he sells an *exact* copy'. The court rejected this suggestion and agreed with West that

Since Skelt started his business in the mid-1830s, he could not have been the unnamed person who created the prints in dispute in the 1822 litigation.

24 The defendant's identity is also unclear. *Johnstone's London Commercial Guide* (London: Barnard and Farley, 1818) includes James Frances, a stationer and bookseller in Hatton Garden, and James Francis, a stationer and bookseller in Lambeth (pp. 68, 152, 679). Whether the defendant was either of these, or someone else, may be impossible to discover, given the limited information in the court report.

the prints included only 'small variations from the main design' of the original.[25]

The decision therefore offers little guidance on how substantial the copying must be, to count as infringing, and it might have been forgotten, if one of the judges had not explained that '[a] copy is that which comes so near to the original as to give every person seeing it the idea created by the original'.[26] Read in context, this is simply a way of rejecting the defendant's attempted distinction between 'exact' copies and copies with minor variations. When the same issue had arisen in literary copyright cases, however, no one had defined copies in this fashion. Even in disputes over literary abridgements that were merely 'colourable' and were therefore impermissibly close to the original, jurists had not explained the infringement by observing that a copy elicited the same 'idea' in the reader's mind. When William Blackstone, for instance, had written about literary infringement in the 1760s, he explained that it depended on a duplication of both 'the *sentiment* and the *language*'; repeating the sentiment alone was not enough.[27] If images are understood as corresponding with unique ideas in a way that texts do not, this suggests a difference between visual and literary copyright that could impose some limits on the ability to transpose legal standards from one domain to the other.

The same issue at stake in *West* arose again in *Martin* v. *Wright*, decided in 1833, with the significant distinction that the defendant had rendered the work in an entirely different format.[28] John Martin, a prominent painter of religious scenes, had achieved a notable success with his large-scale painting of 'Belshazzar's Feast' in 1821. More than 5,000 people paid to see it. According to one commentator, it was 'the first canvas the Royal Academy was forced to cordon off due to public over-excitement'.[29] Capitalizing on this success, Martin made a mezzotint engraving based on the painting and measuring 28 by 18.5 inches; proofs were sold in

25 *West*, 1 Dowl. & Ryl. at 400.

26 *West*, 5 B. & Ald. at 737.

27 William Blackstone, *Commentaries on the Laws of England, Book II: Of the Rights of Things*, ed. by Simon Stern (Oxford: Oxford University Press, 2016), p. 275.

28 Martin v. Wright (1833) 6 Sim. 297, 58 Eng. Rep. 605.

29 Michael J. Campbell, *John Martin: Visionary Printmaker* (York: Campbell Fine Art, 1992), p. 90; David Gange, *Dialogues with the Dead: Egyptology in British Culture and Religion, 1822–1922* (Oxford: Oxford University Press, 2014), p. 60. A very informative discussion of the painting appears in Albert Boime, *Art in an Age of Counterrevolution* (Chicago: University of Chicago Press, 2004), pp. 560–563.

two different states for five or ten guineas, and copies in the regular print edition were sold for two and a half guineas.[30] In 1833, one Wright (seemingly Edward A. Wright), in partnership with the artist Hippolyte Sébron, used the engraving to create a panorama, and exhibited it at the Queen's Bazaar in Oxford Street, admittance one shilling.[31] The advertisements emphasized its massive scale: 'Five times as large as the late Mr. B[enjamin] West's celebrated picture of Death on a Pale Horse [...] [occupying] in magnitude the space of Four Dioramic Views'.[32] The transformation of the engraving into a panorama meant that Wright was not offering an exact copy, but as in *West*, the image was substantially the same as the one in the engraving. Martin went to court, seeking an injunction to shut down the exhibition.[33] Citing the language in the 1777 statute relating to copies that 'var[ied] or add[ed] to the main design', he asked for a preliminary injunction without hearing any argument from the defendants (who had not been notified), because the display interfered with sales of his prints, creating an immediate and irreparable injury.[34] Today, this use of the image would certainly be regarded as infringing, but Martin had no success. At a hearing on 27 July 1833, Vice-Chancellor Shadwell denied Martin's request, observing that the defendants might have valid arguments for opposing the injunction; for instance, '[i]t might be contended that there was a material difference between dioramic views

30 See, e.g., 'Engravings by Mr. Martin', inserted at the end of *Descriptive Catalogue of the Fall of Babylon* (London: Martin, 1832).

31 See Ralph Hyde, et al., *Dictionary of Panoramists of the English-Speaking World* (n.p.: n.d.), p. 498, http://www.bdcmuseum.org.uk/uploads/uploads/biographical_dictionary_of_panoramists2.pdf. Seemingly, Wright commissioned the work; contemporaneous discussions attribute the painting to Sébron. See, e.g., 'Diorama and Physiorama', *The Olio*, 11 (1834), 14. Ads for the exhibit had appeared in the London *Morning Post* starting in January 1834. A journalist commended it as 'very creditably executed', adding that 'from its size (covering 2,000 feet of canvass), and the known illusory effect of dioramic representations, the spectator may, by a slight stretch of fancy, imagine himself a party present at the festival'. 'Belshazaar's Feast — Diorama', *Morning Post* (London), 31 March 1834.

32 Handbill advertising 'Mr. Martin's Grand Picture of Belshazzar's Feast Painted with Dioramic Effect at Queens Bazaar, Oxford Street', quoted in Christopher James Coltrin, 'Apocalyptic Progress: The Politics of Catastrophe in the Art of John Martin, Francis Danby, and David Roberts' (unpublished doctoral thesis, University of Michigan, 2011), p. 32.

33 It was common to use painting exhibitions as a way to sell engravings of the paintings (see the example of Ernest Gambart, discussed below, in the text accompanying note 59). Martin might have been wiser to try to profit from Wright's exhibition instead of attempting to shut it down.

34 *Martin*, 6 Sim. at 297.

and paintings'. He added ungenerously that 'if the view in question was such a daub as had been represented', there was also some doubt as to whether Martin could be entitled to any damages.[35]

The case then proceeded with all parties appearing in court to argue their position, and on 9 August 1833 the injunction was again denied. Martin's lawyers couched their argument in economic terms, contending that 'there was no difference between selling a copy of a print, and exhibiting it for money; as, in both cases, profit was made of that which was appropriated to another'. The Vice Chancellor, similarly, relied on economic logic in rejecting Martin's allegations, concluding that the panorama could not harm the sales of the engraving:

> Here the Defendant is alleged to have made a copy of the Plaintiff's print, in oil colours, and of dimensions different from the Plaintiff's print, not to sell, but to exhibit in a fixed place and in a given manner, so as to produce an optical illusion. Exhibiting for profit is in no way analogous to selling a copy of the Plaintiff's print, but is dealing with it in a very different manner.[36]

Shadwell emphasized both the visual effect of the panorama and the defendants' method of 'dealing' with the public. If the question were simply whether Wright and Sébron had copied 'the main design' 'in the whole or in part', the answer must have been yes; Martin lost, then, because of the 'different manner' of the defendants' use. The reputational argument fared no better: according to Shadwell, the defendants' version 'must be either better or worse [than the original]; if it is better, Martin has the benefit of it; if worse, then the misrepresentation is only a sort of libel, and this Court will not prevent the publication of a libel'.[37] Wright celebrated his legal victory in his advertisements for the exhibit, and he later took it to Boston, where it also met with great success.[38]

Moore v. *Clarke*, in 1842, featured the next plaintiff to raise claims involving partial copying, and he fared no better.[39] In 1839, John Moore, who published prints 'illustrative of the turf and English

35 'Vice-Chancellor's Court — Saturday', *Morning Post* (London), 29 July 1833.

36 *Martin*, 6 Sim. at 298.

37 Ibid. at 299.

38 For the advertisements, see, e.g., *Morning Post* (London), 16 August 1833 (noting that the court had 'refused the Injunction of H. Sebron's inimitable copy' of the image). On the exhibit in Boston, see Coltrin, 'Apocalyptic Progress', p. 32.

39 Moore v. Clarke (1842), 6 Jurist 648; the case is also reported in 9 M. & W. 692, 152 Eng. Rep. 293.

national sports' at his shop in St. Martin's Lane,[40] had commissioned an engraving by Charles Hunt of a prize-winning racehorse called Beeswing.[41] The painting furnished the basis for a print, measuring 18 by 15 inches, which Moore sold at his shop for fifteen shillings as an aquatint, and seven shillings sixpence uncolored.[42] William Mark Clark (the court reports misspelt his last name) was the co-owner of a short-lived newspaper, *Tom Spring's Life in London and Sporting Chronicle.* In early June 1841, Clark's paper included a woodcut image that closely resembled the horse in Moore's print, but that purported to depict Coronation, the horse that had won the Derby a week earlier.[43] In Clark's version, the horse was flipped horizontally, and the jockey and background were altered. Alleging that Clark had copied the print while 'varying the main design', Moore sued for money damages, since an injunction would have been useless by the time the litigation started.[44] He proceeded under the 1777 statute, which provided for 'double costs' (i.e., a successful plaintiff would receive twice the litigation costs).[45] At trial, on 19 February 1842, Moore called 'several engravers and painters [...] as witnesses', who testified that Clark's version differed from the original only in 'reversing [...] the position of the head of the animal, and in the back-ground'.[46] They claimed that the image had been copied so faithfully that it 'adopted the sex of Beeswing', a mare, 'when professing to give a portrait of Coronation', a stallion.[47]

40 Obituary in *Gentleman's Magazine* (n.s.) 42 (1854), 639; see also the obituary in *Illustrated London News*, 7 Oct. 1854, p. 342.

41 Hunt also specialized in sporting scenes; see, e.g., *Benezit Dictionary of British Graphic Artists and Illustrators*, ed. by Stephen Bury (Oxford: Oxford University Press, 2012), vol. 1, p. 595. A later description disparaged Moore's image, saying that his engraving was based on a 'rough sketch taken on a race-course' and that it suffered from 'want of proper time and opportunity'. 'Sporting Obituary', *Sporting Almanack and Oracle of Rural Life* (London: Baily, 1843), p. 56. The article then proceeded to commend a 'splendid' new engraving, just released by Bailey and Co., the publishers of the *Sporting Almanack.*

42 *Hodgson's Annual Catalogue of Books and Engravings Published During 1839* (London: Hodgson, 1840), p. 39.

43 *Tom's Spring's Life in London and Sporting Chronicle*, 6 June 1841. On Clark's paper, see *Dictionary of Nineteenth-Century Journalism in Great Britain and Ireland*, ed. by Laurel Brake and Marysa Demoor (Gent and London: Academia Press and The British Library, 2009), p. 348.

44 *Moore*, 6 Jurist at 648.

45 Engravers' Copyright Act 1777.

46 'Law Intelligence', *Morning Post* (London), 21 Feb. 1842, p. 4.

47 'Veterinary Jurisprudence', *The Veterinarian*, 15 (1842), 238.

However, Lord Abinger, presiding over the trial, found their testimony unpersuasive. In his view, 'the imitation [occurred only] in points where the eye of an artist alone could detect that there had been a copying', and on the whole, 'the two [pictures] seemed very different'. By implication, he suggested that the jury should reject the expert evidence and should instead rely on the perspective of an ordinary observer — such as himself. Only a 'substantial' copy could be infringing, he instructed the jury; if the imitative aspects were 'minute', then they were 'not [...] within the act'. The defendant's lawyers also ridiculed the suggestion that Moore had suffered any financial harm, asking the jury to 'consider whether any sporting gentleman, or any individual', interested in 'a portrait of Beeswing [...] [for] 15s. and 7s. 6d., would buy a work of such manifold inferior merit as a cheap weekly publication'.[48] Although the judge did not emphasize this point, it doubtless carried some weight with the jury: 'racing' or 'sporting' papers like *Tom Spring's* catered mainly to working-class readers, who shared few other commonalities with Moore's clientele besides an interest in horses.[49] In light of this distinction and the judge's instructions, it is hardly surprising that the jury found for the defendant.[50]

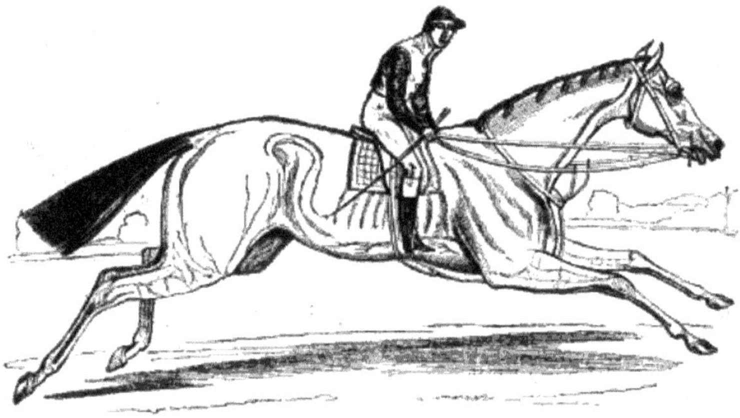

Fig. 2 Charles Hunt, *Beeswing*, engraving commissioned by John Moore (1839).

48 'Law Intelligence', (note 46), p. 4.

49 See, e.g., Andrew August, *The British Working Class, 1832–1940* (New York: Routledge, 2007), p. 93; Susie L. Steinbach, *Understanding the Victorians: Politics, Culture and Society in Nineteenth-Century Britain* (New York: Routledge, 2012), p. 123.

50 'Law Intelligence', *Morning Post* (London), 21 Feb. 1842, p. 1.

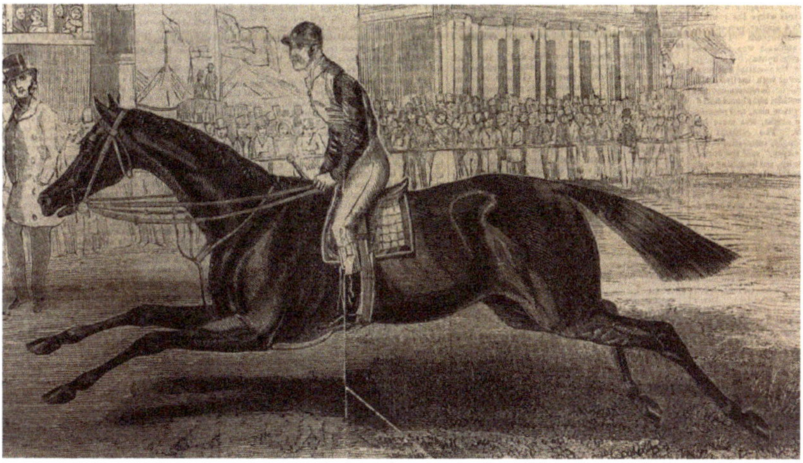

Fig. 3 *Coronation*, from *Tom Spring's Life in London, and Sporting Chronicle*, June 6, 1841 (artist unknown; thanks to Maks Del Mar for providing this image).

Moore appealed, contending that Lord Abinger had misdirected the jury, and reminding the court that 'the piracy [need not] be an exact copy in every respect, because the act says in whole or in part'.[51] Thus the question was what counts as substantial copying: if the image of the horse is the most important element, then varying the background and reversing the direction of the horse are insignificant changes. On the other hand, if one must consider all the features of both images, the horse becomes only one element in a larger arrangement. According to the defendant's lawyer, 'There were hardly two things in which the pictures resembled each other. The size of the two animals was totally different, the position of the horse was different, and the scenery about was essentially different, so that it was difficult to say in which the piracy consisted'.[52] Today, this argument would be seen as specious: infringement depends on the 'nature and quality' of the use, and in these two images, the horse is the most important feature.

The appellate court held that the jury instructions were correct, and added that if a piracy had occurred, Clark would have been 'entitled to nominal damages', but the point '[did] not arise'.[53] However, it would be just as plausible to think that the reasoning underlying the jury's findings

51 *Moore*, 6 Jurist at 648.
52 Ibid.
53 Ibid., at 649.

(and the trial judge's comments) went the other way: Moore could not have suffered any economic loss from Clark's use of the image; therefore, no infringement had occurred. Doubtless, the defendant's lawyers were right about the buying habits of a 'sporting gentleman': few of Moore's customers would have seen the image in Clark's newspaper (which sold for a penny), and even if they had, the version in the newspaper could hardly have diminished the sales of Moore's engravings. The question is whether this consideration has any bearing on the determination of infringement. One may suspect that this economic logic guided both the judge and the jury, but that it remained hidden under the finding that any copying was not 'substantial'.[54]

Viewed as a single episode, Clark's use of the image seems too trivial to justify a lawsuit. Since Moore presented no evidence as to damages, his decision to sue must have been prompted by some other reason. Perhaps he was attempting to set an example. That would make sense if he had already experienced other similar episodes — as we might infer, given his area of specialization. He may, then, have been hoping to induce Clark (and the publishers of other sporting newspapers) to desist from such practices, or to pay for a license instead of using the images without authorization.

The cases of John Martin and John Moore suggest that plaintiffs, in this era, had little hope of success when alleging infringement by altering 'the main design', despite the expanding scope of literary copyright. In an especially notable American case from the latter part of the century, for instance, Augustin Daly successfully sued a producer for staging a play that shared only one feature with Daly's: they both included a scene in which a character is tied to a railroad track and is rescued just as a train is about to run her over.[55] This case marks out an unusually capacious view of the scope of literary copyright — few

---

54 It bears noting that five months after the appellate decision was rendered, Moore's image was reprinted, with thanks for his permission, in the *Illustrated London News*. See 'Beeswing', *Illustrated London News*, 24 Sept. 1842, p. 309. The same issue includes an ad promoting Moore's pictures of 'Beeswing, and other winners'. Ibid., p. 319.

55 Daly v. Palmer, 6 F. Cas. 1132 (C.C.S.D.N.Y. 1868). For discussion, see Matthew Wilson Smith, *The Nervous Stage: Nineteenth-Century Melodrama and the Birth of Modern Theater* (Oxford: Oxford University Press, 2017), pp. 91–93; Bruce E. Boyden, '*Daly v. Palmer*, or the Melodramatic Origins of the Ordinary Observer', *Syracuse Law Review*, 68 (2018), 147–179.

other decisions even came close — but it helps to highlight, by contrast, the very different judicial approach to artistic works, which had to be virtually identical in all respects to justify a finding of infringement.

From the question of partial copying, I turn briefly to another issue involving the scope of copyright — the reproduction of images by photography. The invention of photography made it possible to create inexpensive copies of artworks in a new medium. Photographers contended that such copies were not infringements, because the law covered only copies made by 'lithography, or any other mechanical process by which prints or impressions of drawings or designs are capable of being multiplied indefinitely', and photography was a chemical process, not a mechanical one.[56] The Fine Art Copyright Act of 1862 had provided for copyright in photographs (among other forms), but had not expressly provided that photographs of other images in other media were infringing.[57] The result was an extensive amount of litigation aimed at the problem of photographs, and the arguments resembled those we have already seen.

Thus, for example, an 1866 article on this subject in the *Art Journal* defended the legitimacy of making photographic copies of artworks, which served 'the interests of [...] that portion of the Art-loving public who cannot afford to pay large sums for works they desire to possess'. The markets for engravings and photographs, the author continued, were entirely different: 'It is absurd to argue, as some do, that [any financial loss] follows the sale of a shilling photograph of a print for which two or three guineas must be paid'. The customer for the print is 'a man who can afford to pay more or less expensively for the indulgence of his taste', and he will be 'indifferent to the photograph'. Similarly, hardly anyone willing to buy 'a shilling photograph would ever enter the shop of [...] [an] eminent publishing firm, to buy their high-priced engravings'. Nevertheless, evidently conceding that artists have a right to control this part of the market, the author proposed 'some plan [...] which might meet the exigencies of all parties', by which the publisher of a 'high class and expensive engraving' would arrange to make '*small*

56 International Copyright Act 1852 (15 & 16 Vict. c. 12), s. 14, available in *Primary Sources on Copyright (1450–1900)*, ed. by Lionel Bently and Martin Kretschmer, http://www.copyrighthistory.org/cam/tools/request/showRecord.php?id=record_uk_1852.

57 Fine Art Copyright Act 1862. For discussion of the statute and its treatment of photographs, see Cooper, *Art and Modern Copyright*, pp. 32–48.

photographic copies for sale at a cheap rate', thus helping 'the holder of the copyright, that is, the printseller' and also 'prevent[ing] any photographer from re-producing the work; it would not answer his purpose to attempt it'.[58]

Just a few years before this article appeared, in 1863, the art dealer Ernest Gambart had prevailed in a copyright dispute turning on the issue of photographic copies. Gambart had invested heavily in some of the most popular artists of the day (such as William Powell Frith, Edwin Landseer, and Rosa Bonheur). Expanding on a business model that dated back to the eighteenth century, Gambart promoted the artists' paintings and exhibited them for a fee, and then sold expensive engravings. For example, he bought Rosa Bonheur's *The Horse Fair* for £1600 ('having outbid the French Government') and paid Landseer £800 to make a mezzotint engraving of the painting. Gambart also paid £210 for the copyright of Holman Hunt's *The Light of the World* plus another £130 to borrow the painting from the owner, and commissioned an engraving by William Henry Simmons (for 300 guineas).[59] After investing so heavily in these works, and working so assiduously to publicize them, Gambart expected to control the market for reproductions of them. Photography was a menace to this model. He campaigned vigorously against the dealers who sought to exploit that market, and he engaged in a series of copyright disputes aimed at eliminating this threat.[60] He offers a paradigmatic example of a dealer whose economic interests made this sort of litigation feasible.

58 'Engravings v. Photographs', *The Art-Journal*, 5 (1866), 312–14. For more discussion of this article, see Katherine Haskins, The Art-Journal *and Fine Art Publishing in Victorian England, 1850–1880* (Farnham: Ashgate, 2012), p. 52; Cooper, *Art and Modern Copyright*, pp. 225–226.

59 Cooper, *Art and Modern Copyright*, p. 222; 228–230. Holman Hunt later blamed photographers for driving down the value of engravings: the publisher's investment would be lost 'if the engraving should not sell [...] while, if it should prove a source of profit, photographers in number [would] pirate his property'. Hunt concluded that Britain would do better to emulate France, where 'such piracy is treated as a criminal offence with imprisonment', giving the photographers good reason 'to make terms with the possessor of the copyright before reproducing a favourite work of Art'. W. Holman Hunt, 'Artistic Copyright', *The Nineteenth Century*, 5 (1879), pp. 418–424 (p. 421).

60 Robert Verhoogt, *Art in Reproduction: Nineteenth-Century Prints after Lawrence Alma-Tadema, Josefs Israëls, and Ary Scheffer* (Amsterdam: Amsterdam University Press, 2007), p. 157, notes that 'Gambart instigated more than twenty lawsuits in connection with [...] *The Light of the World* alone'.

In 1863, Gambart sued William Ball, a print-seller based in Middle-Row, Holburn, for selling photographic copies of the Landseer and Simmons engravings of Bonheur and Hunt.[61] Ball rather cynically attempted a defense that blended the reputational and economic arguments, contending that the statutes were concerned only with 'base copies' whose 'sale [...] would injure the reputation of the artist'; his 'little photographs', he insisted, 'could not possibly be bought in mistake for the engraving'. The court rejected this argument: '[T]he statute [...] goes much beyond the evil of lowering [the artist's] estimation by publishing a spurious article under his name. Engravings are, for the most part, made for the purpose of reward by sale — money reward, commercial value', and the statute 'gives to the engraver a protection for the monied value of the products of his mind'.[62] Again, '[t]he purpose of the statute [...] was not to prevent the name of the original engraver being lowered in estimation, but [...] to secure to him the commercial value of his property. He wished to sell a number of his plates; those plates are an object of value, because they give pleasure by the imaginative ideas represented in them'. Therefore, the court reasoned, the aim is to prohibit 'the transferring from the [engraving] the speculative idea placed thereon'.[63] So long as the photograph 'represent[s] to the mind exactly the same ideas that give pleasure and make attraction for the plate taken from the original engraving', it 'give[s] precisely the analogous pleasure to the purchaser'.[64] Accordingly, a photographic copy would interfere 'with the commercial value of [Gambart's] print' and would erode Gambart's sales: if customers could not 'purchas[e] the photograph[ic] copy, they would be likely enough to purchase the other'.[65] Here, as in *West* v. *Francis*, the copy is infringing because it transfers 'exactly the same ideas' from one work to another. No matter

61 Gambart v. Ball (1863), 8 L.T. Rep. N.S. 426, 14 C.B. (N.S.) 306.

62 *Gambart*, 8 L.T. Rep. N.S. at 427.

63 Ibid.

64 Ibid. The *Law Reports* gives a fuller elaboration than the *Common Bench Reports*, which makes substantially the same point, but does not speak about conveying 'the same ideas'; instead it says that 'a photographic copy may excite in the mind of the beholder the same pleasurable emotions' as any other kind of copy. *Gambart*, 14 C.B. (N.S.) at 316. Since the *Law Reports* renders the judges' comments more circumstantially in various other respects, it probably offers the more accurate version of the judgment.

65 *Gambart*, 8 L.T. Rep. N.S. at 428.

that it did so in a new medium: unlike the diorama exhibition in *Martin* v. *Wright*, the photographs were being sold in the same fashion, if not to the same clientele, as Gambart's engravings. The plaintiff and defendant were both 'dealing' with the work in the same manner.

The court's rationale echoes the one in *Daly* v. *Palmer*, the copyright dispute over the melodramatic railroad scene, mentioned above. In *Daly*, the court held that the second play amounted to an infringement because it 'convey[ed] substantially the same impressions to, and excit[ed] the same emotions, in the mind', as the original scene, and that was sufficient for infringement even if the new version was 'performed by [...] different characters, using different language'. All that matters, according to the court, is that 'the spectator' experiences the two in the same way, 'through any of the senses to which the presentation is addressed'.[66] What makes these two cases so remarkable, then, is that a similar theory of infringement could yield such different results. In the case of visual copyright, the infringement resulted from the photograph's power to confer 'the same kind of pleasure' on the viewer, but only because it was identical to the engraving. If Ball had somehow varied the image, introducing some new elements, the result might nevertheless have produced 'the same impressions' and 'the same emotions', but the result would very likely have been held to be permissible. The juxtaposition of the *Gambart* and *Palmer* cases thus helps to underscore the great difference between visual and literary copyright in the nineteenth century. Doctrinally speaking, in both areas, the same conception of 'substantial similarity' defined the grounds of infringement. For visual copyright, however, courts were reluctant to find any infringement except in cases of complete and identical copying, even as the courts significantly expanded the scope of infringement in cases of literary copyright.

Not until the close of the century did artistic copyright catch up with literary copyright in this respect. In *Brooks* v. *Religious Tract Society* (1897), the image in contention was a woodcut that borrowed the central feature of the plaintiff's engraving, but placed it in a different context. George Augustus Holmes's painting *Can't You Talk*, portraying an infant gazing at a collie, became one of the most beloved and frequently reproduced images of the century, largely because of the engraving produced by

66 *Daly*, 6 F. Cas. 1132, 1138.

Benjamin Brooks.[67] Brooks, a prominent fine art publisher with a shop in the Strand, had bought the painting along with the copyright, shortly after seeing it exhibited in 1875, and commissioned an engraving, apparently by George Zobel.[68] The print was an immediate success; piracies were rampant and led to extensive litigation over the following decades.[69] A woodcut with the same collie, now accompanied by two cats, all staring at a tortoise, was used to illustrate the story 'A Strange Visitor' in the November 1896 issue of the *Child's Companion and Juvenile Instructor*, published by the Religious Tract Society. (see Figures 4 and 5). Brooks sued, seeking an injunction to prevent any further printing and sales of the magazine — and he prevailed, unlike Martin, who had lost the suit over the repurposed image of Beeswing. The defendants' counsel argued that the 'meaning of the two [images] is quite distinct'; drawing on the jurisprudence that associated infringement with communication of the same ideas, he insisted that 'the idea conveyed by the picture is not that of the woodcut'. According to the judge, however, the woodcut copied 'not only the dog, but the feeling and artistic character', even the 'sentiment' of the engraving, reproducing exactly the dog's 'sagacious or benevolent appearance'. The judge therefore had little difficulty concluding that the woodcut was 'a direct copy of a substantial portion of [the plaintiff's] work'.[70]

The judgment did not dwell on economic considerations. According to one summary of the case, the defendant's lawyer argued that because the woodcut presented a different idea, 'it would therefore interfere neither with the reputation of the artist [...] nor with the commercial value of his work'.[71] This account makes the economic argument stand or fall with the argument concerning substantial copying, but the two could be separated. Despite the magazine's low price (it sold for a penny an issue), it is difficult to see how the image could have harmed Brooks's

67 Brooks v. Religious Tract Society (1897), 45 WR 476; see also Cooper, *Art and Modern Copyright*, pp. 217–218; Katherine C. Grier, *Pets in America: A History* (Chapel Hill: UNC Press, 2006), pp. 172–174.

68 J. Herbert Slater, *Engravings and Their Value*, 2nd ed. (London: Gill, 1897), pp. 570–571.

69 See, e.g., 'Police Intelligence', *Reynolds's Newspaper*, 2 June 1878, p. 6; 'Singular Copyright Prosecution', *Edinburgh Evening Press*, 18 Nov. 1879, p. 3; 'Police Intelligence', *The Standard*, 11 March 1884, p. 3.

70 *Brooks*, 45 WR 476.

71 'Brooks v. Religious Tract Society', *Legal News*, 20 (1897), 86–87 (p. 87).

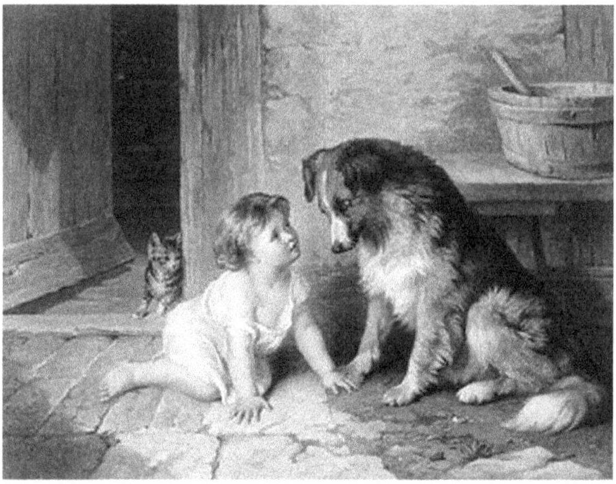

Fig. 4 George Zobel(?), *Can't You Talk?*, engraving commissioned by Benjamin Brooks, after the painting by George Augustus Holmes, 1875.

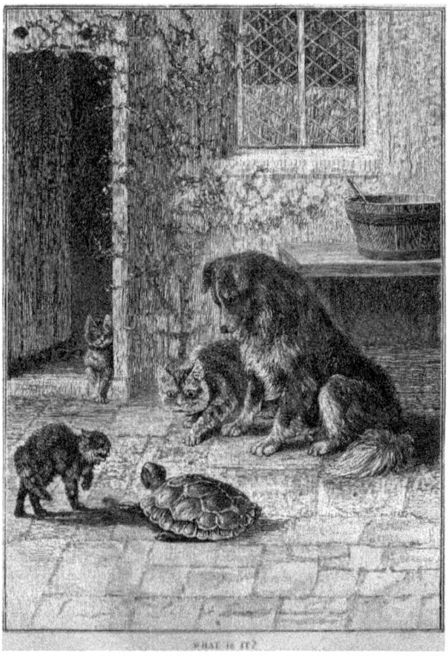

Fig. 5 *What Is It?*, woodcut by unknown artist, 1896.

sales: his very popular image was treasured in Victorian England precisely because of the encounter it staged between the infant and the dog. *Can't You Talk* without the child is like *Hamlet* without the prince — as the defendant's counsel observed, according to one report, 'it could not be supposed for one moment that either the dog or the tortoise would say "Can't you talk?"'[72] Granting that the copy used a substantial part of the source, one might still doubt that anyone who desired the engraving would have been satisfied with the woodcut. Perhaps, having sought unsuccessfully to distinguish the images' different effects, the defense concluded that an attempt to distinguish the markets would also fail. Possibly, given the optics of the case, in which an evangelical society was charged with misappropriating a popular icon of childhood charm and innocence, any talk of lucre would have seemed ignominious. Implicitly, at least, the judgment suggests that 'substantial' copying constitutes infringement regardless of the economic effects on the market for the plaintiff's work.

That implication is significant, because it suggests that the question of infringement turns not on the parties' different manners of 'dealing' with the work, as *Martin* v. *Wright* had held, but rather on the works' similarities, including their ability to convey the same sentiment. The result would be to place the scope of artistic and literary copyright largely on the same footing, and eventually to reintroduce economic questions in a new guise. In modern law, the extension of copyright to various kinds of spinoffs (such as sequels, movies, video games, and fanwear) is typically justified on the view that, even if the plaintiff had not yet exploited that market, the new form represents a potential future market that the plaintiff could have exploited. The broad extension of copyright to 'nonliteral' uses would constitute a crucial chapter in the law's development. For literary works, that process was already under way during the nineteenth century, but for visual works, the seeds for this extension were laid only at the dawn of the twentieth century.

Bibliography

Alexander, Isabella, *Copyright Law and the Public Interest in the Nineteenth Century* (Oxford: Hart, 2010), https://doi.org/10.5040/9781472565013.

Alexander, Isabella, and Cristina S. Martinez, 'The First Copyright Case under the 1735 Engravings Act: The Germination of Visual Copyright?' (Chapter 2 of the current volume).

72 'To-Day's Legal Intelligence', *Pall Mall Gazette*, 5 March 1897, p. 8.

August, Andrew, *The British Working Class, 1832–1940* (New York: Routledge, 2007 (2014)), https://doi.org/10.4324/9781315838809.

'Beeswing', *Illustrated London News*, 24 Sept. 1842, p. 309.

'Belshazaar's Feast — Diorama', *Morning Post* (London), 31 March 1834.

Blackstone, William, 'Book II: Of the Rights of Things' in *Commentaries on the Laws of England*, edited by Simon Stern (Oxford: Oxford University Press, 2016), https://doi.org/10.1093/oseo/instance.00248902.

Boime, Albert, *Art in an Age of Counterrevolution* (Chicago: University of Chicago Press, 2004).

Boyden, Bruce E., '*Daly* v. *Palmer*, or the Melodramatic Origins of the Ordinary Observer', *Syracuse Law Review*, 68 (2018), 147–179.

Bracha, Oren, *Owning Ideas: The Intellectual Origins of American Intellectual Property, 1790–1909* (Cambridge: Cambridge University Press, 2016), https://doi.org/10.1017/9780511843235.

Brake, Laurel, and Marysa Demoor, eds., *Dictionary of Nineteenth-Century Journalism in Great Britain and Ireland* (Gent and London: Academia Press and The British Library, 2009).

'Brooks v. the Religious Tract Society', *Legal News*, 20 (1897), pp. 86–87.

Bury, Stephen, ed., *Benezit Dictionary of British Graphic Artists and Illustrators*, 2 vols. (Oxford: Oxford University Press, 2013 [orig. 2012]), https://doi.org/10.1093/acref/9780199923052.001.0001.

Campbell, Michael J., *John Martin: Visionary Printmaker* (York: Campbell Fine Art, 1992).

Coltrin, Christopher James, 'Apocalyptic Progress: The Politics of Catastrophe in the Art of John Martin, Francis Danby, and David Roberts' (unpublished doctoral thesis, University of Michigan, 2011).

Cooper, Elena, *Art and Modern Copyright: The Contested Image* (Cambridge: Cambridge University Press, 2018), https://doi.org/10.1017/9781316840993.

Cooper, Elena, and Sheona Burrow, 'Photographic Copyright and the Intellectual Property Enterprise Court in Historical Perspective', *Legal Studies*, 39 (2019), 143–65, https://doi.org/10.1017/lst.2018.10.

Deazley, Ronan, 'The Statute of Anne and the Great Abridgement Swindle', *Houston Law Review*, 47 (2010), 793–818.

'Diorama and Physiorama', *The Olio*, 11 (1834).

Duhaime, Douglas, 'Copyright and the Early English Book Market: An Algorithmic Study' (unpublished doctoral thesis, University of Notre Dame, 2019), https://www.earlybookmarket.com/.

'Engravings by Mr. Martin', in *Descriptive Catalogue of the Fall of Babylon* (London: Martin, 1832).

'Engravings v. Photographs', *The Art-Journal*, 5 (1866), pp. 312–14.

Gange, David, *Dialogues with the Dead: Egyptology in British Culture and Religion, 1822–1922* (Oxford: Oxford University Press, 2013), https://doi.org/10.1093/acprof:oso/9780199653102.001.0001.

Grier, Katherine C., *Pets in America: A History* (Chapel Hill: UNC Press, 2006).

Haskins, Katherine, *The Art-Journal and Fine Art Publishing in Victorian England, 1850–1880* (Farnham: Ashgate, 2012).

Hodgson, Thomas, *Hodgson's Annual Catalogue of Books and Engravings Published During 1839* (London: Hodgson, 1840).

Hunt, W. Holman, 'Artistic Copyright', *The Nineteenth Century*, 5 (1879), 418–424.

Hyde, Ralph et al., eds., *Dictionary of Panoramists of the English-Speaking World* (n.p.: n.d.), http://www.bdcmuseum.org.uk/uploads/uploads/biographical_dictionary_of_panoramists2.pdf.

Johnstone, Andrew, *Johnstone's London Commercial Guide* (London: Barnard and Farley, 1818).

Keymer, Thomas and Peter Sabor, *'Pamela' in the Marketplace* (Cambridge: Cambridge University Press, 2005).

'Law Intelligence', *Morning Post* (London), 21 Feb. 1842, p. 1.

Miller, Derek, *Copyright and the Value of Performance, 1770–1911* (Cambridge: Cambridge University Press, 2018), https://doi.org/10.1017/9781108349284.

'Police Intelligence', *Reynolds's Newspaper*, 2 June 1878, p. 6.

'Police Intelligence', *The Standard*, 11 March 1884, p. 3.

Sag, Matthew, 'The Prehistory of Fair Use', *Brooklyn Law Review*, 76 (2011), 1371–1412.

Silbey, Jessica, 'Images in/of Law', *New York Law School Law Review*, 57 (2012), 171–183.

'Singular Copyright Prosecution', *Edinburgh Evening Press*, 18 Nov. 1879, p. 3.

Slater, J. Herbert, *Engravings and Their Value*, 2nd ed. (London: Gill, 1897).

Seville, Catherine, *Literary Copyright Reform in Early Victorian England: The Framing of the 1842 Copyright Act* (Cambridge; Cambridge University Press, 1999).

Slauter, Will, 'Toward a History of Copyright for Periodical Writings: Examples from Nineteenth-Century America' in *From Text(s) to Book(s): Studies in Production and Editorial Processes*, ed. by Nathalie Collé-Bak et al. (Nancy: Éditions universitaires de Lorraine, 2014), pp. 65–84.

Smith, Matthew Wilson, *The Nervous Stage: Nineteenth-Century Melodrama and the Birth of Modern Theater* (Oxford: Oxford University Press, 2017).

'Sporting Obituary', *Sporting Almanack and Oracle of Rural Life* (London: Baily, 1843), p. 56.

Steinbach, Susie L., *Understanding the Victorians: Politics, Culture and Society in Nineteenth-Century Britain* (New York: Routledge, 2012), https://doi.org/10.4324/9780203723654.

Stern, Simon, 'Copyright as a Property Right? Authorial Perspectives in Eighteenth-Century England', *UC Irvine Law Review*, 8 (2018), 461–488, https://scholarship.law.uci.edu/ucilr/vol9/iss2/10/.

——, 'Copyright, Originality, and the Public Domain in Eighteenth-Century England' in *Originality and Intellectual Property in the French and English Enlightenment*, ed. by Reginald McGinnis (New York: Routledge, 2008), pp. 69–101.

——, 'From Author's Right to Property Right', *University of Toronto Law Journal*, 62 (2012), 29–91.

Thomas, Ralph, 'West's Toy-Theatre Prints', *Notes and Queries*, 4th series, 12 (1873), 463.

'To-Day's Legal Intelligence', *Pall Mall Gazette*, 5 March 1897, p. 8.

'Toy Theatre Gallery: History', http://toytheatregallery.com/page12.htm.

Verhoogt, Robert, *Art in Reproduction: Nineteenth-Century Prints after Lawrence Alma-Tadema, Josefs Israëls, and Ary Scheffer* (Amsterdam: Amsterdam University Press, 2007).

'Veterinary Jurisprudence', *The Veterinarian*, 15 (1842), p. 238.

'Vice-Chancellor's Court — Saturday', *Morning Post* (London), 29 July 1833, p. 3.

'William West', The British Museum, https://research.britishmuseum.org/research/search_the_collection_database/term_details.aspx?bioId=12167.

Statutes

N.B. Digital scans of the statutes listed below are available in *Primary Sources on Copyright (1450–1900)*, ed. by Lionel Bently and Martin Kretschmer, http://www.copyrighthistory.org/cam/index.php.

Engravers' Copyright Act 1735 (8 Geo. II, c. 13).

Engravers' Copyright Act 1777 (17 Geo. 3, c. 57).

International Copyright Act 1852 (15 & 16 Vict. c. 12).

Fine Art Copyright Act 1862 (25 & 26 Vict. c. 68).

Legal Cases

Brooks v. Religious Tract Society (1897), 45 WR 476.

Daly v. Palmer, 6 F. Cas. 1132 (C.C.S.D.N.Y. 1868).

Dodsley v. Kinnersley (1761) Amb. 403.

Gambart v. Ball (1863), 8 L.T. Rep. N.S. 426, 14 C.B. (N.S.) 306.

Martin v. Wright (1833) 6 Sim. 297, 58 Eng. Rep. 605.

Moore v. Clarke (1842), 6 Jurist 648; 9 M. & W. 692.

West v. Francis (1822), 5 B. & Ald. 737, 106 Eng. Rep. 1361; 1 Dowl. & Ryl. 400.

5. The 'Death of Chatterton' Case

Reproductive Engraving, Stereoscopic Photography, and Copyright for Paintings ca. 1860

Will Slauter

In 1859, a Dublin photographer named James Robinson visited Thomas Cranfield's gallery on Grafton Street, just a short walk from his own studio. On temporary display at the gallery was Henry Wallis's stunning portrayal of the death of the eighteenth-century poet Thomas Chatterton (see Figure 1). Upon viewing this painting, Robinson thought that the scene would make the perfect subject for a stereoscopic view. By taking two photographs of the same object from vantage points several centimeters apart (to account for the distance between the human eyes) and mounting these photographs side-by-side on a card so that they could be viewed through a stereoscope, it was possible to create the illusion of a three-dimensional experience. Robinson knew that a stereoscopic view could not be produced by photographing the flat surface of a painting. His idea was to recreate the scene as a *tableau vivant* in his own studio, using a live model, furniture, and a painted backdrop, and then take photographs of this scene. He found the idea so compelling that he began running newspaper advertisements announcing that stereo cards depicting 'the Death of Chatterton' would soon be available for purchase (see Figure 2).[1]

1 *Saunders's News-Letter* (Dublin), 22 April 1859, p. 4. For a detailed account, see Denis Pellerin and Brian May, *The Poor Man's Picture Gallery: Stereoscopy versus Paintings in the Victorian Era* (London: The London Stereoscopic Company, 2014), pp. 24–31. The author would like to thank Robert Brauneis, Elena Cooper, Marie-Stéphanie Delamaire, Daniel Foliard, Anthony J. Hamber, Denis Pellerin, and Simon Stern for their comments and assistance, and the late François Brunet for his advice during the writing of this chapter.

 https://doi.org/10.11647/OBP.0247.05

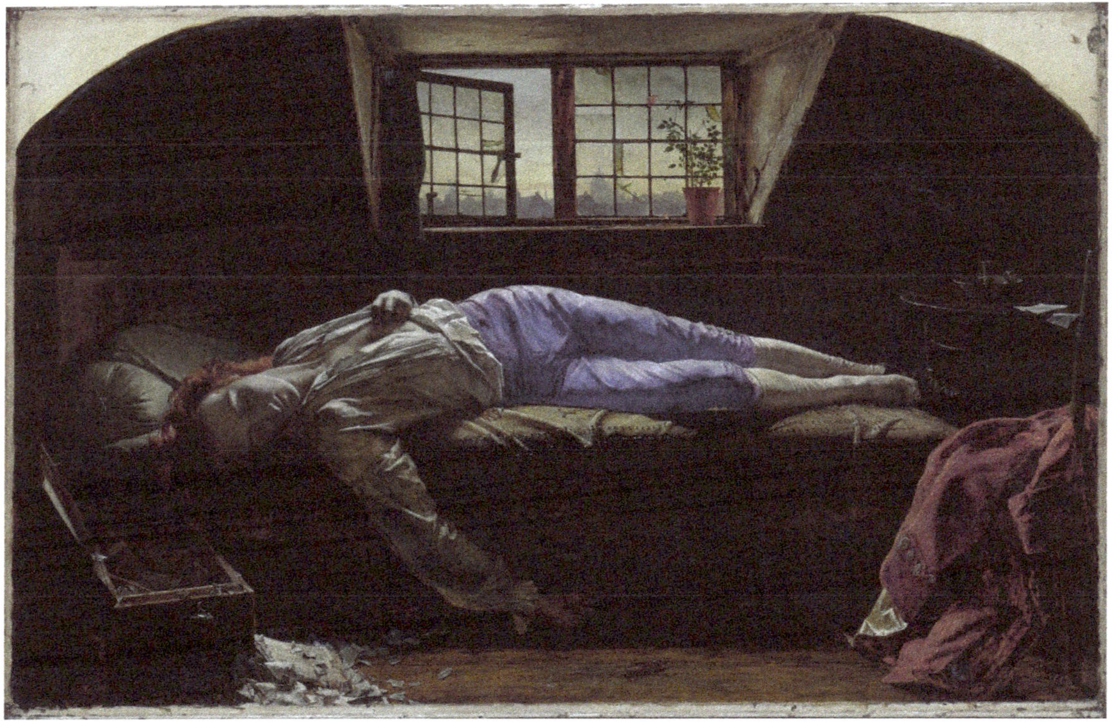

Fig. 1 Henry Wallis, *Chatterton* (1856), Tate, image from Wikimedia Commons, https://commons.wikimedia.org/wiki/File:Henry_Wallis_-_Chatterton_-_Google_Art_Project.jpg.

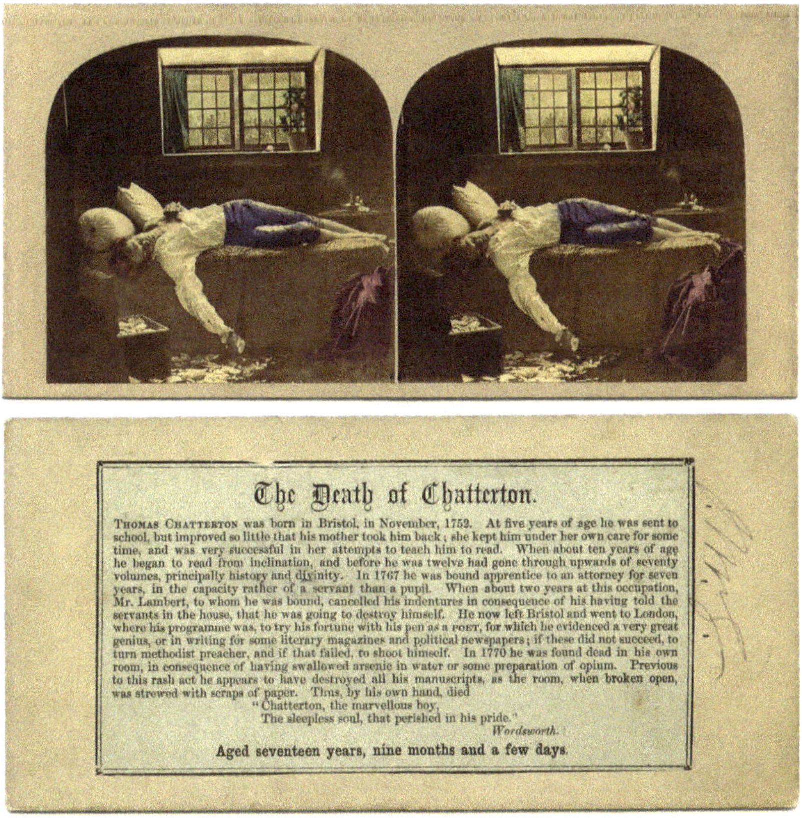

Fig. 2 James Robinson, *The Death of Chatterton*, 1859, two hand-tinted albumen prints on paper, mounted on a stereograph card (front and back). Collection of Dr. Brian May, reproduced by kind permission.

Robinson's advertisements infuriated Robert Turner, a print publisher based in Newcastle who claimed to have the exclusive right to make and sell reproductions of Wallis's painting. At the time, there was no statutory copyright for paintings; along with original drawings and photographs, paintings would be protected by the Fine Arts Copyright Act of 1862.[2] However, for decades prior to the enactment of that law, print publishers had been willing to pay the artist or owner of a painting

2 Fine Arts Copyright Act 1862 (25 & 26 Vict. c. 68), available in *Primary Sources on Copyright (1450–1900)*, ed. by Lionel Bently and Martin Kretschmer, http://www.copyrighthistory.org/cam/tools/request/showRecord.php?id=record_uk_1862.

(if the artist no longer owned the canvas) for the exclusive right to produce an engraving based on it. The resulting engraving could then be protected by copyright thanks to statutes passed in the eighteenth century.[3] But Turner's engraving did not exist yet, and Robinson insisted that the print publisher did not have the right to stop him (or anyone else) from producing his own reproduction of a painting that had been exhibited publicly. The resulting court case, *Turner* v. *Robinson* (1860), considered several important questions: did the owners of paintings enjoy a common law 'copyright' or other cause of legal action (such as breach of confidence) that they could use to stop others from reproducing an artwork? If a common law 'copyright' did exist, would it be lost when a painting was exhibited in a public gallery or published as an engraving?[4]

In the years before and after 1862, photographers struggled to obtain recognition as 'authors' whose works were worthy of copyright protection, rather than as operators of a 'mechanical' process. But *Turner* v. *Robinson* is a reminder that photographers were also defendants in suits brought by print publishers who claimed exclusive rights over a particular painting.[5] The case exposed growing tensions within the

3 See Elena Cooper, *Art and Modern Copyright: The Contested Image* (Cambridge: Cambridge University Press, 2018), pp. 115–117, and 221–222, https://doi.org/10.1017/9781316840993; and Ronan Deazley, 'Commentary on Fine Arts Copyright Act 1862'(2008), in *Primary Sources on Copyright*, ed. by Bently and Kretschmer, http://www.copyrighthistory.org/cam/tools/request/showRecord?id=commentary_uk_1862. On the engraving acts, see also Chapter 2 and Chapter 4 of the present volume. Protection under the engraving acts was extended to Ireland in 1836 (Copyright in Prints and Engravings (Ireland) Act 1836 (6 & 7 Will. IV c.59), available in *Primary Sources on Copyright*, ed. by Bentley and Kretschmer, http://www.copyrighthistory.org/cam/tools/request/showRecord.php?id=record_uk_1836).

4 *Turner v. Robinson* (1860), 10 Ir. Ch. 121 (before the Master of the Rolls), 510 (Court of Appeal in Chancery). See Cooper, *Art and Modern Copyright*, pp. 213–215. A pioneering study is Gillian B. Greenhill, 'The Death of Chatterton, or Photography and the Law', *History of Photography*, 5 (1981), 199–205, https://doi.org/10.1080/03087298.1981.10442668. Note, however, that the stereograph reproduced in Greenhill's article and attributed to Robinson is different than the one in Dr. Brian May's collection reproduced in the present chapter; the former is the work of another photographer, Michael Burr (more on this later in the present chapter). See Pellerin and May, *Poor Man's Picture Gallery*, p. 30.

5 Anne McCauley, '"Merely Mechanical": On the Origins of Photographic Copyright in France and Great Britain', *Art History*, 31 (2008), 57–78, https://doi.org/10.1111/j.1467-8365.2008.00583.x; and Ronan Deazley, 'Struggling with Authority: The Photograph in British Legal History', *History of Photography*, 27 (2003), 236–246,

market for reproductions of fine art, and it led the court to inquire into prevailing commercial arrangements and institutional norms, such as the rules related to copying in public galleries. The dispute raised the thorny question of what constituted a 'copy' of a visual work — especially if it were rendered in a new medium — at a crucial transition period in the history of photography and its relationship to the other arts. It was a hinge moment not only in the development of photography as a business and a generator of new forms of visual culture (such as stereoscopic views) but also in the use of photography to document artworks and make reproductions available to a wider public.

This chapter takes a closer look at *Turner* v. *Robinson*, not so much for its importance as a legal precedent, but for what the dispute reveals about the shifting artistic and commercial landscape in which photographers like Robinson and print publishers like Turner were operating. The chapter draws on contemporary reports of court proceedings — as well as more obscure newspaper accounts, advertisements, and exhibition catalogues — to reconstruct the story of the litigation and its protagonists. It also draws on detailed research by collectors and curators of stereographs and specialists of the history of painting, printmaking, and photography. In doing so, the chapter seeks to situate Robinson's actions and Turner's response in relation to wider cultural and technological trends. It ends by considering the significance of the case and what effects the judgment may have had on contemporary artistic and commercial practices.

The Poet and the Painting

By the time Wallis exhibited his painting in 1856, accounts of Thomas Chatterton's short life and tragic death had made him something of a cult figure for writers and artists, from William Wordsworth and John Keats to the Pre-Raphaelite circle of painters with which Wallis was associated. The usual story is that Chatterton committed suicide in a London garret in 1770. He was seventeen, poor, and largely unknown, despite having published some of his work in newspapers. His unique

---

https://doi.org/10.1080/03087298.2003.10441249. For an analysis of some of the subsequent cases that print sellers brought against photographers, see Cooper, *Art and Modern Copyright*, pp. 219–248.

literary imagination and immense desire for recognition had ended in tragedy. As a boy growing up in Bristol, Chatterton collected remnants of old manuscripts from St. Mary Redcliffe Church and devoured collections of medieval English verse. He was also inspired by the Scottish poet James MacPherson, who in the 1760s published a series of epics that he claimed to be translations from ancient Gaelic works by the legendary Irish poet Ossian. For his part, Chatterton composed a series of mock-medieval writings that he presented as the work of a fifteenth-century figure named Thomas Rowley. After testing out his forged manuscripts on some local antiquarians, Chatterton sought out patronage at the highest levels of the British literary world, writing first to the publisher James Dodsley and then to the writer Horace Walpole, whose own *Castle of Otranto* (1764) Chatterton admired. Walpole initially expressed interest, but after discovering Chatterton's low social status he suspected a trap. Walpole showed the manuscripts to others who concurred that they were forgeries. Disappointed and angry at Walpole, Chatterton moved to London, where he began to eke out a living contributing political essays and satires to local newspapers. Things were looking up until another potential patron — William Beckford, the lord mayor and supporter of the radical John Wilkes — died suddenly. Chatterton desperately took his own life.[6] In line with this story, Wallis inscribed a quotation from Christopher Marlowe's Elizabethan tragedy *Doctor Faustus* on the frame of his painting of Chatterton: 'Cut is the branch that might have grown full straight,/ And burned is Apollo's laurel bough'.[7]

The literary scholar Nick Groom has challenged the assumption that Chatterton committed suicide, suggesting instead that he died of an accidental drug overdose. In Groom's words, 'despite the juggernaut of myth that began almost immediately to roll, obliterating history, this was no proto-Romantic suicide of a starving poet in a friendless garret, his genius cruelly unrecognized'.[8] Yet there is no denying that Chatterton

6 Nick Groom, 'Chatterton, Thomas (1752–1770)', *Oxford Dictionary of National Biography* (2004), https://doi.org/10.1093/ref:odnb/5189; John H. Pittock, 'Thomas Chatterton (10 November 1752–24 August 1770)', in *Dictionary of Literary Biography*, vol. 109: *Eighteenth-Century British Poets: Second Series*, ed. by John Sitter (Detroit: Gale, 1991), pp. 64–83.

7 Frances Fowle, 'Henry Wallis, *Chatterton*, 1856' (2000), Tate, https://www.tate.org.uk/art/artworks/wallis-chatterton-n01685.

8 Groom, 'Chatterton'.

became a hero of the English romantics. A 'Monody on the Death of Chatterton' was one of Samuel Taylor Coleridge's earliest poems, and one he reworked several times over the course of his career. William Wordsworth, in 'Resolution and Independence'(1807), described Chatterton as 'the marvellous Boy,/ The sleepless Soul that perished in his pride'.[9] John Keats, who dedicated his long poem *Endymion* (1818) to Chatterton, went so far as to claim that the fallen poet was 'the purest writer in the English language'.[10] Further admirers included Robert Browning and Dante Gabriel Rosetti. The writer George Meredith actually posed as Chatterton for Wallis's painting. Unfortunately, Wallis soon ran off with Meredith's wife, inspiring Meredith to write a series of fifty sonnets that was published under the title *Modern Love* in 1862.[11]

Chatterton is now one of Wallis's best-known works, and it was already somewhat famous when James Robinson saw it in Dublin in 1859. Exhibited at the Royal Academy in 1856, the painting was then featured in the Manchester Art Treasures Exhibition of 1857, a huge event that drew unprecedented crowds. The critic John Ruskin declared Wallis's painting 'faultless and wonderful' and invited viewers to 'examine it inch by inch: it is one of the pictures which intend, and accomplish, the entire placing before your eyes of an actual fact — and that a solemn one'.[12] Whether he read Ruskin's review or not, Robinson certainly examined the painting 'inch by inch', and he spied an opportunity to profit from the fast-growing demand for stereoscopic views.

The Rise of Stereography

After stereograph cards and viewers mesmerized visitors to the Crystal Palace Exhibition in 1851, opticians tinkered with devices and burgeoning photography firms began to develop products within the

9 William Wordsworth, 'Resolution and Independence', in *Poems in Two Volumes* (London: Longman, Hurst, Rees, and Orme, 1807), I, 89–97 (p. 92).

10 John Keats, *Endymion: A Poetic Romance* (London: Taylor and Hessey, 1818), unpaginated dedication; John Keats to John Hamilton Reynolds, 22 September 1819, quoted in Pittock, 'Thomas Chatterton', p. 81.

11 Linda Kelly, *The Marvellous Boy: The Life and Myth of Thomas Chatterton* (London: Weidenfeld and Nicolson, 1971), pp. 118–119.

12 John Ruskin, *Notes on Some of the Principal Pictures Exhibited in the Rooms of the Royal Academy, and the Society of Painters in Water Colours: No. II — 1856. 6th ed.* (London: Smith, Elder & Co., 1856), p. 26.

reach of middle-class consumers.[13] Meanwhile, uncertainty about the patent claims of William Fox Talbot was resolved at the end of 1854, enabling the widespread use of the wet plate collodion process.[14] Since it could be used to create multiple positive prints on paper, the collodion process is what made possible the mass commercialization of photographs in the form of stereograph cards and the small-format photographs known as *cartes de visite*. Numerous photography studios were started in the late 1850s. In London alone, it has been estimated that the number grew from sixty-six in 1855 to 284 in 1864.[15] The London Stereoscopic Company, founded in 1854, had the ambition (according to the company's own slogan) to place 'a Stereoscope in Every Home'. By 1856, the same year that Wallis first exhibited *Chatterton*, the London Stereoscopic Company claimed to have sold more than 500,000 viewers and have a catalog of over 10,000 stereograph cards. Two years later, they boasted 100,000 different stereo views.[16] Stereography transformed the visual landscape: suddenly a dazzling range of images were available in a format that was both exciting and affordable to middle-class families. Purchasing, exchanging, and viewing stereographs became a craze (see Figure 3).

13 See Laura Claudet, 'Stereoscopy', in *Encyclopedia of Nineteenth-Century Photography*, ed. by John Hannavy. 2 vols. (New York and London: Routledge, 2008), II, 1338–1341.

14 The collodion process was developed by Frederick Scott Archer, who had not patented it, but Fox Talbot insisted that the process was a violation of his own calotype patent. In 1854 Fox Talbot sued the photographer Martin Laroche, but the jury determined that the collodion process being used by Laroche did not infringe Talbot's calotype patent. In the wake of this decision, Talbot also dropped his petition to the Privy Council for an extension of his calotype patent. R. Derek Wood, *The Calotype Patent Lawsuit of Talbot v. Laroche 1854* (Bromley, Kent: privately published by R. D. Wood, 1975), available here: http://www.midley.co.uk/laroche/TalbotvLaroche.htm.

15 Steve Edwards, *The Making of English Photography: Allegories* (University Park: Pennsylvania State University Press, 2006), p. 71. On the 1850s as a turning point, see Ian Jeffrey, 'British Photography from Fox Talbot to E.O. Hoppé', in *The Real Thing: An Anthology of British Photographs 1840–1950* (London: Arts Council of Great Britain, 1975), pp. 5–24; and Mark Haworth-Booth, ed., *The Golden Age of British Photography, 1839–1900* (New York: Aperture, 1984), chaps. 2–4.

16 Claudet, 'Stereoscopy'; Zoe Clayton, 'Sterographs', *V&A Blog*, 29 January 2013, https://www.vam.ac.uk/blog/caring-for-our-collections/stereographs; Colin Harding, 'L is for...London Stereoscopic Company: The Home of 100,000 Views', Science and Media Museum blog, 26 October 2013, https://blog.scienceandmediamuseum.org.uk/a-z-photography-l-is-for-london-stereoscopic-company/.

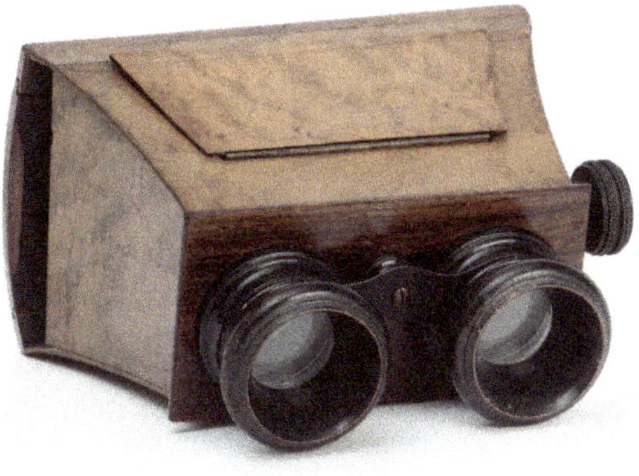

Fig. 3 An example of a Brewster-style stereoscope from around 1870, Museo della scienza e della tecnologia, Milano, CC-BY-SA-4.0, https://commons.wikimedia.org/wiki/File:IGB_006055_Visore_stereoscopico_portatile_Museo_scienza_e_tecnologia_Milano.jpg.

Robinson's business was tiny compared to the London Stereoscopic Company, but he had a good eye: the scene depicted in Wallis's painting was well-suited to the new medium. Viewers of the painting were invited to peer into the bedroom of the young Chatterton, and even to assume the perspective of the landlady who in 1770 opened the door to discover his body. Why not offer spectators the titillating illusion of entering the arch-ceilinged room? Robinson had been familiar with stereoscopy since at least 1853, when the catalogue for the Dublin International Exhibition listed him exhibiting 'stereoscopes of various forms, with diagrams and proofs; cameras for the calotype, daguerreotype and collodion processes; various specimens of photography on paper and on glass'.[17] That Robinson exhibited photographic apparatuses alongside specimens produced using a range of materials was not unusual for international exhibitions meant to showcase technical innovations. Although relatively little is known about Robinson, it should not be assumed that he was just a shady figure trying to make an easy profit by 'copying' Wallis's painting (and 'copy' was a word

17 Catalogue no. 643, 1853 Dublin International Exhibition, in 'Photographic Exhibitions in Britain 1839–1865: Records from Victorian Exhibition Catalogues', ed. by Roger Taylor, http://peib.dmu.ac.uk/index.php. The same database indicates that Robinson exhibited again at the 1865 Dublin International Exhibition, where he showed 'Portraits, coloured and plain; Siamese cartes'.

that Robinson found problematic, as we shall see).[18] Scattered evidence from contemporary newspaper notices and exhibition catalogues as well as extant portraits by him in major collections reveal that over time Robinson built a successful business that combined studio photography and the manufacture and sale of cameras, lenses, and related materials.[19] The lengths he was willing to go to defend himself against Turner, and the legal expenses that would have been involved in the initial trial and the appeal, also suggest that he considered it important to take a public stand at a moment when copyright reform, and the competing interests of engravers and photographers, were being actively discussed.[20]

By the mid-1840s Robinson was advertising that his 'Polytechnic Museum' on Grafton Street stocked a range of chemicals and scientific apparatuses, including microscopes and telescopes, opera and racing glasses, magic lanterns, and 'an extraordinary collection of rational and Amusing Toys, Novelties in Mechanism, Drawing-room Recreations, &c'.[21] As photography developed, Robinson changed the name of his establishment to 'Polytechnic Museum and Photographic Galleries' and sometime in the late 1850s he began to operate a portrait studio. An ambrotype print of a group portrait that has been attributed to Robinson and dated to approximately 1858 was included in a 2010 exhibition at the Gallery of Photography, Ireland.[22] The National Portrait Gallery in London has several *carte-de-visite* portraits by Robinson that curators date to the 1860s; the cards are stamped J. Robinson, Dublin.[23] Appropriately

---

18 On shifting meanings of the 'copy' in relation to copyright law, see also Stina Teilmann-Lock, *The Object of Copyright: A Conceptual History of Originals and Copies in Literature, Art and Design* (London: Routledge, 2016), https://doi.org/10.4324/9781315814476.

19 For more on Robinson, see Pellerin and May, *Poor Man's Picture Gallery*, p. 196. On products manufactured or sold by Robinson and J. Robinson & Sons, see Charles Mollan, *Irish National Inventory of Historic Scientific Instruments* (Blackrock, Ireland: Samton Limited, 1995), pp. 535–536.

20 On the legislative process and debates, see Cooper, *Art and Modern Copyright*, chap. 2.

21 *Freeman's Journal* (Dublin), 20 October 1847.

22 Group portrait of young men, ambrotype print, ca. 1858, attributed to 'Grafton Street Studio of James Robinson', in 'The Collector's Eye: Original Vintage Prints from the Sean Sexton Collection', October-November 2010, Gallery of Photography Ireland, https://www.galleryofphotography.ie.

23 Five portraits attributed to Robinson (and later Robinson & Sons) can be viewed here: https://www.npg.org.uk/collections/search/person/mp82935/james-robinson?role=art. The National Museum of Ireland catalogue indicates that work by James Robinson is included in the Duggan Photographic Collection, though the number and type of photographs is not specified in the online catalogue: http://catalogue.nli.ie/Collection/vtls000194032.

enough, after the Fine Arts Copyright Act of 1862 extended copyright to photographs, Robinson registered some of his portraits. Sometime in the 1870s his sons joined him in the business, and by 1884 they added a London location in Regent Street, while retaining the Dublin address (where James Robinson seems to have remained).[24]

In any case, newspaper reports indicate that by 1859 Robinson was an active member of the Dublin Photographic Society, where he showed some of his own work in addition to showcasing the achievements of more well-known photographers. In March 1859, just before the dispute with Turner, he exhibited magic lantern slides of some of Francis Frith's famous views of Egyptian monuments.[25] By this time such slides were being marketed by the London firm of Negretti and Zambra, and it seems likely that Robinson did not think he was doing anything wrong by showing them to fellow members of the Dublin Photographic Society.[26] He was clearly a practitioner who was up to date with the latest technology, practices, and subject matter of various photographic processes.

Photography and *tableaux vivants*

Robinson's idea to stage Chatterton's death scene as a *tableau vivant* and then photograph it did not occur to him suddenly, nor was it some sort of clever subterfuge to avoid directly photographing the canvas. Robinson would have known that writers and scenes from literary

24 A search of copyright registrations in the online catalogue of the National Archives, UK (http://discovery.nationalarchives.gov.uk/details/r/C5349) reveals that James Robinson registered at least eight photographs in his name (as both author of the work and owner of the copyright) between 1863 (COPY 1/2/493) and 1896 (COPY 1/424/184). J. Robinson and Sons must have existed by 2 September 1882, when the firm registered a photograph of the late Daniel O'Connell using the address of 65 Grafton Street, Dublin (COPY 1/58/394). A pair of photographs registered by J. Robinson and Sons in 1884 listed both the Dublin address and 172 Regent Street, London (COPY 1369/273-274). Almost all registrations after 1882 are in the firm's name, but as late as 1896 James Robinson did register a photograph of the tenor Braxton Smith in his own name using only the Dublin address (COPY 1/424/184).

25 'Fine Art Section', *Freeman's Journal* (Dublin), 26 March 1859.

26 *An Illustrated Descriptive Catalogue of Optical, Mathematical, Philosophical, Photographic and Standard Meteorological Instruments, Manufactured and Sold by Negretti and Zambra* (London, 1859), p. 178, https://archive.org/details/NegrettiAndZambraCatalogue1859/page/n195/mode/2up; 'Photographic Pictures for Dissolving Views and Magic Lanterns', *Cornhill Magazine* 1 (January 1860), unpaginated advertisement for Negretti and Zambra, https://books.google.fr/books?id=pY9UAAAAcAAJ&dq=negretti%20and%20Zambra%20egypt%20magic%20lantern&hl=fr&pg=PP49#v=onepage&q&f=false.

and dramatic works were popular subjects for staged photographs, not least among practitioners who had trained as painters and sought to elevate photography to an art form. A prominent example was William Frederick Lake Price's *Don Quixote in his Study*, which was shown at several exhibitions in the late 1850s and made available as a stereo card (see Figure 4).[27] As evidenced by this and other contemporary stereographs, cluttered interiors enhanced the pleasure of the optical illusion by allowing viewers to inspect each object in turn. Denis Pellerin, a curator and historian of photography, put it this way: 'stereoscopy loves clutter and photographers, who knew their customers well, made the most of it in their compositions'.[28] Working with Brian May, who has a unique collection of Victorian stereographs, Pellerin has shown that the phenomenon of restaging paintings to produce stereoscopic views was quite common in the 1850s and 1860s. Pellerin and May have suggested that much of the appeal came from the idea of making works of art more accessible to the public and allowing individuals to spend time intensely looking at all the details.[29] In the case of Wallis's painting, there was much to work with: Chatterton's partly undressed body stretched out on the bed in a Pietà-like position, his arm dangling down to the floor, his hand still gripping a crumpled manuscript, the vial of poison a few inches away, the chest full of disorderly papers, the recently extinguished candle on the table, the dome of St. Paul's Cathedral and the London cityscape visible through the window — all of these objects could be inspected as viewers took a virtual tour of the room. Those who looked closely at the painting could even see the name of the newspaper on the floor — the *Middlesex Journal; or Chronicle of Liberty* — to which Chatterton had contributed.[30]

---

27 A copy of the stereo card held by the Victoria & Albert Museum may be viewed here: http://collections.vam.ac.uk/item/O1436246/don-quixote-in-his-study-photographs-lake-price-william/.

28 Denis Pellerin, 'From 3D to 2D...and Back', blog post, 1 October 2018, 'Thinking 3D' project, https://www.thinking3d.ac.uk/3Dto2D/.

29 Pellerin and May, *Poor Man's Picture Gallery*. In 2014–2015, Pellerin and May collaborated with the Tate on an exhibition that featured stereographs from May's collection alongside paintings from the Tate. See Carol Jacobi, 'Tate Painting and the Art of Stereoscopic Photography' (2014), https://www.tate.org.uk/whats-on/tate-britain/display/bp-spotlight-poor-mans-picture-gallery-victorian-art-and-stereoscopic/essay.

30 Anne Helmreich, 'Henry Wallis, The Death of Chatterton', in *The Victorians: British Painting, 1837–1901*, ed. by Malcolm Warner (Washington: National Gallery of Art, 1996), pp. 101–102. Wallis's inclusion of the *Middlesex Journal* and other details may

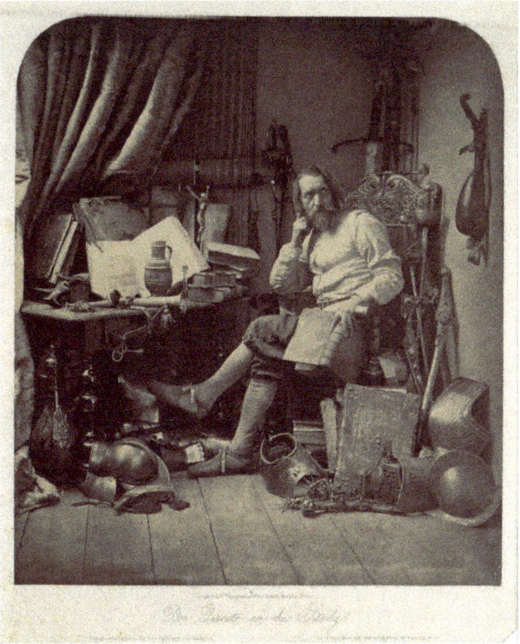

Fig. 4 William Frederick Lake Price, *Don Quixote in his Study*, 1857, albumen silver print from glass negative, Metropolitan Museum of Art, New York, CC0 1.0, https://www.metmuseum.org/art/collection/search/271528.

As a member of a local photographic society and dealer in all things related to the art, Robinson was almost certainly aware of a cultural trend among both professionals and amateurs in which people would recreate scenes from paintings as *tableaux vivants* for the camera.[31] Robinson may have spied a business opportunity, but he was also up

have been influenced by the recent publication of an account of the poet's final year by David Masson (Kelly, p. 118). The inclusion of the London skyline as a backdrop for Chatterton's death was interpreted at the time, in the words of one contemporary review, as evidence of the 'careless city'. Nancy Rose Marshall, *City of Gold and Mud: Painting Victorian London* (New Haven: Yale University Press, 2012), p. 22. On depictions of the city in paintings at this time, see Chapter 10 of the present volume.

31 In addition to Pellerin and May, *Poor Man's Picture Gallery*, see Martin Meisel, *Realizations: Narrative, Pictorial, and Theatrical Arts in Nineteenth-Century England* (Princeton University Press, 1983), pp. 93–94; Grace Sieberling, with Carolyn Blore, *Amateurs, Photography, and the Mid-Victorian Imagination* (Chicago: University of Chicago Press, 1986), p. 86; Quentin Bajac, *Tableaux vivants: Fantaisies photographiques victoriennes (1840–1880)* (Paris: Réunion des musées nationaux, 1999), pp. 10–20; Marta Weiss, 'La photographie mise en scène dans l'album victorien', in *La*

for a technical challenge in line with contemporary aesthetic trends. In his affidavit, Robinson stated that he hired a scene painter to create a backdrop simulating the garret with its window. He placed the bed, table, chest, and other objects as he remembered seeing them in Wallis's painting, and had his own assistant pose as Chatterton.[32] However, given how closely Robinson's stereoscopic view reproduced numerous details from the painting, the court would not be satisfied by Robinson's claim that he worked entirely from memory, and it may well be that he relied in part on an existing wood engraving (discussed later in this chapter).

Reproductive Engravings and the Threat of Photography

Wallis's painting was on display at Cranfield's Gallery for approximately three weeks in April 1859. The exhibition had been arranged by Turner, who was following what was by then a common business model among print sellers: charging a small admission price to see the original painting, then using these viewings to solicit subscribers to the engraved reproduction. Turner had commissioned the highly-respected engraver Thomas Oldham Barlow to carry out the work. But on 22 April, Robinson announced in *Saunders's News-Letter*, a major Dublin newspaper, that his stereo cards of *The Death of Chatterton* would be ready for sale the following Monday; plain copies would cost 1s. 6d. and hand-colored cards 2s. 6d.[33] For Turner, the advertisements must have seemed like a deliberate provocation. Print publishers were growing increasingly concerned about how photography could harm the market for engravings, and here was a photographer who worked in the same street where the painting was being displayed, openly advertising his own version in the local newspaper. Because the purpose of the Dublin exhibition was to attract subscribers (and it was the first such showing),

Photographie mise en scène: créer l'illusion du reel, ed. by Lori Pauli (London/ New York: Merrell, 2006), pp. 81–99.

32 Charles H. Foot, *'The Death of Chatterton' Case. Turner v. Robinson* (Dublin: Edward Ponsonby, 1860), pp. 12–14; *Turner*, 10 Ir. Ch. at 125–126.

33 *Turner*, 10 Ir. Ch. at 124. 22 April 1859 was a Friday, but it appears that the stereographs were not ready the following Monday since Robinson repeated the advertisement in *Saunders's News-Letter* on Tuesday 26 April. On Friday 29 April a notice in *Saunders's News-Letter* stated that the stereographs were on sale.

Barlow had not yet begun the time-consuming and painstaking process of producing his plate. Not only were Robinson's photographs first to market, but they were also significantly cheaper than a quality print of the sort Turner was planning. Barlow's engraving was a mezzotint, with additional tonal effects produced through stipple engraving and etching, a process often referred to as 'mixed-method engraving'(see Figure 5).[34] Although Barlow inserted the year 1860 next to his monogram in the engraving, he did not actually deliver the finished plate to Turner until 1862, a delay that led Turner to sue him (unsuccessfully, it turned out) for violating their contract.[35] In any case, when the engraving was advertised for sale in the spring of 1862, standard prints cost 2 guineas, almost thirty times as much as Robinson's uncolored stereo cards and roughly seventeen times as much as the colored ones (artist's proofs of the engraving cost much more — 8 guineas).[36]

Given this disparity in price, the potential clientele for the engraving was more limited than that of Robinson's stereoscopic view, and one could argue that they were two different products aimed at two different markets. Indeed, evidence presented to the court stated that Turner had circulated prospectuses for the engraving 'among the nobility and gentry of Ireland', and that the admission price of 6d. for viewing the painting at Cranfield's Gallery had been designed to avoid the kinds of crowds that might deter potential subscribers from entering the gallery in the first place.[37] But print publishers like Turner were concerned with how photographic reproductions of works of art could cut into the sales of quality engravings, and there is some evidence that this threat was beginning to reduce the amounts they were willing to pay painters for so-called 'engraving rights'.[38]

34 Allen Staley, *The Post-Pre-Raphaelite Print: Etching, Illustration, Reproductive Engraving, and Photography in England in and around the 1860s* (New York: Miriam & Ira D. Wallach Art Gallery, Columbia University, 1995), pp. 13–14, 33–34.

35 Ibid., pp. 33–34. According to his agreement with Turner, Barlow was to have access to the painting for a total of fourteen months, with interruptions for Turner to be able to display the painting. Barlow proved that he did not have possession for more than fourteen months, and the court found in his favor. 'Art at Law', *Art Journal*, 1 January 1864, p. 30.

36 Staley, *Post-Pre-Raphaelite*, pp. 33–34. Although gold guinea coins had stopped circulating, prices for certain luxury goods and services were still quoted in guineas, the equivalent of 21 shillings.

37 Foot, *'Death of Chatterton' Case*, p. 18.

38 Anthony Dyson, *Pictures to Print: The Nineteenth-Century Engraving Trade* (London: Farrand Press, 1984), p. 67; Lionel Bently, 'Art and the Making of Modern Copyright

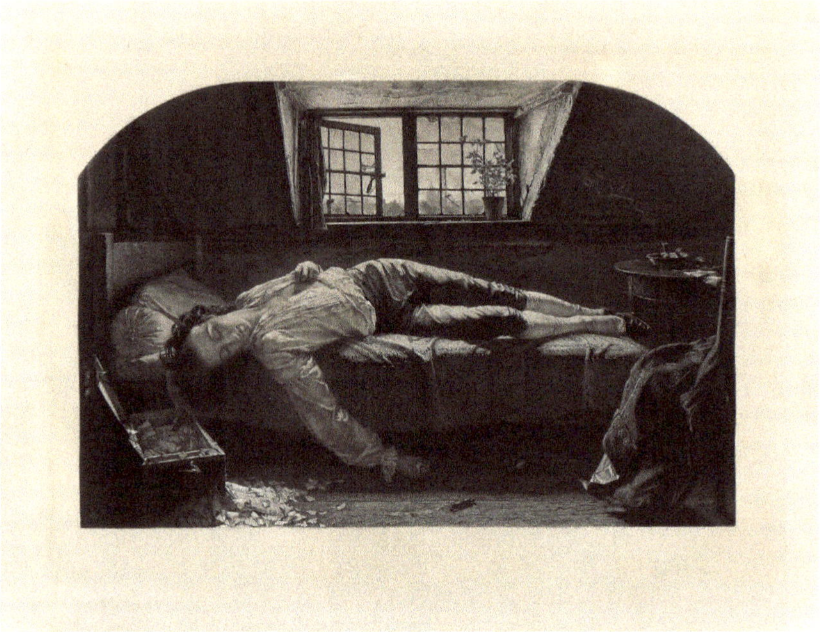

Fig. 5 Thomas Oldham Barlow (after Henry Wallis), *The Death of Chatterton*, 1860, Art Institute of Chicago, CCO Public Domain, https://www.artic.edu/artworks/148404/the-death-of-chatterton.

Turner had in fact anticipated that photographers might be tempted by Wallis's painting, and on 2 April he had the following notice published in *Saunders's News-Letter*:

> CAUTION TO PHOTOGRAPHERS. –Mr. Turner hereby intimates to Photographic Artists and others, that proceedings at law will be immediately instituted against anyone infringing upon his copyright by means of Photography or otherwise. 32, Grey-street, Newcastle, April 1st, 1859.[39]

A short editorial in the same newspaper sympathized with 'the eminent Robert Turner' and other print publishers who had 'very properly

Law', in *Dear Images: Art, Copyright, and Culture*, ed. by Daniel McClean and Karsten Schubert (London: Ridinghouse/ICA, 2002), pp. 331–351 (pp. 342–343).

39 'Notice to Photographers', *Saunders's News-Letter* (Dublin), 2 April 1859. A copy of this advertisement was presented when Turner testified on 24 November 1859 (*Saunders's News-Letter*, 25 November 1859; *Freeman's Journal*, 25 November 1859). The notice was also quoted in the report of the Court of Appeal: *Turner,* 10 Ir. Ch. 510.

taken alarm at the extent to which copies of the finest engravings are multiplied by means of photography'.[40] But since Barlow's engraving did not exist yet, Robinson could not have used photography to create copies of it. Still, Turner saw Robinson's advertisements for *The Death of Chatterton* as proof that the photographer was infringing his right to sell reproductions of the painting. Turner's solicitors wrote to Robinson requesting that he desist from producing or selling any more copies of *The Death of Chatterton*, and threatening legal proceedings 'for pirating said work, and publishing the same'.[41] Turner also complained about Robinson's use of the title *The Death of Chatterton*, which Turner had been using to advertise Wallis's painting and his forthcoming print.[42] Turner's counsel argued that Robinson had 'increased the interest and value of the photograph by representing that it was a copy of the original picture, which he clearly led the public to understand'.[43]

Robinson insisted that his stereoscopic views were not copied directly from the painting and that Turner had no right to interfere in his business. In response to the letter from Turner's solicitors, he published a new advertisement defending himself against the allegations of 'piracy':

> THE DEATH OF CHATTERTON. —
> JAMES ROBINSON begs to announce that he has now ready for Sale the most wonderfully effective and beautiful Stereoscopic Pictures ever yet produced, Photographed by him from the living model, representing
> THE LAST MOMENT AND DEATH OF THE POET CHATTERTON.
> 1s. 6d. each plain, 2s. 6d. coloured.
> J.R. begs most emphatically to deny having copied or pirated his Stereoscopic Slides from any Picture exhibited in Dublin; and it must be obvious to any one that has the slightest knowledge of the principles of the stereoscope that pictures such as he has produced

40 'Photographic Copies of Engravings', *Saunders's News-Letter*, 2 April 1859.

41 Kiernan and McCreight to Robinson, 27 April 1859, quoted in Foot, *'Death of Chatterton' Case*, pp. 9–10.

42 As discussed later in the article, Wallis actually objected to the title 'The Death of Chatterton'.

43 *Saunders's News-Letter*, 7 June 1859. Counsel specifically referenced the law related to trademarks: 'the court ought to interfere, on a principle analogous to that in which the Court interferes to restrain the sale of goods with a trade-mark belonging to another' (*Turner*, 10 Ir. Ch. at 128).

> could not be obtained from the flat surface of any painting or engraving. Polytechnic Museum and Photographic Galleries.
> 65 GRAFTON-STREET[44]

This notice appeared in *Saunders's News-Letter*, immediately underneath an advertisement announcing the public's final opportunity to view Wallis's painting at Cranfield's Gallery. Such dueling newspaper notices no doubt increased interest in Wallis's painting and demand for reproductions of it. The initial trial and the appeal were thoroughly covered in the newspapers and included several days of hearings spread over many months from May 1859 through June 1860 — generating publicity for both Turner and Robinson. In fact, the day after Turner's solicitors wrote to Robinson, Cranfield informed the public that Wallis's painting might be needed in court as a result of Turner having commenced legal proceedings against Robinson 'for infringement on his copyright of the Picture of 'THE DEATH OF CHATTERTON'; consequently, the painting would remain on view for a few additional days at Cranfield's.[45] Once hearings began, Turner was able to enjoy newspaper reports that referred to him as 'the celebrated publisher of engravings'; newspaper readers also learned that 'the beautiful painting was exhibited in court, and was greatly admired by the bar and a very crowded audience'.[46]

Robinson sought support from local photographers. Conveniently for him, the Dublin Photographic Society was scheduled to meet the same evening that he ran the newspaper notice quoted earlier in which he denied the allegation of 'piracy'. After displaying his stereograph of *The Death of Chatterton*, Robinson announced to the Photographic Society that he was being sued for the 'alleged piracy of a celebrated picture of this name', but that his work was 'no copy'; he asserted that he would defend his rights in court, to the apparent approbation of

44 *Saunders's News-Letter*, 29 April 1859. A later advertisement stated that the stereographs were 'not copied from any painting or engraving, but are Photographed from the living model, and when seen in the Stereoscope stand out in bold relief, producing the most extraordinary effect' (*Saunders's News-Letter*, 3 May 1859, 5 May 1859; *Irish Times* (Dublin), 5 May 1859). See also Pellerin, 'From 3D to 2D', which refers to an 1858 article in *The Times* reporting on the successful conversion of an etching into a stereograph.

45 *Freeman's Journal* (Dublin), 28 April 1859.

46 *Dublin Evening Mail*, 9 May 1859; *Dublin Mercantile Advertiser*,13 May 1859.

those present.[47] Turner would not give up either. His petition to the Irish Court of Chancery claimed that Robinson's stereographs were 'piratical imitations and copies of the design and subject' of Wallis's painting, and requested that the court issue an injunction to stop Robinson from exhibiting, publishing, or selling his photographs 'or any other picture, print or engraving, being an imitation of, or a copy from the design of the said picture'.[48]

Turner's Stand on Behalf of Engraving Rights

The case came before the Master of the Rolls in Ireland, the second-highest ranking judge in the Court of Chancery after the Lord Chancellor. The current Master of the Rolls was Thomas Berry Cusack Smith, who was known as a learned and conscientious judge but also for his blunt and colorful courtroom demeaner. In a previous role as Attorney-General for Ireland, Smith led the prosecution of Daniel O'Connell and his followers in 1843–1844, and O'Connell gave him the nicknames 'Alphabet Smith' and 'the Vinegar Cruet'.[49] Smith's personality also seems to have been a factor in *Turner* v. *Robinson*: as we shall see, the defense objected to the strong language that the judge used to characterize Robinson's actions, and to the way Smith personally gathered evidence that he thought would support Turner's case.

On what basis did Turner claim a right to stop Robinson or anyone else from reproducing Wallis's painting? In an arrangement that was common by this time, Turner had contracted with the owner of the painting for the right to produce an engraving, as well as the right to publicly display the painting to attract subscribers.[50] Wallis was no longer the owner, as he had sold the painting to Augustus Leopold Egg, a fellow painter and the organizer of the 1857 Manchester Art Treasures Exhibition. Turner purchased from Egg 'the copyright, or the sole right

47 'Photographic Society', *Freeman's Journal*, 30 April 1859.

48 *Turner*, 10 Ir. Ch. at 125.

49 Daire Hogan, 'Smith, Thomas Berry Cusack (1795–1866)', *Oxford Dictionary of National Biography* (2004), https://doi.org/10.1093/ref:odnb/25916; 'The Late Master of the Rolls', *Dublin Daily Express*, 18 August 1866.

50 *Turner*, 10 Ir. Ch. at 121–124; and Foot, *'Death of Chatterton' Case*, pp. 6–8. On prevailing practices, see Deazley, 'Commentary on Fine Arts Copyright Act'; and Cooper, *Art and Modern Copyright*, pp. 115–117; 221–222.

to engrave and publish an engraving' of Wallis's painting.[51] Although there was no statutory copyright for paintings, for decades artists (and, as in the case of Egg, owners of paintings) had nonetheless sold the exclusive right to produce engravings of their paintings under the so-called Engravers' Copyright Acts passed in the eighteenth century. Also, purchasers of paintings tended to insist that the right to authorize engravings passed to them as part and parcel of their ownership of the physical canvas; moreover, since they controlled physical access to the canvas, they were effectively able to decide whether to allow engravings and on what terms. For certain well-known painters, payments for engraving rights could represent a significant portion of their income, sometimes as much as half.[52]

At trial Turner's counsel gave the example of Sir Edwin Henry Landseer's pair of paintings entitled *Time of Peace* and *Time of War* (1846). Counsel claimed that while Landseer's paintings sold for £1,000, the engraving rights went for £2,500.[53] In the present case, it was reported that Egg had purchased Wallis's painting for 100 guineas (the equivalent of £105) and that Turner had paid Egg £150 for the engraving rights.[54] The contract also provided other benefits for Egg as the owner of the painting. He was to receive twelve artist's proofs of Barlow's engraving for his own use, and in the event that Barlow died or was unable to finish the work, Egg had the right to approve Turner's choice for a new engraver. The engraving plate also had to be delivered to Egg, which would effectively give him control over subsequent prints from that plate.[55] Although not specified in the written agreement, Turner also included a prominent dedication to Egg on the print itself.[56]

---

51 *Turner*, 10 Ir. Ch. at 122.

52 Cooper, *Art and Modern Copyright*, pp. 116–117, 221–222; Deazley, 'Commentary on Fine Arts Copyright Act'; Bently, 'Art and the Making', pp. 337–338.

53 *Saunders's News-Letter*, 7 June 1859. On Landseer and copyright see Dyson, *Pictures to Print*, pp. 64–68. In 1861 D.R. Blaine gave the same example but the figures were £1260 and £3150 respectively. Deazley, 'Commentary on Fine Arts Copyright Act' (in footnote 33). The Master of the Rolls reportedly stated that, 'he understood the value of the engraving of Mr. [Henry Nelson] O'Neill's "Eastward Ho" was ten times greater than that of the painting itself' (*Freeman's Journal*, 14 June 1859).

54 *Turner*, 10 Ir. Ch. at 121–122.

55 Ibid., at 122–123.

56 The inscription on the print was as follows: 'Painted by H. Wallis; Published March 20th, 1862, by R. Turner, 32, Grey St. Newcastle-on-Tyne; Chatterton; — "The Marvellous Boy, the Sleepless Soul that perished in his pride." — Wordsworth.

Controlling access to the physical painting had long been crucial to securing a print publisher's investments, especially before the print was put on sale. Once an engraving of the painting was published, it could be protected by the Engravers' Copyright Acts. These statutes could be used to stop others from copying directly from an existing engraving, but the situation was more problematic in cases where a second engraver made an independent engraving from the original painting. The judgment in *De Berenger* v. *Wheble* (1819) suggested that a print publisher did not have a legally enforceable monopoly on all reproductions of a painting. In that case, a print publisher had purchased the sole right to make engravings of two paintings by Philip Reinagle. He hired an engraver to carry out the work, but the engraver made a sketch of the original painting and used this sketch to reproduce further engravings beyond the one the publisher had commissioned. These additional prints were then published in a periodical called the *Sporting Magazine*. The print publisher sued the engraver for copyright infringement, but the court refused the injunction on the grounds that these prints were copies of the painting rather than the first set of engravings. The court was keen to ensure that the copyright on the first reproduction did not impede further reproductions, because, in the words of Lord Chief Justice Abbott 'it would destroy all competition in the art [of engraving] to extend the monopoly to the painting itself'.[57]

This decision suggested the importance of strictly controlling access to the painting, and over time the law related to breach of trust or confidence provided a means of restricting the activity of individuals who were given temporary access to an artwork. If their access was understood to preclude making copies or even publishing a written description of the artwork (in cases where the creator wanted the very existence of the work to remain unknown), then they could be restrained from doing so, as was decided in the case of *Prince Albert* v. *Strange* (1849). Prince Albert had produced a series of etchings and entrusted the copper plates to a printer to make copies for the royal household's private enjoyment. Unfortunately, an employee of the

Engraved from the original picture in the possession of Augustus Egg, Esqre, R. A. to whom this Engraving is respectfully dedicated. Engraved by T. Oldham Barlow' (*Chatterton*, Metropolitan Museum of Art, https://www.metmuseum.org/art/collection/search/646564).

57 De Berenger v. Wheble (1819) 2 Starkk 548; 171 Eng. Rep. 732.

printer made unauthorized copies and sold them to another individual who announced a public exhibition of the etchings and prepared a printed catalogue with descriptions of each work. Prince Albert sued to prevent the exhibition and the publication of the catalogue. At first instance the court held that the creator of an artwork, like the author of a letter or other unpublished manuscript, had a common law property right that enabled them to decide when and how to publish the work or make its existence known to the public. The court determined that this right enabled Prince Albert to prohibit not only the exhibition, but also the publication of written descriptions of the etchings. *Prince Albert* v. *Strange* thus confirmed that common law 'copyright' existed for unpublished works of art just as it did for unpublished writings. But on appeal the Lord Chancellor added a second grounds for the injunction: since the defendant must have obtained the copies surreptitiously, he was in breach of trust or confidence as well as in violation of Prince Albert's common law property right in the etchings.[58]

For print publishers who sought to stop others from producing an independent engraving from the same painting, it was important to seek an exclusive contract with the owner of the painting, just as Turner had done with Egg. But what was Turner to do about members of the public (such as Robinson) who walked into a gallery and saw the painting on display? One solution would have been to wait until the engraving was completed before exhibiting the painting. A quality engraving took many months to produce. If by the time a major painting was exhibited a print was already on sale and protected by its own copyright (which covered the 'design' that had been engraved, and thus indirectly provided some protection for the painting), then rival publishers would be much less likely to invest in making a competing version even if they had access to the painting.[59] In an 1853 treatise on the current state of copyright law for artistic works, the barrister D. Roberton Blaine advised print publishers to proceed cautiously. He warned that if a painting or drawing were exhibited — either privately or publicly — before the engraving was published, 'then it would seem that the design is public property; and

58 Lionel Bently, 'Prince Albert v. Strange (1849)', in *Landmark Cases in Equity*, ed. by Charles Mitchell and Paul Mitchell (London: Hart Publishing, 2012), pp. 235–268, https://doi.org/10.5040/9781474200790.

59 Deazley, 'Commentary on Fine Arts Copyright Act'.

that the work of the engraver, exclusive of the design, is alone entitled to copyright; in other words, that any one may engrave the subject [i.e. the original painting or drawing] provided they do not copy it from the engraving'.[60]

Although Turner could have waited for Barlow to finish his work before exhibiting Wallis's painting in Dublin, proceeding in this way would have entailed significantly more risk, because exhibitions aimed at attracting subscribers were a means of gauging interest in the engraving.[61] Moreover, in this case Wallis's painting had already been featured in two major public exhibitions. Complicating matters still further, Wallis had already authorized the publication of a wood engraving illustration of his painting in the *National Magazine* in 1856 (see Figure 6).[62] The public exhibitions and the authorized engraving meant that the outcome of the case was uncertain. Turner's counsel had to persuade the court that, contrary to what Blaine had written in his 1853 treatise, and contrary to what Robinson's counsel argued, the design of Wallis's painting was not 'public property' just because it had already been exhibited and reproduced in a magazine.

The fact that there was no statutory copyright for paintings meant that Turner's counsel had to argue the case on the grounds of common law property rights in unpublished works and/or breach of confidence. With respect to the first grounds, Robinson's counsel conceded that Wallis might have enjoyed a common law property right in his painting that would enable him to restrict copying *before* publication, but not after. Therefore, it became crucial for the court to determine whether the wood engraving or the public exhibitions constituted the sort of 'publication' that would terminate the artist's common law rights. Meanwhile, protection against breach of confidence would require showing that

---

60 D. Roberton Blaine, *On the Laws of Artistic Copyright and their Defects* (London: John Murray, 1853), p. 27.

61 The contract specified that Turner was to pay Egg £50 in advance (one third of the total amount), and if Turner decided to abandon the engraving after the exhibition at Cranfield's, he could simply return the painting to Egg and the contract would be void. *Turner*, 10 Ir. Ch. at 122.

62 Ibid., at 121. Intriguingly, the British Museum owns a copy of the same wood engraving on *chine collé* that it labels as a 'proof illustration' for the magazine: https://www.britishmuseum.org/collection/object/P_1875-0710-3739). Did the publishers sell separate prints on *chine collé*, thereby elevating the status of this wood engraving?

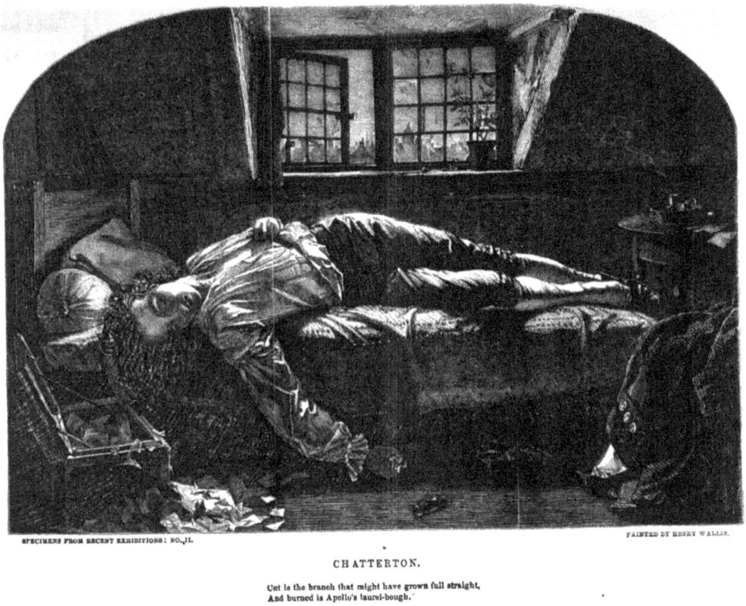

Fig. 6 Wood engraving of Wallis's *Chatterton*, in *The National Magazine*, edited by John Saunders and Westland Marston, 1 (1857), p. 33, https://babel.hathitrust.org/cgi/pt?id=uiug.30112109516473&view=1up&seq=49.

Robinson's viewing of the painting was subject to conditions. The case of *Prince Albert* v. *Strange* confirmed that it was a breach of confidence to make unauthorized copies of a work when the creator wanted them to remain private, but could the same rule apply to a painting that was reproduced in a magazine, shown in major public exhibitions, and described in published reviews?

Robinson's Defense

Just as Turner could be seen as taking a stand on behalf of the interests of the engraving trade, Robinson seems to have seen himself as defending the rights of photographers to co-exist with print publishers and offer their own reproductions of works of art. As his counsel reminded the court, Robinson did not sell his stereographs in secret. He advertised them openly, and when accused of piracy was confident enough to publish a new advertisement explaining that his photographs were not taken from the painting but from a living model.[63] Robinson also defended what he saw as the added value that stereoscopic photography brought to the viewer's experience of an artwork. As he explained in an affidavit, 'the Stereoscopic Pictures were only designed for the instrument, the Stereoscope, and when seen through it, produced an effect, which is not produced by the painting, and which cannot be produced by any painting'.[64] Similarly, some of Robinson's newspaper advertisements highlighted the fact that his photographs 'when seen in the Stereoscope stand out in bold relief, producing the most extraordinary effect'.[65]

Robinson's counsel developed several arguments in his defense. First, they questioned Turner's standing to sue. Turner was neither the artist nor the owner of the canvas, so he had to prove that he had acquired exclusive rights from one or the other. The final judgment suggests that Smith, the Master of the Rolls, took it for granted that the purchaser of an artwork automatically obtained any common law rights to exclude others from making copies.[66] But newspaper reports of proceedings suggest that Smith expressed doubts about whether Wallis had in fact transferred the 'copyright' to Egg as part of the initial sale. As a precaution, Turner had asked Egg to write to Wallis to make sure he did not oppose the engraving. Wallis replied that 'the sum that is to be given for the copyright appears to me to be very mild', but that if Turner thought it was reasonable then he agreed to the engraving.[67] Interestingly, Wallis also asked Egg to 'request that the picture, in being advertised, may not be called *The Death of Chatterton* but *Chatterton Dead*'.[68] Why Wallis objected to *The Death of Chatterton* is

63 *Evening Freeman* (Dublin), 26 November 1859; and *Saunders's News-Letter*, 26 November 1859.

64 Foot, *'Death of Chatterton' Case*, p. 14.

65 *Saunders's News Letter*, 3 May 1859, 5 May 1859; *Irish Times*, 5 May 1859.

66 'It would be a waste of time to add more than that the copyright is incident to the ownership, and passes at the Common Law with a transfer of the work of art' (*Turner*, 10 Ir. Ch. at 142). As Cooper has shown, the competing interests of painters and collectors was an important dimension in nineteenth-century debates about artistic copyright. Cooper, *Art and Modern Copyright*, pp. 115–117; and Elena Cooper, 'How Art was Different: Researching the History of Artistic Copyright', in *Research Handbook on the History of Copyright Law*, ed. by Isabella Alexander and H. Tomás Gómez-Arostegui (Cheltenham: Elgar, 2016), pp. 158–173.

67 Excerpts of letter from Henry Wallis to Augustus Egg quoted in *Saunders's News-Letter*, 28 November 1859.

68 Ibid.

not known, but when the painting was exhibited at the Royal Academy in 1856 the title listed in the catalogue was simply *Chatterton*.[69] Smith interpreted Wallis's request concerning the title and his explicit assent to the engraving in this letter to indicate that Wallis 'had not previously sold the copyright'.[70] Smith was also troubled by the fact that £50 out of the £150 that Turner promised to Egg were in fact delivered to Wallis. According to newspaper reports of the case, Smith stated several times that this payment seemed to be for the engraving right, suggesting that Egg had not automatically acquired this right when he took possession of the painting.[71] Turner was examined in court and his testimony, as reported by a Dublin newspaper, explained why he felt the need to ask Wallis for permission:

> I swore before, and I swear again, that Mr. Wallis sold the copyright when he sold the picture, and the exclusive right to print, engrave and publish same; that is the custom of the trade, the copyright goes with the picture unless it is reserved; Mr. Egg sold me the copyright; I applied for Mr. Wallis's consent merely to strengthen my case; I wanted his consent to the sale of the copyright by Egg to me; my reason for seeking the artist's consent was that the point has never been decided in our courts.[72]

Turner's testimony confirms that the litigation was prompted by a desire to clarify the state of common law protection for paintings in an art market that was evolving as a result of the advent of photography. Although engraving rights were recognized as a 'custom of the trade' and it was generally understood that they were transferred upon sale of the painting, the way photography threatened to disrupt the trade made judicial recognition of common law copyright in paintings urgent. In the final judgement, Smith mentioned that Wallis assented in writing to Egg's contract with Turner; however, he did not state that this consent was necessary for Egg to be able to transfer the rights to Turner. Ultimately, the court found that Turner had legitimate title and standing to sue for piracy as a 'bailee for hire' who enjoyed property in

69 *The Exhibition of the Royal Academy of Arts. MDCCCLVI. The Eighty-Eighth* (London: William Clowes and Sons, 1856), p. 17, https://www.royalacademy.org.uk/art-artists/exhibition-catalogue/ra-sec-vol88-1856.

70 *Freeman's Journal*, 25 November 1859.

71 *Saunders's News-Letter*, 25 November 1859, 26 November 1859, 28 November 1859.

72 *Freeman's Journal*, 25 November 1859.

the painting for the duration and the purpose specified in his contract with Egg.[73]

The second argument for the defense was that Wallis's work was not original and therefore could not be protected against copying. Robinson drew the court's attention to an engraving produced in 1794 by Edward Orme after a painting (now lost) by Henry Singleton (see Figure 7). In an affidavit, Robinson argued that Wallis took 'the idea and design of his picture' from Orme's engraving. He pointed to the similar attic setting with a window above the bed, 'the body in the same costume, and nearly in the same position, the poison bottle on the floor, the box of torn papers, the table, and all the minor details observable in Mr. Wallis' picture'.[74] Turner responded with an affidavit by Wallis stating that his painting was his 'original design and conception' and that he had never previously seen or heard of any picture by another artist representing the same subject.[75] The Orme engraving was produced in court, but from the bench Smith asserted that 'it was absurd to say that this engraving suggested to Mr. Wallis the idea of the picture'.[76]

The defense's third argument was that Wallis's work had already been published; therefore, any common law property rights in the work had been terminated. During the preliminary hearings in the Rolls Court, Smith stated that irrespective of the question of an artist's property rights at common law, he was fairly certain that the court had a duty to intervene because Robinson's actions constituted fraud. Robinson was given the privilege of viewing the painting at Cranfield's Gallery and took advantage of that privilege to produce unauthorized copies of the painting.[77] If Smith had issued an injunction solely on the grounds of breach of confidence, as the Court of Appeal would later do, he could have avoided the whole question of what constituted publication in the case of paintings. But he seems to have been genuinely interested in the

73 *Turner*, 10 Ir. Ch. at 146–147. He also stated that he planned to grant an injunction 'only for the period for which the painting is hired to the petitioner' (at 147). But ultimately the Court of Appeal granted a perpetual injunction on the grounds of breach of confidence rather than common law property rights (more on this later).

74 Foot, *'Death of Chatterton' Case*, p. 14.

75 Ibid., p. 15.

76 *Saunders's News-Letter*, 26 November 1859. See also *Turner*, 10 Ir. Ch. at 144. The hearing in which the engraving was shown is reported in *Saunders's News-Letter*, 7 June 1859.

77 *Freeman's Journal*, 14 June 1859.

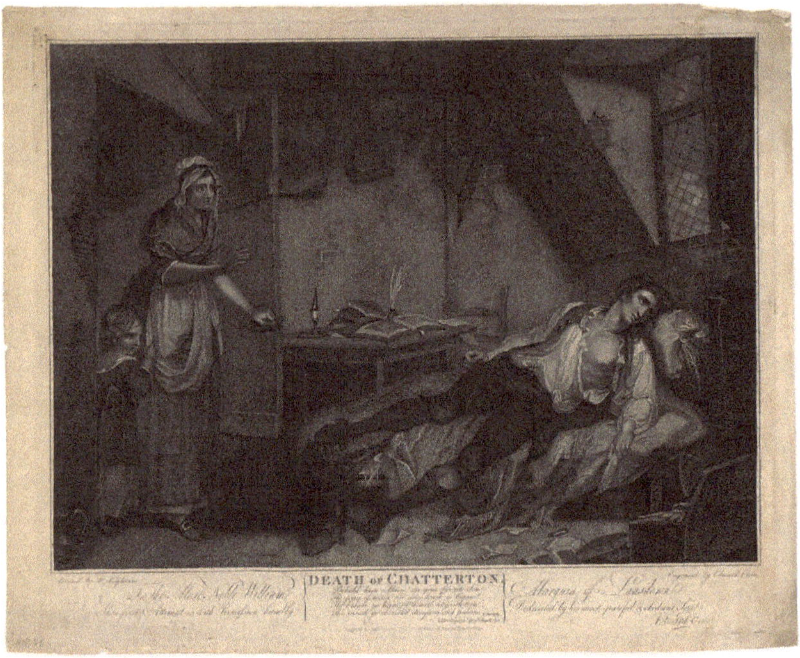

Fig. 7 Edward Orme, after Henry Singleton, *Death of Chatterton*, 1794. Library of Congress. Public Domain, https://www.loc.gov/item/2003674219/.

question and aware of its importance for painters, print publishers, and photographers. He warned Robinson that he was leaning heavily toward issuing an injunction, but allowing the case to go forward so that both sides could present evidence.[78] The legal definition of publication for a painting thus became a central aspect of the case. In the case of literary works, the law was clear: unpublished works were protected by the common law whereas published works could only be protected by the copyright statutes. Since there was no statutory copyright for paintings, the question of what constituted 'publication' was paramount.

What Constitutes 'Publication' of a Painting?

Robinson's lead counsel, a Mr. Sullivan, contended that Wallis's painting had been 'published' at least four times: in the *National*

78 *Saunders's News-Letter*, 14 June 1859.

Magazine, at the Royal Academy, at the Manchester Art Treasures Exhibition, and at Cranfield's Gallery.[79] He said that the magazine had given wide circulation to the design of Wallis's painting, and insisted that 'it had been held over and over again, that when an engraving was published and printed anybody could publish an engraving after the same subject if it were taken from the picture itself'.[80] With respect to the exhibitions, he argued that these were open to the public upon payment of a fee, without any restrictions attached. Referring to the exhibition of Wallis's painting at the Royal Academy, Sullivan proposed that anyone 'could go to the Academy and copy, and, if clever enough, carry away in his recollection the features of the picture, so as to enable him to copy it'.[81]

Turner's counsel argued that Wallis's painting had never been published in an unqualified way. Wallis had given permission to the editors of the *National Magazine* to publish a wood engraving, but his consent in this one instance could not be seen as a dedication to the public. In addition, the engraving in the magazine could not be considered a publication of the painting itself. Turner's counsel noted that many major paintings were now being reproduced in periodicals such as the *Art Journal*, and it would be a serious detriment to the owners of paintings if these illustrations were held to be publications of the paintings.[82] Although this point does not seem to have been elaborated in court, wood engravings were produced with a different process (relief rather than intaglio) and using different techniques and materials (wood rather than copper or steel), creating very different products. The relief process enabled the main features of an artwork to be reproduced as a series of intricate lines, but the carved-out areas of the woodblock would simply appear as white in the finished print. By contrast, the addition of hatchings and other techniques on a metal plate allowed the engraver to approximate effects of light and texture to a much greater extent. In that sense, specialists of nineteenth-century prints have distinguished between 'illustrations' (such as might be

79 *Turner*, 10 Ir. Ch. at 129. Counsel also argued that the sale to Egg constituted publication, which Smith found absurd (Ibid., at 143).
80 *Saunders's News-Letter*, 14 June 1859.
81 'Curious Copyright Case', *Western Daily Press* (Yeovil, England), 23 June 1859.
82 *Turner*, 10 Ir. Ch. at 127–128.

found in a periodical) and 'reproductive engravings' of the sort that Turner published.[83] In addition, wood engravings involved the use of several blocks, which were carved individually (often by several people working simultaneously) and then bolted together before being sent through the press. The borders between the individual wood blocks can often be seen in the printed image (note the clear vertical lines in Figure 6). Such block lines were characteristic of wood-engravings in the illustrated press. They were cheaper to produce and not as finely detailed as intaglio prints of the sort that Barlow produced for Turner.

The Master of the Rolls was receptive to the argument that a wood engraving in a magazine should not be considered a publication of the painting. Unlike a printed book, which Smith said could be considered the publication of the author's manuscript, a wood engraving could not be considered the publication of the painting itself. In the present case, Smith found the difference all the more striking because the illustration in the magazine was uncolored.[84] As he put it in the written judgment, 'a painting and a wood engraving, as imperfect as that published in the *National Magazine*, have but little resemblance to each other'.[85]

As for the exhibitions, Turner's counsel argued that they did not constitute publication because they were restricted: members of the public were allowed to view but not to copy the paintings. Counsel raised the analogy of a theater performance. Courts had held that the performance of a stage play did not terminate the author's right to decide whether and when to sell printed copies of the play. Similarly, an exhibition of a painting did not terminate the artist's right to restrict copying. According to Turner's counsel, Robinson had committed fraud and breach of confidence, 'for he availed himself of a privilege granted to him, to carry away surreptitiously in his mind the details of the picture'.[86] On this point counsel cited not only *Prince Albert* v. *Strange*, but also *Abernethy* v. *Hutchinson* (1825), in which a student had transcribed a lecture by a surgeon, which was then published in the medical journal *The Lancet*. The court granted an injunction on the grounds of breach of trust or contract after it was shown that students were admitted to such lectures on the understanding that they could take notes solely for their

83 Staley, *Post-Pre-Raphaelite Print*, p. 4.
84 *Saunders's News-Letter*, 28 November 1859.
85 *Turner*, 10 Ir. Ch. at 133.
86 Ibid., at 128.

own information.[87] The point of similarity was that Robinson had been admitted to view the painting on the understanding that he was not to make and sell copies of it.

Robinson claimed that the exhibition at Cranfield's was not subject to clear conditions and pointed out that the newspaper advertisements for the showing did not mention any engraving.[88] However, Turner's testimony and supporting affidavits showed that the goal of obtaining subscribers was widely known: 1,500 copies of a prospectus had been printed and distributed, and there was a subscription book in the room where the painting was on view.[89] During a hearing Smith described such exhibitions as an established and well-known practice among print publishers. He cited Henry Nelson O'Neill's *Eastward Ho!* (1857) as a recent example of a famous painting exhibited in Dublin to attract subscribers to an engraving. If counsel for Robinson were correct, Smith said, then anyone who saw *Eastward Ho!* on display might make and distribute copies for their own profit. On behalf of Robinson, Sullivan responded that 'such pictures might stand upon a different ground from that of a painting at the Royal Academy'.[90] His point seems to have been that even if the viewing at Cranfield's would not have constituted a publication of Wallis's painting, surely works exhibited at the Royal Academy could not be said to be 'unpublished'.

Gallery Rules Related to Copying

Unfortunately for Robinson, Smith thought it was important to inquire into the rules governing copying at the Royal Academy. According to Smith, the existence of such regulations would destroy the argument that public exhibition of an artwork constituted dedication to the public. And since neither Turner nor Robinson presented evidence on this subject, Smith announced that before committing his judgment to writing he would make inquiries of the Royal Academy and the organizers of the Manchester Art Treasures Exhibition to determine

87 Ronan Deazley, 'Commentary on Publication of Lectures Act 1835' (2008), in *Primary Sources on Copyright*, ed. by Bently and Kretschmer, http://www.copyrighthistory.org/cam/tools/request/showRecord?id=commentary_uk_1835.

88 Foot, *'Death of Chatterton' Case*, pp. 17–18.

89 Ibid., pp. 18–20.

90 *Saunders's News-Letter*, 14 June 1859.

what regulations were in place when Wallis's painting was displayed.[91] When he delivered his final judgment in January 1860, Smith presented the results of his research and took the opportunity to chastise the opposing parties. Smith suggested that his own reputation, and that of the Irish court system, was at stake:

> In a case of so much public importance, the inquiries which the Court had been obliged to make should have been made instead of giving the Court the trouble of making them; but he did not wish it to be said in England that he had given a judgment without inquiring into the practice, which was well-known, indeed notorious, that permission was not given to copy pictures in the Royal Academy.[92]

Smith's son happened to know the painter and arts administrator Richard Redgrave, who wrote to John Prescott Knight, Secretary of the Royal Academy, for policy details. Knight's reply, which was quoted in court, referred to an 1847 resolution that read: '[A]s much property in copyright is annually entrusted to the guardianship of the Royal Academy, the Council is compelled to disallow all copying within the walls from pictures sent for exhibition'.[93] Knight also cited a more recent resolution prohibiting copying during exhibitions, and gave the telling example of an artist who was refused permission to copy his own picture while it was on display. In addition, Knight confirmed that the Academy employed a guard to prevent anyone from copying surreptitiously. Smith obtained a further letter from Sir Charles Eastlake, President of the Royal Academy and director of the National Gallery. With respect to the Royal Academy, Eastlake confirmed Knight's statements. As for the National Gallery, he reported, 'there is no prohibition to copy pictures which are the property of the nation'.[94] Interestingly, Eastlake was also the first president of the Photographic Society, founded in London in 1853, though the excerpts from his letter quoted by the Master of the Rolls do not allude to photographic reproductions at all.

As Eastlake and Redgrave both knew, the policies of public art galleries with respect to photography were varied and evolving at this time. What is not mentioned in any of the published reports of *Turner*

91 *Saunders's News-Letter*, 28 November 1859.
92 *Saunders's News-Letter*, 31 January 1860.
93 Quoted in *Turner*, 10 Ir. Ch. at 135.
94 Ibid., at 136.

v. *Robinson* is that at this very moment the South Kensington Museum (later renamed the Victoria & Albert Museum) was launching a new program that would make low-cost photographic reproductions of artworks in its collection available to the public. In an initiative that was approved by the Privy Council on Education, the museum's own photography department produced these prints and sold them to the public at cost, a fact that vexed professional photographers who wanted to profit from demand for reproductions of artworks.[95] Redgrave, as the Inspector General for Art in the government's Department of Science and Art and the first Keeper of Paintings at the South Kensington Museum, was one of the initiators of this program. He would have been aware that his own institution's policies with respect to photography differed from those of other museums, which at this point gave much less thought to photography.[96] It is not known if the letters from Redgrave or Eastlake alluded to the work taking place at the South Kensington Museum, but even if they had Smith would have avoided the topic in his judgment. The court was interested in the practices of the Royal Academy with respect to the exhibition of paintings by living artists, not older works that Eastlake referred to confidently as the 'property of the nation'. Any discussion of authorized photographic reproductions would have muddied the waters. For Smith, the letters from Eastlake and Knight confirmed that the exhibition of Wallis's painting at the Royal Academy was 'no publication, as it would have been a breach of trust and a breach of an implied contract to have allowed the painting to be copied'.[97]

With respect to the Manchester Art Treasures Exhibition, Smith obtained similar evidence, with Redgrave once again acting as intermediary. The president of the committee that organized the Manchester exhibition confirmed that copying had not been allowed. The secretary of the same exhibition admitted that the art dealers and print publishers Paul and Dominic Colnaghi had published a series of photographic reproductions featuring 'gems' of the Art Treasures Exhibition, but that they had obtained written permission from all of

95 Ronan Deazley, 'Photography, Copyright, and the South Kensington Experiment', *Intellectual Property Quarterly*, 3 (2010), 293–311.

96 Hamber, '*A Higher Branch*', compares the practices of several institutions.

97 *Turner*, 10 Ir. Ch. at 137.

the owners whose paintings they photographed.[98] Interestingly, one of the photographers that contributed to the Colnaghi project, Leonida Caldesi, actually produced a photograph of Wallis's *Chatterton* during the Manchester exhibition, though this one was not published by the Colnaghis. The existence of this photograph was mentioned at trial; Turner explained that Caldesi had provided Egg with some copies of it for his personal use.[99] A different photograph of Wallis's painting had been taken by Charles Wright around the time of the Royal Academy exhibition in 1856. Wright actually exhibited this photograph at the February 1857 exhibition of the Photographic Society of London.[100] This fact was apparently not mentioned at trial. Had Robinson known about the public exhibition of a photograph of Wallis's *Chatterton*, he most likely would have tried to use the example to reinforce his argument that the painting had already been 'published' in multiple ways.

For the Master of the Rolls, all that mattered was that during the exhibitions of Wallis's painting at the Royal Academy and the Manchester Art Treasures Exhibition rules against copying were being enforced. Consequently, these exhibitions could not be considered publications of Wallis's painting. On behalf of Robinson, Sullivan objected to the way Smith had solicited these letters and relied on them to support his ruling. The letters had not been properly entered as evidence or made available for examination by opposing counsel. After a heated exchange with Sullivan, Smith decided to order a Master (a judicial official) to make an independent investigation of the rules observed at the Royal Academy and at the Manchester exhibition. Smith said that Robinson could appeal, and suspected that he would, since 'there is no species of litigation in which your client is not prepared to embark'.[101] Sullivan objected to Smith's language as prejudicial to his client and found

98 Ibid., at 139. The work referred to is *Photographs of the 'Gems of the Art Treasures Exhibition,' Manchester, 1857, by Signori Caldesi and Montecchi, Modern Series* (London: Paul and Dominic Colnaghi and Co./ T. Agnew and Sons, 1858).

99 *Freeman's Journal*, 5 November 1859; *Saunders's News-Letter*, 25 November 1859.

100 Hamber, *'A Higher Branch'*, 194. The title printed in the catalogue of the Photographic Society's 1857 exhibition was *'Death of Chatterton*, copy of Original Picture by H. Wallis, exhibited at the Royal Academy, 1856' ('Photographic Exhibitions in Britain 1839–1865: Records from Victorian Exhibition Catalogues', ed. by Roger Taylor, http://peib.dmu.ac.uk/index.php).

101 *Saunders's News-Letter*, 31 January 1860.

his personal inquiry into gallery practices to be highly irregular. One newspaper reporter understood Sullivan to say, 'no court of justice should take the conduct of any case into its own hands for the purpose of punishing a suitor'.[102]

What Constitutes an Illegal Copy?

Robinson appealed both the injunction and the order for the Master's formal inquiry into gallery rules. The Court of Appeal determined that the inquiry was not necessary because the case could be decided on the basis of breach of confidence. Robinson did not deny having imitated the composition and details of Wallis's painting. For the Lord Chancellor, it was clear that Robinson did not have the right to do this, and that he knew as much. Turner had published a warning to photographers and Robinson never denied having seen this warning. Robinson's own advertisement, which responded to the allegation of piracy by insisting that he had photographed from a living model, also suggested to the court that Robinson knew that copying the painting was forbidden.[103] The Lord Justice of Appeal also found that Robinson had acted surreptitiously and was in breach of confidence. He cited the fact that Robinson had not copied the painting in Cranfield's Gallery, but reproduced the scene in his own studio, as further proof that he knew that he was not allowed to copy it.[104]

It will be recalled that Robinson denied having copied the painting at all. His goal was not to produce a single-image photograph but a stereoscopic view. Since the photographs that appeared on his stereo cards were taken from a live model and props in his studio, he did not see how they could be considered copies of the painting. His counsel added that the resulting stereo cards could not be said to harm the sale of the engraving because they were produced in a different manner and for a different purpose.[105]

That argument echoed the judge's decision in the case of *Martin v. Wright* (1833), which is fully discussed in Simon Stern's chapter in

102 Ibid.
103 *Turner*, 10 Ch. at 512–518.
104 Ibid. at 519.
105 *Turner*, 10 Ir. Ch. at 130.

this volume.[106] Briefly, the court held that the public exhibition of a diorama reproducing the design of the well-known painting and print of *Belshezzar's Feast* by John Martin did not constitute infringement because 'exhibiting for profit is in no way analogous to selling a copy of the Plaintiff's print, but is dealing with it in a very different manner'.[107] In other words, charging admission to view a representation of Martin's design was not the same as selling copies of the print. But counsel for Turner insisted that in the present case Robinson's stereo cards were in fact copies of Wallis's painting, and that these copies would necessarily harm the sale of Turner's projected engraving.

Martin v. *Wright* was decided on the basis of statutory copyright, whereas in the Irish Rolls Court *Turner* v. *Robinson* was being discussed in terms of common law protection for unpublished works. The scope of protection (what constituted infringement) was understood to be different in these two areas of law. Statutory copyright developed a number of exceptions that made it somewhat more flexible than common law protection for unpublished works, which was generally held to be quite broad.[108] In this context it is not surprising that counsel for Turner made the following argument: 'if persons could pirate the idea of a painting, and publish it as they pleased, the rights of engravers would be very seriously invaded'.[109] Robinson objected to such a broad right in the 'idea of a painting'. He claimed that his stereo cards, though indeed based on the *idea* of Wallis's painting, were not *copies* of the painting itself.

In the Rolls Court, Smith found the fact that Robinson had copied to be obvious, though he insisted that it was highly unlikely that Robinson had worked from memory alone. In newspaper reports of the hearings, Smith is quoted saying that he thought Robinson must have worked from the engraving in the *National Magazine*; how else would he have been able to reconstruct even minor details? His choice of colors, however, indicated to the judge that Robinson had also benefited from his access to the painting at Cranfield's Gallery.[110] Wallis's color choices

106 See Chapter 4 of the present volume.
107 Martin v. Wright (1833), 6 Simm. 297 (at 298–299). See Simon Stern's chapter.
108 See Cooper, *Art and Modern Copyright*, pp. 215–216.
109 *Saunders's News-Letter*, 7 June 1859.
110 *Saunders's News-Letter*, 14 June 1859, 21 November 1859. The possibility that Robinson had worked from a photograph was apparently not broached in court. If

were indeed distinctive — note the red hair, violet breeches, and red coat in Figure 1 — and like other artists associated with the Pre-Raphaelite style, Wallis painted on a white ground, which heightened the vibrancy of the colors. Although Robinson's hand-colored stereo cards (Figure 2) could not possibly reproduce the vividness of the original, the fact that he used similar colors clearly worked against him in court. Smith acknowledged that it was reasonable to doubt whether Robinson's stereo cards would represent 'a serious injury to the owner of this valuable painting', but he insisted that photographic reproductions posed a clear threat, evoking a sort of slippery slope that had to be avoided: 'The photograph might by a very easy process be enlarged to the size of the original, and thus an unimportant piracy might be followed up by the adoption of another mode of piracy which would be most injurious to the owner of the painting'.[111] It will be noticed that the judge consistently referred to the rights of the owner of the painting (in this case Egg, and by extension Turner as 'bailee') rather than to the artist himself.

The Court of Appeal was similarly unreceptive to the idea that Robinson's stereographs should not be considered copies of the painting. The Lord Justice of Appeal stated that Robinson's stereograph 'does not, in my opinion, lose the character of a copy because it has been effected, not in the usual mode, but by an exercise of memory, and by ingenious scientific operations, which, by rendering the likeness more accurate, must or may diminish the demand for engravings, which constitutes so large a proportion of [the painting's] value'.[112] The fact that Robinson did not take the photographs directly from the painting but from a living model and props in his studio did not mean that they were not copies. On the contrary, the Lord Justice of the Appeal stated, 'it is through this medium [i.e. the restaging of the painting as a *tableau*] that the photograph has been made a perfect representation of the painting'.[113] Thus the Court of Appeal held that Robinson's stereographs were copies of the painting, and that it was illegal for him to make these copies regardless of the process or medium involved.

Turner had any evidence that Robinson had taken a photo in the gallery, this most certainly would have been mentioned.

111 *Freeman's Journal*, 14 June 1859; *Irish Times*, 14 June 1859.

112 *Turner*, 10 Ir. Ch. at 519.

113 Ibid. at 521.

The surviving record of proceedings suggests that there was no discussion of the contemporary cultural practice of creating *tableaux vivants*, or of whether it would have been lawful to restage Wallis's painting as a 'living picture' if no photographic prints had been offered for sale. Did the *tableau* in his studio already constitute an illegal copy of the painting, or would it have been too ephemeral to rise to the level of infringement? The fact that Robinson had produced photographic prints that closely resembled the painting may have made such a question moot. But British courts did face this question in the 1890s, when major commercial theaters popularized the staging of 'living pictures' for large paying audiences. The owners of some of the paintings being imitated on stage sued for copyright infringement under the 1862 act. In one case that went all the way to the House of Lords, it was held that a *tableau vivant* performed as part of a stage play and newspaper illustrations of the same *tableau* did not infringe the copyright in the painting itself. The Lord Chancellor acknowledged that an infringing copy could be made from an intermediate work such as a *tableau vivant*, but in the case at hand he found that the newspaper illustrations were not sufficiently similar to the painting. As for the 'living picture' itself, it had already been decided at first instance and affirmed by the Court of Appeal that the live staging of the painting was not infringing because it was only temporary and did not result in any material 'copy' that could be forfeited under the 1862 act. In other words, a painting could be infringed by a drawing, photograph, or another painting, but not by the *tableau vivant* itself.[114] The facts in *Robinson* v. *Turner* were different because the defendant had imitated Wallis's painting so closely, and because he was offering physical copies for sale.

Legal Significance v. Commercial and Cultural Effects

What is the significance of *Turner* v. *Robinson* for the history of artistic copyright? As Elena Cooper has explained, the Master of the Rolls offered an expansive interpretation of common law protection for

114 *Hanfstaengl v. HR Baines and Co.* [1895] AC 20 (HL); Teilmann-Lock, *Object of Copyright*, pp. 105–107; David Lindsay, '*Tableaux Vivants:* Permissible Transformation or Infringing Mimesis?', paper presented at the International Society for the History and Theory of Intellectual Property, Sydney, 2019.

paintings. The scope of this right was held to be quite broad, since the process by which Robinson made his reproductions did not matter to the courts, nor did the fact that stereoscopic views were different media than mezzotint engravings. When copyright protection was extended to paintings in 1862, the statute prohibited unauthorized copies of the painting 'and the design thereof' produced 'by any means and of any size'.[115] In some ways, Smith's judgment anticipated this broad ownership right, though of course he decided the case based on the common law rather than the copyright statute. The common law protection for paintings that Smith recognized was quite durable, since it could not be terminated by the publication of an engraving or by the exhibition of the painting in cases where the display was for a specific purpose (such as to attract subscribers) or subject to restrictions against copying (as at the Royal Academy). Theoretically, this common law protection in paintings could subsist alongside the protection offered by the Fine Arts Copyright Act of 1862. Because the statute protected artworks from the moment of creation rather than 'publication' (as had long been the case with literary works), as long as an artwork was deemed 'unpublished', it could be protected by both common law and statutory copyright.[116] And yet, according to Cooper, the decision in *Turner* v. *Robinson* was not looked to by artists or collectors, in part because its principles were not subsequently endorsed by a higher court, and in part because of uncertainty about who would own the common law copyright. The case law with respect to unpublished writings had clearly established that the author of a letter retained the common law copyright. The recipient owned the physical letter, but did not have the right to publish it without the author's consent. By contrast, Smith held — despite the hesitations he voiced in court — that the common law copyright passed automatically to the purchaser of a painting. Artists did not generally like this principle.[117]

On the question of whether public exhibition of an artwork divested an artist of their rights, *Turner* v. *Robinson* was cited in the United States

115 Fine Arts Copyright Act, sec. 1. The judgment in *Gambart* v. *Ball* (1863), discussed in Chapter 4 of this volume, confirmed that a reproduction in a new medium and in a reduced size (such as a photograph of an engraving) was infringing if it conveyed the same idea or offered the viewer the same pleasure as the original. See also Cooper, *Art and Modern Copyright*, p. 229.

116 Cooper, *Art and Modern Copyright*, p. 214.

117 Ibid., pp. 214–215.

as well as in the United Kingdom.[118] From the perspective of print publishers like Turner, such a ruling had become urgent because of the increased frequency and scale of public exhibitions. In the case of works by well-known artists, it was rarely practical to wait for an engraving to be finished before displaying the work, and photographic reproductions seemed much more threatening than rival engravings. Engravings like Barlow's took a significant amount of time and resources to produce, and major print publishes protected their investments further by making formal or informal agreements not to compete directly on a particular subject or in a given territory.[119] Photography was disruptive not only because it could be used to facilitate the engraving process — significantly reducing the amount of time an engraver needed access to the physical painting — but also because photographic reproductions could compete directly with engravings, as Turner claimed Robinson's stereographs would do. Unauthorized photographic reproductions of the engraving itself constituted another threat, and these were the subject of significant litigation in the 1860s, when major print publishers, especially Ernest Gambart and Henry Graves, turned to the courts to protect their prints against piracy by photographers.[120]

Cooper has suggested that one practical consequence of *Turner* v. *Robinson* is that explicit rules prohibiting copying of works by living artists became more common in major galleries in the British Isles.[121] But did the decision alter the practices of photographers, particularly those inclined to stage scenes from famous paintings? Pellerin and May have shown that stereoscopic photographs of *tableaux vivants* constituted an important but hitherto neglected genre in Victorian photography, and this genre continued to flourish after *Turner* v. *Robinson* and the adoption of the Fine Arts Copyright Act in 1862. So far, no subsequent lawsuit against a photographer for restaging a painting as a tableau vivant has been found.[122] One explanation for this might be that Robinson's *Death of Chatterton* was a rather extreme example: he imitated Wallis's painting

118 American examples include Oertel v. Wood, 40 How. Pr. 10 (N.Y. Sup. 1870); Parton v. Prang, 18 F. Cas. 1273 (C.C. Mass. 1872); and Gross v. Seligman, 212 F. 930 (2d Cir. 1914).

119 Dyson, *Pictures to Print*, pp. 64–65.

120 See Chapter 4; and Cooper, *Art and Modern Copyright*, pp. 219–248.

121 Cooper, *Art and Modern Copyright*, p. 214.

122 Pellerin and May, *Poor Man's Picture Gallery*, 28; Jacobi, 'Tate Painting and the Art of Stereoscopic Photography'.

very closely, whereas most photographers who restaged scenes from paintings introduced variations of one sort or another.[123]

In his study of the symbiotic relationship between Pre-Raphaelite painting and photography, Michael Bartram remarked that the result of Robinson's attention to detail was 'at once bizarre and tawdry, though doubtless photography had been encouraged to turn in this direction by the obsessive literalism of painting at this time. Painting and photography could go no further than this in their exchange of identities'.[124] But as Martin Meisel has explained in his study of the complex relationship between painting and theater during this period, for contemporary audiences much of the appeal of *tableaux vivants* depended upon the spectator being able to recognize a specific painting and judge how closely its details had been recreated.[125] The same could be said for Robinson's remediation of Wallis's painting.

In any case, Robinson's *The Death of Chatterton* clearly inspired other photographers to treat the same subject following the same method. The Birmingham photographer Michael Burr produced at least two versions of a stereograph of the same scene (see Figures 8 and 9). Although it seems likely that Burr got the idea from Robinson's stereographs — or perhaps from newspaper accounts of *Turner* v. *Robinson*? — he did not necessarily work directly from Robinson's cards to recreate the scene. Wallis's painting was exhibited in Birmingham in the spring of 1860 (again as part of Turner's campaign to advertise Barlow's engraving), and Burr may have seen the canvas at that time.[126] Burr does not seem to have been sued (at least no record of a case has been found), but according to Pellerin one of his stereographs was in turn pirated by an unknown photographer.[127] In addition to these stereographs, a *carte-de-visite* version of *The Death of Chatterton* was produced by an unknown photographer in the early 1860s (see Figure 10). The text on the bottom

123 See, for example, the different stereoscopic views based on Philip Calderon's *Broken Vows*, in Pellerin and May, *Poor Man's Picture Gallery*, pp. 20–23.

124 Michael Bartram, *The Pre-Raphaelite Camera: Aspects of Victorian Photography* (London: Weidenfeld and Nicolson, 1985), p. 155.

125 Meisel, *Realizations*, 93.

126 'The Ratcliff Portrait and the *Death of Chatterton*', *Birmingham Journal*, 7 April 1860. On links between Robinson and Burr see Pellerin and May, *Poor Man's Picture Gallery*, pp. 29–30.

127 This is the stereograph that is mistakenly attributed to Robinson in Greenhill, 'The Death of Chatterton'. Denis Pellerin, personal communication, 14 April 2020.

of the card is from a biography of Chatterton published in 1810, but that text was almost certainly copied directly from the back of Robinson's stereo card, which contains a longer extract from the same biography (see Figure 2).[128] We thus know of at least four unauthorized versions of *The Death of Chatterton* that seem to have been directly inspired by Robinson's, though it is quite possible that there were additional versions that have not survived.

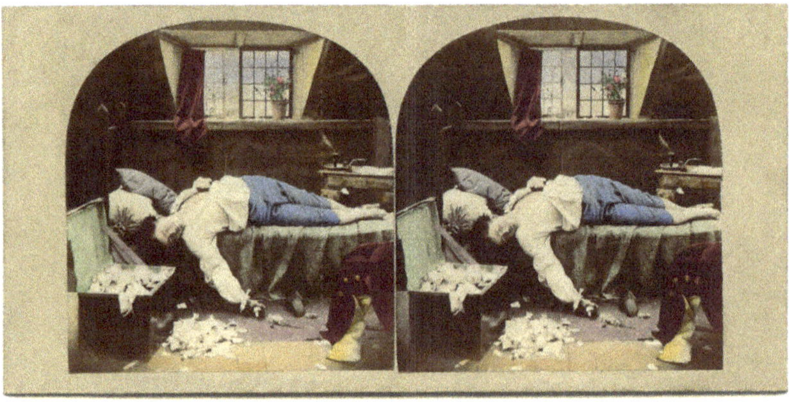

Fig. 8 Michael Burr, *The Death of Chatterton*, ca. 1860, Collection of Dr. Brian May, reproduced with kind permission.

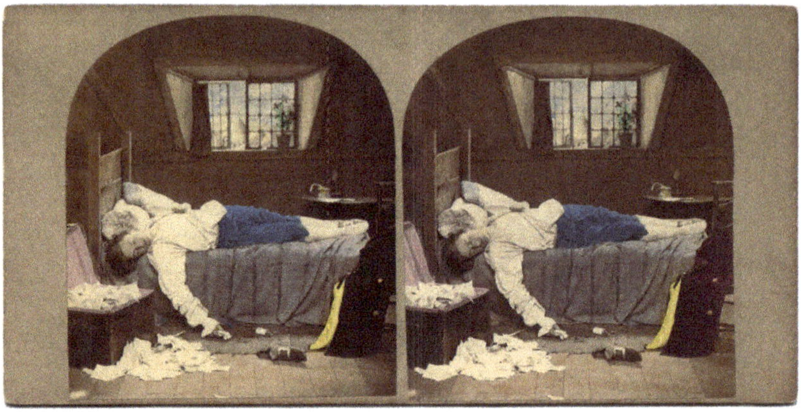

Fig. 9 A second version of *The Death of Chatterton* by Michael Burr, ca. 1860, Collection of Dr. Brian May, reproduced with kind permission.

128 Alexander Chalmers, 'Life of Chatterton', in Chalmers, *The Works of the English Poets, from Chaucer to Cowper*. 21 vols. (London: J. Johnson and others, 1810), vol. 15: 375.

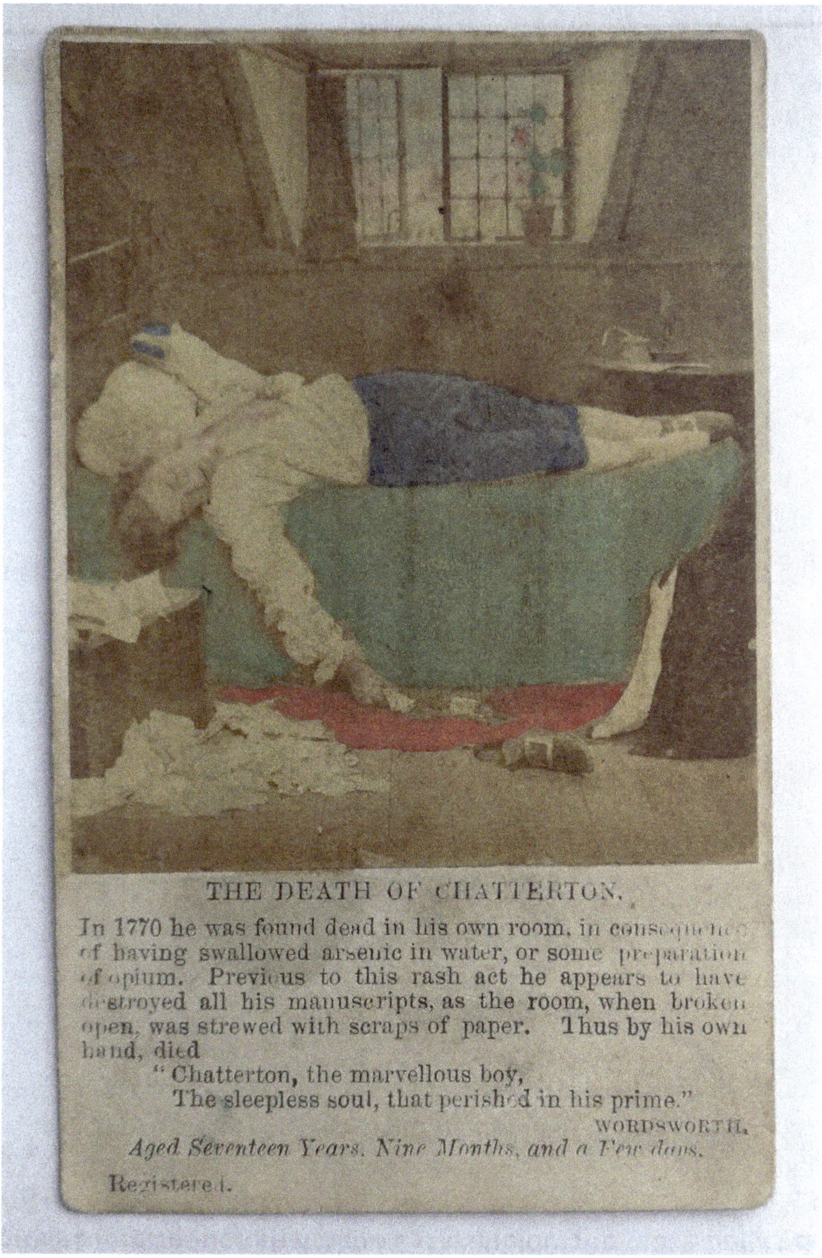

Fig. 10 An anonymous and undated *carte de visite* that closely resembles the Burr photograph in Figure 9, but which uses part of the text printed on the back of Robinson's card (Figure 2). Collection of Anthony Hamber, CC BY.

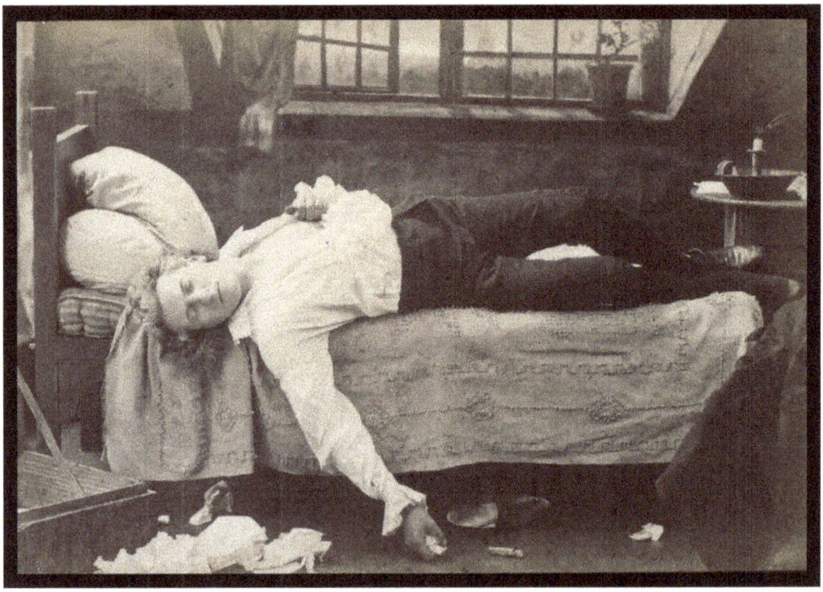

Fig. 11 Herbert Rose Barraud, photograph of Wilson Barrett as Chatterton at the Princess's Theater, 1884, Guy Little Theatrical Photograph Collection, Victoria and Albert Museum, http://collections.vam.ac.uk/item/O227561/guy-little-theatrical-photograph-photograph-barraud-herbert-rose/.

The extent to which Wallis's painting shaped subsequent representations of Chatterton could be the subject of a fascinating study of its own. Only a couple of examples can be mentioned here. In the mid-1880s, the actor Wilson Barrett portrayed Chatterton in a popular one-act play. A series of cabinet-sized photographs of Barrett in this role include one that closely imitates Wallis's painting (see Figure 11). The photographer, Herbert Rose Barraud, was not the one who had the idea to restage Wallis's painting, since that was part of the *mise-en-scène* of the one-act play. But Barraud was unknowingly following in Robinson's footsteps. And though Robinson has been largely forgotten today, recreations of Wallis's painting in the form of photographs from *tableaux vivants* continue to be produced. In 2011, the British Nigerian artist Yinka Shonibare restaged the painting, but substituted the likeness of Admiral Lord Nelson for that of Chatterton.[129] And it will perhaps come as little surprise that

129 Yinka Shonibare, 'Fake Death Picture (Death of Chatterton — Henry Wallis)', 2011, Yale Center for British Art, https://collections.britishart.yale.edu/vufind/Record/4229466.

among the countless photographs of *tableaux vivants* based on classic paintings that circulated on social media during the Covid-19 pandemic in the spring of 2020 (often using the hashtag #GettyChallenge), there were some personalized recreations of Wallis's *Chatterton.*[130]

Conclusion

What explains the fact that Burr and other photographers who restaged paintings were not sued by copyright owners? Should the case against Robinson be seen as an outlier? Insofar as there are many factors explaining why an individual such as Turner would decide to pursue litigation, it may not be possible to provide definitive answers to these questions, but I will offer what I think is a plausible explanation based on the legal and commercial contexts. Turner sued in 1859 because Robinson's actions were provocative and because he wanted to take a stand on behalf of print publishers against photographers at a moment when there was no statutory copyright for paintings. After the Fine Arts Copyright Act was adopted in 1862, print publishers continued to worry about photography, but most of their attention turned to the problem of photographs taken directly from engravings, rather than the more complex case of photographs of *tableaux vivants* based on paintings.[131] It could be that within a few years the extent to which stereoscopic views actually harmed the sale of quality engravings was understood to be less than what Turner and others feared in the late 1850s. The actions of both Robinson and Turner made sense given the legal, cultural, and economic contexts. But the fact that stereoscopic views based on *tableaux vivants* of famous paintings continued to be produced after 1860 should caution us against assuming that *Turner* v. *Robinson* had any direct effect on artistic and commercial practices.

Though decided on the grounds of common law property rights and breach of confidence rather than on the grounds of statutory copyright, the decisions in the Rolls Court and in the Court of Appeal reflected

130 For example, Zoetica Ebb, 'Chatterton Revisited', London, 2020, https://twitter.com/zoetica/status/1249690644991410177.

131 As Cooper explains, after 1862 the print publishers also preferred the new option (which they helped to bring about) of summary proceedings before magistrates rather than litigation in the higher courts. Cooper, *Art and Modern Copyright*, pp. 232–242.

a fairly widespread perception that the lack of statutory protection for paintings represented a gap in the law. Indeed, in the course of his opinion, Smith cited speeches and legal opinions that he thought could be employed effectively to lobby for statutory copyright in paintings.[132] The rulings of the Rolls Court and the Court of Appeal also pointed toward a more expansive view of what constituted an infringing 'copy'. Both courts found that Robinson's stereo cards were illegal 'copies' of Wallis's painting, regardless of the process he used, let alone the very different viewing experience enabled by stereography. Robinson did not have the right to reproduce the 'design' or the 'idea' of Wallis's painting. The fact that the copying was indirect and transposed the subject of *Chatterton* into a new medium was deemed irrelevant by the courts. In that sense, *Turner* v. *Robinson* confirmed an ongoing expansion in the scope of property rights in visual works.

Bibliography

Bajac, Quentin, *Tableaux vivants: Fantaisies photographiques victoriennes (1840–1880)* (Paris: Réunion des musées nationaux, 1999).

Bartram, Michael, *The Pre-Raphaelite Camera: Aspects of Victorian Photography* (London: Weidenfeld and Nicolson, 1985).

Bently, Lionel, 'Art and the Making of Modern Copyright Law', in *Dear Images: Art, Copyright, and Culture*, ed. by Daniel McClean and Karsten Schubert (London: Ridinghouse/ICA, 2002), pp. 331–351.

——, 'Prince Albert v. Strange (1849)', in *Landmark Cases in Equity*, ed. by Charles Mitchell and Paul Mitchell (London: Hart Publishing, 2012), pp. 235–268, https://doi.org/10.5040/9781474200790.ch-008.

Bently, Lionel, and Martin Kretschmer, eds., *Primary Sources on Copyright (1450–1900)*, http://www.copyrighthistory.org.

Blaine, D. Roberton, *On the Laws of Artistic Copyright and their Defects* (London: John Murray, 1853).

Chalmers, Alexander, 'Life of Chatterton', in Alexander Chalmers, *The Works of the English Poets, from Chaucer to Cowper*. 21 vols. (London: J. Johnson and others, 1810), vol. 15: 375.

Claudet, Laura, 'Stereoscopy', in *Encyclopedia of Nineteenth-Century Photography*, ed. by John Hannavy. 2 vols. (New York and London: Routledge, 2008), vol. 2: 1338–1341, https://doi.org/10.4324/9780203941782.

132 *Turner*, 10 Ir. Ch. at 147–148.

Clayton, Zoe, 'Stereographs', *V&A Blog*, 29 January 2013, https://www.vam.ac.uk/blog/caring-for-our-collections/stereographs.

Cooper, Elena, *Art and Modern Copyright: The Contested Image* (Cambridge: Cambridge University Press, 2018), https://doi.org/10.1017/9781316840993.

——, 'How Art was Different: Researching the History of Artistic Copyright', in *Research Handbook on the History of Copyright Law*, ed. by Isabella Alexander and H. Tomás Gómez-Arostegui (Cheltenham, UK: Elgar, 2016), pp. 158–173, https://doi.org/10.4337/9781783472406.00015.

Deazley, Ronan, 'Commentary on Fine Arts Copyright Act 1862'(2008), in *Primary Sources on Copyright*, ed. by Lionel Bently and Martin Kretschmer, http://www.copyrighthistory.org/cam/tools/request/showRecord?id=commentary_uk_1862.

——, 'Commentary on Publication of Lectures Act 1835' (2008), in *Primary Sources on Copyright*, ed. by Lionel Bently and Martin Kretschmer, http://www.copyrighthistory.org/cam/tools/request/showRecord?id=commentary_uk_1835.

——, 'Photography, Copyright, and the South Kensington Experiment', *Intellectual Property Quarterly*, 3 (2010), 293–311.

——, 'Struggling with Authority: The Photograph in British Legal History', *History of Photography*, 27 (2003), 236–46, https://doi.org/10.1080/03087298.2003.10441249.

Dyson, Anthony, *Pictures to Print: The Nineteenth-Century Engraving Trade* (London: Farrand Press, 1984).

Edwards, Steve, *The Making of English Photography: Allegories* (University Park: Pennsylvania State University Press, 2006).

The Exhibition of the Royal Academy of Arts. MDCCCLVI. The Eighty-Eighth (London: William Clowes and Sons, 1856), https://www.royalacademy.org.uk/art-artists/exhibition-catalogue/ra-sec-vol88-1856.

Foot, Charles H., *'The Death of Chatterton' Case. Turner v. Robinson* (Dublin: Edward Ponsonby, 1860).

Fowle, Frances, 'Henry Wallis, *Chatterton*, 1856' (2000), Tate, https://www.tate.org.uk/art/artworks/wallis-chatterton-n01685.

Greenhill, Gillian B., 'The Death of Chatterton, or Photography and the Law', *History of Photography* 5 (1981), 199–205, https://doi.org/10.1080/03087298.1981.10442668.

Groom, Nick, 'Chatterton, Thomas (1752–1770)', *Oxford Dictionary of National Biography* (2004), https://doi.org/10.1093/ref:odnb/5189.

Hamber, Anthony J. *'A Higher Branch of the Art': Photographing the Fine Arts in England, 1839–1880* (Amsterdam: Gordon and Breach Publishers, 1996).

Harding, Colin, 'L is for...London Stereoscopic Company: the Home of 100,000 Views', Science and Media Museum, 26 October 2013, https://blog.scienceandmediamuseum.org.uk/a-z-photography-l-is-for-london-stereoscopic-company/.

Haworth-Booth, Mark, ed., *The Golden Age of British Photography, 1839–1900* (New York: Aperture, 1984).

Helmreich, Anne, 'Henry Wallis, "The Death of Chatterton"', in *The Victorians: British Painting, 1837–1901*, ed. by Malcolm Warner (Washington: National Gallery of Art, 1996), pp. 101–102.

Hogan, Daire, 'Smith, Thomas Berry Cusack (1795–1866)', *Oxford Dictionary of National Biography* (2004), https://doi.org/10.1093/ref:odnb/25916.

Jacobi, Carol, 'Tate Painting and the Art of Stereoscopic Photography' (2014), Tate, https://www.tate.org.uk/whats-on/tate-britain/display/bp-spotlight-poor-mans-picture-gallery-victorian-art-and-stereoscopic/essay.

Jeffrey, Ian, 'British Photography from Fox Talbot to E.O. Hoppé', in *The Real Thing: An Anthology of British Photographs 1840–1950* (London: Arts Council of Great Britain, 1975), pp. 5–24.

Keats, John, *Endymion: A Poetic Romance* (London: Taylor and Hessey, 1818).

Kelly, Linda, *The Marvellous Boy: The Life and Myth of Thomas Chatterton* (London: Weidenfeld and Nicolson, 1971).

Lindsay, David, '*Tableaux Vivants:* Permissible Transformation or Infringing Mimesis?', paper presented at the International Society for the History and Theory of Intellectual Property, Sydney, 2019.

Marshall, Nancy Rose, *City of Gold and Mud: Painting Victorian London* (New Haven: Yale University Press, 2012).

McCauley, Anne, '"Merely Mechanical": On the Origins of Photographic Copyright in France and Great Britain', *Art History*, 31 (2008), pp. 57–78, https://doi.org/10.1111/j.1467-8365.2008.00583.x.

Meisel, Martin, *Realizations: Narrative, Pictorial, and Theatrical Arts in Nineteenth-Century England* (Princeton University Press, 1983).

Mollan, Charles, *Irish National Inventory of Historic Scientific Instruments* (Blackrock, Ireland: Samton Limited, 1995).

Pellerin, Denis, 'From 3D to 2D...and Back', 'Thinking 3D' project, 1 October 2018, https://www.thinking3d.ac.uk/3Dto2D/.

Pellerin, Denis, and Brian May, *The Poor Man's Picture Gallery: Stereoscopy versus Paintings in the Victorian Era* (London: The London Stereoscopic Company, 2014).

Photographs of the "Gems of the Art Treasures Exhibition", Manchester, 1857, by Signori Caldesi and Montecchi, Modern Series (London: Paul and Dominic Colnaghi and Co./ T. Agnew and Sons, 1858).

Pittock, John H., 'Thomas Chatterton (10 November 1752–24 August 1770)', in *Dictionary of Literary Biography*, vol. 109: *Eighteenth-Century British Poets: Second Series*, ed. by John Sitter (Detroit: Gale, 1991), pp. 64–83.

Ruskin, John, *Notes on Some of the Principal Pictures Exhibited in the Rooms of the Royal Academy, and the Society of Painters in Water Colours: No. II — 1856 (6th ed.)* (London: Smith, Elder & Co., 1856).

Sieberling, Grace, with Carolyn Blore, *Amateurs, Photography, and the Mid-Victorian Imagination* (Chicago: University of Chicago Press, 1986).

Staley, Allen, *The Post-Pre-Raphaelite Print: Etching, Illustration, Reproductive Engraving, and Photography in England in and around the 1860s* (New York: Miriam & Ira D. Wallach Art Gallery, Columbia University, 1995).

Taylor, Roger, ed., 'Photographic Exhibitions in Britain 1839–1865: Records from Victorian Exhibition Catalogues', http://peib.dmu.ac.uk/index.php.

Teilmann-Lock, Stina, *The Object of Copyright: A Conceptual History of Originals and Copies in Literature, Art and Design* (London: Routledge, 2016), https://doi.org/10.4324/9781315814476.

Weiss, Marta, 'La photographie mise en scène dans l'album victorien', in *La Photographie mise en scène: créer l'illusion du réel*, ed. by Lori Pauli (London/New York: Merrell, 2006), pp. 81–99.

Wood, R. Derek, *The Calotype Patent Lawsuit of Talbot v. Laroche 1854* (Bromley, Kent: privately published by R. D. Wood, 1975), http://www.midley.co.uk/laroche/TalbotvLaroche.htm.

Wordsworth, William, *Poems in Two Volumes* (London: Longman, Hurst, Rees, and Orme, 1807).

6. Before an Image Was Worth a Thousand Words

Ben-Hur and Copyright's Right of Derivatives

Oren Bracha

In 1834 Justice Joseph Story wrote that in the law of copyright one could get the closest to 'the metaphysics of the law'.[1] Nowhere was this observation truer than with respect to the rules pertaining to the scope of copyright and its infringement. The puzzles strewn across this area of the law went to the core of the modern concept of intellectual property. What does it mean to own an intellectual work of authorship? What are the metes and bounds of this peculiar object of property? And how can one tell when these were transgressed in the absence of 'natural' physical boundaries? The metaphysics involved, however, were of a peculiar kind. Deep theoretical questions about the nature of expressive works of the intellect — and the meaning of ownership of such works — were closely intertwined with the nitty-gritty aspects of commercial practices, and with the ideology of the market embedded in them.

Half a century after Story made his observation, the world of commerce in which intellectual works were immersed transformed considerably, and so did the 'metaphysics' of copyright. The last quarter of the nineteenth century saw the appearance of what soon became the entertainment industry: new expressive technologies with vast commercial potential, new business models for organizing the production and exploitation of creative works (both traditional and

1 Folsom v. Marsh, 9 F. Cas. 342, 344 (C.C.D. Mass. 1841).

 https://doi.org/10.11647/OBP.0247.06

in new formats), and the perfection of techniques for creating and capturing markets for such works. As part of this process, creative works were increasingly commodified. The creation of expressive works came to be supported chiefly by commercial market exchange, existing markets grew dramatically, and new markets for new media opened up. Most importantly, however: each work gradually came to represent multiple streams of value in multiple markets. A novel was no longer merely a prospect for commercial success in the book market. A commercially successful novel represented potential profits in the secondary markets of translations, serializations, abridgments and, soon enough, dramatizations, pictorial-representations, and motion pictures. This was reflected in the logic of property rights in creative works known as 'copyright': if a work, as a commodity, represented multiple sources of exchange value from many markets, the property right had to be extended to enable exchange in these markets and capture their value. Market practices and the ideology of copyrighted 'works' as commodities were mutually constitutive. Commercial pushes to capture new markets led to novel assertions about the scope and nature of the property right as extending to all secondary markets. At the same time, an expanding understanding of the object of property legitimized and naturalized ventures to control new markets. At the heart of this ideology was a new and peculiar concept of the intellectual work that was wrapped in a powerfully circular logic: the intellectual work extends to all the concrete forms it might take in any potential market, and all secondary markets are ones for the work itself, owing to its enduring intellectual essence in the face of changing form.

Caught in this process of ideological transformation was the relationship between text and image. The traditional domain of copyright was text, although some recognition of images as a possible object of proprietary control existed even during the early origins of copyright. By the late nineteenth century, visual subject matter in various forms was already officially recognized as falling within the domain of copyright. The transition from text to image, however, was a different matter. Text and image were generally seen as distinct domains. To claim that a visual representation was a copy of a text and therefore interfered with its ownership was to brush copyright against the grain. Yet in a climate of growing commodification of works, visual 'translations' represented another market to be brought within the fold of copyright, and therefore a new territory to be conquered by the malleable coverage of the 'work'. Pressure to reconceive the relationship between text and image and extend the property right in texts into the domain of images was sure to come.

The novel *Ben-Hur* by Lew Wallace was the perfect site for this process to unfold. Published in 1880, *Ben-Hur* created an unprecedented cultural and economic phenomenon. Moreover, it arrived at a precise transitionary moment: one in which publishers were newly poised to squeeze every drop of value from this new caliber of a bestseller, and when the boundaries of copyright were being pushed to encompass new markets. One legal case, *Wallace* v. *Riley*, acted as a lightning rod that captured these forces at work.[2] The lawsuit at issue was brought by Wallace and his publishers against the Riley Brothers for creating and selling a set of magic-lantern slides based on the novel *Ben-Hur*. It was not a 'great case' in its time and it has been mostly forgotten since. It is, however, an invaluable specimen for studying the changing ideology of copyright. The case is the equivalent of the geologist's stratigraphic column, juxtaposing the different strata of copyright and conveying a clear image of the process of change. It represents a moment in which two conceptions of the relationship between text and image coexisted in copyright. The traditional text-bound and domain-specific conception was already in decline, but the modern logic that extends copyright to all 'derivative' forms and markets did not yet naturalize the transition from text to image.

Exploring this forgotten case allows a glimpse at how the 'metaphysical' assumptions of copyright arose from below through human agency. In *Wallace* v. *Riley* publishers, creators and jurists all took part in a conversation about the nature of creative works and the relationship between text and image. Even as they were making technical legal claims, they were also articulating arguments and making assumptions about the underlying fundamental questions, all in the service of their interests as they understood them against the background of changing market practices and ideology. As they were

2 The case was not reported. The discussion here is based on the case's record and press reports.

doing so, they were shaping the modern copyright ideology of the 'work' as a commodity, within which the bridge of market exchange value spans the chasm between text and image.

All the Profits of Publication Which the Book Can, in Any Form, Produce

By 1880 copyright had traveled a long way. Originating more than three centuries earlier in the trade privileges of publishers, this area of the law retained much of the features of the book trade's unique regulation even after statutes creating general regimes of authors' rights were enacted in 1710 in Britain and in 1790 in the US.[3] Two of these features were a print-bound understanding of the domain of copyright and a narrow concept of its scope centered on the paradigm of literal reproduction of printed text.

Emerging from the regulation of the printing press, early copyright was not seen as based on an abstract principle of authorship, nor as extending to every form of creative expression. While some early printing privileges were given for pictorial prints, the traditional domain of copyright had been that of printed texts, known as 'books'.[4] Adding pictorial subject matter to the sweep of copyright followed, more or less, on the heels of general statutory regimes with the 1735 British Engravers' Act and the US inclusion of prints in 1802.[5] These extensions, while pushing the boundaries of copyright beyond texts and the book trade, did not venture far from the traditional universe of print. As late as 1884, one old-fashioned definition of copyright still

3 Statute of Anne 1710 (8 Anne c. 19); 1790 Copyright Act (Act of May 31, 1790), ch. 15, 1 Stat. 124.

4 For examples of early printing privileges in prints see David Hunter, 'Copyright Protection for Engravings and Maps in Eighteenth Centaury Britain', *The Library*, 6th Ser., 9 (1987), 128–147 (p. 146), https://doi.org/10.1093/library/s6-IX.2.128; For a discussion of continental printing privileges in prints see Lisa Pon, *Raphael, Dürer, and Marcantonio Raimondi: Copying and the Italian Renaissance Print* (New Haven and London: Yale University Press, 2004). The Statute of Anne covered 'Book or Books' (8 Ann., c. 19, § 1). The American 1790 Act covered 'map, chart, book or books' (1 Stat. 124 § 2). Obviously, the latter already extended copyright beyond texts and into the realm of the printed image with its inclusion of maps and charts.

5 Engravers' Copyright Act 1735 (8 Geo. II, c.13); 1802 Copyright Act (Act of Apr. 29, 1802), ch. 36, 2 Stat. 171, § 2.

referred to it as limited to the 'arts of printing in any of its branches'.[6] By this time, however, a series of incremental extensions applied copyright to a variety of subject matters, including dramatic compositions, photographs, paintings, drawings, sculptures, and more.[7] This did not yet entail a crisp and fully developed understanding of the field as based on an overarching principle of property in expressive works of authorship. Copyright now applied to multiple media, but these were generally seen as distinct domains, each loosely connected and governed by similar sets of internal rules. There was copyright in books and copyright in paintings, but it was unclear that the two ever crossed paths.

This fragmentation was apparent in the rules that governed intermedia copying. Here too copyright as the publisher's privilege historically started with a narrow concept of the right's scope. To own a 'copy' literally meant a 'copy-right', meaning an exclusive right to reproduce in print nearly identical as well as 'colorable' or 'evasive' versions of a protected text.[8] An upshot of this understanding was a generally permissive approach toward various secondary uses of copyrighted works even within the textual realm, such as abridgments or translations.[9] That copyright in texts could go beyond textual reproduction was at first hardly contemplated. There was a steadily growing push against these assumptions and in favor of increasing copyright's scope, going at least as far back as the eighteenth century.[10] By the second half of the nineteenth century, with increased

---

6 John Bouvier, *Bouvier's Law Dictionary*, 2 vols. (Boston: Boston Book Co., 1897), I, 436.

7 In the American context see 1865 Copyright Act (Act of Mar. 3, 1865), 13 Stat. 540, §1 (adding photographs); 1870 Copyright Act (Act of July 8, 1870), ch. 230, 16 Stat. 198, § 86 (adding 'painting, drawing, chromo, statue' and other subject matter).

8 See e.g. the entry for 'Copy-right' in William Nicholson, *American Edition of The British Encyclopedia: Or, Dictionary of Arts and Sciences, Comprising An Accurate and Popular View of the Present Improved State of Human Knowledge*, 12 vols. (Philadelphia: Mitchell, Ames and White, 1819), IV.; Oren Bracha, *Owning Ideas: The Intellectual Origins of American Intellectual Property, 1709–1909* (New York: Cambridge University Press, 2016), pp. 147–148, https://doi.org/10.1017/9780511843235.

9 See Gyles v. Wilcox (1740) 26 Eng. Rep. 489; Millar v. Taylor (1769) 95 Eng. Rep. 201, 205. In the American context see Story v. Holocombe, 23 F. Cas. 171 (C.C.D.Oh. 1847); Stowe v. Thomas, 23 F. Cas. 201 (C.C.E.D.Pa. 1853).

10 See Ronan Deazley, 'The Statute of Anne and the Great Abridgment Swindle', *Houston Law Review*, 47 (2010), 793–818; Mathew Sag, 'The Prehistory of Fair Use', *Brooklyn Law Review* 76 (2011), 1371–1412.

commodification of texts and a gradually rising consciousness of ownership to match it, copyright's scope was in a state of flux in the US.

There was still a strong foothold to the traditional narrow understanding of copyright's ambit, the epitome of which was *Stowe* v. *Thomas*.[11] Often considered to be the first bestseller, Harriet Beecher Stowe's *Uncle Tom's Cabin* was prone to attract attempts to develop new markets and control them through copyright, which is precisely what happened when Stowe's and her publisher John P. Jewett's plans for a German translation were disrupted by an unauthorized version that was published by F. W. Thomas.[12] In the ensuing litigation Stowe expressed a broad understanding of copyright ownership, asserting that she 'ever had, and still hath the sole and exclusive right, to translate, print, publish and sell the same, for her own private benefit and advantage' and that she will be 'greatly injured and damnified in respect of and deprived of the receipt of large profits which she reasonably expects to receive from the sale' of the authorized translation.[13] The sentiment also found considerable support in the press with one report asserting the following: 'As for the absolute moral right, we see nothing in the nature of things to limit the ownership of the author. It is his work, and it ought to be for him to say on what terms others shall enjoy it, in whatsoever time, place, or tongue'.[14] Thomas's defense, in turn, was that '[i]n no parlance-either ordinary or legal-does "copy" mean "translation"' and that 'the prohibition is only against printing, publishing or importing "any copy of such book"'.[15] Justice Robert Grier of the US Supreme Court sided with the defendant and with the traditional, narrow understanding of copyright's scope. '[T]he only property' conferred by copyright, he wrote, 'is the exclusive right to multiply the copies of that particular combination of characters which exhibits to the eyes of another the ideas intended to be conveyed. This is what the law terms copy, or copyright'.

11 Stowe v. Thomas, 23 F. Cas. 201 (C.C.E.D.Pa. 1853).

12 See Melissa J. Homestead, '"When I can Read my Title Clear": Harriet Beecher Stowe and the Stowe v. Thomas Copyright Infringement Case', *Prospects*, 27 (2002), 201–45; Oren Bracha, 'Commentary on Stowe v. Thomas (1853)', in *Primary Sources on Copyright (1450–1900)*, ed. by Lionel Bently and Martin Kretschmer (2008), http://www.copyrighthistory.org/commentary/us_1853b.

13 National Archives and Records Administration (NARA), Stowe v. Thomas Case File, Complainant's Bill; Stowe v. Thomas Case File, Affidavit of Harriet Beecher Stowe.

14 '"Uncle Tom" at Law', *New York Weekly Tribune*, 16 April 1853, p. 10.

15 *Stowe*, 23 F. Cas. at 205.

It followed that a 'copy' of a book must be 'a transcript of the language in which the conceptions of the author are clothed; of something printed and embodied in a tangible shape', something which a translation clearly was not.[16]

The old orthodoxy of 'copy-right' embodied in *Stowe* v. *Thomas* was clearly beleaguered by the time the case was decided in 1853. Commentators directed a hail of criticism at the decision.[17] In 1870 Congress overturned its rule by amending the statute to include rights of dramatization and translation.[18] The parallel rule favoring abridgments of copyrighted works was accepted only begrudgingly in American case law, and while never formally rejected, it was well on its way to dissolving.[19] An important landmark was the 1856 creation of a public performance right in dramatic works.[20] Playwrights, motivated by the changing economic organization of American theater and a developing self-consciousness as an authorial class, had been lobbying for such a right for decades.[21] The conceptual significance of the new right was in extending the scope of copyright into the sphere of intermedia reproduction. Plays could traditionally be protected as texts, but with the newly minted public performance right, their copyright could be infringed by a form of non-textual use. In the context of dramatic works, courts, that were faced with the challenge of conceptualizing drama as a form of non-textual expression, began to apply copyright in the interface between text and this different expressive form on a routine basis.[22] Music, whose traditional copyright protection was similarly limited to reprinting, would undergo a similar process, with the statutory creation of a public performance right only in 1897.[23]

---

16 *Id.* at 207.

17 Eaton S. Drone, *A Treatise on the Law of Property in Intellectual Productions in Great Britain and the United States* (Boston: Little, Brown, 1879), pp. 454–455; James O Pierce, 'Anomalies in the Law of Copyright', *Southern Law Review*, 5 (1879), 420–36 (pp. 433–434).

18 1870 Copyright Act, § 86.

19 Bracha, *Owning Ideas*, p. 158.

20 1856 Copyright Act Amendment (Act of August 18, 1856), 11 Stat. 138, 139, §1.

21 See Oren Bracha, 'Commentary on the U.S. Copyright Act Amendment 1856', in *Primary Sources on Copyright (1450–1900)*, ed. by Lionel Bently and Martin Kretschmer (2008), http://www.copyrighthistory.org/commentary/us_1856.

22 See Derek Miller, *Copyright and the Value of Performance, 1770–1911* (Cambridge: Cambridge University Press, 2018), pp. 122–74, https://doi.org/10.1017/978110834 9284.

23 1897 Copyright Act Amendment (Act of Mar. 3, 1897), ch. 392, 29 Stat. 694.

By 1880 the traditional understanding of the legal field as 'copy-right' was under significant pressure. Doctrinal and conceptual incursions had been made, but no general principle extending copyright to intermedia reproduction had appeared. Specifically, images and texts remained distinct. The early treatise writers, however, were busily erecting the intellectual infrastructure that would support such a principle and eventually bring down the barrier dividing image and text. There were three foundations to this new conceptual structure: a market-oriented understanding of the right, a matching concept of the expressive work as an intellectual essence that transcends varying forms, and a sharp distinction between an original creation and derivatives. George Ticknor Curtis launched the attack on the rules that limited copyright to close textual reproductions and shielded secondary uses in his mid-century treatise. Curtis' starting point was defining the authorial entitlement over a work in terms of market profits from all its possible forms: 'to the author belongs the exclusive right to take all the profits of publication which the book can, in any form, produce'.[24] The author's copyright, he argued, 'must be held to have secured to him the right to avail himself of the profits to be reaped from all classes of readers'.[25] An abridgment, for example, is 'a valuable part of the copyright', and '[i]f, during the existence of the copyright, the work is abridged by a stranger, the copyright is shorn of an incident, the loss of which may greatly affect its value as property'.[26] The assumption that copyright covers all 'incidents' of profits led to a rejection of the 'copy' and its replacement with a broader and elusive object of property. Thus, with respect to translations:

> The property of the original author embraces something more than the words in which his sentiments are conveyed... In such cases his right may be invaded, in whatever form his own property may be reproduced. The new language in which his composition is clothed by translation affords only a different medium of communicating that in which he has an exclusive property.[27]

In his influential 1879 treatise, Eaton Drone perfected this vision of copyright's object of property that tied together profits from multiple

---

24 George Ticknor Curtis, *A Treatise on the Law of Copyright* (Boston: C. C. Little and J. Brown 1847), pp. 237–238.

25 Ibid., p. 278.

26 Ibid., p. 279.

27 Ibid., p. 293.

markets and a manifold of forms. Drone insisted that 'It is no defence of piracy that the work entitled to protection has not been copied literally; that it has been translated into another language; that it has been dramatized; that the whole has not been taken; that it has been abridged; that it is reproduced in a new and more useful form'. Rather, '[t]he controlling question always is, whether the substance of the work is taken without authority'.[28] The 'substance of the work' became the linchpin solidifying the control of the owner over all secondary markets for his work. Moreover, the principle of controlling all secondary markets replaced the old concept of the 'copy' with that of 'the substance of the work' as an intellectual essence that persists notwithstanding changes of form. Secondary markets constituted the metaphysics of the 'work', and the 'work' defined these markets as ones to whose value the author was entitled. 'The definition that a copy is a literal transcript of the language of the original finds no place in the jurisprudence with which we are concerned', wrote Drone. 'Literary property', he argued,

> is not in the language alone; but in the matter of which language is merely a means of communication. It is in the substance and not in the form alone. That which constitutes the essence and value of literary composition... may be capable of expression in more than one form of language different than the original.[29]

The logic of reducing all secondary works to mere forms manifesting the same substance — and of subjecting all secondary markets to the property right in the work — also entailed a sharp hierarchy between original and derivative. While earlier views often emphasized the value and merit of secondary works, Drone asserted with confidence that 'the translator creates nothing' but rather 'takes the entire creation of another, and simply clothes it in new dress'.[30] Similarly, he stated that

> the dramatist invents nothing, creates nothing. He simply arranges the parts, or changes the from, of what which already exists... in making this use of a work of which he is not the author, he avails himself of the fruits of genius and industry which are not his own, and takes to himself profits which belong to another.[31]

28 Drone, *A Treatise on the Law of Property in Intellectual Productions*, p. 385.
29 Ibid., p. 451.
30 Bracha, *Owning Ideas*, pp. 148–149; Drone, *A Treatise on the Law of Property in Intellectual Productions*, p. 451.
31 Ibid., p. 464.

This was a fully developed version of the modern logic of 'derivative' works: an original intellectual work is a polymorphic intellectual essence that extends to all secondary creation based on it, no matter how different in form; such secondary creation is merely derivative; from which it naturally follows that the author of the original is entitled to all profits generated by such derivative markets. All of this was an ideological reflection in consciousness of changing market realities. As expressive works were increasingly commodified and right owners sought to squeeze out each drop of market value in every available secondary market, the legal arguments and the metaphysics of the 'work' to support and legitimize extending the reach of property into such markets were accordingly developed. In Drone's version, the main examples of secondary works and markets were still largely text-oriented: translations, abridgments, and (beginning to reach beyond text) dramatizations. With market players ever on the look for new sources of value and image-oriented uses promising exploitable markets, it was only a matter of time before the emerging logic of derivative works would be extended to challenge the division between text and image.

Ben-Hur: My God, Did I Set All of This in Motion?

A recent comprehensive study described 'the Ben-Hur property' as 'an avatar of American popular, artistic commercialism'.[32] The foundation of what became a cultural and commercial empire was the immensely successful novel. Despite a slow start and a cold reception by literary critics, *Ben-Hur's* sales gradually picked up, eventually making it an unprecedented bestseller.[33] There were many reasons related to the content of the novel that account for its vast success. The story had all the right ingredients to appeal to the sensibilities of the era: an epic tale of a Jewish nobleman, betrayed by his friend and enslaved by the Romans, his adventure-packed quest for revenge turned into religious redemption, all intersecting with the life and death of Christ. Literary and cultural historians have explored the many ways in which these elements

32 Jon Solomon, *Ben Hur: The Original Blockbuster* (Edinburgh: Edinburgh University Press, 2016), p. 14.

33 See Robert E. Morsberger and Katharine M. Morsberger, *Lew Wallace: Militant Romantic* (New York: McGraw-Hill 1980), pp. 309–331.

touched the right nerves at the right time: offering a way of embracing modernity without rejecting religion through the personification of Christ; telling a Gilded-Age-apt story of rags to riches achieved through piety and virtue; offering the thrill of action and vengeance combined with the elation of spiritual redemption, and even, as some speculate, helping to reunite the nation in the post-Reconstruction years.[34] Whatever the reasons for its sweeping cultural success, when it came to the world of commerce *Ben-Hur* created a new phenomenon. It was much more than a popular novel sold in many copies. In the two decades following its publication it grew to be a powerhouse, feeding an elaborate network that connected artistic creation, popular culture, and commerce. In this respect *Ben-Hur* was different from bestsellers that preceded it, and was a harbinger of the modern business franchise: one that builds a comprehensive structure of economic exploitation around a successful expressive commodity through complex commercial and legal arrangements in numerous markets.

Following the success of the novel, its publishers, Harper Brothers — in cooperation with Lew Wallace and later his son Henry Wallace — worked to cultivate and exploit demand in various book submarkets. In doing so they employed and perfected techniques that had been developed by book publishers since the mid-nineteenth-century. Harper commissioned a prequel to the book (*The Boyhood of Christ*), released an extended and illustrated version for the gift book market in 1889, published or licensed a variety of excerpted shorter versions such as *The First Christmas* and *The Chariot Race*, and licensed a short Christmas gift-book called *Seekers After 'The Light'*.[35] A special two-volume, extravagant and expansive Garfield edition was issued following the assassination of President Garfield.[36] There was also a Wallace Memorial Edition published after his death. In 1913, in a deal

34 See Solomon, *Ben Hur*, pp. 188–217; Howard Miller, 'The charioteer and the Christ: Ben Hur in America from the Gilded Age to the Culture Wars', *Indiana Magazine of History*, 104 (2008), 153–75; Barbara Ryan, *Chronicling Ben-Hur's Climb, 1880–1924* (London and New York: Routledge, 2019); John Swansburg, 'The Passion of Lew Wallace: The Incredible Story of How a Disgraced Civil War General Became One of the Best-Selling Novelists in American history', *Slate*, 26 March 2013, http://www.slate.com/articles/life/history/2013/03/ben_hur_and_lew_wallace_how_the_scapegoat_of_shiloh_became_one_of_the_best.html.

35 Solomon, *Ben Hur*, pp. 149–151; Ibid., p. 5; Ibid., p. 13; Ibid., pp. 141–142.

36 Ibid., pp. 151–156.

of an unprecedented scale, the mail-order giant Sears, Roebuck & Co. bought the rights to reprint, and sell in an affordable format, one million copies of this edition: a sales operation that it supported with a massive advertisement campaign.[37]

The commercial and cultural power of *Ben-Hur* emanated, however, well beyond print markets. By the early decades of the twentieth century the novel's name and imagery could be found in many corners of the interface between American popular culture and commerce. There were *Ben-Hur* spices, coffee, flour, cigars, oranges, bicycles, and many more products.[38] *Ben-Hur* elements appeared in a plethora of advertisements for anything from cars to fences. Chapters of *Ben-Hur* fraternal organizations appeared.[39] One of them — The Tribe of Ben-Hur — had an insurance scheme for members and eventually became an insurance company.[40] There were chariot races *Ben-Hur* style, river boats named *Ben-Hur,* and even various towns bearing the name (see Figure 1).[41] With American trademark law in its infancy and no broad concept of brand ownership as means for allowing brand owners to fully commodify their commercial insignia, most of these activities were beyond the legal reach of Wallace and his publishers. With the exception of some arrangements for cooperation and endorsement, the brand value of *Ben-Hur* was thus mostly free for all to exploit with little ability by its originator to capture its vast commercial value.

In between the book market and the, still largely un-commodified, brand market, there was a wide variety of expressive activities that drew on *Ben-Hur*'s repository of expressions and meanings. Many of those started as spontaneous cultural activities that were neither coordinated nor controlled by the owner of *Ben-Hur*. Some were quasi or fully commercial. And many would eventually become of interest to Wallace's publishers and licensees, who tried to monetize them as sources of market value or protect adjacent markets they exploited. Beginning in the late 1880s, public recitations and live readings of the novel were becoming a widespread phenomenon. These appeared in many formats and ranged over a spectrum of social, charitable, and

37 Ibid., pp. 174–180.
38 Ibid., pp. 408–490.
39 Ibid., pp. 410–412.
40 Ibid., pp. 412–423.
41 Ibid., pp. 488–489.

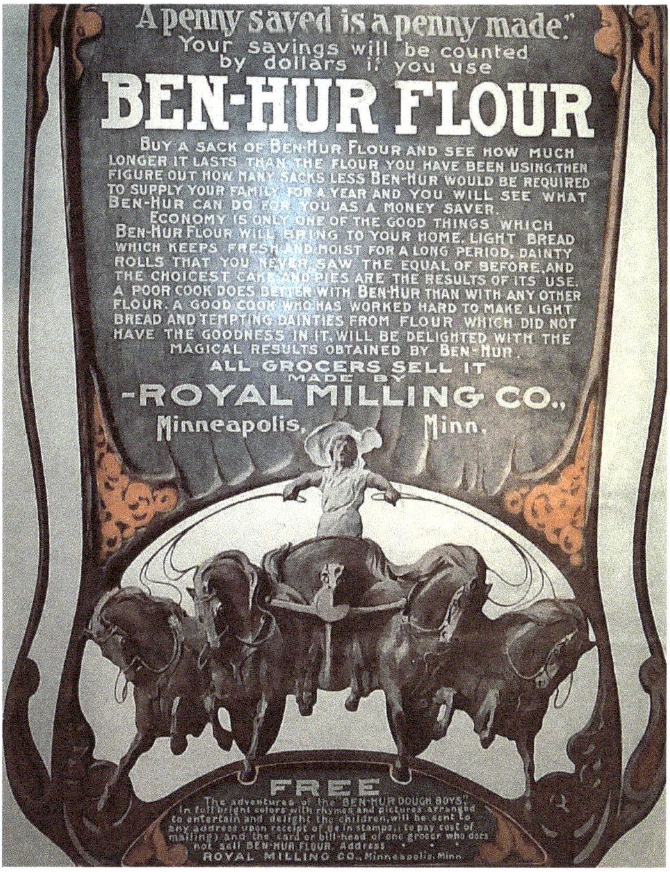

Fig. 1 Ben-Hur Flour, advertisement by unknown creator (item held by the author).

commercial events, as well as everything in between. One instance out of countless similar reading events demonstrates both that *Ben-Hur*'s copyright owner was aware of the phenomenon and that it began to elicit thoughts of proprietary control. In 1894, Virginia Saffel Mercer from Salem, Ohio launched a show named 'The Healing of The Lepers' (see Figure 2). It was advertised as 'An Entire Evening from Ben Hur' and offered to 'Church and College Societies, Lecture Committees and Cemetery Associations'.[42] In a December 1896 letter to Wallace, Mercer

42 Advertisement Pamphlet, in Lew Wallace (1827–1905) Miscellaneous Uncataloged Materials, Lilly Library, Indiana University Bloomington (hereinafter 'Wallace Miscellaneous').

described her show as embracing 'the quieter scenes' (hence no chariot race) and remarked that 'For obvious reasons, the impersonation of the lepers is not close'. She then informed Wallace that she 'should be pleased' to present her act to him 'for charitable purposes or even in your private study' and asked for his endorsement.[43] Wallace, perhaps moved by Mercer's report that she was about 'to secure an agent and make a tour of the cities in this and surrounding states', promptly forwarded the letter to Harper, alerting the publisher to a possible infringement of the novel's copyright.[44]

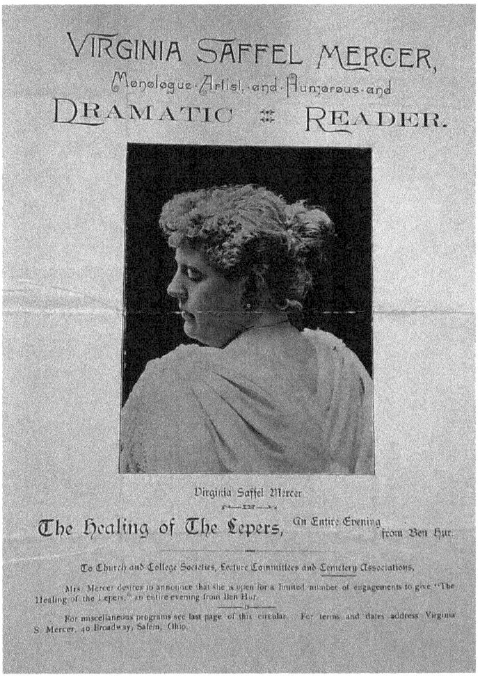

Fig. 2 An Advertisement Poster for Virginia Saffel Mercer's Ben-Hur's Show (author unknown), Lilly Library, Indiana University, Bloomington Indiana.

In addition to public readings, there was a plethora of *Ben-Hur* public lectures and sermons as well as various local dramatizations. In light of the dramatization right created in 1870, a full-scale stage production

43 Letter from Virginia Mercer to Lew Wallace, 20 December 1896, in Wallace Mss. II, Lilly Library, Indiana University Bloomington (hereinafter 'Wallace Mss. II').

44 Letter from Susan Wallace to Harper & Bros., 26 December 1896, Wallace Mss. II.

unambiguously required permission from the copyright owner. Requests for licensing started to flow to Wallace as early as 1882.[45] He adamantly refused all such requests, citing as his main ground the fear that a dramatic adaptation would lack the 'proper spirit of reverence'.[46] Even as late as 1898, Wallace wrote one suitor that in his view 'the subject ought not be put on the stage; that would be a profanation, not of the book but the most sacred of characters to which it must be considered dedicated'.[47] The following year, however, Wallace and Harper were engaged in negotiations with Klaw and Erlanger for a grand theater production, with Wallace shrewdly haggling over his royalties.[48] When an agreement was finally reached the new licensees promised 'to endeavor to give America the greatest production it had ever had'.[49] The play, which opened on Broadway in November 1899 and ran for twenty-one years, marked a new stage in the commercial exploitation of *Ben-Hur* derivatives (see Figure 3).

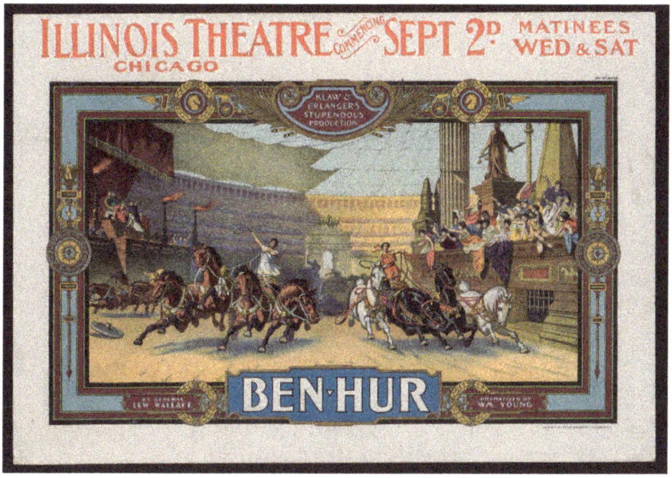

Fig. 3 *Ben-Hur Klaw & Erlanger's Stupendous Production*, advertisement Poster (1901), Strobridge Lith. Co., Library of Congress, https://www.loc.gov/item/2014635366/.

45 Morsberger and Morsberger, *Lew Wallace*, pp. 453–454.
46 Ibid.
47 Letter from Lew Wallace to W.W. Allen, 15 November 1898, Wallace Mss. II.
48 Solomon, *Ben Hur*, p. 315.
49 Letter from Klaw & Erlanger to Lew Wallace, 25 May 1899, Wallace Mss. II.

Being a hefty source of royalties, the play also gave rise to many cross-markets synergies. A quick look at one of the many *Ben-Hur* theatrical programs, in which a list of the characters and scenes is nestled between advertisements for corsets and cigars, demonstrates what a valuable commercial asset the work had become (see Figure 4).

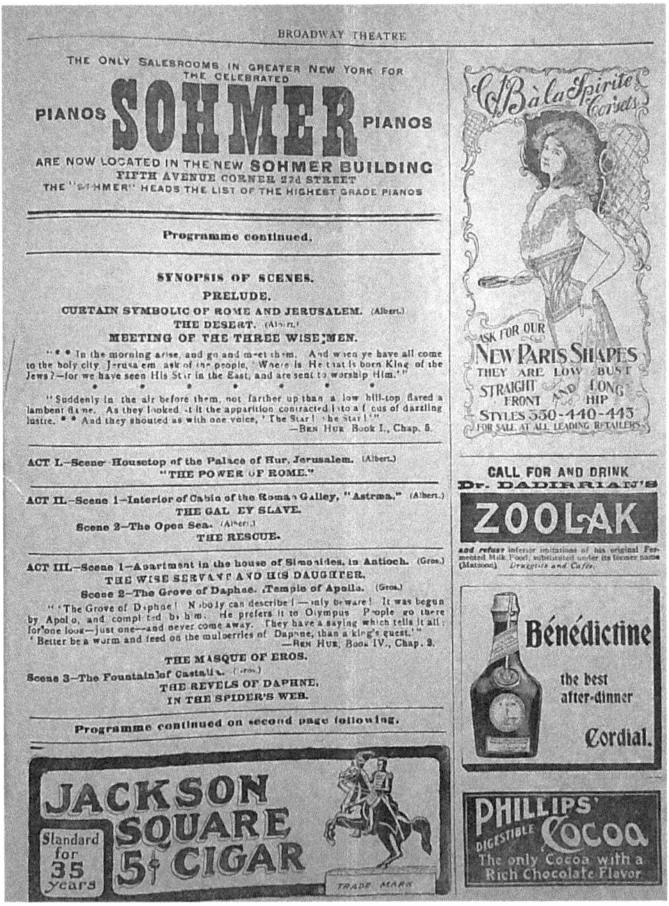

BROADWAY THEATRE

THE ONLY SALESROOMS IN GREATER NEW YORK FOR THE CELEBRATED
PIANOS SOHMER PIANOS
ARE NOW LOCATED IN THE NEW SOHMER BUILDING
FIFTH AVENUE CORNER 22d STREET
THE "SOHMER" HEADS THE LIST OF THE HIGHEST GRADE PIANOS

Programme continued.

SYNOPSIS OF SCENES.

PRELUDE.

CURTAIN SYMBOLIC OF ROME AND JERUSALEM. (Albert.)

THE DESERT. (Albert.)

MEETING OF THE THREE WISE MEN.

"* * In the morning arise, and go and meet them. And when ye have all come to the holy city Jerusalem ask of the people, 'Where is He that is born King of the Jews?—for we have seen His Star in the East, and are sent to worship Him.'"

* * * * * * *

"Suddenly in the air before them, not farther up than a low hill-top flared a lambent flame. As they looked at it the apparition contracted into a focus of dazzling lustre. * * And they shouted as with one voice, 'The Star! the Star!'"
—Ben Hur Book I., Chap. 5.

ACT I.—Scene Housetop of the Palace of Hur, Jerusalem. (Albert.)
"THE POWER OF ROME."

ACT II.—Scene 1—Interior of Cabin of the Roman Galley, "Astræa." (Albert.)
THE GALLEY SLAVE.
Scene 2—The Open Sea. (Albert.)
THE RESCUE.

ACT III.—Scene 1—Apartment in the house of Simonides, in Antioch. (Gros.)
THE WISE SERVANT AND HIS DAUGHTER.
Scene 2—The Grove of Daphne. Temple of Apollo. (Gros.)

"'The Grove of Daphne! Nobody can describe it—only beware! It was begun by Apollo, and completed by him. He prefers it to Olympus. People go there for one look—just one—and never come away. They have a saying which tells it all: 'Better be a worm and feed on the mulberries of Daphne, than a king's guest.'"
—Ben Hur, Book IV., Chap. 2.

THE MASQUE OF EROS.
Scene 3—The Fountain of Castalia. (Gros.)
THE REVELS OF DAPHNE.
IN THE SPIDER'S WEB.

Programme continued on second page following.

JACKSON SQUARE 5¢ CIGAR
Standard for 35 years
TRADE MARK

À la Spirite Corsets
ASK FOR OUR NEW PARIS SHAPES
THEY ARE LOW BUST STRAIGHT FRONT AND LONG HIP
STYLES 330-440-443
FOR SALE AT ALL LEADING RETAILERS

CALL FOR AND DRINK
Dr. DADIRRIAN'S
ZOOLAK
and refuse inferior imitations of his original Fermented Milk Food, substituted under its former name (Matzoon). Druggists and Cafés.

Bénédictine
the best after-dinner Cordial.

PHILLIPS' DIGESTIBLE COCOA
The only Cocoa with a Rich Chocolate Flavor

Fig. 4 Ben-Hur's Play Program (author unknown), Lilly Library, Indiana University, Bloomington.

There were also various multimedia products that monetized the combined power of the novel and the play, such as the *Ben-Hur* Souvenir Album that featured photographs of scenes from the play, short quotations from the novel and matching art work (see Figs. 5 and 6).

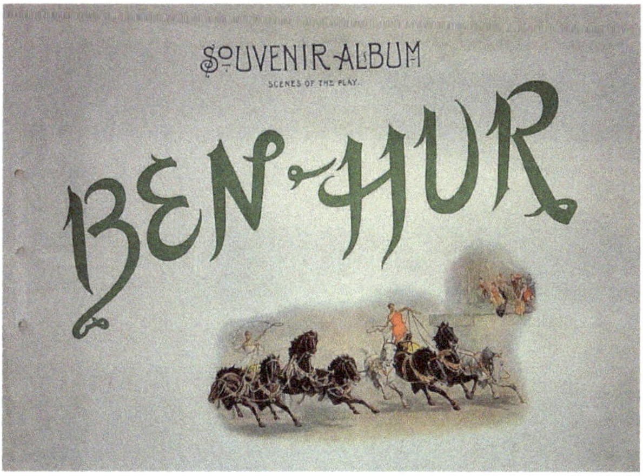

Fig. 5 Ben-Hur Souvenir Album (author unknown), Lilly Library, Indiana University, Bloomington.

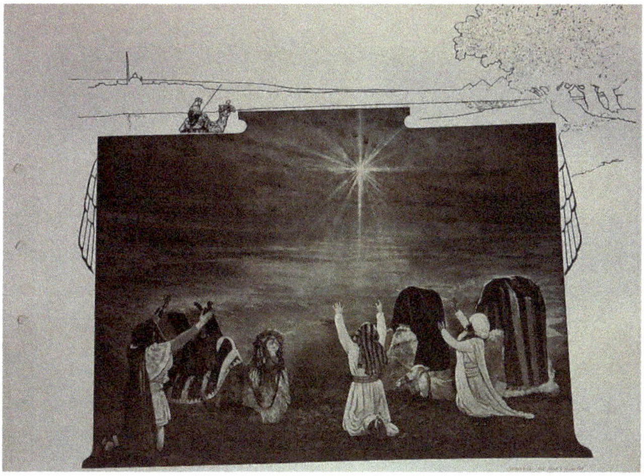

Fig. 6 Ben-Hur Souvenir Album (author unknown), Lilly Library, Indiana University, Bloomington.

It was with respect to the play that Wallace famously remarked 'My God, did I set all of this in motion?'[50] But the comment had a much broader application.

The Klaw and Erlanger production was not, however, the first extension of the *Ben-Hur* licensing network beyond print markets. This

50 Lee Scott Theisen, '"My God, Did I set all of this in Motion?" General Lew Wallace and Ben-Hur', *Journal of Popular Culture*, 18 (1984), 33–41 (p. 38).

had already happened earlier, in 1892 with the authorized show *Ben Hur in Tableaux and Pantomime*.[51] Tableaux-vivant, a brand of performance art consisting of portrayal of silent scenes often accompanied by narration, was a highly popular form of entertainment in the nineteenth century. As the name that translates into 'living pictures' implies, it is an expressive form halfway between drama and visual arts. Tableaux performances of *Ben-Hur* started to appear in the mid-1880s and proliferated in the following years.[52] Like other *Ben-Hur* performances, they span a broad spectrum, from social or amateur events to quasi-commercial productions. A conspicuous example of the latter was the tableaux version by Ellen Knight Bradford. It started in 1887 as a charitable event in Washington D.C., but grew more ambitious in nature. Bradford registered with the Copyright Office *Selections from Ben Hur Adapted for Readings with Tableaux* and toured multiple cities with her successful show, which featured local amateur casts.[53] Wallace learned of the Bradford enterprise and attended an Indianapolis performance. He responded with vitriolic remarks but also acknowledged the possibilities for exploiting the novel.[54]

Wallace also alerted Harper to the possibility of copyright infringement. Harper's belated response was telling. The legal advice Harper received was that it was unclear whether the unauthorized tableaux infringed copyright. If there was such an infringement it was 'only as a violation of the right to dramatize the work'.[55] One uncertainty related to the fact that the 1870 statutory amendment allowed or perhaps required an author to 'reserve' the right of dramatization.[56] More fundamentally, it was an open question whether 'reading from a book and at the same time representing in sight of the audience tableaux composed of figures mentioned and described in the book' was such a dramatization of the work.[57] This was solid legal advice. In a context in which cross-media copyright was not recognized as a general principle,

51 This was the title of the libretto that Wallace wrote for the show which went under different names.
52 Solomon, *Ben Hur*, pp. 220–231.
53 Ibid., pp. 220–226.
54 Ibid., pp. 226–227.
55 Harper & Bros. to Lew Wallace, 29 January 1889, Wallace Mss. II.
56 1870 Copyright Act, § 86.
57 Harper & Bros. to Lew Wallace, 29 January 1889, Wallace Mss. II.

trying to fit the case into the only relevant statutory category was natural. At the same time, the hybrid visual and performative subject matter of tableaux was not a frictionless fit for the category of drama. Given the less-than-ironclad legal case, Harper suggested that making some arrangements 'by which Mrs. Bradford would acknowledge our rights and take a license from us at even a nominal royalty' was preferable to an expensive litigation of an uncertain outcome. Despite Harper contacting Bradford's attorney and her show persisting, there is no indication that such an agreement was ever reached.[58]

By the time Harper sent this response in late January 1889, Wallace had already agreed to another licensing arrangement of *Ben-Hur* for tableaux. The origin of this arrangement was a Crawfordsville charitable production endorsed by Wallace, who advised on costumes and scenery.[59] This local initiative grew into a full-scale traveling company show officially licensed by Wallace. The contract signed between Wallace and the licensees, later to be known as 'Clark and Cox' embodied a calculated and detailed business arrangement.[60] Wallace granted a forty-year exclusive license to produce a tableaux based on the novel and undertook to write a libretto for it — all for royalties of five percent of the revenue from charitable shows and six percent from commercial ones, backed by an accounting duty.[61] There were also a host of other conditions, including the following: making the license unassignable, the licensees refraining from presenting themselves as agents of Wallace 'in the business growing out of the rights', a duty not to exhibit 'the Lord Jesus Christ as a character or person or make any personal representation of Him in any manner', and ample opportunities for Wallace to terminate the contract for various causes.[62] There was also an

58 Indeed, Harper estimated that in the absence of a license Bradford would take the risk and continue her shows. Ibid.

59 Solomon, *Ben Hur*, pp. 235–237.

60 The original licensees were David W. Cox, William S. Brown and Albert S. Miller. Walter Clark joined in later but ended up buying up a full share of the enterprise in 1894.

61 Harper was able to propose granting a tableaux license to Bradford despite the exclusivity of the license to Cox and Clark because the latter agreement contained an exception that reserved for Wallace the right to authorize or prevent shows by churches and congregations in their own towns. This meant that Bradford's license would have had to be limited to such local, church-affiliated performances.

62 Wallace Mss. II.

auxiliary contract with Harper designed to protect their various print interests in *Ben-Hur*.[63]

The Clark and Cox tableaux deal was an important landmark. It extended the commercial exploitation of *Ben-Hur* derivatives under copyright beyond print markets. It also installed a vigilant licensee with a vested interest in protecting this new market, as was evidenced by the legal warnings that Clark and Cox started issuing before long.[64] The turf controlled and protected by the licensee laid on the borderline between performative and visual expression, and thus pictorial uses of the work — at least those that chafed against this market — were now more likely to attract attempts to further extend copyright in this direction. There was also a foreshadowing of the legal tactic that could be used for such an extension: fitting the square peg of an image into the round hole of dramatic copyright.

The Masterpiece of the Nineteenth-Century Illustrated

In the mid-1890s, a new market for *Ben-Hur* derivatives was emerging with the proliferation of magic-lantern slides presentations. The Reverend E. Homer Wellman enticed his potential audience with 'Eighty of the Most Beautiful Pictures by Celebrated Foreign Artists' (see Figure 7).[65] Another advertisement promised 'A rare treat' in the form of 'The celebrated book written by Gen. Lew Wallace brilliantly portrayed by means of one of the finest dissolving stereopticons' accompanied by 'a realistic story' and 'MUSICAL SELECTIONS' with everything 'animated, vivid and glowing' (see Figure 8).[66]

While these popular magic-lantern presentations varied somewhat, many of them were technologically altered versions of tableaux vivants, combining narration and visual effects, with the images no longer being living ones. This was bound to create friction with the tableaux market, regarded by its licensees as their own.

On 11 January 1896, Herbert Riley registered with the Library of Congress 'The Stereopticon Illustrator of "Ben-Hur": A Tale of the

63 Ibid.

64 Solomon, *Ben Hur*, p. 239.

65 Advertisement Pamphlet, Wallace Miscellaneous.

66 Advertisement Pamphlet, Wallace Miscellaneous.

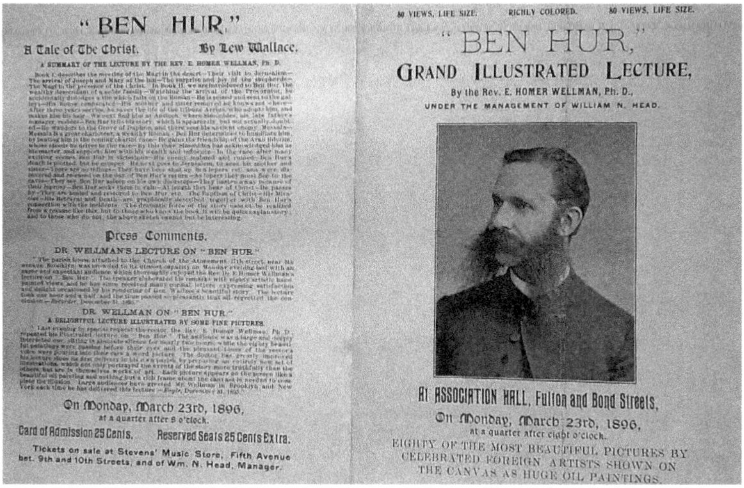

Fig. 7 An Advertisement for a Ben-Hur Magic-Lantern Slides Lecture (1896, author unknown), Lilly Library, Indiana University, Bloomington.

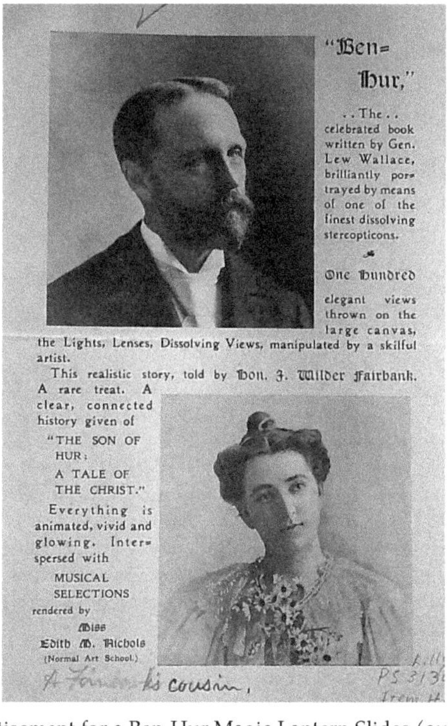

Fig. 8 An Advertisement for a Ben-Hur Magic-Lantern Slides (author unknown), Lilly Library, Indiana University, Bloomington.

Christ by General Lew Wallace'.[67] It did not take long for a warning blip to appear on Wallace's radar. On 8 February he wrote to Harper and alerted the company that he had encountered an advertisement flyer for 'pictures designed to illustrate lectures on Ben Hur'. The enclosed advertisement, he said, should be enough to inform them of the enterprise so they could 'consider its effect on the book'. 'For my own part', he concluded, 'I cannot avoid a feeling that, while they advertise, they cheapen the work' (see Figure 10).[68]

The Riley Brothers, from Bradford, England, had an established magic-lantern business founded in 1884 by Joseph Riley.[69] The enterprise had a New York branch run by Joseph's son, Herbert, who moved there in 1894. Riley, which sometimes claimed to be the 'Largest Lantern Outfitters in the World,' had a broad catalog of slides.[70] Among its most popular were religious and biblically themed sets. *Ben-Hur*, already a cultural phenomenon at the time, promised to be a hit, and Riley treated it accordingly. Riley heavily advertised the set, which it heralded as 'The Masterpiece of the Nineteenth Century Illustrated with Lantern Slides'.[71] The seventy-two slides depicted various scenes from the novel. The set was prepared, according to another Riley advertisement, 'with considerable labor and an enormous cost'.[72] The first twenty-five slides were made by the leading slide artist Frank F. Weeks.[73] In a promotional published in the *Optical Magic Lantern Journal*, Weeks was described as having 'erected studios' at Leytonstone equipped with a 'large stock of costumes, models, scenes, etc.' where he produced the *Ben-Hur* slides 'from living Jewish models'.[74] Weeks used a unique technique

67 Certificate of deposit of 11 January 1896, Wallace Mss. II. Riley deposited a copy of the work as a 'Book'. He was, however, probably trying to obtain copyright protection for the slides. The subtitle of the work was '72 Lantern Pictures by Eminent Artists' and the deposit was of a pamphlet that included a small version of all the images on two pages. The most plausible explanation is that Riley was trying to copyright all 72 slides — but register, deposit, and pay fees only once.

68 Letter from Lew Wallace to Harper Bros., 8 February 1896, Lew Wallace Collection 1799–1972, Indiana Historical Society Manuscript Collection.

69 See Colin Gordon, *By Gaslight in Winter: A Victorian Family History through the Magic Lantern* (London: Elm Tree Books, 1980).

70 This was an occasional boast in the Riley Brothers advertisements. See e.g. *Dominion Medical Monthly and Ontario Medical Journal*, 6 (January-June 1896), 471.

71 Advertisement pamphlet, Wallace Miscellaneous.

72 Advertisement pamphlet, Wallace Miscellaneous.

73 See David Henry, 'Ben-Hur: Francis Fredric Theophilus Weeks and Patent No. 8615 of 1894', *The New Magic Lantern Journal*, 5 (1987), 2–5.

74 'Photique Art', *The Optical Magic Lantern Journal and Photographic Enlarger*, 7 (1896), 175.

that combined photographing his human models and then heavily reworking the image by painting.[75] It may have been this technique that led to 'the slow progress made with the work, and the enormous cost of the process', resulting in the transfer of the project to 'the celebrated Artist' Nannie Preston and a marked change in style beginning with the twenty-sixth slide (see Figure 9).[76]

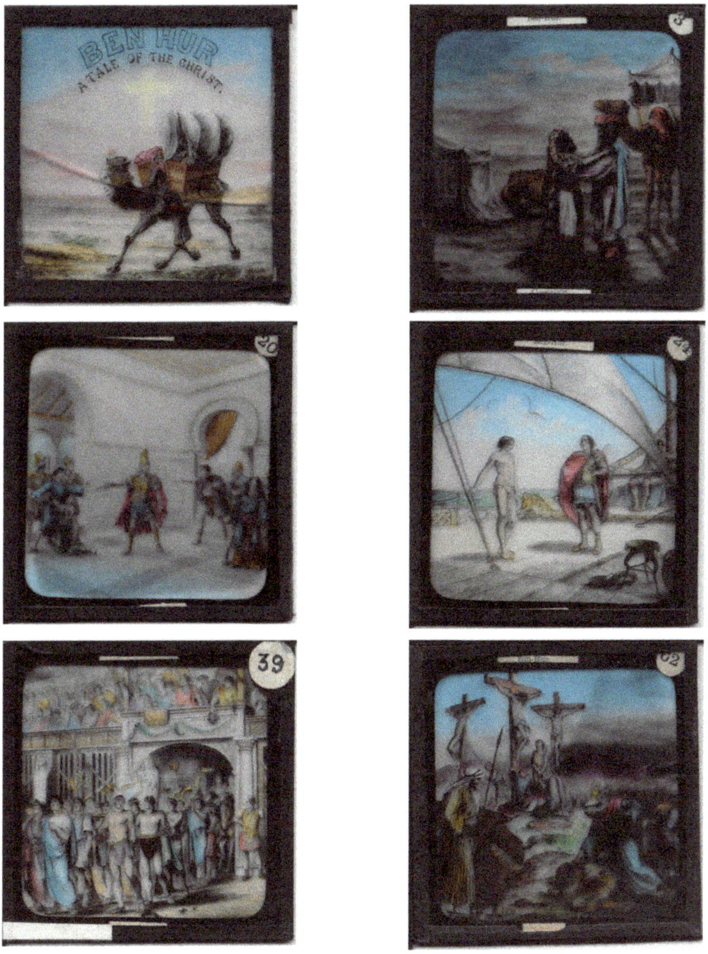

Fig. 9 Frank Weeks and Nannie Preston, Six Slides from Riley Brothers' Ben-Hur Set (1896), Museum of PRECINEMA — Minici Zotti Collection, Padua, Italy.

75 Henry, 'Ben-Hur', p. 3.
76 *Cincinnati Enquirer*, 27 April 1896, p. 9.

Riley sold the slides together with a 'Reading', a forty-page text meant to be read as part of the lantern slides presentation. The text devoted a paragraph to each slide and consisted of condensed versions — and sometimes close paraphrases — of Wallace's own descriptions in the novel. Unsurprisingly, the *Ben-Hur* slides were a big success. They were sold directly from Riley or through dealers and other companies. If Riley's promotion is to be believed, they were sold not only in numerous U.S. locations but also in Britain, Canada, Australia, New Zealand, South Africa, and India.[77] When Walter Clark, Wallace's licensee, went on a snooping mission he was told by the sellers that 'the demand is so high they cannot supply it.'[78]

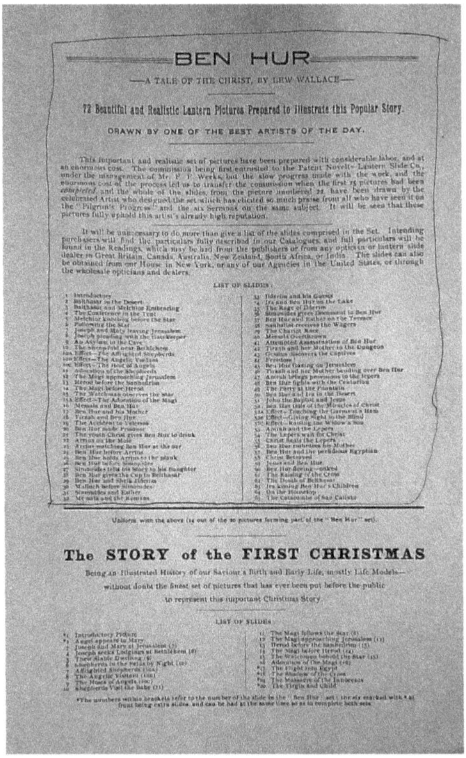

Fig. 10 An Advertisement for the Riley Brothers' Ben-Hur Slides, in Lew Wallace's Papers with the Slide List Marked in Red (author unknown, 1896), Lilly Library, Indiana University, Bloomington Indiana.

77 Advertisement pamphlet. Wallace Miscellaneous.

78 Letter from Augustus Gurlitz to Lew Wallace, 21 March 1896, Wallace Mss. II.

The Riley Brothers' prospering enterprise set off loud alarm bells at Wallace's licensees who identified a potential business threat. Harper referred Wallace's note to Walter Clark, the licensees of the authorized *Ben-Hur* tableaux. On 21 March Augustus T. Gurlitz — a seasoned copyright lawyer representing Clark — wrote Wallace a detailed and concerned letter. He reported that 'Mr. Clark bought a set of the pictures' and warned that 'an examination has disclosed an enterprise which will probably destroy the pantomime and tableaux exhibitions of "Ben-Hur"'.[79] Riley, he said, is 'a large concern'; 'they advertise world-wide' and 'sell lantern out-fits to ministers on the installment system in scholastic institutions'.[80] Gurlitz enclosed a copy of the text that was circulated together with the slides and suggested that Wallace consider, in consultation with Harper, whether it infringed his book copyright. As for his immediate interest — the 'dramatic' rights exploited by his client — he admitted that whether these were infringed by Riley's actions was 'not entirely free from doubt' but expressed his hope that the performance of the slides together with their sale would be found to be such an infringement of dramatic copyright.[81] Warning that unless 'some steps are taken to suppress Riley brothers the country will be overrun with these performances', he suggested initiating a legal action, half of whose cost would be borne by Clark.[82]

Whether Wallace was primarily concerned with preventing the 'cheapening' of his work or also interested in protecting his profits mattered little. He was now connected to a network of business alliances, and his allies were determined to maximize their profits in the markets they controlled. Clark was the main motivating force. His interest was not in entering the magic-lantern market, and the performances of the Riley Brothers' slides were, as Gurlitz admitted in his letter, 'neither tableaux nor pantomimes'. Clark's concern was that magic-lantern slides might divert demand from the market he commanded, or in Gurlitz's words: the slide shows 'interfere with and have a tendency to take the place of tableaux and pantomime performances'.[83] The concern was factually plausible in light of the nature of tableaux performances as

79 Ibid.
80 Ibid.
81 Ibid.
82 Ibid.
83 Ibid.

'living pictures', halfway between drama and still imagery. Clark aimed at protecting a stream of profit in a derivative market and pushing the frontiers of copyright outward was the obvious vehicle of choice for achieving this aim.

Parallel to his correspondence with Gurlitz, Wallace updated Harper, reminded them of their contractual obligation 'to defend that book against all piracies' and encouraged them to file a lawsuit against the Riley Brothers.[84] It took Gurlitz three more weeks to initiate legal proceedings in Equity against the Riley Brothers on behalf of Wallace, Harper and Clark in the U.S. District Court for the Southern District of New York.[85]

It Is a Very Valuable Property

Gurlitz's legal strategy was focused and persistent. Its aim was to cast the defendants' activities as dramatization of the novel. This was perhaps motivated by Clark's interest in protecting the tableaux market. The main logic of the strategy, however, was the same as that of the legal advice Harper received years earlier with respect to unauthorized tableaux. In the context of copyright jurisprudence that did not recognize a general principle of intermedia infringement, fitting the defendant's acts within the statutorily-recognized category of dramatization was the most promising route. This was achieved by presenting the entire set of activities comprising the lantern slide show as the equivalent of a dramatic performance of the novel, and portraying the images as merely an element of this integrated whole.

Clark's affidavit, which used various inflections of the word 'drama' dozens of times, was clearly built around this strategy. Clark described the lantern shows as 'public Dramatic Representation by Tableaux and Recitation of the work'.[86] His verbal gymnastics drew on the flexible meaning of 'tableaux' when he explained that the work was 'represented by tableaux thrown upon a screen upon the stage, by means of stereopticon or similar lanterns, and the person giving such Dramatic Representations then recited with such tableaux the portions

84 Letter from Lew Wallace to Harper Bros., 21 March 1896, Wallace Mss. II.
85 NARA, Wallace v. Riley Case File (hereinafter 'Wallace v. Riley').
86 Affidavit of Walter C. Clark, Wallace v. Riley, p. 2.

of the said work "BEN HUR" appropriate to convey to the audience the dramatic situation represented by each tableaux'.[87] Based on his snooping mission — that included attending one of the lantern shows in Brooklyn — Clark described the setup of the show in great detail, while studiously referring to the narrator as the 'reciting performer' and to the magic-lantern operator as 'the other performer'. The two-hour show, he said, was 'a dramatization and dramatic performance of the entire work of "BEN HUR" as invented, composed and written by General Wallace'.[88] Describing himself as being 'familiar with the business of giving dramatic performances of "BEN HUR" throughout the United States', he warned that 'unless the defendant is at once enjoined and prevented from further infringing on the rights of the deponent and the other complaints, the damage to his said business will be very large, and almost impossible to calculate'.[89]

In his affidavit, James Thorne Harper adapted a stunt from the publishing market: he referred and attached President Garfield's letter of praise for *Ben-Hur* to Wallace (the same one that was reproduced in the Garfield Edition of the book). His two foci, however, were market effects and a theory of dramatization. As for the former, Harper observed that *Ben-Hur* is 'a very valuable property, which, if protected, will give the author ample compensation'.[90] He predicted, however, that if lantern shows continue unchecked, profits would be adversely affected both in the book market and from the authorized tableaux. Harper's argument was that lantern slides 'of character to give most unsatisfactory impression of the genuine work' might dissuade the public from attending the tableaux or purchasing the book.[91] He also offered an elaborate theory to explain why the lantern shows constituted 'dramatizations and dramatic representations of the genuine works of General Wallace'.[92] The argument was that the defendants 'copied, imitated, represented and set in order, by means of living models, the portions of "BEN HUR" containing the most striking dramatic situations and events', and that these live representations were 'photographed and colored' and then

87 Ibid., p.3.
88 Ibid., p. 8.
89 Ibid., pp. 10–11.
90 Affidavit of James Thorne Harper, Wallace v. Riley, p. 1.
91 Ibid., p. 2.
92 Ibid., p. 5.

presented on the screen, accompanied by narration.[93] Harper likened the slide projection to the use of the *ekkylema* in ancient Greek theater where, he also observed, 'the dramatic effect was evidently produced largely by narration, in which, of course, the voice was the main instrument, especially as cumbersome painted masks were then worn by the actor'.[94] According to Harper, dramatization was constituted by the following: dividing the novel into scenes (including the most dramatic events), creating representations of those scenes by live models, photographing the representations, and presenting the images successively on stage in life-sized formats and accompanied by narration. The clever invocations of the special technique of photographing live subjects in creating the slides and of the apparatus, narration and masks used in Greek theater were designed to conceal the main weakness of the dramatization theory: the fact that magic-lantern shows involved no acting by live actors.

The heart of the argument in the Bill of Complaint was twofold. First, the general principle was argued that 'all property of every kind and nature' was held by the plaintiffs.[95] Here Gurlitz emphasized that the plaintiffs 'receive a substantial profit and benefit' from the licensed tableaux, that Clark 'has a large capital invested' in the enterprise, and that 'the said works constitute a most valuable property, and your orators believe that the value of the said property can only be preserved and maintained by preventing any use of said works without the consent and supervision of your orators'.[96] This was a version of the new understanding of copyright's property as protecting the extraction of profit from all possible markets. Since legal doctrine did not yet reflect this principle, however, Gurlitz was astute enough not to stop the argument there, and proceeded to try to squeeze the use into the category of dramatization. On this issue his argument repeated, in cumbersome legalese, the theories developed by Clark and Harper. The effect of the lantern slide projection, he argued,

> is to represent upon the stage before the audience in life size, one of such dramatic situations or events, and these devices are arranged and intended to be used, and are used, commencing with the beginning of

93 Ibid., p. 3.
94 Ibid., pp. 4–5.
95 Bill of Complaint, Wallace v. Riley, p. 10.
96 Ibid., p. 11.

> your orators' work 'BEN HUR' and carried forward in succession in the order in which, and as your orator the said Wallace, has invented and devised his said works, until the whole of his said works has so been represented before the audience.[97]

In the plea for remedy at the end of the bill it became clear that the dramatization argument was merely a strategy for capturing pictorial representation. In addition to accounting and disgorgement of profits, Gurlitz asked for an injunction — both preliminary and permanent — to restrain the defendants from engaging in a broad range of activities, including 'importing, manufacturing, advertising, selling, loaning, or otherwise disposing of any outfits or parts of outfits designed for or capable of being used in giving dramatic representations and recitations' of *Ben-Hur* and from 'copying, printing, reprinting, completing or imitating pictorially or otherwise the work'.[98] In other words, the dramatization right was being used as a means for prohibiting all derivatives of the text, including in the form of images such as the Riley Brothers' slides (see Figure 11).

The Rileys and their attorney William O. Campbell offered a different story.[99] The snide answer and affidavits — the latter kept referring to *Ben-Hur* as 'purporting to have been written by Lewis Wallace' — made two main arguments. The first was that the Riley slides, perhaps with the exception of the first in the set (proudly presenting the title 'Ben Hur: A Tale of the Christ'), are not illustrations of *Ben-Hur* at all, but rather 'original works of art' depicting 'scenes in the Orient illustrative of Biblical history and the history of ancient Eastern people'.[100] Herbert Riley went as far as asserting in his affidavit that Wallace did not 'devise and design all of the scenes, events, situations and incidents in the play or story of Ben Hur' and that if all the elements 'which have been published for centuries in the Bible, in the Histories of Greece, Rome Palestine, Arabia, Egypt and the Ancients' were removed from the novel 'there would remain neither plot nor story'.[101] This was a stretch, given

97 Ibid., p. 12.
98 Ibid., pp. 16–17.
99 This is the attorney of record in the court's documents. The Rileys later referred to 'Mr. Wilber' as their attorney. See 'Letter to the Editor' from Riley Brothers, *The Optical Magic Lantern Journal and Photographic Enlarger*, 7 (1896), 135–136 (p. 136).
100 Answer, Wallace v. Riley, p. 1.
101 Ibid., p. 2.

not only the title of the slides but also their highly detailed depictions of specific scenes from the novel. The argument precipitated angry refutations from plaintiffs in the form of further affidavits by two literary experts, who testified that *Ben-Hur,* while drawing on biblical and historical themes, is a highly original and imaginative work.[102]

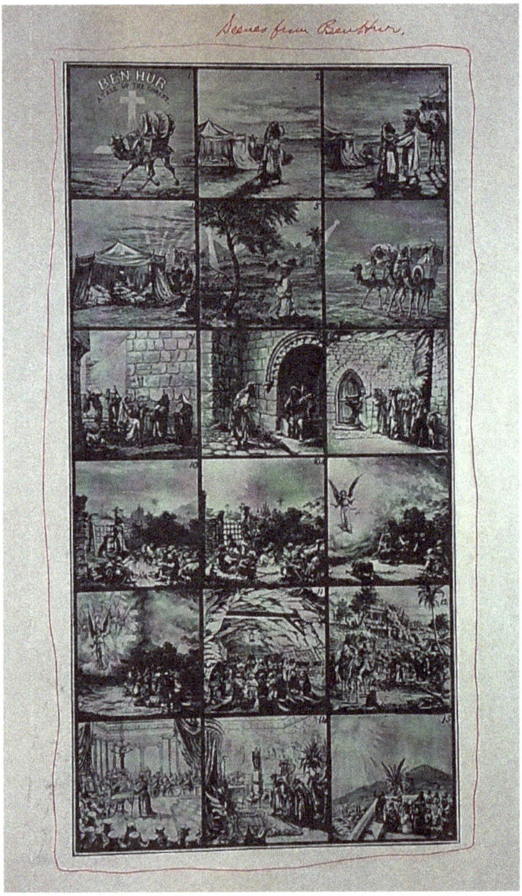

Fig. 11 A Reproduction of the Riley Brothers' Ben-Hur Slides Set as it Appeared in an Advertisement Submitted to the Court (author unknown, 1896), Lilly Library, Indiana University, Bloomington.

The second defense argument was more plausible. The affidavits by both Joseph and Herbert contained an identical paragraph designed 'to

102 Affidavit of Charlton T. Lewis and Affidavit of Laurence Hutton, Wallace v. Riley.

deny once for all [sic] that the words drama, dramatic or dramatically, dramatize or dramatization are correctly used' by the plaintiffs. In other words: 'A Stereoptican illustration is in no sense a drama, and a stereoptican lecture is not a dramatic entertainment'. The passage ends by referring the reader 'to any and all of the standard dictionaries to the English language extant'.[103] In a published letter, the Rileys further explained the definition of drama as 'a representation made by living actors, etc. and must have living voices and movements, etc.'[104] Laying aside the possibility that the slides constituted dramatization, Joseph's affidavit went on to assert that the production of lantern slides could not infringe copyright because 'they are neither copies nor imitations of any cut, print, picture, portrait or drawing in said books'.[105] This was a restatement of the traditional view: an image can only infringe copyright in another image.

In early September 1896 Judge Emile Henry Lacombe issued a preliminary injunction enjoining the Riley Brothers from selling, advertising or distributing copies of their text.[106] Some observers assessed that the injunction 'will put an end to "Ben Hur" stereopticon lectures'.[107] This was a misreading of the situation, since the injunction applied to the text only and not to the lantern slides. When the decision was issued later that month, it became clear that the plaintiffs had suffered a defeat.[108] That Riley was enjoined with respect to the text was no surprise. Half a century earlier an infringement by textual condensation of the entire novel might have been a close question, but not in 1896. Moreover, the argument that Riley drew only on general biblical themes rather than the specific expression of the novel *Ben-Hur* was disingenuous at best. In fact, according to one report, during

103 Affidavit of Herbert Jowett Riley, Wallace v. Riley, p. 1. Affidavit of Joseph Riley, Wallace v. Riley, p. 1.

104 Letter to the Editor from Riley Brothers, *The Optical Magic Lantern Journal and Photographic Enlarger*, 7 (1896), 135–136 (p. 136).

105 Affidavit of Joseph Riley, Wallace v. Riley, p. 4.

106 'A "Ben Hur" Injunction', *The New York Times*, 3 September 1896, p. 9.

107 Ibid., p. 12.

108 The last document in the case file is a decision by Judge Lacombe whose transcript is truncated. It appears that this was the written decision of the motion for a preliminary injunction. There is no indication that the case ever advanced beyond this stage, either in the trial court or as an appeal. See Order for Preliminary Injunction, Wallace v. Riley.

the lawsuit Riley proposed to withdraw the text.[109] With respect to the images, Lacombe was not unsympathetic to the plaintiffs. In a comment that would prove prophetic, he reportedly said that had the issue been a Vitascope presentation 'he could have understood' the argument.[110] But seeing still images as containing the same expressive content as a text was too much for him. He rejected the premise that no one 'might produce and sell copies of drawings, the *motif* of which was suggested in the book', deeming it something that no one would contend.[111] The Riley Brothers were free to go on distributing their slides, which they apparently did.[112]

The borderline separating text and image was not crossed in *Wallace v. Riley*. Learned treatise writers developed a new legal theory of copyright's property right as extending to every expressive form and market. *Ben-Hur* introduced a new economic model of exploiting a successful novel through licensing in multiple media markets, and produced the pressure for extending copyright to capture the exchange value of these derivatives. A clever legal strategy that attempted to squeeze images into the recognized category of dramatization had been devised, and various matching theories of dramatization had been woven. But the courts, still held back by remnants of the traditional understanding of copyright, refused to see images as copies of texts. For a time.

Aftermath: Harper v. Kalem and the Logic of Derivative Works

Images soon came back to haunt American copyright law, this time as moving images. And *Ben-Hur* was again in the thick of it. In 1907 the Kalem Company released a motion picture it advertised as 'A Roman

109 'Wallace and Others v. Riley Brothers, New York', *The Optical Magic Lantern Journal and Photographic Enlarger*, 7 (1896), 166. See also 'Wallace and Others v. Riley Bros.', *Photography*, September 24, 1896, p. 632; 'Infringement of Copyright', *The Photographic News*, 25 September 1896, p. 618; 'Illustrative Slides', *The American Amateur Photographer*, 8 (1896), 483–484.

110 Letter to the Editor from Riley Brothers, *The Optical Magic Lantern Journal and Photographic Enlarger*, 7 (1896), 135, p. 136.

111 'Wallace and Others v. Riley Brothers, New York', p. 167.

112 Solomon, *Ben-Hur*, p. 525.

Spectacle Pictures adapted from Gen. Lew Wallace's Famous Book Ben Hur'.[113] What followed was a reenactment of the Riley Brothers' slides events, only with higher stakes. The main interested party was now Klaw and Erlanger, the licensee and producer of the *Ben-Hur* grand theatrical production. Regarding the motion picture as a threat to its market, it rapidly filed a lawsuit together with Harper and Henry Wallace who following the death of his father took over the management of the commercial empire that *Ben-Hur* had become.[114] The motion picture itself, while being one of the first to have a written script, was nevertheless still a close cousin of the tableaux-vivant and magic-lantern shows. It consisted of a visual presentation of several scenes out of the novel connected by short textual intertitles. This was a pictorial spectacle, literally a 'motion picture' in the original sense of a sequence of images with the added incident of movement.[115] Thus, in light of *Wallace v. Riley* and traditional copyright principles, Kalem had reasons to be cautiously optimistic.

Presiding over the trial in the Southern District of New York was none other than Jude Emile Henry Lacomb. Making good on his comment eleven years earlier, he ruled in a cryptic opinion that the movie infringed the copyright in the novel and issued a broad injunction including a prohibition on Kalem to produce, play, exhibit, copy or advertise the dramatic composition 'Ben Hur' or 'any of its characters, scenes, incidents, plot or story'.[116] Kalem appealed the decision to the U.S. Circuit Court for the Second Circuit and then, after another loss, to the U.S. Supreme Court where it suffered a final defeat. The legal strategies of the opposing parties closely followed those employed in the Riley Brothers litigation. Kalem's lawyers argued that text and image were two different forms of expression and that one could not infringe copyright in the other. Their Supreme Court brief contained a long

113 *The Billboard*, 7 December 1907, p. 100.

114 See Oren Bracha, 'How Did Film Become Property? Copyright and the Early American Film Industry', in *Copyright and the Challenge of the New*, ed. by Brad Sherman and Leanne Wiseman (New York: Wolters Kluwer Law & Business, 2012), pp. 141–77; Peter Decherney, *Hollywood's Copyright Wars: From Edison to the Internet* (New-York: Columbia University Press, 2012), pp. 45–54; Solomon, *Ben-Hur*, pp. 543–552.

115 See Bracha, 'How Did Film Become Property?', p. 171.

116 Permanent Injunction Decision, Kalem Company v. Harper Bros, Transcript of Record, p. 24 (hereinafter 'Kalem v. Harper Bros').

section entitled 'Book and Picture Are Essentially Different', that led to the conclusion that an image could not be a 'copy' of a copyrighted text.[117] The plaintiffs' lawyers, for their part, used the exact same strategy introduced in *Wallace v. Riley*: bringing the images within the scope of copyright in texts through the category of dramatization. Their Supreme Court brief argued that 'What the Kalem Company did was to dramatize "Ben Hur"'.[118]

Ruling in favor of plaintiffs, both the Court of Appeals and the Supreme Court found that the exhibitors of the motion picture were copyright infringers and that Kalem was contributorily liable by facilitating their actions.[119] Indeed, today *Kalem* is often cited as a precedent with respect to secondary liability.[120] Modern lawyers usually find this reasoning puzzling or even backwards: surely, by adapting *Ben-Hur* into a motion picture, Kalem was the primary infringer whose infringement facilitated the further activities of the exhibitors? This anachronistic puzzle fails to understand the reasoning of the decisions and the extent to which recognizing moving images as an infringement of a book copyright was a revolutionary and challenging step for the judges who took it. On neither of the appeals did a court rule that the motion picture adaptation was dramatization or copyright infringement. In fact, the Court of Appeals explicitly ruled that it was not. 'The series of photographs taken by the defendant constitutes a single picture, capable of copyright as such', Circuit Judge Ward wrote, 'and as pictures only represent the artist's idea of what the author has expressed in words [...] they do not infringe a copyrighted book or drama, and should not as a photograph be enjoined'.[121] In other words, on this point the court agreed with the defendant: an image is neither a copy nor dramatization of a text. Dramatization does occur, however, '[w]hen the film is put on an exhibiting machine, which reproduces the action of the actors and animals'.[122] The Supreme Court opinion written by Justice Oliver Wendell Holmes Jr. further elaborated this reasoning:

117 Brief for Appellant. Kalem v. Harper Bros., p. 12.
118 Brief for Appellees. Kalem v. Harper Bros., p. 28.
119 Kalem Co. v. Harper Bros., 222 U.S. 55 (1911); Harper & Bros. v. Kalem Co., 169 F. 61 (2d Cir. N.Y. 1909).
120 See e.g. Metro-Goldwyn-Mayer Studios Inc. v. Grokster, Ltd., 545 U.S. 913, 935 (2005).
121 *Kalem*, 169 F. at 63.
122 Ibid.

> [D]rama may be achieved by action as well as by speech. Action can tell a story, display all the most vivid relations between men, and depict every kind of human emotion, without the aid of a word [...] But if a pantomime of Ben Hur would be a dramatizing of Ben Hur, it would be none the less so that it was exhibited to the audience by reflection from a glass and not by direct vision of the figures — as sometimes has been done in order to produce ghostly or inexplicable effects. The essence of the matter in the case last supposed is not the mechanism employed but that we see the event or story lived.[123]

Since it was only the exhibition of the film rather than the pictorial adaptation by its maker that constituted dramatization and copyright infringement, the courts had to resort to the secondary liability construct.

This reasoning was complex and cumbersome. Moreover, as critics were quick to point out, the theory that exhibition of a motion picture constituted dramatization under the 1870 statute was highly dubious.[124] Laying aside the technical legal maneuvers, when understood in context, what happened in *Kalem* is clear: the judges had already internalized copyright's new ideology as broad control over exchange value in all secondary markets. Yet, still constrained by the old doctrines and categories, they did not feel free to simply rule that a motion-picture adaptation was an infringing reproduction of a text. Instead they relied on the dramatization strategy first introduced in *Wallace* v. *Riley*, and the secondary liability construct. Notwithstanding these remnants of traditional copyright thinking, the *Kalem* courts did cross the text-image Rubicon. Within a few years, the idea that a motion-picture adaptation is an infringement of a novel's copyright was normalized. Future courts simply proceeded on the basis of that assumption and let the dramatization and contributory liability crutches drop.[125] Today, modern copyright lawyers are likely to find the idea that a motion-picture adaptation is not infringement of a copyright in a book alien. And while modern text-to-still-images cases are hard to find, if you asked an American copyright lawyer, her answer is likely to be that

123 *Kalem*, 222 U.S. at 61–62.

124 See e.g. 'Copyright — Moving Pictures as Dramatization', *Central. Law. Journal*, 73 (1911), 442–443.

125 Bracha, *Owning Ideas*, 186–187. For a discussion of the effect of the new regal framework on the film industry see Decherney, *Hollywood's Copyright Wars*, pp. 54–57.

images that embody enough concrete and detailed expression derived from a copyrighted text are infringing.

Recognizing text-to-image copyright infringement had broader implications. The Supreme Court's step in *Kalem* marked the beginning of the acceptance of the logic of derivative works: the deeply-seated assumption that copyright's property stretches across media and fields of expression as a means for allowing the owner to internalize profits from all available markets. American copyright law thus shifted from physicalism to meta-physicalism. In its early days, copyright's limited scope, traceable to its origin as a publisher's privilege, was embodied in the legal concept of the copy. The copy functioned as a quasi-physicalist object, somewhere between the physical book and the intangible work.[126] Understood as encompassing the specific language used by the author, it seemed to supply clear boundaries to the property right, objectively dictated by natural facts. By the dawn of the twentieth century the increased commodification of expressive works, epitomized by *Ben-Hur,* reshaped copyright. It came to be reflected in a new concept of the work as transcending specific expressive forms and spanning all possible markets. These metaphysics of derivative works-cum-markets would make the new logic of copyright seem as inevitable and natural as that of the copy.

Bibliography

Primary Sources

i. Archival Material

Kalem Company v. Harper Bros. Transcript of Record.

Lew Wallace (1827–1905) Miscellaneous Uncataloged Materials, at Lilly Library, Indiana University Bloomington.

Lew Wallace collection 1799–1972, Indiana Historical Society Manuscript Collection.

Stowe v. Thomas Case File, National Archives and Records Administration.

126 Bracha, *Owning Ideas*, pp. 143–145. See also Mark Rose, 'The Author in Court: Pope v. Curll (1741)', *Cardozo Arts & Entertainment Law Journal*, 10 (1992), 475–493 (p. 492).

Wallace Mss. II, Lilly Library, Indiana University Bloomington.

Wallace v. Riley Case File, National Archives and Records Administration.

ii. Legislation

1790 Copyright Act (Act of May 31, 1790), ch. 15, 1 Stat. 124.

1802 Copyright Act (Act of Apr. 29, 1802), ch. 36, 2 Stat. 171.

1856 Copyright Act Amendment (Act of Aug. 18, 1856), 11 Stat. 138.

1865 Copyright Act (Act of Mar. 3, 1865), 13 Stat. 540,

1870 Copyright Act (Act of July 8, 1870), ch. 230, 16 Stat. 198.

1897 Copyright Act Amendment (Act of Mar. 3, 1897), ch. 392, 29 Stat. 694

Statute of Anne 1710 (8 Anne c. 19).

Engravers' Copyright Act 1735 (8 Geo. II c.13).

iii. Cases

Gyles v. Wilcox (1740) 26 Eng. Rep. 489.

Folsom v. Marsh, 9 F. Cas. 342, 344 (C.C.D. Mass. 1841).

Harper & Bros. v. Kalem Co., 169 F. 61 (2d Cir. N.Y. 1909).

Kalem Co. v. Harper Bros., 222 U.S. 55 (1911).

Metro-Goldwyn-Mayer Studios Inc. v. Grokster, Ltd., 545 U.S. 913 (2005).

Millar v. Taylor (1769) 95 Eng. Rep. 201.

Story v. Holocombe, 23 F. Cas. 171 (C.C.D.Oh. 1847).

Stowe v. Thomas, 23 F. Cas. 201 (C.C.E.D.Pa. 1853).

Secondary Sources

Bracha, Oren, 'Commentary on Stowe v. Thomas (1853)', in *Primary Sources on Copyright (1450–1900)*, ed. by Lionel Bently and Martin Kretschmer (2008), http://www.copyrighthistory.org/commentary/us_1853b.

——, 'Commentary on the U.S. Copyright Act Amendment 1856', in *Primary Sources on Copyright (1450–1900)*, ed. by Lionel Bently and Martin Kretschmer (2008), http://www.copyrighthistory.org/commentary/us_1856.

——, 'How Did Film Become Property? Copyright and the Early American Film Industry', in *Copyright and the Challenge of the New*, ed. by Brad Sherman and Leanne Wiseman (New York: Wolters Kluwer Law & Business, 2012) pp. 141–177.

——, *Owning Ideas: The Intellectual Origins of American Intellectual Property, 1709–1909* (New York: Cambridge University Press, 2016), https://doi.org/10.1017/9780511843235.

Curtis, George Ticknor, *A Treatise on the Law of Copyright* (Boston: C. C. Little and J. Brown, 1847).

Deazley, Ronan, 'The Statute of Anne and the Great Abridgment Swindle', *Houston Law Review*, 47 (2010), 793–818.

Decherney, Peter, *Hollywood's Copyright Wars: From Edison to the Internet* (New-York: Columbia University Press, 2012).

Drone, Eaton S., *A Treatise on the Law of Property in Intellectual Productions in Great Britain and the United States* (Boston: Little, Brown, 1879).

Gordon, Colin, *By Gaslight in Winter: A Victorian Family History through the Magic Lantern* (London: Elm Tree Books, 1980).

Henry, David, 'Ben-Hur: Francis Fredric Theophilus Weeks and Patent No. 8615 of 1894', *The New Magic Lantern Journal*, 5 (1987), 2–5.

Homestead, Melissa J., '"When I can Read my Title Clear": Harriet Beecher Stowe and the Stowe v. Thomas Copyright Infringement Case', *Prospects*, 27 (2002), 201–245, https://doi.org/10.1017/s0361233300001198.

Hunter, David, 'Copyright Protection for Engravings and Maps in Eighteenth Centaury Britain', *The Library*, 6th Ser., 9 (1987), 128–47, https://doi.org/10.1093/library/s6-IX.2.128.

Miller, Derek, *Copyright and the Value of Performance, 1770–1911* (Cambridge: Cambridge University Press, 2018), https://doi.org/10.1017/9781108349284.

Miller, Howard, 'The charioteer and the Christ: Ben-Hur in America from the Gilded Age to the Culture Wars', *Indiana Magazine of History*, 104 (2008), 153–175.

Morsberger, Robert E. and Morsberger, Katherine M., *Lew Wallace: Militant Romantic* (New York: McGraw-Hill 1980).

Pon, Lisa, *Raphael, Dürer, and Marcantonio Raimondi: Copying and the Italian Renaissance Print* (New Haven and London: Yale University Press, 2004).

Rose, Mark, 'The Author in Court: Pope v. Curll (1741)', *Cardozo Arts & Entertainment Law Journal*, 10 (1992), 475–493.

Ryan, Barbara, *Chronicling Ben-Hur's Climb, 1880–1924* (London and New York: Routledge 2019), https://doi.org/10.4324/9781315572000.

Sag, Mathew, 'The Prehistory of Fair Use', *Brooklyn Law Review,* 76 (2011), 1371–1412.

Solomon, Jon, *Ben-Hur: The Original Blockbuster* (Edinburgh: Edinburgh University Press, 2016).

Swansburg, John, 'The Passion of Lew Wallace: The Incredible Story of How a Disgraced Civil War General Became One of the Best-Selling Novelists in American history', *Slate,* 26 March 2013, http://www.slate.com/articles/life/history/2013/03/ben_hur_and_lew_wallace_how_the_scapegoat_of_shiloh_became_one_of_the_best.html.

Theisen, Lee Scott, '"My God, Did I set all of this in Motion?" General Lew Wallace and Ben-Hur', *Journal of Popular Culture,* 18 (1984), 33–41.

PART II

AGENTS OF CIRCULATION: ENTREPRENEURS AND RIVALS

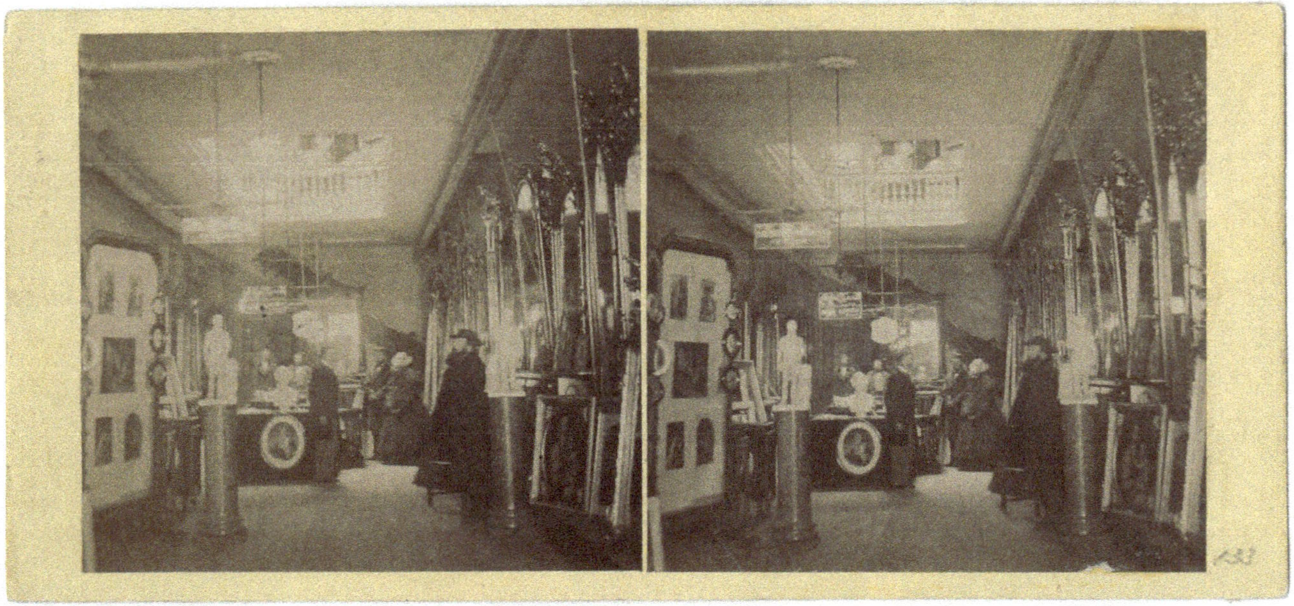

Fig. 1 John Moran, [James S. Earle & Son, looking glasses, 816 Chestnut Street, Philadelphia] (Philadelphia, ca. 1861). Library Company of Philadelphia, https://digital.librarycompany.org/islandora/object/digitool%3A100622.

7. The Frame Maker/Picture Dealer

A Crucial Intermediary in the Nineteenth-Century American Popular Print Market

Erika Piola

In July 1832, in an advertisement published in the *Philadelphia Inquirer*, British-born James S. Earle (1806–1879) begged 'leave to inform his friends and the public ... that he [had] commenced [his] business ...' of a looking glass and picture frame manufactory on the 100 block of South Fifth Street. Earle promoted his moderated rates and prompt attention to 'orders' in which prints received second billing only to looking glasses.[1] During Earle's near fifty years in the business, the entrepreneur who professionally described himself more often as a frame maker, always sold prints. Engravings, often European in provenance, predominantly constituted his picture stock.

Philadelphia frame-maker-turned-picture dealer William Smith also left a visible, if smudgy, professional mark on the mirror of the antebellum American picture trade. Smith, who is less well-documented than Earle, operated on the other end of the spectrum of this bifurcated profession. He entered the field in the 1850s, amid the rise in popularity of the more affordable and efficiently-executed lithographic parlor print. Engravings and lithographs published by him and some including a copyright statement in his, the artist's, or the printer's name, comprised his pictures for sale. Since at least the late eighteenth century, Philadelphia looking glass and frame

1 'Looking-Glass & Picture Frame Manufactory. James S. Earle', *Philadelphia Inquirer*, 26 July 1832, p. 4. Earle was the nephew of James Earle (1770–1855), a Philadelphia glazier, gallery owner, and business partner of Thomas Sully.

 https://doi.org/10.11647/OBP.0247.07

makers who were also picture dealers, publishers, and sometimes printers have played a role in the development of an American print market.[2]

Philadelphia is one of the few American cities able to serve as a focal point to examine the democratization of the nineteenth-century picture market in the antebellum United States. By the early nineteenth century, a national art movement had gained momentum, particularly in the Mid-Atlantic city, spurred by developments in printing, domestic art training, and the art trade's lessening dependence on European imports.[3] Established with missions to foster the cultivation and appreciation of American art, the Pennsylvania Academy of the Fine Arts (PAFA, founded in 1805) and the subscription-based American Art-Union (AAU) of New York and its counterpart the Art-Union of Philadelphia (AUP), chartered in 1842 and 1844 respectively, were integral to the national movement and to the trade practices of the frame maker.

When established as a shareholding institution by several of Philadelphia's wealthiest citizens, and as a classical art academy by three of its most successful artists, PAFA sought to facilitate American training of working artists in tandem with enabling patronage-based professional development. By the 1810s, however, the Academy had evolved into an exhibition space for a paying public to view American art not as purchasers, but as 'middlebrow amateurs'.[4] Art unions lauded as '[having] more effect in producing the growing taste for beauty in forms and colors, among all classes, than all others combined' served a complementary, parallel role in fostering an American art market for the non-elite.[5] Sustained by membership fees affordable by the middle

---

2 For brevity in professional identification, looking glass/frame makers/picture dealers will be referred to here as frame makers or frame makers/picture dealers. Extant business records for Earle and Smith are not known to exist.

3 For a compendium of commentaries contemporary to the period and representative of the movement, see *American Art to 1900: A Documentary History*, ed. by Sarah Burns and John Davis (Berkeley: University of California Press, 2009). See also E. McSherry Fowble, *Two Centuries of Prints in America, 1680–1880: A Selective Catalogue of the Winterthur Museum Collection* (Charlottesville: University Press of Virginia, 1987).

4 Yvette Piggush, 'Visualizing Early American Audiences: The Pennsylvania Academy of the Fine Arts and Allston's Dead Man Restored', *American Art Studies*, 9 (2011), 716–747 (p. 747).

5 'The Fine Arts in Scotland. The Edinburgh Art Union,' *Philadelphia Inquirer*, 23 January 1855, p. 2. Educator and amateur painter J. J. Mapes expressed a similar sentiment in his 1851 essay about the indispensable role of fine arts to civilization, and noted 'Our Academies of Art and Art Unions have done much to improve the public taste, and their influence cannot but prove most beneficial'. J. J. Mapes,

classes, the institutions organized by the socially elite or by artists offered an annual subscription premium of an engraving, purchased paintings by American artists and distributed them as lottery prizes, and oversaw free, public art galleries among their multiple means to create educated consumers of art from a wider socioeconomic base.

Between the 1820s and 1850s, an American market distributing American and European-made prints to the middle- and lower-middle classes more fully developed in concert with the establishment of American art unions, the evolution of PAFA, and the fomenting of implicit trade rules by frame makers. When the *Inquirer* reported in May 1840 on the *Future Prospects of the Fine Arts in America* lecture delivered by literary scholar Rev. George W. Bethune, it underlined the forging synergistic dynamic of the Academy, Unions, and frame makers in creating a viable print market and sustaining the latter's trade. In the lecture, reported to the newspaper's wide readership, Bethune advocated that 'well-executed engravings of good pictures are incomparably better than middling paintings' and when hung on the walls of one's house were means for the 'cultivation of the [American] domestic virtue — love of home'.[6] Delivered at the opening of the new exhibition hall of the Philadelphia Artists' Fund Society, the artists of the Society, like the frame makers, sought the financial rewards of those 'well-executed engravings'. PAFA, AAU, AUP, and Earle, and later Smith worked in concert with and in reaction to this climate, inculcating all classes to appreciate and consume art, particularly American art. These actors helped to create a print market based on reproductions, reprints, and reuses of existing 'good pictures' and 'middling paintings'. Within this culture, graphic material from artists' designs, whether prepared in the context of a professional commission, patronage, or a collaborative endeavour, was produced, distributed, and consumed. The artists involved rarely claimed ownership of their work or initiated litigation.[7]

'Usefulness of the Arts of Design,' *Sartain's Union Magazine*, 8 (1851), 211–213 (p.212).

6 The Artists' Fund Society, formed in 1835, was the first art organization in Philadelphia managed exclusively by artists, with the mission of 'the cultivation of skill, the diffusion of taste, and the encouragement of living professional talent in the arts of Painting, Sculpture, Architecture, and Engraving, as may best conduce the primary purpose of benevolence'. 'Dr. Bethune's Lecture. The Fine Arts'. *Philadelphia Inquirer*, 8 May 1840, p.2.

7 Oren Bracha has argued that a radical transformation of American copyright law occurred during the nineteenth century. An incomplete, convoluted, and

The process for the production and publication of the prints sustaining the emerging market was usually a collaborative one. The execution of the design, drawing, and intaglio engraving/or lithography of a work was not typically completed by the same person. An artist created the design, an engraver or lithographer placed it onto a printing surface, and the printer printed it onto paper with print runs ranging from a few hundred copies to several thousand copies. A publisher, who could be the printer or a frame maker/picture dealer, sold the print through their shop or through canvassers. The reproduced work could be of an original painting commissioned or purchased by the publisher, who would be its owner. Conversely, the artist could commission the publisher to reproduce their painting, of which they were the owner. Prints, frequently after original paintings that were often also displayed in frame makers' warerooms, were mainstays in the stock of these dual-role entrepreneurs.

Whereas intaglio engravings in these dealers' stocks, which could take several months to produce, were described by cultural critics as 'the nearest approach that can be made to the individuality of a painting,' they debated whether the lithographs the tradesmen had for sale, which could take only days to execute, had any 'real claims to art' to the works having a 'spirit ... no merely imitative art can ascertain'.[8]

In 1802, the amendment to the US Copyright Act to include legal protection for the creation of 'historical and other prints' was enacted.[9] Despite being eligible for copyright, antebellum-era prints included in the frame makers' traceable stocks of engravings and later lithographs only sometimes contained a statement of copyright. Historical scenes and the 'other prints' of portraits or views typically encompassed those presented as having been registered for copyright.[10] The visual content of prints, even those originally issued with a copyright statement, often

---

contradictory ideology of romantic authorship and originality emerged. Oren Bracha, 'The Ideology of Authorship Revisited: Authors, Markets, and Liberal Values in Early American Copyright', *The Yale Law Journal*, 118 (2008), 186–271.

8 'Fictitious Engravings', *Cosmopolitan Art Journal*, 4, December 1860, 176 and *United States Gazette*, 14 February 1832, p. 2.

9 See '1802 Amendment (1802)', in *Primary Sources on Copyright (1450–1900)*, ed. by Lionel Bently and Martin Kretschmer, http://www.copyrighthistory.org/cam/tools/request/showRecord.php?id=record_us_1802 (particularly section 3).

10 Deduction made from survey of cataloged prints dated between 1800 and 1860 and with a statement of copyright in the collections of the American Antiquarian Society.

led multiple lives betwixt and between print mediums and publishers. Unclear transfers of copyright, which became more nebulous when a work no longer contained a statement, permeate these multiple iterations. However, copyright infringement cases against antebellum print sellers, as well as those brought forth by antebellum engravers, lithographers, and printers, are not common in the public record.[11] Frame makers/picture dealers appear to have acted within a professional network irrespective to, uninfluenced by, and outside of the confines of a law that was often understood idiosyncratically.

Within this milieu, frame makers, commonly associated with art unions and with their storefronts — geographically clustered together and near art institutions in a given city — imbued prints with artistic, cultural, and commercial value. These nineteenth-century art agents represent a touchstone in unpacking the cultural mechanisms influencing socioeconomic values of copies of art in the form of the mass-produced print. However, despite the enduring presence of frame makers/picture dealers during the nineteenth century, scholars have yet to fully explore the significant intermediary role that such tradesmen had within the popular print market of a major American city.

This chapter explores the cultural field of these overlooked figures, with a focus on the Philadelphia frame maker, and asks the following question: how did these diversified entrepreneurs try to distinguish themselves, yet conform to the structures and patterns that characterized their trade?[12] The professional networks and tools, as well as the interrelationships, of these businessmen within the art world and trade represent underexplored dimensions in the construction and operations of the American popular print market. Frame makers/picture dealers play a consequential role in understanding how the nineteenth-century print consumer came to define and own art.

---

11 Reviews of J. B. (John Bradford) Wallace et al., *Reports of Cases Determined in the Circuit Court United States for the Third Circuit*, 3 vols. (Philadelphia, 1849–1871) revealed no cases focused on infringement of copyright related to prints, engravings, or lithographs in the Philadelphia court between 1801 and 1862. *Binns* v. *Woodruff* is the exemplar case of the period. See Chapter 3 in this volume.

12 Pamela Fletcher, 'Shopping for Art: The Rise of the Commercial Art Gallery, 1850s-90s,' in *The Rise of the Modern Art Market in London: 1850–1939*, ed. by Pamela Fletcher and Anne Helmreich (New York: Manchester University Press, 2011), 47–84 (p. 61). See also Martha Tedeschi, '"Where the Picture Cannot Go, the Engravings Penetrate": Prints and the Victorian Art Market', *Art Institute of Chicago Museum Studies* 31 (2005), 8–19.

Philadelphia Frame Makers' Role in the Print Market

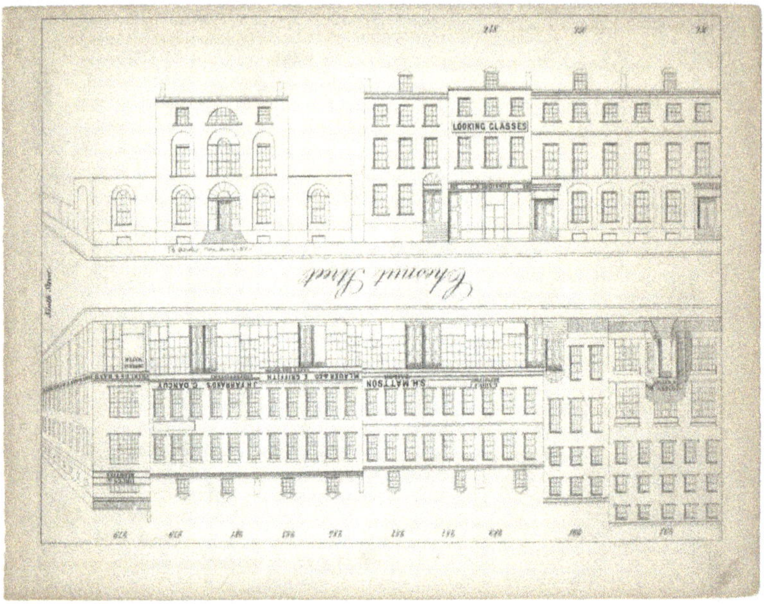

Fig. 2 Julio Rae, *Rae's Philadelphia Pictorial Directory & Panoramic Advertiser. Chestnut Street, from Second to Tenth Streets*, 900 block Chestnut Street (Philadelphia: Julio Rae, 1851). Library Company of Philadelphia, https://digital.librarycompany.org/islandora/object/digitool%3A123507.

When Earle announced the opening of his frame-making business in the early 1830s, the popular print trade in Philadelphia was beginning a new era. Lithographs had entered the market. The first successful Philadelphia commercial lithographic firm had been recently established when the existing print market was essentially equated with intaglio engravings.[13] By the turn of the next decade around twenty-four framers, glaziers, and looking-glass manufacturers, including Earle, C. N. Robinson (b. ca. 1790), Thomas J. (ca. 1805–1859), and later Joseph S. (ca. 1818–1871) Natt, helped the city's denizens to beautify themselves and their walls, operating in shops clustered closely together on Chestnut Street.[14] Their

13 In 1828, gilders David Kennedy and William Lucas established the firm nine years after artist Bass Otis executed the first successful lithograph in the United States in Philadelphia in 1819.

14 A familial relationship has not been determined between Thomas J. and Joseph S. Natt.

businesses were often acknowledged and lauded in the popular press during the height of the AAU's success at mid-century.

Robinson, active in the carver and gilder trade since the 1810s, received consistent mention in the *Philadelphia Inquirer*. In 1849, *Inquirer* columnists noted his store on the 900 block of Chestnut Street as crowded, 'morning, noon, and night' and implied that his reputation and location were so well-established, his address did not need to be stated (see Figure 2). In the October 17 edition of the paper that year, he garnered high praise for his fairness in picture- dealing.[15] Like Robinson, Earle had a presence in the mid-nineteenth century Philadelphia press. 'Fine Arts' articles noted that his gallery, which had relocated to the 800 block of Chestnut Street by 1839, as one for the 'lovers of the ... beautiful', as well as an exemplar of a 'leading print and painting establishment' in the city (Figure 1 and Figure 3).[16]

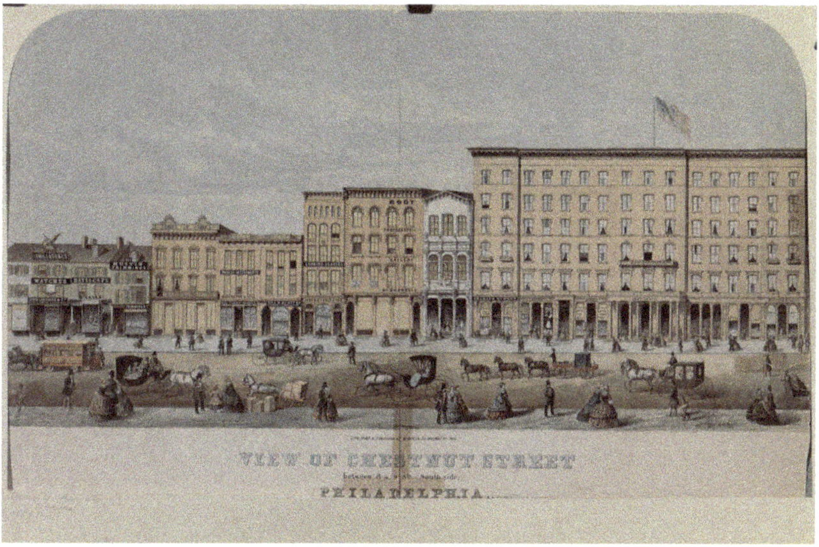

Fig. 3 William Boell, *View of Chestnut Street Between 8 & 9 Sts. (South Side,) Philadelphia* (Philadelphia: W. Boell, 1860). Color lithograph. Bc 87 C 525a, Historical Society of Pennsylvania.

15 'City Notices', *Philadelphia Inquirer*, 9 November, p. 1, and 15 December 1849, p. 1. See also 'The Fine Arts. The American Art Union and the International Art Union. Reprinted from the N.Y. Mirror.' *Philadelphia Inquirer*, 17 October 1849, p. 1.

16 'A Gallery of Paintings', *Philadelphia Inquirer*, 16 April 1849, p. 2; and 'The Fine Arts. Choice and Beautiful Paintings', *Philadelphia Inquirer*, 4 September 1849, p. 2.

For the 'lovers of the beautiful', Philadelphia frame makers'/picture dealers' galleries were free to visit and offered a selection of prints affordable by a cross-section of consumers. Earle's newspaper advertisements capitalized on this rhetoric of affordability, and he often promoted his gallery as constantly open and proffering a 'large collection of Prints, with portrait frames, of the [...] latest patterns' to be disposed 'on the most reasonable terms'.[17] Before the frame makers' free galleries had a palpable presence in the city and press, PAFA at Tenth and Chestnut Streets, located within a block of the AUP and the Earle cohort galleries, served in the preceding decades as the city's major public space catering to art consumers.

Soon after its establishment in 1805, PAFA began to hold ticket-based exhibitions of contemporary American art, including those organized by the Society of Artists formed in 1810 to challenge the ideology of art based on classical models. A means for the institution to remain financially solvent, it was also a means, as Yvette Piggush has shown, for PAFA's paying art spectators, rather than the shareholding patrons or the artists, to control the trajectory of the genres of art produced and exhibited. Spectators who could not necessarily afford to purchase a painting directly from an artist and who were influenced by the popular literary, theatrical, entertainment, and tourism culture of the time became central actors in the type of art seen inside — and bought outside the walls of PAFA. An expanding antebellum art audience wanted and expected artists to produce historical and narrative-themed works, rather than classical ones, that provided something 'sensational to see, to feel, and to write about'.[18]

In turn, the artists wanted to capitalize on that demand and earn the financial benefits of a wider audience seeking an emotional connection with art. Frame makers/picture dealers like Earle literally and figuratively situated themselves as intermediaries whose role it was to transform PAFA viewers of art into purchasers of art. As observed in the 1840s by AUP manager Prof. George Reed, 'lookers-on who belong to every condition of life ...' were thronging print shop windows as a result

17 See *Press* (Philadelphia, Pa.), 23 March 1859, p. 4; and 'Prints, Paintings, and Looking Glasses', *Philadelphia Inquirer*, 11 February 1833, p. 4.

18 Piggush, 'Visualizing Early American Audiences', 716–747 (pp. 725; 747).

of 'the innocent pleasure from works of art [being] felt by increasing numbers'.[19]

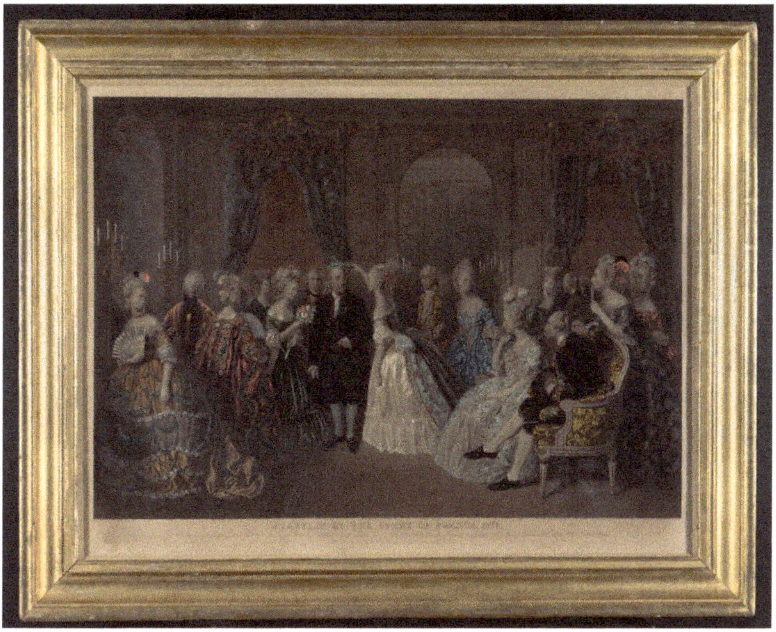

Fig. 4 Example of types of frames and engravings sold by Philadelphia frame makers/picture dealers. William Overend Geller after Baron André-Edouard Jolly, *Franklin at the Court of France, 1778* (Philadelphia: William Jay, Charles J. Hedenberg and William H. Emerson, 1853). Hand-colored engraving on woven paper in gilded, wood frame. Gift of Mr. & Mrs. Donald F. Carpenter, 1980.0042 A B, Courtesy of Winterthur Museum.

Owing to their location in the city, the Chestnut Street frame makers regularly interacted with PAFA's (and later AUP's) middle-class patron base who sought an emotional connection with a framed work of art (painting or print) in their own home, and not only in a public display space.[20] In practical terms, they could also serve the 'lookers-on' who could not afford a painting, nor possibly the admission fee to the Academy, nor a subscription to an art union. Enticed persons could use Earle and his neighboring cohorts as 'gift shops'. Any patron of these tradesmen, for twenty-five cents — about the same price to see

19 *Transactions of the Art-Union of Philadelphia for the Year 1849* (Philadelphia: King & Baird, 1849), p. 69.

20 'Now Exhibiting at the Academy of the Fine Arts, Chestnut Street', *Public Ledger*, 1 January 1849, p. 3.

an exhibition at PAFA — could purchase a framed print suggestive of the paintings at the Academy that they had viewed, felt, read, or heard about (Figure 4). Whether the working-class laborers in Philadelphia who earned nearly $300 a year were one of Reed's noted lookers-on who visited the 'fair' Chestnut Street frame makers for 'lovers of the beautiful' can only be speculated, but they had that choice.[21]

In 1856, when William Smith began to be listed as a frame maker on the 700 block of South Third Street, the trade had grown to thirty-five in the field. He evolved into a frame maker/ picture dealer within a few years. Earle and his long-standing peers worked in the cultural and commercial section of the city and near hotels, the AUP gallery, and PAFA (Figure 2 and Figure 8). Smith worked below the corridor of the city's printing district near Third and Chestnut Streets. Unlike his longstanding Philadelphia peers, he operated close to and en route to printers, print publishers, and coloring establishments, such as John Childs (100 block South Third Street) who provided other professional networking opportunities — including his lithographs being published by Smith.

While Earle relied on direct marketing and good press in the *Philadelphia Inquirer*, a ca. 1863 catalog of steel engravings and lithographs that were published by Smith suggests that he focused on canvassers and the wholesale market.[22] Although a comprehensive list of titles sold by Earle and Smith and the demographics of those who purchased them cannot be compiled from extant records, similarities and differences in both men's stocks of available prints and their patronage are discernible through newspaper ads, Smith's catalog, and extant graphic materials.

Patrons of Earle would be privy to a stock of imported European prints after European artists. Based on Earle's title lists in the press in the 1850s, the picture dealer focused his imported stock on European landscapes, and religious and genre works, and with most priced between one and six dollars. The genre prints were often after popular British, German, and French genre and animal painters, such as Edwin Landseer, Rosa Bonheur, and Thomas Faed, as well as Pre-Raphaelites

21 Income figure extrapolated from United States Bureau of Labor Statistics, *History of Wages in the United States From Colonial Times to 1928* (Washington, D.C: G.P.O., October 1929), p. 253, https://fraser.stlouisfed.org/title/4067.

22 *Washington's Triumphal Entry into New York* (Philadelphia: Published by William Smith, [ca. 1863]). Library Company of Philadelphia.

who strove for realism in their works. In contemporary terms, these were more fine than popular art prints, and ones published in Europe during a period before international copyright agreements came into force.[23]

Usually promoted in the dozens and without sizes or prices in the newspaper notices, the prints' artists, and not their engravers, are typically referenced in the advertisements — and generally by their last names only. The fact that Earle's advertisements mentioned the artists suggests that he thought his (middle-class) audience was familiar with them, perhaps from visiting his and other Philadelphia galleries.[24] By all appearances, the social value of Earle's primary print stock in the market for the middle class and those who emulated them relied on European cachet.[25] Nonetheless, Earle also sold prints after American artists of imagery that was 'sensational to see and to feel'. In 1849, A. C. Smith's lithograph after Philadelphia Artists' Society Fund organizer and artist Joshua Shaw's painting *Travelling of Village Tinker* received high praise.[26] As part of a set, the prints, when promoted without a price in an article in the *Inquirer*, were characterized 'as admirably suited for parlor ornaments ... which cannot but find a response in every feeling heart.'[27]

Unlike Earle, Smith newspaper advertisements are rare. His circa-1863 catalog with retail prices, as well as a 'Notice to Agents and the Trade' suggests he sometimes sold his prints directly to the consumer, but more often through canvassers and at wholesale. Tellingly, in terms of who may have purchased Smith's prints, he advises in his 'Notice' that 'The most successful method to sell these pictures is to allow your

23 The Berne Convention for the Protection of Literary and Artistic Works was adopted in 1886. http://www.wipo.int/treaties/en/ip/berne/summary_berne.html. The United States did not sign the International Copyright Act until 1891.

24 This marketing technique aligns with ones employed by the post-revolutionary Paris art dealers explored by Steven R. Adams. As examined by Adams, the dealers' advertising methods created a narrative for an appreciation of art based on subjective factors that were tied to the personage of the artist and the 'intuitive sensibilities of the consumer'. 'Noising Things abroad": Art, Commodity, and Commerce in Post-Revolutionary Paris', *Nineteenth Century Art Worldwide*, Autumn 2013, http://www.19thc-artworldwide.org/autumn13/adams-on-art-commodity-and-commerce-in-post-revolutionary-paris.

25 See Shearjashub Spooner, *An Appeal to the People of The United States, on Behalf of Art, Artists, and the Public Weal* (New York, 1854), p. 11.

26 An image of Shaw's *Travelling of Village Tinker* in a private collection can be viewed at https://www.the-athenaeum.org/art/detail.php?ID=34460.

27 'Fine Arts', *Philadelphia Inquirer*, 27 August 1849, p. 2.

purchasers to pay for them by weekly instal[l]ments'.[28] Smith courted a retail print consumer with less discretionary income for whom knowing the price upfront and being able to pay in installments was appealing.

The catalog lists over 100 prints with 'size to frame in inches'. They are organized by engravings, lithographs, and 'colored sporting pictures'. Like Earle, Smith 'always [had] on hand' European prints, including works by Bonheur and Landseer. However, these represented a minor part of his advertised stock. From the catalog and his known extant prints, his commercial wheelhouse in terms of his picture dealing by the end of the antebellum era rested on prints published by him, many likely as reprints. Engravings and lithographs, measuring between 8 x 10 and 33 x 44 inches and typically depicting genre, sentimental, religious, historical, political, and portrait views predominated. The engravings sold at retail prices between twelve cents and three dollars, while the lithographs sold for between ten cents and five dollars.

Size, medium, and color variably and seemingly inconsistently affected the price. Plain copies of the same title in color were typically half the price, but a color printed lithograph of *The Court of Death* indicated as being after the renowned painting of American painter Rembrandt Peale was priced less than half (seventy-five cents) of a similarly-sized, plain genre lithograph after the European artist Jacob Eickholtz (two dollars). European cachet was seemingly at play as well with certain Smith prints. However, it also conceivable that the Smith *Court* lithograph was a reprint from the original printing stone of the Peale color lithograph first published by and with a statement of copyright in the name of showman Gordon Q. Colton (1814–1898), the owner of the painting at the time. Through an extensive advertisement in the *Public Ledger* in January 1860, Colton exhorts that since he was able to print 100,000 of the lithographs (which he called engravings), he could sell them by subscription for one dollar each. A price, he notes, that would not be possible if he could only print 5,000.[29] The chromolithographic process afforded such large print runs in a way that the engraving process did not. The Smith seventy-five cent price intimates the market value of the lithograph as a reprint did not decrease substantially in a few years. As will be discussed later, other

28 *Washington's Triumphal*, p. 8.
29 'The Court of Death', *Public Ledger*, 6 January 1860, p. 2.

prints in Smith's stock prompt additional speculation as to how prices emanated in frame makers' stocks of prints.

Whereas Earle's title lists made little effort to introduce his stock to unfamiliar consumers, Smith's catalog employed promotional epithets about the works in an effort to appeal to a wider consumer base. Whether those targeted purchased the prints or not is not known from available sources. The assumption can be drawn that white Philadelphians were the primary purchasers in the print market of a city where the Black population was about four percent at mid-century.[30] However, a broad cross-section of Philadelphia society, including women, African Americans, and the working class, especially with a payment plan, could have acquired *The Cottage Fireside*, 'a charming steel plate for every home' for fifty cents or *We Praise Thee O God!* 'for every Christian home' for one dollar and fifty cents. Similarly, in this vein, an engraved portrait of William Lloyd Garrison captioned as the 'Advocate of Human Rights' selling for twenty-five cents may have enticed persons from the city's white abolitionist community and/or the Black community active in civil rights to purchase it. Frame makers/picture dealers were entrepreneurs active in a growing popular art market. They wanted to leverage this growth, and in Smith's case, he used personal connections through item-specific descriptions of the prints more often than relying on the cachet of an artist's name or a European provenance as a marketing tactic.

Smith and Earle also appealed to niche markets by gender and age to sell their prints (and frames). In 1859, when Earle requested the special attention of ladies to review his spring sale of original art paintings at auction, he could conceivably presume his 'Fine Art' department of engravings, including sentimental prints, would receive the women's attention as well.[31] More middle-class women could

30 Percentage extrapolated from figures listed in *Demographics of Philadelphia* https://en.wikipedia.org/wiki/Demographics_of_Philadelphia and *History of African Americans in Philadelphia* https://en.wikipedia.org/wiki/History_of_African_Americans_in_Philadelphia.

31 See *James S. Earle & Son's Great Spring Sale of Oil Paintings. Catalogue of the Most Extensive and Highest Class Collections of Oil Paintings, Watercolor Drawings, Etc.* (Philadelphia: Earle's Galleries, 1859), https://archive.org/details/collectionofoilp00jame/page/4/mode/2up. Metropolitan Museum of Art. Auction advertised in *Philadelphia Inquirer*, 26 March 1859, p. 3. Josephine Cobb, 'The Washington Art Association: An Exhibition Record, 1856–1860', in *Records of the Columbia Historical Society* 63/65, ed. by Francis Coleman Rosenberger (Washington, D.C.: Historical Society of Washington D.C., 1966), 122–190 (p. 165).

readily and individually purchase a sentimental print like *Grandmother's Darling* after Ernst Meyer (seventy-five cents), one of his least expensive offered, than an original oil painting for hundreds of dollars. In a related manner, Smith published a complementary pair of ten-cent lithographs that appealed to children and depicted a boy in *Morning Prayer. 'God Bless Papa'* and a girl in *Evening Prayer. 'God Bless Mama'* that tugged at parental and juvenile heart strings meant to loosen maternal purse strings. Smith also proactively solicited to the young adult market through the engraving *Sparking* (fifty cents) of a scene of courting that 'Bachelors and Young Ladies should have ...'. Originally issued through the AAU in 1844, the print, as will be discussed later, was one of a number by art collectives that Smith reissued.

Engravings found a second life through Smith's tradesmanship: not only through reprints, but also through the fluid exchange of imagery between mediums that was common in this period. Given the preponderance of titles in Smith's catalog and known prints that were reprints or reiterations, the practices of reuse and appropriation, which were not readily visible in Earle's business, were foundational to Smith's. Although Earle and Smith occupied different positions along a spectrum of frame-making and picture dealing, they could also work in synergistic tandem with each other in the development of their print stock after the same original artwork.

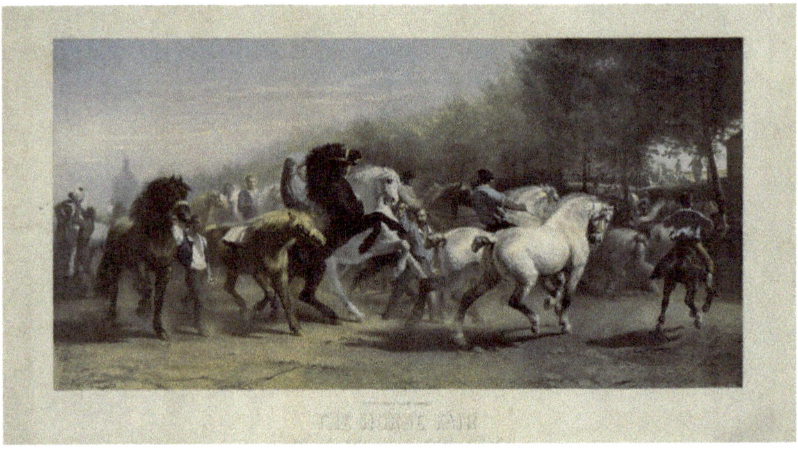

Fig. 5 Rosa Bonheur, *The Horse Fair* (New York: Publ. by J. M. Emerson & Co., 1859). Printed by Sarony, Major & Knapp. Library of Congress, https://www.loc.gov/pictures/resource/pga.02615/.

Rosa Bonheur's most acclaimed painting, *The Horse Fair,* demonstrates this. The painting, which was displayed for a few weeks in fall 1857 at New York frame maker/picture dealer Williams, Stevens, Williams & Co.'s gallery and at Earle's in the spring of 1858, was shown daily until 10PM at the latter. The hour was late enough that it allowed for even the laboring classes to peruse the splendid work as a form of evening entertainment. Engravings of the painting through subscription were available at Earle's in 1858 and advertised at twenty dollars in 1859 (Figure 5). Less than five years later, Smith, in his catalog, advertised seventy-five cent lithographs after the painting.[32] The less-wealthy admirers of the original Bonheur could acquire a print after it by paying in installments over several weeks. When sold by Earle as an engraving that cost several dollars it was likely not financially feasible for them.

Frame makers/picture dealers Earle and Smith employed different business strategies within their place in their trade and capitalized on a liminal space within the print market: one inhabited by an evolving pluralistic base of art consumers. Earle and his longstanding cohort catered to the middle class and their emulators through their location and newspaper advertisements. Smith focused his business on a wider cross-section of society by describing works based on personal connection and a print stock of reprints and reiterations. All frame makers sold prints and frames in a profession rooted in trade practices to cultivate this commercial marriage. But the frame makers would not have been so successful in fostering the development of a market for framed art in the absence of PAFA and the subscription art unions. These institutions also played a crucial role in nurturing the commercial marriage of prints with frames.

32 Williams, Stevens, Williams & Co.'s admission fee was twenty-five cents between the hours 8:30AM and 6:30PM, October-November 1857. *Evening Post*, 26 October 1857, p. 3; 'The Horse Fair Shortly to Close', *New York Daily Tribune,* 7 November 1857, p. 2; 'The Last Day', *Philadelphia Inquirer*, 29 April 1858, p. 2; and 'New Engravings', *Press*, 13 May 1859, p. 3.

'Growing Taste for Beauty in Forms and Colors': Philadelphia Frame Makers and Subscription Art Unions

While frame makers inhabited a liminal space in relation to the Philadelphia picture consumer, allied institutions in their network did not. The Academy and later art unions defined their roles more singularly in the city's visual culture. Companionate actors in broadening the art world, the unions and the Philadelphia frame makers bolstered each other as agents of the art trade.

When the AAU and the AUP were officially chartered in New York in 1842 and Philadelphia in 1844, European models in London, Switzerland, and Germany had been in existence since the late-eighteenth century.[33] The AAU, which was previously called the Apollo Association (1839–1844), was organized by mainly wealthy, politically and socially conservative New York merchants, manufacturers, shippers, and newspaper men such as former Mayor Philip Hone. It sought to define what American art should be through its stated mission of the 'promotion of the Fine Arts in the United States'.[34] The AUP, which was managed by artists, merchants, and philanthropists, including John Sartain, Joseph Sill, and Rev. William Furness, took three years to become active in support of their mission of 'the promotion of the Arts of Design throughout the United States' and to 'feed the eye'.[35] By

33 For histories of art unions in the US, including their cultural relevance, see Jane Aldrich Dowling Adams, *A Study of Art Unions in the United State of America in the Nineteenth Century* (Richmond: Virginia Commonwealth University, MA. Thesis, 1990). For the AAU specifically, recent scholarship includes Kimberly Orcutt, with Allan McLeod, 'Unintended Consequences: The American Art-Union and the Rise of a National Landscape School,' *Nineteenth-Century Art Worldwide*, 18 (2019), https://doi.org/10.29411/ncaw.2019.18.1.14; Patricia Hills et al., *Perfectly American: The Art-Union and Its Artists* (Tulsa, OK: Gilcrease Museum, 2011); and Joy Sperling, '"Art, Cheap and Good:" The Art Union in England and the United States, 1840–60', *Nineteenth-Century Art Worldwide*, 1 (2002), http://www.19thc-artworldwide.org/spring02/196--qart-cheap-and-goodq-the-art-union-in-england-and-the-united-states-184060.

34 Dozens of men sat on the AAU Committee of Management over the Union's life span, and also included physician John W. Francis; lawyer William L. Morris; type founder George Bruce; and banker Francis W. Edmonds. See Jane Adams, pp. 110–113; and Sperling, 'Art, Cheap and Good'.

35 Jane Adams, pp. 21–27, 116–118; and 'Art Union of Philadelphia', *North American*, 7 June 1847, p. 2.

the time each union was established, frame makers and AAU and AUP members Earle, Robinson, and Natt had been in their trade for over a dozen years if not decades.

At its peak in 1849, the AAU distributed nationwide to nearly 19,000 subscribers, who paid the five-dollar membership fee, dozens of prints after American-made paintings the Union had borrowed, purchased, or commissioned. At around the same time, the AUP sustained about 1,900 subscribers, mostly regional. It followed most of the protocols of the AAU, including the price of the subscription fee, holding an annual art lottery, distributing gift prints after the work of American artists, publishing a bulletin, and maintaining a free gallery.[36]

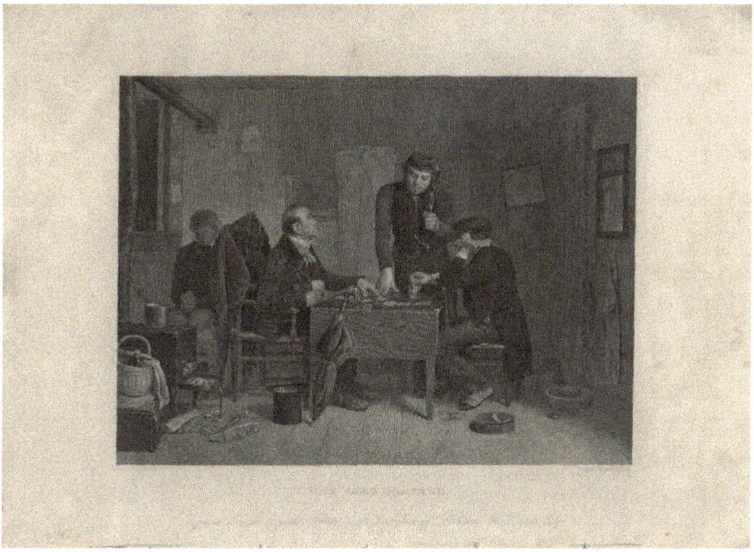

Fig. 6 C. Burt after Richard Caton Woodville, *The Card Player* (New York: American Art Union, 1850). Library Company of Philadelphia, https://digital.librarycompany.org/islandora/object/digitool%3A130650.

In New York, the Art-Union managers chose paintings, including Richard Caton Woodville's *The Card Player* (1846) (Figure 6) and William Ranney's *Marion Crossing the Pedee* (1850), to be engraved. The chosen paintings were often by American artists and composed with a historical or national theme and intended didactic undertone. Other paintings in stock were described in their *Bulletin*, sold at their New York gallery on Broadway, or offered as lottery prizes to the subscribers

36 Jane Adams, p. 23

who helped pay for them. But it was the Union's mass-produced prints, distributed with a statement of copyright in the Union's name, which served as their best instrument to demonstrate the power of art in the formation of a national culture.[37]

Overseen by more artists and engravers than the AAU, the AUP exhibited differing intentions in cultivating the appreciation of art through prints. This is evident in an early edition of the Union's *Transactions* (1848). In a piece about the selected gift print for the year, the AUP managers focused the explanation of their selection more so in terms of the aesthetics of the work than its American subject matter which was typically the reason provided by the AAU for their chosen gift prints. In the choice of their long-awaited first premium (the first of six in total), the Philadelphia managers exhorted that 'Many pictures of the highest grade in composition, colour, and expression, are not well fitted to be reduced unto black and white; and hence, among a large number of works of Art of high excellence examined by the board, it was no easy thing to select such a Picture as would combine the desired requisites.'[38] In the end, local artist Emmanuel Leutzes's painting *John Knox and Mary Queen of Scots* — depicting a defining moment in the United Kingdom's, rather than America's, history — prevailed as the print engraved by manager Sartain. This labored and propagandized rationale suggests that unlike the AAU, the AUP's goal as a national organization — which did not consistently include a copyright statement in the Union's name on their distributed prints — was not ultimately to try to promote 'America' through art, but instead the idea that every American had a right to good art 'to feed the eye'.[39] Whether it represented an art-appreciation mission to promote America or to feed the eye, an art collective's goals were best brought to fruition through a framed print.

---

37 The plan of the AAU published in 1840s-1850s editions of the *Transactions* and then *Bulletin* of the Union regularly included the statement 'The plates and copyright of all engravings and all other publications belong to the institution and are used solely for its benefit'.

38 *Transactions of the Art-Union of Philadelphia for the year 1848* (Philadelphia: Printed by Griggs & Adams, 1848), p. 44.

39 When a copyright statement was included on the prints, it could be in the name of the Union or the owner of the painting after which the print was based.

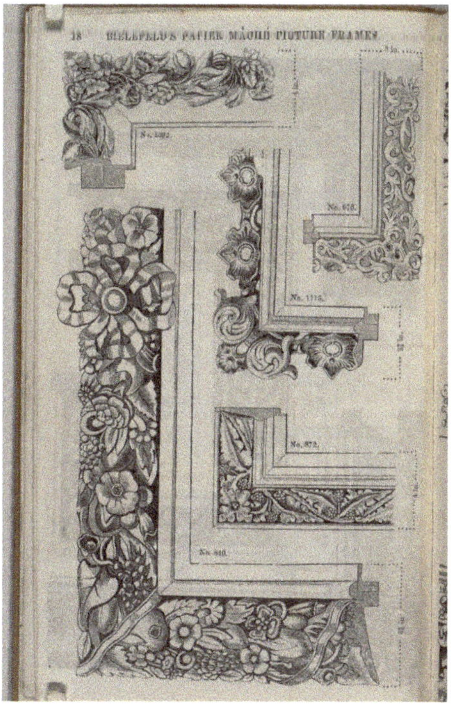

Fig. 7 Page 18 of Charles Frederick Bielefeld, *Illustrated Tariff of the Improved Papier-Mâché Picture Frames* (London, ca. 1847). Metropolitan Museum of Art, Harris Brisbane Dick Fund, 1940, https://www.metmuseum.org/art/collection/search/334058.

By 1847, a New York news article about technical improvements to machine-made ornamental frames attributed to an 'Art Union' proclaimed, 'We consider that to produce good and cheap frames is second only in importance to producing prints good and cheap'.[40] Invented by British frame maker Charles Frederick Bielefeld (1803–1864), the iron-fortified paper mâché frames allowed for the 'meanest wooden shelter in which a work of art ever found refuge...' Priced as low as a shilling (i.e., about twelve cents), ornate frames were now comparable in aesthetics and cost to the print that would fit in them (Figure 7). The Union lauded the invention for its significance to engravings that 'have been deprived of an opportunity of effectively 'doing their spiriting'

40 'Picture Frames by Machinery. (From the Art Union)', *Evening Post*, 16 February 1847, p. 1.

from their circumstance of being unframed …'[41] A print without a frame was demeaned in purpose. The frame gave the print more social cachet. The union of print and frame emulated middle-class décor. The print would not just be seen, but felt. As a discretionary purchase, a frame was justifiable and necessary for the proper cultivation of Bethune's domestic virtue.[42] Art is not art unless displayed, nor complete without a 'wooden shelter'. It was the print consumer's civic duty to purchase an accompanying frame when purchasing a print.

This sentiment was echoed in an August 30, 1849 *Philadelphia Inquirer* article referencing frame maker Robinson. Robinson often announced his display of prints, including ones issued by the AAU, in the press.[43] The columnist adamantly notes:

> The taste for paintings and prints is quite extended as it was formerly, but our citizens do not use them so generally as they did, as decorations for drawing rooms … We think this is an error. There is nothing which imparts to a parlor or drawing room such an air of comfortable elegance as handsomely framed paintings or prints…[44]

The AAU dissolved in 1852. The union was mired in controversy in its final years because its art lotteries were criticized as a form of gambling. Its competition and redundancy with the International Art Union, as well as slow print production and distribution, were also factors in its demise.[45] By this time, the AAU had cast a defining influence over the rationale of the visual culture of the time: one that held that not only painted but also printed works, especially framed, equated to art.

---

41 Ibid.

42 See Joanna Cohen, *Luxurious Citizens: The Politics of Consumption in Nineteenth-Century America (Philadelphia: University of Pennsylvania Press, 2017)* for an in-depth cultural examination of the American civic-consumer in the antebellum period. Cohen asserts that the concept and practices of the antebellum consumer formed from an economy of a collective imaginary as much as from a political one.

43 See 'Looking glasses, etc.', *Philadelphia Inquirer*, 5 March 1834, p. 4; 'American Art-Union', 8 December 1849, p. 1; and *Philadelphia Inquirer*, 7 June 1851, p. 2.

44 'City Notices', *Philadelphia Inquirer*, 30 August, 1849, p. 1.

45 The International Art Union, with support from New York cultural figures such as Washington Irving, formed in 1848 as a veiled commercial enterprise of the French publishing firm Goupil, Vibert & Co. See Jane Adams, pp. 62–64. Newspapers stoked the rivalry with articles about which Union deserved a subscriber's patronage and comparisons between and criticisms of their ideological and economical missions and motives. See for example, 'The Fine Arts. The Two Unions at Loggerheads', *Herald*, 15 October 1849, p. 3.

In Philadelphia, the city's picture dealers worked in tandem with art unions to cultivate this principle so central to their trade.

A distinction between AAU and AUP reinforced this principle. Unlike the AAU, the AUP let a lottery winner 'select for himself' their painting.[46] While it deflected the accusations of gambling often directed toward the AAU, the AUP's self-selection approach also echoed the consumerism requisite to the commercial success of the galleries of the Philadelphia frame makers/picture dealers, who were also Union members. In accordance with the AUP's goal to 'feed the eye' and their established intermediary position with PAFA, Philadelphia frame makers were optimally positioned to take advantage of the mechanisms of their local art trade culture.

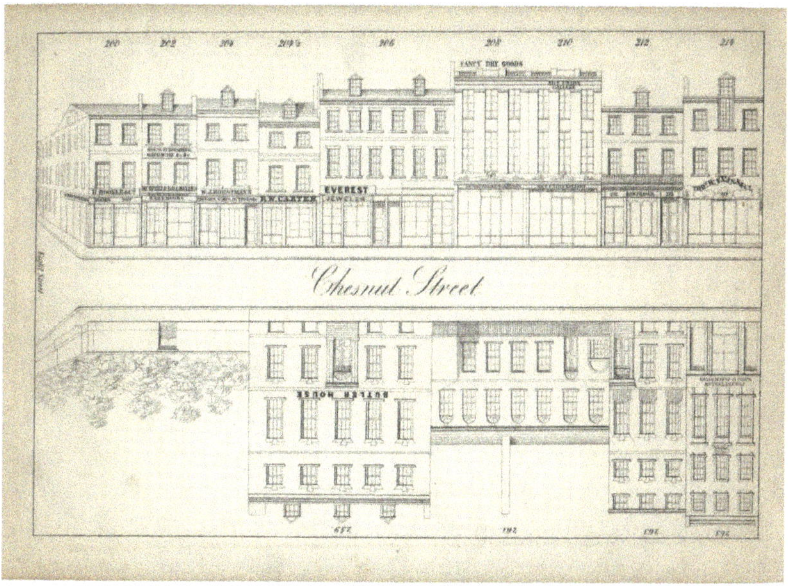

Fig. 8 Julio Rae, *Rae's Philadelphia Pictorial Directory & Panoramic Advertiser. Chestnut Street, from Second to Tenth Streets*, 800 block Chestnut Street (Philadelphia: Julio Rae, 1851). Library Company of Philadelphia, https://digital.librarycompany.org/islandora/object/Islandora%3A61652.

46 'Art Union of Philadelphia', *North American*, 7 June 1847, p. 2. AUP followed the self-selection model of the London Art Union. See Jane Adams, p. 23; and Sperling, 'Art, Cheap and Good'.

In early 1849, soon after attorney and AUP corresponding secretary William Tilghman consulted with the AAU, the AUP opened 'day and evening' its Free Gallery of Art on the 800 block of Chestnut Street (Figure 8). Almost immediately, frame maker/picture dealers were involved in choosing a site. The site was to be close to PAFA so the AUP gallery would 'tend to the prosperity of the Academy ... and the advancement of the objects proposed by the Art Union'.[47] Robinson originally brokered the deal, his son T. J. Robinson was approached and declined to sublet the building, and the frame makers Andrews & Meeser were finally engaged to oversee the site and contribute towards the rent. The firm framed the union's 'specimen engravings', acted as independent picture dealers, and advertised in the Union's monthly periodical the *Art Union Reporter.*[48] This complementary yet independent role shaped the relationship between the Unions and the Philadelphia frame makers. When the name of AAU's honorary subscriptions secretary in Philadelphia, merchant William Goodrich, was announced in the newspaper in 1848, this sentiment of simultaneous independence and mutual benefit was evident. The columnist commented: 'Philadelphia possesses liberality sufficient to do her share to its support, although she has a kindred institution at home'.[49]

This liberality enabled Earle and long-standing colleagues Natt and Robinson to be active in the American and Philadelphia art unions as both members and secretaries, as well as allowing their warerooms to serve as places of distribution for the Unions' premium prints. Earle even rented a room to AUP for their early meetings, and served as secretary for a number of national and international unions, including the AAU, the Edinburgh Art Union, and the London Art Union.[50] This mutually beneficial relationship extended into advertising in the unions' periodicals. In the case of Earle, the Philadelphia union saw no issue with conjointly promoting their Free Gallery and Earle's Free Gallery

47 *Transactions of the Art-Union of Philadelphia for the year 1849* (Philadelphia: King & Baird, 1849), p. 30.

48 Historical Society of Pennsylvania, Joseph Sill Diaries, 13, 20, 23, 25 November 1848; 1, 26, 29 December 1848; and 8, 17, 20, 25, 29 January 1849; *Philadelphia Art-Union Reporter*, 1 (1851), 96; and *Philadelphia Art-Union Reporter*, 1 (1852), 147.

49 'American Art Union', *North American*, 2 September 1848, p. 2.

50 *Art-Union Reporter,* 1 (1851), 32; Sill Diaries, 19 June 1847; 'The Fine Arts in Scotland.,' *Philadelphia Inquirer*, 23 January 1855, p. 2 and 'London Art Union', *Philadelphia Inquirer*, 11 March 1857, p. 2.

of Art that displayed two hundred and fifty paintings,' including 'gems which are ranked among the best productions of our own native, as well as foreign artists.'[51] Both desired art patrons, and Earle also sought consumers of not only paintings and prints, but also the frames needed for the works of art to do their 'spiriting'.

This mutually beneficial competition for consumers of graphic works between frame makers and the AUP was acknowledged in 1849 in *Sartain's Union Magazine,* the Philadelphia literary and art periodical published by AUP manager Sartain. Two years following Joseph S. Natt's rebuilding of his storefront a block away from AUP and Robinson's relocation to the 900 block of Chestnut Street, the magazine observed:

> The large public attendance at the Art Union Gallery and the success of the enterprise [...] soon excited the rivalry of those who had formerly been the agents [...] now we have four large and beautiful picture and looking glass stores, [...] superior to any ever before known in our city.[52]

Earle, whose gallery was also in the neighborhood, was almost certainly one of the four art and picture dealers who distributed engravings described in the same periodical as 'now widely circulated of the best kinds, and instead of the grotesque libels on art which formerly were to be found in every house, we now see works of superior merit'.[53] The "friendly" competition between the frame makers' galleries and that of AUP would not last. The AUP dissolved about 1855.

The unions organized with a mission to cultivate art appreciation among the middle classes supported frame makers and vice versa. Established frame makers, such as Earle, and those who were new to the field, such as Smith, buttressed the cultural missions of the unions to encourage the appreciation and consumption of art. The picture dealer worked to create that need and met it before, during, and following the demise of unions. Individuals of all means could visit their galleries, day or night, and for the frame maker, the patron was an active agent in the choice of a print, rather than merely a passive recipient. In this context, art unions worked in concert with frame makers, fostering a mutable

51 *Art-Union Reporter,* 1 (1851), 109.

52 'City Notices', *Philadelphia Inquirer*, 21 December 1849, p.1; 'Removal', *Philadelphia Inquirer*, 1 November 1849, p.1; and *Sartain's Union Magazine*, 9 (1851), 156–157.

53 J. J. Mapes, 'From Sartains Magazine for March. "Usefulness of the Arts of Design"', *Philadelphia Art Union Reporter,* 1 (1851), 27–28.

relationship between commercial, aesthetic, and material values of prints for their patrons. An article reprinted in an 1866 edition of the *American Art Journal* acknowledges, albeit sarcastically, this outcome and the centrality of the frame maker. With a tone critical of the success of the London art unions, which were deemed to be 'wrong in principle and unserviceable to good art' in their construction of a wider art consumer base with a broader appreciation of what constitutes art, the columnist asserted that '[t]he only people who benefit by these Unions are the picture frame makers'.[54]

Frame Maker/Picture Dealers, Print Values, and Copyright

The art unions and frame makers/picture dealers, along with PAFA, commodified art across socioeconomic classes through their implicit and explicit missions and practices. An increasing number of viewers of art became material consumers of art during the nineteenth century. Through the will of PAFA and its internal and external constituents to cultivate a national art culture through universal access to art, American-made prints after American-made paintings by American-trained artists infused the antebellum print market. Patrons, who through cultural agents like the art unions and frame makers, came to believe that their dwellings were not a home without pictures on the wall, in part constructed this market. While the unions distributed engravings after original works that they denoted as art to their patrons, frame makers Earle and Smith had on hand American and European prints for purchase that their consumers ultimately judged and purchased as such. These buyers were able to acquire a ten-cent lithograph and complementary frame, and they did not need to be members of the middle classes to afford it.

Within this print market culture, we can glean anecdotal traces of trade strategies and agreements, and socioeconomic factors influencing the prices and titles offered within frame makers' stocks of prints. Through contextual analysis of an Earle advertisement of 1859, and particularly through surveying select titles in Smith's catalog, one can

54 'Art Unions', *The American Art Journal*, 5 (1866), 88.

directly and judiciously trace the commercial and social life cycle of a print published and/or sold by dealers in cases where questions of copyright may have been a factor.

As noted, Earle rarely included prices in his newspaper listings. He did so in an April 1859 advertisement for nearly two dozen European engravings.[55] The prints, priced from twenty cents to twenty dollars, were arranged by order of cost. Titles included an engraving after popular German painter Franz Winterhalter's literary painting *Florinde,* priced at $12.50.[56] Exhibited in spring 1857 by Goupil & Co. in New York and reproduced by the company as an engraving, the painting, described by a reviewer as a scene with a 'voluptuous expression', was further exhibited at the gallery of Earle's Boston peer Williams & Everett. Concurrently, Williams solicited subscriptions for a print after the painting at the same $12.50 uncolored price as originally advertised by Goupil and later by Earle in 1859.[57] In other words, a price had been set by Goupil and honored by Earle and Williams. One picture dealer was not undercutting or upselling another in a different city. Implicit trade rules had been derived and followed by the frame makers, who sold high end prints after paintings 'on tour' in their galleries.

In comparison, Smith's advertised stock in his catalog included prints that were often previously published by another publisher, including a number sold by the AAU or Cosmopolitan Art Association (CAA). These prints would have contained statements of copyright in the name of the union when first issued. Although extant engravings of the previous union titles with Smith's imprint have yet to be found, given the known reprinted works by Smith (including engravings by Sartain) and bibliographic notes, he most likely published restrikes of

---

55 'New Engravings', *Press,* 29 April 1859, p. 3.

56 An image of August Charles Lemoine's engraving after Winterhalter's *Florinde* in the collections of the British Museum is viewable at https://www.britishmuseum.org/research/collection_online/collection_object_details/collection_image_gallery.aspx?assetId=373589001&objectId=1615012&partId=1.

57 *Springfield Republican,* 30 May 1857. p.1; *On Exhibition at Williams & Everett's, No. 234 Washington Street, Boston, the Original Painting of Florinde, by Winterhalter (Exhibited in the Royal Academy of Arts, 1852.) Admission 25 cents.* (Boston, [ca. 1857]), https://www.loc.gov/resource/rbpe.06101500/?sp=2. Library of Congress; *New York Tribune,* 9 September 1857, p. 1. 'Winterhalter's "Florinde,"' *Boston Traveler,* 11 November 1858, p. 2.

the union engravings from the original plates.[58] By all accounts, Smith was not a member of a union, but he still profited from their existence.

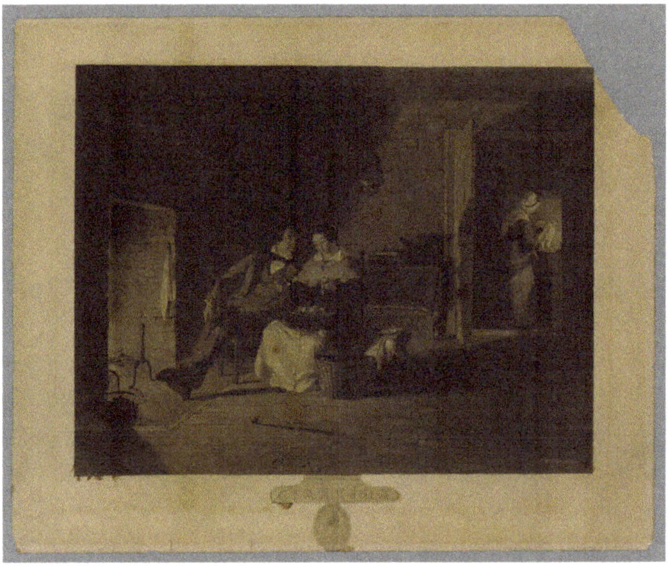

Fig. 9 Alfred Jones after Francis William Edmonds, *Sparking* (New York: American Art Union, 1844). Courtesy of American Antiquarian Society, https://catalog.mwa.org/vwebv/holdingsInfo?bibId=357812.

The aforementioned *Sparking* was one of a number of AAU engravings listed by Smith in his catalog (Figure 9). The catalog shows that Smith transformed the marketing rhetoric used by the Union to expand his consumer base. Advertised by him for 'Bachelors and Young Ladies' and for fifty cents (ten times less than the AAU subscription price for the same work), it displays a scene of polite courtship even beyond the sight of a chaperone. Smith promotes the picture not for American

58 Smith entered the frame-making business three years after the auction of the holdings of the AAU in 1852. Given available evidence, a conclusion has been made that the prints were most likely restrikes from plates in Smith's possession, rather than print remainders. Plate sizes of the AAU prints and framing sizes noted in the Smith catalog were compared in forming this conclusion. The question of how he came to hold the AAU printing plates remains unanswered. The same conclusion has been made for the CAA plates and prints. His method of acquisition of the plates of the CAA which dissolved in 1861 is also uncertain. These conclusions were also informed by bibliographic notes accompanying Smith prints like the following in the online catalog of the American Antiquarian Society which states 'William Smith acquired Cornelius Tiebout's plates and re-struck them'.

homespunness with universal appeal as did the Union in 1844, but by using catalog descriptions and prices that aimed to attract young adults.[59]

As a point of comparison, Smith's catalog also contains a series of titles he notes as previously issued by the CAA, an association established by Ohio publisher Chauncey L. Derby and active between 1854 and 1861, with a branch in New York. The Association, similar to Smith, distributed restrikes from plates engraved for often-failed or bankrupt publishers, or for failed subscription opportunities.[60] In 1858, the CAA acquired the painting, printing plate, and copyright of *The Village Blacksmith* after British artist J. F. Herring from New York frame makers/picture dealers Williams, Stevens, and Williams.[61] The Smith catalog provides a snapshot of the 'third' life of this print in the marketplace.

Within a few years, Smith listed the 28 x 34 inch *Village* as from the 'Cosmopolitan Art Collection' at the previous CAA 'price' of the three-dollar subscriber's fee. The CAA as the earlier publisher of the print proved consequential to its price. The restruck *Sparking* had been divorced from its first life as an AAU print twenty years earlier. Smith did not promote the relationship, and after two decades most consumers likely no longer remembered the connection. And if they did, the print would represent a bargain. The re-actualized and re-contextualized prints kept both unions present at different ends in later nineteenth-century mass visual culture. The reprinted *Village* promoted by Smith as both having 'won the admiration of lovers of art in Europe and America', and as 'Herring's unrivaled Picture' retained a transparent stable price. The print's attributed provenance as a widely-circulated and consumed art union engraving from the recent past informed its market (and social) value.[62] Smith honored a price 'set' by the CAA by

59 'The Subject of the picture is of homely, but of universal interest; one that will appeal to all hearts, and to all understandings, and will require no labelling to make it perfectly understood'. *Transactions of the American Art Union* (1844), p. 9. A copy of the print with Smith's imprint has not been located.

60 See Lauren B. Hewes, '"Dedicated to the lovers of art and literature," The Cosmopolitan Art Association Engravings, 1856–1861', *Imprint*, 31 (2006), 2–17 for a concise, cogent overview of the history and practices of the Association, as well as its relationship with Williams, Stevens, & Williams.

61 *Cosmopolitan Art Journal*, 3 (1858), 67. The fee for the transfer of copyright was not indicated. For context, in 1857 Williams paid two thousand dollars for the painting and three thousand dollars for the copyright of Frederick Edwin Church's *Falls of Niagara*. *Springfield Republican* 30 May 1857, p. 1.

62 Ibid.

capitalizing on the residual socioeconomic presence of the Union with his consumer base from a cross-section of society. Similar to the implicit trade rules followed by Goupil, Williams & Everett, and Earle to honor a set price for *Florinde* with their consumer base on their end of the trade's spectrum, Smith followed a similar strategy on his end of the market.

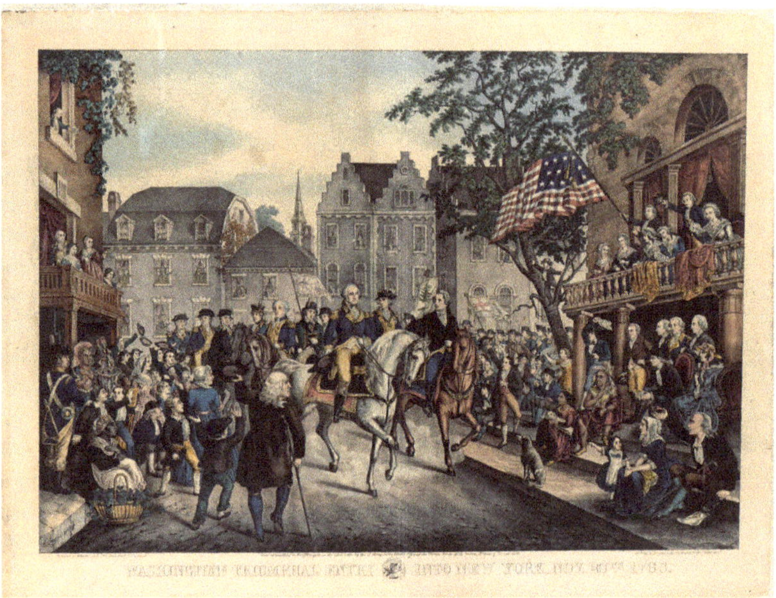

Fig. 10 Christian Inger, *Washington's Triumphal Entry into New York, Nov. 25th, 1783* (Philadelphia: Published by William Smith, 1860). Printed in oil colors by P.S. Duval & Son. Copyright by G. T. Perry. Library Company of Philadelphia, https://digital.librarycompany.org/islandora/object/digitool%3A127816.

Without known extant copies of the aforementioned union prints bearing the Smith imprint, it is uncertain whether the works continued to contain statements of copyright. However, from a sample specimen of Smith titles with a traceable provenance from extant prints, it can be deduced that less than one quarter contained a copyright statement when issued previously. The focus of Smith's catalog *Washington's Triumphal Entry into New York, November 25, 1783* was one of them (Figure 10).[63]

63 Extant Smith prints listed in the circa-1863 catalog are not prevalent in public collections. Deductions were derived from surveys of select, pre-1865 prints in the collections of the American Antiquarian Society and the Library Company of Philadelphia, with William Smith imprints and/ or prints with titles and similar sizes

Whereas copyright status on the prints distributed by Earle can not be easily ascertained, of the known Smith prints, a small number, many portraits or historical images, do include a copyright statement. The statement is not always in Smith's name, however: this is the case with *Triumphal*, which was registered for copyright in 1860 by Philadelphia postmaster George T. Perry. Priced at five dollars, the color historical print with a framing size of around 3 x 4 feet cost the most of all the titles Smith advertised in his catalog.

Described by Smith, and previously by copyright holder Perry, as a 'beautiful print' and the 'best work of its kind ever produced in this country...' the highlighted *Triumphal* represents a case study of the idiosyncrasies of copyright, and an outsider trying to work amid the nuanced dynamics created in the art market by the frame makers and their cohort. Print consumers assumed no overt financial risks when purchasing a 'reprinted' engraving or lithograph even if it violated copyright. Picture dealers and printers who were also publishers, on the other hand, did run a risk of retaliation in the form of costly litigation. However, public shaming of perceived copyright violation through the popular press was the more likely form of retaliation. Such was the case for *Triumphal.*

In January 1862, Perry placed a recurring advertisement with a 'caution' in a Northern newspaper for his 'new national picture' printed in oil colors by P. S. Duval & Son that had been 'duly copyrighted, &c, &c'.[64] The caution warned of a '*badly executed copy*' that did not convey his 'BEAUTIFUL IDEA'. Perry believed his exhortation in the press that he was a copyright holder empowered his caution and it would be heeded by the public he was soliciting.[65] He thought the badly executed

---

listed in Smith's circa-1863 catalog. Review of microfilm of Pennsylvania — Eastern District registration records (Reel 67–70) between January 2, 1854 and November 8, 1864 revealed no deposits by William Smith, nor was he included in the indexes. Consequently, material evidence of Smith as a 'registered' copyright holder is elusive and reasonable deductions are made.

64 The warning message read: 'Caution — A badly executed copy has been thrown out upon the public, which does not in the least convey the BEAUTIFUL IDEA which is carried out in this great work of art published by G.T. Perry, duly copyrighted &c &c and which contains over ONE HUNDRED more figures...' *Massachusetts Ploughman and New England Journal of Agriculture*, 8 February 1862, p. 3.

65 As explored by Isabella Alexander, public interest holds a compelling role in the understanding of copyright. Alexander argues that the 'notion of a "public interest" which diverges from the interests of authors, even if not always opposed to them

copy — a print 'thrown out upon the public' printed by Duval rival Thomas Sinclair — would not be purchased. The 'new and beautiful print' executed and printed by Duval would be. Complicating this narrative, however, is the fact that the Sinclair copy originally also contained a copyright statement in Perry's name. Furthermore, there was also a second Sinclair copy in another publisher's and copyright holder's name in circulation.

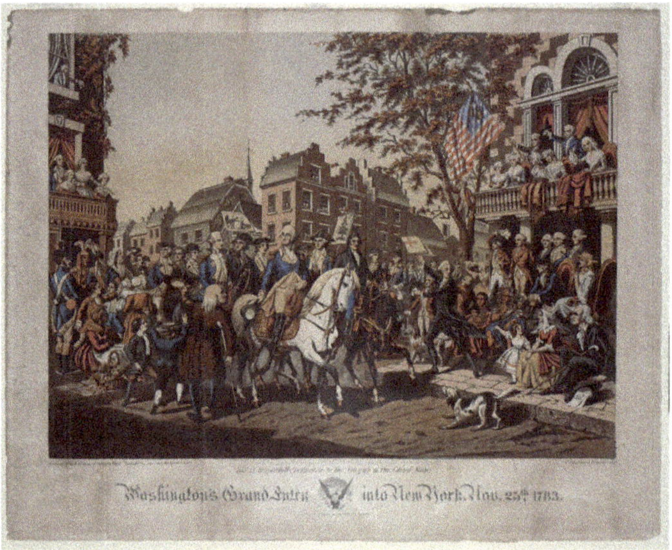

Fig. 11 Alphonse Bigot, *Washington's Grand Entry into New York, Nov. 25th, 1783* (New York: Published by John Smith, 1860). Chromolith. By T. Sinclair. From The New York Public Library, http://digitalcollections.nypl.org/items/5e66b3e8-a61e-d471-e040-e00a180654d7.

Containing the variant title *Washington's Grand Entry* ... and showing a nearly identical visual trope of Washington on horseback and promenading down a crowded New York street, the 'badly executed' print circulated with two different imprints. One named Perry as publisher and copyright holder. The print was registered by him on December 15, 1860. Another included an imprint showing Philadelphia frame maker/print publisher John Smith as publisher and copyright holder (Figure 11). The copyright statement on the print was also dated

has had a significant and rhetorical and discursive impact in shaping the law of copyright'. Isabella Alexander, *Copyright Law and the Public Interest* (Oxford and Portland, OR: Hart Publishing, 2010), p. 4.

1860. Perry possibly transferred his copyright protection of the Sinclair print to John Smith in less than a month, but no transferred registration of copyright is evident.[66] During the same month, as deduced from extant copies of the Duval print and a December 31, 1860 registration deposit, Perry had also copyrighted *Triumphal*, his 'new national picture'.[67] Consequently, three prints with two similar designs, three different imprints, and two different statements of copyright were in circulation. As can be construed from the 1862 advertisement, the prints, and the varying statements of copyright, Perry had opted, through the court of public opinion, to market and reap the profits of his 'duly copyrighted' Duval lithograph. From the print's inclusion and focus in the William Smith catalog, Perry appears to have lost the case he pled in the press. The public shaming to suppress the sale of the Sinclair print did not promote sales of the Duval print. Ultimately, Perry needed a frame maker/picture dealer to sell his print depicting his 'beautiful idea'.

These multiple versions and states with a Perry statement of copyright suggest that Perry, a postmaster by profession, poorly understood the rules of a trade in which copyright did not equal control of a print's circulation. For Perry, copyright leveraged by an 'author' of original art through public shaming (as opposed to litigation) would not prove to be a zero-sum game as he desired. Consequently, Smith, rather than Perry, was selling the print through his two-fold marketing and consumer network, up to a year following the appearance of the Boston ad. Smith sold the color lithograph for one dollar less than was advertised by Perry. Smith leveraged his understanding of the customs of his trade. Litigation of copyright was not an influence. It did not restrict nor promote sales of prints as a marketing tactic. In the world of graphic art, an effective sales strategy hinged on finding the right price point and advertising channel, as well as matching the print with a complementary frame.

66 United States Copyright Office (USCO), entry dated 15 December, 1860; and entry dated 31 December, 1860, Copyright Records, Pennsylvania Eastern District, May 14, 1860-May, 16, 1861, vol. 283, reel 68. A familial relationship between William and John has not been established. A registration in John Smith's name was not located.

67 Copies of *Triumphal* with William Smith's imprint and without Perry's statement of copyright have not been located.

Conclusion

Frame makers/print dealers acted as consequential intermediaries in nurturing art appreciation among mass society during the antebellum era. The picture dealers fostered this role with an evolving consumer base whose taste for prints developed within a cultural nexus of public galleries, the didactic missions of antebellum art unions and institutions, and tradesmen who capitalized on their dual positioning within the worlds of art and trade. As the print market democratized, copyright remained an idiosyncratically understood legal right, and frame maker/picture dealers held an important, yet often forgotten role in the culturally-constructed commercial and social life cycle of antebellum prints. Agents operating within a bifurcated trade, Earle, Smith, and their peers helped to foster the opinion that a print is a work of art, whether fine, popular, or even bad, and especially when placed in a frame. These antebellum men occupied a profession that impelled the creation of a universal appeal for art as a cultural commodity.

Bibliography

Primary Sources

Archival and Graphic Material

Alphonse Bigot, *Washington's Grand Entry into New York No. 25th, 1783* (Philadelphia: George T. Perry, 1860), chromolithograph, Huntington Library, Art collections, Botanical Gardens, Los Angeles. CA, priJLC_POL_002714.

——, *Washington's Grand Entry into New York Nov. 25th, 1783* (Philadelphia: John Smith, 1860), chromolithograph, The Miriam and Ira D. Wallach Division of Art, Prints and Photographs: Print Collection, New York Public Library, New York, Eno 46++.

Christian Schussele, *Washington's Triumphal Entry into New York, November 25, 1783* (Philadelphia: Published by William Smith, ca. 1863), chromolithograph, Library Company of Philadelphia, Philadelphia, ***GC-American Revolution [P.2279].

Joseph Sill Diaries, 1846–1849, v. 7–8, Historical Society of Pennsylvania, Am.1525.

Secondary Sources

Adams, Jane Aldrich Dowling, *A Study of Art Unions in the United State of America in the Nineteenth Century* (Richmond: Virginia Commonwealth University, unpublished MA. thesis, 1990).

Adams, Steven R. Adams, '"Noising things abroad": Art, Commodity, and Commerce in Post-Revolutionary Paris', *Nineteenth-Century Art Worldwide*, 12 (2013), http://www.19thc-artworldwide.org/autumn13/adams-on-art-commodity-and-commerce-in-post-revolutionary-paris.

Alexander, Isabella, *Copyright Law and the Public Interest* (Oxford and Portland, OR: Hart Publishing, 2010).

Bently, L. and M. Kretschmer, eds., *Primary Sources on Copyright* (1450–1900), www.copyrighthistory.org.

Berne Convention for the Protection of Literary and Artistic Works, http://www.wipo.int/treaties/en/ip/berne/summary_berne.html.

Bethune, George W. *The Prospects of Art in the United States: An Address Before the Artists' Fund Society of Philadelphia, at the Opening of their Exhibition*, May 1840 (Philadelphia: Printed for the Artists' Fund Society, 1840).

Bracha, Oren, 'The Ideology of Authorship Revisited: Authors, Markets, and Liberal Values in Early American Copyright', *The Yale Law Journal*, 118 (2008), 186–271.

Bulletin of the American Art-Union (1848–1853).

Burns, Sarah and John Davis, eds., *American Art to 1900: A Documentary History* (Berkeley: University of California Press, 2009), https://doi.org/10.1525/9780520943827.

Cohen, Joanna, *Luxurious Citizens: The Politics of Consumption in Nineteenth-Century America* (Philadelphia: University of Pennsylvania Press, 2017), https://doi.org/10.9783/9780812293777.

Cobb, Josephine, 'The Washington Art Association: An Exhibition Record, 1856–1860', in *Records of the Columbia Historical Society*. 63/65 ed. by Francis Coleman Rosenberger (Washington, D.C.: Historical Society of Washington D.C., 1966), 122–190.

Copyright Records, Eastern District of Pennsylvania, May 14, 1860-May, 16, 1861, vol. 278–283, reel 67–68. United States Copyright Office (USCO).

Cosmopolitan Art Journal, 3 (1858).

——, 4 (1860).

Gaines, Jane G., *Contested Culture: The Image, the Voice, and the Law* (Chapel Hill: University of North Carolina Press, 1991).

Fletcher, Pamela and Anne Helmreich, eds., *The Rise of the Modern Art Market in London: 1850–1939*, eds. (New York: Manchester University Press, 2011).

Fowble, E. McSherry, *Two Centuries of Prints in America, 1680–1880: A Selective Catalogue of the Winterthur Museum Collection* (Charlottesville: University Press of Virginia, 1987).

Green, Nicholas, 'Circuits of Production, Circuits of Consumption: The Case of Mid-Nineteenth Century French Art Dealing', *Art Journal*, 48 (1989), 29–34.

Hewes, Lauren B.,'"Dedicated to the lovers of art and literature," The Cosmopolitan Art Association Engravings, 1856–1861', *Imprint*, 31 (2006), 2–17.

Hills, Patricia et al., *Perfectly American: The Art-Union and Its Artists* (Tulsa, OK: Gilcrease Museum, 2011).

James S. Earle & Son's Great Spring Sale of Oil Paintings. Catalogue of the Most Extensive and Highest Class Collections of Oil Paintings, Watercolor Drawings, Etc. (Philadelphia: Earle's Galleries, 1859). Metropolitan Museum of Art, 199.8 L9, https://archive.org/details/collectionofoilp00jame.

Orcutt, Kimberly with Allan McLeod, 'Unintended Consequences: The American Art-Union and the Rise of a National Landscape School', *Nineteenth-Century Art Worldwide*, 18 (2019), https://doi.org/10.29411/ncaw.2019.18.1.14.

On Exhibition at Williams & Everett's, No. 234 Washington Street, Boston, the Original Painting of Florinde, by Winterhalter (Exhibited in the Royal Academy of Arts, 1852.) Admission 25 cents. (Boston,[ca. 1857]), Library of Congress, Portfolio 61, Folder 15, https://www.loc.gov/resource/rbpe.06101500/?sp=2.

Philadelphia Art-Union Reporter, 1 (1851–1852).

Piggush, Yvette, 'Visualizing Early American Audiences: The Pennsylvania Academy of the Fine Arts and Allston's Dead Man Restored', *American Art Studies*, 9 (2011), 716–747.

Sartain's Union Magazine, 9 (1851).

Sperling, Joy, '"Art, Cheap and Good:" The Art Union in England and the United States, 1840–60', *Nineteenth-Century Art Worldwide*, 1 (2002), http://www.19thc-artworldwide.org/spring02/196--qart-cheap-and-goodq-the-art-union-in-england-and-the-united-states-184060>.

Spooner, Shearjashub, *An Appeal to the People of The United States, on Behalf of Art, Artists, and the Public Weal* (New York, 1854).

Tedeschi, Martha,'"Where the Picture Cannot Go, the Engravings Penetrate": Prints and the Victorian Art Market', *Art Institute of Chicago Museum Studies* 31 (2005), 8–19.

Transactions of the American Art-Union (1844–1849).

United States Bureau of Labor Statistics, *History of Wages in the United States From Colonial Times to 1928* (Washington, D.C: G.P.O., October 1929), https://fraser.stlouisfed.org/title/4067.

Wallace, J. B. (John Bradford), et al. *Reports of Cases Determined In the Circuit Court of the United States for the Third Circuit: (1801–1862)*. Philadelphia, 1819–1871, https://catalog.hathitrust.org/Record/008595371/Home.

Washington's Triumphal Entry into New York (Philadelphia: Published by William Smith, [ca. 1863]). Library Company of Philadelphia, Am 1860 Washi 111635.O.

8. Piracy, Copyright, and the Transnational Trade in Illustrations of News in the Mid-Nineteenth Century

Thomas Smits

The history of the visual representation of news events is often connected to the invention of photography.[1] The half-tone revolution of the early 1880s, which made it possible to reproduce photographs in print media on a mass scale, is presented as the origin of our visual age.[2] However, in recent years, several scholars have argued that the founding of numerous illustrated newspapers in the 1840s might be a better starting point. From a media archeological perspective, Jason Hill and Vanessa Schwartz have proposed a contingent history of 'news pictures' as a separate class of visual representation.[3] Photographs did not acquire their objective status because of any specific affordances of photographic technology, but because, in the nineteenth century, special

1 This chapter is partly based on subsections of the second and third chapters of my book. Thomas Smits, *The European Illustrated Press and the Emergence of a Transnational Visual Culture of the News, 1842–1870* (London: Routledge, 2020). I would like to thank Will Slauter for his insightful comments on this chapter and the paper that preceded it. I would also like to thank him for sharing his research in the National Archives with me.

2 Gerhard Paul, *Das visuelle Zeitalter: Punkt und Pixel* (Göttingen: Wallstein Verlag, 2016), pp. 9–16.

3 Jason Hill and Vanessa Schwartz, *Getting the Picture: The Visual Culture of the News* (London: Bloomsbury Academic, 2015), p. 3.

 https://doi.org/10.11647/OBP.0247.08

(sketch) artists, photographers, draughtsmen, engravers, editors, and publishers developed objective visual discourses and practices.[4]

From this perspective, the publication of the first issue of the *Illustrated London News* on 14 May 1842 fundamentally altered the relationship between publishers, the public, and the news. Although newspapers had informed readers about current events since the early seventeenth century, they only scarcely used images to represent the news.[5] This changed when the *Illustrated London News* began to regularly depict the news to its readers on a weekly basis, becoming, as Lorraine Janzen Kooistra notes, the 'first newspaper to make pictorial reportage its dominant feature'.[6]

The visual world that the London-based periodical presented to its readers quickly became successful. While it only sold 23,000 copies of its first issue, its print run quickly increased to 130,000 copies in 1855. Special supplements, such as the one concerning the Indian Rebellion of 1857, even sold as many as 500,000 copies.[7] Hoping to imitate the success of the British example, European and American publishers quickly copied the format of the *Illustrated London News*. Titles modeled after the British periodical appeared in France (1843), the German state of Sachsen (1843), the Netherlands (1844), Portugal (1844), Russia (1845) and many other countries.

Despite the transnational distribution of the format, scholars have mostly studied illustrated newspapers within a national context, often using Benedict Anderson's concept of the imagined community to connect their images to the production of national identity. However,

4 Hans Jürgen Bucher, 'Ein "Pictorial Turn" im 19. Jahrhundert? Überlegungen zu einer multimodalen Mediengeschichte am Beispiel der illustrierten Zeitungen', in *Historische Perspektiven auf den Iconic Turn. Die Entwicklung der öffentlichen visuellen Kommunikation*, ed. by Stephanie Geise et al. (Köln: Herbert von Halem, 2016), pp. 280–317.

5 Andrew Pettegree, *The Invention of News: How the World Came to Know about Itself* (New Haven: Yale University Press, 2015), pp. 1–17.

6 Lorraine Janzen Kooistra, 'Illustration', in *Journalism and the Periodical Press in Nineteenth-Century Britain*, ed. by Joanne Shattock (Cambridge: Cambridge University Press, 2017), pp. 104–125 (p. 104).

7 These figures are based on notices in the *Illustrated London News* and might be inflated. Figures were more reliable before the abolition of the newspaper stamp in 1855. See 'To Advertisers', *Illustrated London News*, 17 September 1842; 'The Illustrated London News', *Illustrated London News*, 11 August 1855; 'To the Trade', *Illustrated London News*, 28 November 1857; Richard Altick, *The English Common Reader: A Social History of the Mass Reading Public, 1800–1900* (Chicago: University of Chicago Press, 1957), p. 394.

popular European illustrated newspapers were distributed far beyond the national level, and their images were transnational products. A lively transnational trade in images of the news, in the form of metal copies, often called *clichés*, resulted in the emergence of a transnational visual culture of the news in the mid-nineteenth century.[8]

This chapter focuses on an important aspect of the transnational trade in images: the questions of ownership and copyright. After describing the transnational trade in illustrations of the news in general terms, it zooms in on one of the first court cases involving a transnational claim of copyright over images of news. In February 1856, John Cassell (1817–1865), the British publisher of *Cassell's Illustrated Family Paper* (1852–1867), sued his rival, George Stiff (1807–1873) of the *London Journal* (1845–1883) for publishing images from the French illustrated newspaper *l'Illustration* (1843–1944) 'to which the plaintiff claimed having the exclusive right'.[9] Stiff defended himself by stating that the images were 'copied from photographs publicly offered for sale in Paris'.[10]

Cassell v. *Stiff* is an exemplary case in the joint history of the transnational trade in images of the news and that of copyright on visual material published in newspapers and periodicals. This chapter argues that the mid-1850s should be seen as a transitional period in this joint history: one in which new technology, most prominently photographic techniques used to copy images, and new governmental rules put the existing transnational business practices of European illustrated newspapers under pressure.

In his introduction to a recent special issue of the *Victorian Periodicals Review*, Will Slauter noted two gaps in research concerning copyright and nineteenth-century periodicals. First, he observed a limited focus on visual material, 'despite the fact that the growing presence of images in print raised important questions for copyright law'. Second, he discerned the need for more study of the 'international and colonial dimensions of copyright' for newspapers and periodicals.[11] By discussing *Cassell* v. *Stiff*,

8 Smits, pp. 6–9.

9 'Newspaper copyright — Cassell v. Stiff', *Herts Guardian, Agricultural Journal, and General Advertiser*, 2 February 1856.

10 Ibid.

11 Will Slauter, 'Introduction: Copying and Copyright, Publishing Practice and the Law', *Victorian Periodicals Review*, 51.4 (2018), 583–596 (p. 584), https://doi.org/10.1353/vpr.2018.0044.

a case which stands at the crossroads of copyright, news, visual material, new technology, new governmental regulation and transnational trade, this chapter hopes to take a first step in filling these gaps.

Trading Visual News, 1842–1860

In recent years, often aided by digital methods, scholars have pointed to the national and transnational circulation of articles in newspapers and periodicals in the nineteenth century.[12] Focusing on 'reprint' or 'scissor-and-paste' practices, they not only underlined the intrinsically networked nature of the nineteenth-century press but also reframed our understanding of the production of news.[13] Articles were often not original pieces but instead copied or translated from other publications.

Although new methods are being developed, we have, as of yet, no viable technique which can be used to automatically trace the reprinting of images.[14] Even without these techniques, the lack of interest in the transnational distribution of images, as compared to text, is striking, especially if we consider the fact that images seem to make for better transnational products than texts. First, in the mid-nineteenth century, images were often presented and perceived as speaking a universal language. During the World Exhibition of 1851, the *Illustrated London News* wrote: 'The artist speaks a universal language [...] Pictures, then, have a great advantage over words, that they convey immediately much new knowledge to the mind: they are equivalent, [...] to seeing the

12 David A. Smith, Ryan Cordell, and Abby Mullen, 'Computational Methods for Uncovering Reprinted Texts in Antebellum Newspapers', *American Literary History*, 27:3 (2015), 1–15, https://doi.org/10.1093/alh/ajv029; Melody Beals, 'Scissors and Paste: The Georgian Reprints, 1800–1837', *Journal of Open Humanities Data*, 3.0 (2017), 1, https://doi.org/10.5334/johd.8.

13 Stephan Pigeon, 'Steal It, Change It, Print It: Transatlantic Scissors-and-Paste Journalism in the Ladies' Treasury, 1857–1895', *Journal of Victorian Culture*, 22:1 (2017), 24–39, https://doi.org/10.1080/13555502.2016.1249393; Bob Nicholson, '"You Kick the Bucket; We Do the Rest!": Jokes and the Culture of Reprinting in the Transatlantic Press', *Journal of Victorian Culture*, 17:3 (2012), 273–86, https://doi.org/10.1080/13555502.2012.702664; Andrew Walker, 'The Development of the Provincial Press in England c. 1780–1914', *Journalism Studies*, 7:3 (2006), 373–386, https://doi.org/10.1080/14616700600680674.

14 Melvin Wevers and Thomas Smits, 'The Visual Digital Turn. Using Neural Networks to Study Historical Images', *Digital Scholarship in the Humanities*, 35:1 (2020), 194–207, https://doi.org/10.1093/llc/fqy085.

objects themselves; and they are universally comprehended'.[15] Second, the production of images was more expensive than that of texts. In 1885, Mason Jackson, a former art director of the *Illustrated London News*, described the production of illustrations of the news in five stages: sketching, drawing, engraving, electrotyping and printing. Every stage, from the taking of on-the-spot sketches by 'special artists' to the teams of engravers working round the clock in order to provide timely visual material, depended on highly skilled labor and substantial investment.[16]

There had been a transnational market for images, in the form of woodblocks, before the nineteenth century. However, the advent of mass-media print formats, partly made possible by the invention of the steam press, and the invention of new techniques which could be used to copy images, transformed the transnational trade in images. In the 1830s, Charles Knight (1791–1873), the publisher of the famous British *Penny Magazine* (1832–1845), already sold stereotyped copies of engravings to eleven different European publications.[17] In order to make a stereotype, an engraving was covered with grease and brushed with a mixture of plaster, mostly consisting of gypsum. After the engraving was gently taken out, a negative matrix of the original image in plaster appeared. Subsequently, a mixture of iron and antimony was poured into the mold, leaving an exact copy of the original engraving. The more efficient process of electrotyping, which, because of its use of electric current, required less metal, enabled illustrated newspapers to sell relatively cheap copies of their engraved images on the international market.[18] As the *London Standard* remarked in 1855:

> The quickened process of engraving, together with divided work upon blocks, and, most of all, the electro-type, in all its various forms, have

15 'Speaking to the eye', *Illustrated London News*, 24 May 1851.

16 For excellent accounts of the production of Victorian illustrations (of the news) see: Brian Maidment, 'Illustration', in *The Routledge Handbook to Nineteenth-Century British Periodicals and Newspapers*, ed. by Andrew King, Alexis Easley, and John Morton (Abingdon: Routledge, 2016), pp. 102–124; Janzen Kooistra; Jennifer Tucker, '"Famished for News Pictures": Mason Jackson, The Illustrated London News, and the Pictorial Spirit', in *Getting the Picture. The Visual Culture of the News*, ed. by Vanessa Schwartz and Jason Hill (London: Bloomsbury Academic, 2015), pp. 213–221.

17 Jean-Pierre Bacot, *La presse illustrée au XIXe siècle. Une histoire oubliée?* (Limoges: Presses universitaires de Limoges, 2005), p. 211.

18 Smits, *The European Illustrated Press*, p. 79.

> combined to render pictorial journalism what it is at the present day, when its international character is emphasized by the interchange of *clichés*.[19]

Crucially, up until the late 1850s, the transnational trade in images of the news required a transaction of a physical object, the stereo- or electrotyped *cliché*, between the original producer of the image and a foreign partner. The *cliché* had to be transported from the original producer to the publication that planned on reprinting it. As opposed to texts, which could be translated or copied directly from a printed copy, the need for a physical transaction between the original producer and the publisher planning on printing a *cliché* diminished the need for protection under law, for example in the form of bilateral or international copyright agreements. After all, copying an illustration from a printed copy always entailed the costly redrawing and re-engraving of the illustration. Copying without the use of stereo- or electrotype technology not only made little economic sense, but was also too time-consuming for the fast-moving pace of illustrated newspapers.

It is hard to find historical evidence of the transnational trade in images. Publishers did not advertise the fact that they obtained illustrations from foreign publications. However, besides the obvious evidence of the same images being republished in different European illustrated newspapers, a couple of cases point to the intensive business relations between different European publishers.[20] In 1847, for example, *il Mondo Illustrato* (1847–1849, 1860–1861), the first Italian illustrated newspaper, provided its readers with an overview of its production costs. Its publisher Giuseppe Pomba (1795–1876) spent 8,000 lira, or roughly 315 pounds, on 'engravings and *clichés* purchased from English and French newspapers'.[21] In comparison, the production of original 'Italian' images was a very prominent item on the budget: 'drawers on paper and wood' and 'engravers in Turin' were paid almost 12,000 and roughly 26,500 lira respectively, while 'boxwood for engraving, its preparation, tools and other expenses of the engraving workshop' cost another 2,400 lira.[22]

---

19 'New Books: the pictorial press', *London Standard*, 26 May 1855.
20 For more examples see: Smits, *The European Illustrated Press*, pp. 91–116.
21 'Al public Italiano', *Mondo Illustrato*, 13 November 1847.
22 Ibid.

Around 1860, some publishers were accused of using newly developed photographic techniques, often described as photoxylography, to print unauthorized copies of illustrations from other publications. In the mid-1850s, several photographers in Britain and in the United States claimed to supply — or were accused of having supplied — well-known illustrated newspapers with the technique to photographically copy images directly on a woodblock.[23] An 1882 book about these new techniques described how they had changed the transnational trade in illustrations:

> Our cheap illustrated newspapers cannot pay for wood blocks [...] and a less expensive substitute is imperative. Photography stands ready to lend a hand in the dilemma. Any picture that appears in the foreign illustrated journals of sufficient interest is made to do duty again over here.[24]

The most important consequence of the new techniques for the transnational trade in illustrations was the fact that they eliminated the necessity of exchanging a *cliché* between its owner and the publication planning on reusing it.

The new techniques especially altered the relationship between British and American publishers of illustrated newspapers. In 1843, the *Illustrated London News* could still somewhat smugly note: 'Our own Journal, [...] is got up in such an expensive form that the Yankees cannot reprint it, and the American artist would not attempt to copy our fine engravings: we are, therefore, our own cure against a reprint'.[25] Seventeen years later, a British newspaper described how the Bostonian *Ballou's Pictorial Drawing-Room Companion* used 'a detestable invention of transferring daguerreotypes to plate for engraving' to copy British illustrations.[26] By that time, the photographic copying of images was already widespread. As the *Worcester Journal* noted: 'The proprietors of the *Illustrated London News, Punch*, and other English illustrated publications, should memorialize [petition] the Senate for the protection against the Yankee robbers, who reproduce their work as original drawings'.[27]

23 Smits, *The European Illustrated Press*, pp. 80–81.

24 Henry Baden Pritchard, *The Photographic Studios of Europe* (London: Piper & Carter, 1882), p. 124.

25 'Post-office, Boston, U.S', *Illustrated London News*, 26 July 1843.

26 'Literature: Phoenixiana', *Lloyds Weekly Newspaper*, 26 August 1860.

27 'Protection', *Worcester Journal*, 9 March 1867.

In 1870, an article in an American magazine discussed the large-scale copying of continental illustrations by American publishers: 'Piracy of this kind is practised by all the illustrated papers in America, just as it is practiced by the editors and publishers of literary periodicals and books'.[28] However, the article made an important distinction between *Harpers Weekly* (1857–1916), which photographed 'the [British] *Graphic* upon wood-blocks, engraves and prints them as its own', and *Frank Leslie's Illustrated Newspaper* (1855–1922), which published copies of images from several European illustrated newspapers on the same page. However, by reducing the images in size, which became relatively easy using the photographic techniques, and placing them under the header 'The Spirit of the European Press' *Leslie's* actively acknowledged its copying. In a letter to the editor of the *Gentleman's Magazine*, Leslie explained that he was not guilty of piracy because nobody could own descriptions of news events: 'We take these pictures on the same principle that the European newspapers copy out from American newspapers such American intelligence and criticism on current affairs as, it is supposed by them, may interest their readers, and *vice versa*'.[29]

In the mid-1850s, the application of a range of new photographic techniques to copy images resulted in the fact that the production process of illustrations of the news alone no longer sufficiently protected publishers against the reuse of their images. The article in the *Gentleman's Magazine* argued that producers of illustrations of the news could only remedy this situation by seeking *legal* protection under copyright law: 'The absence of an international copyright law, places the whole of the English press at the disposal of the American publishers. And they avail themselves right merrily of everything worthy their attention'.[30] *Cassell v. Stiff* is one of the first cases where internationally-operating publishers sought protection under the law for a trade that had been previously been protected from piracy by its production process.

28 'Illustrated newspapers', *Gentleman's Magazine*, new series vol. IV (1870): 452–470; 'Illustrated newspapers. From the *Gentleman's Magazine*', *Littell's Living Age*, 23 April 1870.

29 Ibid., 754.

30 'Illustrated newspapers', *Gentleman's Magazine*, new series vol. IV (1870): 452–470; 'Illustrated newspapers. From the *Gentleman's Magazine*,' *Littell's Living Age*, 23 April 1870.

The Parties

Cassell v. *Stiff* involved three periodicals, two published in London and one in Paris, and four publishers. Started in 1843, the French periodical *l'Illustration,* the first continental imitator of the *Illustrated London News,* was *the* illustrated newspaper of the French-speaking, world-wide *beau monde*. The *London Journal,* started in 1845, and *Cassell's Illustrated Family Paper,* started in 1853, each targeted a mass audience with a cheap price and a combination of news, penny fiction and 'popular' illustration.[31] Especially during the Crimean War (1853–1856), the two periodicals and their publishers were fierce competitors, hoping to profit from the huge interest in everything related to the war, and an almost insatiable public appetite for visual material relating to it.

After publishing copies of British images in the early 1840s, *l'Illustration* started to produce its own illustrations on a large scale at the end of the decade. The engraving firm ABL, a joint venture of the Paris-based British engraver John Andrew and the French engravers Jean Best and Isodore Leloir, produced the majority of these images.[32] Because of their quality, the French illustrations were in high demand. As a result, *l'Illustration* increasingly sold electrotyped copies of its images all over Europe. In 1863, Paul Schmidt, a German printer who worked in Paris, noted in a trade journal: '*L'Illustration* provides *clichés* from its woodcuts for two centimes per square centimeter and *galvanos* for three centimes, and sells them for roughly 40,000 Fr. a year in total'.[33] The publication also sold the 'exclusive right' to buy its illustrations to publishers in other countries. As we will see, this meant that publishers wishing to print *l'Illustration*'s images, like Cassell, had to pay the French periodical for exclusive rights in their respective countries.

In contrast to the venerable *l'Illustration,* the *London Journal* and *Cassell's* have received considerably less scholarly attention. Most studies

31 Laurel Brake and Marysa Demoor, *The Lure of Illustration in the Nineteenth Century: Picture and Press* (New York: Palgrave Macmillan, 2009), p. 155.

32 Paul Jobling and David Crowley, *Graphic Design. Reproduction and Representation since 1800* (Manchester: Manchester University Press, 1996), p. 36.

33 'L'Illustration gibt *Clichés* von ihren Holzschnitten zu 2 Centimen den Quadratzentimeter, und *Galvanos* zu 3 Centimen, und verkauft deren ungefähr für 40,000 Fr. das Jahr': P. Schmidt, 'Pariser Illustrirte Journale. L'Illustration', *Journal für Buchdruckerkunst, Schriftgiesserei und verwandte Fächer*, 17 June 1863.

have focussed on popular fiction in both publications.[34] In both cases, the substantial and sustained publication of images of the news has mostly been overlooked. This is especially surprising for *Cassell's*, because, as Andrew King noted, the periodical was explicitly designed to 'look like a version of the *ILN* [*Illustrated London News*], comprising the same newspaper-sized page [and] the same extravagant size of illustrations on its front pages'.[35] While the second or new series of *Cassell's* started in 1857 certainly focused on fiction, the three volumes of the first series (December 1853–December 1856) were centred on a single news event: the Crimean War. Around fifty percent of all the illustrations and articles in the first three volumes concerned the war, while many other images were indirectly related to it.[36]

The *Illustrated London News* was not the only example for Cassell. The business model of his periodical, which focused on selling high volume and maintaining low cost, was partly an imitation of the *London Journal*. Its publisher George Stiff, who worked as a foreman for the engravers of the *Illustrated London News* in the mid-1840s, started his career in 1843 by publishing the *Illustrated Weekly Times*, a cheap imitation of the famous illustrated newspaper. Although this venture quickly failed, the *London Journal*, which Stiff started in 1845, became a tremendous success, selling close to 500,000 copies a week in the mid-1850s.[37]

It seems that *Cassell's* was especially started to ride the wave of interest in the Crimean War with high-quality images of the news. Its circulation quickly rose from around 150,000 copies after its launch in 1853 to an astonishing 500,000 copies at the end of 1854. These numbers are even more significant if we contrast them to the 150,000 copies that the *Illustrated London News* sold each week, or the 50,000 copies sold by

---

34 Josef Altholz, *The Religious Press in Britain, 1760–1900* (New York: Greenwood Press, 1989), p. 88; Flora Armetta, 'Cassell's (Illustrated) Family Paper (1853–1867) and Cassell's Magazine (1867–1932)', in *The Dictionary of Nineteenth Century Journalism*, ed. by Laurel Brake and Marysa Demoor (Ghent: Academia Press, 2009), p. 101 (p. 101); Catherine Delafield, *Serialization and the Novel in Mid-Victorian Magazines* (Farnham: Ashgate, 2015), pp. 86–91; Toni Johnston-Woods, 'The Virtual Reading Communities of the London Journal, the New York Ledger and the Australian Journal', in *Nineteenth-Century Media and the Construction of Identities*, ed. by Laurel Brake, Bill Bell, and David Finkelstein (Basingstoke: Palgrave, 2000), pp. 350–361.

35 Andrew King, *The London Journal, 1845–83: Periodicals, Production and Gender* (Aldershot: Ashgate, 2004), p. 100.

36 Smits, p. 131.

37 Johnston-Woods, p. 351.

The Times each day in the same year. Based on these figures, it could be argued that *Cassell's* was the most important shaper of the image of the Crimean War in Britain, meaning that no other (illustrated) news publication reached a comparable audience.[38]

During the Crimean War, *Cassell's* constantly outperformed its main competitor the *London Journal*. As King noted, it

> reported and depicted events earlier than the *Journal*, with larger cuts, and even *ILN*-type supplements. [...] The prints in *Cassell's* recall the urgent sense of immediacy characteristic of the *ILN* much more successfully than the *Journal*'s new attempts at the same.[39]

However, being the cheapest, most newsworthy and most popular illustrated publication in Britain did not mean that the content of Cassell's flagship publication was particularly British. In 1854 the cheapness of *Cassell's* left the reviewer of the *Kerry Examiner and Munster General Observer*, a provincial newspaper in the Southeastern Irish city of Tralee, confused.[40] How was Cassell able to supply his readers with beautiful illustrations 'of many of the scenes referred to in the present war between the Russians and the Turks' for only a single penny?'[41] The answer to this question is simple: he bought electrotyped clichés from images first published in *l'Illustration*.[42]

The Case

On 2 February 1856, articles appeared in several provincial British newspapers, discussing *Cassell* v. *Stiff*.[43] Cassell sued Stiff to restrain him from 'publishing certain numbers of his journal, containing views of the

38 Smits, p. 131.

39 King, p. 100.

40 'Cassell's Illustrated Family Paper', *Kerry Examiner and Munster General Observer*, 31 January 1854.

41 Ibid.

42 King suggests that Cassell's illustrations were made by former employees of the *Illustrated London News*. While some images were indeed made by the engravers he mentions, the vast majority, 295 of the total 361 illustrations of the war, were bought from *l'Illustration*. Furthermore, many articles concerning the war were word-for-word translations from the French periodical King, p. 100; Smits, p. 156.

43 'Newspaper copyright — Cassell v. Stiff', *Herts Guardian, Agricultural Journal, and General Advertiser*, 2 February 1856; 'Newspaper copyright — Cassell v. Stiff', *Wells* Journal, 2 February 1856.

Paris exhibition, on the ground that they were copied from sketches in the French paper, *L'Illustration. Journal Universelle*, to which the plaintiff claimed having the exclusive right'.[44] According to newspaper reports, Stiff defended himself by stating that he copied the illustrations of the Paris exhibition 'from photographs publicly offered for sale in Paris and that none of the sketches in question were copied by him from the French paper referred to'.[45]

King correctly sees the case as one of the fronts in a fierce battle for control of the penny market between Cassell and Stiff in the mid-1850s. He notes that the 'judge accepted Cassell's case without even listening to Stiff's defence'.[46] However, a report on the case in *The Times* suggests the opposite outcome. Vice-Chancellor William Page Wood, the judge in the case, 'without calling on the counsel for the defendants, said that the question was far too doubtful a one for an injunction till the plaintiff's right had been tried at law'.[47] In other words, Cassell had asked the judge to issue an injunction banning the sale of issues of the *London Journal* that contained illustrations copied from *l'Illustration*, prohibiting the same journal from using copies of illustrations from the French periodical in the future, and giving Cassell the right to a part of the profits of the sale of the issues containing the French illustrations. Furthermore, Cassell also demanded that Stiff pay all the legal fees. However, VC Page Wood refused to issue the injunction but allowed Cassell to establish his claim through trial in a court of law.[48]

What was the exact nature of the deal between Cassell and French publishers, which enabled him to provide his readers with high-quality images of the Crimean War? We can piece together the specifics from various reports of the court case. In June 1855, Cassell paid Armand le Chevalier and Jean-Baptiste-Alexandre Paulin, the then-publishers of the French publication, for the exclusive right to reproduce material from *l'Illustration* in the United Kingdom.[49] An article in the *Art Journal*

---

44 'Newspaper copyright — Cassell v. Stiff', *Herts Guardian, Agricultural Journal, and General Advertiser*, 2 February 1856.

45 Ibid.

46 'Cassell v. Stiff and Vickers', *The Times*, 25 January 1856. Cited in King, p. 100.

47 'Cassell v. Stiff and Vickers', *The Times*, 25 January 1856.

48 Edward Ebenezer Kay and Henry Robert Vaughan Johnson, *Reports of Cases Adjudged in the High Court of Chancery, before Sir W.P. Wood, Vice-Chancellor. 1855 to 1856.* (London: W. Maxwell, 1856), II, p. 281.

49 Kay and Johnson, *Reports of Cases*, II, p. 279.

(1850–1880) notes that Cassell paid the French publishers the heavy sum of 12,500 francs, or around 500 pounds, annually for the exclusive right to publish in Britain all texts and illustrations first appearing in *l'Illustration*.[50] The British publisher claimed that this agreement entitled him to the 'exclusive right and liberty of printing, publishing and translating, and selling within the dominions of her said present Majesty' to all the 'original articles and papers, prints, drawings, woodcuts therein respectively from time to time appearing' in *l'Illustration*.[51]

It is important to note that, since its foundation in December 1853, *Cassell's* already contained many copies from *l'Illustration* but that both publications only deemed it necessary to formalize their agreement in the summer of 1855. This discrepancy of eighteen months can mean two things. It is possible that, before June 1855, *l'Illustration* sold copies of its illustrations to more than one British publication. In this scenario, hoping to get an edge over a prominent competitor, Cassell paid the French publishers to acquire exclusive access to their illustrations. In the second scenario, Cassell noticed, or was alerted to the fact, that Stiff had started to print unauthorized copies of illustrations from *l'Illustration*. In other words, using photographic techniques himself, or relying on the services of others, Stiff published copies of the illustrations without paying the French publishers. The last scenario seems the most plausible. As Slauter notes, in the summer of 1855 fear of unfair competition reached unprecedented heights, following the decision to abolish the stamp duty — a tax of one penny per issue on publications that sold for less than six pence and contained news. Cassell's efforts to seek protection for his visual news can be seen as a part of a broader legislative push by London newspapers to enact a special copyright for news in general.[52]

According to the bill of complaint filed at the Court of Chancery on 19 December 1855, Cassell discovered on 1 November 1855 that the *London Journal* had published illustrations that were copied from *l'Illustration*. The bill specifically mentions the issues of the *London Journal* of 25 Augustus, 15 September, 29 September, and 3 November. Some images

50 'Copyright in Engravings', *Art Journal*, 1 March 1856.

51 Kay and Johnson, II, p. 280.

52 Will Slauter, *Who Owns the News? A History of Copyright* (Stanford: Stanford University Press, 2019), pp. 143–163.

were 'exact copies' and even included the names of the French artists and engravers, who often signed their work in the lower-left and right corners of the illustrations. However, other images were 'reduced in size, and others being altered or varied in merely a colourable manner, and the names or designations affixed to such pirated prints, (...) being altered or varied in merely a colourable manner'.[53] The reference to the altered sizes of the illustrations suggests that Cassell claimed that Stiff, or the parties he bought the illustrations from, used photographic techniques to transfer the French illustrations onto new woodblocks. As the practices of Frank Leslie mentioned earlier suggest, it was relatively easy to alter the size of illustrations using photographic techniques.

The description of the case in the *Art Journal* suggests that the VC Page Wood, did not immediately grant an injunction because he argued that 'the question of construction on these Copyright Acts, in connection with the facts, were much too doubtful to be decided upon a motion for an injunction, until the plaintiff had established his legal right in action'.[54] Cassell needed to prove that he had legal title, or ownership, over the images in question, that he had adhered to the provisions of the law, and that Stiff's actions constituted an infringement of copyright. As a result of the transnational dimensions of the case, these three elements were hard to prove. The description in the *Art Journal* referenced these difficulties, noting that the judge had especially 'grave doubts upon the 15th. and 16th. Vict., c.12, sec. 7'.[55] Here the judge referred to the International Copyright Act of 1852.

In the history of copyright legislation, the 1852 act, which was based on the French-Anglo Copyright Treaty of 1851, is primarily discussed in relation to translations of literary works.[56] The treaty served as a model for several bilateral copyright agreements: for example between the United Kingdom and the German city-state of Hamburg (1853)

53 Kay and Johnson, II, p. 280.

54 'Copyright in Engravings', *Art Journal*, 1 March 1856.

55 Ibid.

56 Catherine Seville, *The Internationalisation of Copyright Law: Books, Buccaneers and the Black Flag in the Nineteenth Century* (Cambridge: Cambridge University Press, 2009), pp. 51–52; Ronan Deazley, 'Commentary on International Copyright Act 1852' (2008), in *Primary Sources on Copyright (1450–1900)*, ed. by Lionel Bently and Martin Kretschmer, http://www.copyrighthistory.org/cam/tools/request/showRecord?id=commentary_uk_1852.

and between the United Kingdom and the Kingdom of Spain (1857).[57] Ronan Deazley notes that several provisions in the 1851 treaty between the United Kingdom and France 'sought to delineate certain uses of protected work that would not otherwise be considered to be unlawful'.[58] Article 5 of the treaty, which provided that 'articles extracted from newspapers or periodicals published in either of the two countries, may be republished or translated in the newspapers or periodicals of the other country, provided the source from whence such articles are taken be acknowledged' and subject to a right of the author to specifically forbid the republication of the same, is especially important here.[59] When this provision of the treaty was incorporated in domestic legislation — the 1852 act — the British legislature considerably changed the substance of Article 5, making a distinction between 'political' and 'non-political' material in newspapers and periodicals. Foreign articles containing 'political discussion', could always be reprinted in Britain, regardless of 'whether the authors had "signified his intention of preserving the copyright therein"'.[60] This meant that foreign authors could only claim copyright on articles that were of a 'non-political' nature.

Cassell hoped to use the 1852 act to protect his exclusive right to reproduce images from *l'Illustration*. To do so, he not only had to prove that these illustrations were 'non-political' in nature, which would allow the French publishers to lay claim to their copyright; the plaintiffs, Cassell and the French publishers, also had to satisfy what Deazley calls a 'series of considerably burdensome practical and legal conditions'.[61] First, the owner of the original work had to signify 'his Intention of preserving the Copyright therein, and the Right of translating the same, in some conspicuous Part of the Newspaper or Periodical in which the

57 'Bilateral Treaty between Hamburg and Great Britain, Hamburg (1853)', in *Primary Sources on Copyright*, ed. by Bently and Kretschmer, http://www.copyrighthistory.org/cam/tools/request/showRecord.php?id=record_d_1853; José Bellido, Raquel Xalabarder, and Ramón Casas Vallés (2011) 'Commentary on Bilateral Copyright Convention between Spain and UK (1857)'(2011), in *Primary Sources on Copyright*, ed. by Bently and Kretschmer, http://www.copyrighthistory.org/cam/tools/request/showRecord?id=commentary_s_1857.

58 Deazley, 'Commentary'.

59 Ibid.

60 Ibid.

61 Deazley.

same was first published'.[62] This first provision explains the message that had started to appear on the front page of *l'Illustration* since the summer of 1855: 'Regarding international treaties, the editors reserve the right of reproduction and translation abroad'.[63] Second, within three months after the publication abroad, a copy of the original work had to be deposited at Stationers' Hall. The description of the case in the *Art Journal* notes how Chevalier and Paulin travelled to London to register the copyright and deposit the most recent issue of *l'Illustration* at the Stationers' Company. And, finally, the person claiming the copyright had to exercise his right by publishing the work in the UK within three years after the registration and deposit; otherwise, the work would fall into the public domain.

Why did VC Page Wood refuse to grant Cassell an injunction after the initial hearing in the case? As mentioned above, it was especially the seventh section of the act that made him hesitant. This section explicitly deals with the distinction between 'political' and 'non-political' material in newspapers and periodicals, so one might wonder whether the judge was concerned that illustrations of the news could be considered 'political' material. If they were of a political nature, then the French publishers, and Cassell by extension, could not have established their rights under the 1852 act.

From a published report of the case, it becomes clear that VC Page Wood did not focus on the distinction between political and non-political content. In his ruling, he first argued that Cassell and his French partners had sufficiently signified their 'intention of preserving the copyright' of *l'Illustration* in Britain.[64] However, he believed that Cassell had failed to 'comply with the requisitions of the act'.[65] He and his French partners only registered the latest issue of *l'Illustration* in June 1855, which did not contain any of the illustrations in question, and, on the basis of this single entry, claimed copyright on the material in all subsequent issues. As Slauter notes of national copyright, both the Copyright Act of 1814

62 'International Copyright Act, London (1852)', in *Primary Sources on Copyright*, ed. by Bently and Kretschmer, http://www.copyrighthistory.org/cam/tools/request/showRecord.php?id=record_uk_1852.

63 'Vu les traites internationaux, les éditeurs se réservent le droit de reproduction et de traduction à l'étranger': 'Frontpage', *l'Illustration*, 4 August 1855.

64 Kay and Johnson, II, p. 284.

65 Ibid.

and the Literary Copyright Act of 1842 only required the first issue of a periodical to be registered in order to 'enjoy the benefits of the statute for all subsequent numbers'.[66] Considering the fact that *l'Illustration* had been published since 1843, the judge argued that, in this case, the first issue as meant in the act could only mean the first number of *l'Illustration* published after the act came into effect in 1852. However, the French publishers had only registered one issue in the summer of 1855 and, as a result, could claim copyright only for this specific issue and not for subsequent issues.

This ruling must have left Cassell confused and angered, not only since he had gone to great lengths to meet the criteria of the act, but also because the description of the case in *The Times* notes how he had in fact tried

> to cause an entry to be made in the registry-books of the Stationer's Company of the four numbers of the periodical *l'Illustration* from which the alleged piracies had been taken, but such an entry had been refused by the company as being unnecessary.[67]

However, Vice-Chancellor Wood stated that 'the public' could not

> be bound if there is any neglect at the Stationers' Hall as to registration. [...] if there be any neglect to register, the remedy of the publisher must be against the parties causing such neglect. It cannot affect those who are thereby kept in ignorance of the existence of the copyright.[68]

In other words, Cassell was free to sue Stationers' Hall, but their mistake would not be taken into account in his case against Stiff.

VC Page Wood did not grant Cassell an injunction, but allowed him to press forward with a trial in order to establish his case. This seems to have been his intention, which is not surprising considering the trouble he already went through. However, it also seems that Stiff managed to successfully stall the proceedings. After the hearing at the end of January, VC Page Wood granted Stiff's lawyers an extra fourteen days to prepare their arguments. Several additional two-week extensions were

66 Slauter, 'Introduction', p. 587.

67 'Cassell v. Stiff and Vickers', *The Times*, 25 January 1856.

68 Kay and Johnson, II, p. 287.

granted in February, March, and April 1856.[69] Following this period, the trail in the archive goes cold. Cassell might have dropped the case or settled the matter out of court. In addition to stalling the case, Stiff also started several countersuits, in what King describes as a 'clear *quid pro quo*'.[70] In one of them, Stiff claimed that *Cassell's* contained a copy of an illustration of the main building of the 1857 Art Treasures of Great Britain Exhibition in Manchester, which had originally appeared in the *London Journal*. The tables had turned. A newspaper description of the case noted how Stiff complained of 'the practice in this country of using copies of engravings published in France, which, in fact, were borrowed from English journals, the proprietors of which had a copyright in them'.[71] Now it was Cassell's turn to claim that he had bought the illustration in Paris, having been assured 'that these representations ... were original, and not derived from an English work'.[72] However, because the illustration was originally produced in Britain and national British copyright law did not involve the same burdensome formalities as the 1852 International Copyright Act, the judge granted Stiff an injunction.[73]

Conclusion

John Cassell's success as a publisher of books and periodicals was to a large extent based on his contacts with foreign publishers, authors, artists, and engravers. A contemporary biography notes how he often travelled overnight to Paris to 'see a number of friends and transact business with artists and engravers'.[74] Another biography remarks that he often visited Paris 'where he was well known, and where he was thus enabled to effect a very considerable business in the exchange and purchase of illustrations for his various works'.[75] After Cassell died in 1865, his wife remembered how several French friends, including Jean

69 Kew, The National Archives, Chancery, Entry Books of Decrees and Orders, C33/1033 fol 387v; C33/1034 fols 602v, 607v, 672.
70 King, p. 100.
71 'Stiff v. Cassell', *Standard*, 19 March 1857.
72 Ibid.
73 'Stiff v. Cassell', *The Times*, 18 March 1856.
74 Holden Pike, *John Cassell* (London: Cassel and Company, 1894), p. 108.
75 Henry Curwen, *A History of Booksellers, the Old and the New.* (London: Chatto and Windus, 1873), p. 272.

Best of the engraving firm that supplied *l'Illustration*, members of the influential Hachette publishing family, and Michel Lévy the owner of *l'Univers Illustré*, came to pay their respects at his funeral in London.[76]

On the basis of the 1852 International Copyright Act, Cassell and his French partners tried to protect one of their arrangements formally and claim the right to exclusive use of French illustrations of the news in Britain. However, according to VC Page Wood, they failed to comply with the requirements of the act. The court case shows that the 1852 act was designed to provide copyright protection in Britain and France for (translations) of literary works, including non-political articles and illustrations in newspapers and periodicals. However, the provisions concerning the distinction between political and non-political material as well as the formalities required by the act were discouraging to say the least. VC Page Wood interpreted them in such a way that it became unpractical to claim exclusive use over content in any foreign periodical that was started before 1851. After all, if the very first issue of a publication could not be registered, the act apparently required registering every single issue at Stationers' Hall.

Cassell v. *Stiff* sheds light on an important transitional phase in the history of visual news culture. First, it underlines the fact that Cassell and his French partners had to resort to copyright laws, which had always been focussed on texts, to protect their agreement in the first place. In the 1840s and early 1850s, illustrated newspapers were protected from unauthorized reuse by their production process. Because publishers had to exchange money for *clichés*, the transnational trade of illustrations always necessitated contact and a physical transaction. *Cassell* v. *Stiff* shows that some publishers already started using photographic techniques to copy illustrations in the mid-1850s. It is likely that Stiff, who was always looking to cut costs, was an early adopter of these new techniques. This explains the fact that Cassell only claimed copyright and started to pay the French publishers for exclusive rights in the summer of 1855, more than three years after the International Copyright Act was approved by Parliament and eighteen months after he started publishing French illustrations of the Crimean War.

76 Curwen, p. 272.

Moreover, *Cassell* v. *Stiff* shows that, around 1850, the history of reproduction techniques and new laws on copyright jointly shaped the trade in illustrations. This chapter demonstrated that we can only truly understand this history from a transnational perspective. The pirating of illustrations of news often went unnoticed, because publishers were careful to copy only foreign illustrations. This is not only true for contemporary readers, but also for historians studying the nineteenth-century illustrated press. We often assume that images of the news were produced for a certain periodical, because we fail to look beyond national borders.

Bibliography

Altholz, Josef, *The Religious Press in Britain, 1760–1900* (New York: Greenwood Press, 1989).

Altick, Richard, *The English Common Reader: A Social History of the Mass Reading Public, 1800–1900* (Chicago: University of Chicago Press, 1957).

Armetta, Flora, 'Cassell's (Illustrated) Family Paper (1853–1867) and Cassell's Magazine (1867–1932)', in *The Dictionary of Nineteenth Century Journalism*, ed. by Laurel Brake and Marysa Demoor (Ghent: Academia Press, 2009), p. 101.

Bacot, Jean-Pierre, *La presse illustrée au XIXe siècle. Une histoire oubliée?* (Limoges: Presses universitaires de Limoges, 2005).

Beals, Melody, 'Scissors and Paste: The Georgian Reprints, 1800–1837', *Journal of Open Humanities Data*, 3.0 (2017), 1, https://doi.org/10.5334/johd.8.

Brake, Laurel, and Marysa Demoor, *The Lure of Illustration in the Nineteenth Century: Picture and Press* (New York: Palgrave Macmillan, 2009).

Bucher, Hans Jürgen, 'Ein "Pictorial Turn" im 19. Jahrhundert? Überlegungen zu einer multimodalen Mediengeschichte am Beispiel der illustrierten Zeitungen', in *Historische Perspektiven auf den Iconic Turn. Die Entwicklung der öffentlichen visuellen Kommunikation*, ed. by Stephanie Geise, Thomas Birkner, Klaus Arnold, Maria Löblich, and Katharina Lobinger (Köln: Herbert von Halem, 2016), pp. 280–317.

Curwen, Henry, *A History of Booksellers, the Old and the New.* (London: Chatto and Windus, 1873).

Deazley, Ronan, 'Commentary on International Copyright Act 1852'(2008), in *Primary Sources on Copyright (1450–1900)*, ed. by Lionel Bently and Martin Kretschmer, http://www.copyrighthistory.org/cam/tools/request/showRecord?id=commentary_uk_1852.

Delafield, Catherine, *Serialization and the Novel in Mid-Victorian Magazines* (Farnham: Ashgate, 2015).

Hill, Jason, and Vanessa Schwartz, *Getting the Picture: The Visual Culture of the News* (London: Bloomsbury Academic, 2015).

Janzen Kooistra, Lorraine, 'Illustration', in *Journalism and the Periodical Press in Nineteenth-Century Britain*, ed. by Joanne Shattock (Cambridge: Cambridge University Press, 2017), pp. 104–125.

Jobling, Paul, and David Crowley, *Graphic Design. Reproduction and Representation since 1800* (Manchester: Manchester University Press, 1996).

Johnston-Woods, Toni, 'The Virtual Reading Communities of the London Journal, the New York Ledger and the Australian Journal', in *Nineteenth-Century Media and the Construction of Identities*, ed. by Laurel Brake, Bill Bell, and David Finkelstein (Basingstoke: Palgrave, 2000), pp. 350–361.

King, Andrew, *The London Journal, 1845–83: Periodicals, Production and Gender* (Aldershot: Ashgate, 2004).

Maidment, Brian, 'Illustration', in *The Routledge Handbook to Nineteenth-Century British Periodicals and Newspapers*, ed. by Andrew King, Alexis Easley, and John Morton (Abingdon: Routledge, 2016), pp. 102–124.

Nicholson, Bob, '"You Kick the Bucket; We Do the Rest!": Jokes and the Culture of Reprinting in the Transatlantic Press', *Journal of Victorian Culture*, 17:3 (2012), 273–86, https://doi.org/10.1080/13555502.2012.702664.

Paul, Gerhard, *Das visuelle Zeitalter: Punkt und Pixel* (Göttingen: Wallstein Verlag, 2016).

Pettegree, Andrew, *The Invention of News: How the World Came to Know about Itself* (New Have: Yale University Press, 2015).

Pigeon, Stephan, 'Steal It, Change It, Print It: Transatlantic Scissors-and-Paste Journalism in the Ladies' Treasury, 1857–1895', *Journal of Victorian Culture*, 22:1 (2017), 24–39, https://doi.org/10.1080/13555502.2016.1249393.

Pike, Holden, *John Cassell* (London: Cassel and Company, 1894).

Pritchard, Henry Baden, *The Photographic Studios of Europe* (London: Piper & Carter, 1882).

Seville, Catherine, *The Internationalisation of Copyright Law: Books, Buccaneers and the Black Flag in the Nineteenth Century* (Cambridge: Cambridge University Press, 2009).

Slauter, Will, 'Introduction: Copying and Copyright, Publishing Practice and the Law', *Victorian Periodicals Review*, 51:4 (2018), 583–96, https://doi.org/10.1353/vpr.2018.0044.

——, Who Owns the News? A History of Copyright. (Stanford: Stanford University Press, 2019).

Smith, David A., Ryan Cordell, and Abby Mullen, 'Computational Methods for Uncovering Reprinted Texts in Antebellum Newspapers', *American Literary History*, 27:3 (2015), 1–15, https://doi.org/10.1093/alh/ajv029.

Smits, Thomas, *The European Illustrated Press and the Emergence of a Transnational Visual Culture of the News, 1842–1870* (London: Routledge, 2020).

Tucker, Jennifer, '"Famished for News Pictures": Mason Jackson, The Illustrated London News, and the Pictorial Spirit', in *Getting the Picture. The Visual Culture of the News*, ed. by Vanessa Schwartz and Jason Hill (London: Bloomsbury Academic, 2015), pp. 213–221.

Walker, Andrew, 'The Development of the Provincial Press in England c. 1780–1914', *Journalism Studies*, 7:3 (2006), 373–386, https://doi.org/10.1080/14616700600680674.

Wevers, Melvin, and Thomas Smits, 'The Visual Digital Turn. Using Neural Networks to Study Historical Images', *Digital Scholarship in the Humanities*, 35:1 (2020), 194–207, https://doi.org/10.1093/llc/fqy085.

9. (Re)Assembling Reference Books and Recycling Images

The Wood Engravings of the W. & R. Chambers Firm

Rose Roberto

The *Memoir of William and Robert Chambers* (1872) narrates the story of two brothers, William (1800–1883) and Robert (1802–1871) Chambers, who created a publishing empire over several decades through personal initiative, hard-work, and promoting the philosophy of self-improvement and utilitarian progress derived from long-standing Scottish educational and culture values. Through their editorials, publications, and works of philanthropy, the brothers promoted both formal and informal education, as a means of lifting oneself out of poverty.[1] Their long-lasting legacy was W. & R. Chambers, established in 1832, which successfully operated as a family business until 1992 when it merged with George G. Harrap Limited, and became Chambers Harrap Publishers Ltd (CHPL).[2] After the firm's first twenty years, Chambers formed a partnership with J. B. Lippincott, a Philadelphia-based firm, in order to expand further into North American markets. Between 1859 and 1892, both publishers collaborated to produce the

1 The author thanks the Bibliographic Society for the Barry Bloomfield Award, the Catherine Mackichan Trust for travel assistance, and Jeff Loveland for advice on *Encyclopaedia Britannica* sources; Robert J. Schnolick, 'Intersecting Empires: W. & R. Chambers and Emigration, 1832–1844', *The Biblotheck: A Journal of Scottish bibliography and book history*, 24 (1999), 5–16 (p. 5).

2 The firm is currently part of the international Hachette Livre conglomerate.

 https://doi.org/10.11647/OBP.0247.09

heavily-illustrated *Chambers's Encyclopaedia: A Dictionary of Universal Knowledge for the People,* 1860–1868 and *Chambers's Encyclopaedia: A Dictionary of Universal Knowledge, New Edition,* 1888–1892. Throughout this chapter, these books will be referred to respectively as the First Edition and the Second Edition of *Chambers's Encyclopaedia.* Examining these encyclopedia editions provides insight into the workings of a major Scottish publishing house and its dealings with an important American publishing firm, covering a period in which laws and international treaties were evolving, contested, and subject to interpretation. Given Chambers's significance, its concerns and working practices can be applied more widely to other nineteenth-century publishing firms.

This chapter will address several questions related to the themes of copyright, image production, and image circulation during the second half of the nineteenth century. Namely: Where did illustrations come from, and what explanations can be found for publishers' reliance on existing illustrations? What strategies did publishers such as W. & R. Chambers develop to combat unauthorized reproductions of their own works, while at the same time making use of others' images. Finally, how were images adapted into reference works, such as encyclopedias, and modified as they were reproduced?

Examining these questions through several case studies of images that appeared in the two editions of Chambers's *Encyclopaedia*, this chapter begins with an exploration of illustrations in the context of publishers' culture, which habitually borrowed and copied older and widely circulating content.

Sources for Visual Material in *Chambers's Encyclopaedia*

Between January 1862 and January 1863, a Japanese delegation consisting of 40 men — ambassadors and their aides — visited London, Paris, Berlin and St. Petersburg.[3] They also made shorter visits to the Netherlands and Portugal. Led by Takenouchi Yasunori, who served as governor of Shimotsuke Province prior to the mission, the ambassador had two goals that he completed successfully: to negotiate a delay of five years before Japan would have to officially open up its port cities

3 '*The Times*, 3 May 1862', in *The Library of Nineteenth-Century Photography* from the collection of Paul Frecker, 19th Century Photos, http://www.19thcenturyphotos.com/Japanese-envoy-122059.

to the West for trade, and to research the different European nations that would be their trading partners.[4] As Edo Japan transitioned into the Meiji Empire, this trip was seen as highly influential on the next five decades of Japanese foreign policy.[5] While they were traveling, the Japanese ambassadors were frequently photographed, and featured in major newspapers such as *The Times* in London and *Le Siècle* in Paris.

The entry for `Japan' in the First Edition of *Chambers's Encyclopaedia* contains a reproduction of a widely circulated photograph by London-based photographer Robert Vernon Heath showing three of the Japanese ambassadors, whose image was not only featured in *The Times*, but was also turned into a *carte de visite* that was sold widely.[6] A direct connection can be made between the encyclopedia's entry with its wood engraved print, translated onto a wood block by an unknown employee of the Chambers firm, and the *carte de visite* produced by Robert Vernon Heath. (See Figures 1a and 1b). First, the caption beneath the wood-engraving copies the spelling and diacritics of the ambassadors' names on the *carte de visite*. Second, the caption states that the image was 'from a photograph' produced by Heath. However, it does not look completely identical. A practical consideration when designing the page layout was to make the image fit the space allocated for the 'Japan' encyclopedia entry. Therefore, the image layout was altered from portrait to landscape to fit the format, as can be seen on the woodblock and its print.

This image provides some insight into the production of the First Edition, communicating two things. First, it demonstrates that the Chambers firm was capable of sourcing images within a lead time of only one year. Appearing in 1863, Volume 5 incorporated a photograph taken in April 1862, shortly before the French leg of the ambassadors' journey. By including this relatively current and popular image of people in their pages, the publishers could directly connect with potential audiences. It also shows that the Chambers firm was not averse to copying visual material produced by others.

4 Mayako Shimamoto, Koji Ito, & Yoneyuki Sugita, *Historical Dictionary of Japanese Foreign Policy* (London: Rowman and Littlefield, 2015), p. 79.

5 Andrew Cobbing, *The Japanese Discovery of Victorian Britain: Early Travel Encounters in the Far West* (London: Routledge, 2013), p. 173, https://doi.org/10.4324/9781315073491.

6 Many popular nineteenth-century albumen prints are online at: www.19thcenturyphotos.com.

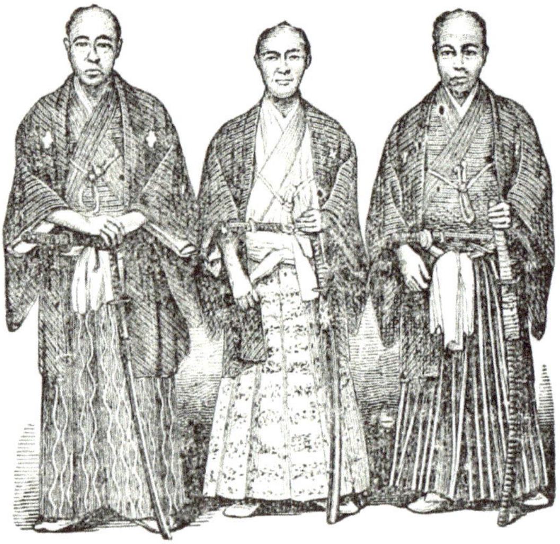

1 2 3

The Japanese Ambassadors to Europe in 1862.

Fig. 1a Print of 1862 Japanese Delegation to Europe with caption in *Chambers's Encyclopaedia*, 1863, Volume 5, based on a *carte de visite* by Vernon Heath, 1862.

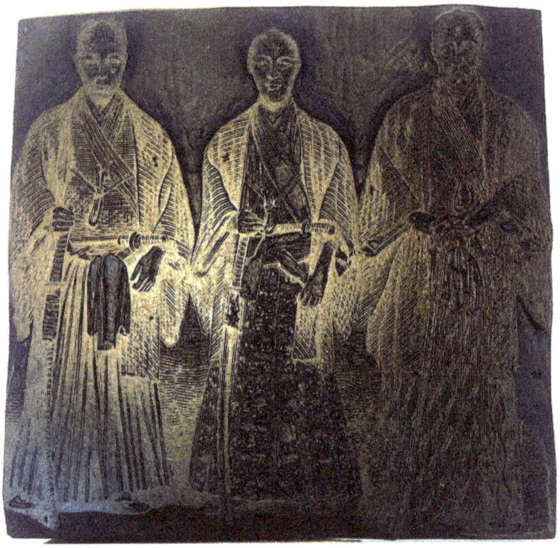

Fig. 1b Woodblock for print (T.2011.56.318), National Museums Collection Centre, Edinburgh, photo by Rose Roberto.

Second, the image itself was consistent with the narrative of 'Western progress' reflected in many Chambers publications. Not only is the inevitability of technological progress explicitly discussed in the text of this and other entries, but the caption reference 'from a photograph' reinforces this message by directly showing the technologies of image reproduction and rapid international travel available through steam-powered ships. Many scholars have debated the documentary evidence around the inventive aspects of photographs contesting the idea of their inherent authenticity.[7] However, the Chambers' position seems to reflect the belief that the mechanical nature of photography imbued its images with objectivity. Their captions and editorial commentary state photographs provided more accurate information to their readers.[8] At the same time, the subjects depicted in the photographs — foreign dignitaries traveling around Europe on a trade mission — testified to an interconnectedness of the mid-nineteenth century world, and the expansion of capitalism. This image further implies the inevitability of European expansion in Asia.

Arguably, the Japanese elite recognized that expansion by Western powers was imminent, and were politically astute enough to begin establishing economic and political relationships with Europe to avoid their own country's colonization. This diplomatic mission seemed to be aimed at adapting to and learning from the Western countries they were visiting, as well as endearing themselves to the public through the medium of illustrated newspapers. By 1865, only three years later, business entrepreneurs in Europe were exporting objects promoting Japanese aesthetics and visual imagery. With the approval of the Japanese government, shops were set up in Paris and other cities which specialized in selling prints and albums made in Japan, proving to be very popular and influential on European art.[9] There were also books published to describe Japan and its culture.

Michael Bhaskar, a writer and expert on publishing and the media, argues that all publishers undertake four activities: framing, modeling, filtering, and amplifying.[10] He states that content cannot be uncoupled

7 Geoffrey Belknap, *From a Photograph: Authenticity, Science and the Periodical Press, 1870–1890* (Bloomsbury: London, 2016).

8 David Patrick, 'Preface', in *Chambers's Encyclopaedia: A Dictionary of Universal Knowledge, New Edition.* Volume I, 2nd edition, ed. by David Patrick (Edinburgh: W. & R. Chambers, 1888).

9 Linda G. Zatlin, *Beardsley, Japonisme, and Perversion of the Victorian Ideal* (Cambridge: Cambridge University Press, 1997), pp. 32–36. Vincent Van Gogh frequented shops selling Japanese art.

10 Michael Bhaskar, *The Content Machine: Towards a Theory of Publishing from the Printing Press to the Digital Network* (London: Anthem Publishing Studies, 2013), p. 89.

from publishing; the way an audience experiences a given work is a critical part of what defines the latter. Content must be framed or packaged for distribution and presented to a specific audience, and it is packaged according to a model. Models help publishers organize and market their content.[11] When enough publishers follow similar models, new genres emerge; ones that are reinforced when other publishers replicate the model's format(s) in new works.

According to Bhaskar's theory of publishing, 'the encyclopedia' is a specific model for a type of publication, that can only exist in a specific time and place, according to the technologies and knowledge of that time. While the idea of an encyclopedia goes back to Roman antiquity, from 1690 to 1830, the scope of encyclopedias kept pace with expanding knowledge of the world.[12] By the 1840s, the encyclopedia genre stabilized into a specific form and average size, owing to economics and publisher intent. Prior to 1840, works of reference such as encyclopedias were aimed at elite audiences.[13] When more men of business became publishers, their commercial interests transformed the previously-standard, subscription-based publishing model requiring a handful of patrons interested in funding an encyclopedia upfront, into publishing models that sought to take advantage of economies of scale. Wider social factors, such as the rise of literacy and population shifts into cities also incentivized the publishing trade to create products appealing to a mass market.[14]

Combining business expertise in the publishing world with nineteenth-century printing technology, publishers experimented with reframing similar content and repackaging it for different markets. Many images eventually used in the First Edition came from an older publication, Chambers's *Information for the People* (1833–1834). Released

11 Bhaskar, *The Content Machine*, p. 139.

12 Robert Collison, *Encyclopaedias: Their History Throughout the Ages, A bibliographical guide, with extensive historical notes, to the general encyclopedias issued throughout the world from 350 B.C. to the present day* (New York: Hafner Publishing Co Ltd, 1966). Also see: William A. Katz, *Cuneiform to Computer: A History of Reference Resources*, 4 (The History of the Book) (London: The Scarecrow Press, Inc, 1998).

13 Jeff Loveland, 'Why Encyclopedias Got Bigger... and Smaller', *Information and Culture: A Journal of History*, 47:2 (2012), 233–254.

14 Rose Roberto, 'Democratising Knowledge and Visualising Progress: Illustrations from *Chambers's Encyclopaedia*, 1859–1892' (unpublished doctoral thesis, University of Reading, 2018), pp. 88–90

in serial form over forty-eight weeks, with each pamphlet-sized part covering a different topic, each part sold for a half-penny, and included attractive wood-engraved illustrations. In 1842, *Information for the People* was repurposed from a serial publication into a bound two-volume set. This bound format is considered to be the direct precursor to *Chambers's Encyclopaedia*.[15] Besides the First Edition of their encyclopedia, parts of *Information for the People* were also initially reused in *Chambers's Education Course*, a schoolbook series first issued in 1835, ultimately containing over one hundred titles.[16]

Jeff Loveland, a noted historian of encyclopedias, documents various types of copying or recycling that European encyclopedia publishers historically engaged in over a 400-year period, finding numerous cases where older versions of other encyclopedias were raided. Dictionaries, atlases, and periodicals were also readily cannibalized to produce 'new' encyclopedic works. In his survey of various encyclopedias, Loveland notes the blurred lines between publishers compiling and revising older encyclopedias, which in many cases included word-for-word copying, abridgement, and paraphrasing.[17]

Editors and publishers sometimes made contractual arrangements for translations of significant and well-known encyclopedias into different languages but they also self-plagiarized and recycled parts of longer works into shorter and 'updated' editions.[18] Charles Knight, a nineteenth-century publisher often compared with Chambers, also transformed his famous, twenty-seven-volume *The Penny Cyclopaedia of the Society for the Diffusion of Useful Knowledge* (1833–1843) into the shorter *English Cyclopaedia: A New Dictionary of Universal Knowledge* (1854–1862); the latter divided the original *Penny Cyclopaedia* content into themed sets

---

15 Aileen Fyfe, 'The Information Revolution' in *The Cambridge History of the Book in Britain, Vol. VI, 1830–1914*. ed. by David McKitterick (Cambridge: Cambridge University Press, 2009), pp. 567–594 (p. 581).

16 William Chambers and Robert Chambers, eds., *Chambers's Information for the People* (Aug. 8, 1840) IX 44, p. 23.

17 Jeff Loveland, *The European Encyclopedia: From 1650 to the Twenty-First Century* (Cambridge: University of Cambridge Press, 2019), p. 146.

18 Loveland, *The European Encyclopedia*, p. 147; Andrew Findlater, 'Preface', in *Chambers's Encyclopaedia: A Dictionary of Universal Knowledge*, vol. 1, ed. by Andrew Findlater (Edinburgh: W. & R. Chambers, 1860). *Chambers's Encyclopaedia* was initially meant to be only a revised version of Brockhaus's German-language *Conversations-Lexicon*.

focused on geography, natural history (NH), biography, and arts and sciences. Each of these divisions were sold separately, and contained between four and eight volumes. The marketing and sales potential for these smaller encyclopedia divisions, especially the NH division which contained nearly 60% of the total images, allowed them to reach larger global audiences. British biologist Alfred Russel Wallace, known for independently discovering evolution by natural selection, valued these illustrated books, carrying the NH division around Asia during his field research.[19]

Indeed, natural history illustrations were considered important, and book publishers frequently used artists' paintings and drawings without their permission or acknowledgement before passage of the Fine Arts Copyright Act of 1862. Christine Jackson, a historian of visual representations of the natural world, sees the new copyright act having a knock-on effect on publishing practice after 1864.[20] An example Jackson provides is *A History of British Birds*, a natural history work for adults and children, that was authored by Rev. F. O. Morris, and published in 1870. The engraver, Benjamin Fawcett, copied the original designs by Thomas Bewick who lived a century earlier.[21]

A large portion of the Chambers's First Edition birds, mammals, fish, reptiles and amphibians, the most frequent subjects chosen by editors to be illustrated, were copied from or heavily influenced by Charles Knight's *Penny Cyclopaedia*.[22] A detailed comparison of the illustrations in the First Edition of *Chambers's Encyclopaedia* with those in the *Penny Cyclopaedia* reveals strong correlations between their visual, subject, and compositional elements. Examples of the ways in which the First Edition of Chambers visually emulated illustrations from *Penny Cyclopaedia,* are shown in Figures 2a and 2b, and in Figures 3a and 3b.[23]

---

19 Wallace's letter to Stevens, 12 May 1856 in *Alfred Russel Wallace: Letters from the Malay Archipelago*, ed. by J. Van Whye and K. Rookmaaker (Oxford: Oxford University Press, 2013), pp. 79–83. Wallace mentions acquiring the four volumes of Knight's encyclopedia on natural history. N4:12ff; vols. 1–2 t. Annotated copies of vols. 1–2 are in the Linnean Society Library.

20 Christine Jackson, *Bird Etchings: the illustrators and their books*, 1655–1855 (Cornell: Cornell University Press, 1989) p. 28; Ronan Deazley, 'Commentary on Fine Arts Copyright Act 1862', in *Primary Sources on Copyright (1450–1900)*, ed. by Lionel Bently and Martin Kretschmer, www.copyrighthistory.org.

21 Jackson, *Bird Etchings*, p. 28.

22 Rose Roberto, 'Democratising Knowledge' pp. 122–125.

23 Roberto, 'Democratising Knowledge', pp. 164–165

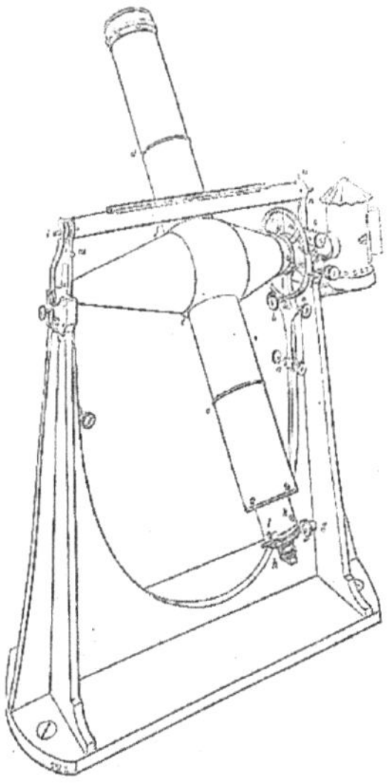

Fig. 2a 'Transit' illustrations found in *Penny Cyclopaedia*, Volume 25, 1843, p. 123.

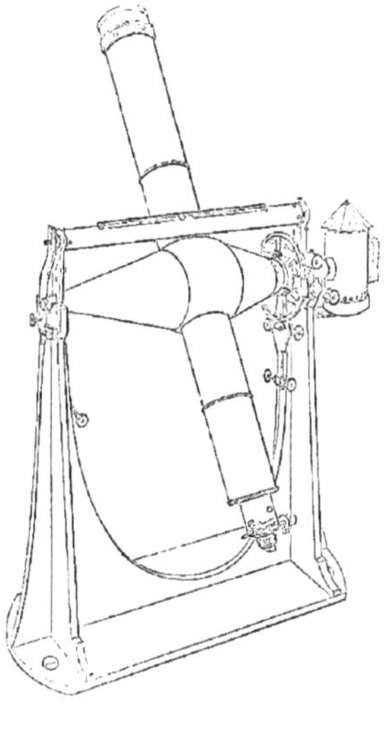

Fig. 2b 'Transit' illustration found in *Chambers's Encyclopaedia*, vol. 9, 1868, p. 512. Images are not to scale.

As can be seen in Figure 2b, the telescope illustration found in the entry for 'transit instrument' used in Volume 9 on page 512 of *Chambers's Encyclopaedia* First Edition looks nearly identical to the telescope found in Volume 5, page 123 of *Penny Cyclopaedia* as shown in Figure 2a. The major differences are related to size. In the *Penny Cyclopaedia* the illustration is presented on a much larger scale, taking up an entire page of the encyclopedia's layout, while Chambers's smaller telescope illustration fits neatly into one of its two-column page layouts. While there are older encyclopedias with transit instrument illustrations, the Chambers and Penny illustrations are both wood engravings that were integrated into the page layout along with the text. Previous illustrations of this telescope, such as the eighth edition of *Encyclopaedia Britannica,* were made using the metal engraving technique which required images to be printed on separate paper from the paper that the text was printed on. The result of using separate printing techniques is that readers viewed illustrations as a fold-out plate. Inclusion of fold-out plates added paper and labor costs for the publishers who passed on the cost of making illustrations to their readers. The eighth edition of *Encyclopaedia Britannica,* as well as its earlier editions, were aimed at audiences who could afford to pay for a higher end product. *Chambers's Encyclopaedia* is more closely linked with Penny when considering production techniques and audience markets.

Comparisons between *Chambers's Encyclopaedia* and the *Penny Cyclopaedia* show that most of the same species of plants and animals that were illustrated in Chambers's had previously appeared in the *Penny Cyclopaedia.* While there are many cases of nearly identical illustrations, such as the transit instrument, some images are *nearly* alike. For instance, the entry for 'dragon', a common name applied to various saurian reptiles, demonstrates the visual equivalent of plagiarism by textual paraphrasing. While these representations of reptiles many not exactly match, both illustrations present the animal in a G or reverse G formation, with long tails arranged in a stylized manner at the bottom of the picture's composition. The differences between the pictures are minor: the Chambers dragon is posed in what seems to be its habitat — with foliage as part of its background — while the Penny specimen has close-up details of the head and claws. If one remembers that wood engraved illustrations print in reverse, their poses facing opposite directions provide evidence of wood engravers copying another publication's images.

The entry for 'tattoo' in both Penny and Chambers (see Figures 3a and 3b, respectively), provides another example of a different type of copying by textual and visual paraphrasing. Despite the Chambers entry being shorter, both Penny and Chambers cover certain main points in their respective articles, which state that tattoos are a practice of 'uncivilised societies', that the English word 'tattoo' comes from the Polynesian word 'ta' which means 'to strike', and that New Zealanders tattoo their faces as a sign of achieving adult status. Both encyclopedia articles further report that tattooing was practiced in Ancient Rome and pre-Roman Britain, and that there is a Biblical passage in Leviticus prohibiting the practice of tattooing. Additionally, both Penny and Chambers list the contemporary ethnic groups that continue to engage in its practice, speculating that it can be seen as a form of initiation within these ethnic groups. It is worth noting that other encyclopedias pre-dating the First Edition of Chambers do not include an entry for 'tattoo.'[24] It is only Charles Knight's encyclopedia that contains this information, again indicating how the *Penny Cyclopaedia* influenced Chambers.

Figure 3a shows one of the two illustrations used for the entry 'tattoo' in Volume 24 of the *Penny Cyclopaedia.* Figure 3b shows an illustration in Volume 9 of Chambers. While the images feature differing illustration styles (discussed in the next section), the visual information presented in both editions has similar content, in that both depictions focus on highlighting areas of the face where New Zealand Maori were tattooed.

The most likely explanation for the number of times that Chambers appears to be copying the *Penny Cyclopaedia* imagery and text was that Chambers's was *actually copying* portions of it. The business records in the Chambers archives show that Chambers had access to the *Penny Cyclopaedia* electrotype plates. In 1854, William Somerville Orr, the former London agent of the Chambers's firm, went into debt,

24 Other British encyclopedias examined for 'tattoo' entries include: *Encyclopaedia Britannica* (1853–1860), eighth edition, and the *London Encyclopaedia* (1826). The latter stops at 'S'. *Imperial Dictionary* (1850), contains an illustrated 'tattoo' entry, but *Penny Cyclopaedia* is where it appears first.

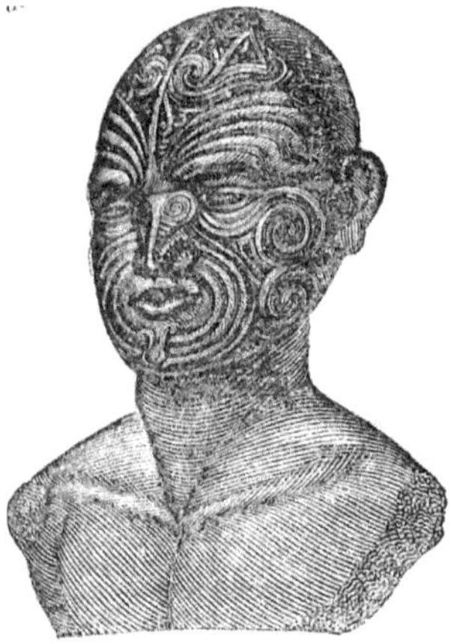

Fig. 3a 'Tattoo' illustrations in *Penny Cyclopaedia*, vol. 24, 1842, p. 100. Image is not to scale.

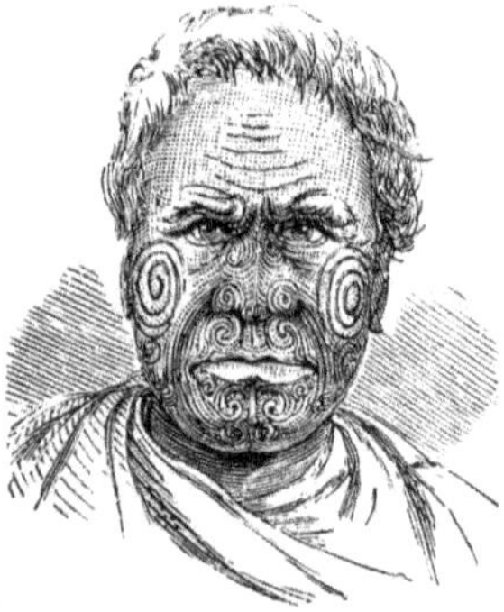

Fig. 3b 'Tattoo' illustration in entry for *Chambers's Encyclopaedia*, vol. 9, 1867, p. 313. Image is not to scale.

owing the firm approximately £10,000.[25] Orr paid part of his debt by giving Chambers stereotype plates for various publications from Charles Knight, including the *Penny Cyclopaedia*, which Orr had in his

25 Sondra Miley Cooney, 'William Somerville Orr, London Publisher and Printer: The Skeleton in the W. & R. Chambers's Closet', in *Worlds of Print: Diversity in the Book Trade*. Ed. by John Hinks and Catherine Armstrong (London: The British Library, 2006), p. 144. The total amount of money still owed to the Chambers firm after transfer of Orr's property was £3930/17s/2d. This chapter provides a longer account of the business dealings between Orr and the Chambers firm.

possession and was intending to publish himself. While Chambers did re-publish several of Knight's works, ultimately the firm decided against re-publishing the *Penny Cyclopaedia*, because Orr had not received copyright from Knight — only permission to update and reprint it.[26]

From a business standpoint, the Chambers editors made a wise decision to carry on production of the firm's own encyclopedia, begun in 1852.[27] Charles Knight himself experienced problems when producing *Penny Cyclopaedia*, which was not ideally organized nor a profitable venture. In the 1830s, Knight wanted to produce an eight-volume encyclopedic work, which he thought should be sold for approximately 72 pence in total.[28] Recalling the *Penny Cyclopaedia* project years later, Knight stated with much regret that unlike the *British Almanack* (begun 1828) and the *Penny Magazine* (1832–1845) which he produced in collaboration with the Society for the Diffusion of Useful Knowledge (SDUK), he could not manage the encyclopedia project effectively because he did not have complete control over it.[29] This was due to a `well-intentioned' but `interfering advisory board'.[30] Many SDUK board members were academics from University College London, who insisted on including numerous topics that Knight, and later Chambers, thought 'unfit for the middle and working classes' because inclusion of so much material made it prohibitively expensive, putting it out of reach for them.[31] While salaries varied during the mid-nineteenth century according to region and type of employment, in the 1860s, an engineer (considered middle class) could earn £110 per year, a footman would

26 Advertisement for reprinted versions of Knight's works published in 1854, in *Miscellaneous correspondence and other papers concerning the publication of various works e.g., 'The Pictorial History of England', 'The Pictorial Bible', 'The Penny Cyclopaedia', 1854*, vol. 132 (unpublished W. & R. Chambers Archives, Deposit 341, National Library of Scotland).

27 Chambers paid Brockhaus for translation rights for its unillustrated *Conversations Lexicon* (10th edition) from German into English.

28 Padraig S. Walsh, *Anglo-American general encyclopedias: a historical bibliography, 1703–1967* (New York: Bowker, 1969), p. 142. Each individual volume was meant to cost 9 pence each. However the cost went up to 18 pence in 1836 and continued to increase, ultimately costing nearly £8 in total.

29 Charles Knight, *Passages of a Working Life During Half a Century: Prelude of Early Reminiscences* (London: Bradbury and Evans, 1864), p. 334.

30 Valerie Gray, *Charles Knight: Educator, Publisher, and Writer* (Aldershot, Hampshire: Ashgate, 2006), p. 55.

31 Chambers and Chambers, *Information for the People*, Volume 2, ed. by William and Robert Chambers (Edinburgh: W. & R. Chambers, 1842), p. 637.

earn just under £30 per year, and a maid about £3 5s per year. At £4 10 shillings, *Chambers's Encyclopaedia,* could be in reach of a footman's salary.[32] In contrast, the *Penny Cyclopaedia* took over a decade to complete because the encyclopedia project ballooned into a twenty-seven-volume set, finally costing the impatient subscribers nearly £8 for the entire set.[33]

By not reissuing the *Penny Cyclopaedia,* the Chambers firm also avoided a market clash with Knight in the 1850s, who was publishing the aforementioned *English Cyclopaedia*. Although the subject coverage of the *English Cyclopaedia* was repackaged into self-contained divisions with updated text, the *English Cyclopaedia* carried previous illustrations initially appearing in the *Penny Cyclopaedia*.[34] It is perhaps for this reason that Chambers saw no marketing value in acknowledging the Penny's visual influence on its own encyclopedia. Another disincentive for publicizing the connection came five years prior to the release of their encyclopedia, when Chambers tentatively announced an updated *Penny Cyclopaedia* reprint. Various letters from the public expressed concern over the level of inaccurate or outdated information Penny contained.[35] Chambers's response to this feedback is reflected in a letter dated 28 November, 1854 to Lippincott:

> ...You will have heard that we have abandoned the intention of bringing out a reissue of the *Penny Cyclopaedia*; our reason for this step being the timely discovery that its proprietors were financially unable to keep up with the publication. We have bought from them the Pictorial Bible and the Pictorial History of England [...] Your best endeavours are asked on behalf of these works, as it would be a matter of first importance to us to reckon in a certain sale in America.[36]

32 Roberto, 'Democratising Knowledge', p. 232. An alternative to purchasing encyclopedias were subscription libraries. Library records show *Chambers Encyclopaedia* available in Cumbria, Dumfriesshire, Devon, Exeter, Essex, Flintshire, Innerpeffray, London, Leeds, Manchester, Newcastle, Nottingham, and Stirling.

33 Fyfe, *Steam-Powered Knowledge*, p. 69.

34 Charles Knight, 'Preface', in *English Cyclopaedia: A new dictionary of universal knowledge, Arts & Sciences*, vol. 1, ed. by Charles Knight (London: Bradbury and Evans, 1859), pp. vii–viii.

35 Chambers firm to R.S. Burn, in *Miscellaneous correspondence and other papers concerning the publication of various works e.g., 'The Pictorial History of England', 'The Pictorial Bible', 'The Penny Cyclopaedia', 1854,* vol. 132 (Unpublished W. & R. Chambers Archives, Deposit 341, NLS).

36 Chambers firm to Lippincott, in *Miscellaneous correspondence and other papers concerning the publication of various works* (Unpublished W. & R. Chambers Archives, Deposit 341, NLS).

The Chambers firm was aware that reprinting Penny could lead to problematic copyright issues, could entail a difficult production schedule, and would lead to tepid public reception made the editors decide undertaking it was financially risky, and a waste of their resources. However, since *The Pictorial Bible* and *The Pictorial History of England* were one-volume works, not requiring revising, the Chambers firm did issue them, but they were not profitable.[37]

It is worth noting here that both Chambers and Knight used wood engraving for their illustrated publications. By choosing this form of relief printing — which allows images to be printed alongside text — rather than by metal engraving processes, which required different paper and separate printing processes, they were choosing to produce works aimed at the middle class (and those aspiring to join it). Metal engraving incurs extra costs for additional paper and extra production time, due to added labor required to assemble works with illustrations due to the additional labor required to make the quality print and integrate it into the bound volume. Typically, added production costs are passed down to consumers as noted earlier. However, with integrated printing technology, money saved on production could then be passed down to *Chambers's Encyclopaedia* customers. The price for the entire ten-volume set of the First Edition was £4 10 shillings, which could be paid in installments. The cost for the eighth edition of *Encyclopaedia Britannica* was 30 shillings per volume, and there were twenty-five volumes in the series.

The Culture of Copying Among Encyclopedia Publishers

While the previous section shows how the Chambers firm engaged in copying, this next section discusses how others copied from Chambers, and how unauthorized copying was generally quite widespread. Loveland's survey states that before the early twentieth century, when international copyright agreements were in place, publishers

37 Cooney, Sondra, p. 145. By 1868, *The Pictorial Bible* only made Chambers a profit of £889, and *The Pictorial History of England* incurred a £500 loss. Lippincott also mentioned that *Pictorial History* did not sell well.

rationalized copying on the following grounds. First, *all* encyclopedias copied content from older sources. Second, the editors stated they were serving the public's best interests because abridged versions and translations could add value to the original material.[38] Finally, European intellectuals and writers increasingly considered there to be a body of classical works of literature that simply belonged to everyone — what we now regard as public domain material.[39] This supports the findings of Meredith McGill, a scholar of American literature. In her study of the American 'culture of reprinting' between 1834 and 1853, she finds that numerous publishers argued against registering fact-based works for copyright on the grounds that texts with factual information, 'were not copyrightable because they were based on facts, which were public property'.[40] In addition, because many reference works were marketed as 'useful works', there was widespread doubt around the creative properties behind their composition, unlike the more obvious originality required for composing fiction or poetry. For publishers, practical works were seen as appealing commodities and good long-term investments, since historically, they 'had broad appeal' to diverse audiences.[41]

In 1879, the text of the First Edition of *Chambers's Encyclopaedia* was over twenty years old, yet still contained 'useful facts'. Because of the First Edition's age, it is clear that William Harrison De Puy, editor of *The People's Cyclopaedia of Universal Knowledge,* considered the Chambers text to be up for grabs in the United States. Furthermore, as a work by a British author who was not resident in the United States, the work was, indeed, not protected by American copyright law. De Puy, a reprinter working for Phillips & Hunt, an imprint of Methodist Tract Society, found a market for repackaging (or re-framing according to Bhaskar) and printing encyclopedias.[42] De Puy was also responsible for editing the *Methodist Yearbook, The Methodist Almanac,* and other reprinting

38 Loveland, *The European Encyclopaedia,* p. 150.

39 Ibid.

40 Meredith L. McGill, *American Literature and the Culture of Reprinting* 1834–1853 (Philadelphia: University of Pennsylvania, 2003), p. 71.

41 McGill, p. 340. Her study cites James Gilreath, 'American Literature, Public Policy, and the Copyright Laws before 1800', in *Federal Copyright Records 1790–1800* (Washington, DC: Library of Congress, 1980), xv–xxv.

42 The Methodist Tract Society had several book imprints. In the 1870s, two were Phillips & Hunt, based in New York and Walden & Stowe, based in Cincinnati.

projects, including *An American Dictionary of the English Language* originally complied by Noah Webster in 1828.[43]

In his *People's Cyclopaedia of Universal Knowledge,* De Puy engaged in a combination of word-for-word copying and abridgement, taking text from Chambers while simultaneously copying illustrations from Webster's dictionary. On average, De Puy standardized its entries into three or fewer paragraphs of plagiarized text from the Chambers's First Edition. This abridgement meant that the ten volumes of *Chambers's Encyclopaedia* could be condensed into two volumes for *The People's Cyclopaedia of Universal Knowledge.* This smaller version was also made possible because dictionary illustrations are typically smaller than encyclopedia illustrations.

Why would De Puy cannibalize two different reference works? First, it kept costs down. Overall, the First Edition contained over 4,000 images, and the majority of them were larger than illustrations typically found in standard dictionary entries. As the nineteenth century unfolded, dictionaries tended to squeeze entries into a three-column page layout or resorted to other typographical means to fit more material in the available space.[44] The 1865 edition of *Webster's Dictionary* also appears to use woodcuts rather than wood engravings, which would have contributed to bringing costs for *The People's Cyclopaedia of Universal Knowledge* down even more because less paper was needed for smaller illustrations. Woodcuts were also easier to reproduce than wood engravings, because generally they are simpler and less detailed than the latter.[45] However, *The People's Cyclopaedia of Universal Knowledge* claims it contains more than 5,000 illustrations, and a few dozen of them are larger than most standard dictionary images, leading to a second theory: De Puy simply chose to use illustrations from *Webster's Dictionary* because as a reprinter of this work, he had access to the Webster images and it was convenient

---

43 W. H. De Puy (1821–1901) also seems to have worked on two other encyclopedia projects which may have also been cheap reprints, namely the *Encyclopaedia Britannica* and the *World-Wide Encyclopaedia and Gazetter.* University of Pennsylvania Online Books Page, http://onlinebooks.library.upenn.edu/webbin/book/lookupname?key=De%20Puy%2C%20W.%20H.%20(William%20Harrison)%2C%201821-1901.

44 Paul Luna, 'Marks, Spaces and Boundaries', *Visible Language*, 45 (2011), 139–160.

45 Paul Luna, 'Picture This: How Illustrations Define Dictionaries' in *Typography Papers, Volume 9.* (London: Hyphen Press, 2013), p. 158.

for him, since the small-scale images worked adequately in *The People's Cyclopaedia's* more compact layout.

Until the mid-nineteenth century, some American publishers specialized in mid-priced or cheap textbooks, or practical manuals produced by taking British-authored texts and reprinting them on less-expensive paper with cheap binding, and selling them at a fraction of the cost of British originals, which was perfectly legal since American copyright law for most of the century did not protect works by authors who were not citizens or residents of the US.[46] According to the New York-based Methodist Episcopal Church's magazine, the Methodist Tract Society committee was established in order to produce and sell inexpensive material from their Methodist Book-Room.[47] Very boldly, the 'Publisher's Announcement' in the opening pages read:

> The publishers of *The People's Cyclopaedia of Universal Knowledge* make no apology for adding another work of its class to the number already in the market. Long experience and close observation of the wants of the public have led them to believe that, in offering to the people a complete Cyclopaedia in a thoroughly condensed form, divested of much of the verbiage found in larger and more costly works, they are supplying a real and generally recognized want. Another reason for issuing this work is the high price of all other Cyclopaedias. The present is the first successful attempt to put upon the market a really desirable work of this character at a price within reach of all.[48]

Not much more is known about editor W. H. De Puy aside from his involvement with the *People's Cyclopaedia.* However, library records do link his name to several later reprinted encyclopedia projects: among them, unauthorized American versions of the ninth edition of *Encyclopaedia Britannica,* published by R. S. Peale and Company of Chicago in 1891, and a reprint of the Peale reprint version by the Werner

46 Aileen Fyfe, *Steam-powered Knowledge: William Chambers and the Business of Publishing, 1820–1860* (Chicago: The University of Chicago Press, 2012), p. 191. The law changed in 1891 but the procedures were still complicated for foreign authors and publishers, who looked for protectionist policies.

47 The Methodist Episcopal Church. *Methodist Magazine: Designed as a compend* [sic] *of useful knowledge and of religious and missionary intelligence for the year of our Lord, 1826,* vol. 9 (New York: N. Bangs and J. Emory, 1826). p. 141–143. Publications in 1826 were sold for 10 cents for each 100 pages.

48 William H. De Puy, 'Preface for Fourth Edition Supplement' *The People's Cyclopedia of Universal Knowledge* (New York: Phillips & Hunt, 1881).

Company of Akron in 1893.[49] The relief images in the unauthorized *Encyclopaedia Britannica* published by R. S. Peale and Company match those found in the authorized A & C Black version, with the addition of fold-out color maps.[50] It seems that De Puy moved around the United States working to compile, repurpose, and reissue earlier standard reference books for various low-priced publishers.

The People's Cyclopaedia of Universal Knowledge sold 40,000 volumes before 1882.[51] While the extensive unauthorized copying found in *The People's Cyclopaedia of Universal Knowledge* does not seem to have financially hurt W. & R. Chambers whose sales figures of their First Edition by 1880 numbered 80,000 sets as the official American publisher of *Chambers's Encyclopaedia*, J. B. Lippincott took issue with whom they called 'third-rate publishers' (such as Phillips & Hunt) affecting Lippincott's profit and reputation for quality.[52] It seems they had reason for concern.

Until 1891, there was no American copyright protection for works by authors who were not citizens or residents of the US. This resulted in American works being unprotected abroad and domestic publishers competing with each other to produce cheap editions of foreign works. Paul Robert Kruse documents copyright cases between 1875 and 1905 filed by A & C Black, the Edinburgh-based publisher of the *Encyclopaedia Britannica's* 7th, 8th, and 9th editions, showing that Britannica was pirated at least twelve times — with multiple lawsuits overlapping in American courts before ownership of Britannica passed to American

49 Paul Kruse, 'Piracy and the Britannica: Unauthorized Reprintings of the Ninth Edition', *The Library Quarterly*, 33 (1963), 313–328, https://doi.org/10.1086/619159; John M. Ockerbloom, 'De Puy, W. H. (William Harrison), 1821–1901', in The Online Books Page, University of Pennsylvania Libraries, and Internet Archive (n.d.)

50 A cursory comparison of images was conducted in Volume XIII of the A & C Black edition of the *The Encyclopaedia Britannica* volume containing entries for the letter 'T', published in 1888, with Volume XIII of the R.S. Peale reprint edition of *The Encyclopaedia Britannica,* published in 1893 by the Werner Company. While new maps and additional American entries were later added, the wood-engraved illustrations were consistent with those found in the original Black edition. There is further scope for investigation of all images in the 9th edition of *Encyclopaedia Britannica.*

51 De Puy, 'Preface for Fourth Edition Supplement', no page number.

52 *Pub. Ledger No.2, 1845–67*, vol. 275 (unpublished W. & R. Chambers Archives, Deposit 341, NLS). Lippincott Company to Chambers, 17 September 1893, in *Correspondence files, Letter pressed book, half calf binding with red sides,* Volume 10.3 (unpublished W. & R. Chambers Archives, Deposit 341, NLS).

businessmen.[53] In the United States, American reprinters vastly outsold editions by A & C Black. Kruse estimates that while 50,000 sets of the *Encyclopaedia Britannica's* 9th edition were sold by 1897 in US markets, about 100,000 sets of unauthorized editions by American reprinters were sold by that time.[54]

Despite the efforts of several authors and their official American publishers for copyright protection, many American publishers did make a profit from reprinting in the United States. Since reprinting benefited them directly, these publishers lobbied the US Congress against protecting foreign works. In the absence of copyright protection for foreign works, publishers resorted to several strategies to try to protect their interests. First, major American publishers established professional courtesy agreements with each other. In the nineteenth century a group consisting of nine major American publishers was formed, and it included the Lippincott firm. All nine firms agreed to a set of norms in order to avoid ruinous competition with each other. The first firm to reprint a work by a British author would claim the field, and the others would agree to respect that arrangement by not undercutting them. This was effective for the most part.[55] Lippincott alludes to the American professional courtesy agreement between D. Appleton of New York and themselves in this 1871 letter to Chambers.

> It should [...] be known to you that when we arranged with your firm to take up work [on printing *Chambers's Encyclopaedia*] the Messrs Appleton, of New York had already commenced in the re-publication, and it is not too much perhaps to claim that but for our instrumentality in forcing them to abandon the field...you [Chambers] would hardly have realized the sum of £1800.[56]

---

53 Kruse, 'Piracy and the Britannica', p. 314. This article is an extract of Kruse's doctoral thesis: 'The Story of the Encyclopaedia Britannica, 1768–1943' (unpublished doctoral thesis, University of Chicago, 1958); Loveland, *The European Encyclopaedia*, p. 149.

54 Kruse, 'Piracy and the Britannica', p. 328.

55 Robert Spoo, 'Courtesy Paratexts: Informal Publishing Norms and the Copyright Vacuum in Nineteenth-Century America', *Stanford Law Review* 69 (2017), 637–710 (pp. 660–661). The nine publishing houses mentioned are: J. B. Lippincott and Co; J. R. Osgood and Co.; D. Appleton and Co.; Roberts Brothers; G. P. Putnam's Sons; Harper and Brothers; Macmillan and Co.; E. P. Dutton and Co.; Henry Hold and Co., pp. 653–654, 660, 662

56 Lippincott Company to Chambers, 17 August 1874, in *Correspondence 1865–1874, Letter pressed book, bound in leather*, vol. 1.9, pp. 71–76 (unpublished J. B. Lippincott

As the authorized publisher and printer of *Chambers's Encyclopaedia* in the United States, Lippincott was positioned to pressure D. Appleton not to reprint the First Edition.[57] Considering the revenue that A & C Black lost due to the unauthorized reprinting of Britannica, this is no small achievement by Lippincott.

Another option available to a major publisher would be to engage in more informal means of shunning novice publishers and smaller firms, so that they never had a national American audience. Loveland provides several examples where this strategy of publishers complaining loudly in public worked, with potential customers purchasing official editions rather than reprints.[58] Ultimately, despite the impressive sales figures reported for *The People's Cyclopaedia of Universal Knowledge*, the publication was forever linked to the Methodist Episcopal Church mission in America, which concentrated on producing cheap educational material for Christian audiences.[59] Arguably, although Lippincott raised concerns in letters to Chambers, the Methodist Episcopal Church and its imprint of Philips & Hunt occupied a different part of the market than J. B. Lippincott or D. Appleton.

Finally, another strategy employed by major publishers to prevent reprinting was to flood the market with updated versions or entirely new editions of a reference work. The Chambers firm, in association with Lippincott, employed this strategy, and images were to be a crucial part of updating the *Chambers's Encyclopaedia* brand.

On-the-Ground Book Production Management

The business relationship and personal rapport between Chambers and Lippincott was established in December of 1853, when William Chambers was in Philadelphia and met Joshua Ballinger Lippincott, founder of J. B. Lippincott, face to face. The men found that they had much in common. Both operated family-run businesses, and they both

Company Archives, Collection 3104, The Historical Society of Pennsylvania).

57 D. Appleton would publish its own encyclopedia, *Johnson's Universal Cycloapedia*, in 1874.

58 Loveland, *The European Encyclopaedia*, p. 155.

59 Oliver S. Baketel, ed., *Methodist Year-book 1921* (New York: The Methodist Concern, n.d.), pp. 160–163.

entered the printing and publishing trade before they had reached the age of twenty. Joshua B. Lippincott was remembered as 'genial' with 'frank and simple' manners [...] inspiring the stranger with confidence and winning for him many friends'.[60] William Chambers writes about how he had been impressed with Joshua personally and the Lippincott's business overall, and saw wide sales potential for Chambers publications through the Lippincott's book trade distribution network.[61]

After William's visit, Robert Chambers also begun corresponding with Joshua B. Lippincott, and in 1860, Robert stayed at the Lippincott home when he visited Philadelphia. Joshua B. Lippincott initially acted as an American distributor for Chambers's publications, including bound versions of *Information for the People, Chambers's Miscellany,* and the Knight reprints. He eventually also published American versions of *Chambers's Cyclopaedia of English Literature* and *Chambers's Book of Days.* When work began in earnest on the First Edition of *Chambers's Encyclopaedia,* Lippincott put Chambers in touch with US-based contributors who could write entries on American subjects.[62] The rationale for this was twofold. Americans would know their subjects better (and by the Second Edition, many were well-known experts in various fields). Additionally, entries written by Americans could be covered by US copyright, and this would enable them to sue for any infringements in US courts.

Copyright was a topic that came up in many letters between the Lippincott and Chambers firms, even when it was not the main issue under discussion. A heated epistolary exchange between the two firms occurred during the end of 1873 and 1874 over the encyclopedia project, showing that the working relationship was not entirely smooth. This was especially true when the next generation of Lippincott and the Chambers family members took over the business from their fathers.[63]

60 'Obituary of Joshua B. Lippincott, 1886', Philadelphia's *Evening Bulletin,* cited in J. S. Freeman, *Toward a Third Century of Excellence: An Informal History of the J. B. Lippincott Company* (Philadelphia: J. B. Lippincott Company, 1992), p. 15.

61 William Chambers, *Things As They Are In America* (Edinburgh: W. & R. Chambers, 1854), p. 321.

62 Fyfe, *Steam-powered Knowledge*, p. 231.

63 Two sons, Craige Lippincott and J. Bertram Lippincott, would go on to run the J. B. Lippincott firm after Joshua Ballinger's passing. Robert Chambers's son Robert

Letters reveal misunderstandings related to editorial roles around the encyclopedia project. Four questions arose that would shape the future of the encyclopedia partnership: Who should have the final editorial say in content when it came to publishing *Chambers's Encyclopaedia*? How would profits be divided? Who would 'own' the final intellectual content of the published work? Finally, how should copyright be claimed in different countries?

The Appendix to this chapter contains a transcript of the 1887 contract to produce an international encyclopedia in 10 volumes, consisting of 520 sheets of 16 pages each.[64] The contract attempts to resolve the most contentious issues between the two firms raised after the First Edition was published. The agreement addressed three areas: copyright, payments, and production schedule. Copyright was claimed by Chambers for the encyclopedia outside the United States, while Lippincott claimed copyright within the United States until 1912. At the end of this period, Lippincott agreed to transfer copyright back to the Chambers firm, along with the plates themselves. Lippincott retained the right to alter and update subsequent print-runs of this edition subject to final editorial approval from the Chambers firm.[65] Both firms agreed to protect and uphold copyright for each other in American and British territories respectively. Both agreed on a payment schedule which included Lippincott paying for importation fees of electrotype plates into the United States and Chambers agreeing to providing fees for American encyclopedia contributors. The Second Edition was not eligible for copyright production under the International Copyright Act of 1891, because all ten volumes of the encyclopedia counted as one work, dating from the release of its first volume in 1888. In an 1876 case involving the *Encyclopaedia Britannica*, Judge Butler had ruled that US copyright protection could not be awarded retrospectively.[66] Nevertheless, Lippincott had already claimed US copyright with the

---

Chambers Jr, and later his grandson Charles Edward Stuart Chambers, also succeeded as editors and owners of W. & R. Chambers.

64 Contract of New Encyclopaedia by W. & R. Chambers and J. B. Lippincott (1887), in *Contract between J. B. Lippincott and Chambers*, vol. 444 (unpublished W. & R. Chambers Archives, Deposit 341, NLS).

65 An updated version of *Chambers's Encyclopaedia* (Second Edition) was printed in 1901.

66 Scribner v. Stoddart, 21 Fed Cases 876 (1879) ruling in case of *Encyclopaedia Britiannica*, quoted in Kruse, 'Piracy and the Britannica', pp. 315–316.

release of each volume on the grounds that *Chambers's Encyclopaedia* was manufactured in Philadelphia.[67]

The 1887 contract is a testament to how precise some aspects of publishers' planning could be in terms of page layouts and illustrations that must have already been calculated in advance, and how they attempted to resolve potential problems inherent to working transnationally. What is notable about this contract is that images were an integral component of negotiations for all three areas of copyright, payment, and production schedules. What's more, the images played a significant role in the publishers' strategy to differentiate the First Edition, which was being reprinted in unauthorized versions by William De Puy (and likely others), and what they began referring to in correspondence with each other as their 'New Edition'.[68]

How New Illustration Styles Presented the Face of 'Modernity'

The Second Edition of *Chambers's Encyclopaedia* has a larger physical layout than the First Edition. The First Edition page size is 25.5 cm x 17 cm, while pages in the Second Edition measure 26.5 cm x 18 cm. The Second Edition was also printed on calendared paper.[69] This means that when potential customers picked up a volume in the late 1880s, and leafed through its pages, they would have immediately felt the smooth surface, noticing that the text was more readable and that the images on the page had crisper lines. The illustrations in the Second Edition also seemed to be radically reimagined by W. & R. Chambers's art department headed by J. R. Pairman, as shown in Figures 4a and 4b, depicting illustrations in 'Arabian Architecture' entries.

67 Lippincott to Chambers, 21 July 1891, in *Penn Letter Book*, Volume 5.7, p. 309 (unpublished J. B. Lippincott Company Archives, Collection 3104, The Historical Society of Pennsylvania).

68 Chambers to Craige Lippincott, 4 October 1886, in *Correspondence between J. B. Lippincott and W. & R Chambers*, Volume 211 (unpublished W. & R. Chambers Archives, Deposit 341, NLS).

69 Calendared paper is achieved mechanically by hard pressure and heated rollers used to smooth it, often leaving it with a shiny, even surface. Calendared paper was commonly used in Britain by the 1880s.

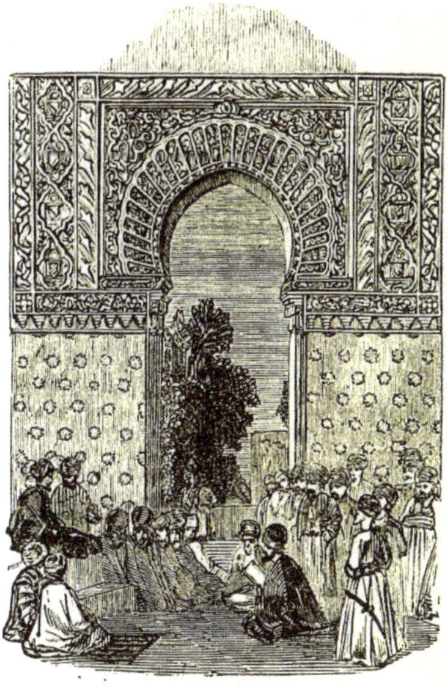

Moorish Gateway.

Fig. 4a 'Arabian Architecture' entry, with caption, *Chambers's Encyclopaedia*, First Edition, vol. 1, p. 346. Image is not to scale.

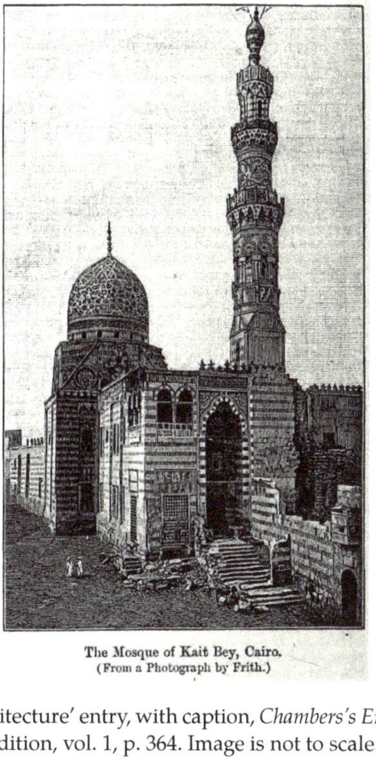

The Mosque of Kait Bey, Cairo.
(From a Photograph by Frith.)

Fig. 4b 'Arabian Architecture' entry, with caption, *Chambers's Encyclopaedia*, Second Edition, vol. 1, p. 364. Image is not to scale.

Viewed side-by-side, these examples show that in comparison to First Edition images, a large number of Second Edition images emulate the aesthetics of photography, and have moved away from illustrating a general concept to instead depict a specific place, animal, or item that served as a model for the illustration. The Preface of the Second Edition of *Chambers's Encyclopaedia* provides a partial explanation for this visual make-over:

> ...In the twenty years [since the completion of *Chambers's Encyclopaedia*] much has happened to call for a completely different treatment of many articles. New subjects have emerged; many have become of greater importance [...] The publishers have therefore resolved to issue a thoroughly new edition of the Encyclopaedia.
>
> [...] The illustrations, a department superintended by Mr J. R. Pairman, are mostly new, and will be found much in advance of the old, alike in accuracy and in artistic character. A large number are from photographs taken for this work.
>
> The Publishers are confident that they are offering to the English-speaking world a really new and greatly improved edition of a work which has in the past received a large measure of popular approval.[70]

Many of the emerging subject areas referred to above by David Patrick, the Second Edition's editor, can be tracked by examining the subjects chosen to be illustrated. In both editions the most frequently illustrated depictions were of animals, plants, machines and vehicles, architectural and built environments, and medical and anatomical structures.[71] These subjects reflect the wider popularity of the natural world, but also the Victorian fascination with technology and appreciation for new mechanical devices related to transport and communication, which changed their lives and shaped their experiences in growing urban centers.

The world looked different between the 1860s and the 1890s, and the editorial staff for *Chambers's Encyclopaedia* chose illustrations which they saw as visually reflecting improvements in the world around them.

70 Patrick, 'Preface'.

71 Roberto, 'Democratising Knowledge', pp. 122–123. Twenty-seven subject categories were identified and classified using CCO (Cataloguing Cultural Objects), a cataloguing standard developed by the Visual Resources Association (VRA) in association with the J. Paul Getty Museum. The top seven categories are vertebrates, botanical specimens, machines/vehicles, architecture, medical specimens, and invertebrates.

For instance, the depiction of two subject areas — microorganisms and human figures — changed significantly between the First and Second Edition. While there were only twenty-nine illustrations in the First Edition of microscopic life forms such as amoebae and various parasites, the Second Edition reflects the growth of Germ Theory in the 1870s by including illustrations based on the work of Robert Koch and Louis Pasteur.[72] While there were 133 depictions of people and human forms in the First Edition represented in historical portraits, religious portraits, mythical creatures and as part of decorative flourishes, by the Second Edition only sixty-seven illustrations of people were retained in entries related to ancient civilizations, foreign countries, or as schematic representations demonstrating a medical or technical concept. Additionally, with the exception of schematic depictions of humans, illustrations mimic the aesthetics of photographs. This is called 'facsimile-style illustration'.[73]

Arguably, the technique for making and using facsimile-style illustrations was not a completely new one for *Chambers's Encyclopaedia*. There are instances of facsimile-style illustrations in the First Edition, such as the portrait of the Japanese Ambassadors (see Figure 1b) and the Maori man with tattoos (see Figure 3b). What does change between editions is the frequency with which one style of illustration is employed over another.

Overall, three types of illustration styles were found in both editions of *Chambers's Encyclopaedia*: schematic, facsimile, and pictorial.[74] Table 1 provides a comparative chart of all three styles next to one another. A schematic illustration shows the main form and features of an object or person, usually in reflected in a simplified drawing aiming to help readers understand a more complex concept or an abstraction. For instance, a medical diagram that explains where internal organs are

72 Louis Pasteur contributed the 'Hydrophobia' entry to the Second Edition of *Chambers's Encyclopaedia*, vol. 6. Hydrophobia is an older term for the rabies virus.

73 Roberto, 'Democratising Knowledge', p. 118

74 The terms `pictorial' and 'facsimile' are widely used by Gerry Beegan, *The Mass Image: A Social History of Photomechanical Reproduction in Victorian England* (Basingstoke: Palgrave Macmillan, 2008), and 'schematic' is used by by Michael Twyman: 'A schema for the study of graphical language' (tutorial paper), in *Processing Visible Language*, ed. by P. A. Kolers (New York, Springer, 1979), pp. 117–150. Other histories of print scholars use 'pictorial' interchangeably with 'interpretive', but I find the term problematic because facsimile-style also requires the interpretation of a three-dimensional object in two-dimensional space.

located in the body, or a map or plan of a city that only illustrates certain highlighted features. Examples of schematic-style illustrations in Table 1 compare skull sizes and main features of extinct mammals of different of different species or show different fencing stances and positions.

Table 1 Examples of schematic, facsimile and pictorial illustration styles found in *Chambers's Encyclopaedia*. Further information is presented on the National Museums Scotland webpage: https://www.nms.ac.uk/collections-research/our-research/highlights-of-previous-projects/chambers-collection/research/illustration-styles-and-subjects/.

Schematic Style	**Facsimile Style**	**Pictorial Style**
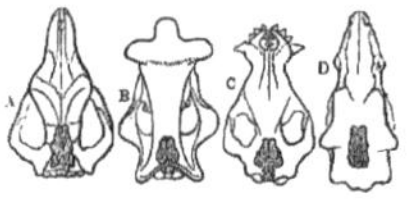 Fig. 3.—Skulls and Casts of Brains of Eocene Mammals: A, *Tillotherium fodiens*; B, *Brontotherium ingens*; C, *Coryphodon hamatus*; D, *Dinoceras mirabile*. (After Marsh.)	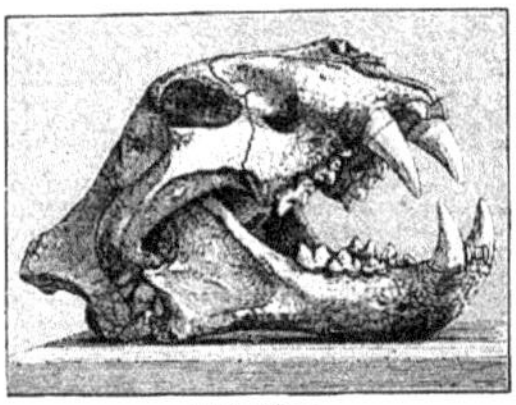 Skull of Tiger.	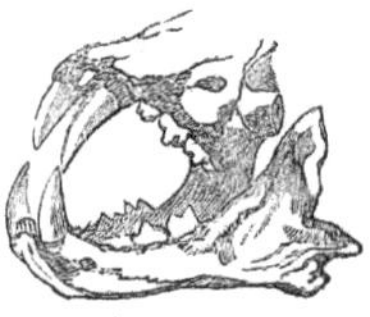 Carnivora: Jaws and Teeth of Lion.
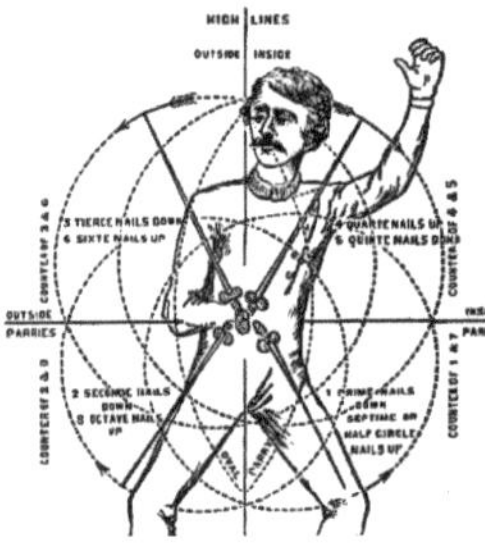	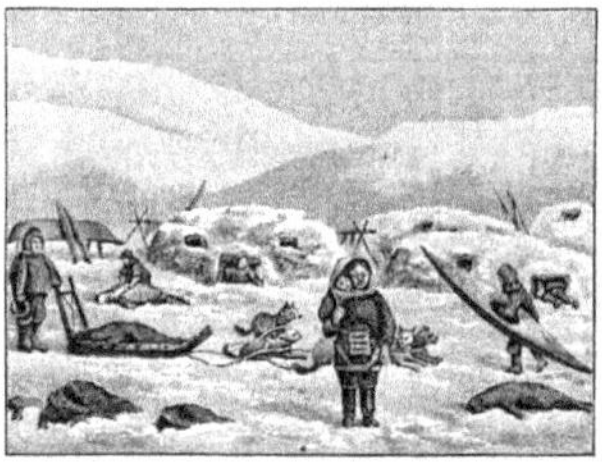	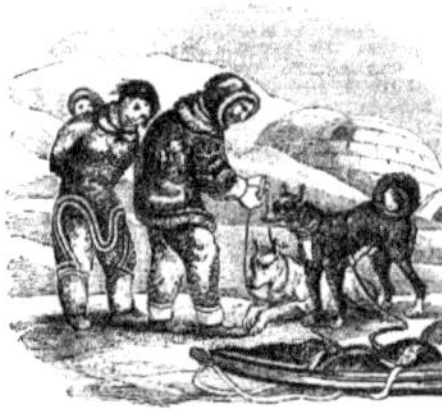

The goal for the use of a facsimile-style illustration is verisimilitude, which depicts an object, person or place in a way that is as realistic as possible, or reproduces how it might be encountered in the physical world. Table 1 provides examples of facsimile-style illustrations based on photographs taken of the places or objects exiting in the real world for the Second Edition, contrasted with First Edition images. For instance, Figure 4b shows the Mosque of Kait Bey in Cairo, which took up one quarter of the page layout in the Second Edition volume in which it appeared.

Furthermore, photographic printing technology was not advanced enough in the 1880s to print actual photographs, so many wood engravers were still being employed to translate photographs onto woodblocks that were then printed with text or as templates for electrotypes. This is why captions based on actual photographs were attributed to an actual photographer who originally composed, chemically developed a negative, and made a print of a photograph.

Finally, what print scholars classify as pictorial style has roots in eighteenth-century aesthetics, when concepts of the beautiful, the sublime, and the picturesque were tied to ideas of 'good taste' in visual art, literature, and music. Pictorial-style illustrations were highly influential and tied to the visual aesthetics of eighteenth-century copper-plate engravings; they also profoundly influenced wood engraving, not only in books but in illustrated newspapers, journals, and magazines. Many celebrated wood engravers in the late 1700s and early 1800s, such as Thomas Bewick, founder of the Newcastle tradition of wood engraving, and John Thurston and Allen Robert Branson, associated with the London School of wood engraving, initially trained as copper-plate engravers. They and their apprentices, William Harvey, John Jackson, Ebenezer Landells, Joseph Swain, George Dalziel, and later William James Linton, formed a direct line of descent from the first generation of wood-engraving masters of the trade to the creators of popular illustrated books and periodicals.[75] William Harvey incidentally worked on Charles Knight publications in the 1830s, including the *Penny Cyclopaedia*. Woodblocks from the Dalziel Brothers were commissioned for Chambers publications as well.

For most of the earlier part of the nineteenth century, pictorial-style illustration was connected with high culture and fine-art prints. There was also a widespread belief among influential art critics such as John Ruskin and publishers such as Charles Knight that illustrations could not only educate lower classes, but provide beauty that was morally uplifting, communicating deeper universal truths revealed through imagination and artistic expression.[76]

By the 1880s, Ruskin's Romantic sensibilities and dislike for what he called the `mechanical aspects' of industrialization were seen as

75 Brian Maidment, 'The *Illuminated Magazine* and the Triumph of Wood Engraving', in *The Lure of Illustration in the Nineteenth Century*, ed. by Laurel Brake and Marysa Denmoor (Basingstoke: Palgrave-Macmillan, 2009), pp. 17–39.

76 Letter from John Ruskin to Rev. W. L. Brown, September 28, 1847. Quoted in Michael Sprinker, 'Ruskin on the imagination', *Studies in Romanticism*, 18:1 (1979), 115–139.

old-fashioned by the editors of *Chambers's Encyclopaedia*; they saw the Second Edition as an opportunity to update a large portion of the illustrations found in Chambers and reevaluate what images it would contain. A comprehensive study of both encyclopedias revealed that the First Edition contained 4,066 illustrations, while in the Second Edition there were only 3,256 illustrations.[77] Table 2 presents the proportion of different styles of illustrations per edition, showing schematic style illustrations remained relatively unchanged. However, the proportion of facsimile-style illustrations increased from seven percent in the First Edition to thirty-six percent in the Second Edition, while proportionally the pictorial style illustrations decreased from nearly half at forty-five percent in the First Edition to fifteen percent. To compensate for 800 fewer illustrations in the Second Edition, editorial staff at Chambers included more fold-out maps and tables.[78]

Table 2 Comparison of illustration styles found in the first two editions of *Chambers's Encyclopaedia*. The First Edition contained 4,066 images. The Second Edition had 3,256. Proportional pie chart based on data of sampling five of ten volumes across both editions.

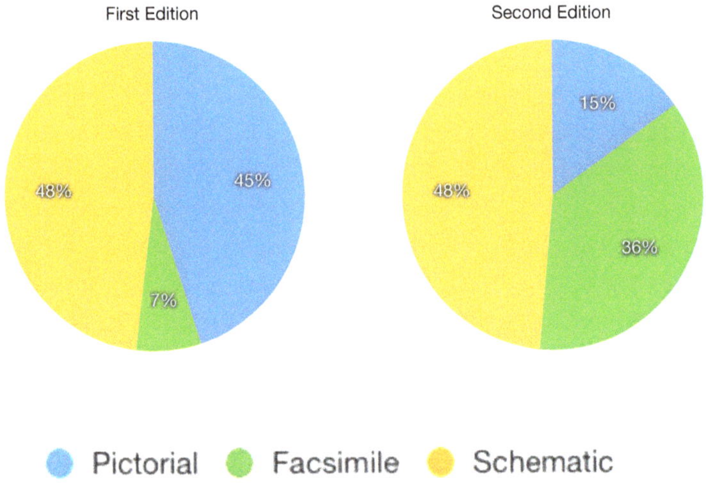

77 Roberto, 'Democratising Knowledge', p. 111.

78 The First Edition had thirty-three fold-out maps; while the Second Edition's number rose to fifty-eight. The First Edition used 506 tables to present information, while in the Second Edition more than sixty were added at 567 tables.

At first it seems counterintuitive for there to be fewer illustrations (overall) in the Second Edition, given that the cost of paper and labor declined by the end of the 1800s, and technological methods for duplicating images had improved in terms of speed and fidelity to the original(s).[79] However, considering the complicated logistics needed to transport electrotype plates across the Atlantic in a timely manner as per the contractual agreement with Lippincott, Chambers streamlining as many processes as possible was a reasonable step. A practical way to do this was by commissioning fewer illustrations for the Second Edition, and being selective in choosing what was to be illustrated.

The commissioning of new engravings with a predominantly different illustration style also served a useful marketing purpose: Chambers could claim their new images were 'much in advance of the old'.[80] The Second Edition notably relied on emulating images in the style of popular photographers, among them Francis Frith and Gambier Bolton. Francis Frith was an English photographer and the founder of Francis Frith & Co, the first firm dedicated to publishing and selling photographs of foreign places as well as cities and vistas around the United Kingdom. Frith's photographic postcards were on sale in 2,000 shops in England by the end of the mid-nineteenth century.[81] Another example of a well-known photographer was Gambier Bolton, a fellow of the Royal Geographical Society, and member of both the Zoological Society and the Royal Photographic Society. Bolton is remembered as an animal photographer who frequently photographed zoo animals across Europe and North America. Bolton's work regularly appeared in popular Victorian magazines. He also published several books illustrated with his own photographs including: A *Book of Beasts and Birds* and *The Animals of the Bible*.[82]

79 Alexis Weedon, *Victorian Publishing: The Economics of Book Production for a Mass Market, 1836–1916* (Aldershot, Hampshire: Ashgate, 2003), p. 71.

80 Patrick, ed. 'Preface', *Chambers's Encyclopaedia*, 1888, Volume 1 [n.p.]

81 Bill Jay, *Victorian Cameraman, Francis Frith's views of Rural England 1850–1898* (Newton Abbot, Devon: David & Charles, 1973), p. 30; Patrick, 'Preface'. No evidence has been found in the Chambers archives that suggest Bolton or Frith objected to use of their work. Based on the editorial acknowledgement from Patrick to J. Pairman for 'sourcing' so many images in his role as Art Director, Pairman could very well have contacted different photographers or publishers. There are records he was in contact with the Dalziel Brothers' firm to commission woodblocks for the *Chambers's Book of Days*.

82 Ken Jacobson and Anthony Hamber, *Etude d'Après Nature: 19th Century Photographs in Relation to Art* (Petches Bridge: Ken & Jenny Jacobson, 1996), p. 171.

While the 'moorish gateway' illustration in Figure 4a looks similar to images in older Chambers publications, the Second Edition illustration presents a more modern aesthetic based on a photo by Frith, taken in Cairo. Ten illustrations in the Second Edition can be directly attributed to Frith.[83] In contrast to an illustration for the `Rhinoceros' entry in the First Edition which is visually similar to the *Penny Cyclopaedia's Rhinoceros Indicus,* the illustration of *Rhinoceros unicornis* found in the Second Edition emulates a photograph by Bolton circa 1882 at the Breslau Zoo, in former Prussia.[84]

In the Second Edition, photographic sensibility was such a priority in visual presentation that even when illustrations were not based on actual photographs, the volume contains illustrations staged to look like them. Among the birds in the Second Edition, images of different species of pigeons have been traced to (pictorial-style) illustrations in *An Illustrated Manual of British Birds* (1889), by Howard Saunders, including illustrations for 'Kite', 'Quail,' and 'Woodpecker' entries, the volumes published between 1890 and 1892.[85] In Table 1, there is a facsimile- style illustration used in the Second Edition for the 'Eskimo' entry. The Second Edition illustration was based on drawings by the author of the Second Edition's 'Eskimo' entry, Dr. Henrich Johannes Rink.[86] Dr. Rink was a pioneer in the study of glaciology, and later a long-term resident of Greenland while serving as a Danish government administrator. Rink and his wife, ethnographer Nathalie Sophia Nielsine Caroline (Signe Rink), researched and published findings on the Greenland

---

83 'The Moors of Spain', in *Chambers's Miscellany of Useful and Entertaining Tracts*, ed. by William and Robert Chambers (Edinburgh: W. & R. Chambers, 1846), p. 106; Roberto, 'Democratising Knowledge', pp. 215–216. The Second Edition specifically credits his work 10 times, although a further handful of illustrations look very similar to Frith's widely circulated photographs.

84 Roberto, 'Democratising Knowledge', p. 216.

85 Howard Saunders, *An Illustrated Manual of British Birds, Rock Dove*, London: Gurney and Jackson. p. 471, Stock Dove, p. 469, King-Dove or Wood-Pigeon, p. 467); A digitized version of *An Illustrated Manual of Birds* is online at the Biodiversity Heritage Library: https://www.biodiversitylibrary.org/bibliography/13544.

86 David Patrick, ed., *Chambers's Encyclopaedia: A Dictionary of Universal Knowledge*, vol. 4, 2nd edition (Edinburgh: W. & R. Chambers, 1889), p. 422; S.M. Cooney, 'A Catalogue of Chambers's Encyclopaedia 1868', *The Bibliotheck: A Journal of Scottish Bibliography and Book History*, 24 (1999), p. 106; Andrew Findlater, ed., *Chambers's Encyclopaedia: A Dictionary of Universal Knowledge*, vol. 4 (1865), pp. 129–130. 'Esquimaux or Eskimo' is the actual title of the First Edition entry.

native population's language and culture.[87] The Chambers illustration depicts a winter station in Greenland with details such as the physical scale of a kayak in relation to a person who might use it, and reveals details of actual Eskimo igloos that were not perfect domes, and are partially dugout structures. People can be seen emerging and entering from underground entrances. Due to many visual elements — such as a border surrounding the image — and the framing perspective of human foreground figures in relation to the animals and distant snow-covered mountains, the illustration has photographic qualities.

These photographic cues show that Chambers embraced the marketing strategy to provide readers of the New Edition with information written by subject experts, whose names were presented to readers at the opening of each Second Edition volume. The verisimilitude style of illustration adopted also communicated the more modern, technical sensibility of photography. For this reason, Chambers and Lippincott publicized the Second Edition as being superior to the older edition, and by extension superior to unauthorized editions copying the First Edition.

Conclusion

Sources for encyclopedia illustrations changed between the 1860s and the 1890s. Most illustrations came from older sources, and encyclopedia publishers relied on them for market appeal — but also because illustrations communicated two types of messages to their audiences. First, they visually communicated didactic information relevant to the entry in question, or helped readers to better understand the entry they had just read. Second, illustrations communicated indirect information about the publisher, which today we might call brand marketing.

From the 1830s to the 1850s, founders of W. & R. Chambers promoted individual and societal progress, and provided tools in the form of low-priced publications for individuals to improve their minds and better their circumstances. Although the First Edition was published in the 1860s, production of *Chambers's Encyclopaedia* began in the late 1850s, and therefore the work reflects the working practices and values of both William and Robert to promote high morals, good taste, and practical

87 Mark Nuttall, *Encyclopedia of the Arctic* (Abingdon, Oxon: Routledge, 2012), p. 158.

ways to an intellectually rewarding life. This is reflected visually in the pictorial illustration style chosen for a large portion of the images, which Chambers repurposed from its own, earlier publications, and from images commissioned by fellow publisher Charles Knight, who shared the former's values and aims, but whose works were more popular in the 1830s.

By the late 1880s, the Chambers firm had been in business for over 50 years and the next generation had taken over major responsibilities of running the firm. The illustration style promoted in the Second Edition was verisimilitude, which tied into a marketing strategy that advertised the Second Edition as having up-to-date information in the form of more tables of data, additional newly designed maps, and a visual aesthetic mimicking photographs. In the promotional language of the encyclopedia, editors took for granted that fin-de-siècle audiences would appreciate how photographic facsimiles provided current and authoritative information.

Indeed, the illustrations in Chambers proved to be commercially valuable. Before the last two volumes of the Second Edition were issued, Lippincott asked Chambers to purchase the right to reuse some 400 images for two of their upcoming textbooks: *A Course on Zoology: Designed for Secondary Education*, and *Home Life in all Lands*. The Chambers firm charged $1 per image for copyright permission and their use in the named publications. *A Course on Zoology*, published in 1893, used nearly 300 images originating from Britain, but with text translated from a French-language book co-written by a French educator and natural history expert. *Home Life in all Lands* was published circa the 1890s and had a fifth reprinting between 1907 and 1911. The text was provided by prolific American history textbook writer Charles Morris, who wrote dozens of books for the Lippincott firm. The preface of the Zoology book states:

> The illustrations form an important feature of [this work]. We desire to extend our thanks to Messrs. W. & R. Chambers for permission to use these [illustrations] from the new *Chambers's Encyclopaedia*, without which it would have been extremely difficult to give the book its present value in this respect [...] Many [illustrations] are from photographs, and of special scientific value.[88]

88 C. de Montmahou and H. Beauregard, Translated by Wm. H. Green, 'Preface', in *A Course on Zoology Designed for Secondary Education* (Philadelphia: J. B. Lippincott Company, 1893), p. 3.

In *Home Life in all Lands,* Charles Morris records a similar sentiment, noting that he had 'the privilege of using so many of the illustrations' from *Chambers's Encyclopaedia.*[89]

Through agreements and business practices, American versions of *Chambers's Encyclopaedia* were printed by Lippincott in the US. While the firms argued that the contributions by authors resident in the US were protected for the First Edition, they recognized material that had already been published in the UK would not have been protected. A contract drawn in 1887 attempted to allow the works to gain US copyright protection, and was mutually the profitable for both publishers, because it provided clear guidance for both firms in terms of production and claims for intellectual property. As publishers, Chambers, and later Lipponcott, treated encyclopedia content as a commodity, while text and images were viewed as separate entities that could be easily assembled, repurposed, printed and reprinted on an industrial scale. Images were crucial to amplifying specific content, they were components to be recycled and reframed with different text, and repackaged into a new book for a different market. This was, and is, a successful publishing strategy that continues today.

Bibliography

Advertisement [for reprinted versions of Knight's works published in 1854], in *Miscellaneous correspondence and other papers concerning the publication of various works e.g.,'The Pictorial History of England', 'The Pictorial Bible', 'The Penny Cyclopaedia', 1854,* vol. 132 (unpublished W. & R. Chambers Archives, Deposit 341, National Library of Scotland).

Contract of New Encyclopaedia by W. & R. Chambers and J. B. Lippincott (1887), in *Contract between J. B. Lippincott and Chambers,* vol. 444 (unpublished W. & R. Chambers Archives, Deposit 341, National Library of Scotland).

'The Moors of Spain', in *Chambers's Miscellany of Useful and Entertaining Tracts,* ed. by William and Robert Chambers (Edinburgh: W. & R. Chambers, 1846).

Baketel, Oliver S., ed. *Methodist Year-book 1921* (New York: The Methodist Concern, n.d.).

Beegan, Gerry, *The Mass Image: A Social History of Photomechanical Reproduction in Victorian England* (Basingstoke: Palgrave Macmillan, 2008).

89 Charles Morris *Home Life in all Lands* (Philadelphia: J. B. Lippincott, 1907), p. vi.

Belknap, Geoffrey, *'From a Photograph': Authenticity, Science, and the Periodical Press, 1870–1890* (London: Bloomsbury, 2016).

Bhaskar, Michael, *The Content Machine: Towards a Theory of Publishing from the Printing Press to the Digital Network* (London: Anthem Publishing Studies, 2013).

Chambers, William, *Things As They Are In America* (Edinburgh: W. & R. Chambers, 1854).

Chambers, William and Robert Chambers, eds., *Information for the People*, Volume 2 (Edinburgh: W. & R. Chambers, 1842).

——, *Chambers's Information for the People*, Volume IX, 44, Aug. 8, 1840.

Cobbing, Andrew, *The Japanese Discovery of Victorian Britain: Early Travel Encounters in the Far West* (London: Routledge, 2013), https://doi.org/10.4324/9781315073491.

Collison, Robert, *Encyclopaedias: Their History Throughout the Ages, A bibliographical guide, with extensive historical notes, to the general encyclopedias issued throughout the world from 350 B.C. to the present day* (New York: Hafner Publishing Co Ltd, 1966).

Cooney, Sondra Miley, 'William Somerville Orr, London Publisher and Printer: The Skeleton in the W. & R. Chambers's Closet', in *Worlds of Print: Diversity in the Book Trade*, ed. by John Hinks and Catherine Armstrong (London: The British Library, 2006), pp. 135–147.

——, `A Catalogue of Chambers's Encyclopaedia 1868', *The Bibliotheck: A Journal of Scottish Bibliography and Book History*, 24 (1999), 17–110.

de Montmahou, Camille and Henri Beauregard, translated by William. H. Green, 'Preface', in *A Course on Zoology Designed for Secondary Education* (Philadelphia: J. B. Lipponcott Company, 1893).

Deazley, Ronan, 'Commentary on Fine Arts Copyright Act 1862', in *Primary Sources on Copyright (1450–1900)*, ed. by Lionel Bently and Martin Kretschmer, www.copyrighthistory.org.

DePuy, William H., 'Preface for Fourth Edition Supplement', in *The People's Cyclopedia of Universal Knowledge* (New York: Phillips & Hunt, 1881).

Findlater, Andrew, ed., *Chambers's Encyclopaedia: A Dictionary of Universal Knowledge*, Volume 9 (Edinburgh: W. & R. Chambers, 1868).

——, *Chambers's Encyclopaedia: A Dictionary of Universal Knowledge*, Volume 5 (Edinburgh: W. & R. Chambers, 1866).

——, *Chambers's Encyclopaedia: A Dictionary of Universal Knowledge*, Volume 4 (Edinburgh: W. & R. Chambers, 1865).

——, 'Preface', in *Chambers's Encyclopaedia: A Dictionary of Universal Knowledge*, vol. 1, ed. by Andrew Findlater (Edinburgh: W. & R. Chambers, 1860).

Freeman, J.S., *Toward a Third Century of Excellence: An Informal History of the J. B. Lippincott Company* (Philadelphia: J. B. Lippincott Company, 1992).

Fyfe, Aileen, *Steam-Powered Knowledge: William Chambers and the Business of Publishing, 1820–1860* (Chicago: The University of Chicago Press, 2012), https://doi.org/10.7208/chicago/9780226276540.001.0001.

——, 'The Information Revolution' in *The Cambridge History of the Book in Britain,* vol. VI, 1830–1914., ed. by David McKitterick (Cambridge: Cambridge University Press, 2009), pp. 567–594, https://doi.org/10.1017/CHOL9780521866248.018.

Gray, Valerie, *Charles Knight: Educator, Publisher, and Writer* (Aldershot, Hampshire: Ashgate, 2006).

J. B. Lippincott Company to W. & R. Chambers, 17 September 1893, in *Correspondence files, Letter pressed book, half calf binding with red sides,* Volume 10.3 (unpublished W. & R. Chambers Archives, Deposit 341, National Library of Scotland).

J. B. Lippincott Company to W. & R. Chambers, 17 August 1874, in *Correspondence 1865–1874, Letter pressed book, bound in leather,* vol. 1.9, pp. 71–76 (unpublished J. B. Lippincott Company Archives, Collection 3104, The Historical Society of Pennsylvania).

J. B. Lippincott Company to W. & R. Chambers, 21 July 1891, in *Penn Letter Book,* Volume 5.7, p. 309 (unpublished J. B. Lippincott Company Archives, Collection 3104, The Historical Society of Pennsylvania).

Jackson, Christine, *Bird Etchings: The Illustrators and Their Books, 1655–1855* (Cornell: Cornell University Press, 1989).

Jacobson, Ken, and Anthony Hamber, *Etude d'après nature: 19th Century Photographs in Relation to Art* (Petches Bridge: Ken & Jenny Jacobson, 1996).

Jay, Bill, *Victorian Cameraman: Francis Frith views of Rural England 1850–1898* (Newton Abbot, Devon: David & Charles, 1973).

Katz, William A., *Cuneiform to Computer: A History of Reference Resources* (History of the Book: 4) (London: The Scarecrow Press, Inc, 1998).

Knight, Charles, *Passages of a Working Life During Half a Century: Prelude of Early Reminiscences* (London: Bradbury and Evans, 1864).

——, 'Introduction', in *English Cyclopaedia: A new dictionary of universal knowledge, Arts & Sciences,* vol. 1, ed. by Charles Knight (London: Bradbury and Evans, 1859).

——, ed., *The Penny Cyclopaedia of the Society for the Diffusion of Useful Knowledge,* Volume 19 (London: Charles Knight and Co., 1841).

Kruse, Paul, 'Piracy and the Britannica: Unauthorized Reprintings of the Ninth Edition', *The Library Quarterly,* 33 (1963), 313–328, https://doi.org/10.1086/619159.

The Library of Nineteenth-Century Photography, n.p., www.19thcenturyphotos.com

Loveland, Jeff, 'Why Encyclopaedias Got Bigger... and Smaller', *Information and Culture: A Journal of History*, 47 (2012), 233–254.

——, *The European Encyclopedia: From 1650 to the Twenty-First Century* (Cambridge: Cambridge University Press, 2019), https://doi.org/10.1017/9781108646390.

Luna, Paul, 'Marks, Spaces and Boundaries', *Visible Language*, 45 (2011), 139–160.

——, 'Picture This: How Illustrations Define Dictionaries', *Typography Papers*, 9 (2013), 153–172.

Maidment, Brian, 'The *Illuminated Magazine* and the Triumph of Wood Engraving', in *The Lure of Illustration in the Nineteenth Century*, ed. by Laurel Brake and Marysa Denmoor (Basingstoke: Palgrave-Macmillan, 2009), pp. 17–39, https://doi.org/10.1057/9780230233867_2.

McGill, Meredith L., *American Literature and the Culture of Reprinting 1834–1853* (Philadelphia: University of Pennsylvania Press, 2003), https://doi.org/10.9783/9780812209747.

The Methodist Episcopal Church, *Methodist Magazine: Designed as a compend* [sic] *of useful knowledge and of religious and missionary intelligence for the year of our Lord, 1826*, 9 (New York: N. Bangs and J. Emory, 1826), pp. 141–143.

Nuttall, Mark, *Encyclopedia of the Arctic* (Abingdon, Oxon: Routledge, 2012).

Ockerbloom, John M., 'De Puy, W. H. (William Harrison), 1821–1901' in *The Online Books Page*, University of Pennsylvania Libraries, and Internet Archive (n.d.)

Fine Arts Copyright Act (1862) or Bill for amending Law relating to Copyright in Works of Fine Art, 1862, Paper No. 53, I.493–502 (20 March 1862) in *Primary Sources on Copyright (1450–1900)*: www.copyrighthistory.org.

Pasteur, Louis, 'Hydrophobia' in *Chambers Encyclopaedia Chambers Encyclopaedia: A Dictionary of Universal Knowledge, New Edition,*Volume 6, 2nd edition, ed. by David Patrick (Edinburgh: W. & R. Chambers, 1890).

Patrick, David, 'Preface', in *Chambers Encyclopaedia: A Dictionary of Universal Knowledge, New Edition,* Volume 1, 2nd edition, ed. by David Patrick (Edinburgh: W. & R. Chambers, 1888).

——, ed., Chambers Encyclopaedia: A Dictionary of Universal Knowledge, Volume 4, 2nd edition (Edinburgh: W. & R. Chambers, 1889).

Pub. Ledger No.2, 1845–67, vol. 275 (unpublished W. & R. Chambers Archives, Deposit 341, National Library of Scotland).

Roberto, Rose, 'Democratising Knowledge and Visualising Progress: Illustrations from *Chambers's Encyclopaedia*, 1859–1892' (unpublished doctoral thesis, University of Reading, 2018), consultable at the CentAUR institutional repository, University of Reading, http://centaur.reading.ac.uk/85483/.

Ruskin, John, letter to Rev. W. L. Brown, September 28, 1847. Quoted in Michael Sprinker, 'Ruskin on the imagination,' *Studies in Romanticism*, 18:1 (1979), 115–139.

Saunders, Howard, *An Illustrated Manual of British Birds* (London: Gurney and Jackson, 1889), https://doi.org/10.5962/bhl.title.13544.

Schnolick, Robert J., 'Intersecting Empires: W. & R. Chambers and Emigration, 1832–1844', *The Biblotheck: A Journal of Scottish bibliography and Book History*, 24 (1999), 5–16.

Scribner v. Stoddart, 21 Fed Cases 876 (1879) ruling in case of *Encyclopaedia Britiannica*, quoted in Kruse, *Piracy and the Britannica*, pp. 315–316.

Spoo, Robert, 'Courtesy Paratexts: Informal Publishing Norms and the Copyright Vacuum in Nineteenth-Century America', *Stanford Law Review*, 69 (2017), 637–710.

Twyman, Michael, 'A schema for the study of graphical language (tutorial paper)', in *Processing Visible Language*, ed. P. A. Kolers (New York: Springer, 1979), pp. 117–150.

W. & R. Chambers firm to Craige Lippincott, 4 October 1886, in *Corrrespondence between J. B. Lippincott and W. & R Chambers*, Volume 211 (unpublished W. & R. Chambers Archives, Deposit 341, National Library of Scotland).

W. & R. Chambers firm to R. S. Burn, in *Miscellaneous correspondence and other papers concerning the publication of various works e.g. "The Pictorial History of England", "The Pictorial Bible", "The Penny Cyclopaedia"*, 1854, vol. 132 (Unpublished W. & R. Chambers Archives, Deposit 341, National Library of Scotland).

W. & R. Chambers firm to J. B. Lippincott, in *Miscellaneous correspondence and other papers concerning the publication of various works* (Unpublished W. & R. Chambers Archives, Deposit 341, National Library of Scotland).

Van Whye J. and K. Rookmaaker, eds., *Alfred Russel Wallace: Letters from the Malay Archipelago* (Oxford: Oxford University Press, 2013), pp. 79–83.

Walsh, S. Padraig, *Anglo-American General Encyclopedias: A Historical Bibliography, 1703–1967* (New York: Bowker, 1968).

Weedon, Alexis, *Victorian Publishing: The Economics of Book Production for a Mass Market, 1836–1916* (Aldershot, Hampshire: Ashgate, 2003).

Tegg, Thomas, and Thomas Curtis, ed. 'Tattoo', in *London Encyclopaedia* (1826).

Traill, Thomas Stewart, ed. 'Tattoo', in *Encyclopaedia Britannica* (1853–1860), eighth edition.

Zatlin, Linda G., *Beardsley, Japonisme, and Perversion of the Victorian Ideal* (Cambridge: Cambridge University Press, 1997).

Appendix

Contract for New Encyclopaedia by Lippincott and Chambers 1887

It is minuted and agreed upon between William and Robert Chambers Publisher, Edinburgh, Scotland hereinafter termed, the first party on the first part and J. B. Lippincott Company Publishers, Philadelphia, United States, hereinafter termed the Second Party on the Second Party in manner fall owning that is to say, the said parties, considering that they have entered into arrangements relative to the publication of Chambers International Encyclopaedia in (10) volumes consisting of five hundred and twenty (520) sheets of sixteen (16) pages each with maps and which the first party is the owner. And now seeing that in order to regulate their respective rights and interests and prevent disputes and differences the parties hereto have resolved to execute these pursuits. Therefore the said 'parties' have agreed and do heartily agree and bind and oblige themselves, and their respective presentations and successors as follows: [?]

(First) The First party agrees to supply the Second party with Electrotype plates of the text and wood engravings of said work at the rate of two pounds thirteen shillings (£2.13.0) for each sixteen (16) pages [?] of and the said first party agrees to have the plates of the first volume completed if possible not later than October one thousand and eight-hundred and eighty seven (1887) The succeeding volumes to be furnished at such periods thereafter as may be found, practicable, and to supply impressions of the maps and other illustrations pertaining to the work as, from the wood engravings at the rate of one shilling and three pence (1 1/3), if the maps and other illustrations don't exceed fifty (50) any maps above fifty (50) in number to be charged at the same profitable rate. All expense of packing, shipping, freight, insurance duties etc. to be paid by the second party, the payments to be made quarterly as in clause three of this agreement. The first party further gives the sole and exclusive right of publication and of sale of the said ten in the United States of America to the Second Party during the continuance of this agreement. This right-shall be limited to the United States of America. It is agreed that the expense of alteration on the American plates that may be made from time to time to keep the work up to date shall be paid by the Second party (Second). It is further agreed that the first part shall pay the cost of preparation of such American Articles as the parties hereto shall deem advisable, this cost of preparation shall include the following items: payment to authors; cost of procuring copyrights, and of any assignments of said rights and such legal expenses as are directly connected, with the procuring and assigning of the said copyrights; and it is further agreed that the copyright of the same in the British Empire shall be the property of the first party. The American copyright to be the property of the Second Party during the continuance of this agreement, the Second party agrees to transfer the American copyright to the First Party on termination of this agreement. It also agrees that these American articles shall be subject to Editorial Revision of the first party, before being incorporated.

[Second Page]

III Incorporated in the Work (Third) The Second Party in consideration of the foregoing stipulations agrees to manufacture the work in appropriate style from the aformentioned electrotype plates and the maps and furnished and to use their facilities for its sale, and to pay the first party a royalty of one and half (1 1/2) gold dollars of present weight and fineness for every ten (10) volumes of the work sold by the said Second Party equal to fifteen (15) cents for each volume, containing fifty two (52) sheets of sixteen (16) pages with maps, sold during the continuances as in volumes the Royalty, at the same rate of fifteen (15) cents for every fifty two (52) sheets of sixteen (16) pages sold, the amount of sales to be certified annually by the Secretary of J. B. Lippincott Company verified by this affidavit before a notary public. Accounts to be rendered and payments to be made quarterly, by Bank Bill at the sixty (60) days sight in February, May, August and November of each year. (Fourth) it is further agreed between the two parties that each shall take the necessary action regarding the simultaneous of the other issue of the different volumes of the work to protect, the Second party in the copyright of the aforesaid American Articles (Fifth). It is agreed that i/i at any time it many be deemed advisable by the Second party to import the sheets of the British printed edition of the said work, the first party shall supply the same in terms — of not less than two thousand (2000) copies of any one volume at two (2) shillings per volume in sheets unfolded, subject to advance of price corresponding to any material advance, in the price of paper of All expense of packing, shipping, freight- insurance quarterly as in clause three (Sixth) On the termination of this agreement it is agreed that the Electrotype plates shall be returned to the first Party who shall pay for them to the Second party then value at the price of stereotype metal. The first party agreeing that the said plates shall be immediately destroyed. (Seventh) This agreement shall continue for the term of twenty (20) years from the date of the issue of the last volume of the work unless terminated by mutual consent or unless either of the parties ceases to fulfil its stipulations. In the event of any disputes or differences arising as to the meaning of this agreement, or as to the rights and interests of the parties under if both parties agree to refer the source to the Lord advocate for Scotland when failing to the Solicitor General for Scotland for the time being? and they agree to accept his decision as final. This submission shall be made by written or printed briefs and neither party shall...

[Third Page]

have the right to appear before the arbiter either in person or for legal representative only attorney of any kind. The expenses of this arbitration to be paid equally by both parties (Lastly) the parties hereto agree and bind and oblige themselves, and their respective fore- said to implement this agreement in all its parts the one to the other. In Witness thereof these pursuits writt en upon this and the two preceding pages of stamped paper, William Frederick McAlpine apprentice to Lindsay McKeny, written to the Signet-Edinburgh.

Signatures

William & Robert Chambers
Robert P. Morton Secretary of J. B. Lippincott Company

[Original document held at National Library of Scotland, W. & R. Chambers Archives, Dep 341–444]

PART III

NAVIGATING INTELLECTUAL PROPERTY: ARCHITECTS, SCULPTORS, AND PHOTOGRAPHERS

10. Architectural Copyright, Painters and Public Space in Mid-Nineteenth-Century Britain

Elena Cooper and Marta Iljadica[1]

Introduction

A premise of mid-nineteenth century copyright debates culminating in the passage of the Fine Arts Copyright Act 1862 (the first UK copyright legislation expressly to protect paintings, drawings and photographs) was the aesthetic parity of painting with literature, grounded in the notion of the 'fine arts'.[2] Books were longstanding subject matter of copyright, protected by statute since the early eighteenth century. By the mid-nineteenth century, the aesthetic equivalence of new subject matter to literature was part of the case in favor of copyright protection for paintings, and raised further questions as regards the protection of photographs (as photography's fine art status was unclear).[3] This chapter

1 The authors are grateful for comments on an earlier draft by participants of the Workshop of the International Society for the History and Theory of Intellectual Property, Sydney, 2019 (particularly Charles Rice) and the Conference 'Images, Copyright and the Public Domain in the Nineteenth Century', Paris, 2019, as well as the specific comments of the editors of this volume. Elena Cooper is grateful to The Leverhulme Trust (grant no: ECF-2016–016).

2 Fine Arts Copyright Act 1862 (25 & 26 Vic. c.68); Lionel Bently, 'Art and the Making of Modern Copyright Law', in *Dear Images: Art, Copyright and Culture*, ed. by Daniel McClean and Karsten Schubert (London: Ridinghouse RCA, 2002), pp. 331–351; Elena Cooper, *Art and Modern Copyright: The Contested Image* (Cambridge: Cambridge University Press, 2018) p. 12.

3 Bently, 'Art and the Making', p. 332; Cooper, *Art and Modern Copyright*, Chapter 2.

 https://doi.org/10.11647/OBP.0247.10

considers a hitherto unconsidered facet of the artistic copyright debates of the 1850s and early 1860s: the resistance of painters to unsuccessful proposals put forward by architects for copyright protection for three-dimensional buildings (unprotected by copyright until 1911). As we later explain in detail, by the late 1850s, the hub for copyright reform was the Copyright Committee of the Society of Arts, Manufactures and Commerce, and painters soon came to dominate its discussions; photographers and engravers were members of the same Committee, but had significantly less influence. Architecture had long been accepted to be a fine art.[4] Yet, though painters invoked the rhetoric of the 'fine arts' when seeking to establish the case for their own protection, they emphatically resisted similar claims made by architects as regards protection for their three-dimensional works. This chapter explores this seeming contradiction within the copyright debates of the 1850s and early 1860s, focusing on tensions between painters (as the dominant lobby group in the Society of Arts' Committee) and architects. In so doing, we link copyright to nineteenth-century concepts that might be seen as forerunners to later ideas about the 'right to the city'. This relates both to arguments in favor of architectural copyright (asserting that copyright would improve public experience of architecture) as well as painters' opposition to architectural copyright (contending that image-making in the public space should not be restricted by new copyright subject matter). In this respect, the debates considered in this chapter differ from the tensions between painters and photographers during the same period which, as has been shown elsewhere, became intertwined with questions of creative status.[5]

Building Nineteenth-Century Public Spaces

The nineteenth century marked the expansion of British cities, and strong activity as regards urban building in response to industrialization and social and economic change. As a result, and as the historian Donald J. Olsen describes in *The City as a Work of Art*, cities became

4 Paul Oskar Kristeller, 'The Modern System of the Arts: A study in the History of Aesthetics Part I', *Journal of the History of Ideas*, 12 (1951), 496–527 (p. 497), https://doi.org/10.2307/2707484.

5 Cooper, *Art and Modern Copyright*, Chapter 2.

monuments — enduring representations of identity — rather than merely spaces containing monumental works.[6] In London, the central city layout changed strikingly, implemented by the architect John Nash. His additions included a new broad street, Regent Street (see Figure 1), and a new square, Trafalgar Square (completed in the 1830s), as well as the new National Gallery on the Square's north side, opening in 1838. New bridges and railway stations were also built: for instance, Tower Bridge was built between 1886 and 1894 and Baker Street station (see Figure 2), part of the first underground (the Metropolitan Railway) opened in 1863. There were also new Government buildings at Whitehall: buildings were constructed in the 1860s and 1870s to house the Foreign Office, India Office, Colonial Office, and Home Office. In Westminster, the Houses of Parliament had burned down in 1834, and the new building was largely completed in 1860; between the Strand and Carey Street, a new Royal Courts of Justice building was opened in 1882. South Kensington was also a site for new construction funded by the profits of the Great Exhibition of 1851, including the buildings that today house the Victoria and Albert Museum, the National History Museum, and Imperial College. The Royal Albert Hall was erected between 1867 and 1871.[7]

This new-built environment sought to endow London with imperial status and authority and resonate ideologically with its inhabitants.[8] Indeed, historians of architecture have noted that architectural changes of the nineteenth century were accompanied by a growing discourse about the experience of architecture by the public. As H. Horatio Joyce and Edward Gillin argue in *Experiencing Architecture in the Nineteenth Century*:

> In the nineteenth century, more than ever before, architecture was built to be experienced [...] how individuals experienced buildings around them was central to society and culture. How architecture was seen, smelt, felt, heard in, interpreted [...] was inseparable from the ways in which contemporaries perceived their rapidly industrializing societies to

6 Donald J. Olsen, *The City as a Work of Art: London, Paris, Vienna* (New Haven and London: Yale University Press, 1986) p. 9.

7 Stephen Porter, *London: A History in Painting and Illustrations* (Gloucestershire: Amberley Publishing, 2014) pp. 103–105, 225, 232.

8 Nancy Rose Marshall, *City of Gold and Mud: Painting Victorian London* (New Haven and London: Yale University Press, 2012) p. 26.

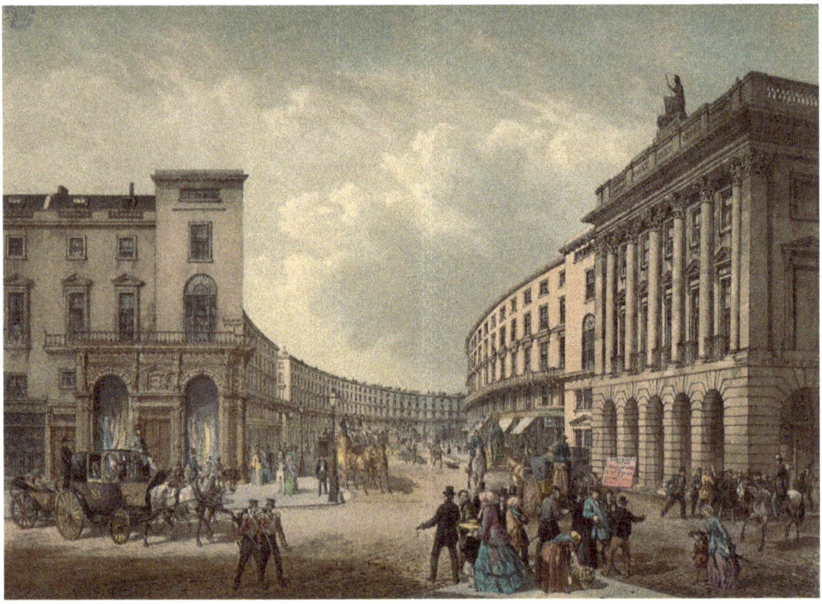

Fig. 1 The Quadrant, Regent Street, 1852, City of Westminster Archives Centre.

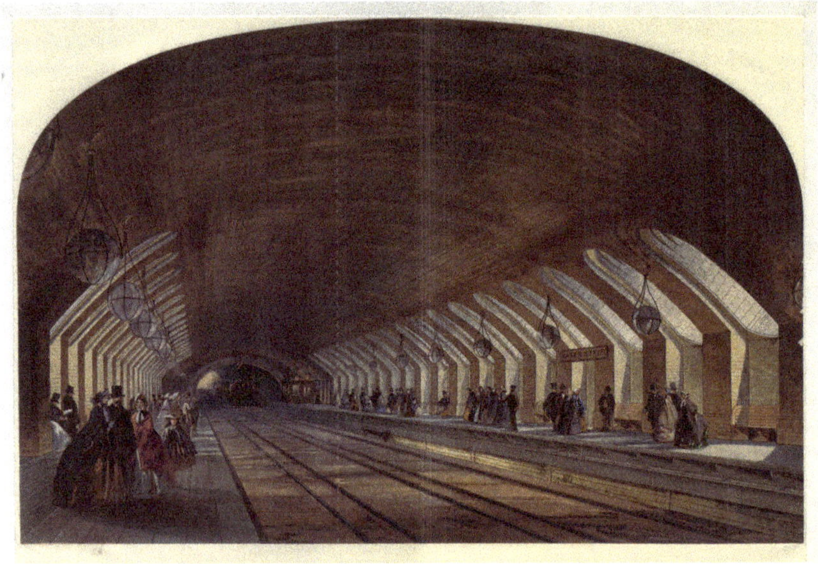

Fig. 2 Metropolitan Railway, Baker Street Station, c.1864, City of Westminster Archives Centre.

> be modern and progressive. [...] This was a moment of profound social and economic change, through rapid industrialization, urbanization and population growth [...] And the built environment was very much part of this changing world.[9]

These observations about architecture in the nineteenth century share much, argue Joyce and Gillin, with the philosopher Henri Lefebvre's twentieth-century theorization of the inhabitation of space as productive: a physical and mental category produced through human agency.[10] In the nineteenth-century architectural press, this heightened awareness of the experience of architecture gave rise to increasing commentary about the merits and weaknesses of new building on the urban space, as well as critical analysis of competing ideas for future changes, and these were sometimes written from the perspective of the anonymous 'critical lounger about town' as the observer of urban change.[11] These commentaries can be placed in the wider context of the 'public language of city exploration' which art historians have noted to be present in Britain as early as the 1820s, pre-dating the later, nineteenth-century French discourse of the *flâneur*: the gentleman who wandered the streets of the city absorbing its spectacles, and usually attributed to the writing of Charles Baudelaire.[12] Such constructions of the experience of the city are dependent on assumptions about gender, class and race and,

9 Edward Gillin and H. Horatio Joyce, 'Introduction', in *Experiencing Architecture in the Nineteenth Century: Buildings and Society in the Modern Age*, ed. by Edward Gillin and H. Horatio Joyce (London: Bloomsbury Visual Arts, 2019), pp. 1–12 (p. 1), https://doi.org/10.5040/9781350045972.

10 Ibid, p. 4, citing Henri Lefebvre's influential 1974 book *La production de l'espace.* On the construction of space in Britain see also Colin G. Pooley, 'Patterns on the ground: urban form, residential structure and the social construction of space', in *The Cambridge Urban History of Britain,* Volume 3: 1840–1950, ed. by Martin Daunton (Cambridge: Cambridge University Press, 2000), pp. 429–465, https://doi.org/10.1017/CHOL9780521417075.

11 For example, Lynx Eye, 'New Buildings in the City of London, No 1', *Builders' Weekly Reporter*, 27 July 1861, p. 2521; 'Our New Year's Address', *The Builders' Weekly Reporter*, 13 January 1862, p. 2857; 'Our New Year's Address', *The Builders' Weekly Reporter*, 20 January 1862, p. 2873 describing one new building as 'distinguished by its novelty of treatment'; 'Important New Buildings of the Metropolis' *Builders' Weekly Reporter*, 7 April 1862, p. 3049; 'New Blackfriars' Bridge', *The Builders' Weekly Reporter*, 27 January 1862, p. 2907: assessing various designs put forward for a new bridge at Blackfriars. 'A Critical Lounger About Town' was the title of a series of articles published in *The Builders' Weekly Reporter,* starting in 1861: 'A Critical Lounger About Town, No.1', *The Builders' Weekly Reporter,* 14 October 1861, p. 2675.

12 Marshall, *City of Gold and Mud*, p. 29.

consequently, the representation of the city promoted and reinforced particular identities, over others.[13]

The architectural development of the city and the public experience of the individual moving around town was prominent in the context of the development of parks such as Victoria Park in London.[14] Crucially, building projects were not necessarily purely aesthetic projects but also reflected a more general concern with the health of the city.[15] For example, the Metropolitan Board of Works, created in 1855, was tasked with effecting necessary practical improvements such as London's sewage system. This in turn gave (literal) cover to city beautification projects: for example, the Victoria Embankment project produced a beautiful public space that in reality is a fancy sewer lid.[16]

Architects seemed to be aware of the significance of architecture beyond its existence as an object. The understanding of the public experience of architecture, including public space generally, is implicit in architectural trade publications of the time (e.g. *The Builder*) and demonstrates a keen awareness of architecture being more than for architects, but about public spaces and public benefit. Thus, for example *The Building News*, in an item about expenditure on London parks observes in 1860: 'Kew-gardens are so admirably managed, and productive of so much enjoyment as well as of instruction to all classes of society'.[17] Art and architecture were also discussed in terms of offering advantage to the working class, as we see in the justification of parks for leisure as improving the health of the working class.[18]

---

13 On the female perspective on the idea of the flâneur noting that it is 'necessarily male' in allowing the walker to proceed unnoticed, see Janet Wolff, 'Gender and the Haunting of Cities (or, the retirement of the flâneur)' in *The Invisible Flâneuse? Gender, Public Space, and Visual Culture in Nineteenth-Century Paris*, ed. by Aruna D'Souza and Tom McDonough (Manchester University Press, 2006) pp. 18–31 (p. 19) and Lynda Nead, *Victorian Babylon: People, Streets and Images in Nineteenth-Century London* (New Haven: Yale University Press, 2000), p. 9.

14 On the occasion of the opening of the park's fountain in ('once-tabooed') east London: 'Opening of the Victoria Fountain', *The Builders' Weekly Reporter*, 14 July 1862, p. 3286. See also, on Cremorne Park: Nead, *Victorian Babylon*, p. 109.

15 In nineteenth-century Glasgow this entailed the wholesale destruction of areas of the city: Micheline Nilsen, *Architecture in Nineteenth-Century Photographs: Essays on Reading a Collection* (Abingdon and New York: Ashgate, 2011), p. 45.

16 Olsen, *The City as a Work of Art*, p. 24.

17 'Public Works and Buildings', *The Building News*, 6 July 1860, p. 539.

18 See for example: 'The Advantages and Use of a Knowledge of Art to the Working Classes', *The Builders' Weekly Reporter*, 20 January 1862, p. 2863.

Attention was paid more widely to the aesthetics of the city that was being produced. Architectural influences of the time were varied, with *The Builders' Weekly Reporter* carrying an opinion piece in 1861 querying the extensive adoption of an Italian style of architecture over the preceding two years, and the presentation of different architectural styles next to each other instead of showing a uniformity of style.[19] We see here a clear conception of architectural works mattering because they produce a particular image of public space. Architectural style may, furthermore, be considered as part of a political project, something to which a correspondent to *The Building News* alluded, privileging a specific type of person: 'With proper direction, the characteristics of the Englishman and *his present civilization* can sure be expressed in national architectural features'.[20] Moreover, there is a suggestion in the architectural press of the time that architecture is not (only) a thing but produces movement. The style of streets matters because of what it says about the city and the country in question. For example, *The Builders' Weekly Reporter* allegedly quotes an Italian visitor criticizing London sculpture and architecture:

> [I]t is a town of monstrosities, and the amateurs of the fine arts are not able to decide whether they should wonder most at the want of good taste, or the patience of the *people who night and morning pass such wretched performances* and allow them to remain.[21]

The criticism is perhaps beside the point, but the movement of people, alluded to above, matters; it is useful as a reflection of the understanding of British cities (in the above criticism, London) as public spaces that are not static: they both produce and are produced by movement. In short, architecture (and also architects' views of their role) would seem to echo the Lefebvrian concept of space as a 'lived experience'.[22] Architecture

19 'Lynx Eye', *The Builders' Weekly Reporter*, 27 July 1861, p. 2521.

20 'Victorian Architecture' (Correspondence), *The Building News*, 23 November 1860, p. 900 (emphasis in original).

21 'The Critical Lounger about Town no. 2', *The Builders' Weekly Reporter*, 27 July 1861, p. 2717 (emphasis added).

22 See Henri Lefebvre, *The Production of Space*, trans. by Donald Nicholson-Smith (Oxford: Blackwell Publishing, 2009), noting also the understanding of 'lived experience' as 'flux' or 'non-knowledge' (pp. 4, 6). Lefebvre distinguishes between the 'problematic' of space and 'spatial practice', the latter including architecture (p. 413). Elsewhere, Lefebvre notes: 'Perhaps... the producers of space have always

creates an encounter between the work of architecture and the city's inhabitants.[23] A distinct feature of architecture is that inhabitants could move through and use a building (in the case of private housing, physically inhabit it) whereas a painting or photograph could only be viewed. Accordingly, buildings, as elements of public space, were viewed simultaneously as objects and as sites of activity by the public. Such activity would include image-making and, as we explain in the next section, by the 1840s and 1850s the depiction of urban public space had acquired great importance.

Image-Making and Public Space

Public access — such as walking, viewing — and engagement with city spaces made architecture a ready subject for representation in paintings (our focus due to the nature of the composition of the Society of Arts' Copyright Committee, explained below), as well as in photographs and engravings. For example, urban development projects such as the building of municipal offices and museums were a practical response to a growing population, but also became the subject of photographs to help tourists distinguish new buildings from 'ancient' ones.[24] Thus, the physical manifestation of the city — its aesthetics and the attendant controversies over appropriate architectural style — mattered precisely because these buildings would be reproduced in two-dimensional images. In a discussion of how cities are represented, the art historian Caroline Arscott summarizes the position as follows, considering in particular the aesthetic theories of the nineteenth-century critic John Ruskin:

> The choice of a classical façade and gothic form became a vexed question. A beautiful vista or a fine building could figure prominently in an engraved or painted scene and lend the represented cityscape the

---

acted in accordance with a representation, while the 'users' passively experienced whatever was imposed upon them...' (p. 43).

23 See *Experiencing Architecture*, ed. by Joyce and Gillim, on Lefebvre and the concept of space as experience: 'When we deal with experience, we do not just examine how architecture could be encountered by inhabitants, but that the act of experiencing a building or a built environment contributed and shaped the architecture itself' (p. 4).

24 Nilsen, *Architecture in Nineteenth-Century Photographs*, p. 103.

> aesthetic merits and ethical connotations of the environment or building. Or else an image could alter, cancel or marginalise the architectural components of the urban fabric.[25]

What we can see here is an expectation that the city will be open to visual representation. While the concept of public space is not referred to, it is implicit in the view presented above. Indeed, the artistic practice of the period was, we argue, built on a conception that the city's public spaces — its views and vistas, its buildings and squares — should be available for reproduction.[26]

It is thus helpful to place the dispute between painters and architects within the context of not only the rapid industrialization of the period, but also aesthetic experiences within the mid-nineteenth-century city. Two aspects of aesthetic experience are relevant: the capture of views (especially via panoramic entertainment) and the paintings of streetscapes and elements of street life. Both aspects feed into the constitution of the individual — the city's inhabitant, who is both viewer and viewed — during this period.

The reproduction of the city as panoramic entertainment in the early nineteenth century included paintings exhibited in rotundas, an experience that became very popular and gained its inventor patent protection.[27] Such panoramas usually had a 'moatlike area surrounding [a] viewing platform' which had the effect of fully immersing the viewer in the view.[28] Panoramas of this nature, such as *A View of London and the Surrounding Country Taken from the Top of St Paul's Cathedral* (ca. 1845), represented a fast-changing urban environment to its inhabitants.[29]

---

25 Caroline Arscott, 'The representation of the city in the visual arts', in *The Cambridge Urban History of Britain, Volume III 1840–1950*, ed. by Martin Daunton (Cambridge: Cambridge University Press, 2000), pp. 811–831 (p. 813) https://doi.org/10.1017/CHOL9780521417075.

26 Nead, *Victorian Bablylon*: 'London was itself a web of representations and the site for the circulation of representations' (p. 57).

27 Robert Barker applied for a patent in 1787 and first exhibited his *Panorama of Edinburgh* in 1788. Bernard Comment, *The Panorama* trans. by Anne-Marie Glasheen (London: Reaktion Books, 1999), p. 23. On the history of panoramas, see also Michael Charleseworth, *Landscape and Vision in Nineteenth-Century Britain and France* (Abington and New York: Ashgate, 2008), Chapter 1. On panoramas: Comment, *Panorama*, p. 25.

28 Jonathan Crary, 'Géricault, the Panorama, and Sites of Reality in the Early Nineteenth Century', *Grey Room*, 9 (2002), 5–25 (p. 19).

29 Comment, *Panorama*, pp. 145, 165.

Crucially, such panoramas sought to be highly realistic; Robert Barker defended himself against an accusation that his Edinburgh panorama was inauthentic by seeking certification from the city's Provost that he had accurately represented the city.[30] This objective of truthful representation required that the buildings forming part of the cityscapes were free to be reproduced.

The art historian Nancy Rose Marshall describes nineteenth-century images of London as existing on a 'continuum between the panorama and the vignette', reflecting interest in not just the bird's eye view, but also street-level representations of the urban environment which depicted the public's relationship to the city.[31] In the 1820s and 1830s, as the art historian Alex Werner explains, there were 'relatively few paintings of urban contemporary life'.[32] However, by the 1840s and 1850s, 'urban modern life settings became popular subjects within the tradition of genre painting'.[33] Such paintings included the representation of particular people in 'street-cry' paintings and illustrations, such as *London Cries and Public Edifices* (1847) by John Leighton and *Covent Garden Market: The West End* (1859) by William McConnell.[34] They also comprised documentary pictures, for instance paintings by George Elgar Hicks, such as *Billingsgate Fish Market* (1861), which echoed the written social commentary work of the journalist Henry Mayhew (published as *The London Labour and the London Poor* in installments between 1849–1852, and as a book in 1861–2).[35] *Billingsgate Fish Market* was praised by the *Athenaeum* in 1861 as exemplifying the importance of documenting modern life in the City:

---

30 Ibid., pp. 145, 129.

31 Marshall, *City of Gold and Mud*, p. 32, referring to the categories in Michel de Certeau in *The Practice of Everyday Life*. On 'the poetic space of the pedestrian' see Nead, *Victorian Babylon*, p. 7.

32 Alex Werner, 'The London Society Magazine and the Influence of William Powell Frith on Modern Life Illustration of the Early 1860s', in *William Powell Frith: Painting The Victorian Age*, ed. by Mark Bills and Vivien Knight (New Haven and London: Yale University Press, 2006), pp. 95–108 (p. 95).

33 Ibid.

34 Marshall, *City of Gold and Mud*, p. 39.

35 Mark Bills, ''The line which Separates Character from Caricature...': Frith and the Influence of Hogarth', in *William Powell Frith*, ed. by Mark Bills and Vivien Knight, pp. 41–55 (p. 48). *George Elgar Hicks: Painter of Victorian Life*, ed. by Rosamond Allwood and Rosemary Treble (London: Geffrye Museum, 1982–3), p. 4. See also Christopher Wood, *Victorian Panorama: Paintings of Modern Life* (London: Faber & Faber, 1976) which includes a review of works by Hicks.

> Mr G.E. Hicks hit upon a good idea when he resolved to paint for us the scenes which take place at some well-known places of business in the City of London [...] Such pictures, even if less well painted than these really are, will be interesting for the future time, and therefore we shall be thankful to get them as creditably executed as this one is.[36]

Street-level pictures were also popular magazine illustrations, such as the *London Society* magazine's series of pictures entitled *The Artist in the London Streets* — the first of which was published in June 1862 depicting Oxford Street.[37] Further, as we explain in more detail later, the 1850s and early 1860s saw the exhibition of ground-breaking paintings depicting modern life by the Royal Academician William Powell Frith, a member of the Society of Arts' Copyright Committee, which firmly established modern life as an important subject of 'high art'.

The production and reproduction of the British city described above is the context in which the copyright debates (to which we now turn) took place. It suggests that this dispute is an example of the ways in which copyright too was the terrain for a contest not, or at least not only, over the protection of works but about the production and inhabitance of public space.

Architecture and Copyright in the Nineteenth Century

Copyright protection, as is well known, was expanded gradually to artistic subject-matter such as engraving and sculpture, through piecemeal legislation passed in the eighteenth and nineteenth centuries. This followed the first copyright Act, the Statute of Anne 1710, which protected books.[38] By the mid-nineteenth century, two-dimensional works of architecture were protected by copyright in a number of ways. The Engraving Acts expressly protected 'architectural prints' produced by engraving,[39] and the Literary Copyright Act 1842 included within the protection for books, 'charts, maps or plans' which were separately published.[40] The Fine Arts Copyright Act 1862, as mentioned earlier,

36 *Athenaeum*, 25 May 1861, p. 699, quoted in *George Elgar Hicks*, ed. by Allwood and Treble, p. 11.

37 A. Werner, 'The London Society Magazine', p. 100.

38 An Act for the Encouragement of Learning (Statute of Anne) 1710 (8 Anne c.19).

39 Engravings Act 1767 (7 Geo. III c.38), s. 1.

40 Literary Copyright Act 1842 (5 & 6 Vict. c.45), s. 1.

was the first legislation to protect 'drawings' as well as paintings and photographs; it was uncontroversial in the debates that preceded its passage that 'drawings' would encompass architectural drawings.[41] As we will explain, controversies instead lay with proposals for the protection of three-dimensional works of architecture, which were outside the scope of the 1862 Act, and not protected until 1911.[42]

From the vantage point of today, it may appear strange that the same objections made against the protection of three-dimensional buildings were not also levelled against two-dimensional architectural drawings; today, in the UK, copyright infringement can be established where copying is not only indirect (through copying an intermediate copy of a copyright work) but also copying a three-dimensional work (e.g. a building) may infringe a two-dimensional work (e.g. a drawing) and vice versa.[43] By contrast, in the nineteenth century, copyright in two-dimensional works was more limited. The courts readily accepted that copying could be indirect: in *Re Beal's Case*, the Court of Queen's Bench held that 'a copy from an intervening copy', such as an engraving of a painting, would infringe copyright in a painting.[44] However, it was generally understood that copying a three-dimensional work would not infringe copyright in a two-dimensional work and vice versa, and this position remained until the passage of the Copyright Act 1911.[45]

Notwithstanding this legal position, in the case of sculpture — three-dimensional works which had been protected since the late eighteenth century — the general consensus of the copyright debates of the mid to late nineteenth century was that the law should be changed to provide

41 Unlike protection under the Literary Copyright Act 1842, which commenced on publication, protection under the Fine Arts Copyright Act 1862 commenced on creation, and therefore would encompass unpublished architectural drawings. See further Cooper, *Art and Modern Copyright*, p. 214.

42 Copyright Act 1911, c.46, section 1(1) and 35(1), protecting 'architectural works of art'. The 1911 Act also introduced an exception allowing the two-dimensional copying of such 'architectural works of art': section 2(1)(iii) Copyright Act 1911, discussed in Cooper, *Art and Modern Copyright*, p. 219. On the campaign for the protection of architecture from the 1870s to 1911 see: Kimberlee Weatherall, 'Bringing Architecture into the Copyright System in the UK', unpublished paper presented at Emmanuel College, Cambridge, 2009.

43 Copyright Designs and Patents Act 1988, section 16(3)(b) and 17(3).

44 *Re Beal's Case* (1868) L.R. 387, 394, per Blackburn J., with whom Mellor J. and Lush J. agreed.

45 Cooper, *Art and Modern Copyright*, pp. 218–19. Section 1(2) of the Copyright Act 1911 restricted reproduction in 'any material form whatsoever'.

that two-dimensional reproductions (for example photographs of sculpture) would infringe copyright in three-dimensional sculpture.[46] This was accepted, for instance, by the Report of the majority of the Royal Commission on Copyright of 1878, endorsing the evidence given by the sculptor Thomas Woolner, and was a generally accepted premise in the copyright debates that followed thereafter to 1911.[47] This consensus reflected the principle that copyright should not be restricted to protecting the author against cases of harm, but should enable the author to 'reap the benefits' of the 'money value in reproduction'.[48] That sculpture should be protected against copying in two dimensions was also an accepted tenet of the copyright debates of the 1850s. It was the application of the same principle to architecture, which caused painters difficulty. To uncover the nature of these debates, we now introduce the 'hub' of copyright reform initiatives in the 1850s and early 1860s: the copyright committee of the Society of Arts, Manufactures and Commerce.

Architects and the Society of Arts Copyright Committee

The Artistic Copyright Committee of the Society of Arts was established in November 1857, under the chairmanship of Sir Charles Eastlake (President of the Royal Academy of Arts). As originally composed, the Committee brought together a broad range of representatives from the art world: painters, photographers, engravers, art collectors, and art administrators. However, the original records of the meetings of the Committee, show that it was painters — Royal Academicians and watercolourists — that soon came to dominate the Committee.[49]

46 Sculpture was protected by the Sculpture Copyright Act 1798 (38 Geo. III c.71) and Sculpture Copyright Act 1814 (54 Geo. III, c.56). On nineteenth century debates regarding the infringement of sculpture copyright see Cooper, *Art and Modern Copyright*, p. 218.

47 Copyright Commission, *The Royal Commissions and the Report of the Commissioners*; PP 1878 C-2036, C-2036-1 XXIV 163, 253, para. 97–98, and Thomas Woolner's evidence at Q.4058.

48 William Reynolds-Stephens giving evidence to the Gorell Committee. See Report of the Committee on the Law of Copyright; PP 1909 Cd 4976, at Q.2285-92.

49 Cooper, *Art and Modern Copyright*, p. 23 and p. 30. The inclusion of architects on the Committee is discussed below.

The Committee articulated the general principles of its proposals in its Report to the Council of the Society of Arts published in March 1858. This outlined two categories of protection. The 'chief' object was 'to secure a Copyright... for such of the designs of an artist as he may himself have conceived, and as have been produced by his own hands, or those of his assistants'.[50]

This denoted 'works of which the artist's own brain may be considered as the inventor and primary source... however first embodied' but applying 'especially' to, amongst others, painters, sculptors and architects.[51] The 'next object' was protection for works of a 'more imitative character, and not necessarily embodying design' against their reproduction and sale by competitors; such protection would not extend to the 'original design or other source'.[52] Engravers, photographers, and plaster cast-makers were specified as the groups who would be 'principally' protected in this way.[53] While the inclusion of architecture within the first category of protection might reflect the equivalence of architects' claims to protection to those of painters and sculptors, the Report also envisaged different treatment for architecture as compared to sculpture as regards the scope of protection. It was to this that architects objected.

How did the Society of Arts' Report envisage that architecture was to be differently treated to sculpture? The 1858 Report made clear that copyright protection for sculpture should restrict two-dimensional reproductions. However, to accommodate the interests of painters and engravers, who wished to be free to depict sculptures located in the public space, the Report stated that there should only be infringement where 'the original design as the sole or chief end of the publication' was reproduced. The Report continued with an example:

> No stranger ought to engrave one of the statues at the entrance of the House of Lords as a work *per se*. While a picture of the whole scene, including the set of statues as incidents would be within the rule known as to Copyright books, permitting legitimate extracts not being competitions with the original work or design.[54]

---

50 Society for the Encouragement of Arts, Manufactures and Commerce, *Report of the Artistic Copyright Committee to the Council* (London: 1858), p. 4.

51 Ibid.

52 Ibid.

53 Ibid.

54 Ibid.

The 'rule known as to Copyright books' is a reference to infringement case law under the Literary Copyright Act 1842 which accommodated certain fair uses of copyright works; until the Copyright Act 1911, there were no express statutory defenses to infringement.[55]

A different approach, however, was recommended as regards works of architecture. First, the Report is ambiguous as to whether three-dimensional buildings were to be protected as works in their own right; the Report refers to the protection of 'architectural plans, models etc.' and does not specify that buildings also were to be protected. In any event, the Report made clear that nothing would 'prevent new drawings etc. being taken from executed buildings', suggesting that two-dimensional reproduction of buildings would not be restricted.[56]

Indeed, in the dossier of evidence collected by the Society of Arts' Committee following the publication of the Report — intended to illustrate the problems which legislative reform should address — the only example concerning architecture related to an incident where an architect's plan had been copied (rather than copying from the building itself). Charles Robert Cockerell, an architect who was also a Royal Academician, joined the Society of Arts' Committee in 1858, following the publication of the Society's Report.[57] The evidence which he gave, accepted for inclusion by the Society of Arts in its dossier, concerned the unauthorized copying of architectural plans submitted to architectural competitions. As Cockerell explained:

> ...piracy of ideas and inventions from rejected designs [...] is notorious, and the work executed is constantly the composition of the ideas and inventions of the several competitors, without scruple, reward, or acknowledgment of any kind.[58]

---

55 See further: Kathy Bowrey, 'On Clarifying the Role of Originality and Fair Use in Nineteenth Century UK Jurisprudence: Appreciating "the humble grey which emerges as the result of long controversy",' in *The Common Law of Intellectual Property: Essays in Honour of Professor David Vaver*, ed. by Catherine Ng, Lionel Bently and Giuseppina Agostino (Oxford: Hart Publishing, 2010), p. 45–72, https://doi.org/10.2139/ssrn.1402444.

56 Ibid.

57 David Watkin, 'Cockerell, Charles Robert (1788–1863)' *Oxford Dictionary of National Biography*, https://doi.org/10.1093/ref:odnb/5781. Artistic Copyright Committee Minutes, 3 November 1858, RSA Archive, London.

58 E.M. Underdown, *The Law of Art Copyright* (London: John Crockford, 1863), p. 184.

As mentioned above, 'charts, maps or plans' were expressly included in the definition of 'books' protected under the Literary Copyright Act 1842, but this did not apply to unpublished works, as would have been the case in plans submitted to an architectural competition. While unpublished works were protected at common law, it was assumed by the Society of Arts' Committee that it was not an infringement to reproduce unpublished plans as a building in three dimensions. As Cockerell concluded referring to an example of a public competition:

> The direct consequence of this failure of protection was, in that instance, that the most important feature of my design, and of other designs in this public competition, were pirated and put into execution in a great or public work.[59]

The Society of Arts proposals, then, in providing protection for two-dimensional drawings from the moment of their creation (rather than publication), met certain concerns of architects as regards the copying in two-dimensions of plans submitted to competitions. As an article in *The Building News* stated, by protecting drawings through copyright, 'the system of public competition will be ameliorated'.[60] However, architects wanted proposals that went further. As the same article continued, 'it does seem strange that the architect is to have no copyright in the design when realised; that is, in the work itself...'[61]

Indeed, as another article in the same journal concluded, referring to the paragraphs of the 1858 Report concerning architecture: 'The profession will probably not see very clearly how or in what manner [the Report's proposals] will or can confer benefit upon them'.[62] In this way, as an article in *The Builder* expressed in 1859, 'the depreciation of just rights to the profession is greater than is involved' in the case of competitions; architects, as we will now explain, also sought protection for their three-dimensional works.[63] However, repeated attempts by architects to secure this principle were adamantly opposed by the Society of Arts' Committee.

---

59 Ibid.
60 'Art Copyright', *The Building News*, 24 May 1861 p. 429.
61 Ibid.
62 'Property in Art', *The Building News*, 30 March 1860, pp. 241, 242.
63 'Architectural Copyright', *The Builder*, 11 June 1859, p. 385.

Architectural Copyright and the RIBA Copyright Committee

The increasing professionalization of architectural practice in the nineteenth century, and its independence from noble patronage formed an important context for the copyright initiatives of architects.[64] The nineteenth century saw a boom in the construction of housing, and architects were keen to consolidate their professional position and fend off the challenges posed by a number of new players in the building world, in particular, the builder. Builders were general contractors that would oversee construction work, often with mere financial interests in building, rather than being workmen or having any real skills in their own right. By at least the late 1850s, architects were calling for copyright protection in three-dimensional buildings, owing to the activities of this new class of builder in the field of suburban housing. An architect would be engaged to produce the design, and the builder (sometimes, but not always, one who had overseen the work of the original design) would often subsequently produce countless other houses to the same design, at times working from the original plans, but more often from the three-dimensional buildings itself.[65] The result, argued the architects, was bad architecture: the designs were badly executed by builders, to the extent — to quote an article from *The Builder* in 1859 — that the architect 'may be disgusted with his own work'.[66] Therefore, for architects, copyright in three-dimensional buildings was an essential element in establishing their professional authority over the building trades.[67]

64 See further, Martin S. Briggs, *The Architect in History* (Oxford, Clarendon Press, 1927), Frank Jenkins, *Architect and Patron* (Oxford: Oxford University Press, 1961), B. Hanson, *Architects and the Building World' from Chambers to Ruskin: Constructing Authority* (Cambridge: Cambridge University Press, 2003).

65 'Architectural Copyright', *The Builder*, 11 June 1859, p. 385: 'many of the speculative builders even work entirely without drawings'. Therefore, the article concluded that only protection for three-dimensional works could 'prevent that sort of imitation or perversion of an original design' which was 'one of the chief sources of annoyance and of injury to the reputation of architects'.

66 Ibid.

67 We deal below with the public-interest dimension to architectural copyright, which was also articulated by architects at this time. Note, also, that *The Builder* carried a report in 1858 of a meeting in Brussels the summary of which included the following point: '7. Works of design, painting, sculpture, *architecture*, and engraving to be placed on the same footing as regards copyright as works of literature.' 'Copyright Congress at Brussels' *The Builder*, 9 October 1858, p. 680 (emphasis in original).

What specific action did architects take in an attempt to secure such rights? As we mentioned above, the architect Charles Robert Cockerell joined the Society of Arts' Copyright Committee in 1858, following the publication of the Society of Arts' Report; he attended its meetings in April 1858.[68] However, dissatisfied with the Society of Arts' proposals, architects sought to promote their interests instead through their own professional body, the Royal Institute of British Architects (RIBA) — which at that time was much concerned with the consolidation of architects' professional status more generally.[69] The first step taken by the RIBA, in May 1858, was the drafting of a petition to Parliament, which was presented by Lord Lyndhurst to the House of Lords in July 1858, the occasion of the first parliamentary debate on the subject of artistic copyright in the campaign culminating in the 1862 Act.[70] The petition, after reciting the need for architectural copyright, as 'architects are liable to injury in the piracy of their designs', specified: 'that such copyright should extend to their executed works, as well as to their publications'.[71] The House of Lords appointed a Select Committee, but this was abandoned in 1859 for reasons unconnected with the protection of architecture.[72]

Then, in April 1859, the RIBA Council formed its own Copyright Committee with the express purpose of continuing to press for architectural copyright reform in the form of the 1858 petition.[73] The Committee included Charles Robert Cockerell amongst its membership, in addition to the following architects: Thomas Leverton Donaldson (a founder of the RIBA and Professor of Architecture at University College London), George Godwin (an architect who was also the editor of the architectural journal *The Builder*), Robert Kerr (who was also Professor of construction arts at King's College London), John Woody Papworth

68 Artistic Copyright Committee Minutes, 8 April 1858 and 15 April 1858, RSA Archive, London.

69 See further in Angela Mace, *The Royal Institute of British Architects: A Guide to its Archive and History* (London: Mansell Publishing, 1986). The Institute of British Architects was founded in 1834 and received a Royal Charter in 1837.

70 'Royal Institute of British Architects', *The Builder*, 8 May 1858, p. 310; *Journal of the House of Lords* Volume XC, 26 July 1858, p. 468–469.

71 'Royal Institute of British Architects', *The Builder*, 8 May 1858, p. 310.

72 Cooper, *Art and Modern Copyright*, pp. 32, 129.

73 RIBA Council Minutes, 1 April 1859, RIBA Archive. See also 'The Royal Academy; The Franchise; and Copyright; At the Institute of Architects', *The Builder*,19 March 1859, pp. 199, 200.

(a frequent contributor to *The Builder*) and John Norton (who was also President of the Architectural Association).[74] In May 1860, the RIBA Committee again forwarded their petition of 1858 to the Society of Arts' Copyright Committee, asking that the Society of Arts' proposals 'be altered so as to be in accordance with the said petition' through the protection of three-dimensional works.[75] As the RIBA Council reported to the RIBA Annual Meeting in May 1860, the RIBA's grievance was that the Society of Arts scheme 'legalises the copying of Architects' executed works, while it affords protection to their publications'.[76]

A petition affirming the same principle — the protection of three-dimensional works of architecture — was also presented by the RIBA to Parliament in 1861, expressed to be 'essential to the bestowal of a protection to architects similar to that contemplated to be given to other artists'.[77] In view of these tensions, when the Fine Arts Copyright Bill of 1862 was introduced (again, on the initiative of the Society of Arts' Committee) dealing only with paintings, drawings and photographs, the RIBA Council concluded that it was 'undesirable to take any active steps with respect to it' in view that 'no direct reference has been made to works of Architecture'.[78]

Tensions between Painters and Architects

As noted in the opening of this chapter, there was, at first glance, a contradiction in the Society of Arts' treatment of architects' claims. On the one hand, as Lionel Bently has shown, the rhetoric of the 'fine arts' and the parity of painting to literature was invoked as an argument in

74 L.A. Fagan, revised by Anne Pimlott Baker, 'Donaldson, Thomas Leverton (1795–1885)', *DNB*, https://doi.org/10.1093/ref:odnb/7806. GB Smith, revised by Ruth Richardson and Robert Thorne, 'Godwin, George (1813–1888)', *DNB*, https://doi.org/10.1093/ref:odnb/10891. Paul Waterhouse revised by Geoffrey Tyack, 'Kerr, Robert (1823–1904)', *DNB*, https://doi.org/10.1093/ref:odnb/34304. Arthur Cates revised by John Elliott 'Papworth, John Woody (1820–1870)', *DNB*, https://doi.org/10.1093/ref:odnb/21256. Paul Waterhouse revised by John Elliott, 'Norton, John (1823–1904)', *DNB*, https://doi.org/10.1093/ref:odnb/35259.

75 RIBA Copyright Committee Minutes, 12.5.1860, RIBA Archive. RIBA Petition 23.5.1860, RSA Archive.

76 Report of the Council to the Annual Meeting, 7 May 1860, RIBA Proceedings (1859–1860), RIBA Archive.

77 RIBA Copyright Committee Minutes, 20 June 1861, RIBA Archive.

78 Report of the Council to the Annual Meeting, 5 May1862, RIBA Proceedings (1861–1862), RIBA Archive.

favor of the Society of Arts' proposals regarding painting.[79] Architects sought to justify protection for three-dimensional buildings, with analogous reasoning. As one article in *The Builder* published in 1859 expressed:

> Works of design, paintings, sculpture, architecture and engraving were to be placed on the same footing as regards copyright, as works of literature. Nothing else can satisfy the justice of the case, and give the architect the reward for his labour, or effect the improvement which is demanded in our architecture [...] We, architects, want a demonstration by the law, of the fact that there is a right to property in architectural invention, as in all works of mind.[80]

As the same article later noted, literary copyright protected 'results from the labour of the pen guided by the intellect' and 'the rights of architects' were 'strictly analogous'.[81] In this way, the RIBA petition was characterized as seeking 'the assimilation of the position of architects' to authors, and reflecting architects' 'identity of claim' to copyright to those of other artists, including painters.[82] The injury to painting and painters which resulted from the circulation of 'spurious copies', was 'equally[...] true of buildings and architects' work.'[83]

It was curious then, that the Society of Arts' Committee should oppose the same principle applied to architecture. As an article in *The Building News* remarked:

> If [painters and sculptors] are to have copyright in the embodiment of their conception, ideas, or compositions, which they ought to have, so should architects have copyright in their ideas when embodied in construction.[84]

What lay behind the resistance of the Society of Arts to conceding to architects' proposals for protection of their three-dimensional works? As we have already noted, while the Society of Arts' Committee began as a broadly constituted body — spanning representatives from across the art-world — the Committee soon came to be dominated by painters,

79 Bently, 'Art and the Making', p. 332.
80 'Architectural Copyright', *The Builder*, 11 June 1859, p. 385.
81 Ibid.
82 Ibid.
83 Ibid.
84 'Art Copyright', *The Building News*, 24 May 1861, p. 429.

led by the President of the Royal Academy Sir Charles Eastlake, who was also the Committee's Chairman.[85] It was the objections of painters, Royal Academicians and watercolorists that explained the Committee's resistance. The problem as regards the reception of 'the claims of architects', argued *The Builder* in 1859, lay with:

> ...those professors of the sister branches of art who have made themselves heard loudest in the matter of copyright. The title which is the proper subject for protection, is that to *design*; and it is impossible for us to understand that there can be clear views in this respect amongst persons who would attach less importance to work of architecture than to that of painting.[86]

What arguments were advanced by painters and architects? Architectural copyright intersected with ideas about the public's experience of architecture in two ways. On the one hand, arguments advanced by architects for architectural copyright, concerned the resulting public benefit of improved architecture to ordinary members of the public. As *The Builder* reported in 1859, with the exception of architectural projects of 'a higher order', such as 'public buildings and in localities like the city of London [...] where circumstances are specially favourable', the 'general state of architecture' was that 'it has not a tendency to become worse'.[87] Accordingly, as the article concluded:

> ...the corrective for the large amount of bad design in buildings, which is exhibited in suburban London, in fashionable watering-places, and in almost every town and populous district, would be supplied by a system of architectural copyright.[88]

Copyright, then, would result in 'the improvement which is needed in the aspect of our streets and our places of abode'[89] by producing greater 'originality' in architectural designs, such that 'there would be greater variation in street architecture than is at present apparent'.[90] These were arguments which reflected the public placement of architecture, accessible to the public in the widest sense. As an article from *The*

85 Cooper, *Art and Modern Copyright*, p. 30.
86 'Architectural Copyright', *The Builder*, 11 June 1859, p. 385.
87 Ibid.
88 Ibid.
89 Ibid.
90 'Art Copyright', *The Building News*, 24 May 1861, p. 429.

Building News commented in 1860: 'Architecture standeth in the streets and public ways and welcometh, and exhibiteth herself to all alike, — to the million just as freely as to the millionaire'.[91] What is interesting here is the appeal not, as we see elsewhere, to public spaces such as Trafalgar Square and the like, but more humbly to the suburban house:

> The architect is employed to design say an ordinary suburban residence [...] He will see, however, houses built to the very pattern, sometimes by the builder who had worked from his drawings: he will see his enrichments multiplied; and in unsuitable positions; and in every time a degree worse in execution. [...] The rights of architects, and the interest of the public in the maintenance, form a case which is strictly analogous.[92]

Accordingly, the multiplicity of poor copies becomes a broader *spatial* problem. This is made more explicitly in an appeal for copyright protection for works of architecture because of the inherently public nature of architecture:

> The question [of copyright] affects not only architects, but those who might be benefited by becoming their clients and it affects vastly the future of architecture. Piracy actually tends to the destruction of the profession, in what should be its widest field. Let the corrective be applied ...[and] architects will find it then their interest to attend to the smaller class of houses; [...] and architecture may be advanced with benefit to all parties...[93]

In the hands of architects, then, the public placement of architecture — the experience of architecture by the public — was part of the case in favor of copyright protection for three-dimensional works. By contrast, from the perspective of painters, who wished to be free to depict the changing urban landscape in their two-dimensional works, the place of architecture in the public space explains their opposition to architectural copyright. As Nancy Rose Marshall shows in her monograph *City of Gold and Mud: Painting Victorian London*, the mid-nineteenth century saw the emergence of a 'self-conscious attempt to

91 'Vox Populi' and the Million', *The Building News*, 30 November 1860, p. 918.
92 'Architectural Copyright', *The Builder*, 11 June 1859, p. 385.
93 Ibid., p. 386. Similarly, the following year, as the dispute raged on, stating that '[i]t is desirable, nevertheless, to keep the question open...' with protection for drawings only described as unsatisfactory both for architects and the public: 'Architects' Copyright', *The Builder*, 28 June 1860, p. 386.

create an "art of modern life"' through the painting of 'contemporary urban subjects' on a grand scale. This reflected the Victorian awareness of London's status as a 'hub of global economic, political and social enterprise', bringing together the elements of 'modernity'. The result was a new reportage style of painting where 'there was no obvious distance in space and time between the subjects depicted and the viewers themselves'.[94] Mid-nineteenth century painting, then, was dominated by 'realist strategies of representation', 'with its crisp apparent transcription of the world'.[95] Painting played an important role in reproducing public space and simultaneously producing the public (or at least a certain public) that gazed upon itself in paintings of public spaces. In this way, as Marshall argues, image-making in Victorian Britain was as much part of the experience of the city as other practices, whether moving or mapping the city (which Henri Lefebvre was later to articulate), and to which Marshall adds the practice of 'image-making to concretize [city] identities'.[96]

The depiction of modern life, particularly the urban environment, then, was generally accepted as an important ambition for painting by the mid-nineteenth century. As the art historian Rosemary Treble explains:

> ...it is clear that there was in the mid-century a common impulse to immortalise the City and its life in paint as a reaction against Romanticism and Naturalism, and a conscious assertion of new values over old.[97]

A particularly important contribution was the work of the Royal Academician painter William Powell Frith (1819–1909). Frith was formally a member of the Society of Arts' Committee; he signed the Society's petition to Parliament and attended the Committee's deputation to the Prime Minister, Viscount Palmerston in 1860.[98] Frith was a pioneer in painting crowd-scenes capturing everyday

94 Marshall, *City of Gold and Mud*, p.1.

95 Ibid., p. 3.

96 Ibid., p. 11 referring to Henri Lefebvre, *The Urban Revolution* trans. by Robert Bonanno (Minnesota: University of Minnesota Press, 2003), pp. 118–119.

97 Rosemary Treble, 'Victorian Painting of Modern Life', in *George Elgar Hicks*, ed. by Allwood and Treble, p. 7.

98 'Court Circular', *The Times*, 30 April1860, p. 9. William Powell Frith was elected to the membership of the Copyright Committee on 11 March 1858: Minutes of the Artistic Copyright Committee, RSA Archive.

life, and established the importance of such 'modern life' subjects and their undisputed status as 'high art', particularly by presenting his approach as in the tradition of the street-scenes painted by the venerated eighteenth-century English painter William Hogarth (albeit adapted to suit Victorian sensibilities).[99] Frith's first crowd-scene, set at the seaside and entitled *Ramsgate Sands* (1854), was purchased by Queen Victoria in recognition of its significance.[100] A second picture of a crowd at the races, entitled *Derby Day* (1856–8) followed. The copyright debates of 1862 were contemporaneous with the much-awaited unveiling (in April 1862) of Frith's most ambitious panoramic picture, *The Railway Station*, which was his first crowd picture set in the urban environment (at Paddington railway station in London). Over 21,000 spectators viewed the picture over the seven weeks it was displayed, and it was praised by the art press of the time for capturing all 'the sparkle of modern life', 'the illustration of contemporary life' being 'one of the most valuable functions of art'.[101] Following on from this success, in the summer of 1862, the printseller Ernest Gambart commissioned Frith for a large sum (£10,000) to produce three London street-scenes entitled *The Streets of London*, comprising *Morning* (to be set in Covent Garden), *Noon* (depicting Regent Street) and *Night* (set in Haymarket), echoing Hogarth's famous picture *The Times of Day* (1736–1738). Only small-scale pictures were produced (today held in private hands) as Frith abandoned the project in 1863, to paint a picture of the Prince of Wales' Wedding.[102] However, the importance of art representing the urban environment would have undoubtedly been recognized by members of the Society's Committee who opposed protection for architecture. Copyright subject-matter debates, then, constituted a further terrain that registered the importance of the unencumbered freedom to experience public urban space through image-making.

---

99 Bills, 'The line which Separates Character from Caricature...', in *William Powell Frith*, ed. by Bills and Knight, pp. 41–55.

100 Mary Cowling, 'Frith and his Followers: Painters and Illustrators of London Life', in *William Powell Frith*, ed. by Bills and Knight, pp. 57–77 (p. 57).

101 *The Athenaeum*, 12 March 1862, pp. 502–504; and *Illustrated London News*, 3 May 1863, p. 457.

102 W.P. Frith, *My Autobiography and Reminiscences*, vol. 1 (Cambridge: Cambridge University Press, 2012) [originally published in 1887], pp. 338–340.

Conclusion

The dispute between painters and architects uncovered in this chapter is not one about authorship, or whether new categories of author and work can (and ought to) be recognized, but rather represents a point of conflict between painters and architects over public space. In short, both painters and architects recognized that buildings were in some respect special for being publicly experienced. They differed, however, in what the implications of this should be for copyright protection. Painters saw buildings as subject matter for their paintings — paintings which would give back to the public, images of themselves and their world — while architects saw buildings as necessarily for the public to experience. For the former, copyright protection for architecture would prevent the viewing of the city in ways that would record modern life, and so help inhabitants conceptualize themselves. For copyright to prevent the reproduction of buildings would thus, the argument might run, not only represent an affront to the painter seeking freedom to exercise their aesthetic tastes, but would also harm the public itself. The latter, of course, situated the public differently: public buildings, public squares, gardens and parks, private housing has an indisputably public element because such buildings and spaces are necessary for public health, leisure, enjoyment or in the case of private houses, safety. Copyright protection would thus, for example, prevent detrimental, poor-quality copies of houses. More broadly, people's inhabitance of spaces — the ways spatial practices in effect create architecture through movement — is privileged. The tension becomes again one between the building as subject matter for a painting, and a building's use — the static and the dynamic — but where both aspects produce public experience of the mid-nineteenth century city and indeed mould *who* the public was.

Bibliography

Allwood, Rosamond and Rosemary Treble, *George Elgar Hicks: Painter of Victorian Life* (London: Geffrye Museum, 1982–3).

Arscott, Caroline, 'The representation of the city in the visual arts' in *The Cambridge Urban History of Britain, Volume III 1840–1950*, ed. by M. Daunton (ed.) (Cambridge: Cambridge University Press, 2000), pp. 811–831, https://doi.org/10.1017/CHOL9780521417075.

Bently, Lionel, 'Art and the Making of Modern Copyright Law' in *Dear Images: Art, Copyright and Culture*, ed. by Daniel McClean and Karsten Schubert (London: Ridinghouse RCA, 2002), pp. 331–351.

Bills, Mark, ''The line which Separates Character from Caricature...': Frith and the Influence of Hogarth', 1860s' in *William Powell Frith: Painting the Victorian Age*, ed. by Mark Bills and Vivien Knight (New Haven and London: Yale University Press, 2006), pp. 41–56.

Bowrey, Kathy, 'On Clarifying the Role of Originality and Fair Use in Nineteenth Century UK Jurisprudence: Appreciating "the humble grey which emerges as the result of long controversy"' in *The Common Law of Intellectual Property: Essays in Honour of Professor David Vaver*, ed. by Catherine Ng, Lionel Bently and Giuseppina Agostino (Oxford: Hart Publishing, 2010), pp. 45–72, https://doi.org/10.2139/ssrn.1402444.

Briggs, Martin S., *The Architect in History* (Oxford, Clarendon Press, 1927).

Charleseworth, Michael, *Landscape and Vision in Nineteenth-Century Britain and France* (Abington and New York: Ashgate, 2008).

Cates, Arthur revised by John Elliott 'Papworth, John Woody (1820–1870)', *DNB*, https://doi.org/10.1093/ref:odnb/21256.

Comment, Bernard, *The Panorama* translated by Anne-Marie Glasheen (London: Reaktion Books, 1999).

Cooper, Elena, *Art and Modern Copyright: The Contested Image* (Cambridge: Cambridge University Press, 2018), https://doi.org/10.1017/9781316840993.

Cowling, Mary, 'Frith and his Followers: Painters and Illustrators of London Life' in *William Powell Frith: Painting the Victorian Age*, ed. by Mark Bills and Vivien Knight (New Haven and London: Yale University Press, 2006), pp. 57–77.

Crary, Jonathan, 'Géricault, the Panorama, and Sites of Reality in the Early Nineteenth Century' *Grey Room* 9 (2002), https://doi.org/10.1162/152638102320989498.

Fagan, L.A. revised by Pimlott Baker, Anne, 'Donaldson, Thomas Leverton (1795–1885)', *DNB*, https://doi.org/10.1093/ref:odnb/7806.

Frith, W.P. *My Autobiography and Reminiscences*, vol. 1 (Cambridge: Cambridge University Press, 2012) [originally published in 1887], https://doi.org/10.1017/CBO9781139343923.

Gillin, Edward. and H. Horatio Joyce, 'Introduction' in *Experiencing Architecture in the Nineteenth Century: Buildings and Society in the Modern Age*, ed. by Edward Gillin and H. Horatio Joyce (London: Bloomsbury Visual Arts, 2019), pp. 1–12, https://doi.org/10.5040/9781350045972.

Hanson, Brian, *Architects and the Building World' from Chambers to Ruskin: Constructing Authority* (Cambridge: Cambridge University Press, 2003).

Jenkins, Frank, *Architect and Patron* (Oxford: Oxford University Press, 1961).

Kristeller, P.O., 'The Modern System of the Arts: A study in the History of Aesthetics Part I', *Journal of the History of Ideas*, 12 (1951).

Lefebvre, Henri, *The Production of Space* translated by Donald Nicholson-Smith (Oxford: Blackwell Publishing, 2009).

Mace, Angela, *The Royal Institute of British Architects: A Guide to its Archive and History* (London: Mansell Publishing, 1986).

Marshall, Nancy Rose, *City of Gold and Mud: Painting Victorian London* (New Haven and London: Yale University Press, 2012).

Nead, Lynda, *Victorian Babylon: People, Streets and Images in Nineteenth-Century London* (New Haven: Yale University Press, 2000).

Nilsen, Micheline, *Architecture in Nineteenth-Century Photographs: Essays on Reading a Collection* (Abingdon and New York: Ashgate, 2011).

Olsen, Donald J., *The City as a Work of Art: London, Paris, Vienna* (New Haven and London: Yale University Press, 1986).

Pooley, Colin G., 'Patterns on the ground: urban form, residential structure and the social construction of space' in *The Cambridge Urban History of Britain, Volume III 1840–1950*, ed. by Martin Daunton (Cambridge: Cambridge University Press, 2000), pp. 429–65, https://doi.org/10.1017/CHOL9780521417075.

Porter, Stephen, *London: A History in Painting and Illustrations* (Gloucestershire: Amberley Publishing, 2014).

Smith, G.B. revised by Richardson, Ruth and Thorne, Robert, 'Godwin, George (1813–1888)', *DNB*, https://doi.org/10.1093/ref:odnb/10891.

Treble, Rosemary, 'Victorian Painting of Modern Life', in *George Elgar Hicks: Painter of Victorian Life*, ed. by Rosamond Allwood and Rosemary Treble (London: Geffrye Museum, 1982–3).

Underdown, E. M., *The Law of Art Copyright* (London: John Crockford, 1863).

Waterhouse, Paul revised by Tyack, Geoffrey, 'Kerr, Robert (1823–1904)', *DNB*, https://doi.org/10.1093/ref:odnb/34304.

Waterhouse, Paul revised by Elliott, John, 'Norton, John (1823–1904)', *DNB*, https://doi.org/10.1093/ref:odnb/35259.

Weatherall, Kimberlee, 'Bringing Architecture into the Copyright System in the UK', unpublished paper presented at Emmanuel College, Cambridge, 2009.

Werner, Alex, 'The London Society Magazine and the Influence of William Powell Frith on Modern Life Illustration of the Early 1860s' in *William Powell Frith: Painting the Victorian Age*, ed. by Mark Bills and Vivien Knight (New Haven and London: Yale University Press, 2006), pp. 95–110.

Wolff, Janet, 'Gender and the haunting of cities (or, the retirement of the flâneur)' in *The Invisible Flâneuse? Gender, Public Space, and Visual Culture in Nineteenth-Century Paris*, ed. by Aruna D'Souza and Tom McDonough (eds.) (Manchester University Press, 2006), pp. 18–31.

Wood, C., *Victorian Panorama: Paintings of Modern Life* (London: Faber & Faber, 1976).

11. Nineteenth-Century American Sculpture and United States Design Patents

Karen Lemmey

On 7 July 1849, Hiram Powers submitted a design patent application through the American consulate in Livorno, Italy for his sculpture *The Greek Slave*.[1] As an expatriated American artist living in Florence, Powers desperately wished to protect his work in Europe and the United States. For unknown reasons, however, Powers's petition appears to have failed, leaving his most important work vulnerable to piracy. His fears were justified, and unauthorized reductions of *The Greek Slave* (see Figure 1) soon abounded in plaster and Parian ware, a mass-produced porcelain.

The search for anything relating to Powers's application in the archives of the United States Patent and Trademark Office (USPTO), in preparation for a 2016 exhibition on *The Greek Slave* at the Smithsonian American Art Museum (SAAM), sowed the seeds for this essay. It is especially ironic that this hunt for evidence was initiated by SAAM.

1 This essay is dedicated to Dr. William H. Gerdts. The author is grateful to the United States Patent and Trademark Office, especially D. Lawrence Tarazano and Elizabeth Dougherty for their invaluable assistance and guidance in accessing and interpreting the archival records of nineteenth-century design patents. The author is also grateful to Thayer Tolles, Debra Pincus, Kimberly Orcutt, and Ann Boulton for their insights on the material presented here, and to Grace Yasumura for her assistance locating critical nineteenth-century sources. Gratitude is also due to the anonymous peer reviewer who offered such helpful insights. Powers stated he paid a $15 application fee to the US Treasury. '*Greek Slave* Patent Application, 7 July 1849. Hiram Powers Papers, 1819-1953, Bulk 1835-1883. Archives of American Art, Smithsonian Institution.' https://www.aaa.si.edu/collections/items/detail/greek-slave-patent-17307.

 https://doi.org/10.11647/OBP.0247.11

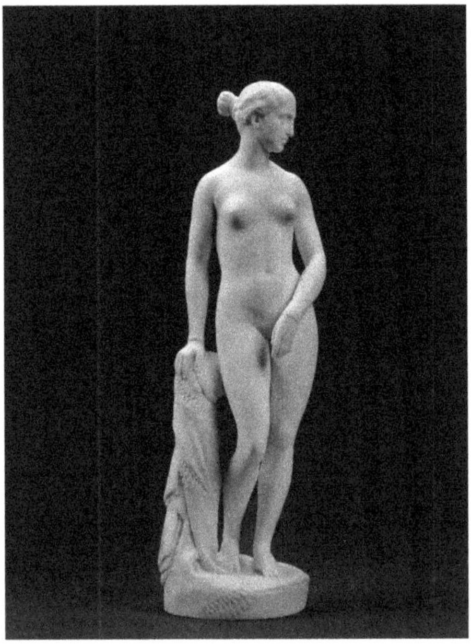

Fig. 1 Minton and Company after Hiram Powers, *The Greek Slave* (after 1849), porcelain, Smithsonian American Art Museum, Washington, D.C.

After all, the museum is housed in the Old Patent Office Building in Washington, D.C. — the very place where Powers had directed his ill-fated application in 1849. The building also contains the largest collection of Powers's sculptures, including several working models of *The Greek Slave* that the artist used to replicate his sculpture.[2] No patent for *The Greek Slave* came to light, but the search generated a broader exploration of nineteenth-century design patents for sculptures registered through the United States Patent Classification system within Class D11 ('Jewelry, Symbolic Insignia, and Ornaments'). This classification included 'sculptures, table or wall ornaments', some of which are described by the subcategories 'Simulative, Animate, Equestrian, Humanoid, Winged, Plural': terms likely devised by Patent Examiners functioning in their capacity as government officials, rather than artists.[3]

2 The historic structure occupies a city block in Washington, D.C. bounded by F, G, 8, 7, and 9th Streets Northwest.

3 All design patents references in this essay may be found online by conducting a search using the design number (prefaced by 'D') in this search engine, 'United States Patent and Trademark Office Search Engine' http://patft.uspto.gov/

This essay offers the first overview of the USPTO's records for Design Patents classified in D11 issued for sculptures between 1842 and 1902, the years in which patent law offered the most significant protection for this art form.[4] Prior to 1842, sculptures lacked any significant form of intellectual property protection in the United States and copying was rampant. In response, the Patent Act of 1842 created 'Design Patents' which provided protection for sculpture and ornamental design. This ended in 1902, when sculptures were no longer protected by design patents and sculptors instead availed themselves of copyright protection, made available in 1870.[5] Between 1842 and 1902, the USPTO issued more than 400 design patents for sculptures that ranged from bust and figures commemorating venerated statesmen to ornaments that were sculptural in nature, such as coffin handles, clock cases, cake decorations, hat stands, and umbrella stands. The records underscore sculpture's fluidity across the fine and decorative arts in the nineteenth century, especially as a significant number of patents were issued to designers affiliated with major decorative arts manufacturers. These include Karl L. Muller and his bother Nicholas, both of whom worked with Union Porcelain Company in Brooklyn, New York.[6] Similarly, many patents were assigned to firms in Meriden, Connecticut, which earned the appellation Silver City owing to the numerous decorative arts manufactures based there. This remarkable body of patent documents does not offer an accurate or comprehensive history of nineteenth-century American sculpture; indeed, the majority of sculptors did not patent their designs.

---

netahtml/PTO/srchnum.htm. For a list of United States Patent Classification (USPC) system as it relates to Design Patents see https://www.uspto.gov/web/patents/classification/uspcd11/schedd11.htm.

4 This essay offers my perspective as an art historian; a legal scholar would surely have different and valuable observations around the selection of design patents. For an overview of the history of the US design patent, see Mark D. Janis and Jason J. Du Mont, 'The Origins of American Design Patent Protection', *Indiana Law Journal*, 88:3 (2013), 837-880, https://www.repository.law.indiana.edu/ilj/vol88/iss3/1/.

5 The Copyright Act of July 8, 1870, defined copyrightable subject matter to include 'statuary, and . . . models or designs intended to be perfected as works of the fine arts'. *Copyright Act of 1870, ch. 230, § 86, 16 Stat. 198, 212* (1870).

6 See Brooklyn Museum for an example of Muller's *Statuette of Blacksmith* produced by Union Porcelain Works. Karl Muller, 'Design Patent for a Statuette (Blacksmith)', 1868, http://patft.uspto.gov/netacgi/nph-Parser?patentnumber=D2919.

Nineteenth-century sculptors critically depended on selling replicas of their compositions, at times in large editions. The iterative nature of sculpture echoed the practices of photography, etching, engraving, and other serial art forms addressed elsewhere in this volume. Yet the copyright laws that protected such print editions did not historically apply to sculptural ones. The passing of the Patent Act of 1842 offered new protections, but the design patent was not self-enforcing, and its effective extent had yet to be tested in court. Moreover, while the Act of 1842 was expansive enough to include sculpture, it was not written specifically *for* that particular medium, and thus unevenly served the needs of sculptors according to their individual business models, preferred material, and studio practices. Initially, the design patent was only available to US citizens and foreign nationals who had resided in the US for one year who had pledged to become a citizen; this citizenship requirement was removed in 1870. Essentially, one had to submit a petition describing the design and arguing for its novelty and innovation, along with an illustration and the associated fee.[7] Between 1836 and 1861, applicants for utility patents were generally required to submit a model that could be returned once it was reviewed, but it is unclear whether all design patents strictly required a model or the illustration alone sufficed. One could choose to hire a patent lawyer to draft the petition and a patent agent to render and deliver the model, or draw the design on behalf of the applicant; however, there is no specific evidence of sculptors contracting these services. If the petition was approved, the designer would take the required oath declaring the originality of his design in any number of places, including clerks of the court, magistrate

7 I am grateful to Robert Berry, Manager Patent and Trademark Resource Center (PTRC) Program (USPTO) for his guidance on resources on the history of the patents. For general information on patents in this period see: John L. Kingsley and Joseph P. Pirsson, 'Practice in Procuring Patents in United States', in *Laws And Practice of All Nations And Governments Relating to Patents for Inventions: with Tables of Fees and Forms. Also, an Editorial Introduction, With Explanations of Practice And Proceedings Used In Procuring Patents Throughout the World* (New York: Kingsley and Pirsson, 1848), pp. 51–64; United States Patent Office, 'Rules and Directions for Proceedings in the Patent Office', in *Rules of Practice In Patent Cases*, 1867, https://babel.hathitrust.org/cgi/pt?id=mdp.35112103497923&view=1up&seq=15; Thomas B. Hudson, 'A Brief History of the Development of Design Patent Protection in the United States', *Journal of the Patent Office Society*, 30:5 (1948), 380–99, https://www.ipmall.info/sites/default/files/hosted_resources/DesignPatentAct/Articles/30%20JPTOS%20380.pdf.

offices, and US consulate offices abroad. Application fees and the term of the patent changed to some degree, with a benchmark established in 1861 that included options to protect a design for three-and-half ($10), seven ($15), or fourteen years ($30).[8]

This essay focuses on case studies to show how select sculptors used the design patent to protect their work and advance their careers. In addition to Powers, key artists addressed in this essay include John King, Thomas Ball, John Rogers, Dayton Morgan, Leonard Volk, and Clark Mills, each of whom benefited from the patent in various ways and degrees. This essay also considers the implications of patenting a likeness of a sitter who does not typically profit from the commodification of his portrait, a point that is all the more urgent in the case of the self-emancipated Frederick Douglass, who took extreme care to control the replication and diffusion of his portrait.

Hiram Powers

With so many patents assigned to sculptors, one wonders why Powers's attempt to patent *The Greek Slave* failed, especially as this work was fast becoming the best-known American sculpture of the nineteenth century.[9] His application may have been doomed from the start, since the US Patent Act of 1836 prohibited patenting anything that had been 'on sale with the applicant's consent', and Powers had already sold several replicas of *The Greek Slave* between 1844 and 1849, by the time he applied to patent this design.[10] Powers may have also misunderstood the protections a patent was meant to offer. His primary intention may have been to prevent the replication of *The Greek Slave* altogether. Had he succeeded in obtaining a patent, it is unlikely that he would have ever agreed to license reproduction of *The Greek Slave* to anyone else, at any price. Yet the design patent was most useful as a tool for authorizing

---

8 Hudson, 384; *Rules of Practice In Patent Cases*, 1867, 25.

9 Powers's correspondence attests that he contemplated and may have applied to patent his sculpture *The Fisher Boy*, 'Patent Documents, Hiram Powers Papers, 1819-1953, Bulk 1835-1883. Archives of American Art, Smithsonian Institution', https://www.aaa.si.edu/collections/hiram-powers-papers-7255/series-4/box-10-folder-47.

10 I am grateful to D. Lawrence Tarazano of the USPTO for bringing this to my attention. *United States Patent Act, Ch. 357, 5 Stat. 117* (1836), https://patentlyo.com/media/docs/2008/03/Patent_Act_of_1836.pdf.

reproductions. Powers appreciated the concept of licensing when applied to his designs for vices, rasps, and other tools, for which he successfully secured utility patents in order 'to enable others skilled in the arts to make and use my invention'.[11] When it came to his sculptures, however, Powers could hardly imagine entrusting the execution of his designs to anyone outside his studio, much less a manufacturer. The translation of his design into marble required considerable labor, which he conscientiously confined to his studio where he directly supervised production, paying a premium to carvers who pledged to work exclusively for him.[12] In the case of *The Greek Slave*, he was not trying to issue a large edition, but rather protect a handful of exquisite life-sized marble replicas.[13]

Significantly, Powers's failed patent application specified 'a statue of a 'Greek Slave' in marble', suggesting his primary objective was to protect his finished work, rather than its design. Powers may have unwittingly condemned his application by specifying marble as the medium.[14] By contrast, most other applicants suggested a range of possible materials for those who intended to reproduce the design, stating that it might for example 'be made of metal, papier-maché, plaster, or other suitable material, painted, stained, bronzed, or colored, as may be desired'.[15]

11 'Patent Documents, Hiram Powers Papers, 1819-1953, Bulk 1835-1883. Archives of American Art, Smithsonian Institution', https://www.aaa.si.edu/collections/hiram-powers-papers-7255/series-4/box-10-folder-47; Hiram Powers, 'Utility Patent for File and Rasp, Patent No. 10088', 1853, http://patft.uspto.gov/netacgi/nph-Parser?patentnumber=10088; Hiram Powers, 'Utility Patent for Metal Punch, Patent No. 31476', 1861, http://patft.uspto.gov/netacgi/nph-Parser?patentnumber=31476.

12 By contrast, other sculptors in Florence sent their clay or plaster models to carving shops for replication, or hired carvers as needed, sharing the skilled artisan's time with other sculptors.

13 Powers ultimately produced just six examples, each one a singular masterpiece personalized to the tastes and demands of the individual patron who commissioned its translation into stone. For details on these marble examples see Karen Lemmey, 'From Skeleton to Skin: The Making of the *Greek Slave*(s)', *Nineteenth-Century Art Worldwide*, 15:2 (2016), http://www.19thc-artworldwide.org/summer16/lemmey-on-from-skeleton-to-skin-the-making-of-the-greek-slave.

14 It follows that Powers did not pursue patents for works that he sold in large plaster editions, for example his busts of *The Greek Slave* or *Proserpine*. See Richard P. Wunder, *Hiram Powers: Vermont Sculptor, 1805-1873* (Newark: University of Delaware Press, 1991), ii, pp. 187–204 and 168–177.

15 Otto Kornemann and Julius Jungbluth, 'Design Patent for a Statuette, Design Patent No. 3517', 1869, http://patft.uspto.gov/netacgi/nph-Parser?patentnumber=D3517.

Indeed, the great expense and specialized skill required to replicate a life-sized sculpture in marble inherently made it an unlikely material for counterfeiters.[16] It follows that the majority of unauthorized copies of *The Greek Slave* were plaster or Parian ware, materials that were far cheaper than marble and could be used to quickly churn out large editions. In 1851, soon after Powers's failed patent petition, the first marble example of *The Greek Slave* became the gateway for illicit copies. Powers's patron Captain John Grant, who had purchased this sculpture in 1844, allowed plaster artisan Domenico Brucciani to make a mold of the sculpture. Brucciani, in turn, cast a life-sized plaster replica and collaborated with prominent Parian ware producer William T. Copeland of Sheffield, England, to create reductions of the sculpture, much to Powers's vexation.[17]

Only a handful of American art patrons could afford to tour Europe and commission works in marble from artists like Powers. At midcentury, Americans were just beginning to cultivate a taste for sculpture, and most aspiring patrons in the United States were satisfied purchasing finished plasters—a medium that prevailed until the mid-1850s due to the absence of bronze foundries and lack of locally sourced statuary marble. The low cost of plaster, and the ease with which it could be faithfully copied, prompted professional sculptors to sell their finished work in larger editions than if they had been working in bronze or marble. Yet these circumstances made it relatively easy for counterfeiters to release illicit plaster casts into the market, and most consumers were not able to distinguish between the authentic plasters and their knock-offs. Thus, the protections offered under the new patent law of 1842 particularly appealed to sculptors who primarily used plaster as the medium for their finished works.

---

16 Significantly, other sculptors who worked in marble did not typically patent their work, even those who issued large editions. For example, Randolph Rogers, who served as a witness on Powers's patent application for *The Greek Slave*, did not patent his compositions, notwithstanding *Nydia*, of which he issued more than 168 marble replicas.

17 For a detailed account of this this event see chapter 'Brucciani's *Greek Slave* and the International Exhibition of 1862' (pp. 48-54) in Rebecca Wade, *Domenico Brucciani and the Formatori of Nineteenth-Century Britain* (London: Bloomsbury Visual Arts, 2019).

John King and Thomas Ball

One of the first American sculptors to patent his work was John Crookshanks King, a Scottish immigrant who was largely self-taught. King received a patent for his portrait bust of Daniel Webster (see Figure 2) in September 1850.[18]

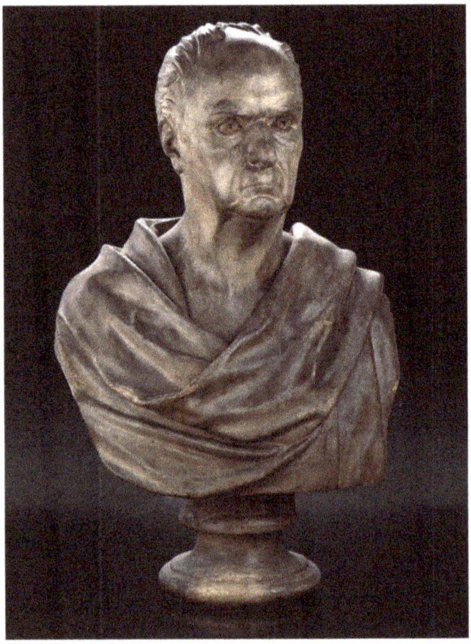

Fig. 2 John Crookshanks King, *Daniel Webster* (patented 1850), plaster, Smithsonian American Art Museum, Washington, D.C.

The Boston-based sculptor inscribed the work 'MODELLED AT WASHINGTON (MARCH) 1850', suggesting that his effort to travel to the capital to directly observe the New England statesman added to the portrait's authenticity. Significantly, during the artist's visit to Washington D.C., he may have also been introduced to officials who could have helped him with the application. (Up to this point, since the passing of the 1842 law only two other patents had been issued to sculptors, in New Orleans and Philadelphia, suggesting that most sculptors were unfamiliar with the process of filing a petition for a

18 John C. King, 'Design Patent for Bust of Daniel Webster, Design Patent No. 313', 1850, http://patft.uspto.gov/netacgi/nph-Parser?patentnumber=D313.

patent). After the beloved statesman's death in October 1852, King sold numerous life-size plaster casts, which were usually cast with the inscription 'Patented 1850,' suggesting this novel government-issued protection may have made the portrait seem more official.[19] In June 1853, King arranged to edition smaller replicas of the bust in porcelain through Copeland's factory in England, perhaps emboldened to send his work to an industrial manufacturer in a foreign country because he had secured a US patent for his design.[20]

King's experience with patents likely influenced his protégé Thomas Ball to protect his own models. Ball was an up-and-coming painter specialized in miniature portraits in Boston in the late 1840s, when King suggested he try sculpting.[21] Ball completed his first sculpture in 1851, a portrait of the popular singer Jenny Lind. It was an instant success, and Ball quickly established a market for plaster copies of his works. However, his progress was immediately threatened by piracy as he recounted, 'for a time I could not produce the plaster copies fast enough to supply the demand [...] But soon an Italian pirate in New York got possession of one of them...flooding the market at starvation prices'.[22] Ball patented his bust of Lind in April 1852, lamenting how the application process entailed many supporting documents, 'almost as many as would be required to patent a steam-engine'.[23] He subsequently patented several other compositions in the 1850s, but it is unclear if these patents successfully discouraged counterfeiters, a reminder that the patent was not self-enforcing and less effective if the holder was unwilling to take legal action against his imitators.[24]

19 Wayne Craven, *Sculpture in America* (New York: Cornwall Books, 1984), p. 192. King also made at least two examples of the bust in marble, one located in Faneuil Hall, Boston. For examples in plaster see Hood Museum, https://hoodmuseum.dartmouth.edu/objects/s.939.22; Boston Athenaeum, https://cdm.bostonathenaeum.org/digital/collection/p16057coll35/id/34; and SAAM, https://americanart.si.edu/artwork/daniel-webster-13747.

20 The porcelain version measures approximately 17 x 12 x 8 inches (see example in the New Hampshire Historical Society, https://www.nhhistory.org/object/137355/bust) and is a reduction of the plaster examples that measure 25 x 19 x 14 inches.

21 Craven, p. 191.

22 Thomas Ball, *My Threescore Years and Ten: An Autobiography* (Boston: Roberts, 1892), p. 130.

23 Ball, *My Threescore Years and Ten*, p. 130.

24 Thomas Ball, 'Design Patent for Bust of Jenny Lind, Design Patent No. 369', 1851, http://patft.uspto.gov/netacgi/nph-Parser?patentnumber=D369; Thomas Ball, 'Design Patent for Bust of Napoleon Bonaparte, Design Patent No. 894', 1857,

Ball's piercing encounter with plaster pirates likely motivated him to reevaluate his studio practice. In a short time, he stepped out of the plaster business altogether, and the D11 patent gave him the means to do so. In 1853, Ball's plaster statuette of Daniel Webster (Figure 3) caught the eye of George Ward Nichols, a young artist and burgeoning entrepreneur who purchased the sculpture along with the rights to reproduce it.[25]

Ball used his patent, dated 9 August 1853, to complete this transaction by listing Nichols as the assignee. Nichols paid Ball $500, a considerable sum that afforded the sculptor the opportunity to move to Florence, Italy, where he would refine his skills, develop an international clientele, and increasingly work in marble. Ball arrived in Italy with his wife in October 1854, setting his career on a new path. He patented one more design on his own in 1857, a bust of Napoleon Bonaparte, but only a single, marble example of this composition is known, suggesting the artist found it more efficient to leave replication and marketing concerns to Nichols.[26]

Through Nichols's skillful marketing, sales of the Webster statuette soared along with Ball's reputation. Between 1858 and 1865, during which time Ball was in Boston, he no longer relied on the marginal profits gained through the sales of plaster casts and turned his attention instead to a commission for a monumental equestrian bronze sculpture for the Boston Public Garden.[27] Indeed, in 1858 when Ball patented his

---

http://patft.uspto.gov/netacgi/nph-Parser?patentnumber=D894; Thomas Ball, 'Design Patent for Bust of Daniel Webster, Design Patent No. 548', 1853, http://patft.uspto.gov/netacgi/nph-Parser?patentnumber=D548; Thomas Ball, 'Design Patent for Statuette of Daniel Webster, Design Patent No. 590', 1853, http://patft.uspto.gov/netacgi/nph-Parser?patentnumber=D590]; Thomas Ball, 'Design Patent for Statuette of Henry Clay, Design Patent No. 1060', 1858, http://patft.uspto.gov/netacgi/nph-Parser?patentnumber=D1060.

25 For a thorough history and analysis of Ball's relationship with Nichols see, Ann Boulton, 'The Dealer and Daniel Webster', *Gilcrease Journal*, 20:1 (2013), 46–63 (p. 54).

26 An example of this appeared at Christie's in London on 19 October 2005, sale 7109, lot 11. Thomas Ball, *Bust of Napoleon*, 1856, https://www.christies.com/lotfinder/Lot/napoleon-i-1769-1821-an-4587488-details.aspx.

27 A stereograph of the interior of the shop of James S. Earle & Son in Philadelphia prominently displays plaster casts of Ball's statuettes of Clay and Webster. For more on Earle's business practice see Erika Piola's essay in this anthology. John Moran, photographer, [*James S. Earle & Son, Looking Glasses, 816 Chestnut Street, Philadelphia.*], ca. 1861, Library Company of Philadelphia, https://digital.librarycompany.org/islandora/object/digitool%3A100622.

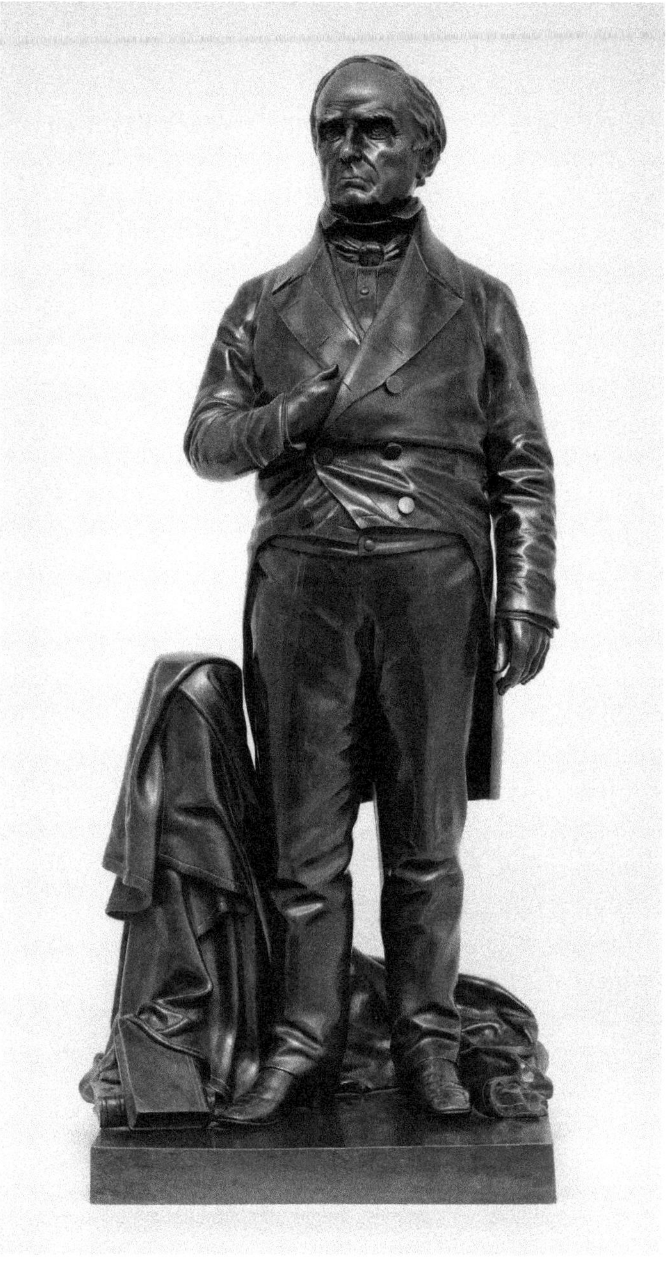

Fig. 3 Thomas Ball, *Daniel Webster* (1853), bronze, The Metropolitan Museum of Art, New York.

statuette of Henry Clay, his last statue to receive a patent, he again listed Nichols as the assignee.

Nichols was empowered to replicate Ball's designs as he saw fit. Without needing to further consult Ball, Nichols single-handedly made decisions about the scale and medium, as well as the size of the editions. Nichols even took the liberty to change the compositions, eliminating the draped column on some editions of the statuettes of Clay and Webster, which had been itemized as a separate element in their respective patents, in an effort to reduce production costs for these simplified versions and to create a tiered market for the sculptures. It seems that 'the final expression of [Ball's] idea was not a necessary aspect of the sculptor's task'; rather, it was the design concept that mattered most.[28] When Ball reflected on the transaction for the Webster statuette years later he conceded, perhaps with some regret, that Nichols was a 'shrewd art dealer [...] who must have made five thousand dollars out of it [...] I could not have done it', fully crediting Nichols with the execution, marketing, and success of the sculpture.[29]

Nichols's large editions of Ball's statuettes in plaster and Parian ware were a popular novelty, but he launched a new chapter in the history of American sculpture by deciding to cast hundreds of the statuettes in bronze at the Ames Manufacturing Company in Chicopee, Massachusetts, making these the first mass-produced American bronze sculptures (see Figure 4). Ames was primarily a firearms foundry that had opened a special division for casting art in the early 1850s, through the sustained encouragement of sculptor Henry Kirke Brown.[30] Ames became the first bronze foundry in the United States to reliably cast art bronzes. Earlier generations of American sculptors were forced to send their models to European foundries, or settle with inferior casts that were riddled with casting flaws. Nichols perceptively recognized Ames's unique capacity to execute large editions of high-quality bronze

28 Michele Helene Bogart, 'Attitudes toward Sculpture Reproductions in America, 1850-1880' (unpublished doctoral dissertation, University of Chicago, 1979), p. 157.

29 Ball, *My Threescore Years and Ten*, p. 142.

30 For Henry Kirke Brown's involvement with Ames see Michael Edward Shapiro, *Bronze Casting and American Sculpture: 1850–1900* (Cranbury, NJ: Associated University Presses, Inc., 1985), pp. 34–60; Karen Yvonne Lemmey, 'Henry Kirke Brown and the Development of American Public Sculpture in New York City, 1846-1876' (unpublished doctoral dissertation, The City University of New York, 2005), pp. 126–134.

casts. The foundry's business records show it cast at least 200 statuettes of Webster, each inscribed with Nichols's name alongside that of the artist. Nichols issued casts in several sizes between 36 and 76 inches high, with or without drapery, and with an 'ordinary' or 'fine' finish, so they could be variously priced to reach a range of consumers.[31]

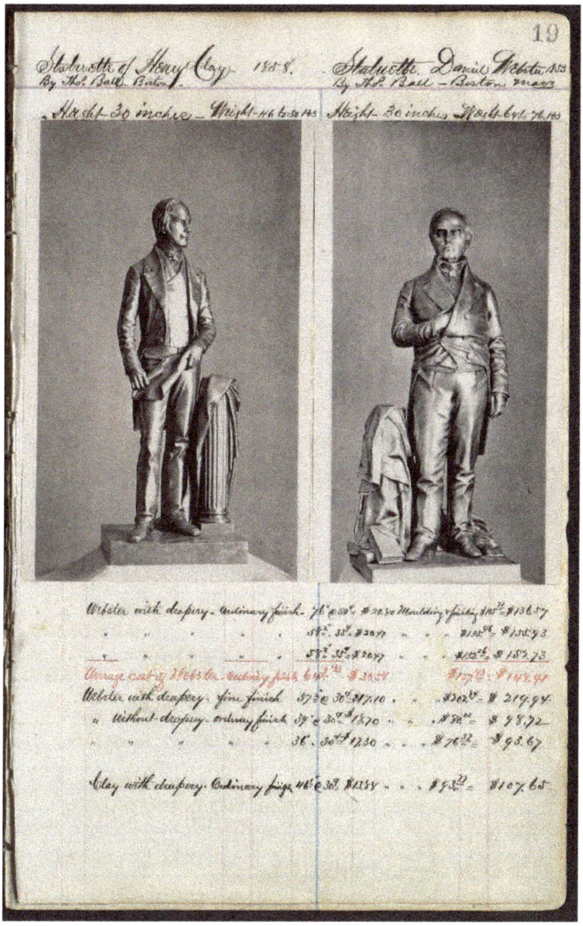

Fig. 4 Bronze Casting Record (Henry Clay and Daniel Webster), Ames Manufacturing Company, Bronze Foundry after Thomas Ball (1853–ca. 1877), Archives of American Art, Washington, D.C.

31 The associated costs of production ranged from $93 to $219, 'Bronze Casting Records, 1853-ca. 1877, from the Stearns-Ames Collection, [ca. 1838–1894]', p. 17, Archives of American Art, https://www.aaa.si.edu/collections/items/detail/bronze-casting-records-16695.

Despite the critical importance of patents early in his career, Ball did not patent any other work after assigning the statuette of Henry Clay to Nichols in 1858. Significantly, the bulk of Ball's small-scale sculpture after this period was made in marble or limited editions of bronze. For Ball, the design patent proved an important means through which the artist could formally separate design from production, a contractual agreement that allowed him to monetize the creative aspect of his practice by selling production rights to an assignee.

John Rogers

A third sculptor from Boston, John Rogers, made exceptional use of the D11. Between 1862 and 1888, he secured 63 patents for his sculptures — approximately eight percent of the total number of patents issued for sculptures in the nineteenth century, far more than any other sculptor.

His body of patents is useful for charting changes in how artists presented their designs. For example, after about 1862, Rogers began replacing simple line drawings of his designs (see Figure 5) with photographs of his models, and around 1866 he switched from handwritten submittals to typed applications.

For nearly four decades, Rogers flourished as an artist of the people, selling tens of thousands of Rogers Groups (as his works were known) and generally issuing two new groups each year.[32] He targeted his art to an expanding market of middle-class consumers by making affordable, small-scale, plaster compositions depicting a range of accessible themes, from humorous vignettes of young courtship, to more politicized scenes of military troops in camp or advancing the Union cause. Rogers's consistent choices about the scale, medium, and marketing of his artworks led to a highly standardized production process that made the design patent especially important to his practice.

Rogers was born to a prominent Boston family that had fallen into financial difficulty, and as a consequence he received a limited formal education. While working as a machinist in 1849, he began filling his leisure time modelling clay figures inspired by the work of Scottish genre painter Sir David Wilkie. In 1859, Rogers traveled to Europe to

32 New-York Historical Society, 'John Rogers: American Stories', 2010, http://www.johnrogers-history.org/artist/index.html.

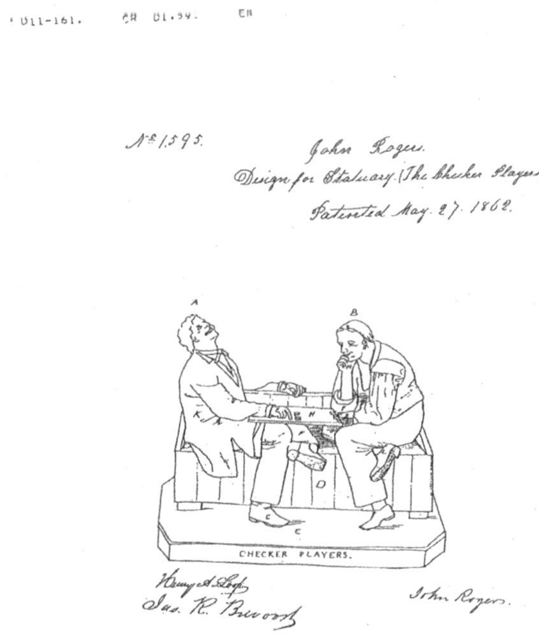

Fig. 5 John Rogers, line drawing accompanying application for 'Design for Statuary (*The Checker Players*)', 1862, United States Patent and Trademark Office, Washington, D.C.

pursue more formal training in the arts, studying in Paris with Antoine-Laurent Dantan, and in Rome with the English sculptor Benjamin Edward Spence. Rogers soon realized he was uninterested in both the prevailing neoclassical aesthetic and quintessential medium of Carrara marble, both of which had enchanted Powers, Ball, and other expatriate artists in Italy. He returned to the United States after just seven months abroad, eager to create small-scale genre scenes in plaster, his medium of choice.[33]

As Rogers's career advanced, he employed numerous specialized laborers to focus on each of the steps required to produce a Rogers Group. The artist began each new composition in clay, which was then molded and cast in plaster as needed to fulfill orders. The cast was finely

33 For details of Rogers's early career and his formative decision to reject Neoclassicism see Kimberly Orcutt, 'Neoclassicism and the Artist's Ideal', in *John Rogers: American Stories*, ed. by Kimberly Orcutt et al. (New York: New-York Historical Society, 2010), pp. 41–57.

finished to remove mold seams, and dipped in specially formulated coatings that protected the surface and gave it the color of terracotta, a material more closely associated with fine art.[34] At the height of his career in the 1870s, Rogers's studio in New York was a well-run factory buzzing with sixty assistants. Early on, however, he had neither the skills nor the means to oversee this multi-step production, and necessarily relied on professional plaster casters. These were mainly Italian immigrants, whom he regarded with wariness. Fearing they would steal his designs, he bluntly proclaimed 'I believe all these Italian casters are thieves and rascals'.[35] In fact, these highly skilled *formatori* (mold-makers) had carried the centuries-old craft from Italy, where they likely apprenticed at a young age in preparation for their essential role in the marble statuary industry. As immigrants to the United States, they were often characterized as mere street peddlers who sold cheap casts, such as the one Ball described selling illicit copies of his bust of Jenny Lind. Rogers demeaned them, but he needed their valuable knowledge of their métier. This was a point made plain by Rogers's conniving plan to advertise for a workman. 'I may find one that I can employ but my main object is to pump them all day when they apply and find out all they know –Mean trick, isn't it?'[36]

Rogers's business plan required that he sell many multiples to turn a profit, which meant tapping every available market. To reach more clients, he often sold his work through local shops in Chicago, Philadelphia, Boston, and other northern cities where his vignettes of Union troops, such as *The Pickett Guard*, *Camp Life*, and *Wounded to the Rear* (see Figure 6), held the greatest appeal.

Early in his career, in the late 1850s and early 1860s, Rogers arranged to have his works cast close to the point of sale to minimize breakage of works when shipping them from his New York studio. This meant trusting his models to plaster casters in other cities. For example, he arranged for his Boston retailer Williams and Everett to cast his models

34 Thayer Tolles, 'A Union of Art and Industry: How Rogers Groups Were Made', in Orcutt et al, pp. 135–152.

35 John Rogers to SEDR, New York, 1 December 1861, 'Rogers Family Papers, 1719-1955', New-York Historical Society Library, Manuscript Collection. All subsequent letters cited for Rogers may be found in this collection.

36 Bogart, p. 157.

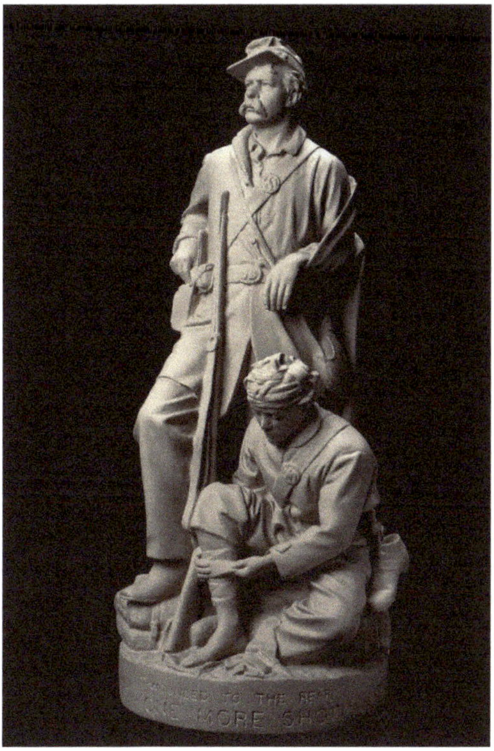

Fig. 6 John Rogers, *Wounded to the Rear, One More Shot* (1864), painted plaster, Smithsonian American Art Museum, Washington, D.C.

with a local caster named Gariboldi.[37] The need to 'trust to [the] honor' of both his retailer and craftsman irritated Rogers to no end. He was especially concerned about Gariboldi's 'Italian friends getting hold of the models'.[38] Writing from New York in 1861, he asked his father in Boston to check on the replication process, and the following year, he

37 Rogers is likely referring to Pietro Gariboldi, who is listed as a statuary manufacturer in the 1855 Boston City Directory. George Adams, *The Boston Directory. Embracing the City Record, a General Directory of the Citizens, and a Special Directory of Trades, Professions, &c.*, 1855 digitized version at Tufts Digital Library, https://bcd.lib.tufts.edu/view_text.jsp?urn=tufts:central:dca:UA069:UA069.005.DO.00002&chapter=d.1855.su.Gariboldi.

38 Rogers also notes that Gariboldi charges $2 per cast. By contrast, it costs the artist $1.25 to cast them. John Rogers to Sarah Ellen Derby Rogers, 10 November 1861, New-York Historical Society.

pleaded with his father to check again 'whether the "original" that Gariboldi [had] been destroyed'.[39]

During this time, Rogers constantly weighed the cost benefits of patenting his models. As early as 1856, he expressed interest in patents, asking his father to contact fellow Bostonian Thomas Ball for guidance on the application process as he wondered how 'a patent is managed at Washington, whether the commissioners decide for themselves or whether lawyers are employed like a case in court'.[40] His eagerness to patent his work was tempered by limited means to pay the application fees, and he deliberated over which composition to protect first. In January 1860, Rogers wrote of his intention to patent his group *The Slave Auction*, 'so as to present it being copied [and] to enable me to sell the right in other places'.[41] Rogers hoped to reach new clients in Boston's vibrant abolitionist community by making 'some bargain with [Nathan Davies] Cotton', whose art supply store on Boston's Tremont Row had been known for selling J. C. King and Ball's plaster sculptures in the 1840s and 50s.[42]

Rogers yearned for Cotton to 'either exhibit [*The Slave Auction*] and take orders on commission or to buy the rights and [cast the plasters] in Boston. In the latter case I should have to get a patent right to secure him and there is so much risk and trouble in transporting them that I prefer the latter course'.[43] Rogers ultimately decided not to patent *The Slave Auction*, once he realized that its emphatically abolitionist message would attract a limited number of customers. He instead targeted direct sales in New York neighborhoods that were known for their abolitionist sympathies, and decided 'to send a negro round' with the casts as a way of bringing to life and exploiting the composition's tragic narrative.[44]

---

39 [1862? Undated, possibly misfiled as 1861] John Rogers to Sarah Ellen Derby Rogers, 15 June 1861, New-York Historical Society.

40 It is unclear whether Ball ever responded to Roger's plea for his counsel. JR to [father], Hannibal, 3 November 1856; JR to [Mother], Chicago, 29 October; JR to [mother] Chicago, 5 November 1859, Rogers Family Papers, 1719-1955.

41 JR to Mary Jane Derby Peabody [aunt], New York, 19 January 1860, Rogers Family Papers, 1719-1955.

42 For example, this broadside showing Cotton and King jointly advertising King's work, John Crookshanks King and Nathan Davies Cotton, *A Bust of Dr. Samuel B. Woodward, Which Has Just Been Finished by John C. King, to Be Placed in the State Asylum at Worcester ... Is Now on Exhibition for a Few Days, at the Store of N.D. Cotton, No. 13 Tremont Row* (Boston: s.n., 1847).

43 JR to Mary Jane Derby Peabody [aunt], New York, 19 January 1860, Rogers Family Papers, 1719-1955.

44 JR to MJDP, New York, 31 January 1860, Rogers Family Papers, 1719-1955.

As his business grew, Rogers increasingly took measures to protect his designs. In 1861, he moved to a more spacious studio in the Dodsworth Building, where he was surrounded by accomplished artists. He employed more hands in order to keep the casting process in his New York studio, and ceased sending models to plaster casters in other cities. His improved packing and crating methods allowed him to sell Rogers Groups directly through mail-order catalogues, shipping them to 'all parts of the World'.[45] A year later, he began patenting his designs, obtaining six patents over the span of a few weeks in the spring of 1862.[46] He grumbled about how the application fees were 'quite a drain on my stock of cash', but admitted that securing these documents was 'the only way I can feel safe'.[47]

Rogers's commitment to patenting his work marked a professional milestone that signaled a new phase in his career. Fellow sculptors John Quincy Adams Ward, whose studio was also in the Dodsworth building, and Charles Calverley signed as witnesses on these first applications, testifying to the originality of Rogers's designs. Ward worked primarily in bronze and Calverley in marble, and neither of them patented any works of their own; yet their service as witnesses underscores the professional respect Rogers earned from his fellow artists. From this point on, the design patent became a crucial part of Rogers's business plan, especially as he widened the roster of retailers around the nation beyond art stores, bookstores, jewelry shops, and other points of sale.[48]

For all its benefits, the design patent offered incomplete protection. It did not shield Rogers's groups against unauthorized photographic

45 Quoted from Kimberly Orcutt, 'Selling the John Rogers Brand,' in Orcutt et al., p. 160.

46 John Rogers, 'Design Patent for Statuary: The Camp Fire, Design Patent No. 1597', 1862, http://patft.uspto.gov/netacgi/nph-Parser?patentnumber=D1597; John Rogers, 'Design Patent for Statuary: The Checker Players, Design Patent No. 1595', 1862, http://patft.uspto.gov/netacgi/nph-Parser?patentnumber=D1595; John Rogers, 'Design Patent for Statuary: The Town Pump, Design Patent No. 1598', 1862, http://patft.uspto.gov/netacgi/nph-Parser?patentnumber=D1598; John Rogers, 'Design Patent for Statuary: The Village Schoolmaster, Design Patent No. 1596', 1862, http://patft.uspto.gov/netacgi/nph-Parser?patentnumber=D1596; John Rogers, 'Design Patent for Statuette Group of the Camp Life, Design Patent No. 1559', 1862, http://patft.uspto.gov/netacgi/nph-Parser?patentnumber=D1559; John Rogers, 'Design Patent for Statuette Group of the Picket Guard, Design Patent No. 1558', 1862, http://patft.uspto.gov/netacgi/nph-Parser?patentnumber=D1558.

47 John Rogers to Sarah Ellen Derby Rogers, 28 April 1862, New-York Historical Society.

48 Kimberly Orcutt, 'Selling the Rogers Brand', in Orcutt et al., pp. 159–160.

or other printed reproductions. As Kimberly Orcutt has noted, Rogers struggled 'to maintain control over the commercial proliferation of his images', leading the artist to inscribe a warning on the base of some of his patented sculptures, reading 'The right to photograph this group is not sold with it'.[49] Ironically, Rogers took full advantage of advances in photography and print culture to advertise his works in catalogues and periodicals, and increasingly relied on portrait photography to serve as references for his groups representing statesmen and their advisors. This included *Council of War*, which shows Abraham Lincoln with Secretary of War Edwin M. Stanton and Ulysses S. General Grant.[50]

With few exceptions, Rogers Groups depicted stock characters and generic figures who typified specific roles or groups of people, but there were many sculptors who sought patents for their work in portraiture: a category of art that presents distinctive questions, as patenting the likeness of another human is fundamentally different than patenting a character type or idealized, allegorical figure. It prompts us to consider the following questions: what legal claim could an artist expect to have over reproductions of another person's face; furthermore, did the sitter have any authority over the authenticity or proliferation of his portrait; finally, how much should an artist profit from another person's likeness?

Elected officials such as Daniel Webster could reasonably assume artists might patent and market their portraits for public consumption. But what of private citizens who achieved celebrity? What control might they effectively assert over their portraits, especially as sculptors increasingly relied on photographs to create portraits from a distance, without the intimate contact with subjects that happened when modelling a person from life?

Dayton Morgan

These concepts of consent and control are most poignant when considering Dayton Morgan's patented bust of Frederick Douglass, a man who risked his life to self-emancipate in 1838. Douglass believed positive visual representations had the power to change majority opinions

49 See illustration of *Challenging the Union Vote* (patented 1869) in Michael Leja, 'Sculpture for a Mass Market', in Orcutt et al., p. 23; Orcutt et al., p. 164.

50 Orcutt, 'Selling the Rogers Brand' in Orcutt et al., p. 164.

about the nation's Black population. He recognized that 'photographic portraits bore witness to African Americans' essential humanity, while also countering the racist caricatures that proliferated throughout the North'.[51] Throughout his life, Douglass took care to ensure he was represented accurately and with dignity; his 'likeness embodied his cause of racial equality'.[52] There is no documentation to suggest that Morgan ever asked Douglass to sit for a portrait bust, and it seems unlikely the orator would have accepted such an invitation as he was skeptical of depictions that were not photographic, observing, 'Negroes can never have impartial portraits at the hands of white artists...It seems to us next to impossible for white men to take likenesses of black men, without most grossly exaggerating their distinctive features'.[53]

Morgan probably relied on one or several photographs made between 1864, when Douglass shaved his beard in favor of a handlebar mustache, and August 1868, when the sculptor patented the bust.[54] The bust evidently met the approval of Douglass's son Charles R. Douglass, who wrote to his father on 9 June 1868, 'I am proud to see you honored in the way the Cincinnati people have inaugurated, and I predict that in other localities the same steps will be taken to show the people's appreciation of you and your service in the cause of the oppressed'.[55] Since this letter predates Morgan's patent, it is unclear whether the Douglass family was aware of the artist's intentions to commodify reproductions of this bust. In these early dates of Reconstruction, Douglass was a legendary figure who was well on his way to becoming 'the most photographed American in the nineteenth century'. By the time Douglass died in 1895, he had posed for at least 168 photographs, prompting the *Chicago Tribune* to write, 'No man, white or black, has been better known for nearly half a

51 John Stauffer et al., *Picturing Frederick Douglass: An Illustrated Biography of the Nineteenth Century's Most Photographed American* (New York: Liveright Publishing Corporation, 2015), p. xiii.

52 Ibid., p. xv.

53 Ibid., p. xvii.

54 The catalogue raisonné in Stauffer et al., pp. 171-175, includes Morgan's bust (entry no. 59) and photographs of Douglass from the period in which Morgan made this bust. Dayton Morgan, 'Design for a Bust of Frederick Douglas [sic], Design Patent No. 3151', 1868, http://patft.uspto.gov/netacgi/nph-Parser?patentnumber=D3151.

55 Quoted in Celeste-Marie Bernier, '"To Preserve My Features in Marble": Post-Civil War Paintings, Drawings, Sculpture, and Sketches of Frederick Douglass. An Illustrated Essay', *Callaloo*, 39:2 (2016), 372–399 (p. 380), https://doi.org/10.1353/cal.2016.0042.

century in this country'.[56] Morgan, a relatively obscure artist who hailed from Ohio, clearly hoped to capitalize on Douglass's fame by patenting his bust.[57] By the time he patented his bust of Douglass, his most notable artwork had been a bust of Abraham Lincoln (1861) that was displayed at a bookstore in Washington, D.C. in 1865.[58] Morgan was active in the capital from 1877 to 1891, and likely returned to Ohio afterwards, as records show he was buried there in 1914.[59] Morgan's bust of Douglass was one of only two sculptures made of the orator during his lifetime,[60] yet only one example has come to light. This suggests that the edition was very small, and in turn prompts us to wonder whether Morgan ever profited from patenting the sculpture.[61]

A good portrait is expected to capture more than the line and form of its subject's face; it should express the essence of a sitter's character. Nevertheless, the primary criterion for judging a portrait's success in the nineteenth century was its faithful likeness. To achieve maximum verisimilitude, many sculptors relied on life and death masks that were made from molds cast directly from a subject's face, an artefact that promised an indexical record of one's visage. A sculpted portrait that was based on a mask was, arguably, as much the product of the sitter as the artist, since the sitter necessarily participated in its making. Patents, however, were granted solely to the sculptor, regardless of how much or how little artistry went into producing the portrait in question.

56 Stauffer et al., p. ix.

57 The article also notes Morgan was working at the marble firm of 'Messrs Brownell' and had exhibited marble, plaster, and clay sculptures at the local fair, 'Ross County Fair, 1860', *The Scioto Gazette* (Chillicothe, Ohio), 19 October 1860, 43 edition.

58 It was shown at Hudson and Taylor bookstore on Pennsylvania Avenue, 'City News', *Daily National Intelligencer* (Washington, DC), 22 September 1865, 16, 566 edition.

59 *Who Was Who in American Art, 1564-1975: 400 Years of Artists in America*, ed. by Peter H. Falk, Georgia Kuchen, and Veronika Roessler, 3 vols (Madison, CT: Sound View Press, 1999), II, p. 2328; The artist's grave is in Toledo, Ohio 'Dayton Morgan (1836-1914) - Find A Grave Memorial', https://www.findagrave.com/memorial/132323233/dayton-morgan.

60 The other portrait bust was sculpted by Johnson M. Mundy in the 1870s. See Stauffer et al., p. 74.

61 An example in plaster was sold at Swann Auction, New York, sale 2342, lot 47, 27 March 2014, Dayton Morgan, *Frederick Douglass*, 1868, https://www.lotsearch.net/lot/slavery-and-abolition-douglass-frederick-frederick-douglass-41770160?perPage=50&page=6.

Leonard Volk

Leonard Volk's statuette of statesman Stephen A. Douglas introduces an unusual degree of agency on the part of the sitter, since the latter served as a witness to the sculptor's patent application. The senator from Illinois was related to the sculptor through marriage and supported his work in numerous ways, even sponsoring Volk's studies in Europe.[62] Volk completed a life-size marble statue of Douglas in 1859, a commission from former Illinois governor Joel Matteson. The large sculpture was used as a campaigning prop and accompanied Douglas as he canvased the South for votes in the 1860 presidential election.[63] Volk noted, 'I spent most of the winter of 1860 in Washington, publishing a statuette of Senator Douglas', by which he meant securing a patent for his reduction of the life-size marble.[64] Volk received the patent in February 1860, having secured Douglas's signature as one of his witnesses. In this unusual case, the patent document provided a means for the sitter to show his approval of the portrait and endorse its authenticity.

Douglas had introduced Volk to his political opponent Abraham Lincoln in 1858. The sculptor convinced Lincoln to sit for his portrait, an arrangement that was delayed until April 1860, when Lincoln visited the sculptor's studio in Chicago. Volk made a plaster mold of Lincoln's face, regaling him with disparaging anecdotes of how he 'occasionally employed a little black-eyed, black-haired, and dark skinned Italian as a *formatore* in plaster work', to amuse and put his sitter at ease before requiring him to sit immobile as the plaster mask set.[65] Volk subsequently used the mask to create a bust of Lincoln (Figure 7), which he patented in June 1860, after the young statesman had won the nomination as Republican candidate, and before his election as president.[66]

62 On Volk see *American Sculpture in the Metropolitan Museum of Art*, ed. by Thayer Tolles, 2 vols (New York: Metropolitan Museum of Art, 1999), i, pp. 122–124; Craven, pp. 240–242.

63 'Stephen A. Douglas' Missing Finger', *SangamonLink*, 2015, http://sangamoncountyhistory.org/wp/?p=6891; Leonard W. Volk, 'Design Patent for Statuette of Stephen A. Douglas, Design Patent No. 1203', 1860, http://patft.uspto.gov/netacgi/nph-Parser?patentnumber=D1203.

64 Leonard W. Volk, 'The Lincoln Life Mask and How It Was Made', *The Century, Illustrated Monthly Magazine*, November 1881, 223–228 (p. 225).

65 Ibid.

66 Leonard W. Volk, 'Design Patent for Bust of A. Lincoln, Design Patent No. 1250', 1860, http://patft.uspto.gov/netacgi/nph-Parser?patentnumber=D1250.

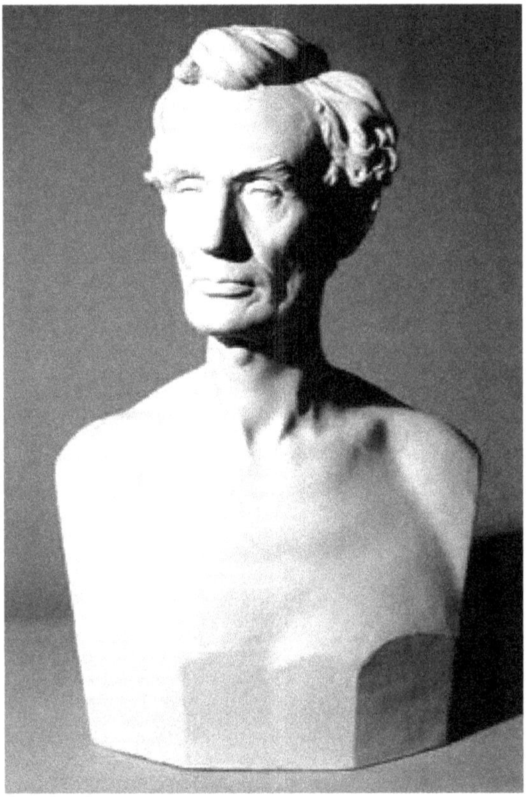

Fig. 7 Leonard Wells Volk, *Abraham Lincoln* (1860), plaster, National Portrait Gallery, Washington, D.C.

Volk was the only sculptor to patent a portrait of Lincoln during the president's lifetime. Almost immediately after Lincoln's death in April 1865, and as the nation mourned, some eleven sculptors secured patents for their portraits of the first American president to be assassinated. Nine of these were issued within a year of Lincoln's death, including one to sculptor Sarah Fisher Ames—one of only two women to obtain a D11 patent in the nineteenth century.[67]

67 The only other design patents issued to a woman in this period were: Celia M. Smith, 'Design Patent for Statuette of Baby, Design Patent No. 22967', 1893, http://patft.uspto.gov/netacgi/nph-Parser?patentnumber=D22867; Celia M. Smith, 'Design Patent for Statuette of Cat, Design Patent No. 21680', 1892, http://patft.uspto.gov/netacgi/nph-Parser?patentnumber=D21680.

Clark Mills

Perhaps the most significant of these sculptural renderings of Lincoln is a life mask made by Clark Mills on 14 February 1865, just two months before the President's death (see Figure 8).

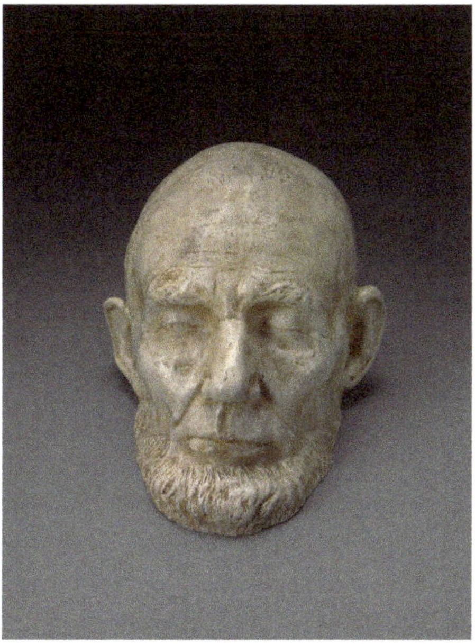

Fig. 8 Clark Mills, *Abraham Lincoln* (cast in 1917 after 1865 original), plaster, National Portrait Gallery, Washington, D.C.

In contrast to the youthful, beardless face shown in Volk's *Lincoln*, Mills captured a grizzled, war-weary commander-in-chief. Fisk Mills, the sculptor's son, secured a patent for his father's work in June 1865, noting that it was

> modeled from a cast taken from the living face [of Lincoln] [...] and differs from all other likenesses as being a perfect facsimile [...] physiologically and phrenologically speaking. The calipers being applicable to the cast for minute exactness of the features and organs.[68]

This description suggests that Mills intended his sculpture as a tool for *other* artists seeking to sculpt monuments to the martyred leader. Indeed,

68 Fisk Mills, 'Design Patent for Bust of A. Lincoln, Design Patent No. 2082', 1865, http://patft.uspto.gov/netacgi/nph-Parser?patentnumber=D2082.

it is improbable that Mills, who used slave labor to run his foundry on Bladensburg Road in the District of Columbia, was motivated to depict Lincoln out of admiration, and it is telling that the Mills family opportunistically patented the mask after Lincoln's death, after realizing there would be a market for memorials.

Clark Mills also patented a design for an equestrian monument: one based on his colossal bronze sculpture of Andrew Jackson (see Figure 9), that was dedicated in Lafayette Park in front of the White House on 8 January 1853.[69]

A largely self-taught artist, Mills had entered the arts through his work as an ornamental plaster craftsman. Through a combination of circumstances and outsized ambition, he won the enviable commission for the Jackson monument in 1847. Equestrian bronze monuments have proven technically challenging for many civilizations, and Washington society enthusiastically celebrated Mill's work as the first equestrian bronze monument to be cast in the United States. Yet while it marked a technological milestone, it was roundly dismissed by other artists and critics for its artlessness. Mills rigged his lifeless figure of Jackson to sit rigidly at a ninety-degree angle on an equally lifeless horse, in order to balance the weight of the bronze entirely on the hind legs of the horse. Mills ignored these critiques and patented his design in May 1855. His application reveals that his priority was neither his portrait of Jackson nor the overall aesthetic of the monument. Instead, he asserted his ingenuity, and the originality of the technical achievement of balancing the horse 'rampant, and so poised as to be supported on its hind legs only, and mounted by a rider [...] the hind legs [...] of the horse are embedded or otherwise secured so as to avoid all other vertical supports which detract from the general effect of the statue'.[70]

In an era when there were only a handful of monuments in the United States, most of them imported from Europe, Mills had good reason to believe his patented design for an equestrian statue might serve other monument campaigns. In essence, he had patented a generic model for a monument. He admitted his design was formulaic, 'The trappings being of a character suited to the design, and the size of the whole

69 Clark Mills, 'Design Patent for an Equestrian Statue or General Andrew Jackson, Design Patent No. 704', 1855, http://patft.uspto.gov/netacgi/nph-Parser?patentnumber=D704.

70 Ibid.

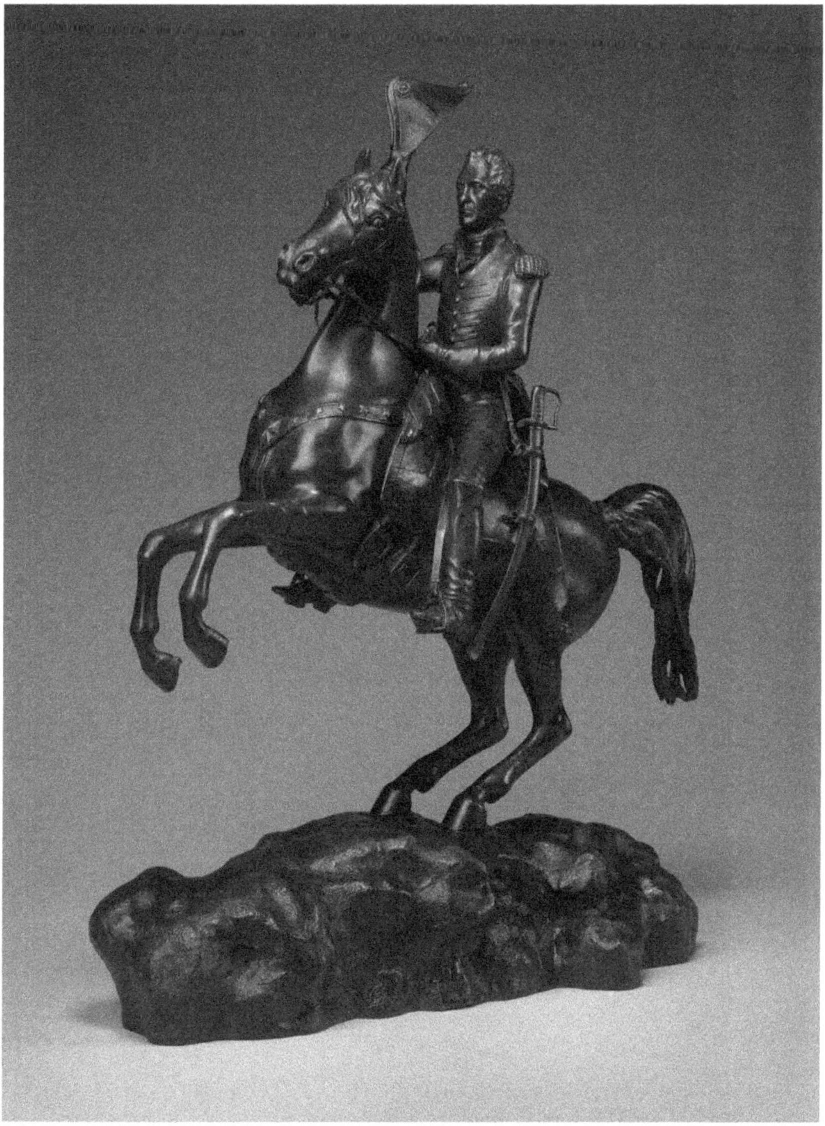

Fig. 9 Cornelius & Baker after Clark Mills, *Andrew Jackson* (1855), bronze, National Portrait Gallery, Washington, D.C.

depending upon the fancy of the maker or user', encouraging others to replace Jackson with their chosen hero and modify the accoutrements as needed.[71]

71 Although Mills patented a design for a general, equestrian monument, statuette replicas after his Andrew Jackson monument were commercially issued in bronze.

After the Civil War, as the country fell into the grip of monument mania, several manufacturing firms, such as J. W. Fiske Ironworks in New York, indiscriminately filled orders for public and private memorials throughout the North and South. Fiske notably patented a generic life-size figure of a 'soldier at rest [...] thus furnishing an ornamental figure for military monuments, grounds, buildings and similar places'.[72] In subsequent decades Fiske patented various other 'stock' figures for a range of commemorative and decorative purposes — from a fireman holding a child to ornamental lions and Newfoundland dogs, which it sold through its catalogue.[73] With few exceptions, the most important monuments of the last quarter of the nineteenth century were not patented, with the notable exclusion of the *Statue of Liberty* — a reminder that US design patents were available to foreign applicants in some instances.[74] The record for patents classified in D11 continued to grow, but the applications tended towards small-scale decorative objects of lesser importance, figurines and statuettes, a number of which document the ubiquity and popularity of racist caricatures in everyday objects, and which equally bear the imprimatur of an official federal patent.[75]

The firm Cornelius & Baker of Philadelphia, for example, issued a cast now in the National Portrait Gallery, Washington, D.C. that is stamped 'PATENTED/MAY 15/1855'. Other casts in lesser metals (such as zinc and 'pot metal' alloys) were also replicated by unknown manufacturers and inexplicably left unmarked, such as this example in the collection of SAAM, https://americanart.si.edu/artwork/general-andrew-jackson-24788.

72 Joseph W. Fiske, 'Design Patent for Statue (Soldier), Design Patent No. 9396', 1876, http://patft.uspto.gov/netacgi/nph-Parser?patentnumber=D9396.

73 J. W. Fiske was listed as assignee on this document: Charles G. Demuth, 'Design Patent for a Statue of a Fireman, Design Patent No. 20426', 1890, http://patft.uspto.gov/netacgi/nph-Parser?patentnumber=D20426; Joseph W. Fiske, 'Design Patent for a Cast, Design Patent No. 8214', 1875, http://patft.uspto.gov/netacgi/nph-Parser?patentnumber=D8214; J. W. Fiske Iron Works, *Illustrated Catalogue of Iron Fountains and Statuary* (Cushing, Bardua & Co., 1875).

74 These patents for the Statue of Liberty suggest the designs could be made in a range of materials, perhaps anticipating the souvenir culture that it would inspire. August Bartholdi, 'Design Patent for a Bust, Design Patent No. 10893', 1878, http://patft.uspto.gov/netacgi/nph-Parser?patentnumber=D10893; August Bartholdi, 'Design Patent for a Statue (Statue of Liberty), Design Patent No. 11023', 1879, http://patft.uspto.gov/netacgi/nph-Parser?patentnumber=D11023.

75 A selection of racist depictions are referenced in 'Revised Patently Black: An Exhibit of Black Images Appearing on United States Patents (1864-1956)', 2008, https://view.officeapps.live.com/op/view.aspx?src=http%3A%2F%2Fptrca.org%2Ffiles%2Fhandouts%2FPATENTLY_BLACK.doc. Additional examples include John G.

Conclusion

As the nineteenth century drew to a close, American sculptors became increasingly organized, especially after the founding of the National Sculpture Society in 1893, their first professional association. The most successful sculptors no longer concerned themselves with direct sales, especially casts in plaster. Their finest small-scale work was sold through the expanding network of international art dealers and galleries, some of which were directly operated by bronze foundries, such as Gorham, that had vested interests in protecting the quality and size of editions. The most prominent sculptors were focused on winning major commissions for the new civic buildings of the City Beautiful movement, Beaux-Arts urban projects, and robber-baron mansions, all of which marked the end of the nineteenth century. Many participated in the ambitious sculptural programs featured at various world fairs and expositions that were regularly staged in cities around the nation. Moreover, as the twentieth century began, most sculptors turned away from the patent altogether, preferring to protect their designs through copyright, which was cheaper and simpler to obtain. Indeed, fin-de-siècle sculptors Augustus Saint-Gaudens, Frederick MacMonnies, and A. Phimister Proctor worked with multiple foundries at home and in Europe to release numerous copyrighted reductions of their monumental bronzes, as a way of expanding private sales of their designs for public sculptures.

In hindsight, the design patent offered critical rights to nineteenth-century American sculptors and helped them establish their burgeoning field as a respected creative profession. The protection granted through the design patent was always temporal, and most works from this period have been in the public domain for a long time. As today's 3D digital scanning and printing technologies continue to improve, and institutions increasingly digitize their historical collections, nineteenth-century sculpture stands on the precipice of a new world of reproductive possibilities entirely unimagined by the sculptors of the past. (It is hard to know what Clark Mills might make of seeing his mask of Lincoln for

Hicks and John McGreer, 'Design Patent for a Statuette, Design Patent No. 16167', 1897, http://patft.uspto.gov/netacgi/nph-Parser?patentnumber=D28054; Nicholas Muller, 'Design Patent for Statuette [Indian Warrior in the Act of Throwing a Tomahawk], Design Patent No. 4187', 1870, http://patft.uspto.gov/netacgi/nph-Parser?patentnumber=D4187.

sale on Walmart.com.[76]) Limitless modern editions of the nineteenth-century sculptures whose replication was once so strictly controlled can now be readily fabricated with variations in medium and scale to meet any market demand.

Bibliography

Patent Archives

Ball, Thomas, 'Design Patent for Bust of Daniel Webster, Design Patent No. 548', 1853, http://patft.uspto.gov/netacgi/nph-Parser?patentnumber=D548.

——, 'Design Patent for Bust of Jenny Lind, Design Patent No. 369', 1851, http://patft.uspto.gov/netacgi/nph-Parser?patentnumber=D369.

——, 'Design Patent for Bust of Napoleon Bonaparte, Design Patent No. 894', 1857, http://patft.uspto.gov/netacgi/nph-Parser?patentnumber=D894.

——, 'Design Patent for Statuette of Daniel Webster, Design Patent No. 590', 1853, http://patft.uspto.gov/netacgi/nph-Parser?patentnumber=D590.

——, 'Design Patent for Statuette of Henry Clay, Design Patent No. 1060', 1858, http://patft.uspto.gov/netacgi/nph-Parser?patentnumber=D1060.

Bartholdi, August, 'Design Patent for a Bust, Design Patent No. 10893', 1878, http://patft.uspto.gov/netacgi/nph-Parser?patentnumber=D10893.

——, 'Design Patent for a Statue (Statue of Liberty), Design Patent No. 11023', 1879, http://patft.uspto.gov/netacgi/nph-Parser?patentnumber=D11023.

Demuth, Charles G., 'Design Patent for a Statue of a Fireman, Design Patent No. 20426', 1890, http://patft.uspto.gov/netacgi/nph-Parser?patentnumber=D20426.

Fiske, Joseph W., 'Design Patent for a Cast, Design Patent No. 8214', 1875, http://patft.uspto.gov/netacgi/nph-Parser?patentnumber=D8214.

——, 'Design Patent for Statue (Soldier), Design Patent No. 9396', 1876, http://patft.uspto.gov/netacgi/nph-Parser?patentnumber=D9396.

Hicks, John G., and John McGreer, 'Design Patent for a Statuette, Design Patent No. 16167', 1897, http://patft.uspto.gov/netacgi/nph-Parser?patentnumber=D28054.

King, John C., 'Design Patent for Bust of Daniel Webster, Design Patent No. 313', 1850, http://patft.uspto.gov/netacgi/nph-Parser?patentnumber=D313.

76 'Mills' Abraham Lincoln Life Mask,' *Walmart.Com,* https://www.walmart.com/ip/Mills-Abraham-Lincoln-Life-Mask/22427174.

Kornemann, Otto, and Julius Jungbluth, 'Design Patent for a Statuette, Design Patent No. 3517', 1869, http://patft.uspto.gov/netacgi/nph-Parser?patentnumber=D3517.

Mills, Clark, 'Design Patent for an Equestrian Statue or General Andrew Jackson, Design Patent No. 704', 1855, http://patft.uspto.gov/netacgi/nph-Parser?patentnumber=D704.

Mills, Fisk, 'Design Patent for Bust of A. Lincoln, Design Patent No. 2082', 1865, http://patft.uspto.gov/netacgi/nph-Parser?patentnumber=D2082.

Morgan, Dayton, 'Design for a Bust of Frederick Douglas [sic], Design Patent No. 3151', 1868, http://patft.uspto.gov/netacgi/nph-Parser?patentnumber=D3151.

Muller, Carl, 'Design Patent for a Statuette (Blacksmith), Design Patent No. 2919', 1868, http://patft.uspto.gov/netacgi/nph-Parser?patentnumber=D2919.

Muller, Nicholas, 'Design Patent for Statuette [Indian Warrior in the Act of Throwing a Tomahawk], Design Patent No. 4187', 1870, http://patft.uspto.gov/netacgi/nph-Parser?patentnumber=D4187.

Rogers, John, 'Design Patent for Statuary: The Camp Fire, Design Patent No. 1597', 1862, http://patft.uspto.gov/netacgi/nph-Parser?patentnumber=D1597.

——, 'Design Patent for Statuary: The Checker Players, Design Patent No. 1595', 1862, http://patft.uspto.gov/netacgi/nph-Parser?patentnumber=D1595.

——, 'Design Patent for Statuary: The Town Pump, Design Patent No. 1598', 1862, http://patft.uspto.gov/netacgi/nph-Parser?patentnumber=D1598.

——, 'Design Patent for Statuary: The Village Schoolmaster, Design Patent No. 1596', 1862, http://patft.uspto.gov/netacgi/nph-Parser?patentnumber=D1596.

——, 'Design Patent for Statuette Group of the Camp Life, Design Patent No. 1559', 1862, http://patft.uspto.gov/netacgi/nph-Parser?patentnumber=D1559.

——, 'Design Patent for Statuette Group of the Picket Guard, Design Patent No. 1558', 1862, http://patft.uspto.gov/netacgi/nph-Parser?patentnumber=D1558.

Powers, Hiram, 'Utility Patent for File and Rasp, Patent No. 10088', 1853, http://patft.uspto.gov/netacgi/nph-Parser?patentnumber=10088.

——, 'Utility Patent for Metal Punch, Patent No. 31476', 1861, http://patft.uspto.gov/netacgi/nph-Parser?patentnumber=31476.

Smith, Celia M., 'Design Patent for Statuette of Baby, Design Patent No. 22967', 1893, http://patft.uspto.gov/netacgi/nph-Parser?patentnumber=D22867.

——, 'Design Patent for Statuette of Cat, Design Patent No. 21680', 1892, http://patft.uspto.gov/netacgi/nph-Parser?patentnumber=D21680.

Volk, Leonard W., 'Design Patent for Bust of A. Lincoln, Design Patent No. 1250', 1860, http://patft.uspto.gov/netacgi/nph-Parser?patentnumber=D1250.

——, 'Design Patent for Statuette of Stephen A. Douglas, Design Patent No. 1203', 1860, http://patft.uspto.gov/netacgi/nph-Parser?patentnumber=D1203.

Other Sources

Adams, George, 'The Boston Directory. Embracing the City Record, a General Directory of the Citizens, and a Special Directory of Trades, Professions, &c.', 1855 in *Tufts Digital Library*, https://bcd.lib.tufts.edu/view_text.jsp?urn=tufts:central:dca:UA069:UA069.005.DO.00002&chapter=d.1855.su.Gariboldi.

Ball, Thomas, *Bust of Napoleon*, 1856, marble, 31 x 24 inches, https://www.christies.com/lotfinder/Lot/napoleon-i-1769-1821-an-4587488-details.aspx.

——, *My Threescore Years and Ten: An Autobiography* (Boston: Roberts, 1892).

Bernier, Celeste-Marie, "To Preserve My Features in Marble': Post-Civil War Paintings, Drawings, Sculpture, and Sketches of Frederick Douglass. An Illustrated Essay', *Callaloo*, 39:2 (2016), 372–399, https://doi.org/10.1353/cal.2016.0042.

Bogart, Michele Helene, 'Attitudes Toward Sculpture Reproductions in America, 1850-1880' (unpublished doctoral dissertation, University of Chicago, 1979).

Boulton, Ann, 'The Dealer and Daniel Webster', *Gilcrease Journal*, 20:1 (2013), 46–63.

'Bronze Casting Records, 1853-ca. 1877, from the Stearns-Ames Collection, [ca. 1838-1894]', Archives of American Art, https://www.aaa.si.edu/collections/items/detail/bronze-casting-records-16695.

'City News', *Daily National Intelligencer* (Washington, District of Columbia, 22 September 1865), 16, 566 edition.

Copyright Act of 1870, Ch. 230, § 86, 16 Stat. 198, 212.

Craven, Wayne, *Sculpture in America* (New York: Cornwall Books, 1984).

Falk, Peter H., Georgia Kuchen, and Veronika Roessler, eds., *Who Was Who in American Art, 1564-1975: 400 Years of Artists in America*, 3 vols (Madison, CT: Sound View Press, 1999), II.

Hudson, Thomas B., 'A Brief History of the Development of Design Patent Protection in the United States', *Journal of the Patent Office Society*, 30:5 (1948), 380–399, https://ipmall.law.unh.edu/sites/default/files/hosted_resources/DesignPatentAct/Articles/30%20JPTOS%20380.pdf.

J. W. Fiske Iron Works, *Illustrated Catalogue of Iron Fountains and Statuary* (Cushing, Bardua & Co., 1875).

Janis, Mark D., and Jason J. Du Mont, 'The Origins of American Design Patent Protection', *Indiana Law Journal*, 88:3 (2013), 837-880, https://www.repository.law.indiana.edu/ilj/vol88/iss3/1/.

Powers, Hiram, '*Greek Slave* Patent Application, 7 July 1849. Hiram Powers Papers, 1819 1953, Bulk 1835 1883. Archives of American Art, Smithsonian Institution', https://www.aaa.si.edu/collections/items/detail/greek-slave-patent-17307.

King, John Crookshanks, and Nathan Davies Cotton, *A Bust of Dr. Samuel B. Woodward, Which Has Just Been Finished by John C. King, to Be Placed in the State Asylum at Worcester ... Is Now on Exhibition for a Few Days, at the Store of N.D. Cotton, No. 13 Tremont Row* (Boston: s.n., 1847).

Kingsley, John L., and Joseph P. Pirsson, 'Practice in Procuring Patents in United States', in *Laws and Practice of All Nations and Governments Relating to Patents for Inventions: with Tables of Fees and Forms. Also, an Editorial Introduction, with Explanations of Practice and Proceedings Used in Procuring Patents Throughout the World* (New York: Kingsley and Pirsson, 1848), pp. 51–64.

Lemmey, Karen, 'From Skeleton to Skin: The Making of *The Greek Slave*(s)', *Nineteenth-Century Art Worldwide*, 15:2 (2016), http://www.19thc-artworldwide.org/summer16/lemmey-on-from-skeleton-to-skin-the-making-of-the-greek-slave.

——, 'Henry Kirke Brown and the Development of American Public Sculpture in New York City, 1846-1876' (unpublished doctoral dissertation, The City University of New York, 2005).

New-York Historical Society, 'John Rogers: American Stories', 2010, http://www.johnrogers-history.org/artist/index.html.

Orcutt, Kimberly, Michael Clapper, John Rogers, New-York Historical Society, Palmer Museum of Art, Dixon Gallery and Gardens, et al., eds., *John Rogers: American Stories* (New York: New-York Historical Society, 2010).

'Patent Documents, Hiram Powers Papers, 1819-1953, Bulk 1835-1883. Archives of American Art, Smithsonian Institution', https://www.aaa.si.edu/collections/hiram-powers-papers-7255/series-4/box-10-folder-47.

'Revised Patently Black: An Exhibit of Black Images Appearing on United States Patents (1864-1956)', 2008, https://view.officeapps.live.com/op/view.aspx?src=http%3A%2F%2Fptrca.org%2Ffiles%2Fhandouts%2FPATENTLY_BLACK.doc.

Rogers Family Papers, 1719-1955., 'Rogers Family Papers, 1719-1955', New-York Historical Society Library, Manuscript Collection.

'Ross County Fair, 1860', *The Scioto Gazette* (Chillicothe, Ohio, 19 October 1860), 43 edition.

Shapiro, Michael Edward, *Bronze Casting and American Sculpture: 1850-1900* (Cranbury, NJ, London, UK, & Ontario, CA: Associated University Presses, Inc., 1985), pp. 34–60.

Stauffer, John, Zoe Trodd, Celeste-Marie Bernier, Henry Louis Gates, and Kenneth B Morris, *Picturing Frederick Douglass: An Illustrated Biography of the Nineteenth Century's Most Photographed American* (New York: Liveright Publishing Corporation, 2015).

'Stephen A. Douglas' Missing Finger', *SangamonLink,* 2015, http://sangamoncountyhistory.org/wp/?p=6891.

Tolles, Thayer, ed., *American Sculpture in the Metropolitan Museum of Art*, 2 vols (New York: Metropolitan Museum of Art, 1999), i.

United States Patent Act (1836), ch. 357, 5 Stat. 117, https://patentlyo.com/media/docs/2008/03/Patent_Act_of_1836.pdf.

United States Patent Office, 'Rules and Directions for Proceedings in the Patent Office', in *Rules of Practice In Patent Cases,* 1867, https://babel.hathitrust.org/cgi/pt?id=mdp.35112103497923&view=1up&seq=15.

Volk, Leonard W., 'The Lincoln Life Mask and How It Was Made', *The Century, Illustrated Monthly Magazine*, November 1881, 223–28, https://archive.org/details/lincolnlifemask00volk/mode/2up.

Wade, Rebecca, *Domenico Brucciani and the Formatori of Nineteenth-Century Britain* (London: Bloomsbury Visual Arts, 2019).

Wunder, Richard P., *Hiram Powers: Vermont Sculptor, 1805-1873* (Newark: University of Delaware Press, 1991), ii.

12. New or Improved?

American Photography and Patents ca. 1840s to 1860s

Shannon Perich

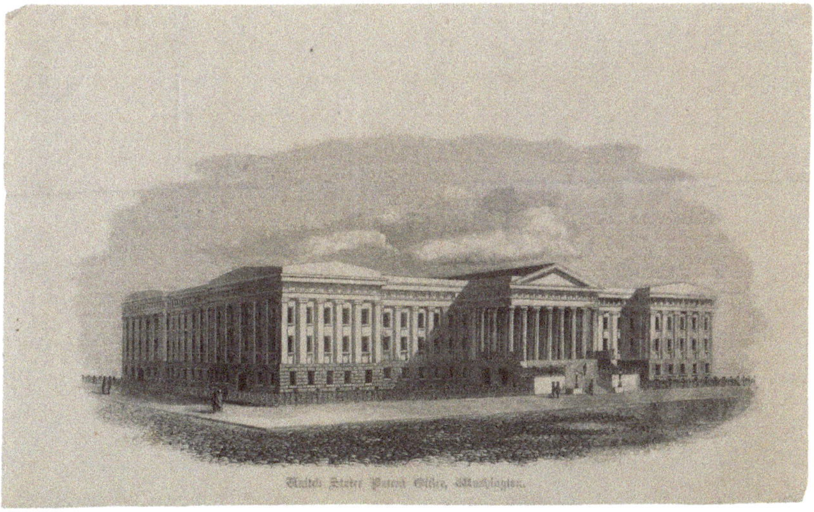

Fig. 1 Howland Brothers, *United States Patent Office, Washington* (1840), engraving included in Titian Ramsay Peale Album, Washington, DC, Smithsonian's National Museum of American History, Photographic History Collection, catalog number PG.66.25A.24, https://ids.si.edu/ids/deliveryService?max=800&id=NMAH-ET2017-14021-000001.[1]

1 All images in this chapter are from the Photographic History Collection at the Smithsonian's National History Museum of American History, Washington, DC unless otherwise noted. Most images can be found at https://collections.si.edu.

 https://doi.org/10.11647/OBP.0247.12

Photography was not, and is not, the brainchild of one person. It emerged after curious and persistent individuals tinkering with known facts about chemistry and optics — alongside new discoveries — were able to stabilize images created by rays of light on sensitized surfaces. In the nineteenth century, individuals endeavoring to produce processes we now describe as photographic were dependent on combinations of chemical, scientific, and manufacturing achievements; some of these were common practice, some were shared without patent infringements, and some patents were held tightly with hopes of financial renumeration. As such, the medium of photography, before an image is even produced, is shaped by a variety of factors, including whether certain aspects of the apparatus and processes are controlled by patent claims.

Although most histories of photography hold 1839 as a benchmark year owing to Louis Jacques Mandé Daguerre's demonstration of the daguerreotype process, successful and not-so-successful experiments had been produced and shared privately and publicly prior to that date, as would be the case for several subsequent photographic processes. In late 1839, the naturalist Hercule Florence, a Frenchman working in Brazil, posted a press release in a São Paulo newspaper, *A Phenix,* in response to the announcement of Daguerre's process. Asserting that he had been making paper-based photographs for nine years as a means to print and distribute his work, he nevertheless wrote, 'I will not dispute anyone's discoveries, because one same idea can come to two persons and because I always considered my findings precarious'.[2]

Meanwhile, the international rivalry between France's Daguerre (see Figure 3) and the United Kingdom's William Henry Fox Talbot (see Figure 4), who both claimed to be the first inventor of a photographic process, is storied and well-documented.[3] One of the ways in which primacy and legitimacy were debated, and perceived as validated, was through the receipt of patents. For Daguerre, retaining the patent to the photographic equipment offered him the possibility of additional financial benefits and international recognition. Daguerre's

2 'The Niépce Heliograph', https://www.hrc.utexas.edu/niepce-heliograph/; Natalia Brizuela, 'Light Writing in the Tropics', *Aperture* no. 215 (2014), pp. 32–37 (p. 35), https://aperture.org/editorial/light-writing-tropics/.

3 Sarah Kate Gillespie, *The Early American Daguerreotype: Cross-Currents in Art and Technology*, Lemelson Center Studies in Invention and Innovation (Cambridge, Massachusetts: The MIT Press, 2016), pp. 26–27.

agent was awarded a patent in the UK for his process. The terms for licenses were restrictive, thus becoming the first example in the history of photography in which a patent prevented the production of a certain type of photography to thrive because of scientific and international competition.[4] Talbot, was not issued a patent until 1841 and spent years chasing perceived patent infringements. His own process, once patented, also restricted who could use his patent and thereby potentially hindered the development of photography as a process and business. Across the Atlantic in the United States, patents would play their own role in shaping early American photography.

This chapter explores a group of photographic processes and patent claims in the US, beginning with the calotype in the 1840s. It then turns to examine ambrotypes in the 1850s, ending with the tintype in the 1860s. The early history of photography, especially from 1839 and through 1865, is significantly shaped by the materiality of the medium. Contemporary written histories of early photography privilege art historical pedagogies, without fully acknowledging how processes and practices — which created historical photographs as images and objects — were shaped by patents. Patent application approvals were made based on government-imposed processes and policies, patent examiner decisions, the nascent state of the photography as a medium, and individual decisions about whether to apply for or claim patent rights. The resulting processes and materials that were used to create, form, and hold photographic images embody a host of underpinning histories that might shape how we understand photographic possibility, creativity, and control.

As Karen Lemmey's chapter in this volume points out, not all arts and artists benefited equally from the award of patents. The usefulness of a patent may vary depending on the creative endeavor and legal effectiveness of the patent. In the emerging field of photography, shrewd business skills, scientific knowledge, and technological abilities were more important than artistic prowess. Patents afforded some photographers a level of prestige, serving as a stamp of legitimacy from which they could benefit financially through improved reputation.

4 Naomi Rosenblum, 'The Early Years: Technology, Vision, Users 1839–1875', in Naomi Rosenblum, *A World History of Photography* (New York: Abbeville Press, 1984) (2007, Fourth ed.), pp. 14–37 (pp. 17–18).

This resulted in more studio sales, the licensing of the patent rights, and maintaining control over a line of products. However, the road to acquiring a photography-related patent and reaping its benefits was neither straightforward nor always beneficial.

The Smithsonian Institution, the Patent Office and Innovation History

The history of the Smithsonian Institution (SI) and the United States Patent Office (USPO) are intertwined as federal government agencies and collectors of knowledge. The Patent Act of 1836 established the USPO as a standalone agency with a Commissioner, afforded grantees fourteen years of protection with the possibility of an extension of seven years, insisted copies of patents would be made available through libraries to improve the quality of the patent applications, allowed foreigners to file, and began a renumbering system starting with the number '1'. As a submission requirement, the applicant included a model of the patent so the examiner might better understand the proposed invention and prove its utility or improvement upon an existing patent.[5]

The Smithsonian Institution, founded in 1846, is now a repository for many historical patent models that provides researchers with opportunities to see physical manifestations of designs, apparatuses, and processes to complement the written portion of a patent application. As early as 1858, Smithsonian curators selected some patent models to become part of the Smithsonian's collection.[6] The keeping of USPO history, along with selected artifacts and documents held at the USPO, uniquely documents the shaping of national culture, federal policy, and intellectual endeavors.[7] Studying the patent model collection reveals that not all patents granted were viable or unique products or processes.

Today, of the 810 photography patents issued by the USPO between 1840 and 1880, the patent models for some 230 photography-related

5 United States Congress, 'United States Statutes at Large, Volume 1', Wikisource, https://en.wikisource.org/wiki/United_States_Statutes_at_Large/Volume_1/2nd_Congress/2nd_Session/Chapter_11.

6 Frederick True, 'An Account of the United State National Museum', *Annual Report of the Board of Regents of the Smithsonian Institution* (Washington, DC: Government Printing Office, 1895), p. 290.

7 'James Smithson, Founding Donor', *Smithsonian Institution Archives*, 2011, https://siarchives.si.edu/history/james-smithson.

patents now reside in the Photographic History Collection (PHC) at the NMAH.[8]

The Patents

The first patent issued by the USPO for photographic apparatus went to Alexander Walcott on 8 May 1840: patent number 1582, awarded for his camera using a concave reflector (see Figure 2). However, it would be several years before there was an abundance of applications for photography apparatus and processes. From 1840 to 1854, there were between one and six photography patents per year. In 1844, 1845, and 1848, there were none. The awarded patents were for improvements in daguerreotype apparatus for preparing and developing plates, as well as adding color to enliven photographs. 1847 marks the beginning of patents for non-daguerreotype photography.[9] This modest number of patents belies the number of innovations, published and unpublished common practices, and experimentation that took place during that period. However, the patent model collection helps us understand how photographers, case makers, doctors, dentists, opticians, machinists, cabinet makers, painters and colorists, framers, and many others understood how they might contribute to, benefit from, and imagine an impact on the visual culture of their era.

Among the multi-disciplinary personalities that engaged with photography was the inventor of the telegraph key, Samuel F. B. Morse (see Figure 5). While in Paris demonstrating his own invention, he met with Daguerre and famously wrote about the meeting in a published letter. Morse's brother, Sidney Morse, published it in the *New York Observer*. It was there, on 20 April 1839, that Americans first learned about the daguerreotype.[10] Morse ends the letter indicating that 'the

---

8 NMAH accession 48866; Barbara Suit Janssen, *Patent Models Index: Guide to the Collections of the National Museum of American History, Smithsonian Institution: Listings by Patent Number and Invention Name, Vol. 1* (Washington, DC: Smithsonian Institution Scholarly Press, 2010), https://doi.org/10.5479/si.19486006.54-1.

9 Janice Schimmelman, *The Tintype in America 1856–1880* (Philadelphia: American Philosophical Society, 2007), pp. 4–6.

10 Samuel F. B. Morse, 'The Daguerreotype', *New York Observer* 17:16 (20 April 1839), p. 62, http://www.daguerreotypearchive.org/texts/N8390002_MORSE_NY_OBSERVER_1839-04-20.pdf.

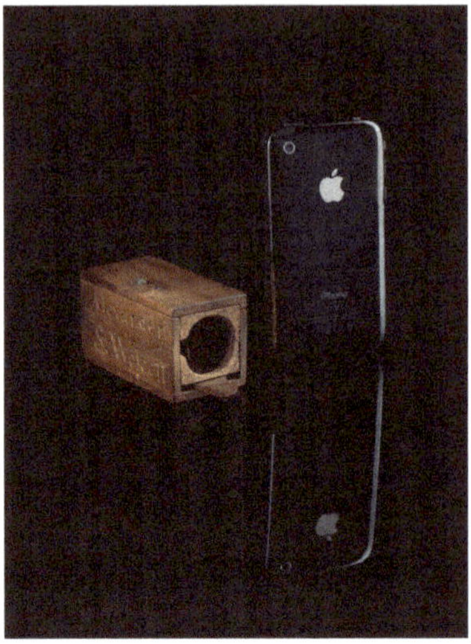

Fig. 2 Alexander Walcott patent model camera (1840) and photographer John Paul Caponigro's iPhone (about 2009), catalog numbers PG.000697 and 2012.0049.13, https://ids.si.edu/ids/deliveryService?max=800&id=NMAH-ET2012-14187.

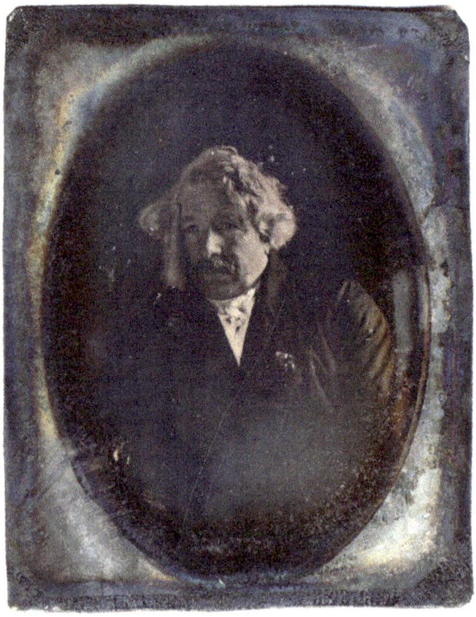

Fig. 3 Meade Brothers, *Louis Jacques Mandé Daguerre* (1848), daguerreotype, catalog number PG.000953, https://ids.si.edu/ids/deliveryService?max=800&id=NMAH-2009-10914-000001.

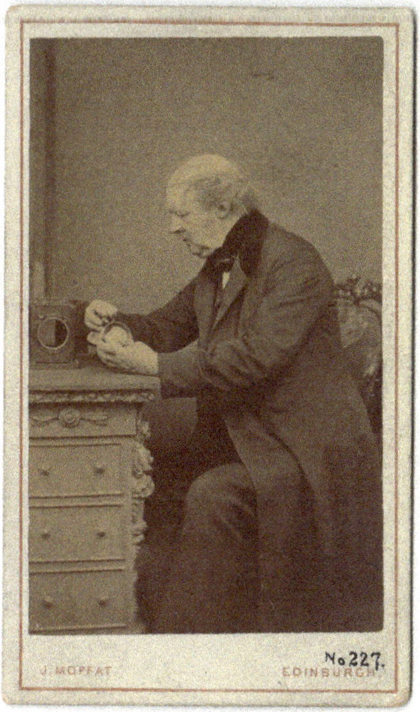

Fig. 4 John Moffat, *William Henry Fox Talbot* (1864), carte-de-visite, catalog number PG.000227, https://ids.si.edu/ids/deliveryService?max=800&id=NMAH-AHB2020q046154.

French Government did act most generously toward Daguerre'.[11] With support from François Arago at the French National Academy of Sciences, Daguerre surrendered the rights to his process, in which a highly polished silver plate is sensitized with bromine and exposed in camera, to the French government in exchange for an annuity. Morse's note about the French government's involvement gave photography legitimacy. In the US, scientists, dentists, professors, tinkerers and others did not wait for instructions, demonstrations or licenses to arrive before beginning their own experiments and making photographs[12]

11 Samuel Finely Breese Morse, and Edward Lind Morse, *Samuel F.B. Morse, His Letters and Journals* (United States: Houghton Mifflin Company, 1914), pp. 128–130.

12 MP Simmons, 'The Early Days of Daguerreotyping', *Anthony's Photographic Bulletin*, V, 21 (September 1874), pp. 309–311. (Reprinted in *Scientific American* (14 November 1874) pp. 311–312).

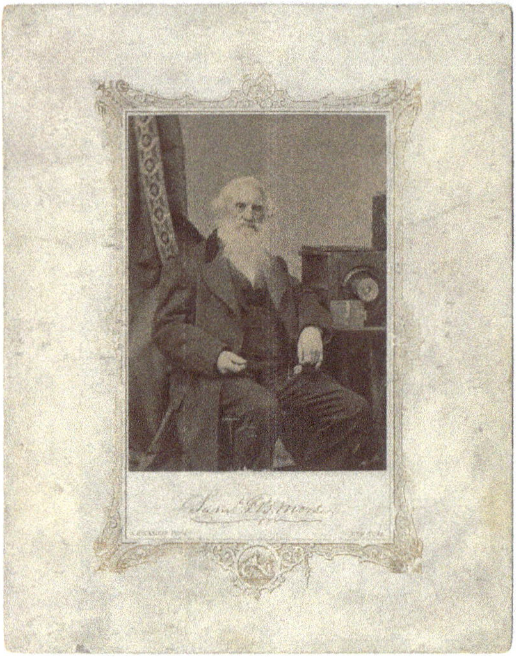

Fig. 5 Abraham Bogardus, *Samuel F. B. Morse* (1871), mounted photograph on cardstock, catalog number PG.000006. Note, Morse is depicted with the camera (turned on its side) seen in Fig. 6, https://ids.si.edu/ids/deliveryService?max=800&id=NMAH-AHB2020q046158.

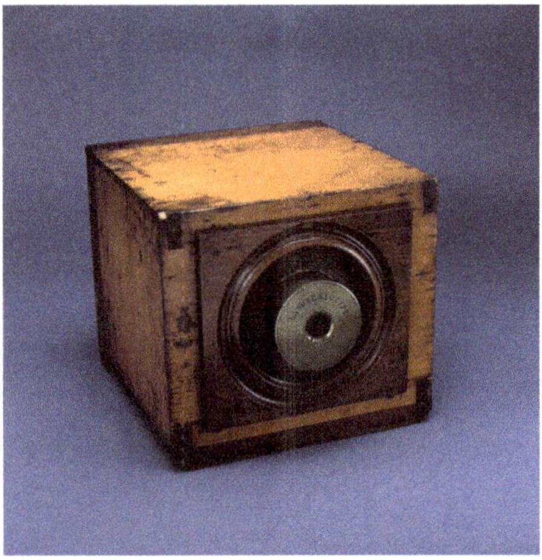

Fig. 6 George W. Prosch, *Morse's Daguerreotype Camera* (1839), catalog number PG.000004, https://ids.si.edu/ids/deliveryService?max=800&id=NMAH-2003-36149.

The hubris that some American innovators held regarding the work of others was not necessarily attributed solely to individual curiosity or disdain for European inventions. In his essay, 'Patent Models: Symbols of an Era', historian Robert C. Post, describes 'Yankee Ingenuity', a phenomenon of American national pride that spurred entrepreneurial and technological innovation.[13] In early 1833, Morse writes to the American author James Fenimore Cooper about the state of art and science in the US and notes that '[i]mprovement is all the rage'.[14] Demonstrating this himself, Morse brought a daguerreotype lens with him when he returned from France in 1839. There were no camera manufacturers yet, so he hired a cabinet maker to construct the body of the camera (see Figure 6). Morse exemplified the American attitude around invention and innovation to just 'go ahead' and do it.[15] In fact, 'doing things better' or making 'improvements' was a sufficient standard for the award of new patents granted by the US government. Between 1836 and 1880, the Patent Office described the threshold for award as 'novelty, originality, and utility'.[16] However, as the following examples demonstrate, these terms were not clearly defined or evenly applied, resulting in the granting of patents that caused confusion and anger among photographers, and shaped photographic products. In some cases, rights to photographic processes stifled or perpetuated the making and introduction of some types of photographs. Some patents incorporated or were aligned with existing patents. And still in other cases, crafty language and slightly altered approaches allowed for creative work arounds.

The Calotype in America

Brothers William and Frederick Langenheim, German immigrants working and living in Philadelphia, experimented in photography by exploring processes and various business models from the 1840s until their deaths in the 1870s. Their enthusiasm was evident in their

13 Robert C. Post, 'Patent Models: Symbols of an Era', *American Enterprise: Nineteenth-Century Patent Models* (United States: Smithsonian Institution, 1984), pp. 8–13 (p. 10).

14 Morse, *His Letters*, p. 22.

15 Gillespie, *The Early American Daguerreotype*, p. 135.

16 Post, 'Patent Models', p. 11.

advertising texts, but also in the way they succeeded in producing quality daguerreotypes while investing in emerging paper processes and inventing their own forms of photography. As such, they highlight the trial and error that was needed to find commercial success and the ways in which patents might have worked against them.

The Langenheims began their lives in the United States as journalists for a German-language newspaper, *Die Alte und Neue Welt*. They began experimenting, and quickly perfecting, the daguerreotype process in 1842, opening a studio in the Merchants' Exchange Building (see Figure 7).[17] William (see Figure 8) oversaw the business while Frederick (see Figure 9) was the primary image-maker. In his article 'Prospects of Enterprise: The Calotype Venture of the Langenheim Brothers', David R. Hanlon notes that the brothers earned an average of about $95 a week in late summer to early fall 1844. Following an aggressive advertising campaign, they increased earnings to $232 a week from 1 May to 7 June 1845. In 1845, Frederick opened a studio in New York City with Alexander Beckers.[18]

Fig. 7 Walter Johnson, *Philadelphia Exchange* (1840), daguerreotype, catalog number PG.000167, https://ids.si.edu/ids/deliveryService?max=800&id=NMAH-JN2020-00034-000001.

17 Sarah Weatherwax, 'Part 1: A Philadelphia Snapshot from When Daguerreotypes Were New', *National Museum of American History*, 2015, https://americanhistory.si.edu/blog/part-1-philadelphia-snapshot-when-daguerreotypes-were-new.

18 David R. Hanlon, 'Prospects of Enterprise: The Calotype Venture of the Langenheim Brothers', *History of Photography*, 35:4 (2011) pp. 339–354, https://doi.org/10.1080/03087298.2011.606729.

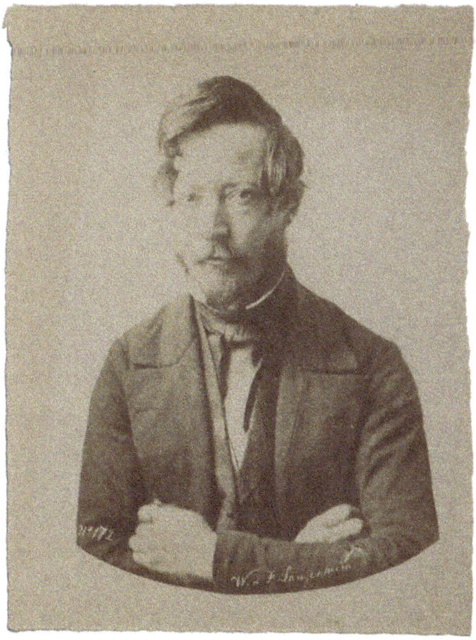

Fig. 8 Frederick Langenheim, *William Langenheim* (1840s), calotype, catalog number PG.003864.12, https://ids.si.edu/ids/deliveryService?max=800&id=NMAH-JN2020-00037-000001.

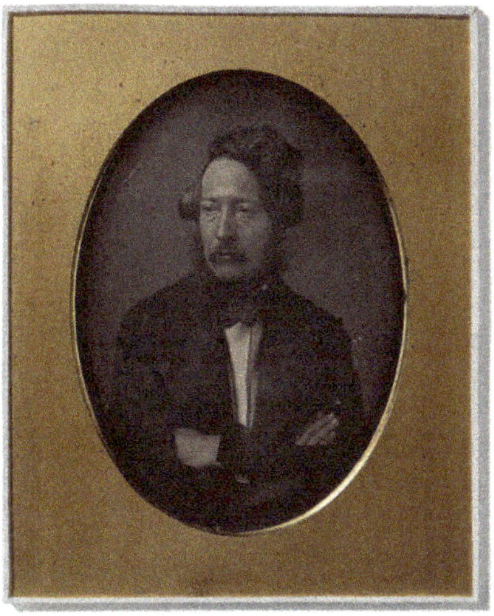

Fig. 9 Unidentified maker, *Frederick Langenheim* (1840s), daguerreotype, catalog number PG.000203, https://ids.si.edu/ids/deliveryService?max=800&id=NMAH-JN2020-00037-000001.

Frederick Langenheim and Beckers began garnering individual patents. Between 1849 and 1877, Beckers would be granted eleven patents, including a block to hold daguerreotype plates while polishing them and an improvement in stereoscopes. Langenheim would be granted three patents, including one for pictures on glass. In 1850, he invented the hyalotype, a transparent positive on an albumen-coated piece of glass (see Figure 10).[19] While the hyalotype was somewhat successful when made on a larger piece of glass for store window decorations, it was extremely short-lived as a viable commercial medium, as collodion on glass would prove to be a somewhat more practical process.[20] Note that Langenheim's patent model depicts the very building in which the patent examiner reviewing his application would have been sitting.

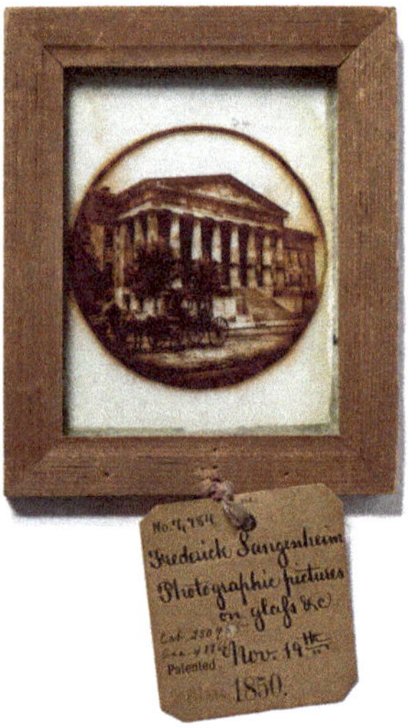

Fig. 10 Frederick Langenheim, *Photographic Pictures on glass*, patent number 7754 (19 November 1850), wooden frame with attached Patent Office tag and albumen photograph on glass, catalog number PG.000887, https://collections.si.edu/search/detail/edanmdm:nmah_1022700.

---

19 Janice G. Schimmelman, *American Photographic Patents, The Daguerreotype & Wet Plate Era 1840–1880* (Nevada City, NV: Carl Mautz Publishing, 2002) pp. 4–5, 12, 30, 32, 49.

20 'Hyalotype', *Encyclopedia of Photography*, ed. by International Center of Photography, 1st ed (New York: Crown, 1984) p. 285; Marissa Fessenden, 'This Is the First Known Photo of the Smithsonian Castle', *Smithsonian Magazine* https://www.smithsonianmag.com/smart-news/smithsonian-celebrates-169th-birthday-image-castles-construction-180956212/. The first known image of the Smithsonian's first building, the Castle, is a Langenheim hyalotype.

Throughout the 1840s and 1850s in the United States, the daguerreotype was deeply entrenched as the favored form of photography. In the UK, William Henry Fox Talbot was busy clamoring for recognition and renumeration with his paper-based photography, the Talbotype, or calotype.[21] His efforts in the UK to litigate were often perceived as wasteful, excessive, and too far-reaching. An article from the *London Art Journal* wryly critiqued his approach: 'he appears to imagine [he] secures to himself a complete monopoly of the sunshine'. The article complains that as a man of wealth Talbot 'can play with the law', and feels free to assert claims that were actually 'the discoveries of earlier laborers than himself' in an effort to protect what he perceived within his patent rights.[22] The question as to how far Talbot's rights extended would be settled when he lost an 1854 lawsuit, *Talbot* v. *Laroche*. The verdict did not dismiss his claim to the rights as inventor of the calotype patent; but it did find that Laroche had not infringed on Talbot's right, thereby confirming other photographers had the right to use collodion processes.[23]

In 1845, William Langenheim may have seen some of Talbot's calotypes from *The Pencil of Nature* (considered the first book with photographic illustrations and published in installments between 1844 and 1846) as they circulated in Philadelphia, as well as examples of a paper process by a Mr. Tilghman, that in turn, inspired Frederick to experiment. As early as 1844, the brothers advertised that their studio carried chemical supplies to produce calotypes, should customers desire them.[24] As newspaper men, it must have occurred to the Langenheims that images produced on paper could be less expensive to make, purchase, and distribute. Having multiple copies could be appealing for customers, and paper photography produced in numbers would not require bulky cases. With his New York partner, Beckers, Langenheim experimented with waxed paper negatives from their studio window to

21 *How Was It Made? Calotypes| V&A*, https://www.youtube.com/watch?v=5jCWQTNWgyM.

22 'The Photographic Patents', *The Photographic and Fine Art Journal* VII, IX (1854), p. 277.

23 'The Great Photographic Lawsuit of 1854', *British Journal of Photography*, 52 (15 December 1905), p. 985.

24 David R. Hanlon, *Illuminated Shadows: The Calotype in Nineteenth Century America*, 1st Ed (Nevada City, CA: Carl Mautz Pub, 2013) p. 64.; 'The Pencil of Nature| Home Page', https://www.thepencilofnature.com/.

make some of the first paper photography views of Manhattan in 1848 (see Figure 11). The studio was in close proximity to Phineas T. Barnum's American Museum, and just two doors away from Mathew Brady's and Edward Anthony's respective businesses at 205 and 207 Broadway.[25]

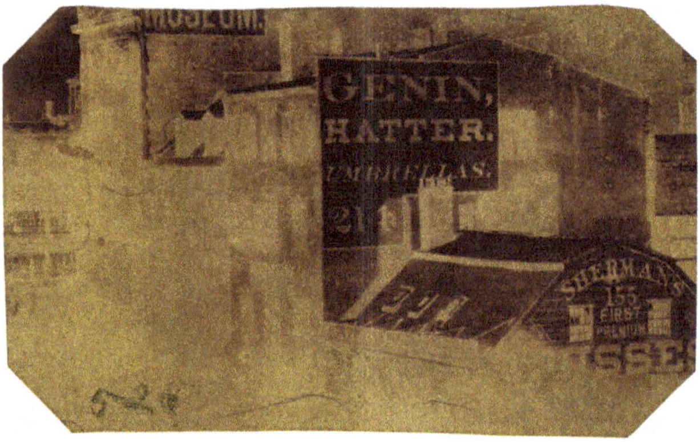

Fig. 11 Frederick Langenheim and Alexander Beckers, *Buildings on the East Side of Broadway* (1848–1849), waxed paper negative, catalog number PG.000526, https://collections.si.edu/search/detail/edanmdm:nmah_1399434.

Edward Anthony, an American photographic materials supplier and well-established member of the photographic community in New York City, spent nearly a year beginning in 1846 negotiating with Talbot, trying to buy the patent rights for the United States.[26] Meanwhile, Talbot was granted patent number 5171 by the USPO on June 26, 1847, the only photographic patent for that year (see Figure 12).[27] Anthony, still eager to be at the vanguard of a new wave of paper-based photography, persisted, inquiring about acting as Talbot's agent for the 'sale of licenses, Talbotype views', and more. Talbot declined.[28] Hanlon makes the case that Talbot, whose litigation efforts in the UK centered around attempts to recover his financial investments, missed an opportunity with Anthony as one of the most successful and savvy photography suppliers in the United States. William Welling in, *Photography In*

25 Hanlon, *Shadows*, p. 67.
26 Ibid., p. 61.
27 Schimmelman, *American Photographic Patents*, p. 5.
28 Hanlon, *Shadows*, p. 61. Quoted from letter from Anthony to Talbot, 12 July 1847, London, British Library, Fox Talbot Collection, LA-47-066; Talbot Correspondence Project, document #5977.

America: The Formative Years, 1839–1900, asserts that in 1847, American photographers had little interest in paper negatives, suggesting that even if Anthony, a supplier to most photographers had garnered the Talbot calotype license, it might have been a wasted effort.

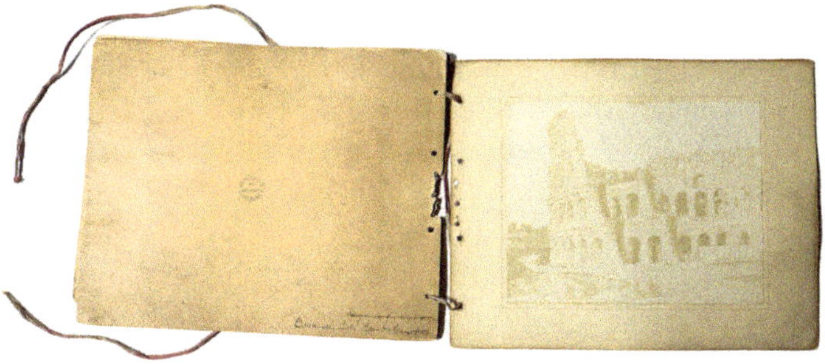

Fig. 12 William Henry Fox Talbot, *Patent 5171 for Improvement in Photographic Pictures* (26 June 1847), calotype catalog number PG.000890. Note the stamp on left, https://collections.si.edu/search/results.htm?q=PG.000890.

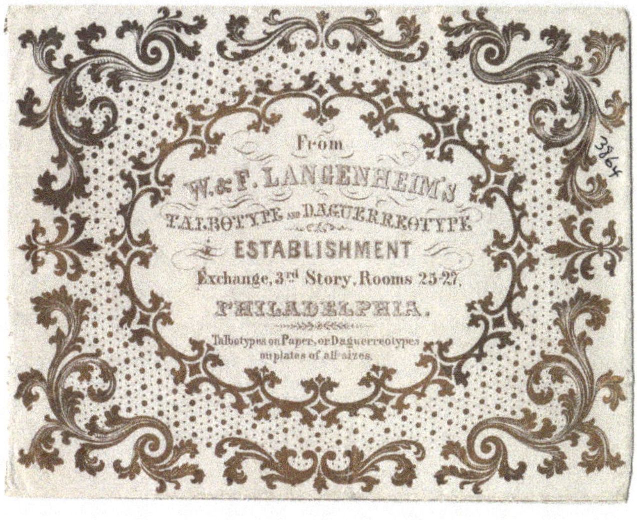

Fig. 13 William and Frederick Langenheim, *Envelope* (1849), catalog number PG.003864.33, https://collections.si.edu/search/detail/edanmdm:nmah_1971477?q=PG.003864.33&record=1&hlterm=PG.003864.33.

The forward-looking Langenheim brothers were also eager to strike a deal with Talbot for the US rights to the calotype process. They configured several offers and suggested financial arrangements beginning in February 1849. One proposal included selling licenses to individuals in the range of $50-$100 and retaining a twenty-five percent commission. They claimed:

> We know that a great many of the numerous Daguerreotype operators here would embrace your art with the enthusiasm of true Yankees if they could learn the art in a short time to a reasonable degree of perfection and if the expense for tuition and the right to exercise it was moderate.[29]

William went to Lacock Abbey, Talbot's home near Bath, England, to negotiate with Talbot while Frederick stayed in the US to promote and build excitement for the new process in which they were about to be heavily invested. In May 1849, for a sum of 1,000 pounds sterling ($6000), Talbot sold them the US rights (see Figure 13). With at least 150 daguerreotypists in the United States, if they sold sixty licenses, they would be able to cover the biannual payments of £200.[30] However, by September they had not sold a single license. They worked hard and advertised widely, as they always had, banking in part on their reputations as well-respected gentlemen, deeply knowledgeable photographers, and savvy businessmen. Unfortunately, the Langenheims' calotype endeavor failed. They attempted to use profits from their daguerreotype business to pay the debt to Talbot, but it was not enough. By the end of 1851, the brothers dissolved their business. Hanlon cites a number of reasons why the calotype failed at that particular moment in the United States, including bad timing as the US was just coming out of a war with Mexico, and a number of urban areas were struggling with a cholera epidemic. But perhaps most pointedly, 'studio owners were not interested in paying to use an unproven process, especially when the populace continued to endorse a method [the daguerreotype] that had no patent restrictions'.[31] Despite the fact that the Langenheim brothers anticipated the rise of paper-based photography and could see

29 Hanlon, *Shadows*, p. 65. Hanlon quotes from Letter from W&F Langenheim to Talbot, 5 February 1849, National Media Museum Bradford, 1937–4971; Talbot Correspondence Project, document #6210.

30 Ibid., p. 88.

31 Ibid., p. 97.

its popularity in Europe, there was no incentive to move to a process that was less detailed and more restricted than the daguerreotype. Even with their expertise in the field, they did not see clearly how committed photographers and consumers were to daguerreotypes.[32]

The brothers were not alone in their frustration about the state of photography being held back by patents, especially when some patent claims were perceived as questionable. In 1852, the author of an article entitled 'Photography-Its Origin, Progress, and Present State' complained about the quality of evaluation of Talbot's patents, noting: 'Several of these patents would never have been granted had there been a scientific board to examine the merits of them and test their originality'.[33] Others shared his concern for how patents were issued without thorough research from patent examiners.

While one might think that a government issued patent would come with a certain level of scrutiny, in fact in the United States, that very process was muddied by USPO itself. US patent examiners were given the daunting task of deciding which patent applications offered utility and novelty, though applications did not have to demonstrate both. The attitude among the examiners at the USPO towards innovation was cultural and political. In her introduction to *The Early American Daguerreotype: Cross-currents in Art and Technology*, Sarah Kate Gillespie argues that '[i]n the middle of the nineteenth century, the idea that certain knowledge would become accessible only to the specialized few went against American ideals'.[34] Welling writes, 'It appears that the thought of using collodion for photography may have occurred to a number of people at the same time'.[35] Taken together, Gillespie and Welling describe the gap between intellectual generosity and a cultural propensity described earlier as 'Yankee Ingenuity' that perhaps shaped risk assessment when deciding whether to infringe upon patent rights. We can see this in the controversies surrounding the ambrotype patents awarded to James Ambrose Cutting.

---

32 Jeremiah Gurney, *Etchings on Photograph* (New York, 1856), pp. 1–27 (p. 8). In his pamphlet, Gurney asserts that there were 4,000 daguerreotypists and a $10,000,000 business that included the studio, manufacturers, and other associated business.

33 'Photography — Its Origin, Progress, And Present State', *The National Magazine; Devoted to Literature, Art, and Religion*, 1, 6 (Dec 1852), p. 510.

34 Gillespie, *Early American Daguerreotype*, p. 5.

35 William Welling, *Photography in America: The Formative Years, 1839–1900* (New York: Crowell, 1978), p. 59.

Two key processes that spurred photography were shared freely by their creators. Sir John Hershel and Frederick Scott Archer shared or published key formulas without financial compensation or stated protection of those ideas. Sir John Hershel shared the benefits of sodium thiosulfate, or hypo, which halts the reaction of light on silver halides that ensured the success of Daguerre's and Talbot's processes.[36] Frederick Scott Archer published his recipe for collodion in 1850, then, more widely with some improvement of the formula, as a manual in 1854.[37]

Archer's collodion process, in which gun-cotton is dissolved in ether with additional silver nitrate to make a clear sticky substance that is spread on to a variety of substrates, became a base recipe in which photographers could experiment and adapt as they saw fit.[38] Archer did not patent his process. By openly publishing the recipe, it was widely adapted with modifications and sometimes by others who then patented an 'improvement'. Sadly, Archer died penniless while others financially profited from his generosity.

Two of these collodion-based processes would take different trajectories because one restricted the actions of photographers and the other restricted the actions of manufacturers. The ambrotype required makers to create a hand-coated, photographic negative made by following a light-sensitive collodion recipe that was then assembled with other elements to complete the presentation of the photograph. The ambrotype was debated and contested for fourteen years in part because individual photographers were singled out for infringement of the process. Mass manufactured tintype plates, in which the light-sensitive emulsion was applied at the factory, relieved photographers from possible infringements. The patent was for the manufacture of the tintype plate and there were no restrictions that prevented a photographer from making his own tintype plates if they wished. In the case of ambrotypes, patents associated with the process would create significant confusion and frustration. Even as they rejected calotypes,

36 Larry J. Schaff, 'To Fix or Not to Fix? — Sir John Herschel's Question', https://talbot.bodleian.ox.ac.uk/2016/01/22/to-fix-or-not-to-fix-sir-john-herschels-question/.

37 'Frederick Scott Archer', *The British Journal of Photography*, XXII (28 February 1873), p. 102, https://archive.org/embed/britishjournalof22unse.

38 *The Wet Collodion Process*, https://www.youtube.com/watch?v=MiAhPIUno1o.

photographers' insistence on producing ambrotypes despite the challenges were explained in part by a reminiscence by A. R. Gould: '...how we hailed with joy the advent of the ambrotype as a Godsend to relieve us from the fumes of mercury and bromine [while making daguerreotypes]...'. A less chemically toxic environment, in addition to a quicker and less expensive process, was appealing. Gould went on to say that tintypes were even better: '...but excellence and beauty were easier reached when the ferrotype [tintype] plate was found in our sanctum'.[39] Not only were tintypes rapidly adopted; they also inspired additional successful patents that applied to manufacturers rather than to individual photographers.

The Ambrotype

An ambrotype is a unique cased image in which a photographic negative on glass is backed by a dark cloth, varnish, or paper (see Figure 14) to make it appear as a positive image (see Figure 15).[40] The contest between ambrotype patentee Cutting and patent examiner Titian Ramsay Peale, illuminates how Cutting's patents were awarded with an eye toward bureaucracy rather than integrity, and how those faulty patents shaped the business of photography for specific photographers (see Figure 16).

Cutting was awarded three ambrotype related patents on 11 July 1854 (patents 11213, 11266, 11267), two of which caused controversy for the photographic community from 1854 to 1868. The first was for the addition of camphor to collodion. While qualifying as 'novel', it had no actual utility; therefore, although it was awarded, the patent was worthless. The second patent was for the use of balsam of fir, a common adhesive of the era, to secure a second piece of glass to the image side of a negative.[41] The third patent was for Cutting's formula

39 A. R. Gould, 'A Few Leaves From My Diary', *The Philadelphia Photographer*, XIX, 217 (January 1882), pp. 13–14, http://archive.org/details/philadelphiaphot1882phil.

40 'Art & Architecture Thesaurus Full Record Display (Getty Research)', http://www.getty.edu/vow/AATFullDisplay?find=ambrotype&logic=AND&note=&english=N&prev_page=1&subjectid=300127186. The term 'ambrotype' is used predominately in the US. Cutting attempted to trademark 'ambrotype' in the UK where the process is usually called collodion glass positives.

41 Larry J. Schaaf and William Henry Fox Talbot, *Records of the Dawn of Photography: Talbot's Notebooks P & Q* (Cambridge [England]; New York, USA: Cambridge University Press, in cooperation with the National Museum of Photography, Film & Television, 1996), p. 396.

for collodion, in which bromide was added to decrease exposure time, making portraiture on glass more viable.

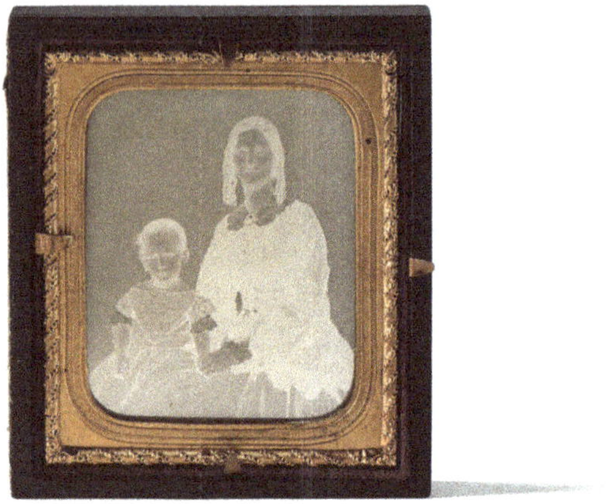

Fig. 14 Unidentified maker (possibly Mathew Brady), *Negative of Unidentified sitters*, late 1850s to early 1860s, ambrotype, catalog number PG.75.17.892, https://collections.si.edu/search/detail/edanmdm:nmah_1971422.

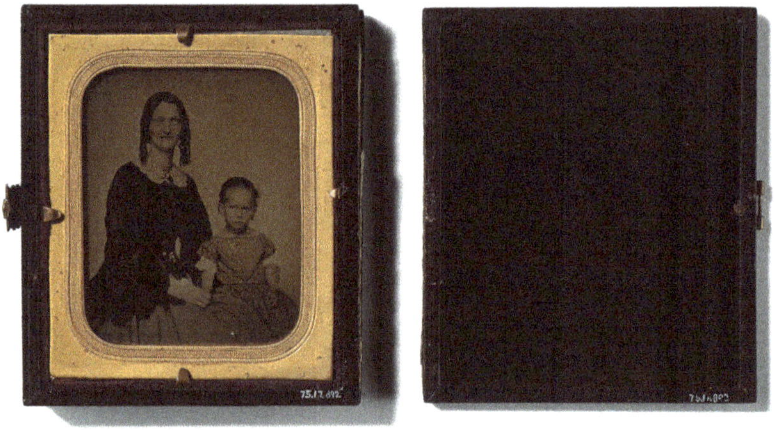

Fig. 15 Unidentified maker (possibly Mathew Brady), *Positive of Unidentified sitters*, late 1850s to early 1860s, ambrotype, catalog number PG.75.17.892, https://collections.si.edu/search/detail/edanmdm:nmah_1971422.

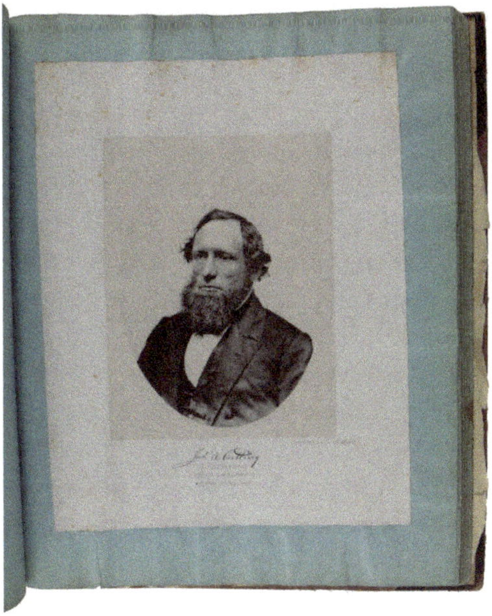

Fig. 16 Cutting and Bradford, James Ambrose Cutting (about 1858), photolithograph, included in Peale's album, catalog number PG.66.21.55, https://collections.si.edu/search/detail/edanmdm:nmah_1403396?q=PG.66.21.55&record=1&hlterm=PG.66.21.55.

Cutting had a practice of acquiring patents, then selling them. Prior to his photographic patents, Cutting had experience with the patent application process, and was awarded a patent for a new kind of beehive that he sold in the 1830s. Later, in the 1840s, he patented railroad switches and sold those patents as well.[42] When he applied for the three ambrotype patents, it was during a period in which the Patent Office Commissioner often awarded patent claims with more leniency than previous administrations.[43] The late stages of a patent application review might ask for clarification, a partial rejection that allowed the applicant to revise, or an outright rejection with the possibility of

42 USA House of Representatives, *House Documents* (U.S. Government Printing Office, 1866). Patent 8077 for spark arresters 1851.

43 Mazie McKenna Harris, 'Inventors and Manipulators: Photography as Intellectual Property in Nineteenth-Century New York' (doctoral thesis, Brown University, 2014), p. 125, available through *History of Art and Architecture Theses and Dissertations*, Brown Digital Repository, Brown University Library, https://doi.org/10.7301/Z0CF9NF2.

appealing to the Commissioner. During the review of Cutting's patent assignment request, one of his applications needed only to add the words 'for photography' to be accepted as novel. However, the other two were initially rejected for their lack of originality by patent examiner Titian Ramsay Peale. Despite Peale's rejection based on his research and strong understanding of common photographic image production practices, Commissioner Charles Mason approved the patents under a questionable presumption that more patent awards ensured the United States appeared as innovative and productive, thus making Cutting's weak patent claims legally binding.[44]

In her doctoral dissertation and in the exhibition catalogue *Paper Promises,* photography historian and curator Mazie Harris illuminates the patent request process, particularly as it relates to Peale.[45] Peale, known as stringent and tough, often annoyed commissioners, solicitors, potential patentees, and his own fellow examiners when he double-checked their approvals. Peale refused bribes and wrote long responses to submissions. Harris notes that Peale's rejection letters often provided detailed and specific references to period literature from a wide range of subjects.[46]

Peale rejected Cutting's applications with an abundance of proof and an exchange of letters asserting that his patent submissions were derivatives of common and previously published processes. Peale had deep knowledge in the field and was an amateur photographer who tested photographic formulas and processes. He kept records of his experiments, associated with practicing photographers, and came from a long line of erudite, patriotic artists all of which rounded out his breadth of knowledge and experience (see Figures 17 and 18).[47]

---

44 Harris, 'Inventors and Manipulators', p. 124.

45 Harris, 'Inventors and Manipulators'; Mazie M. Harris, Matthew Fox-Amato, and Christine Hult-Lewis, *Paper Promises: Early American Photography* (Los Angeles: The J. Paul Getty Museum, 2018).

46 Harris, 'Inventors and Manipulators', p. 116.

47 Peale-Sellers families, 'Peale-Sellers Family Collection, 1686–1963', https://search.amphilsoc.org/collections/view?docId=ead/Mss.B.P31-ead.xml#bioghist. Charles Willson Peale (1741–1827) was an influential painter and socialite who helped set a national iconography related to American culture, politics, and science. His ten children, most named after well-known artists, continued his legacy in the worlds of museums, art, and commerce. Titian Ramsay Peale (1799–1885) was the youngest, making a name early in life for his scientific illustrations of butterflies; he also worked with Charles Darwin on the latter's second expedition. Peale joined the US Patent Office seeking a regular income to support his family; NMAH accession 263090, gift of Jacqueline Hoffmire, 11 October 1965.

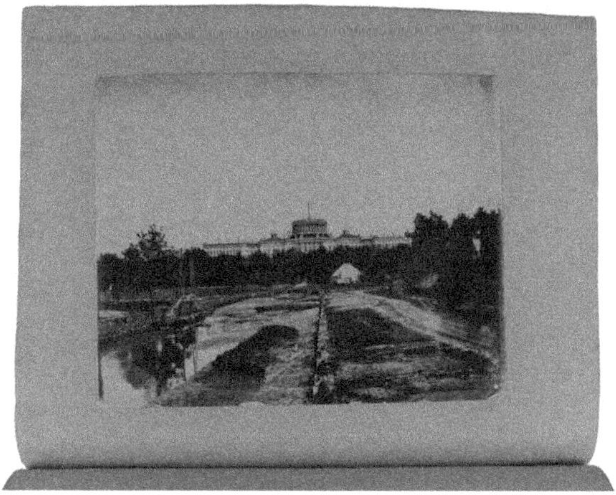

Fig. 17 John Wood, *The US Capitol Under Construction* (July 1860), salted paper print, included in Peale's album, catalog number PG.66.21.58, https://collections.si.edu/search/detail/edanmdm:nmah_1403399.

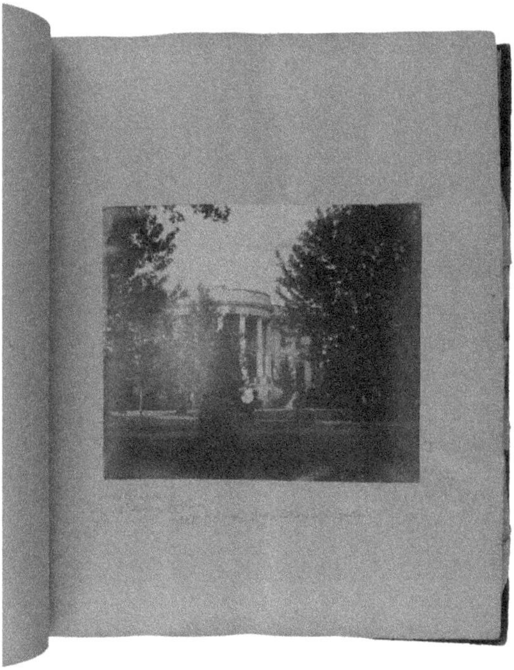

Fig. 18 Titian Ramsay Peale, *White House Portico, Albumen, 12' exposure 4pm TRP* (*A drop of perspiration on the portico!*) (1850s) salted paper print, included in included in Peale's album, catalog number PG.66.21.23, https://collections.si.edu/search/detail/edanmdm:nmah_1403377?q=number+PG+66.21.23&record=1&hlterm=number%2BPG%2B66.21.23.

Peale and other photographers had been adding bromide or bromine to photo sensitive surfaces since the Daguerreian era to speed exposure time. Cutting's bromide-related patent, however, created a situation in which any practitioner adding bromide to his collodion — as was common practice — might suddenly find himself infringing on Cutting's patent.

In 1854, many photographers were incensed that Cutting's patent had been approved. *Humphrey's Journal* declared, 'As regards the claim of Bromide of Potassium, it is wholly worthless, having been published and used long before Mr. Cutting's application was filed'.[48] Photographer and photography manual publisher Marcus Aurelius Root, who gave the name 'ambrotype' to the process and format, initially supported Cutting, but after conducting his own patent research at the USPO he withdrew his support.[49]

To further complicate the landscape, in addition to selling individual licenses himself, Cutting sold shares of the patent to individuals who could then set their own licensing fees and pursue patent infringement lawsuits. Acquiring a portion of Cutting's shares of the patents required a hefty sum. In 1868, lawyers from Howson & Son went to court to seek an annulment of the Cutting ambrotype patent and prevent its renewal. At that time, it was revealed how much Cutting had made from selling shares of the patent. In the *Arguments Before the US Patent Office and Justices of the Supreme Court* (the validity of awarded patents could be brought to federal court for resolution) it was reported that Jesse Briggs paid $10,000 to Cutting for the right to license Cutting's process, and Asa Millet paid $1,100 for the same rights in Maine and New Hampshire. Some rights holders were reported to have paid up to $20,000.[50] William A. Tomlinson purchased rights to license the process in New York, a potentially lucrative locale with a high concentration of photographers, manufacturers, and supply distributers. The high sums paid gave some a grand sense of control over the ambrotype process.

48 'Correspondence upon Cutting's Patents', *Humphrey's Journal*, VIII, 21 (1 March 1857) p. 326. Some of the correspondence between Peale and Cutting was published.

49 James S. Jensen, 'Cutting's Edge' in *The Collodion Journal*, 5, 19 (Summer 1999), p. 5. Quoted by Jensen.

50 *Arguments Before the U.S. Patent Office and Justices of the Supreme Court, D.C.: With Decisions, Comments, &c* (Howson & Son, 1871) pp 343–365 (p. 347). The sums of money and the tangled distribution of rights and shares were revealed by the Philadelphia lawyers Howson & Son, who opposed (on behalf of Edward Wilson) the reissue of Cutting's patent.

Tomlinson took Virginia photographer M. P. Simons to court for using the word 'ambrotype' in his advertisements. A US District Court judge did not issue an injunction and explained to Tomlinson that the name of the process and format, even if included in the patent, was not an infringement; the judge added that Tomlinson needed to learn the definition of trademark.[51]

With an improved understanding of the patent and how it might be held up in court, Tomlinson targeted New York City photographer Abraham Bogardus in 1858.[52] Bogardus had enough evidence to go to court to fight the patent, but he opted to settle out of court and pay the $100 licensing fee to make ambrotypes, instead of losing business during the height of the photography season. He later regretted the decision, as did others, since by default, Tomlinson was considered to have won the case thus making it possible to sue other photographers.[53] The outcome was wide-reaching and benefitted Cutting and his assignees, as most published formulas contained bromide; furthermore, it seemed that he could expand the legal scope of patent infringement beyond photographers to include manufacturers.[54] This left photographers with one of four options. They could choose not to make ambrotypes, thus avoiding the issue altogether. They could take the risk of making ambrotypes and hope not to be sued; this choice may explain, in part, why so many ambrotypes are not stamped with a specific maker's name. Photographers could purchase the license because they believed it was the right thing to do, or they could purchase the license even if they disagreed with the principle, because it was the financially expedient choice. Well-known photographers who had been holding out, such as Mathew Brady and Jeremiah Gurney, recognized they would be legal targets like Bogardus and therefore paid for the license, even though they believed it to be a poorly awarded patent.[55]

51 'The Ambrotype Patent Case', *The Photographic and Fine Art Journal*, X, II (1857) p. 56.

52 Note that Abraham Bogardus photographed Samuel F. B. Morse (see Figure 5 in this chapter).

53 'The Cutting Patents Denounced! New York Photographers assemble for defence [sic]!' in *American Journal of Photography*, 2, 19 (1 March 1860), 289–292 (p. 291); Abraham Bogardus, *The Experiences of a Photographer*, Lippincott's Magazine (May 1891).

54 'The Cutting Patents Denounced!', p. 292.

55 Mathew Brady's ambrotypes were often seen in publications and identified as such as engraved likenesses after his portraits of his celebrity and well-known sitters,

Charles D. Fredericks, another New York City photographer, was itching to take Tomlinson to court to debunk the patents; he was scheduled for a hearing on 18 May 1859.[56] Tomlinson delayed the court date, indicating that he needed more time to gather evidence. Photographers and photography journal editors gathered and began building a defense fund to support Fredericks' legal battle. But after a year and a half, only about $750 of the $5,000 needed had been raised, according to treasurer Edward Anthony. Some photographers did not contribute to the campaign as they felt that only those photographers of sufficient means could afford the license, therefore those making only a modest income from ambrotypes might be priced out of the market. The lawsuit was delayed during the Civil War, leaving photographers in possible legal limbo for five years.[57]

By March 1865, just before the end of the war, Cutting signed all but one-eighth of his rights over to his lawyer, WEP Smyth, and to a former Daguerreian named Timothy Hubbard. They both believed that if they pursued infringements that occurred during the war years, it would be lucrative. Their threat of lawsuits and efforts to chase several years' worth of retroactive compensation put a number of rural New England photographers out of business. The lawsuit between Tomlinson and Fredricks that had been on hold during the war was settled for $900, leading the way for others to do the same, including manufacturers. 'It is very humiliating to acknowledge defeat, but it may be better than to fight when there is no chance of success', wrote Charles Seely in *The American Journal of Photography*.[58] After a meeting to restart the unified resistance that had existed before the Civil War, he lamented, 'half our army has gone to the enemy... the proprietors of the patents have so perfected their plans that they consider their position impregnable'.[59] Despite legal threats by Tomlinson, and other rights holders, only one case went to court. The judgment was in favor of the ambrotype patent holders, and ruled against Maine photographer Enoch H. McKinney in August 1867.[60]

---

including *Ballou's Drawing Room Pictorial Companion* between 1857 and 1858; 'The Cutting Patents Denounced!', p. 292.

56 'The Cutting Patents Denounced!', p. 291.

57 Jensen, 'Cutting's Edge', p. 5.

58 *American Journal of Photography*, 15 November 1865, 239–240.

59 *Ibid.*

60 Jensen, 'Cutting's Edge', p. 7.

When it was learned that Smyth and Hubbard were going to attempt to renew the patents for another seven years, Edward L. Wilson, founder, editor and publisher of the *Philadelphia Photographer*, led the charge to prevent the renewal of Cuttings' patents. A three-month process with Philadelphia lawyers Furman Sheppard and Henry Howson, from Howson & Son, included seventeen witnesses and a preponderance of evidence thanks to a Detroit photographer who retained a trove of American and European journals and books, each marked with pages that showed the use of collodion with bromides before 1853. The Acting Commissioner A. M. Stout denied the extension and pronounced the patent dead one day before it was due to expire on 11 July 1868.[61] The legal victory was anticlimactic for the photography community after much money, time, and debate had been invested. The ambrotype process was rapidly waning commercially in favor of other types of photography, such as the tintype and carte-de-visite. These latter forms of photography were faster, less expensive, and physically lighter; they could also be placed in albums and collected. Cartes-de-visite were mounted paper prints made in multiples from glass plate negatives. Tintypes could be made outside of the studio, offering new types of images and targeting a wider consumer market.

While the ambrotype patent shares and licenses may have been lucrative for a few holders, others piggybacked on existing patents including those secured by the Spooner Brothers of Springfield, Massachusetts. They were awarded a patent for adding color to ambrotypes (see Figure 19). The Spooner Brothers noted the Cutting's license on the ambrotype of their own patent submission to the USPO (see Figure 20). Note how the girl's bow and the tablecloth are subtly tinted red in a modest and tasteful style.

Tintypes

Archer's collodion formula was modified and adjusted by many, or 'improved', to use the USPO's nomenclature. Among the processes

61 Sheppard, Furman and Henry Howson, 'Opposition to and Refusal of James A. Cutting's Patent,' *Arguments Before the U.S. Patent Office and Justices of the Supreme Court, D.C.: With Decisions, Comments, &c.* (United States, Philadelphia, 1871), pp. 343–365 (p. 360), https://www.google.com/books/edition/Arguments_Before_the_U_S_Patent_Office_a/UZZBAQAAIAAJ?hl=en&gbpv=0.

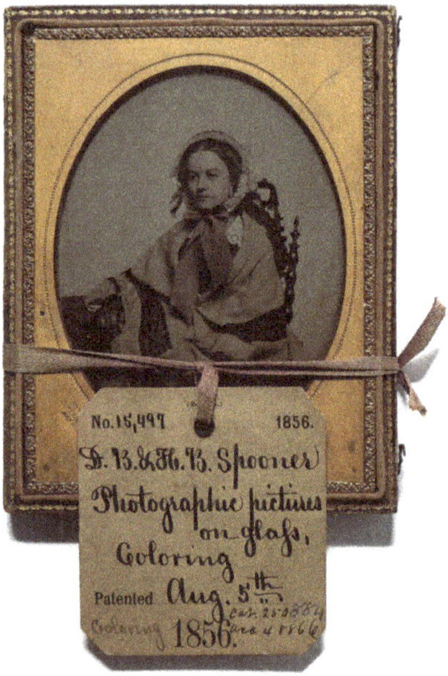

Fig. 19 Spooner Brothers, Patent model for 15497 for Photographic Pictures on Glass, Coloring (5 August 1856), ambrotype, catalog number PG.000817, http://collections.si.edu/search/results.htm?q=PG.000817.

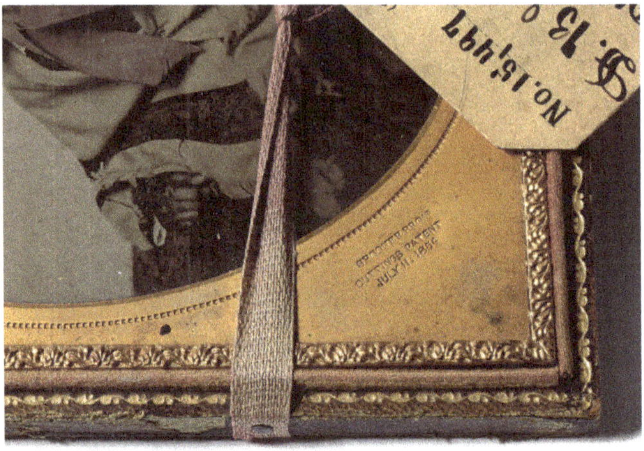

Fig. 20 Spooner Brothers, Patent model for number 15497, *Detail of Cutting patent notification* (5 August 1856), brass mat over ambrotype glass plate negative, catalog number PG.000817, http://collections.si.edu/search/results.htm?q=PG.000817.

that built on Archer's formulas were tintypes. Known in their era by several names, but generally known as tintypes today, their history demonstrates how photographic processes could be moved from individual and small-scale production to mass manufacturing. Tintypes are unique images printed on thin iron sheets coated with collodion-based emulsions. When the image is developed, it appears as a positive and requires no additional printing and only modest packaging though it can be found cased like daguerreotypes and ambrotypes. Hamilton Smith's melainotype patent, his name for a tintype, was assigned to Peter Neff, Jr. Competition with Victor M. Griswold forced him to improve his own product, making it more affordable to consumers.[62] Ultimately, Neff sold his plates to the Waterbury Button Company, which began mass producing photographic images.[63]

Smith, a professor of natural sciences at Kenyon College in Ohio, developed a process of applying a collodion emulsion to a thin iron plate coated prepared with a black varnish, often called a japanned surface, that renders the image as a positive. It was quick, inexpensive, and less cumbersome than other processes, enabling photographers to take the camera outside of the studio.

Smith was granted patent number 14300 on 19 February 1856 for the 'production of pictures on japanned surfaces'. His former student and darkroom assistant, Peter Neff, and his father bought the patent and began manufacturing plates in Cincinnati, Ohio (see Figure 21). By October 1856, Neff was advertising plates, sending out representatives to teach and demonstrate the process, and distributing an instruction manual, *The Melainotype Manual, Complete.* He also secured four agents, including Edward Anthony, to sell his product. Henry H. Snelling, the editor of *Photographic and Fine Art Journal*, would declare, 'This style of picture [tintypes] we have spoken of in a former number, and we can only add here, that our prediction as to the capability of superceding [sic] the *Ambrotype* [his emphasis], is fast becoming realized'.[64] Some photographers specialized in making just ambrotypes or tintypes. Yet others, produced both and offered customers a choice.[65] Today, tintypes

62 The name 'tintype' is a misnomer as there is no tin involved; however, tinsnips (a variety of scissors) are used to trim the metal plates.

63 Schimmelman, *Tintype in America*, p. 46.

64 'The Melainotype' in *The Photographic and Fine Art Journal*, X, II (February 1857) 64.

65 *Singleton's Nashville Business Directory*, p 5. *Polk's Nashville (Davidson County, Tenn.) City Directory... 1865* ([Nashville] R. L. Polk & co., 1865), http://archive.org/details/

are perhaps the most abundant of the non-paper processes found in archives and collections.

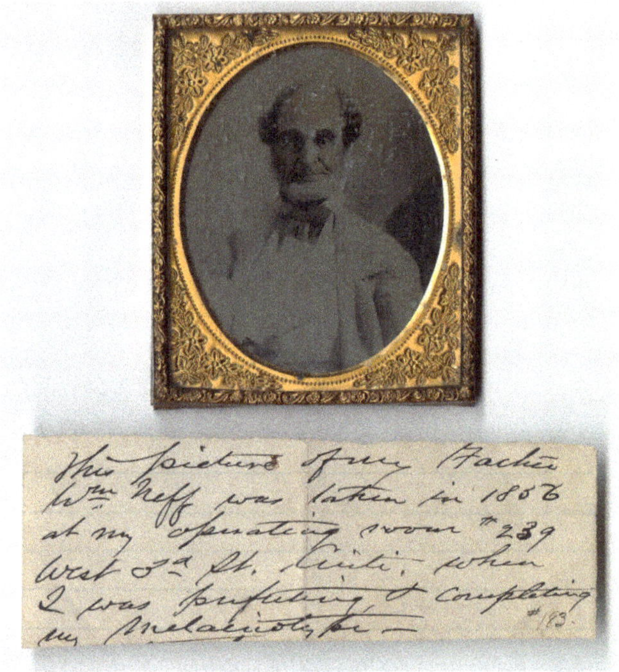

Fig. 21 Peter Neff, *William Neff* (1856), melainotype (tintype), catalog number PG.000183.[66] https://collections.si.edu/search/detail/edanmdm:nmah_751624.

On 21 October 1856, Victor M. Griswold, also one of Smith's students, was granted patent number 15924 for 'bituminous ground for photographic pictures', a modification to an earlier patent. He enameled his plates differently and called the format 'ferrotype'. Neff's patent was for the process of making the images on the surfaced plates, while Griswold's was for the surfacing of the plates.[67] Neither was legally stepping on the

polksnashvilleda00nash; NMAH, PHC. Ephemera collections (advertisements, business cards, broadsides, etc.) reveal the scope of a photographer's business.

66 NMAH, PHC, Accession number 24366. Handwritten note, 'This picture of my father Wm. Neff was taken in 1856 at my operating room #239 West 3d St. Cinti [Cincinnati, Ohio] when I was perfecting and completing my melainotype — '. This is one of several dozen tintypes acquired from Neff in 1891.

67 Robert Taft, 'The Tintype', *Photography and the American Scene* (New York: MacMillan Company, 1938), pp. 153–157.

other's toes, so the competition for the favored product had to take place in the marketplace rather than in a court of law.

Both men undertook the manufacturing of plates amid several challenges. Photographic innovation and invention held an east-coast bias whereas both Neff and Griswold were from Ohio. News from the east was more easily gathered and distributed than when it came from the reverse direction. Consequently, Neff moved his production to Middletown, Connecticut in 1857 to be in closer proximity to New York City. With additional experts in manufacturing in proximity, he made lighter plates on a larger scale. In summer 1859, Griswold substantially cut the prices of his plates to try to counter Neff's improvements.[68]

But Neff need not have worried, as another Connecticut business, the Waterbury Button Company that would become part of Scovill Manufacturing, was beginning to mass-manufacture photographic buttons and political medals. *Humphrey's Journal* wrote, 'Politics will help our friend Neff...There is no knowing who will be President until after the election. Therefore, the admirers of "Old Uncle Abe" [Abraham Lincoln], Breckenridge, Douglas and all the other candidates... want pictures of their leaders'.[69] The company produced hundreds of thousands of button images in 1860 using Neff's plates.

Abraham Lincoln's campaign buttons bring together an interesting example of mass manufacturing and questions about copyright, or at least the reuse of images. The image of Lincoln takes on a series of iterations that begins with one of the poses from his famous session with Mathew Brady after the Cooper-Union address on 27 February 1860.[70] Brady made numerous paper copies in the form of cartes-de-visite that were easily produced and readily sold by his studio, his distributors, and Lincoln's campaign (see Figure 22).[71] Currier and Ives used Brady's photograph as the basis for their lithograph, *Abraham Lincoln...Our Next President* (see Figure 23). The Waterbury Button Company used a multi-lens camera,

68 Schimmelman, *Tintype in America*, pp. 37–52.

69 Taft, *Photography and the American Scene*, p. 158. Quoted by Taft from *Humphrey's Journal*, September 1860.

70 Abraham Lincoln won the nomination to be the Republican Party in May 18, 1860. The election was held on November 6, 1860, and he was inaugurated on March 4, 1861. It is interesting to note the patent awarded on August 14, 1860 using Abraham Lincoln's and Hannibal Hamlin's images. The buttons were likely manufactured before the patent was awarded.

71 Marie Cordié Levy, 'Matthew [sic] Brady's Abraham Lincoln', http://www.asjournal.org/60-2016/matthew-bradys-abraham-lincoln/#.

such as one like Thomas Barbour's, with a repeating back to photograph a detail from the lithograph (see Figure 24). Depending on the camera and the size of the plate between sixteen and seventy-two very small images could be produced (see Figure 25). The gem tintypes, the name for the small coin-sized image, were cut and placed in the button or medal. Photographing the lithographic prints eliminated the cost of making a small engraving or requiring a person to pose for multiple exposures. It also necessarily reduced the size of the image on the plate to fit the button's size. This rapid process meant that hundreds of small portraits of Lincoln could be made within just a few hours (see Figure 26).

Notice how the highlight in Lincoln's bowtie matches the print, and that the flick of hair over his ear and lock on his forehead are the same across all the images. In Douglass F. Maltby's designs for his patent specifications, he included the portrait of Hannibal Hamlin (whose image is on the obverse of the actual button) and Lincoln, both of whom are rendered in reverse from the original source material (see Figure 27). Lincoln won the Presidency and led the country and the Union Army during the Civil War.

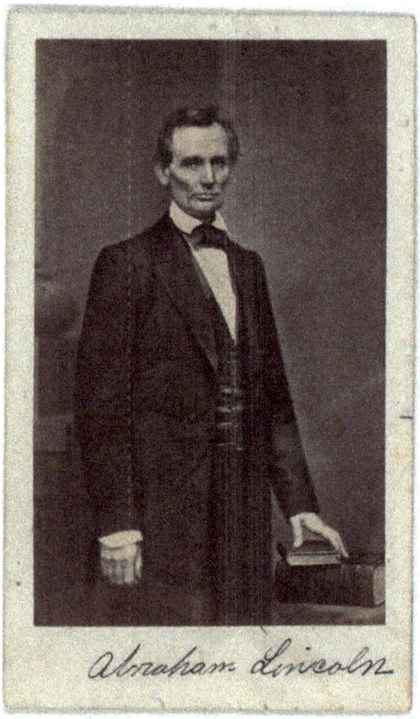

Fig. 22 Mathew Brady, *Abraham Lincoln* (1860), carte-de-visite, Washington, DC, Library of Congress, LC-MSS-44297-33-001, https://www.loc.gov/item/mss4429700001/.

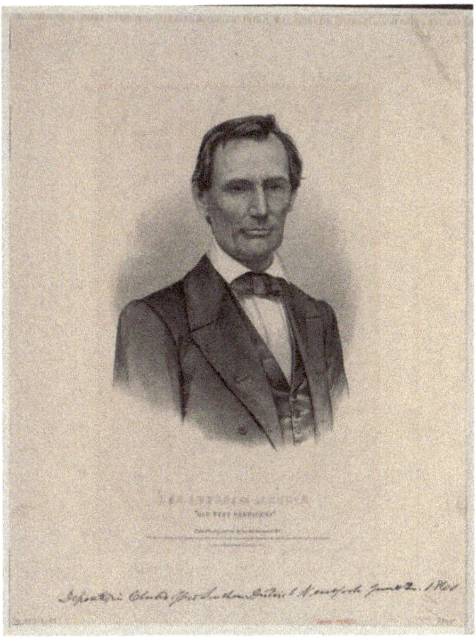

Fig. 23 Currier & Ives, *Hon. Abraham Lincoln, Our Next President* (1860), lithograph, Washington, DC, Library of Congress, LC-USZC2-2593, https://www.loc.gov/item/2002695894/.

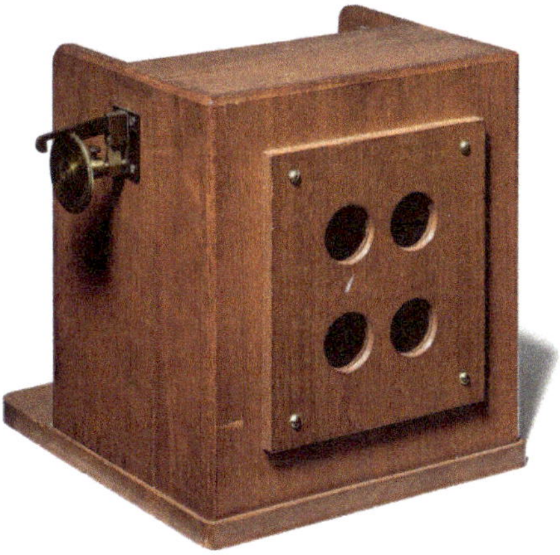

Fig. 24 Thomas Barbour, *Patent model 61,139, Four Lens Tintype Camera* (15 January 1867), catalog number PG.001041, https://collections.si.edu/search/detail/edanmdm:nmah_1101428.

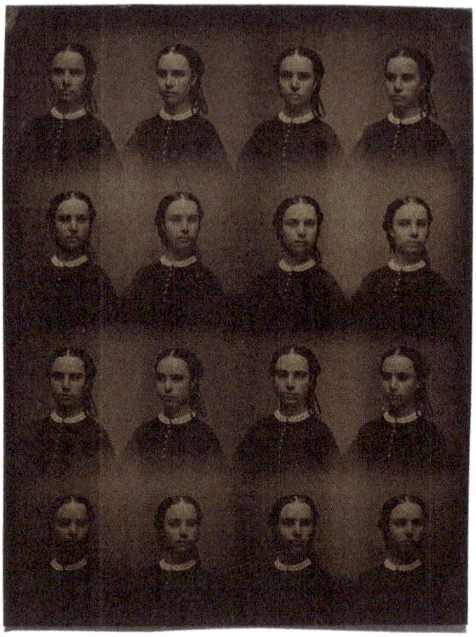

Fig. 25 Thomas Barbour, *Multiple images of portrait of girl made with Barbour's four lens tintype camera* (1866–1867), tintype, catalog number PG.001041A, http://collections.si.edu/search/results.htm?q=PG.001041A.

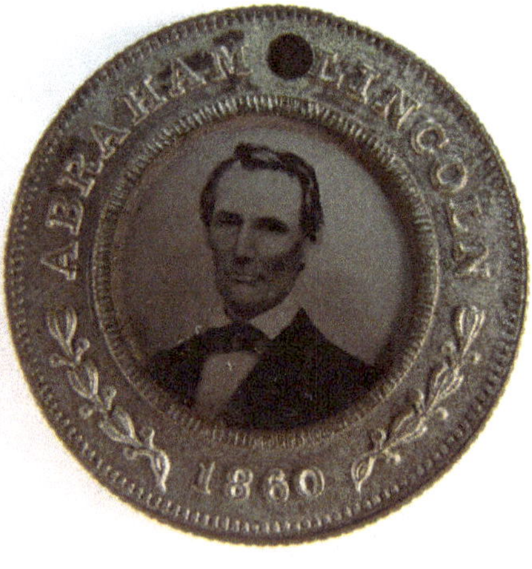

Fig. 26 Scovill Manufacturing Co. *Abraham Lincoln/Hannibal Hamlin* (1860), tintype political campaign pin, Washington, DC, Smithsonian's National Museum of American History, Division of Work & Industry, catalog number 1981.0296.1295, http://collections.si.edu/search/results.htm?q=1981.0296.1295.

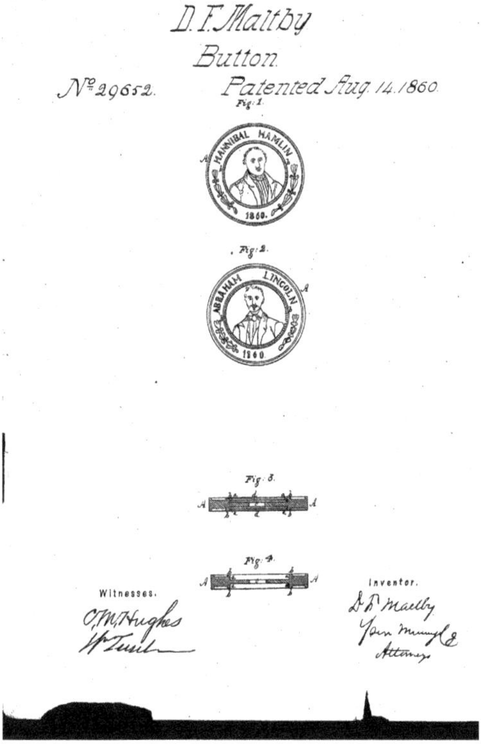

Fig. 27 Douglass F. Maltby, *Specifications for Patent Number 29652 Button* (14 August 1860), patent drawing specifications, Washington, DC, United States Patent and Trademark Office, https://pdfpiw.uspto.gov/.piw?docid=00029652.

The beginning of the Civil War was good for the tintype business. The durability of the plates and the ease of production increased. The number of newly enlisted soldiers increased, as did their desire to be photographed lest they not return. Photographers made tintypes in studios but were also able to take the studio to the battlefield.[72] Neff's and Griswold's businesses were joined by four other manufacturers. The competition drove down prices and improved quality; however the

72 'Civil War Photography| Bibliographies of Selected Sources| Articles and Essays| Civil War Glass Negatives and Related Prints| Digital Collections| Library of Congress', *Library of Congress, Washington, D.C. 20540 USA*, https://www.loc.gov/collections/civil-war-glass-negatives/articles-and-essays/bibliographies-of-selected-sources/civil-war-photography/. Photographers who made wet-plate collodion negatives tended to photographed landscapes and battlefields. Tintypes were predominately used for portraiture.

late stages of the war itself diminished trade, amid a national economic downturn and fewer troop deployments. With fortuitous timing, Neff sold his business to his Connecticut manufacturing partner James O. Smith in 1863. Griswold produced plates until 1867, when he sold the company to John Dean & Company. Paper-based photography and the introduction of the dry plate negative in the 1870s would supersede the tintype. Griswold's legacy would be remembered as the name of his plates, ferrotype, became the preferred term for the remainder of the nineteenth century.

Keeping and Embellishing Photographs

Designs and methods for the preservation and presentation of images in frames, cases, albums, viewers, and more were also within the purview of the USPO.[73] Here, we see that not only function and process was protected by patents, but also some aesthetics. Maltby's housings for portraits of those running for office sat at the intersection of a long history of campaign buttons and medals, and the need to house and protect photographic images.[74] The circa 1861 photograph showing the interior of frame maker James S. Earle's shop (see Chapter 7, Figure 1) showcases the importance of frames as aesthetic objects. They reflect the style and fashion of the day through their designs, materials, and hanging or mounting structures, some of which received patents. The artistic attributes of these objects situate the photograph as part of the practice of collecting, displaying and incorporating visual culture into everyday life as one could 'afford a beautiful parlor ornament'.[75] Samuel Peck was one such person who patented and sold frames, mats, and cases for photographs (see Figure 28).[76] Usually hidden under an image, the listed patents indicate Peck's contribution to shaping aesthetics found in homes of the era. These patents are for the design and construction

73 Schimmelman, *American Photographic Patents*, pp. 115–116. There were no less than thirty-eight photographic-related patents that include frames, cases, levelers for making picture frames, mats, and more. There was a separate category at the USPO for frames and such that were not listed as photography specific.

74 Edmund B. Sullivan, *American Political Badges and Medals 1789–1892* (Massachusetts: Quarterman Publications, 1981).

75 AVD Honeyman, 'Matters of the Month' in *The Photographic Times and American Photographer*, V, 58, 1875, p. 241.

76 *Price List. Samuel Peck and Co.'s Union Goods*, advertisement. *The Photographic Times and American Photographer*, II, 16 (1872), p. 57.

of the case that is both functional and aesthetic (see Figure 29).[77] As one considers material culture of the nineteenth century, some artifacts are comprised of patents that may or may not be visible.

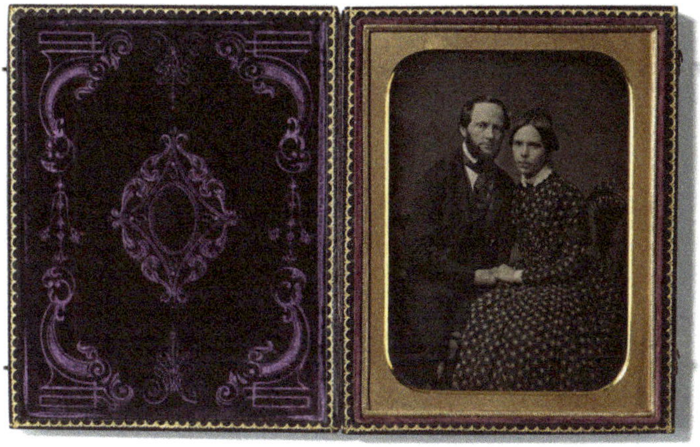

Fig. 28 Unidentified maker, *Samuel Peck and his second wife* (about 1847), daguerreotype, catalog number PG.75.17.931, http://collections.si.edu/search/results.htm?q=PG.75.17.931.

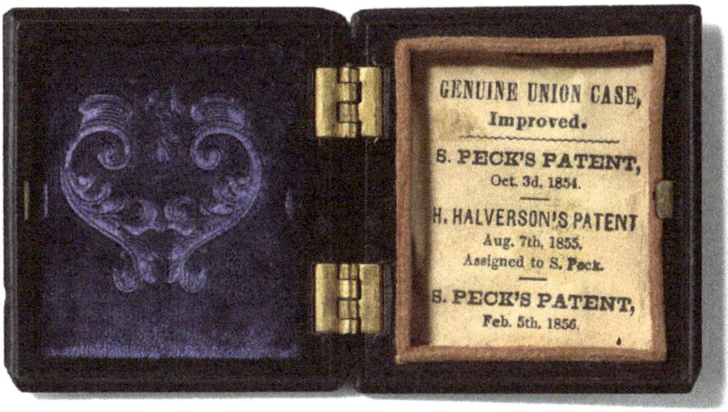

Fig. 29 Samuel Peck, *Case interior showing list of Peck's case patents* (late 1860s), interior of open case, catalog number PG.75.17.798, http://collections.si.edu/search/results.htm?q=PG.75.17.798.

77 Paul Berg, *Nineteenth Century Photographic Cases and Wall Frame* (United States, Berg, 2003); Clifford Krainik, Michele Krainik, and Carl Walvoord, *Union Cases: A Collector's Guide to the Art of America's First Plastics* (Grantsburg, WI, USA: Centennial Photo Service, 1988).

Conclusion

Though not always obvious or visible because they are outshined by the aesthetics, use, and ideas of the pictures they support, the calotype, the tintype, the ambrotype and other image-making processes transmit and embody a host of nineteenth-century national policies, photographic practices, and manufacturing and intellectual histories that shaped the material and physical aspects of the picture. In 1889, F. V. Butterfield read his widely republished paper to the Chemists' Assistants' Association in London, expressing his understanding of the state of photography. In it he notes: 'Boasting of barely half a century's existence, photography has made such rapid and gigantic strides that the position it holds to-day [sic] is one of the highest importance'.[78] His commentary is not one of the great strides in the democratization of images, but rather conveys an amazement with human ingenuity and the ability to harness science for art and usefulness: one that was often reflected in the tensions that surrounded patents. As we study images, their meanings, circulation, and consumption, the very format of their existence also transmits a series of controlled choices made by innovators, national policies, and commercial interests. These histories that envelope images can serve to deepen our understanding of the complicated ways in which people living in the nineteenth century created and experienced visual culture.

Bibliography

'The Ambrotype Patent Case', *The Photographic and Fine Art Journal*, X, II (February 1857), p. 56, https://archive.org/embed/photographicfine1018newy.

American Journal of Photography, 15 November 1865, pp. 239–240.

'Art & Architecture Thesaurus Full Record Display (Getty Research)', http://www.getty.edu/vow/AATFullDisplay?find=ambrotype&logic=AND&note=&english=N&prev_page=1&subjectid=300127186.

Berg, Paul, *Nineteenth Century Photographic Cases and Wall Frame* (United States, Berg, 2003).

Bogardus, Abraham, 'The Experiences of a Photographer', *Lippincott's Magazine* (May 1891).

78 F. V. Butterfield, 'Photography' *American Journal of Pharmacy*, 61 (Jan 1889), 45.

Brizuela, Natalia, 'Light Writing in the Tropics', *Aperture*, 215 (2014), pp. 32–37, https://aperture.org/editorial/light-writing-tropics/.

Butterfield, F. V., 'Photography', *American Journal of Pharmacy*, 61 (Jan 1889), p. 45.

'Civil War Photography| Bibliographies of Selected Sources| Articles and Essays| Civil War Glass Negatives and Related Prints| Digital Collections| Library of Congress', *Library of Congress, Washington, D.C. 20540 USA*, https://www.loc.gov/collections/civil-war-glass-negatives/articles-and-essays/bibliographies-of-selected-sources/civil-war-photography/.

'Correspondence upon Cutting's Patents', *Humphrey's Journal*, VIII, 21 (1 March 1857), p. 326.

'The Cutting Patents Denounced! New York Photographers assemble for defence [sic]!', *American Journal of Photography*, 2, 19 (1 March 1860), pp. 289–292.

Encyclopedia of Photography, ed. by International Center of Photography, 1st ed (New York: Crown, 1984), p. 285.

Fessenden, Marissa, 'This Is the First Known Photo of the Smithsonian Castle', *Smithsonian Magazine*, https://www.smithsonianmag.com/smart-news/smithsonian-celebrates-169th-birthday-image-castles-construction-180956212/.

'Frederick Scott Archer', *The British Journal of Photography*, XXII (28 February 1873), p. 102, https://archive.org/embed/britishjournalof22unse.

Gillespie, Sarah Kate, *The Early American Daguerreotype: Cross-Currents in Art and Technology*, Lemelson Center Studies in Invention and Innovation (Cambridge, Massachusetts: The MIT Press, 2016).

Gould, A. R., 'A Few Leaves From My Diary', *The Philadelphia Photographer*, XIX (January 1882) 217, pp. 13–14, http://archive.org/details/philadelphiaphot1882phil.

'The Great Photographic Lawsuit of 1854', *British Journal of Photography* 52:15 (December 1905) p. 985.

Gurney, Jeremiah, *Etchings on Photograph* (New York, 1856), pp. 1–27.

Hanlon, David R., 'Prospects of Enterprise: The Calotype Venture of the Langenheim Brothers', *History of Photography*, 35:4 (2011), 339–354, https://doi.org/10.1080/03087298.2011.606729.

——, *Illuminated Shadows: The Calotype in Nineteenth Century America*, 1st Ed (Nevada City, CA: Carl Mautz Pub, 2013).

Harris, Mazie McKenna, 'Inventors and Manipulators: Photography as Intellectual Property in Nineteenth-Century New York' (doctoral thesis, Brown University, 2014), available through *History of Art and Architecture Theses and Dissertations*, Brown Digital Repository, Brown University Library, https://doi.org/10.7301/Z0CF9NF2.

Harris, Mazie, Matthew Fox-Amato, and Christine Hult-Lewis, *Paper Promises: Early American Photography* (Los Angeles: The J. Paul Getty Museum, 2018).

Honeyman, AVD, 'Matters of the Month', *The Photographic Times and American Photographer*, V, 58 (1875), p. 241.

How Was It Made? Calotypes| V&A, https://www.youtube.com/watch?v=5jCWQTNWgyM.

'James Smithson, Founding Donor', *Smithsonian Institution Archives*, 2011, https://siarchives.si.edu/history/james-smithson.

Janssen, Barbara Suit, *Patent Models Index: Guide to the Collections of the National Museum of American History, Smithsonian Institution: Listings by Patent Number and Invention Name, Vol. 1* (Washington, DC: Smithsonian Institution Scholarly Press, 2010), https://doi.org/10.5479/si.19486006.54-1.

Jensen, James S., 'Cutting's Edge', *The Collodion Journal*, 5:19 (Summer 1999) pp. 5–9.

Krainik, Clifford, Michele Krainik, and Carl Walvoord, *Union Cases: A Collector's Guide to the Art of America's First Plastics* (Grantsburg, WI: Centennial Photo Service, 1988).

Levy, Marie Cordié, 'Matthew [sic] Brady's Abraham Lincoln', http://www.asjournal.org/60-2016/matthew-bradys-abraham-lincoln/#.

Lind, Edward, *Samuel F.B. Morse, His Letters and Journals*. (United States: Houghton Mifflin Company, 1914).

'The Melainotype', *The Photographic and Fine Art Journal*, X, II (February 1857), p. 64.

Morse, Samuel F. B., 'The Daguerreotype', *New York Observer*, 17:16 (20 April 1839), http://www.daguerreotypearchive.org/texts/N8390002_MORSE_NY_OBSERVER_1839-04-20.pdf.

Morse, Samuel Finely Breese and Edward Lind Morse, *Samuel F.B. Morse, His Letters and Journals*. (United States: Houghton Mifflin Company, 1914), pp. 128–130.

'The Niépce Heliograph', https://www.hrc.utexas.edu/niepce-heliograph/.

Peale-Sellers families, 'Peale-Sellers Family Collection, 1686–1963', https://search.amphilsoc.org/collections/view?docId=ead/Mss.B.P31-ead.xml#bioghist.

'The Photographic Patents', *The Photographic and Fine Art Journal*, VII, IX (1854), p. 277, https://archive.org/embed/photographicfine12185newy.

'Photography — Its Origin, Progress, And Present State', *The National Magazine; Devoted to Literature, Art, and Religion*, 1, 6 (Dec 1852), p. 510.

Post, Robert C., 'Patent Models: Symbols of an Era', *American Enterprise: Nineteenth-Century Patent Models.* (United States: Smithsonian Institution, 1984), pp. 8–13.

Price List. Samuel Peck and Co.'s Union Goods, advertisement. *The Photographic Times and American Photographer*, II, 16 (1872), p. 57.

Rosenblum, Naomi, 'The Early Years: Technology, Vision, Users 1839–1875', *A World History of Photography* (New York: Abbeville Press, 1984) (2007, Fourth ed.).

Schaaf, Larry J. and William Henry Fox Talbot, *Records of the Dawn of Photography: Talbot's Notebooks P & Q* (Cambridge [England]; New York, USA: Cambridge University Press in cooperation with the National Museum of Photography, Film & Television, 1996).

Schimmelman, Janice G., *American Photographic Patents, The Daguerreotype & Wet Plate Era 1840–1880* (Nevada City, NV: Carl Mautz Publishing, 2002).

——, *The Tintype in America 1856–1880* (Philadelphia: American Philosophical Society, 2007).

Sheppard, Furman and Henry Howson, 'Opposition to and Refusal of James A. Cutting's Patent,' *Arguments Before the U.S. Patent Office and Justices of the Supreme Court, D.C.: With Decisions, Comments, &c.* (United States, Philadelphia, 1871), pp. 343–365.

Simmons, MP, 'The Early Days of Daguerreotyping', *Anthony's Photographic Bulletin*, V, 21 (September 1874), 309–11. Reprint, *Scientific American* (14 November 1874), pp. 311–312.

Singleton's Nashville Business Directory, p 5. *Polk's Nashville (Davidson County, Tenn.) City Directory... 1865* ([Nashville] R. L. Polk & co., 1865), http://archive.org/details/polksnashvilleda00nash.

Suit Janssen, Barbara, *Patent Models Index: Guide to the Collections of the National Museum of American History, Smithsonian Institution: Listings by Patent Number and Invention Name, Vol. 1* (Washington, DC: Smithsonian Institution Scholarly Press, 2010), https://doi.org/10.5479/si.19486006.54-1.

Sullivan, Edmund B., *American Political Badges and Medals 1789–1892* (Massachusetts: Quarterman Publications, 1981).

Taft, Robert, 'The Tintype', *Photography and the American Scene* (New York: MacMillan Company, 1938), pp. 153–157.

True, Frederick, 'An Account of the United State National Museum', *Annual Report of the Board of Regents of the Smithsonian Institution* (Washington, DC: Government Printing Office, 1895) p. 290.

USA House of Representatives, *House Documents* (U.S. Government Printing Office, 1866).

US Congress, *Page: United States Statutes at Large Volume 1.djvu/443* (wikisource.org, 1793), https://en.wikisource.org/wiki/Page%3AUnited_States_Statutes_at_Large_Volume_1.djvu/443.

Weatherwax, Sarah, 'Part 1: A Philadelphia Snapshot from When Daguerreotypes Were New', *National Museum of American History*, 2015, https://americanhistory.si.edu/blog/part-1-philadelphia-snapshot-when-daguerreotypes-were-new.

Welling, William, *Photography in America: The Formative Years, 1839–1900* (New York: Crowell, 1978).

The Wet Collodion Process, https://www.youtube.com/watch?v=MiAhPIUno1o.

Wikisource contributors, 'United States Statutes at Large/ Volume 1/2nd Congress/ 2nd Session/Chapter 11', *Wikipedia, The Free Encyclopedia* (1845, last rev. 18 March 2021), https://en.wikisource.org/wiki/United_States_Statutes_at_Large/Volume_1/2nd_Congress/2nd_Session/Chapter_11.

13. King Tāwhiao's Photograph

Copyright, Celebrity, and the Commercial Image in Nineteenth-Century New Zealand

Jill Haley

On 19 January 1882, the Māori king Tūkāroto Pōtatau Matutaera Tāwhiao arrived in Auckland for a two-week sojourn.[1] His visit had been eagerly awaited, and an enormous, animated crowd turned out to the wharf to greet the King and his party. As a Māori celebrity and guest to the city, a reception committee had been organized to entertain Tāwhiao, escorting him to various locations around town. That first afternoon, he visited the Supreme Court building, a cabinetmaker's premises, and Elizabeth Pulman's photographic studio where he inspected photographs of Māori chiefs.[2] Tāwhiao went back to the Pulman studio several days later to select some of the photographs he had seen, and on a third trip, he sat for his portrait. One of the images from that session was selected and produced for commercial sale (see Figure 1).[3] Little did Tāwhiao or the Pulman studio know that seven months later, this image would be the center of New Zealand's first photographic copyright lawsuit.

1 Māori are the indigenous people of New Zealand. Historically tribal, most prefer to identify themselves with their *iwi* (tribal) name rather than the generic term 'Māori'. Not all tribes recognized Tāwhiao as king, and his influence was limited to a region of New Zealand's North Island.

2 *New Zealand Herald* (Auckland), 20 January 1882, p. 6.

3 The Museum of New Zealand Te Papa Tongarewa holds the original glass plate negative as well as several copies of the photograph.

 https://doi.org/10.11647/OBP.0247.13

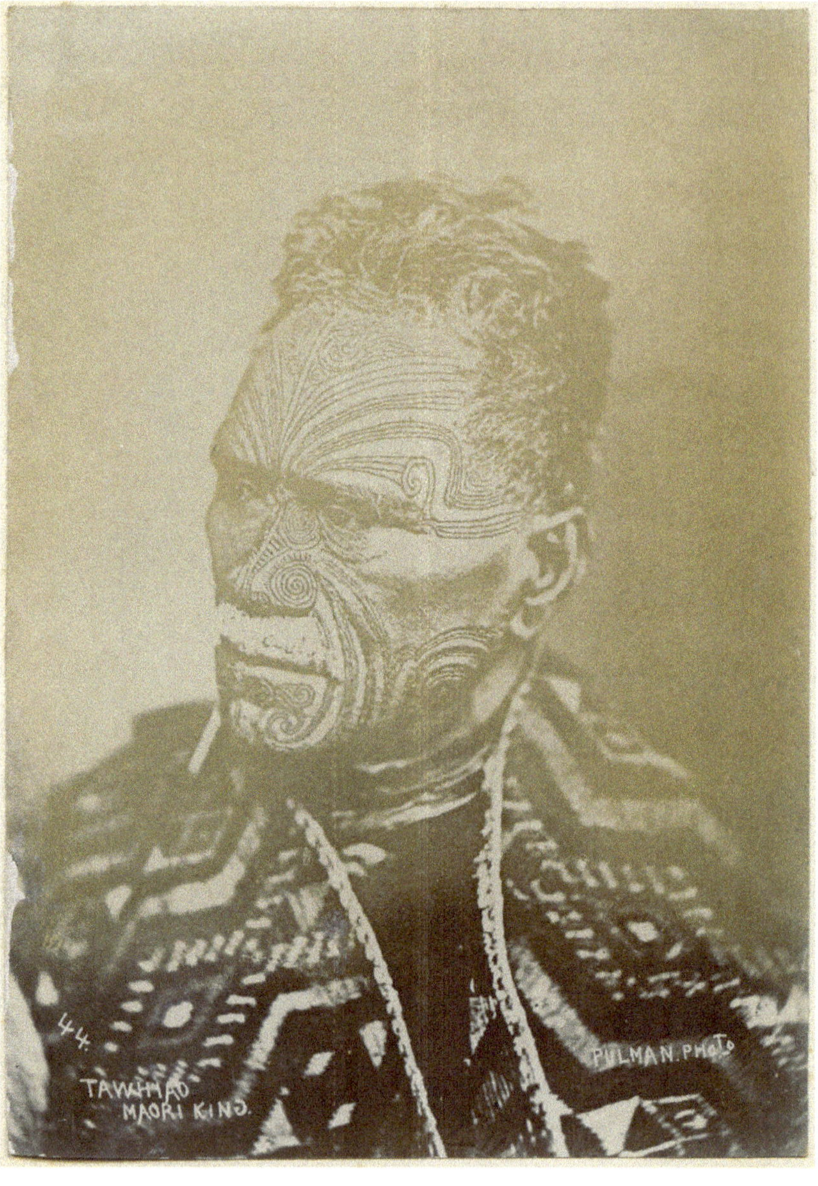

Fig. 1 E. Pulman studio, *Tūkāroto Pōtatau Matutaera Tāwhiao* (1882), Canterbury Museum, Christchurch, New Zealand, 1968.209.5.

Modelled on Britain's Fine Arts Copyright Act 1862, the New Zealand Fine Arts Copyright Act 1877 protected original works of art, defined as paintings, drawings, engravings, useful and ornamental designs, sculptures, photographs, and negatives made by New Zealand residents.[4] Despite the fact that the colony of New Zealand was not covered by Britain's Act, it had taken the colonial government fifteen years to produce its own protective legislation for artworks.[5] Rumours about an impending imperial copyright act in the mid-1870s were partly to blame for the delay.[6] Mounting pressure, some from photographers who had concerns about photographic piracy, finally motivated the New Zealand government to act. Member of Parliament and amateur photographer William Travers drafted the Bill, and in November 1877 the Act was passed.[7] It was not legally tested for photographs until August 1882 when the studio of Elizabeth Pulman, owned by Elizabeth and her second husband John Blackman, sued Charles Henry Monkton for unlawfully copying the portrait of Tāwhiao.

This chapter explores the case of *Blackman* v. *Monkton*. In the first instance, it was a test for the new copyright legislation, finding flaws and weaknesses that would be rectified several years later with a new act. However, an examination of its context highlights a number of factors related to image production and circulation in nineteenth-century New Zealand beyond copyright law. Commercial photography during the

4 Fine Arts Copyright Act 1877 (41 Victoriae 1877 No 17), http://www.nzlii.org/nz/legis/hist_act/faca187741v1877n17337/. For a discussion of the British Fine Arts Copyright Act, see Ronan Deazley, 'Breaking the Mould? The Radical Nature of the Fine Arts Copyright Bill 1862', in *Privilege and Property: Essays on the History of Copyright*, ed. by Ronan Deazley et al. (Cambridge: Open Book Publishers, 2010), pp. 289–320, https://doi.org/10.11647/obp.0007. For a discussion of photography and copyright in Britain, see also Ronan Deazley, 'Struggling with Authority: The Photograph in British Legal History', *History of Photography*, 27 (2003), 236–246 (p. 236), https://doi.org/10.1080/03087298.2003.10441249. For more on the background of New Zealand's Fine Art Copyright Act 1877, see Geoff McLay, 'New Zealand and the Imperial Copyright Tradition', in *A Shifting Empire: 100 Years of the Copyright Act 1911*, ed. by Uma Suthersanen and Ysolde Gendreau (Cheltenham: Edward Edgar, 2013), pp. 30–51, https://doi.org/10.4337/9781781003091.00007.

5 Books were protected by copyright in New Zealand through an ordinance passed in 1842. Copyright Act 1842 (5 Victoriae No 18), http://www.nzlii.org/nz/legis/hist_act/ca18425v1842n18253/.

6 *Evening Post* (Wellington), 5 July 1875, p. 2.

7 Christine Whybrew, 'The Burton Brothers Studio: Commerce in Photography and the Marketing of New Zealand, 1866–1898' (Doctoral thesis, University of Otago, 2010), p. 81.

period was closely tied to the rise of celebrity images and the public's demand for them. Māori chiefs were New Zealand's homegrown celebrities, and there was intense competition among photography studios for a piece of the lucrative Māori celebrity image market. Tāwhiao and other Māori were active and collaborative participants in their own image-making, and their agency is clearly evident in their dealings with studios.

Blackman v. *Monkton*

During the 1860s, photography was a burgeoning business in the recently established colony of New Zealand. English immigrant George Pulman, who trained as a draughtsman, turned his hand to the trade and established a commercial studio in Auckland in 1867. After his death in 1871, his widow Elizabeth retained control of the business and ran it under her own name.[8] When she married John Blackman in 1875, he managed the studio with her, but it continued to operate under the name E. Pulman (later Pulman and Son). The studio developed a brisk trade in photographs of Māori — images that were in high demand in New Zealand, and therefore highly profitable. In the 1880s, the Pulman studio registered many images of Māori chiefs, legally securing their copyright. Although the records no longer exist, we know that the studio registered the image of Tāwhiao because a case for its copyright infringement appeared in court in 1882.[9] This was not the first time that Elizbeth Pulman had encountered piracy. Shortly after George's death in 1871, she wrote to Auckland's *Daily Southern Cross* newspaper about a photograph of a map produced by her husband that was being copied and sold by a third person without her permission. While an unethical act, it pre-dated New Zealand's photographic copyright legislation and was not illegal. Pulman's only recourse was the court of public opinion. In her letter to the newspaper, she begged the public not to buy the

8 It is not known whether Elizabeth Pulman was a photographer. It is likely that she, like many wives of photographers during the period, assisted in the studio. Keith Giles posits that when Elizabeth's husband died, family friend and professional photographer George Steel stepped in to assist her. It is possible that Elizabeth owned the business while Steel operated the camera. Keith Giles, 'Fairs and Steel: Their Impact on Auckland Photography', *New Zealand Legacy*, 19 (2007), 8–12.

9 The registrations for the years 1877 to 1886 were lost in a fire in 1952 that destroyed numerous public records.

photograph of the map, which was her principal source of income for supporting herself and her seven young children.[10] Newspapers such as the *Auckland Star* supported her, threatening that if the sale of the 'pirated maps' continued, it would publish the name of the man 'who has committed such a dastardly act'.[11]

When Elizabeth and John Blackman discovered that Charles Henry Monkton, operating as the London Photographic Company, had been copying and selling their studio's copyrighted photograph of Tāwhiao, they acted.[12] On 23 August 1882, Monkton was charged with a breach of the Fine Arts Copyright Act 1877 which, according to the prosecutor Mr. Cotter, was the first case in New Zealand brought under the Act with regard to photographs.[13] The complaint was with regard to a 'certain work of art, to wit, a photograph of an aboriginal native, called King Tawhiao'.[14] The prosecution claimed that Monkton had violated Section 6 of the Act by 'unlawfully, and without the consent of John Blackman, the proprietor of such copyright, copy for sale the said work, on the 16th August, 1882'.[15] Monkton's lawyer, Edward Cooper, entered a plea of 'not guilty' for his client.[16]

The evidence from the prosecution was voluminous, and a number of witnesses testified.[17] George Steel, the manager of the Pulman studio, deposed that he had taken the photograph on 28 January 1882.[18] The distinctive cloak around the King's shoulders, he pointed out, was a prop owned by the studio. John Blackman confirmed that the image of Tāwhiao was taken by Steel and had been duly registered with the government in April. Frederick Pulman, Elizabeth's son and

10 *Daily Southern Cross* (Auckland), 9 June 1871, p. 2.

11 *Auckland Star*, 10 June 1871, p. 2.

12 No examples of Monkton's version of the portrait of Tāwhiao have been located. This is not surprising given the short amount of time that he was pirating it and the small number that would probably have made it into circulation.

13 Cotter's first name was never mentioned in any of the news reports. *New Zealand Herald*, 11 September 1882, p. 5.

14 *New Zealand Herald*, 21 August 1882, p. 3.

15 *Auckland Star*, 16 September 1882, p. 2; *New Zealand Herald*, 7 September 1882, p. 3.

16 *Auckland Star*, 9 September 1882, p. 2. Although not expressly stated, Monkton was also in breach of Section 7 which outlined the actions considered fraudulent with regards to copyrighted works.

17 *Taranaki Herald*, 11 September 1882, p. 2. For newspaper summaries of the case, see *Auckland Star*, 9 September 1882, p. 2; *New Zealand Herald*, 11 September 1882, p. 5.

18 The report in the *Auckland Star* incorrectly states that it was February 28. *Auckland Star*, 9 September 1882, p. 2.

partner in the business, stated that he had purchased a portrait of King Tāwhiao from Monkton's wife on 11 August. Mortimer Fairs, a friend of Blackman's, testified that he had visited Monkton's studio on 16 August and purchased nine photographs for four shillings and six pence.[19] He was adamant that Monkton himself had sold them. Several witnesses agreed that from the quality of the photographs purchased from Monkton, they were clearly copies. When examined by Blackman's lawyer, Monkton testified that he did not sell any photographs belonging to other studios. However, when presented with a cabinet card of the King produced by the Pulman studio and smaller *cartes de visite* marked with his studio's name, he agreed that the smaller ones were copies.[20] In his defense, he attested to the fact that he often signed his cards before the photographs were mounted onto them but could not account for the photograph appearing on his signed cards. He implied that an incompetent photographer he had employed for a brief period might have produced them while he was away from Auckland.

The judge dismissed the case, finding that although there was ample evidence that Monkton sold the photographs of Tāwhiao, it had not been proven that he had made the copies. Even if he had, it had not been shown that they were made after the image was registered. Section 5 of the Act made it clear that it was not illegal to copy a work of art that had not been registered for copyright, stating that 'no proprietor of any such copyright shall be entitled to the benefit of this Act until such registration, and no action shall be sustainable, nor any penalty recoverable, in respect of anything done before registration'.[21] The Pulman studio was unable to prove when Monkton had made the copies, and the judge surmised that it was possible that he had lawfully made them between the end of January when the photograph was taken and early April when it was formally registered.[22] It was a test case for

19 *New Zealand Herald*, 11 September 1882, p. 2. Fairs was the son of Thomas Armstrong Fairs, a photographer and associate of George Pulman in the 1860s.

20 *Cartes de visite* are paper photographs mounted on card backings measuring approximately 60 mm by 90 mm, roughly the size of a Victorian visiting card. They became the standard form for photographic portraiture throughout the 1860s. Larger format cabinet cards measuring approximately 110 mm by 165 mm appeared after 1870. Both formats were used during the 1870s and 1880s, but cabinet cards had largely replaced *cartes de visite* by 1890.

21 Fine Arts Copyright Act 1877, s. 5.

22 *Auckland Star*, 16 September 1882, p. 2.

photographs under the New Zealand Fine Arts Copyright Act 1877 and a setback for the Pulman studio. If it had won, the studio stood to receive an immediate financial settlement. According to the Act, upon conviction the offender was to pay the copyright holder a sum not exceeding ten pounds and surrender to them all illegal copies of the work of art. In addition, the copyright holder was entitled to recover damages. It is not known whether Monkton continued selling the photograph.

Why did Monkton risk breaking the law and copy the Pulman studio's image of Tāwhiao? It might have been a simple matter of ignorance, but it seems unlikely that he was unfamiliar with the Act. During late 1877 and early 1878, its passing was reported on widely in the newspapers. In February 1880, shortly after an amendment in late 1879 that added dramatic works to protection under the Act, the first of several court cases for its infringement reached the press.[23] In *Gillon* v. *Lumsden*, E. T. Gillon, the New Zealand agent for the English Dramatic Authors Society, took the Invercargill Garrick Club to court for staging the copyrighted play *Hunting a Turtle* without paying the licensing fee.[24] J. T. Lumsden, the secretary for the club, admitted liability and paid the minimum penalty of forty shillings. In the months following, Gillon went on a litigious rampage, successfully bringing cases against several other dramatic groups under the Act.[25] If he read the papers, Monkton would have been aware of this flurry of cases, and if he were illiterate, he no doubt would have heard the news through community gossip. Even though no photographic copyright cases had been brought to court yet, he would have had fair warning that the new Act was being exercised successfully.

In all likelihood, Monkton was simply engaging in the widespread practice of copying the work of other photographers, especially images of Māori. There was no requirement under the 1877 Act to mark photographs as having been registered for copyright, so Monkton would have had difficulty knowing that the Tāwhiao image was protected. In fact, a very low percentage of photographs were registered, making

23 Fine Arts Copyright Act 1877 Amendment Act 1879 (43 Victoriae No. 35), http://www.nzlii.org/nz/legis/hist_act/faca1877aa187943v1879n35438/.

24 *New Zealand Times* (Wellington), 19 March 1880, p. 2.

25 *Gillon* v. *De Lias*, *New Zealand Mail* (Wellington), 8 May 1880, p. 18; *Gillon* v. *Lucas*, *Evening Post*, 20 May 1880, p. 2; *Gillon* v. *Geddes*, *New Zealand Herald*, 31 August 1880, p. 5.

most copying legal. And if a copyrighted image had been unlawfully copied, the onus was on the owner of the copyright to discover this and take action as the Pulman studio had. The situation was rectified in 1896 with the passing of the Photographic Copyright Bill, a piece of legislation that addressed the shortcomings of the 1877 Act with regard to photographs.[26] Section 2 of the 1896 Act stipulated that in order to be covered, the word 'Protected', the name of the photographer or studio, and the date the photograph was taken had to be inscribed on the original negative and appear clearly on the photographic print.

In taking Monkton to court, the Pulman studio was attempting to use the Fine Arts Copyright Act 1877 to protect its commercial interests. Kathy Bowrey and Elena Cooper have likewise found in the United Kingdom that the Fine Arts Copyright Act 1862 was often used to protect commercial rather than creator rights with regards to images.[27] Pulman had invested financially in the Tāwhiao image in several ways that Monkton had not. Similar to the British system, in order to secure copyright, the studio had to register the image with the government.[28] In New Zealand, this entailed completing a form and paying a fee. The application form cost one shilling, and submitting the form and having it registered was an additional two and a half shillings (equivalent to about twenty dollars in today's money). Many photographic studios found the registration fee expensive and the application process cumbersome. Commercial photographers who produced landscape or celebrity photographs could have hundreds of images to register, and the registration fees on poorly-selling photographs could exceed profits. The Burton Brothers studio was one of the most prolific and successful landscape photography businesses in New Zealand, and the studio photographed some of the most remote places in New Zealand,

26 Photographic Copyright Bill 1896 (89–3), http://www.nzlii.org/nz/legis/hist_bill/pcb1896893267/.

27 Kathy Bowrey, '"The World Daguerreotyped — What a Spectacle!" Copyright Law, Photography and Commodification Project of Empire', conference paper presented at the Third International Society for the History and Theory of Intellectual Property (ISHTIP) Workshop, Griffith University, 5–6 July 2011; Elena Cooper, *Art and Modern Copyright: The Contested Image* (Cambridge: Cambridge University Press, 2018).

28 For a discussion of the British system of registrations, see John Plunkett, 'Celebrity and Community: The Poetics of the Carte de Visite', *Journal of Victorian Culture,* 8 (2003), 55–79 (p. 63), https://doi.org/10.3366/jvc.2003.8.1.55.

spending large sums of money doing so. Surprisingly, of the hundreds of photographs Burton Brothers produced in the period between 1887 and 1911, only fifty-two were registered.[29] Such a low number suggests that only images that were expected to have commercial success were registered. Copyright registration, it seems, was the exception rather than the rule. However, when they registered their images, studios expected to own the exclusive right to produce them, reap all profits from their sale, and have the courts protect their commercial interests. The advertising of Tāwhiao's portrait in the *Auckland Star* and *New Zealand Herald* newspapers was another outlay the Pulman studio made.[30] The first advertisement appeared on the same day that Tāwhiao sat for his portrait and would have been placed and paid for in anticipation of the sitting and before the photograph was actually taken.[31] The studio clearly expected the image would be a profitable one worth promoting immediately.

Celebrity, Consumers, and the Circulation of Images

Modern celebrity became established as a part of cultural life during the nineteenth century.[32] According to Tom Mole, who traces the origins of celebrity to the late eighteenth century, it required three components — an individual, an industry, and an audience — which combine to 'render an individual person fascinating'.[33] Sharon Marcus notes that these three must work in collaboration for celebrity to exist.[34] The phenomenon of the celebrity image that emerged in the 1860s was the result of a convergence of the famous (and infamous), the industry

29 Whybrew, p. 83.

30 *Auckland Star*, 28 January 1882, p. 3; *New Zealand Herald*, 30 January 1882, p. 1.

31 *Auckland Star*, 28 January 1882, p. 3.

32 John Plunkett, 'Celebrity Culture', in *The Oxford Handbook of Victorian Literary Culture*, ed. by Juliet John (Oxford: Oxford University Press, 2016), pp. 539–560, https://doi.org/10.1093/oxfordhb/9780199593736.013.21.

33 Tom Mole, *Byron's Romantic Celebrity: Industrial Culture and the Hermeneutic of Intimacy* (Basingstoke and New York: Palgrave Macmillan, 2007), p. 1, https://doi.org/10.1057/9780230288386. See also Plunkett, 'Celebrity Culture', p. 540; Hannah-Rose Murray, 'A "Negro Hercules": Frederick Douglass' Celebrity in Britain', *Celebrity Studies*, 7 (2106), 264–279 (p. 265), https://doi.org/10.1080/19392397.2015.1098551.

34 Sharon Marcus, *The Drama of Celebrity* (Princeton: Princeton University Press, 2019), p. 4, https://doi.org/10.2307/j.ctvc772z0.

of photography (especially the development of cheap *cartes de visite*), and consumer demand for these photographs. As print and visual media grew, the access to and circulation of information, gossip, and images of famous people increased, fuelling a popular desire to see and know more about them. The celebrity image became big business.[35] An article published in the British weekly magazine *Once a Week* commented on the 'commercial value of the human face' and that sudden fame could send up the value of one's image 'to a degree they never dreamed of'.[36] In the trade at the time, celebrity images were referred to as 'sure cards' because their high demand guaranteed their commercial success.[37] Marion & Co. in England was the major wholesale supply point for celebrity *cartes de visite* in that country, and in 1862 they claimed that they dealt with 50,000 every month.[38] In the week after Prince Albert's death, 70,000 of his photographs were ordered from them, and a portrait taken in 1868 of his daughter-in-law Princess Alexandra carrying her daughter Louise on her back sold 300,000 copies.[39] In the United States in 1863, Anthony and Company produced up to 3,600 celebrity photographs daily and had 4,000 subjects available.[40] These weren't just celebrities — they were profitable commodities.

In New Zealand, Māori represented home-grown celebrities, and many studios marketed them as such: John McGarrigle, J. Low, Monkton and the Pulman studio all advertised that they sold photographs of 'Maori Celebrities'.[41] Photographers were not inventing the idea of the Māori celebrity as a marketing tactic; they were tapping into the

---

35 For classic works on the development of commercial photography and the emergence of celebrity images, see Elizabeth Anne McCauley, *A. A. E. Disdéri and the Carte de Visite Portrait Photograph* (New Haven: Yale University Press, 1985); Elizabeth Anne McCauley, *Industrial Madness: Commercial Photography in Paris, 1848–1871* (New Haven: Yale University Press, 1994).

36 'Cartes de Visite', reprinted in *Otago Daily Times*, 22 April 1862, p. 5.

37 Ibid.

38 John Plunkett, *Queen Victoria: First Media Monarch* (Oxford: Oxford University Press, 2003), p. 153.

39 *Otago Daily Times*, 22 April 1862, p. 5; *The Photographic News*, 29 (1885), 136.

40 Vicki Goldberg, *The Power of Photography: How Photographs Changed our Lives* (New York: Abbeville Press, 1991), p. 105; Michael Pritchard, 'Edward Anthony and Henry Tiebout', in *Encyclopedia of Nineteenth-Century Photography*, ed. by John Hannavy (New York: Routledge, 2008), pp. 48–50 (p. 50), https://doi.org/10.4324/9780203941782.

41 *Auckland Star*, 19 February 1873, p. 2; *Waikato Times*, 17 May 1877, p. 1; *Taranaki Herald*, 24 April 1883, p. 3; *Auckland Star*, 26 July 1881, p. 3.

general attitude holding that important Māori, particularly chiefs, were celebrities. New Zealand newspapers abound with reports about 'Maori celebrities' and their activities. The events of the New Zealand Wars between Māori and the colonial government during the 1860s drew attention to the exploits of many individuals such as Tāwhiao and made them household names.[42] In 1879, the *New Zealand Herald* claimed that the 'most famous man in New Zealand' was chief Rewi Maniapoto for his role in helping to bring peace to the country at the end of the war period.[43] There was great consumer demand for putting a face to the name, and portraits of these celebrities were eagerly purchased.

Portraits of Māori were one of the Pulman studio's specialties. In 1864, a few years before setting up his own studio, George Pulman sold photographs of Māori taken by the Auckland studio of Fairs and Steel alongside European celebrities such as Shakespeare and Macauley.[44] George established the Pulman studio in 1867 and continued selling portraits of Māori. One example marked 'G. Pulman' shows an elderly Māori chief with intricate *moko* (facial tattooing) (see Figure 2).[45]

In an 1879 advertisement, the Pulman studio boasted that it had on hand 2,000 'portraits of natives' but listed only eighty views of Auckland, suggesting that the sale of Māori images was a particularly profitable aspect of the business.[46] The studio was not alone in investing in a large stock of Māori images; in an insurance claim John McGarrigle placed for a fire that destroyed his studio in 1876, he claimed to have had 200 negatives and 31,000 mounted and unmounted Māori prints, which he supplied wholesale to shopkeepers at an average rate of 1,000 a month.[47] During the 1880s when Tāwhiao's portrait was taken, the Māori celebrity image market was fiercely competitive. In 1881 and 1882, the Pulman

42 The New Zealand Wars were a series of armed conflicts between some Māori tribes and the New Zealand government over land rights and sovereignty from 1845 to 1872, peaking in the 1860s.

43 *New Zealand Herald*, 28 May 1879, p. 5; 30 May 1879, p. 5.

44 *Daily Southern Cross*, 13 January 1864, p. 2. Macauley was Thomas Babbington Macauley, First Baron Macauley, a well-known nineteenth-century British historian and politician.

45 This portrait has been incorrectly identified as Ngāti Manu leader Whētoi Pōmare (Whiria). However, Pomare died in 1850 before Pulman could have taken his portrait. For a fuller discussion, see Keith Giles, 'The Problematic Portraits of Pomare II', *New Zealand Memories*, 26 (2014), 20–21.

46 *Auckland Star*, 2 January 1879, p. 4.

47 *New Zealand Herald*, 17 January 1877, p. 3.

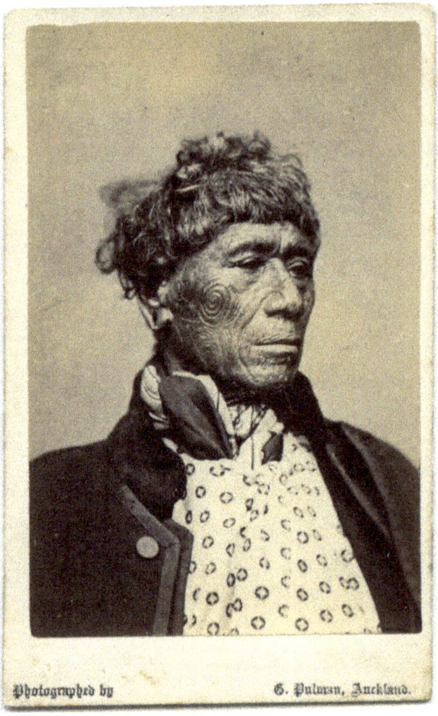

Fig. 2 George Pulman, *Māori Chief* (ca. 1870), Canterbury Museum, Christchurch, New Zealand, 19xx.2.3826.

studio boldly asserted that it had the 'greatest variety of Original Portraits of Maori Celebrities in New Zealand'.[48] Thomas Price made a similar claim, advertising that he had the 'Largest and Best Assortment of Maori Photographs in New Zealand', while the Foy Brothers studio likewise asserted that it sold the 'Best Collection of Maori Photos in New Zealand'.[49]

Monkton also advertised and sold photographs of Māori. In May 1881, he photographed Tāwhiao, his wife Hera, and other members of the royal family at a meeting of Māori at Whatiwhatihoe (see Figure 3).

Four days after Monkton was charged with copyright infringement in 1882, he advertised that he was selling photographs from the Whatiwhatihoe meeting and stressed that they were 'taken by me, and

48 *Auckland Star*, 27 July 1881, p. 3.
49 *Wairarapa Daily Times*, 8 June 1881, p. 3; *Thames Advertiser*, 21 December 1883, p. 2.

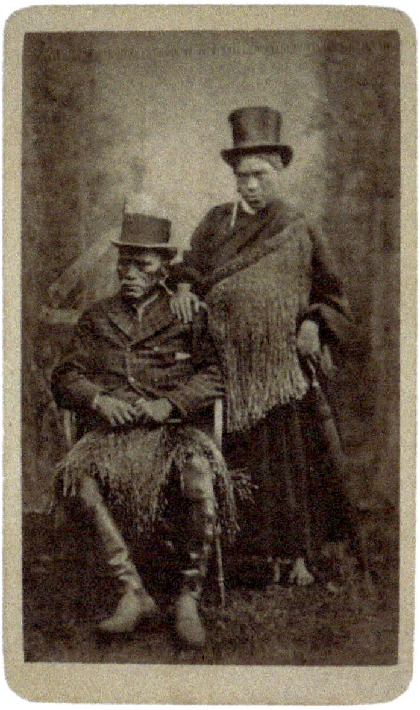

Fig. 3 Charles Henry Monkton, *Tāwhiao and his Wife Hera* (1881), Auckland Libraries Heritage Collections, Auckland, New Zealand, 589–4.

no other photographer'.[50] His newspaper advertisement implied his innocence in the accusation by the Pulman studio and attempted to minimize the impact of the bad publicity he was receiving. However, a few weeks earlier, on August 11, he advertised 'Photographs of King Tawhio and all the Maori Royal Family, from 3/ per dozen', but there was no specific mention of the Whatiwhatihoe meeting.[51] This likely alerted the Pulman studio to the possibility that Monkton was selling their image. On that day, Elizabeth's son Frederick visited Monkton's studio and purchased a copy of the portrait from Monkton's wife, confirming the Pulman studio's suspicion.[52] On August 16, Monkton placed the advertisement a second time, prompting Blackman's friend Mortimer Fairs to immediately visit the studio where he purchased more copies of Pulman's photograph directly from Monkton.[53]

50 *Auckland Star*, 28 August 1882, p. 3.
51 *Auckland Star*, 11 August 1882, p. 3.
52 *Auckland Star*, 9 September 1882, p. 2.
53 *Auckland Star*, 16 August 1882, p. 3; *Auckland Star*, 9 September 1882, p. 2.

Photographs of Māori were not always regarded as celebrity images and, in fact, defy such neat classification. Ultimately, the viewer defined the image, and individual images could have multiple meanings depending on what viewers wanted to see. Teresa Zackodnik argues that with photographs of American abolitionist and activist Sojourner Truth, there is a discrepancy between Truth's intentions with her image and the 'uses and assumed meanings' of her photographs by consumers.[54] In her study of Eugéne Appert's photographs of the French Communards of 1871, Jeannene M. Przyblyski points out the variety of interpretations possible from a single photograph of one of the men: a mother saw evidence of her son's survival, police saw a suspect, and Parisians saw an infamous celebrity.[55] Māori photographs also had many meanings and were simultaneously images of local celebrities, anonymous ethnographic type specimens, and everything in between. In his investigation of representations of Māori in photography and art, Roger Blackley argues that these images represent a variant of European orientalism and embodied a form of colonial fantasy.[56] They were also, he points out, images that both celebrated colonialism and served as memorials for a dying Māori culture. Images of Māori in customary clothing were sought by some collectors as visual trophies and assembled into albums of ethnographic specimens. An album in the collection of Canterbury Museum compiled during the 1870s holds over two dozen of these portraits.[57] Each has been carefully catalogued on the back with information such as 'Te Mamaku a rebel native of Taranaki' or more salacious details such as 'The two native women who ate the heart and drank the blood of Revd Volkner missionary of Opotiki'.[58]A leather-bound example from the 1860s in the collection of

54 Teresa Zackodnik, 'The "Green-Backs of Civilization": Sojourner Truth and Portrait Photography', *American Studies*, 46 (2005), 117–143 (p. 119).

55 Jeannene M. Przyblyski, 'Loss of Light: The Long Shadow of Photography in the Digital Age', in *The Oxford Handbook of Film and Media Studies*, ed. by Robert Kolker (Oxford: Oxford University Press, 2015), pp. 158–186 (p. 166), https://doi.org/10.1093/oxfordhb/9780195175967.013.0006.

56 Roger Blackley, *Galleries of Maoriland: Artists, Collectors and the Māori World, 1880–1910* (Auckland: Auckland University Press, 2018).

57 Canterbury Museum, Album 213, E161.50.

58 In 1865, during the New Zealand Wars, German missionary Carl Sylvius Völkner was executed by the Te Whakatōhea tribe for acting as a spy for the British government. New Zealand History, 'Carl Völkner', https://nzhistory.govt.nz/people/carl-volkner.

the Museum of New Zealand Te Papa Tongarewa features the title 'New Zealand Chiefs' in tooled gold lettering on the front cover.[59] In addition to photographs of Māori, its compiler John Henry Eaton added images of Aboriginal Australians, Fijians, and views of Auckland. The desire for Māori photographs as examples of ethnographic types extended beyond New Zealand. In a letter to Canterbury Museum Director Julius Haast in 1873, Italian anthropologist Enrico Giglioni asks him to send some 'good typical photographs of the New Zealand natives' that he could use for 'ethnological studies'.[60] Recognizing this overseas demand, photography studios like George Hoby's marketed Māori images for sending 'home', the term commonly used in New Zealand to refer to Great Britain.[61] But people overseas did not have to wait for New Zealanders to send them photographs of Māori; celebrity image publishers in England such as Marion & Co. also stocked 'New Zealand Chiefs'.[62]

Collecting images of Māori strictly as ethnographic specimens seems to have been a limited practice in New Zealand. Images of Māori are usually encountered in Victorian photograph albums alongside the compiler's family and friends, suggesting that their meaning was more about curiosity and whimsy — and closer to celebrity — than scientific specimen. Priscilla Smith, daughter of a New Zealand businessman and wife of a sheep station owner, included four photographs of Māori in her family album among her visual menagerie that included Hawai'ian royalty, Peruvian veiled women, the dwarf couple General Tom Thumb and Lavinia Warren, and a portrait of Abraham Lincoln.[63] Still others used photographs of Māori as sources of humor. In a letter written in 1877 from Tannie Fidler in New Zealand to her friend Georgy in Scotland, Tannie describes a joke she was planning to make at her sister's expense with a photograph of Māori women: 'There was a carte of four Maori ladies which I told Fanny I was going to send Robt as my young sister and three friends. She took it from me and crushed it all but I just put it in'.[64]

---

59 Museum of New Zealand Te Papa Tongarewa, AL000208, https://collections.tepapa.govt.nz/object/575310.

60 Canterbury Museum, related documents, EA1988.

61 *Taranaki Herald*, 21 July 1866, p. 2.

62 Michael Graham-Stewart and John Gow, *Negative Kept: Maori and the Carte de Visite* (Auckland: John Leech Gallery, 2013), p. 189.

63 Toitū Otago Settlers Museum, Album 8, 1959/20/43.

64 Tannie Fidler to Georgy, 1877, Toitū Otago Settlers Museum, AG-305.

King Tāwhiao

During the case of *Blackman* v. *Monkton*, neither side called Tāwhiao as a witness, and missing from the court case was any consideration of him other than as the passive subject of the contested photograph. What was his standpoint on the making and circulation of his image? According to the New Zealand Fine Arts Copyright Act, the copyright of any work of art made for another person for 'valuable consideration' was not retained by the artist unless the commissioner agreed to it in writing to cede the copyright to the artist.[65] If Tāwhiao had paid for his sitting and not transferred copyright to the studio, he would have been the one entitled to register his image under the Act. However, if this had been the case, Tāwhiao might not have been aware of his right to his image. Artists and others who stood to gain from copyright would have been familiar with the Act's content but Tāwhiao, who lived in a remote, isolated Māori community and spoke te reo Māori as his first language, would have been less connected to European legal matters. It is possible that the studio took advantage of his ignorance and fraudulently registered itself as the copyright holder. Rather than commissioning their photographs, some nineteenth-century celebrities were instead paid by the studio for their visit, thus giving the photographer copyright and control of the image. Depending on their marketability, some notable sitters in the United States were paid between 25 and 1,000 dollars.[66] Tāwhiao appears to have sat for his portrait for free. During the hearing, it was mentioned that it was common practice to take photographs of Māori celebrities without 'pecuniary consideration', suggesting that this had been the case with the King.[67] If so, the Pulman studio, not Tāwhiao, was entitled to the copyright.

65 According to Section 2 of the Fine Arts Copyright Act 1877, works of art 'made or executed for or on behalf of any other person for a good or valuable consideration, the person so selling or disposing of or making or executing the same, shall not retain the copyright thereof, unless it be expressly reserved to him by agreement in writing, signed at or before the time of such sale or disposition by the vendee or assignee thereof'.

66 Alison Hearn, '"Sentimental Greenbacks of Civilization": Cartes de Visite and the Pre-History of Self-Branding', in *The Routledge Companion to Advertising and Promotional Culture*, ed. by Matthew P. McAlister and Emily West (New York: Routledge, 2013), pp. 24–38 (p. 33), https://doi.org/10.4324/9780203071434.

67 *New Zealand Times*, 11 September 1882, p. 2.

While Māori engaged with photography and visited studios to have their portraits taken, this was not the type of portrait that Tawhiao would have commissioned for himself. It has all the hallmarks of one staged by a studio for the commercial market. Tāwhiao wears a finely woven flax cloak known as a *kaitaka,* but visible beneath it is his everyday clothing — the European-style shirt and cravat-like tie that he wore to the studio. By the 1880s when this photograph was taken, most Māori wore European-style clothing in their everyday life, and hundreds of studio portraits ordered by Māori show that they preferred everyday clothing rather than customary garments for their portraits. In fact, the cloak is not Tāwhiao's but a prop owned by the Pulman studio that features in several other portraits it produced of Māori chiefs. Items such as cloaks and traditional weapons were standard items in studios that produced commercial images of Māori. Adorning a sitter with these accoutrements accentuated his or her 'Māori-ness' and created a more interesting, saleable image. *Kaitaka* like the one Tāwhiao wears have chiefly associations, and posing the King in it emphasized his royal status to viewers. However, he wears it incorrectly upside down so that the decorative, geometric-patterned *taniko* hem is visible in the frame and becomes a feature in the composition. Tāwhiao's elaborate *moko* (facial tattooing) further increased the marketability of his image. Not only did it signify his chiefly status, this exotic cultural practice was also a great curiosity to Europeans. The wet plate collodion process that produced this photograph had difficulty picking up the blue and green shades of Māori tattoos, and as a result, photographers had to re-touch negatives to bring out the intricate designs chiselled into the sitter's skin.[68] The lines on Tāwhiao's face have been re-drawn by the Pulman studio to make them visible.

Portraits of Māori staged in customary clothing similar to Tāwhiao's were produced for a European market, but Māori were also consumers, and these images circulated in their world. For them, such photographs signified personal connections and cultural affiliation. On one of his visits to the Pulman studio, Tāwhiao viewed photographs of Māori chiefs and expressed his pleasure at seeing some old familiar faces such

68 Donna-Lee Biddle, 'Wet-plate Photography and the Resurgence of Tā Moko', https://www.stuff.co.nz/national/106652213/wetplate-photography-and-the-resurgence-of-t-moko.

as Rewi Maniapoto, whom the studio had photographed in 1879, and he selected several photographs to take away.[69] He also felt some nostalgia at seeing many of the chiefs he had known in his earlier days who had since died. Like the Europeans who collected ethnographic type images of Māori and other indigenous people as records of a dying race, late nineteenth-century Māori also recognized the period as one of twilight for their culture in the face of European modernization.[70] Portraits such as Maniapoto's and Tāwhiao's captured and preserved their rapidly disappearing world.

Scholarship on photography of Māori has pointed to a degree of exploitation perpetrated by photographers. Michael Graham-Stewart and John Gow maintain that Māori were unable to control how they were depicted and photographers acted in their own commercial self-interest, and William Main describes Māori as being 'commercially exploited' by photographers such as John Nicol Crombie.[71] While not denying the spectre of exploitation that would have been present in some situations, collaboration and agency marked the creation of much Māori visual representation. Unlike indigenous people in other colonial societies who lacked control over their image production, Māori had engaged with the European world since the early nineteenth century and had an understanding of photography.[72] As clients and consumers, they were familiar with the production and distribution of images.[73] They would also have been familiar with the commercial photographs that were displayed in studio windows as a form of advertising and public portrait gallery amusement.[74] Literate Māori would have read newspaper advertisements for Māori photographs like Pulman's and Monkton's. One photography session was reported in detail in the

69 *Auckland Star*, 20 January 1882, p. 3.

70 See Blackley for further information.

71 Graham-Stewart and Gow, p. 190; William Main, *Maori in Focus: A Selection of Photographs of the Maori from 1850–1914* (Wellington: Millwood Press, 1976), p. 5.

72 Debra Poole's work on photography in Peru is one study that examines the unequal power relations between photography studios and their indigenous sitters. Debra Poole, *Vision, Race and Modernity: A Visual Economy of the Andean Image World* (Princeton, NJ: Princeton University Press, 1997). For a discussion of Māori and modernity, see Megan Pōtiki, 'Me Tā Tāua Mokopuna: The Te Reo Māori Writings of H. K. Taiaroa and Tame Parata', *New Zealand Journal of History*, 49 (2015), 31–49.

73 Museum and archival collections in New Zealand hold hundreds of privately commissioned studio portraits of Māori that attest to their engagement with photography.

74 'Looking in at Shop Windows', *All the Year Round*, 12 June 1869, pp. 42–43.

Wellington Independent newspaper in 1866. High-ranking chief Wiremu Tāmihana Tarapipipi Te Waharoa (known as the Kingmaker for his role in having Tāwhiao's father declared the first Māori king) and his retinue visited Wellington to speak to the New Zealand Parliament and stopped at the Swan and Wrigglesworth studio for a sitting. In addition to having their portraits taken for personal use, the newspaper reported that 'These Maoris have doffed the European costume, for the sake of effect, and shew themselves in "fighting trim" and "eager for the fray"'.[75] For the commercial images the studio wanted to produce, the men posed as New Zealand warriors with traditional weapons and in clothing described as 'purely Maori'. These images were added to the studio's range of other local celebrities such as members of parliament who had recently honoured the studio with sittings. In 1879, chief Rewi Maniapoto had his portrait taken by the Pulman studio (see Figure 4), and he took away 50 copies to distribute, paid for by the government Native Office.[76]

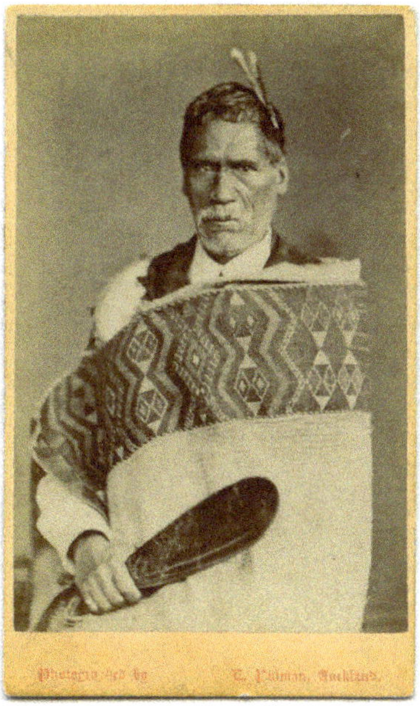

Fig. 4 E. Pulman studio, *Rewi Maniapoto* (1879), Canterbury Museum, Christchurch, New Zealand, 19xx.2.3828.

75 *Wellington Independent*, 28 August 1866, p. 5.
76 *Auckland Star*, 21 June 1879, p. 2; *New Zealand Herald*, 11 December 1879, p. 6.

At a meeting later that year, he showed other chiefs his photograph. They offered their admiration at the image that was so lifelike, compliments that pleased Maniapoto.[77] By the time Tāwhiao visited the Pulman studio in 1882, New Zealand photographers had been selling images of Māori celebrities commercially for nearly twenty years.[78]

Tāwhiao was no stranger to photographic studios, having had his portrait taken several times before visiting Pulman in 1882. He went to the studio twice in the days before his sitting, inspecting the photographs it stocked of Māori. In return, Elizabeth Pulman presented him with several photographs of chiefs, and he promised to return to the studio for a session, which he did on January 28. Having acquainted himself with the studio's range of Māori photographs on his previous visits, it is clear that Tāwhiao co-operated in the production of his portrait. This is not to say that he had full agency with its composition; it is likely that George Steel, the photographer, staged the scene to produce a marketable commercial image. However, Tāwhiao had voluntarily come to the studio, and it was in the studio's best interest to work collaboratively with him. In lieu of being paid for his sitting, it is likely that he was given copies of his photograph as Maniapoto had been.[79]

It was not just the studio that gained by this arrangement; Tāwhiao and other Māori sitters benefitted from the commercialisation of their images in several ways. Recent scholarship on the use of photography by African Americans during the nineteenth century has shown not only their agency but also their use of images to serve their cultural and political needs.[80] Frederick Douglass was possibly the most photographed American in the nineteenth century, and he used the production and distribution of his image to craft his own public identity and change

77 *Auckland Star*, 26 June 1879, p. 2.

78 The first newspaper advertisement found for Māori photographs is George Pulman's from 1864, a few years after *cartes de visite* were introduced in New Zealand and around the time that celebrity *cartes* became popular. *Daily Southern Cross*, 13 January 1864, p. 2.

79 Some Māori were paid models for commercial portraits by painters. Pātara Te Tuhi was reportedly paid eight shillings a day by artist Charles Goldie in 1901 for his sitting. Blackley, p. 100.

80 Jasmine Nichole Cobb, *Picture Freedom: Remaking Black Visuality in the Early Nineteenth Century* (New York: New York University Press, 2015); Maurice O. Wallace and Shawn Michelle Smith, eds., *Pictures and Progress: Early Photography and the Making of African American Identity* (Durham: Duke University Press, 2012), https://doi.org/10.1215/9780822394563.

white perceptions of African Americans.[81] It was a similar situation in New Zealand. The circulation of portraits of Māori chiefs helped to promote, enhance, and legitimize their chiefly status to European settlers and other Māori. This also helped strengthen their *mana*, the Māori concept of personal power and prestige that is an integral part of their culture. No doubt while looking at photographs of other chiefs at the Pulman studio, Tāwhiao envisaged his own photograph joining this respected group and bolstering his own *mana*. Such images could also be used for identity creation. Māori historian Michael Belgrave has described Tāwhiao's own attempts at self-promotion, noting that his physical appearance was deliberately choreographed to reflect his 'cultural and political objectives'.[82] When Tāwhiao visited the Pulman studio in 1882, he had political motivation for crafting and disseminating his image. As the Māori King, he had been at the centre of the New Zealand Wars between Māori and the Crown in the 1860s and was declared a rebel by the New Zealand Colonial Government. In 1881, he and his followers capitulated, and Tāwhiao embarked on a public relations offensive to promote his new identity as a king willing to work with, rather than against, the Crown. His successful tour of Auckland had been to promote his leadership and demonstrate that war was in the past.[83] Through the photographs it took of him, the Pulman studio facilitated Tāwhiao's attempts at this personal reinvention. With his eyes averted from the camera, he is depicted as a peaceful, non-threatening man as opposed to other portraits of archetypal Māori warriors such as chief Tomika Te Mutu whose direct and defiant stare at the camera invites confrontation with the viewer (see Figure 5).

With regard to circulation, it is true that Māori celebrities lost control of their images, but this was not necessarily due to exploitation. Such loss of control was, in fact, a common situation for all celebrities. By the 1860s, photographs were infinitely reproducible, and market factors such as high demand and potential profit compelled photographers and others who sold photographs to capitalize on this. While many artists, actresses, politicians, and other celebrities found the widespread

81 John Stauffer et al., *Picturing Frederick Douglass* (New York: Liveright, 2015); Murray, 264–279.

82 Michael Belgrave, *Dancing with the King: The Rise and Fall of the King Country, 1864–1885* (Auckland: Auckland University Press, 2017), p. 431.

83 Belgrave, p. 198.

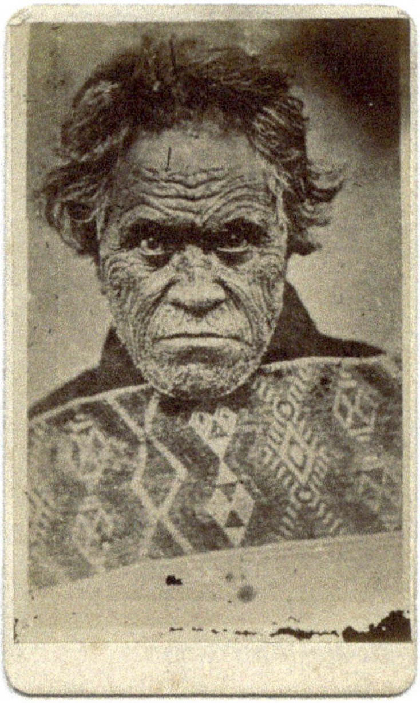

Fig. 5 John Nicol Crombie (attributed), *Chief Tomika Te Mutu* (ca. 1860), Canterbury Museum, Christchurch, New Zealand, E161.50.

circulation of their images of professional benefit, not all were pleased at becoming a commodity that could be owned and gazed at by strangers. British artist Elizabeth Thomson, who skyrocketed to fame through her 1874 painting *The Roll Call*, was reticent about having her portrait taken and appalled when her aunt saw it in a costermonger's barrow.[84] For Māori, losing control of their image had deeper concerns. In Māori culture, the head is *tapu* (sacred) and its treatment follows strict cultural protocols. For some, seeing Queen Victoria's head minted on coins was a dangerous practice, and having their own photograph taken for distribution was equally distressing.[85] The pacifist prophet Te Whiti-o-Rongomai resisted having his photograph taken for many years, remarking once, 'you never know how a photo may be treated; it may be reproduced on paper, and that paper may be put to most ignoble uses'.[86] Artist William F. Gordon found a way around Te Whiti's refusal.

84 Patrizia di Bellow, 'Elizabeth Thompson and "Patsy" Cornwallis West as *Carte-de-visite* Celebrities', *History of Photography*, 35 (2011), 240–249, https://doi.org/10.1080/03087298.2011.592406.

85 Blackley, p. 163.

86 Quoted in Blackley, p. 164.

During a speech in 1880, he surreptitiously sketched the prophet on his shirt cuff and later re-drew the sketch and had it photographed (see Figure 6).[87]

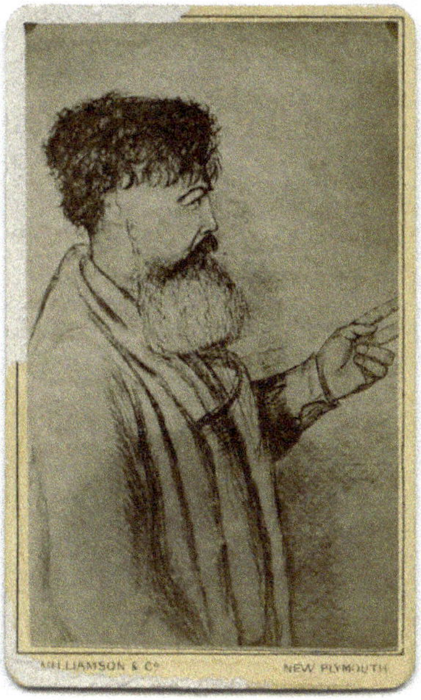

Fig. 6 William F. Gordon (artist) and Williamson & Co. (photographer), *Te Whiti-o-Rongomai* (1880), Canterbury Museum, Christchurch, New Zealand, E161.50.

It quickly made it into circulation. In 1875, Chief Rewi Maniapoto purchased photographs of chiefs from the studio of J. Low but refused to have his taken because he thought it improper for a chief's image to be sold. He relented a few years later and posed for the Pulman studio, among others.[88] Tāwhiao, as discussed above, found personal advantage in having his photograph taken and in 1884 even put his own image into circulation when he passed it on for presentation to the Belgian King.[89] Reconciling traditional attitudes with the advantages of photography had been a gradual but inevitable process for Māori during the nineteenth century.

87 *New Zealand Herald*, 16 July 1928, p. 14.
88 Blackley, p. 172; *Taranaki Herald*, 11 September 1875, p. 2.
89 *New Zealand Herald*, 17 September 1884, p. 5.

Conclusion

The case of *Blackman* v. *Monkton* tested the ability of the New Zealand Fine Arts Copyright Act 1877 to protect registered photographs from pirating, and revealed loopholes that left the legislation weak and ineffective. These were partly rectified by the Photographic Copyright Bill 1896 with its stronger means of demonstrating copyright through inscription. However, there was more to the case than testing the law. An examination of the context surrounding it reveals factors relating to image production and circulation in New Zealand that drove the Pulman studio to register their photographs and take Monkton to court. Commercial interests were at the heart of the case with both sides trying to capitalize on the profits from the portrait of Tāwhiao. Māori were New Zealand celebrities whose faces had commercial value, and photography studios were in fierce competition with each other for a piece of that market. Although not included in the courtroom proceedings, Tāwhiao was a key player in the matter. The creation of his image required his collaboration, as was the case with many commercial portraits of Māori in New Zealand. However, his involvement was more than simply co-operation with the studio to produce a commercial photograph for them. He recognized the value of his portrait for serving his own cultural and political interests.

Bibliography

Archives and Museums

Canterbury Museum, Christchurch, New Zealand.

Museum of New Zealand Te Papa Tongarewa, Wellington, New Zealand.

Toitū Otago Settlers Museum, Dunedin, New Zealand.

Primary Sources

All the Year Round (London).

Auckland Star.

Daily Southern Cross (Auckland).

Evening Post (Wellington).

New Zealand Herald (Auckland).

New Zealand Mail (Wellington).

New Zealand Times (Wellington).

Otago Daily Times.

Taranaki Herald.

Thames Advertiser.

The Photographic News (London).

Waikato Times.

Wairarapa Daily Times.

Wellington Independent.

Legislation

New Zealand Copyright Act 1842 (5 Victoriae No 18), http://www.nzlii.org/nz/legis/hist_act/ca18425v1842n18253/.

New Zealand Fine Arts Copyright Act 1877 (41 Victoriae 1877 No 17), http://www.nzlii.org/nz/legis/hist_act/faca187741v1877n17337/.

New Zealand Fine Arts Copyright Act 1877 Amendment Act 1879 (43 Victoriae No.35), http://www.nzlii.org/nz/legis/hist_act/faca1877aa187943v1879n35438/.

New Zealand Photographic Copyright Bill 1896 (89–3), http://www.nzlii.org/nz/legis/hist_bill/pcb1896893267/.

Secondary Sources

Belgrave, Michael, *Dancing with the King: The Rise and Fall of the King Country, 1864–1885* (Auckland: Auckland University Press, 2017).

Biddle, Donna-Lee, 'Wet-plate Photography and the Resurgence of Tā Moko', https://www.stuff.co.nz/national/106652213/wetplate-photography-and-the-resurgence-of-t-moko.

Blackley, Roger, *Galleries of Maoriland: Artists, Collectors and the Māori World, 1880–1910* (Auckland: Auckland University Press, 2018).

Bowrey, Kathy, '"The World Daguerreotyped — What a Spectacle!" Copyright Law, Photography and Commodification Project of Empire', conference paper presented at the Third International Society for the History and Theory of Intellectual Property (ISHTIP) Workshop, Griffith University, 5–6 July 2011.

Cobb, Jasmine Nichole, *Picture Freedom: Remaking Black Visuality in the Early Nineteenth Century* (New York: New York University Press, 2015).

Cooper, Elena, *Art and Modern Copyright: The Contested Image* (Cambridge: Cambridge University Press, 2018.

Deazley, Ronan, 'Breaking the Mould? The Radical Nature of the Fine Arts Copyright Bill 1862', in *Privilege and Property: Essays on the History of Copyright*, ed. by Ronan Deazley, et al. (Cambridge: Open Book Publishers, 2010), pp. 289–320, https://doi.org/10.11647/obp.0007.

——, 'Struggling with Authority: The Photograph in British Legal History', *History of Photography*, 27 (2003), 236–246, https://doi.org/10.1080/03087298.2003.10441249.

Di Bello, Patrizia, 'Elizabeth Thompson and "Patsy" Cornwallis West as *Carte-de-visite* Celebrities', *History of Photography*, 35 (2011), 240–249, https://doi.org/10.1080/03087298.2011.592406.

Giles, Keith, 'Fairs and Steel: Their Impact on Auckland Photography', *New Zealand Legacy*, 19 (2007), 8–12.

——, 'The Problematic Portraits of Pomare II', *New Zealand Memories*, 26 (2014), 20–21.

Goldberg, Vicki, *The Power of Photography: How Photographs Changed our Lives* (New York: Abbeville Press, 1991).

Graham-Stewart, Michael and John Gow, *Negative Kept: Maori and the Carte de Visite* (Auckland: John Leech Gallery, 2013).

Hearn, Alison, '"Sentimental Greenbacks of Civilization": Cartes de Visite and the Pre-History of Self-Branding', in *The Routledge Companion to Advertising and Promotional Culture*, ed. by Matthew P. McAlister and Emily West (New York: Routledge, 2013), pp. 24–38, https://doi.org/10.4324/9780203071434.

Marcus, Sharon, *The Drama of Celebrity* (Princeton: Princeton University Press, 2019), https://doi.org/10.2307/j.ctvc772z0.

McLay, Geoff, 'New Zealand and the Imperial Copyright Tradition', in *A Shifting Empire: 100 Years of the Copyright Act 1911*, ed. by Uma Suthersanen and Ysolde Gendreau (Cheltenham: Edward Edgar, 2013), pp. 30–51, https://doi.org/10.4337/9781781003091.00007.

McCauley, Elizabeth Anne, *A. A. E. Disdéri and the Carte de Visite Portrait Photograph* (New Haven: Yale University Press, 1985).

——, *Industrial Madness: Commercial Photography in Paris, 1848–1871* (New Haven: Yale University Press, 1994).

Main, William, *Maori in Focus: A Selection of Photographs of the Maori from 1850–1914* (Wellington: Millwood Press, 1976).

Mole, Tom, *Byron's Romantic Celebrity: Industrial Culture and the Hermeneutic of Intimacy* (Basingstoke and New York: Palgrave Macmillan, 2007), https://doi.org/10.1057/9780230288386.

Murray, Hannah-Rose, 'A "Negro Hercules": Frederick Douglass' Celebrity in Britain', *Celebrity Studies*, 7 (2016), 264–79, https://doi.org/10.1080/19392397.2015.1098551.

New Zealand History, 'Carl Völkner', https://nzhistory.govt.nz/people/carl-volkner.

Plunkett, John, 'Celebrity and Community: The Poetics of the Carte de Visite', *Journal of Victorian Culture*, 8 (2003), 55–79.

——, 'Celebrity Culture', in *The Oxford Handbook of Victorian Literary Culture*, ed. by Juliet John (Oxford: Oxford University Press, 2016), pp. 539–60, https://doi.org/10.1093/oxfordhb/9780199593736.013.21.

——, *Queen Victoria: First Media Monarch* (Oxford: Oxford University Press, 2003).

Poole, Debra, *Vision, Race and Modernity: A Visual Economy of the Andean Image World* (Princeton, NJ: Princeton University Press, 1997).

Pōtiki, Megan, 'Me Tā Tāua Mokopuna: The Te Reo Māori Writings of H. K. Taiaroa and Tame Parata', *New Zealand Journal of History*, 49 (2015), 31–49.

Pritchard, Michael, 'Edward Anthony and Henry Tiebout', in *Encyclopedia of Nineteenth-Century Photography*, ed. by John Hannavy (New York: Routledge, 2008), pp. 48–50, https://doi.org/10.4324/9780203941782.

Przyblyski, Jeannene M, 'Loss of Light: The Long Shadow of Photography in the Digital Age', in *The Oxford Handbook of Film and Media Studies*, ed. by Robert Kolker (Oxford: Oxford University Press, 2015), pp. 158–186, https://doi.org/10.1093/oxfordhb/9780195175967.013.0006.

Stauffer, John, et al., *Picturing Frederick Douglass* (New York: Liveright, 2015).

Wallace, Maurice O. and Shawn Michelle Smith, eds., *Pictures and Progress: Early Photography and the Making of African American* Identity (Durham: Duke University Press, 2012), https://doi.org/10.1215/9780822394563.

Whybrew, Christine, 'The Burton Brothers Studio: Commerce in Photography and the Marketing of New Zealand, 1866–1898' (unpublished Doctoral thesis, University of Otago, 2010).

Zackodnik, Teresa, 'The "Green-Backs of Civilization": Sojourner Truth and Portrait Photography', *American Studies*, 46 (2005), 117–143.

14. 'Photography VS the Press'

Copyright Law and the Rise of the Photographically Illustrated Press

Katherine Mintie

Introduction

In September of 1895, an article entitled 'Photography VS the Press' appeared in *Wilson's Photographic Magazine,* a popular American photography journal. Written by Benjamin J. Falk, a successful studio photographer based in New York City, the article begins, surprisingly, with effusive praise for the modern periodical press. As Falk writes,

> The modern newspaper is yearly becoming more wonderful, more interesting, and more powerful. Not content with giving its readers a daily record of events [...] it now amplifies and beautifies this colossal task by illustrating its descriptions with actual pictures, marvelous alike in their accuracy and in the speed of their production.[1]

The 'actual pictures' that Falk marvels at in this passage are halftone reproductions after photographs (see Figure 1). Broadly adopted by publishers in the 1890s, the halftone printing process allowed photographs to be reproduced swiftly and affordably in the popular press as they never had been before.[2] Neil Harris has called the embrace of this

---

1 Benjamin J. Falk, 'Photography VS the Press', *Wilson's Photographic Magazine* (Sept. 1895), p. 389.

2 The *New York Daily Graphic* published the first halftone reproduction after a photograph in 1880. However, the printing technology was still being refined, and halftones did not become common features of the press until the 1890s. See Michael L. Carlebach, *American Photojournalism Comes of Age* (Washington, D.C.: Smithsonian Institute Press, 1997), p. 1.

 https://doi.org/10.11647/OBP.0247.14

printing technology the 'halftone revolution', for halftones transformed the character and expectations of periodical illustrations.[3] As Falk notes, 'accuracy' and 'speed' were emerging as key characteristics of this new illustration process, and these qualities of objectivity and immediacy are now central to our conceptions of press photography.[4] Indeed, it is difficult today to imagine newspapers illustrated with anything but photographs.

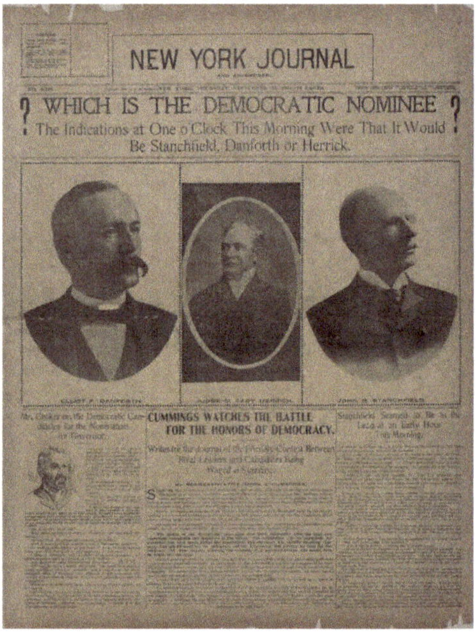
NEW YORK JOURNAL

? WHICH IS THE DEMOCRATIC NOMINEE ?

The Indications at One o'Clock This Morning Were That It Would Be Stanchfield, Danforth or Herrick.

CUMMINGS WATCHES THE BATTLE FOR THE HONORS OF DEMOCRACY.

Fig. 1 Three halftone illustrations after unattributed studio photographs embellishing the front page of the *New York Journal*, Sept. 29, 1898 (Library of Congress).

3 Neil Harris, 'Iconography and Intellectual History: The Halftone Effect', in *Cultural Excursions: Marketing Appetites and Cultural Tastes in Modern America* (Chicago: University of Chicago Press, 1990), pp. 307–308 (p. 316). It is important to note, as Harris does, that the advent of halftone printing did not spell the end of earlier forms of popular illustration, such as wood engraving. On the persistence of wood engraving as a form of periodical illustration in the United States, see Joshua Brown, *Beyond the Lines: Pictorial Reporting, Everyday Life, and the Crisis of Gilded-Age America* (Berkeley: University of California Press, 2002), pp. 239–242.

4 On claims of the accuracy of halftone reproductions, see Carlebach, *American Photojournalism Comes of Age*, pp. 28–30. Michael Gaudio also remarks on the 'mechanical objectivity' ascribed to halftones during the end of the nineteenth century. See Gaudio, *Engraving the Savage: The New World Techniques of Civilization* (Minneapolis: University of Minnesota Press, 2008), p. 137.

The compliments end there, however, and Falk swiftly shifts to his grievances with the photographically illustrated press. His main contention stems from the lack of credit and remuneration accorded to professional photographers like himself for their contributions to the increasingly 'interesting' content of the press and the 'powerful' status it had attained in the US. As Falk asserts, 'The camera being thus so closely allied to the printing-press in the production of the highest forms of modern journalism, it would seem only natural that the photographer and publisher should work harmoniously together'. However, Falk notes with frustration that 'it is nevertheless true that up to now the press, with rare exceptions, has most grudgingly accorded to the photographer proper credit for his share of the work'.[5] While we might imagine, as Falk suggests, that the proliferation of halftones in the popular press would have provided professional photographers with new opportunities to sell and circulate their work, he assures us that such a 'harmonious' relationship had not materialized. Rather, he argues the opposite: that photographers were denied or only 'grudgingly' given 'proper credit' both economic and authorial, for their contributions to the success of the photographically illustrated press at the turn of the twentieth century.

Falk's use of the litigious title 'Photography VS the Press' is not accidental, for debates over the illicit reproduction of studio and other professional photographs by the press were waged through copyright litigation and legislative reform during this period. On the side of 'Photography', Falk and others turned to copyright law to curb the rampant uncredited reproduction of their photographs by the press and to assert their value by demanding steep monetary penalties from infringers. In opposition, 'the Press' leveraged copyright laws in order to disincentivize photographers from suing and thereby maintain a ready, low-cost source of professional photographs to enliven their pages.[6] To evoke the key terms of this volume, photographers turned to copyright

5 Falk, 'Photography VS the Press', p. 389.

6 The desire of the press to transform photographic copyright laws to their advantage is summarized by a frank comment from Don Carlos Seitz, one of the business managers of the New York *World*: 'As a matter of fact, the copyright law is a hindrance to the newspaper business and prevents our taking things [photographs] we have seen and admire, which we would like to have'. See 'Second Meeting: November 1–4, 1905', *Legislative History of the 1909 Copyright Act*, ed. by E. Fulton Brylawski and Abe Goldman, 6 vols (South Hackensack, NJ: Fred B. Rothman and Co., 1976), II, 202.

laws for control over their images while the press sought to use the same legislation to enhance the circulation of the news.

This chapter examines these cases and legislation in order to chart an often-neglected period and set of figures in the early history of the photographically illustrated press. Most accounts focus on the rise of photojournalism in the early twentieth century and the heroics of press photographers, a novel figure within the news ecosystem.[7] Before the emergence of photojournalists, however, press publishers of the late 1880s and 1890s frequently reproduced the work of established studio photographers like Falk, especially their portraits of celebrities to accompany columns devoted to politics and gossip. Because press publishers frequently published professional photographs without permission or credit, they proved a very economical source of images. For photographers like Falk, this clear exploitation of their work was intolerable, leading them to pursue vigorous legal action against press publishers, who fought back equally hard to maintain a cheap and ready body of appealing photographs to reprint. These contentious, and often bitter, copyright cases indicate that the emergence of the photographically illustrated press did not smoothly follow the rise of halftone technology — as histories of the periodical press often claim.[8]

While a number of professional photographers pursued copyright cases against the press and participated in lobbying efforts to reform copyright legislation, this chapter will focus on the efforts of Falk. Though little remembered today, Falk was lauded as one of the premier portrait photographers of turn-of-the-century America, and was a tireless promoter of photographic copyright law.[9] Falk ran a fashionable

7 On the rise of photojournalism, see Thierry Gervais, in collaboration with Gaëlle Morel, *The Making of Visual News: A History of Photograph in the Press* (New York: Bloomsbury, 2017); Michael L. Carlebach, *The Origins of Photojournalism in America* (Washington, D.C.: Smithsonian Institution Press, 1992); and Carlebach, *American Photojournalism Comes of Age*.

8 An exception is Thierry Gervais, who has noted the initially uneasy fit between photography and the press in terms of printing technology and the layout of periodicals. See Gervais, 'Witness to War: The Uses of Photography in the Illustrated Press, 1855–1904', *Journal of Visual Culture* 9 (2010), 370–384 (p. 371) https://doi.org/10.1177/1470412910380343.

9 Few scholars have examined Falk's work and his promotion of more robust photographic copyright laws. Cultural historian Jane Gaines briefly considers the case *Falk* v. *Donaldson Lithographic Co.* in the context of her discussion of *Sarony* v. *Burrow-Giles Lithographic Co.* See Jane Gaines, *Contested Culture: The Image, The Voice, and the Law* (Chapel Hill: University of North Carolina Press, 1991), pp. 75–77. Legal

studio in New York City, initially with locations in the theater district and later in the solarium atop the glamorous Waldorf Astoria Hotel.[10] He specialized in portraits of theater actors and actresses, called theatrical portraits, which enjoyed immense popularity in the United States during the late nineteenth century.[11] Falk's success in the genre of theatrical portraits, however, made his work especially attractive to press publishers looking to capitalize on the celebrity of his sitters. In response to the frequent uncredited and unpaid for reproduction of his work by the press, Falk devoted much of his career to campaigning for more robust photographic copyright laws. From the late 1880s to the 1910s, he initiated numerous lawsuits against publishers that reproduced his work without permission, wrote frequent articles encouraging fellow photographers to apply for and enforce their copyrights, founded the Photographers' Copyright League of America, and traveled to Washington, D.C. to lobby on behalf of professional photographers. Given his sustained efforts to protect photographers' copyrights against the image-hungry press, Falk is an ideal figure for tracing the conflicts that played out between professional photographers and the periodical press at the turn of the twentieth century.

To document the rocky merger of photography and the press in the US, this essay will examine photographers' concerns about halftone reproductions, as well as copyright cases and legislation that pitted the interests of photographers against those of the press. First, the business practices of professional photographers like Falk will be considered to understand why he and many others saw the photographically illustrated press as a threat. The chapter will then turn to the 1895 Amendment of the Copyright Act, which press publishers lobbied for

scholar Christine Haight Farley mentions Falk's copyright activism in her article, 'The Lingering Effects of Copyright's Response to the Invention of Photography', *University of Pittsburgh Law Review* (2003–2004), pp. 439–443. David S. Shields considers Falk's work as a precursor to Hollywood film stills. See Shields, *Still: American Silent Motion Picture Photography* (Chicago: University of Chicago Press, 2013), pp. 46–47. See also Shields' richly illustrated website related to theatrical photography of the late nineteenth century. See Shields, *Broadway Photographs: Photography and the American Scene* (University of South Carolina, 2006), http://broadway.cas.sc.edu/.

10 See Shields, 'Benjamin J. Falk' in *Broadway Photographs*, http://broadway.cas.sc.edu/content/benjamin-j-falk.

11 On theatrical portraits, see Shields, *Still*, pp. 31–50 and Barbara McCandless, 'The Portrait Studio and the Celebrity: Promoting the Art', *Photography in Nineteenth-Century America*, ed. by Martha Sandweiss (New York: Abrams, 1991), pp. 49–72.

in response to photographers' initial success in pursuing copyright cases against them. Finally, it will examine two copyright cases, *Bolles v. Outing Co.* (1899) and *Falk v. Curtis Publishing Co.* (1900), in which the power of the press was further solidified. Though Falk and other photographers sought to constrain the press through the legal system, their strategy backfired; ultimately, it was shifts in copyright law that in part permitted the photographically illustrated press to thrive.

Sales Killers: Halftones and the Business of Professional Photographers

To grasp Falk and other professional photographers' litigious response to the escalating use of photographs by the press, it is important to understand their business practices and the significance of print sales to their bottom lines. The daily operations of Falk's studio can be glimpsed in the detailed account books he kept with information for the numerous customers who came for portrait sittings, the size and number of prints they desired, and other pertinent details.[12] These account books document the wide range of sitters that flocked to Falk's studio for portraits: theater actors, prominent members of New York society, and tourists drawn to his glamorous studio with the hope of glimpsing stars of the stage up close. Though Falk was well paid for individual portrait sessions, his success depended on the profits he made from the subsequent sale of photographic prints, primarily of popular theater actors, to the public.[13] Many professional photographers who specialized in fields other than theatrical photography, such as travel or maritime photography, followed this business model, for the sale of prints to a wide audience offered higher rewards than one-off commissions.[14]

12 Benjamin Falk, 'Record Books, Vols. 1–6, 1881–1917.' Boxes 1–4. B.J. Falk Papers, 1881–1917. Rare Books and Manuscript Division, New York Public Library, New York.

13 To secure profits from his portraits of theater actors, Falk followed a standard procedure that emerged in this period. Falk would photograph the actor in his studio for free or at a reduced rate and agree to provide him or her with complimentary copies of the resulting photographs. In exchange for his services, Falk secured the exclusive right to sell copies of the portraits to the public. Falk and actress Marie Jansen describe the terms of this arrangement, which seems to have been secured by 'custom' rather than formal legal contracts, in the case *Press Publishing Co. v. Falk* (1894), C.C.S.D.N.Y 59 F. 324.

14 The career of Charles E. Bolles, considered later in this chapter, is a case in point. Bolles specialized in maritime photography, primarily picturing ships and yachts.

To ensure that his prints reached a large number of customers, Falk relied on a range of salesmen: specialized dealers, stationers, and street hawkers.[15] Falk kept sample books crammed with miniature versions of his numerous celebrity portraits for this very purpose (see Figure 2).[16] Dealers would leaf through these hefty volumes, note which portraits they wanted copies of, and Falk would provide the requested prints.[17] Barbara McCandless has estimated that, for celebrity portraits alone, dealers of the late nineteenth century sold several hundred thousand dollars' worth of prints per year and that street hawkers brought in over a million dollars annually.[18] As this assessment suggests, the trade in photographic prints was a lucrative business that allowed photographers like Falk to flourish.

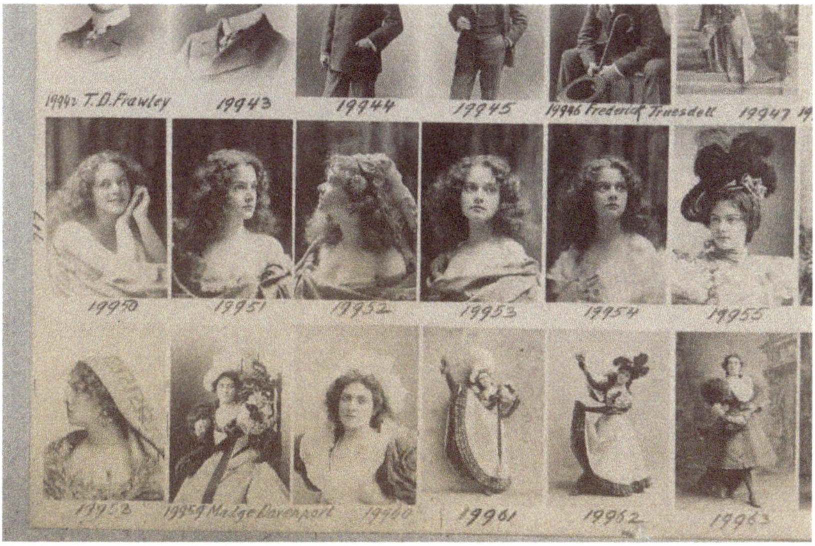

Fig. 2 A series of photographs of Minnie Ashley among other actors, from Benjamin J. Falk, 'Illustrated Catalogue of Photographer's Negatives', vol. 1, ca. 1895 (New York Public Library).

His business depended on his sale of photographic prints through prominent dealers and publishing firms, like the Detroit Photograph Company.

15 On the network of dealers in celebrity portraits that emerged in the 1880s, see McCandless, p. 68.

16 Benjamin J. Falk, 'Illustrated Catalogue of Photographer's Negatives, v. 1–4,' ca. 1881–1900. Performing Arts Research Collections (Theater), New York Public Library, New York.

17 In some instances, dealers took more than a look at these sample books. In the case of *Falk* v. *Gast Lithograph and Engraving Co.*, a dealer re-photographed a sample image of well-known actress Julia Marlowe and then attempted to sell enlarged versions. See *Falk v. Gast Lithograph and Engraving Co.* (1891) C.C.S.D. N.Y 48 F. 262.

18 McCandless, p. 68.

Given that Falk and other professional photographers made a substantial portion of their profits from the sale of prints, it was damaging to their business when cheap, low-quality halftones of their work circulated in the popular press without permission or a credit line. During this period, a single mounted photograph of a well-known celebrity could cost up to five dollars, a substantial sum that was out of reach for many consumers.[19] In contrast, a newspaper replete with halftone reproductions of photographs in various genres could be purchased for pennies. Competition with press halftones thus entailed a significant loss of profits for professional photographers, a fact that Falk emphasized in a report to the professional photographic community in 1899:

> [W]e call your attention again to the anomalous condition existing in this country to-day, whereby illustrated magazines, periodicals, and newspapers secure their most valuable illustrations by reproducing our work without remuneration to us — a remuneration which might, in some measure, counteract the loss we sustain by reason of their cheap reproductions having almost killed the sale to the public of our photographic originals.[20]

As Falk argues here, photographers were not only denied 'remuneration' in the form of a reproduction fee from the press but also lost potential profits from the sale of their photographic prints. Adding insult to injury, the illicit and 'cheap' halftone reproductions boosted the demand for periodicals while they 'killed' sales for photographers.

In addition to lamenting the loss of profits from the wide circulation of halftones, some professional photographers viewed the poor quality of early halftones as detrimental to their professional reputations. Indeed, halftones lacked the high aesthetic and material qualities of photographic prints. This is evident in a comparison between one of Falk's aristotype prints of actress Julia Marlowe posing in the role of Parthenia (Figure 3) and a credited halftone reproduction (Figure 4) that appeared in an 1896 issue of *Godey's Magazine*, a popular women's periodical that prided itself on the quality of its illustrations. In the photographic print, the details of Marlowe's face and costume are sharp, the image possesses an even texture, and the lustrous print surface adds

19 McCandless, p. 67.

20 Falk, 'Annual Meeting and Report of the Copyright League', *Wilson's Photographic Magazine* (Mar. 1899), p. 136.

to the allure of Marlowe's youthful beauty. In contrast, the halftone print has rendered the actress's smooth skin blotchy, the shadows that model her face and hair appear blocky and obscure her features, and the overall grainy texture of the image (a product of the halftone screen) diminishes the perception of details. Even when published with permission by a leading periodical, photographs lost a considerable degree of quality when reproduced as halftones. These deficiencies were not lost on readers, and some complained of being 'nauseated' by the lamentable 'dullness' of halftone reproductions.[21]

Photographers' fears that halftone reproductions would harm the perceived quality of their prints and their professional reputations is clearly communicated in an article entitled 'Magazine Illustration Work' that appeared in *The American Annual of Photography and Photographic Times Almanac* in 1900. The author bemoans the low quality of halftone reproductions after photographs, dismissing them as 'smudges in black and white' that depict 'nothing so much as an upset inkstand'.[22] For the author, these pitiable 'smudges' gave a bad impression of the skill and aesthetic sensibilities of contemporary photographers. Concerns about the visual and material qualities of photographs were especially keen in the 1890s, when numerous American photographers, led by Alfred Stieglitz, argued vigorously for the recognition of photography as a fine art.[23] Roughly reprinted halftones in the press did little to further this cause. Moreover, the author grumbles about the photographs selected for reproduction in the press, writing that they 'cater to the taste for the sensational to the extent of publishing the greater part of their illustrations from the very poorest class of photographic work and consider only the title'.[24] Though newspapers and magazines were potential sites for professional photographers to showcase their best work to large audiences, the author complains that only the 'very poorest'

21 'Question and Answer', *Century Illustrated Magazine* (Jan. 1899), pp. 474–475.

22 Robert E.M. Bain, 'Magazine Illustration Work', *The American Annual of Photography and Photographic Times Almanac* (1900), pp. 152.

23 On the 1890s as a period of transition in American photography and the renewed push for photography to be recognized as a fine art, see Sarah Greenough, 'Of Charming Glens, Graceful Glades and Frowning Cliffs: The Economic Incentives, Social Inducements and Aesthetic Issues of American Pictorial Photography 1880–1902', in *Photography in Nineteenth-Century America*, ed. by Martha Sandweiss (New York: Abrams, 1991), pp. 259–278.

24 Bain, p. 151

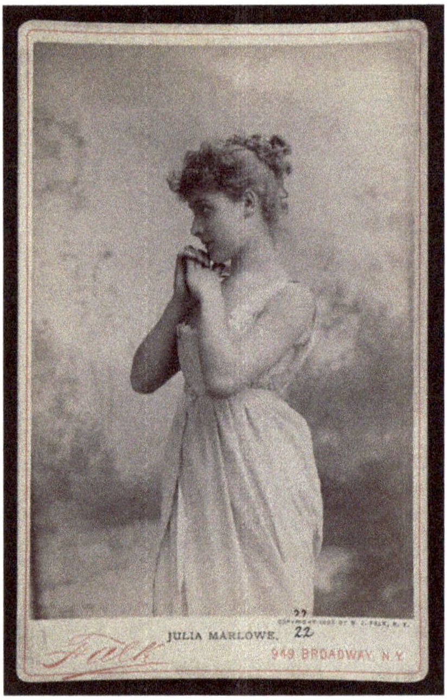

Fig. 3 Benjamin J. Falk, *Julia Marlowe*, 1888, aristotype print (Library of Congress).

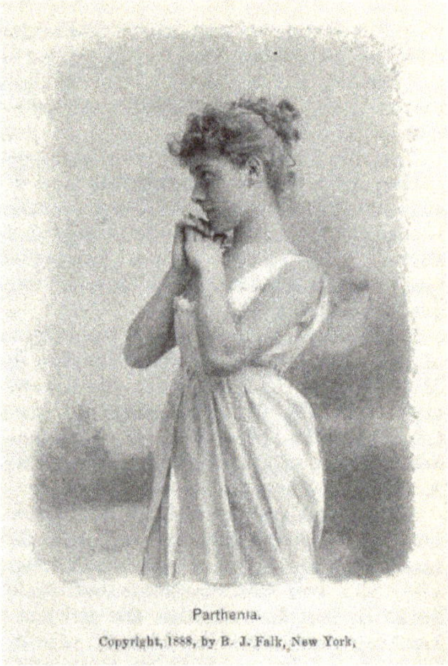

Fig. 4 Benjamin J. Falk, *Julia Marlowe*, in *Godey's Magazine*, June 1896, halftone reproduction after a gelatin silver print (New York Public Library).

photographs were chosen for inclusion and for reasons of convenience or entertainment rather than aesthetic merit. While the author expresses optimism that press publishers would eventually improve the quality of their photographic selections, he concludes with the lament: 'The kind of work we offer now, for the most part, we should be ashamed of.'[25]

Despite protests that halftone reproductions in the press were cheap, of poor quality, and reflected badly on the state of the photographic profession, Falk and other photographers did not entirely shun the business of periodicals. Falk allowed his photographs to be reproduced as halftones with his credit line in a number of periodicals, particularly those devoted to theater.[26] Falk likely received licensing fees in these cases, and may have attracted some new customers who sought out his prints after seeing them reproduced as halftones. However, reproduction fees do not seem to have been a major source of income for him. As he bluntly put it in an article from 1900: 'In how many instances does the photographer profit by this use [by the periodical press] of his work? We venture the answer: not in one instance out of ten.'[27] For Falk, the vast majority of half-tone reproductions published by press publishers were bad for business.

American Newspaper Publishers Association v. Photographers' Copyright League of America: The 1895 Amendment to the Copyright Act

Prominent studio photographers like Falk not only wrote about the damage that press halftones had on their profession, but also began to take publishers to court for copyright infringement. In the late 1880s and early 1890s, a number of studio photographers triumphed in copyright cases and were well compensated for their efforts. Their initial success in extracting financial settlements from infringing publishers was due in part to the procedure for calculating monetary penalties during

25 Ibid., p. 153.

26 Falk appears to have developed a good relationship with *Godey's Magazine* in the 1890s, for halftones after his theatrical portraits appear regularly and are accompanied by his name and copyright notice. His work also appeared regularly in the *New York Dramatic Mirror*, a theatrical trade journal.

27 Benjamin J. Falk, 'Copyright and the American Photographer', *Wilson's Photographic Magazine* (Sept. 1900), pp. 385–387.

this period. Called the 'per-sheet penalty', this method of accounting required the infringer to forfeit one dollar for each 'sheet' or copy of the reproduced image found in his or her possession.[28] This method of accounting applied to all media protected by copyright (with the exception of fine artworks) and the dollar rate had been in place since 1802.[29]

The per-sheet penalty system of accounting was deeply unpopular with press publishers because it often resulted in steep penalties. Such was the case in *Press Publishing Co.* v. *Falk* (1894) in which the company that owned the New York *World,* one of the most widely circulated newspapers of the day, attempted to prevent Falk from bringing an infringement case after reproducing one of his portraits of actress Marie Jansen. Falk alleged that the *World* had printed 260,183 copies of the newspaper containing the unauthorized reproduction of his photograph and was thus owed damages amounting to the dizzying sum of $260,183. When the judge rejected Press Publishing Company's attempt to dismiss the case, the *World* chose to settle with Falk for $5,000 rather than risk paying the full penalty that Falk had levelled against the paper.[30]

The fact that an individual photographer like Falk could confidently allege such high penalties from the press was no small feat, for the press wielded incredible power in the United States during the late nineteenth century. William Randolph Hearst, millionaire publisher of the *New York Journal,* asserted the influence of his newspaper in its motto: "While others talk, the *Journal* Acts." Indeed, Hearst not only reported the news but sought to create it — most famously agitating for the Spanish-American War — through the paper's ability to sway public opinion.[31] Compared to the political and economic clout of the

28 'An Act to amend section forty-nine hundred and sixty-five, chapter three, title sixty, of the Revised Statutes of the United States, relating to copyright, March 1895, Sec. 4965', in *Copyright Enactments: Laws Passed in the United States Since 1783 Relating to Copyright* (Washington, D.C.: Library of Congress, 1973), pp. 55–56.

29 Legal scholars Pamela Samuelson and Tara Wheatland note that the per-sheet penalty was developed in lieu of accounting for the actual monetary damage done to the injured party, which could be difficult to establish. Pamela Samuelson and Tara Wheatland, 'Statutory Damages in Copyright Law: A Remedy in Need of Reform', *William and Mary Law Review,* 51 (2009), 439–511 (p. 447 at fn. 22).

30 Will Slauter, *Who Owns the News? A History of Copyright* (Stanford: Stanford University Press, 2019), p. 222.

31 Hearst is thought to have telegrammed newspaper artist Frederic Remington, who was stationed in Cuba awaiting the first signs of action, 'You furnish the pictures,

newspapers, studio photographers' power was insignificant. During the 1880s and early 1890s, however, the law afforded a unique arena in which photographers could take on the giants of the press. In the words of Falk, these copyright cases were a struggle of 'Might against Right'.[32]

In the wake of high-profile and high-stakes cases like *Press Publishing Co.* v. *Falk*, publishers began to organize to limit the monetary penalties that photographers could seek in court.[33] The American Newspaper Publishers Association (ANPA), a conglomerate of powerful newspaper publishers primarily based in New York City, started lobbing Congress to limit monetary penalties in photographic copyright cases.[34] The ANPA found a receptive audience in the Committee on Patents of the US House of Representatives, which issued a report in January 1895 in favor of penalty reform in the case of photographs reproduced by the periodical press. The report, written by James M. Covert of New York, stated that the 'excessive penalties' that newspapers often paid as a result of the per-sheet penalty system were not only 'unduly harsh' but also 'extremely hazardous'.[35] The harm of such high penalties extended not only to periodicals themselves, the report argued, but to consumers, for the 'value of illustrated news articles naturally depends very largely upon their early publication and illustration' of current events.[36] In other words, the value of the press lies in its ability to inform the public of the news in a timely manner, which, as the report admits, sometimes entailed 'haste of preparation' and oversights in securing rights to reproduce images by even 'the most careful and reputable publishers'.[37]

---

and I'll furnish the war'. Though several scholars have contested this story as legend, it nonetheless suggests the wide-ranging power ascribed to the popular press and Hearst's influence during this period. See Christopher Daly, *Covering America: A Narrative History of a Nation's Journalism* (Amherst: University of Massachusetts Press, 2012), pp. 132–134.

32 Falk, 'Photography VS the Press', pp. 389.

33 Don Carlos Seitz recalled another high-stakes copyright case involving a reproduced photograph by the Pach Brothers, popular studio photographers based in New York City, as motivating the formation of the ANPA's copyright committee. See 'Stenographic Report of the Proceedings of the Librarian's Conference on Copyright, 1st Session, in New York City, May 31-June 2, 1905', in *Legislative History of the 1909 Copyright Act*, I, 22.

34 For more on the ANPA and the perspective of the newspaper publishers on photographic copyright law during this period, see Slauter, pp. 221–223.

35 House Report No. 1733 (1895), 1.

36 Ibid.

37 Ibid.

To 'moderate the rigors of the penalties' that could be alleged against the press, the Committee on Patents proposed a cap of $5,000 'in case of any such infringement of the copyright of a photograph made from any object not a work of fine arts'.[38] This proposal was approved by Congress with little debate and became law in March of 1895.[39] It was a clear win for the ANPA. With penalties capped at $5,000, publications with high circulations no longer had to worry about paying staggering sums to photographers in court.

For studio photographers like Falk who had previously wielded the unlimited per-sheet penalty as a means to deter press publishers from reproducing their work and to recover payment for the uncredited use of their work, this amendment amounted to nothing less than having 'the right to steal from photographers legalized by the United States Government'.[40] From their perspective, this cap gave large publishers less reason to pause before reproducing copyrighted photographs. Further, because the new restrictions on penalties applied only to photographs, the amendment suggested that photographs were not as esteemed as other media protected by copyright law, such as prints or books. Indeed, the amendment was met with little opposition outside a small segment of the professional photographic community. For photographers, this was a worrisome indicator that their prints were losing value in the eyes of lawmakers and the broader public as cheap halftone reproductions abounded.

In response to the perceived injustice of the 1895 Amendment to the Copyright Act, a group of concerned photographers led by Falk established the Photographers' Copyright League of America (PCLA) in 1895.[41] This association was modelled on the Photographic Copyright Union, an organization founded by professional photographers in the United Kingdom only a year earlier to fight infringements by the press,

38 Act of March 2, 1895, in *Copyright Enactments*, p. 56.

39 Covert presented the same arguments from his report to the House when the amendment was passed. See Congressional Record — House 3212 (March 2, 1895) and Congressional Record — Senate 3136 (March 2, 1895).

40 Photographers' Copyright League of America, 'Concerning Copyright', *Wilson's Photographic Magazine* (Mar. 1895), p. 221.

41 Falk, 'Concerning Copyright', p. 221. Falk had been trying to organize US photographers around the issue of copyright since the late 1880s. See, for example, Falk, 'Improved Copyright for Photographers', *The Photographic Times and American Photographer* (Nov. 1888), pp. 511–512.

and that had achieved some success in establishing standard licensing fees for the use of their images.[42] Founding members of the PCLA included some of the most prominent New York-based photographers of the time: Napoleon Sarony, George G. Rockwood, James L. Breese, and Charles E. Bolles.[43] Membership soon expanded to include professional photographers from across the United States. The stated mission of the PCLA was to present a 'united front' against the powerful press and other copyists. To do so, the PCLA proposed to pool resources to prosecute infringers who violated the copyright of members. As the PCLA stated, the organization would 'defray all expenses' when members pursued a case and 'in return, so as to make it [the PCLA] self-supporting, a fair percentage of all recoveries so obtained be turned into the treasury of the organization'.[44] Though a clever system for enforcing the copyrights of members, the PCLA encountered difficulty in recruiting dues-paying members and was never able to match the power of the ANPA.

While the ANPA wielded considerable influence in Washington, stalwart members of the PCLA were able to fight and defeat legislative proposals aimed at further weakening their copyrights. One of the PCLA's most important victories over the ANPA was the beating back of the Hicks Amendment. Flush from its success in 1895, the ANPA attempted to go one step further and push through this amendment that would have, in Falk's apt summary, 'give[n] newspapers, periodicals, etc., the absolute right to use any of our photographs, whether copyrighted or not, without our consent and without any compensation to us'.[45] In other

42 On the efforts of his British colleagues, Falk wrote: 'In England, photographers have already done much to protect their interests in this regard by conjointly adopting resolutions and binding themselves not to supply any newspaper or periodical with any of their pictures for reproduction unless they receive adequate pay for the same. In this way, an income is provided for them, which partially, at least, reimburses them for the losses they sustain owing to the decrease in the sales to the public of their own prints because of these reproductions'. See Falk, 'Suggestion', *Wilson's Photographic Magazine* (Dec. 1896), p. 562. On the founding and lobbying efforts of the Photographic Copyright Union, see Elena Cooper, *Art and Modern Copyright: The Contested Image* (Cambridge: Cambridge University Press, 2018), pp. 74–77, 94–98, https://doi.org/10.1017/9781316840993. See also Elena Cooper and Sheona Burrow 'Photographic Copyright and the Intellectual Property Enterprise Court in Historical Perspective', *Legal Studies* (Dec. 2018), pp. 158–160, https://doi.org/10.1017/lst.2018.10.

43 Falk, 'Concerning Copyright', p. 223.

44 Ibid., p. 222.

45 Falk, 'Annual Report of the Copyright League,' p. 136. The exact wording of the proposed Hicks Amendment read: '*That a line production* [i.e. a halftone] *published*

words, the Hicks Amendment would have allowed press publishers to reproduce photographs without seeking permission from, or paying, photographers. To stop this clearly damaging amendment from passing, Falk, along with Bolles and Rockwell of the PCLA, travelled to Washington, D.C. three times to make their case before the Patents Committee of the House of Representatives and ultimately defeated the amendment.[46] The PCLA's success in this instance suggests the limits of the ANPA's power and the benefits to professional photographers of collective action. Indeed, if not for the attention of Falk and fellow PCLA members to copyright legislation like the Hicks Amendment, the course of photographic copyright law and press photography in the United States would likely look radically different today.

Loopholes and Letdowns: *Bolles* v. *Outing Co.* (1899) and *Falk* v. *Curtis Publishing Co.* (1900)

Despite the vigorous efforts of the PCLA, further restrictions on the monetary penalties photographers could seek in copyright cases emerged following the decision in the US Supreme Court case *Bolles* v. *Outing Co.* (1899). This lawsuit was initiated in 1894 by Charles Bolles, a Brooklyn-based maritime photographer and PCLA member. After discovering that a popular sports magazine called *The Outing* had reproduced without permission or a credit line a halftone of his copyrighted photograph of a yacht called The Vigilant (see Figure 5), Bolles sued the publisher. To prove that his copyright had been violated, Bolles purchased a single copy of the magazine that featured the infringing halftone.

As the case worked its way through the lower courts and on to the US Supreme Court, lawyers and judges alike zeroed in on questions regarding when and where infringing copies needed to be found in order to count towards the per-sheet penalty. The clause of the Copyright Act that received the most scrutiny read:

> he [the infringer] shall forfeit to the proprietor all the plates on which the same [the copyrighted image] shall be copied, and every sheet thereof,

---

in a daily newspaper of a photograph made from an object not a work of the fine arts, shall not be considered as a violation of the copyright of such photograph.' See Charles E. Bolles, 'A Copyright Crisis,' *Wilson's Photographic Magazine* (Mar. 1898), p. 97.

46 Falk, 'Annual Report of the Copyright League,' p. 136.

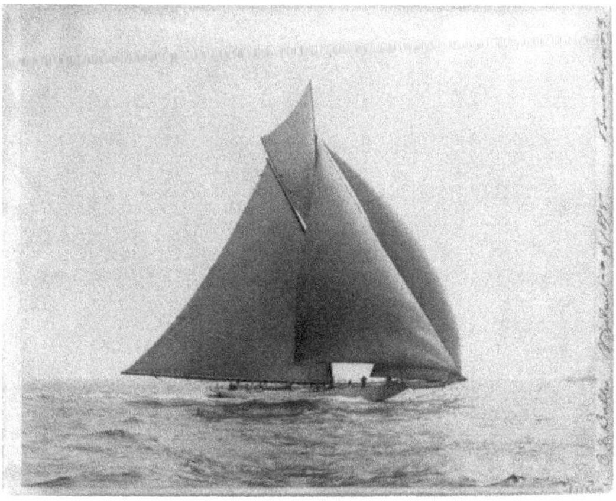

Fig. 5 Charles E. Bolles, *The Vigilant*, ca. 1895, copy print (Library of Congress).

either copied or printed, and shall further forfeit one dollar for every sheet of the same found in his possession.[47]

Particular attention was paid to the phrase 'found in his possession'. Did this mean all copies put into circulation by the infringer? Or only those physical copies found on the premises of the infringer? And when did the copies need to be found?

Ultimately, the justices of US Supreme Court determined that the penalty was 'limited to such [copies] as are found in, and not simply traced to, the possession of the defendant'.[48] Thus, monetary penalties would no longer be calculated by the circulation of a publication as they had been in previous cases like *Press Publishing Co.* v. *Falk* (1894). Going forward, only those copies found physically in the possession of the infringer would count toward the calculation of the per-sheet penalty. The opinion in *Bolles* v. *Outing Co.* also outlined a new limit regarding when the infringing copies were to be found. The justices supported the position of the Circuit Court, which stated: 'We are of the opinion that the section meant to affix the penalty only when the sheets are shown to have been discovered or detected in the possession of the defendant

47 'An Act to amend section forty-nine hundred and sixty-five, chapter three, title sixty, of the Revised Statutes of the United States, relating to copyright, March 1895, Sec. 4965', in *Copyright Enactments: Laws Passed in the United States Since 1783 Relating to Copyright* (Washington, D.C.: Library of Congress, 1973), pp. 55–56.

48 Ibid.

prior to the bringing of the suit'.[49] As the justices reasoned, the copyright owner needed to retrieve the infringing copies before filing suit, because a case could not proceed without first establishing evidence of infringement. Henceforth, photographers could not report the finding of additional copies after filing a complaint but must have already found them.

In accordance with this new interpretation for calculating monetary penalties in copyright cases, Bolles could seek only $1 from Outing Co., based on the single copy of the magazine he had purchased before filing the complaint. Given that just five years earlier Falk and other photographers were able to seek monetary penalties as high as $260,183 in cases like *Press Publishing Co.* v. *Falk*, the opinion in *Bolles* v. *Outing Co.* struck many as a major blow to their ability to profit from and control the circulation of their work. An anonymous writer, possibly Falk or another PCLA member, explained the negative effects of the opinion in an article for *Wilson's Photographic Magazine*, stating: 'Not only does it [the Copyright Act] fail to adequately protect the photographer's rights in his own work, but it also affords several loopholes whereby infringers of the law may escape the consequences of piracy'.[50] The 'loopholes' that the infringers could leverage to avoid 'the consequences' of paying steep penalties were, for the author, a direct result of the decision in *Bolles* v. *Outing Co.* As the writer elaborates:

> In the case of an infringement of copyright by a weekly newspaper, for instance, the infringement is rarely known to the photographer until the paper is published and scattered broadcast, after which, of course, comparatively few copies of the paper may be found in possession of the publisher or his agents.[51]

As the writer suggests, it was often difficult for photographers to detect instances of copyright infringement in the robust press culture of the late nineteenth century. Even when a photographer like Bolles did discover and choose to prosecute an infringer, copies of the offending periodical has already been 'scattered' widely and were no longer physically 'in possession of the publisher or his agents'. Given these obstacles to obtaining recompense for the illicit reproduction of their work by the

49 *Bolles v. Outing Co., 77 F. 966, 968 (2d Cir. 1897)*. Emphasis mine.

50 'A New Copyright Bill', *Wilson's Photographic Magazine* (Apr. 1900), p. 171.

51 Ibid.

press, it is unsurprising that photographers felt that the legal system had 'fail[ed] to adequately protect' their work and did not recognize its value.

Falk felt the immediate consequences of the 'loopholes' made possible through *Bolles* v. *Outing Co.* in a copyright case that he filed in 1899 against Curtis Publishing Company. Falk initiated this suit soon after discovering that one of his portraits of the actress Minnie Ashley had been reproduced as a halftone (see Figure 6) without his permission in the October 1899 issue of *The Ladies' Home Journal,* a widely-read women's magazine owned by Curtis Publishing Company. In response, Falk's lawyer, Samuel Hyneman, issued two writs simultaneously to the publisher: one was a summons to appear in court for allegedly violating Falk's copyright and the other was a replevin, a legal order, to retrieve the copies of the reproduced photograph in possession of Curtis Publishing Company. Through the power of the replevin, Curtis Publishing Company forfeited to Falk over 5,000 copies of the offending issue of *The Ladies Home Journal,* which enabled him to sue for $5,000, the maximum penalty permitted after the 1895 Amendment to the Copyright Act. Despite this strong show of evidence, Falk was not awarded any monetary penalties because, as the recent opinion in *Bolles* v. *Outing Co.* stated, Falk's lawyer needed to gather the infringing copies of the periodical '*prior to* the bringing of the suit'.[52] It is not difficult to imagine Falk's frustration following this loss that hinged on the strict enforcement of a technicality following the Supreme Court's decision.

While Falk and members of the PCLA lamented the decision in *Bolles* v. *Outing Co.*, the periodical press cheered the new regime for determining penalties in copyright cases. The victorious position of the press is strikingly articulated in a *Scientific American* article titled 'New Practice in Photographic Copyright' that appeared in February 1900.[53] In contrast to its bland title, the article includes a number of fiery accusations, including the notion that photographers had used copyright law to extract unearned profits from the press: 'It has been

52 *Bolles,* 77 F. at 968. Emphasis mine.

53 The article states that portions of the article were reproduced from a 'recent edition' of the *New York Sun,* suggesting the broader interest among the periodical press in the issue of photographic copyright law and the penalties applied in cases of infringement. 'New Practice in Photographic Copyright', *Scientific American* (17 Feb. 1900), p. 102.

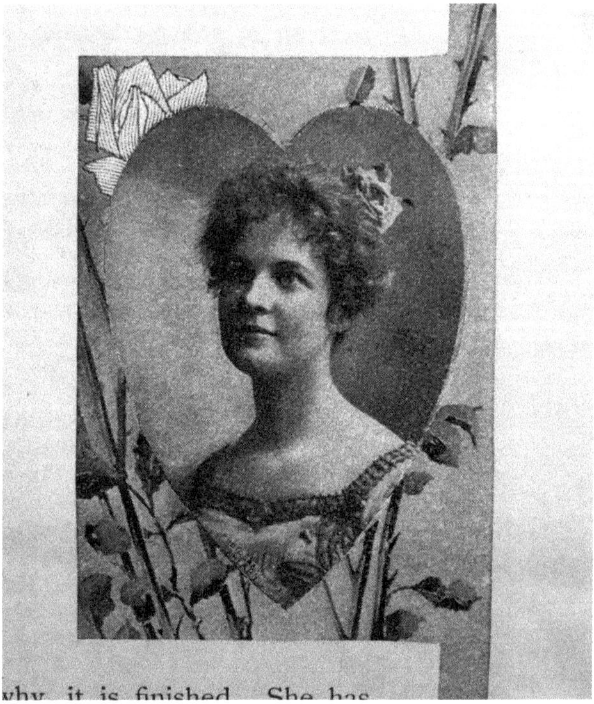

Fig. 6 Benjamin J. Falk, *Minnie Ashley*, in *The Ladies Home Journal*, October 1899, halftone after a silver gelatin print (collection of the author).

a notorious fact for a long time that many photographic establishments have made a regular practice of levying a species of blackmail upon publishers, who have, unwittingly perhaps, published a copyrighted photograph without permission'. Further, the anonymous author asserts that 'the penalty in many cases would amount to many thousands of dollars, while the photograph had, perhaps, no value whatever'.[54] For the author, the per-sheet penalty had allowed photographers to perform a kind of perverse alchemy. Photographs 'with no value whatever', once reproduced by unsuspecting publishers, were converted into 'thousands of dollars' of undeserving profits for the photographer. However, the author notes that *Bolles* v. *Outing Co.* had turned the tides against the supposedly scheming photographers and observes with satisfaction that judges had finally begun 'reducing the exorbitant damages' that

54 'New Practice in Photographic Copyright', p. 102. As Slauter notes (p. 222), the accusation that photographers used copyright to blackmail the press was a common refrain among newspaper publishers.

photographers could extract from publishers in copyright cases.[55] In sum, press publishers had gained the upper hand in the ongoing contest of 'Photography VS the Press'.

Conclusion

At the dawn of the halftone era, the relationship between professional photographers and the photographically illustrated press changed dramatically, as did photographic copyright laws. When the press first began to reproduce the work of photographers as halftones, Falk and others were able to use copyright law and the per-sheet penalty to assert control over and affirm the value of their photographs. Undaunted by these early losses, the press leveraged their political and economic power to weaken the areas of copyright law that photographers had levied against them — especially the per-sheet penalty. As we have seen, this strategy was successful, and led even stalwart Falk to seeming hopelessness over the state of photographic copyright laws and the inaction on the part of his fellow photographers. As he wrote in another article for *Wilson's Photographic Magazine*:

> Why should the publisher profit by selling the photographer's work, and the photographer be content with "glory?" Does the publisher pay the photographer for his use of his productions? Sometimes, where he is compelled to do so; never, if he can avoid it. Why? Because the photographer has not yet learned to appreciate the value of his work to the world.[56]

Though Falk and others associated with the PCLA continued to advocate for stronger copyright protections into the twentieth century, it was shifts in press illustration practices, rather than the legal system, that began to limit the illicit reproduction of professional photographers' work by the press.[57] In the first decade of the twentieth century,

55 'New Practice in Photographic Copyright', p. 102.

56 Falk, 'Annual Meeting and Report of the Copyright League', p. 135.

57 Members of the PCLA lobbied for stronger protections and increased penalties during the meetings and hearings convened by the Librarian of Congress and the Joint Committee on Patents between 1905–1907 in preparation for an overhaul of US copyright law that resulted in the 1909 Copyright Act. Members of the press also participated in these meetings and continued to denigrate professional photographers and their work as 'mechanical maker[s] of kodak snap shot[s]'. See

periodicals increasingly began to hire specialized photojournalists as part of their staffs, sending them out in the field to capture images of newsworthy people and events.[58] This period also saw a rise, in the US, of picture libraries like Bain News Service, which offered periodicals an array of newsworthy images taken by photojournalists for publication.[59] Accompanying the emergence of photojournalism as a profession was the rise of photojournalism as a style. As early press photographer Gilson Willets described the aims of news photography in 1900:

> A poor picture of a public personage at a crucial, newsy moment is worth its weight in gold, while the finest, most artistic photograph of the same person at an unimportant moment, is not worth the paper it is printed on [...] Get the subject in the act, get action in the scene; these are the main objects.[60]

As Willets suggests, news photography, with its emphasis on capturing a scene at a 'crucial, newsy moment' was the opposite of carefully staged and 'artistic' studio photography that Falk practiced. With these developments in photojournalism as a profession and aesthetic, press publishers no longer turned to the work of established photographers like Falk to illustrate their pages.

As photojournalism professionalized in the early twentieth century, photographers began to profit from and be recognized for their contributions to the press. Falk himself predicted this outcome in 'Photography VS the Press', speculating that 'The history of the photographer's struggle for fair recognition whenever his work is used by others will someday [sic] be written, and will show up many curious phases of inconsistency and even of pettiness, practiced during

---

'Copyright Hearings, December 7 to 11, 1906. Arguments before the Committees on Patents of the Senate and House of Representatives, Conjointly', *Legislative History of the 1909 Copyright Act*, vol. 4, p. 169. For more on how the battle of 'Photography VS the Press' played out in the lead up to the 1909 Copyright Act, see Slauter, pp. 223–224.

58 A few photographers, like Jimmy Hare, were offered positions on periodical staffs in the late 1890s. See Gervais, *The Making of Visual News*, pp. 26–37 and Carlebach, *American Photojournalism Comes of Age*, p. 30 and 65–66.

59 On Bain's News Service, see Michael Carlebach, *Bain's New York: The City in Pictures, 1900–1925* (New York: Dover Publications, 2011).

60 Gilson Willets, 'News Photography', *The American Annual of Photography and Photographic Times Almanac* (1900), p. 59.

the past five years by the greatest journals'.[61] The early history of the photographically illustrated press and professional photographers' 'struggle for fair recognition' recounted here is indeed marked by 'inconsistency' and change as publishers, photographers, and copyright law adapted to the arrival of halftone printing, the possibilities of this new illustration process, and the emergence of new business models to source photographs for reproduction. There was certainly a fair amount of 'pettiness', too. While the triumph of the press is not surprising from the vantage of today and our photography-saturated news cycles, the legal resistance on the part of Falk and the PCLA suggests that the alignment of photography and the periodical press was far more 'curious' and contentious than is often understood.

Bibliography

Primary Sources

'A New Copyright Bill', *Wilson's Photographic Magazine* (Apr. 1900), 171–172.

Bain, Robert E.M., 'Magazine Illustration Work', *The American Annual of Photography and Photographic Times Almanac* (1900), 151–153.

Bolles v. Outing Co., 77 F. 966 (2d Cir. 1897).

Bolles v. Outing Co., 175 U.S. 262 (1899).

Bolles, Charles E., 'A Copyright Crisis,' *Wilson's Photographic Magazine* (Mar. 1898), 97–98.

Brylawski, E. Fulton, and Abe Goldman, eds., *Legislative History of the 1909 Copyright Act*, 6 vols (South Hackensack, NJ: Fred B. Rothman and Co., 1976).

Copyright Enactments: Laws Passed in the United States Since 1783 Relating to Copyright (Washington, D.C.: Library of Congress, 1973).

Congressional Record — House 3212 (March 2, 1895).

Congressional Record — Senate 3136 (March 2, 1895).

Falk v. Curtis Publishing Co. 107 F. 126 (3d. Cir. 1901).

Falk, Benjamin J., 'Annual Meeting and Report of the Copyright League', *Wilson's Photographic Magazine* (Mar. 1899), 135–137.

61 Falk, 'Photography VS the Press', p. 390.

——, 'Copyright and the American Photographer', *Wilson's Photographic Magazine* (Sept. 1900), 385–387.

——, 'Improved Copyright for Photographers', *The Photographic Times and American Photographer* (Nov. 1888), 511–512.

——, 'Photography VS the Press', *Wilson's Photographic Magazine* (Sept. 1895), 389–390.

——, 'Record Books, Vol. 1–6, 1881–1917.' Boxes 1–4. B.J. Falk Papers, 1881–1917. Rare Books and Manuscript Division, New York Public Library, New York.

——, 'Suggestion', *Wilson's Photographic Magazine* (Dec. 1896), 561–562.

House Report No. 1733 (1895), 1.

'New Practice in Photographic Copyright', *Scientific American* (17 Feb. 1900), p. 102.

Photographers' Copyright League of America, 'Concerning Copyright', *Wilson's Photographic Magazine* (Mar. 1895), pp. 221–224.

Press Publishing Co. v. Falk C.C.S.D.N.Y 59 F. 324 (1894).

'Question and Answer', *Century Illustrated Magazine* (Jan. 1899), pp. 474–475.

Willets, Gilson. 'News Photography', *The American Annual of Photography and Photographic Times Almanac* (1900), pp. 53–60.

Secondary Sources

Brown, Joshua, *Beyond the Lines: Pictorial Reporting, Everyday Life, and the Crisis of Gilded- Age America* (Berkeley: University of California Press, 2002), https://doi.org/10.1525/9780520939745.

Carlebach, Michael L, *American Photojournalism Comes of Age* (Washington, D.C.: Smithsonian Institute Press, 1997).

——, *The Origins of Photojournalism in America* (Washington, D.C.: Smithsonian Institution Press, 1992).

Cooper, Elena, *Art and Modern Copyright: The Contested Image* (Cambridge: Cambridge University Press, 2018), https://doi.org/10.1017/9781316840993.

Cooper, Elena and Burrow, Sheona, 'Photographic Copyright and the Intellectual Property Enterprise Court in Historical Perspective', *Legal Studies,* 39 (Dec. 2018), 143–165, https://doi.org/10.1017/lst.2018.10.

Daly, Christopher, *Covering America: A Narrative History of a Nation's Journalism* (Amherst: University of Massachusetts Press, 2012).

Gervais, Thierry, in collaboration with Gaëlle Morel, *The Making of Visual News: A History of Photograph in the Press* (New York: Bloomsbury, 2017).

——, 'Witness to War: The Uses of Photography in the Illustrated Press, 1855–1904', *Journal of Visual Culture*, 9 (2010), 370–384, https://doi.org/10.1177/1470412910380343.

Greenough, Sarah, 'Of Charming Glens, Graceful Glades and Frowning Cliffs: The Economic Incentives, Social Inducements and Aesthetic Issues of American Pictorial Photography 1880–1902', *Photography in Nineteenth-Century America*, ed. by Martha Sandweiss (New York: Abrams, 1991), pp. 259–278.

Harris, Neil, 'Iconography and Intellectual History: The Halftone Effect', in *Cultural Excursions: Marketing Appetites and Cultural Tastes in Modern America* (Chicago: University of Chicago Press, 1990), pp. 304–317.

McCandless, Barbara, 'The Portrait Studio and the Celebrity: Promoting the Art', *Photography in Nineteenth-Century America*, ed. by Martha Sandweiss (New York: Abrams, 1991), pp. 49–72.

Samuelson, Pamela and Wheatland, Tara, 'Statutory Damages in Copyright Law: A Remedy in Need of Reform', *William and Mary Law Review*, 51 (2009), 439–511.

Shields, David S., *Broadway Photographs: Photography and the American Scene*. University of South Carolina. 2006, http://broadway.cas.sc.edu/.

——, *Still: American Silent Motion Picture Photography* (Chicago: University of Chicago Press, 2013), https://doi.org/10.7208/chicago/9780226013435.001.0001.

Slauter, Will, *Who Owns the News? A History of Copyright* (Stanford: Stanford University Press, 2019), https://doi.org/10.1515/9781503607729.

List of Illustrations

Chapter 2

Chapter 3

Chapter 4

Chapter 5

Chapter 6

Chapter 7

Chapter 9

Chapter 10

Chapter 11

Chapter 12

Chapter 13

Chapter 14

Index

About the Team

Alessandra Tosi was the managing editor for this book.

Melissa Purkiss performed the copy-editing and proofreading.

Anna Gatti designed the cover. The cover was produced in InDesign using the Fontin font.

Luca Baffa typeset the book in InDesign and produced the paperback and hardback editions. The text font is Tex Gyre Pagella; the heading font is Californian FB. Luca produced the EPUB, MOBI, PDF, HTML, and XML editions — the conversion is performed with open source software freely available on our GitHub page (https://github.com/OpenBookPublishers).

This book need not end here...

Share

All our books — including the one you have just read — are free to access online so that students, researchers and members of the public who can't afford a printed edition will have access to the same ideas. This title will be accessed online by hundreds of readers each month across the globe: why not share the link so that someone you know is one of them?

This book and additional content is available at:

https://doi.org/10.11647/OBP.0247

Customise

Personalise your copy of this book or design new books using OBP and third-party material. Take chapters or whole books from our published list and make a special edition, a new anthology or an illuminating coursepack. Each customised edition will be produced as a paperback and a downloadable PDF.

Find out more at:

https://www.openbookpublishers.com/section/59/1

You may also be interested in:

Image, Knife, and Gluepot
Early Assemblage in Manuscript and Print
Kathryn M. Rudy

https://doi.org/10.11647/OBP.0145

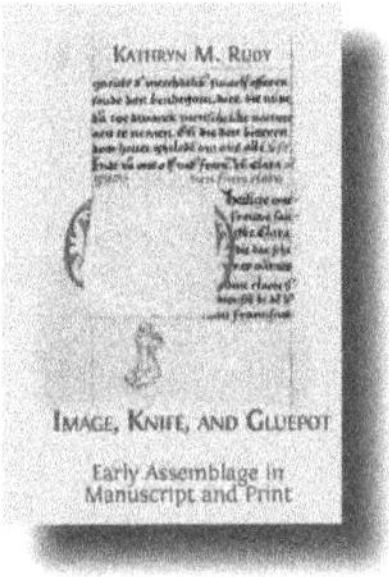

Photography in the Third Reich
Art, Physiognomy and Propaganda
Christopher Webster (ed.)

https://doi.org/10.11647/OBP.0202

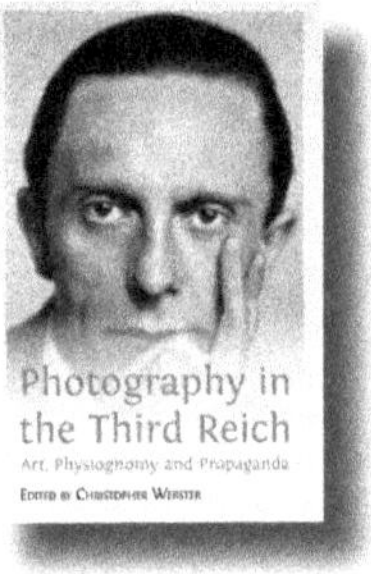

Thomas Annan of Glasgow
Pioneer of the Documentary Photograph
Lionel Gossman

https://doi.org/10.11647/OBP.0057

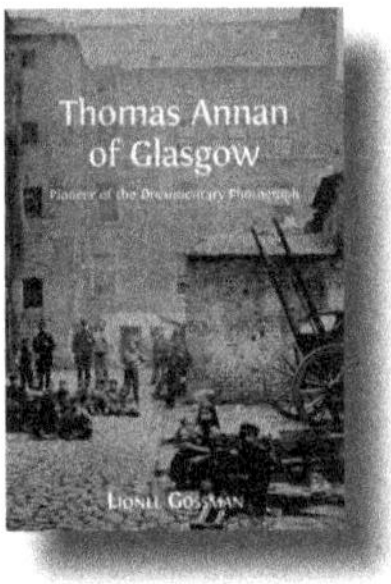

www.ingramcontent.com/pod-product-compliance
Ingram Content Group UK Ltd.
Pitfield, Milton Keynes, MK11 3LW, UK
UKHW020423061026
15625UKWH00006B/381

9 781800 64147